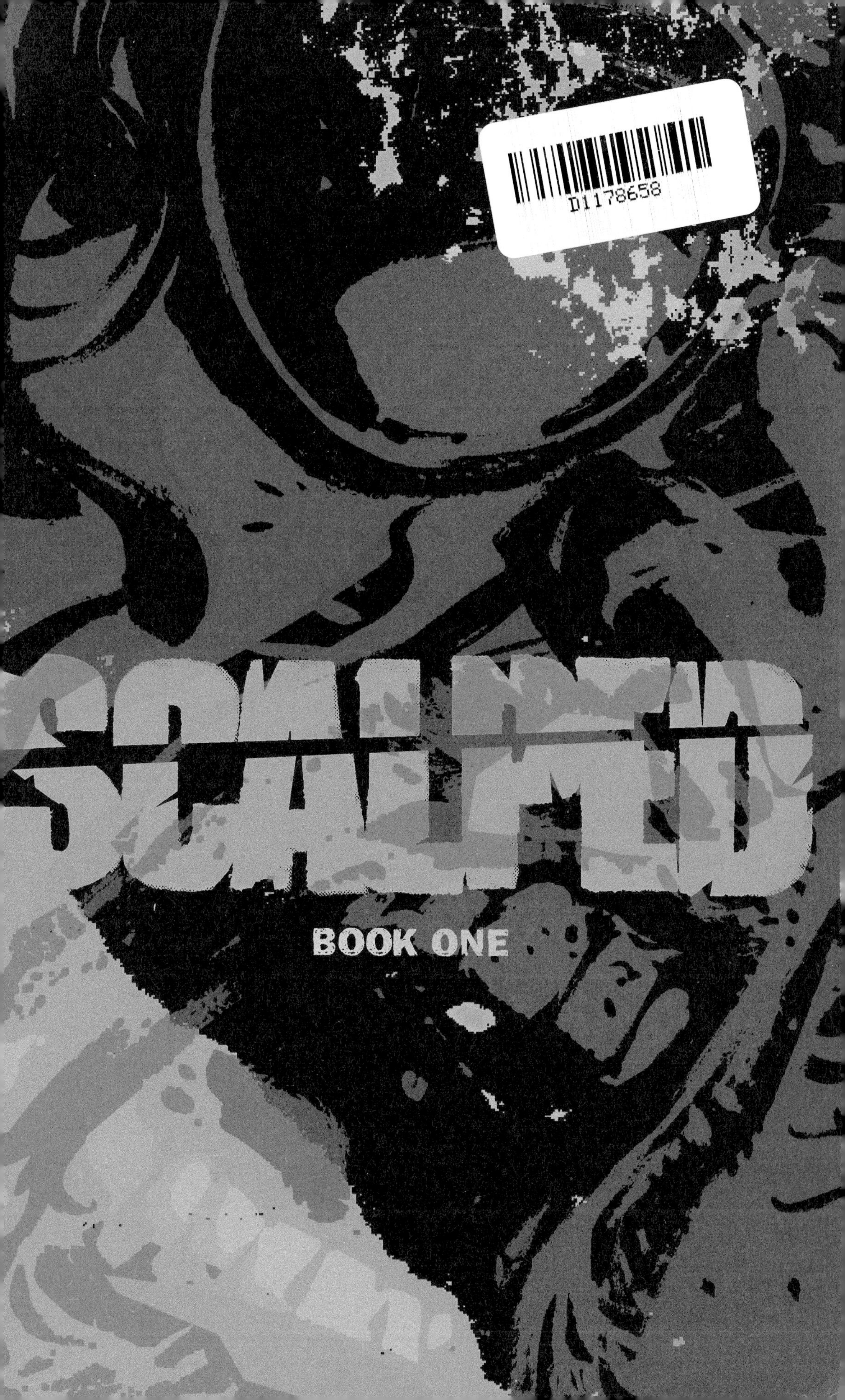
SCALPED
BOOK ONE

JASON AARON
Writer

R. M. GUÉRA
Artist

LEE LOUGHRIDGE
GIULIA BRUSCO
Colorists

PHIL BALSMAN
Letterer

R. M. GUÉRA
Cover Art

Original series covers by **JOCK**

Introduction by **BRIAN K. VAUGHAN**

SCALPED created by
JASON AARON and **R. M. GUÉRA**

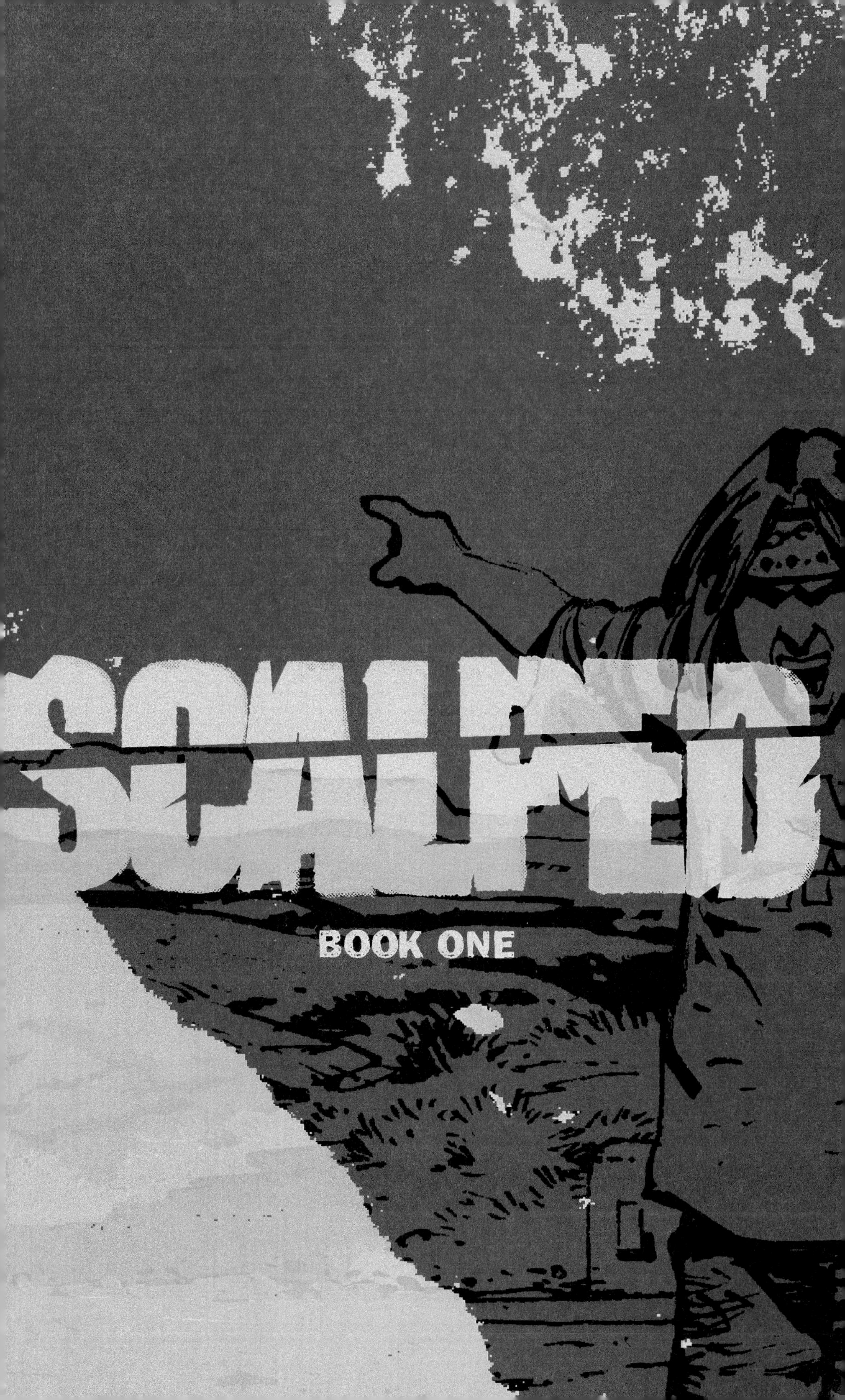
SCALPED
BOOK ONE

WILL DENNIS Editor - Original Series
CASEY SEIJAS Assistant Editor - Original Series
JAMIE S. RICH Group Editor - Vertigo Comics
JEB WOODARD Group Editor - Collected Editions
SCOTT NYBAKKEN Editor - Collected Edition
STEVE COOK Design Director - Books
DAMIAN RYLAND Publication Design

DIANE NELSON President
DAN DiDIO Publisher
JIM LEE Publisher
GEOFF JOHNS President & Chief Creative Officer
AMIT DESAI Executive VP - Business & Marketing Strategy, Direct to Consumer & Global Franchise Management
SAM ADES Senior VP - Direct to Consumer
BOBBIE CHASE VP - Talent Development
MARK CHIARELLO Senior VP - Art, Design & Collected Editions
JOHN CUNNINGHAM Senior VP - Sales & Trade Marketing
ANNE DePIES Senior VP - Business Strategy, Finance & Administration
DON FALLETTI VP - Manufacturing Operations
LAWRENCE GANEM VP - Editorial Administration & Talent Relations
ALISON GILL Senior VP - Manufacturing & Operations
HANK KANALZ Senior VP - Editorial Strategy & Administration
JAY KOGAN VP - Legal Affairs
THOMAS LOFTUS VP - Business Affairs
JACK MAHAN VP - Business Affairs
NICK J. NAPOLITANO VP - Manufacturing Administration
EDDIE SCANNELL VP - Consumer Marketing
COURTNEY SIMMONS Senior VP - Publicity & Communications
JIM (SKI) SOKOLOWSKI VP - Comic Book Specialty Sales & Trade Marketing
NANCY SPEARS VP - Mass, Book, Digital Sales & Trade Marketing

Logo design by JOCK

SCALPED BOOK ONE

DC Comics, 2900 West Alameda Avenue, Burbank, CA 91505
Printed in the USA. First Printing. ISBN: 978-1-4012-7126-8

Library of Congress Cataloging-in-Publication Data is available

Introduction

Most American comics writers suck.

At least, that's what you might think if you
looked back at the vast majority of creators who
helped forge Vertigo, one of the best imprints
in the history of the medium. Moore, Gaiman,
Morrison, Milligan, Millar, Ellis, Ennis...dirty foreigners,
every one of them. This U.K. invasion had already moved on
to innovative new adult fiction while we lowly Yanks were still
trying to figure out how they beat us at our own superhero game.

And while the scales have started to even out over the last few years, it was still a particular
thrill for a U.S. citizen with a nasty inferiority complex like mine to discover the work of a young
guy named Jason Aaron. See, Jason isn't just a great writer who happens to be American,
he's a great writer largely because he *is* American.

And before all the international readers out there start tucking their Euros back into their
wallets, let me be clear that I'm not talking about rah-rah jingoistic bullshit. If you've read *The
Other Side*, Jason's staggeringly brilliant Vietnam story, you know that he's able to write about
the United States with both the burning passion and the uniquely vitriolic rage that's difficult
to balance if you didn't gestate inside the loving belly of this cruel beast.

And speaking of natives, SCALPED is Jason's distinctly American Western-slash-crime story
about the people who had this country first. Starring Dashiell Bad Horse, the rare film noir
protagonist who's actually as cool as his name, this is the riveting tale of one mean cop with
a big damn secret. It's about a lot more than that, of course, but the skeleton in Dash's closet
(which you'll meet for yourself at the end of the first chapter) is so perfect and so satisfying,
you might not even notice all the tough questions this comic is asking about race, vice, class,
family, and sex.

Okay, you'll probably notice the sex, thanks largely to R.M. Guéra, whose visceral artwork will drive to your house, throw you into the back of a pickup, and haul your ass straight onto the Reservation. This book has got some of the best cliff hangers on the stands, and Guéra nails every one of them. Just awesome.

Well-researched yet imaginative, funny but serious, political and politically incorrect, SCALPED is further proof that the most exciting new writer in comics is an American.

Don't hold it against him.

Brian K. Vaughan
May 2007

Along with writing for the television series Lost *and* Under the Dome, *Vaughan is the co-creator of* Y: THE LAST MAN, EX MACHINA, PRIDE OF BAGHDAD *and* Saga. *He was born and raised in the States but married a Canadian, which has got to count for something.*

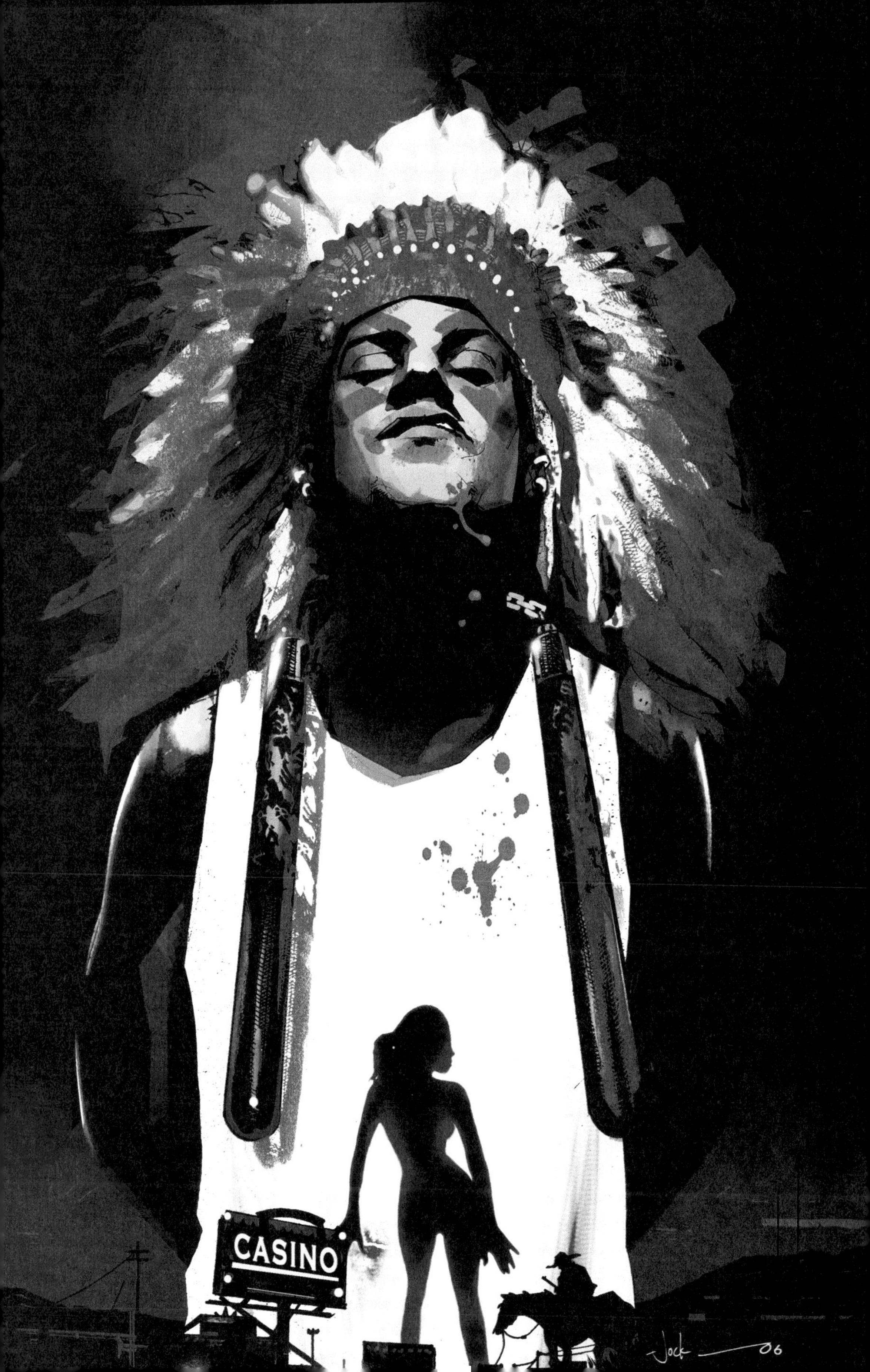
CASINO

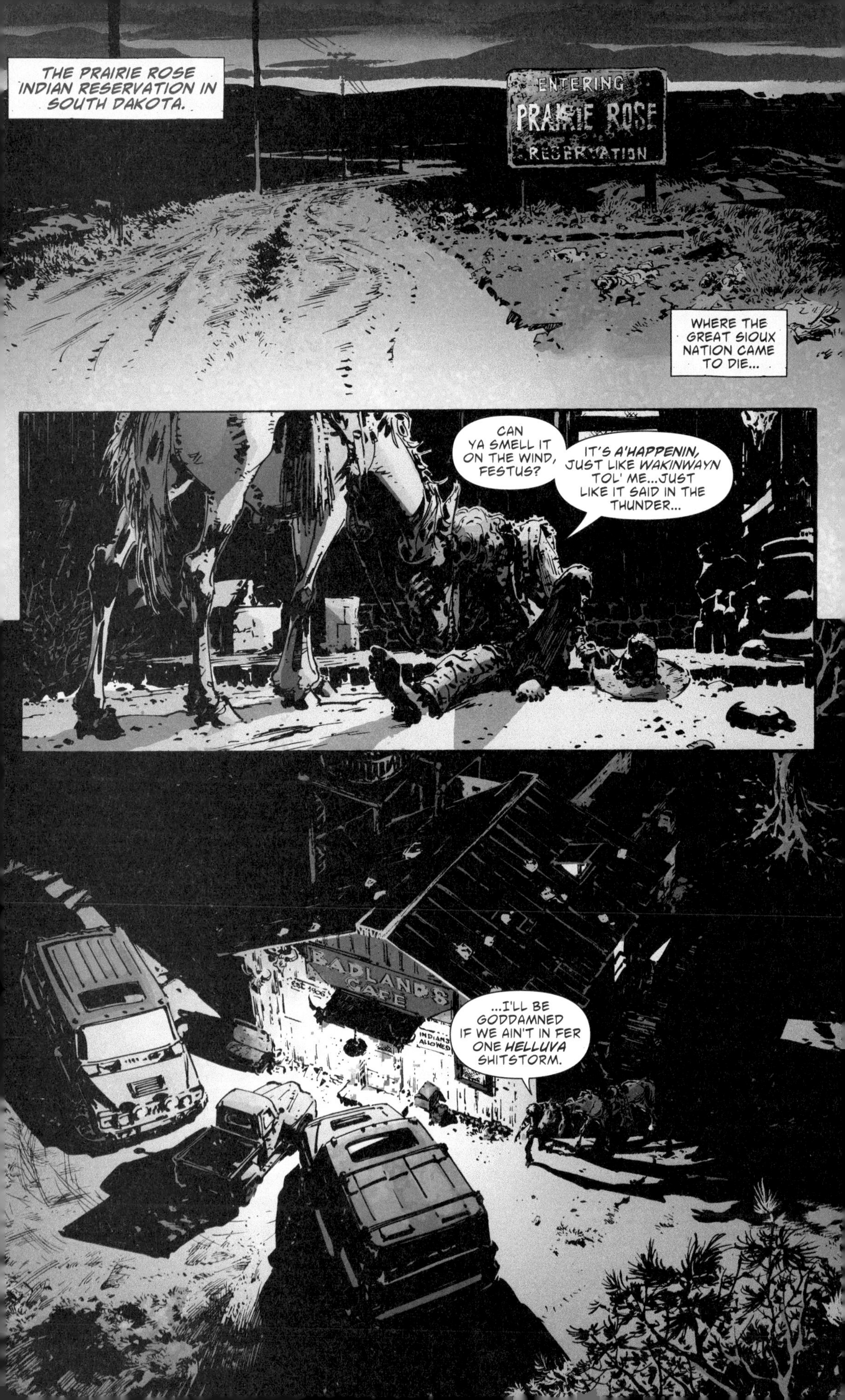
THE PRAIRIE ROSE INDIAN RESERVATION IN SOUTH DAKOTA.
ENTERING PRAIRIE ROSE RESERVATION
WHERE THE GREAT SIOUX NATION CAME TO DIE...
CAN YA SMELL IT ON THE WIND, FESTUS?
IT'S *A'HAPPENIN,* JUST LIKE *WAKINWAYN* TOL' ME...JUST LIKE IT SAID IN THE THUNDER...
BADLANDS CAFE
INDIANS ALLOWED
...I'LL BE GODDAMNED IF WE AIN'T IN FER ONE *HELLUVA* SHITSTORM.

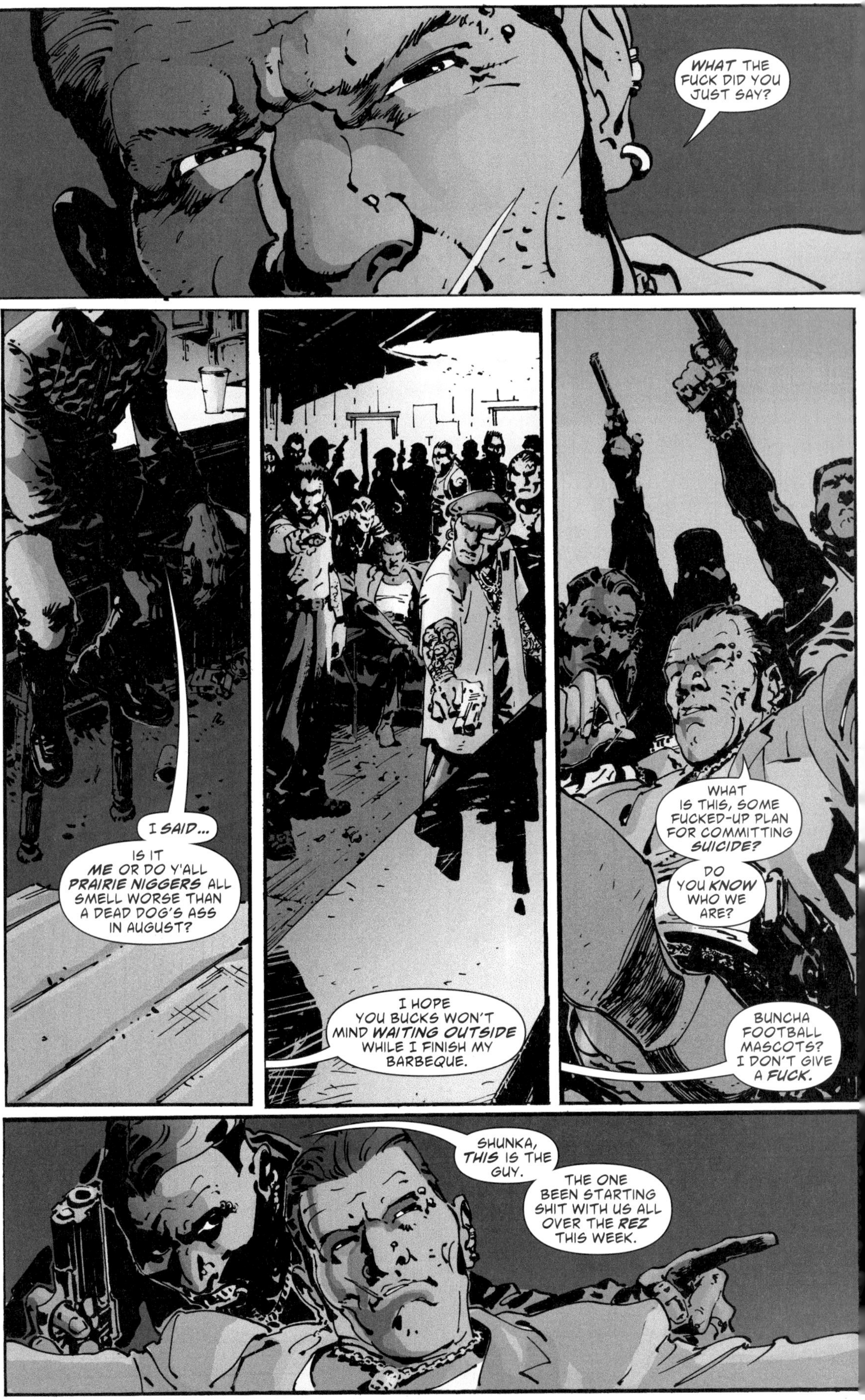

WHAT THE FUCK DID YOU JUST SAY?
I SAID...
IS IT ME OR DO Y'ALL PRAIRIE NIGGERS ALL SMELL WORSE THAN A DEAD DOG'S ASS IN AUGUST?
I HOPE YOU BUCKS WON'T MIND WAITING OUTSIDE WHILE I FINISH MY BARBEQUE.
WHAT IS THIS, SOME FUCKED-UP PLAN FOR COMMITTING SUICIDE?
DO YOU KNOW WHO WE ARE?
BUNCHA FOOTBALL MASCOTS? I DON'T GIVE A FUCK.
SHUNKA, THIS IS THE GUY.
THE ONE BEEN STARTING SHIT WITH US ALL OVER THE REZ THIS WEEK.

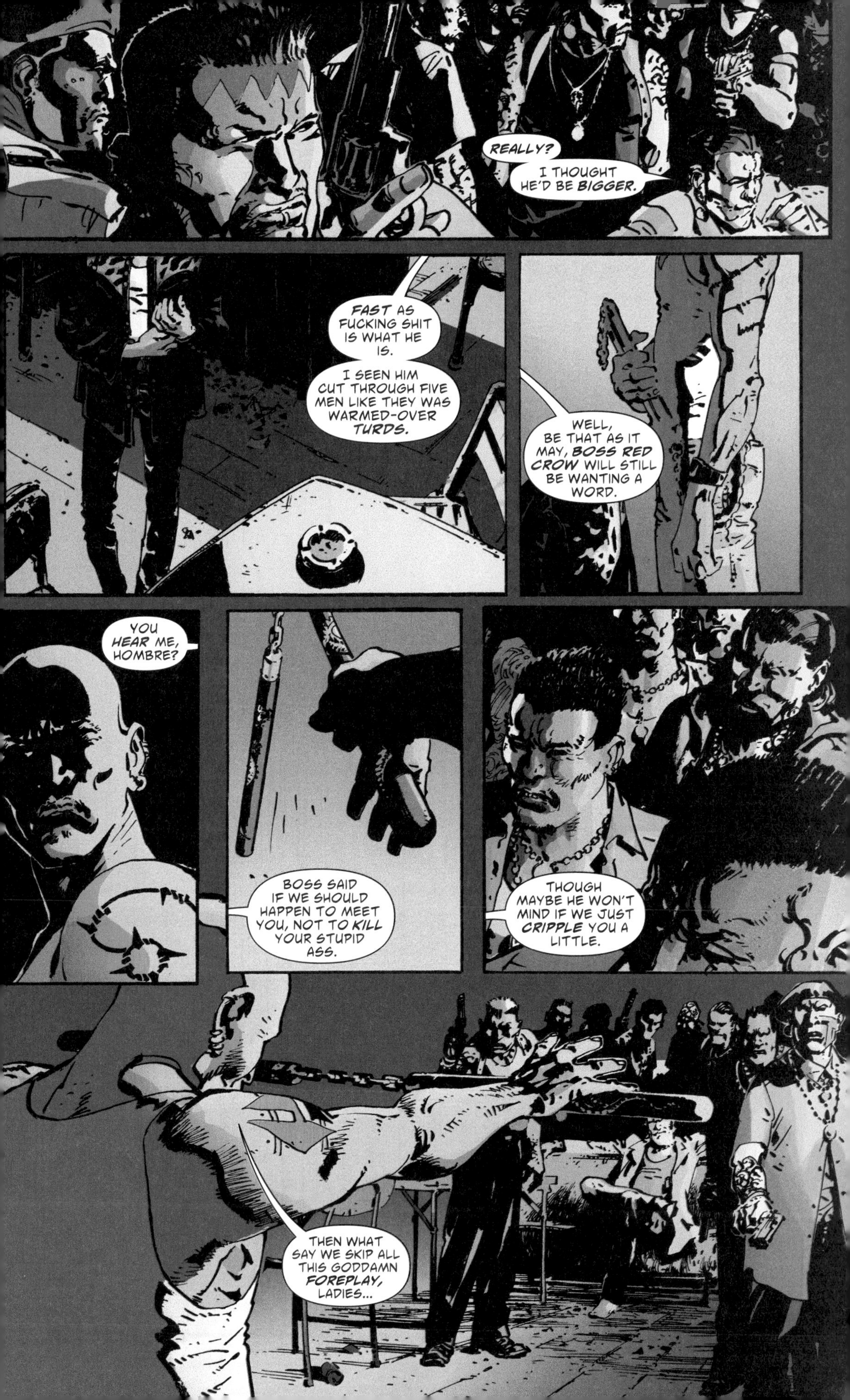
REALLY?
I THOUGHT HE'D BE BIGGER.
FAST AS FUCKING SHIT IS WHAT HE IS.
I SEEN HIM CUT THROUGH FIVE MEN LIKE THEY WAS WARMED-OVER TURDS.
WELL, BE THAT AS IT MAY, BOSS RED CROW WILL STILL BE WANTING A WORD.
YOU HEAR ME, HOMBRE?
BOSS SAID IF WE SHOULD HAPPEN TO MEET YOU, NOT TO KILL YOUR STUPID ASS.
THOUGH MAYBE HE WON'T MIND IF WE JUST CRIPPLE YOU A LITTLE.
THEN WHAT SAY WE SKIP ALL THIS GODDAMN FOREPLAY, LADIES...

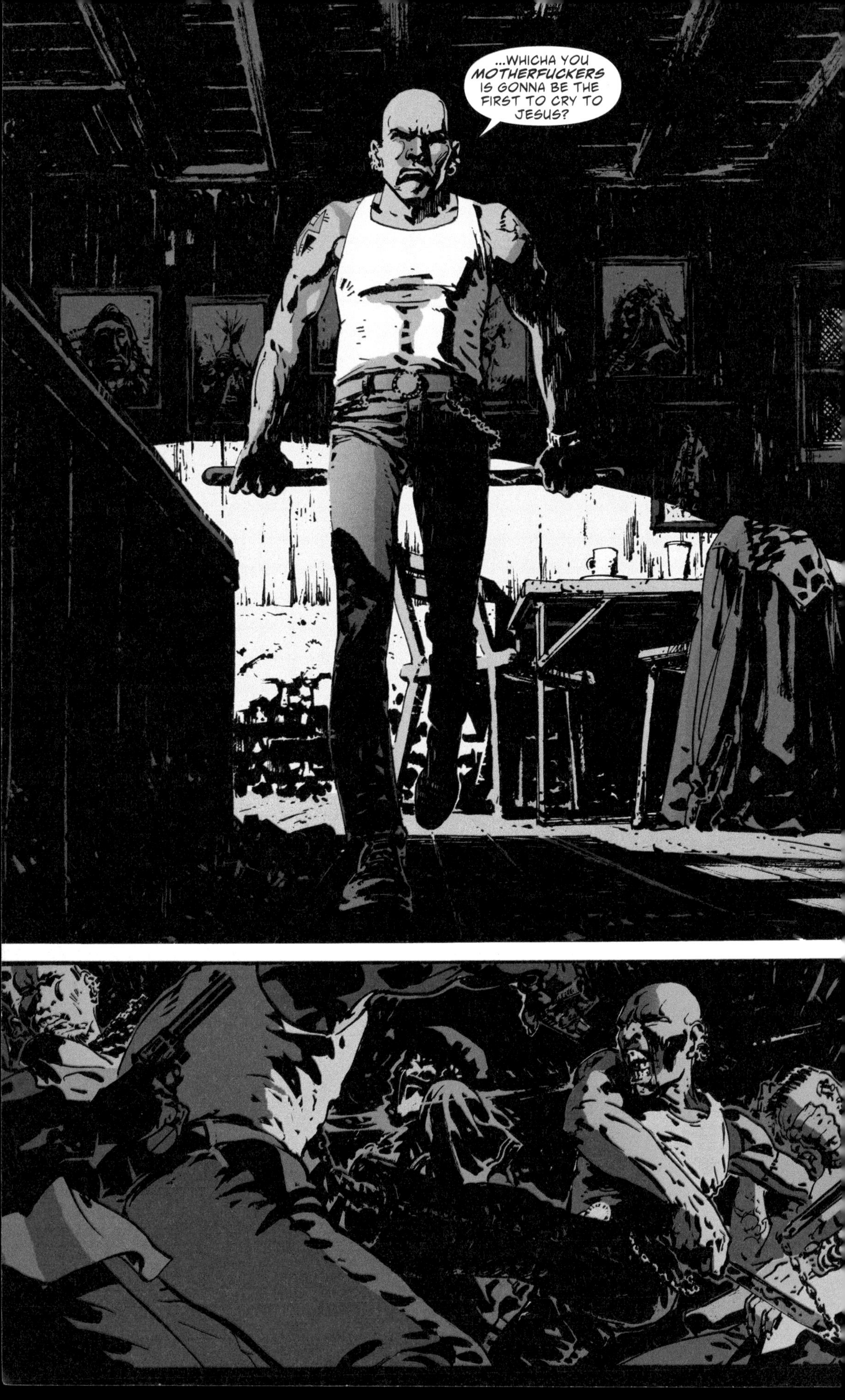
...WHICHA YOU MOTHERFUCKERS IS GONNA BE THE FIRST TO CRY TO JESUS?

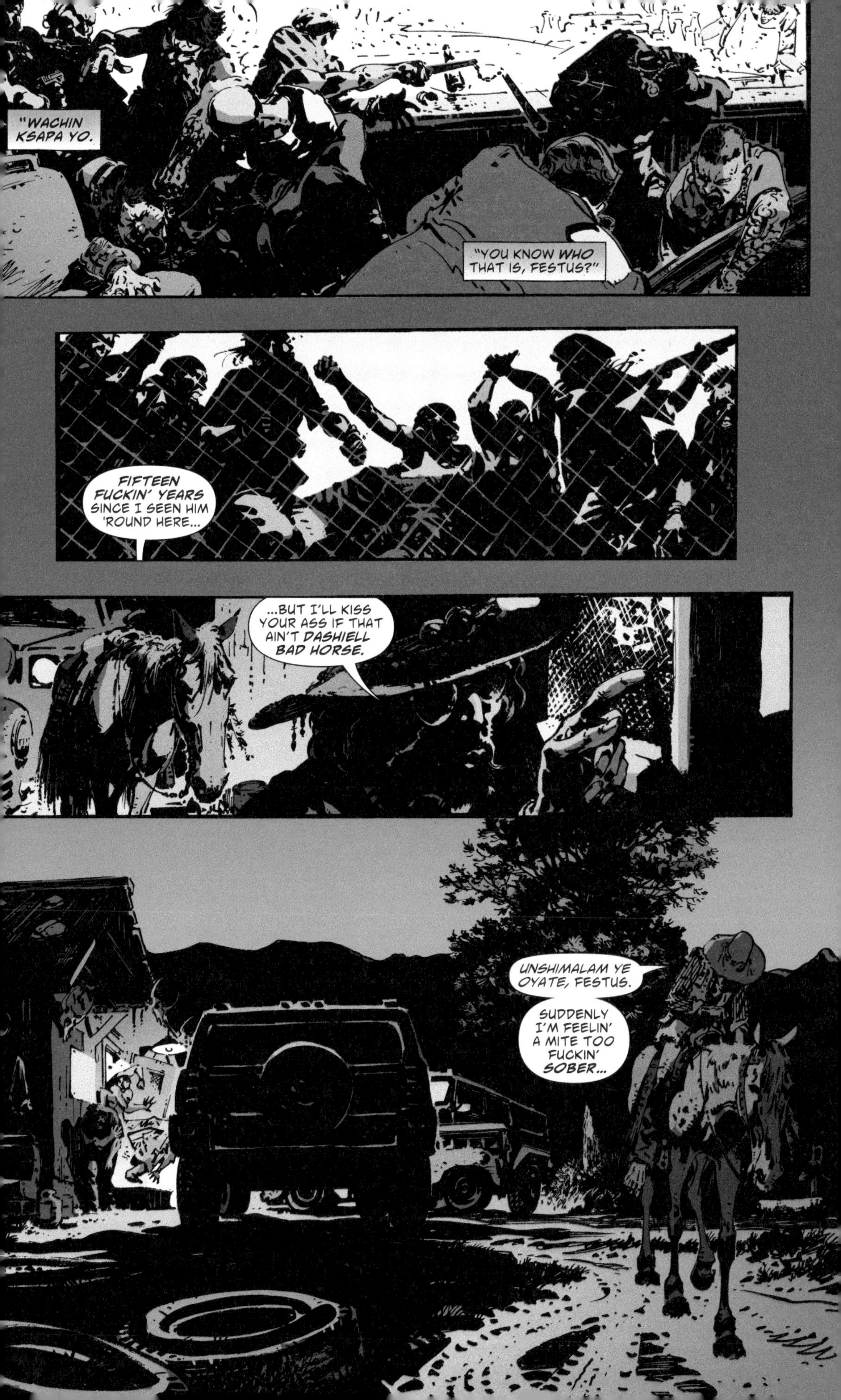
"WACHIN KSAPA YO.
"YOU KNOW WHO THAT IS, FESTUS?"
FIFTEEN FUCKIN' YEARS SINCE I SEEN HIM 'ROUND HERE...
...BUT I'LL KISS YOUR ASS IF THAT AIN'T DASHIELL BAD HORSE.
UNSHIMALAM YE OYATE, FESTUS.
SUDDENLY I'M FEELIN' A MITE TOO FUCKIN' SOBER...

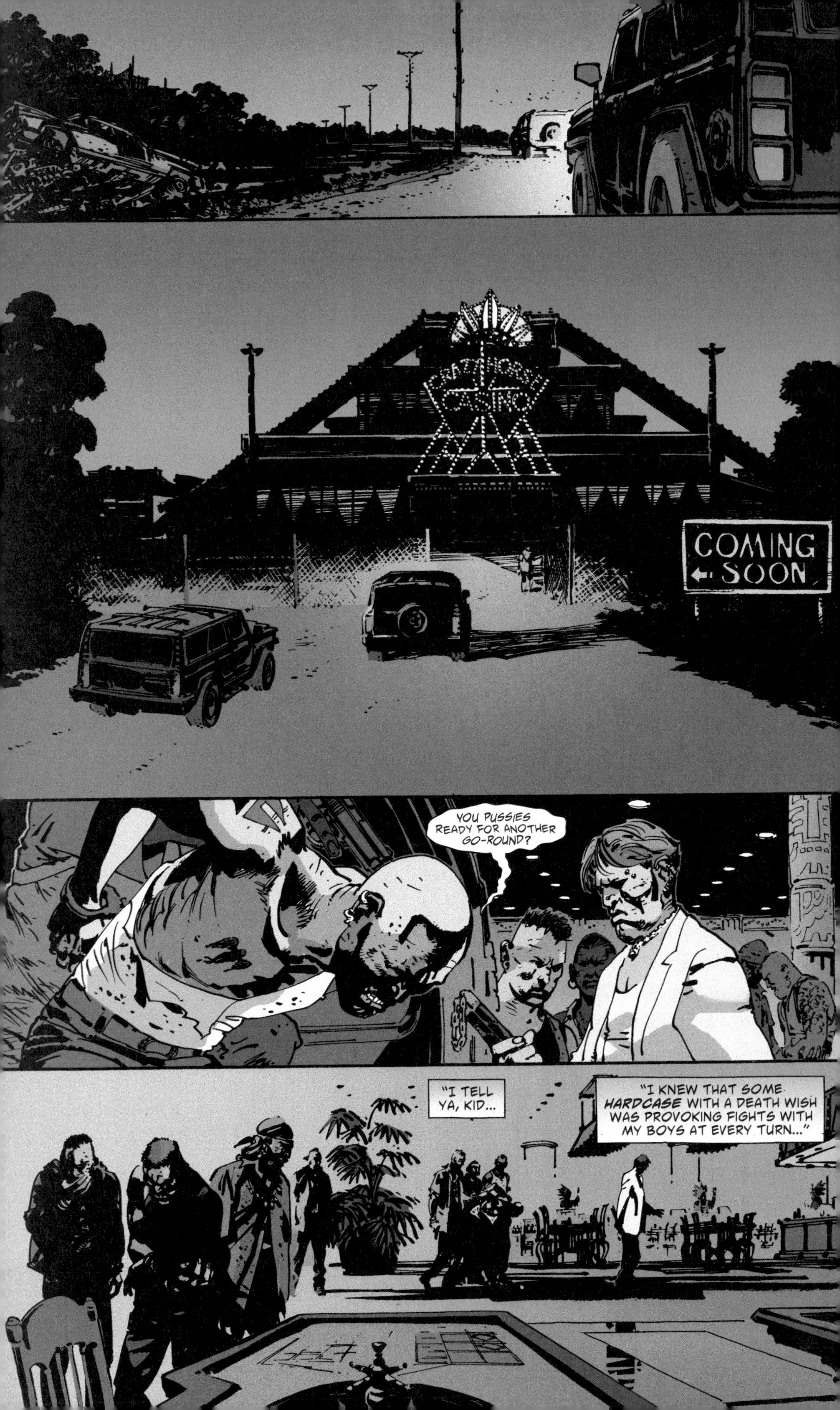

CRAZY HORSE CASINO
COMING SOON
YOU PUSSIES READY FOR ANOTHER GO-ROUND?
"I TELL YA, KID...
"I KNEW THAT SOME HARDCASE WITH A DEATH WISH WAS PROVOKING FIGHTS WITH MY BOYS AT EVERY TURN..."

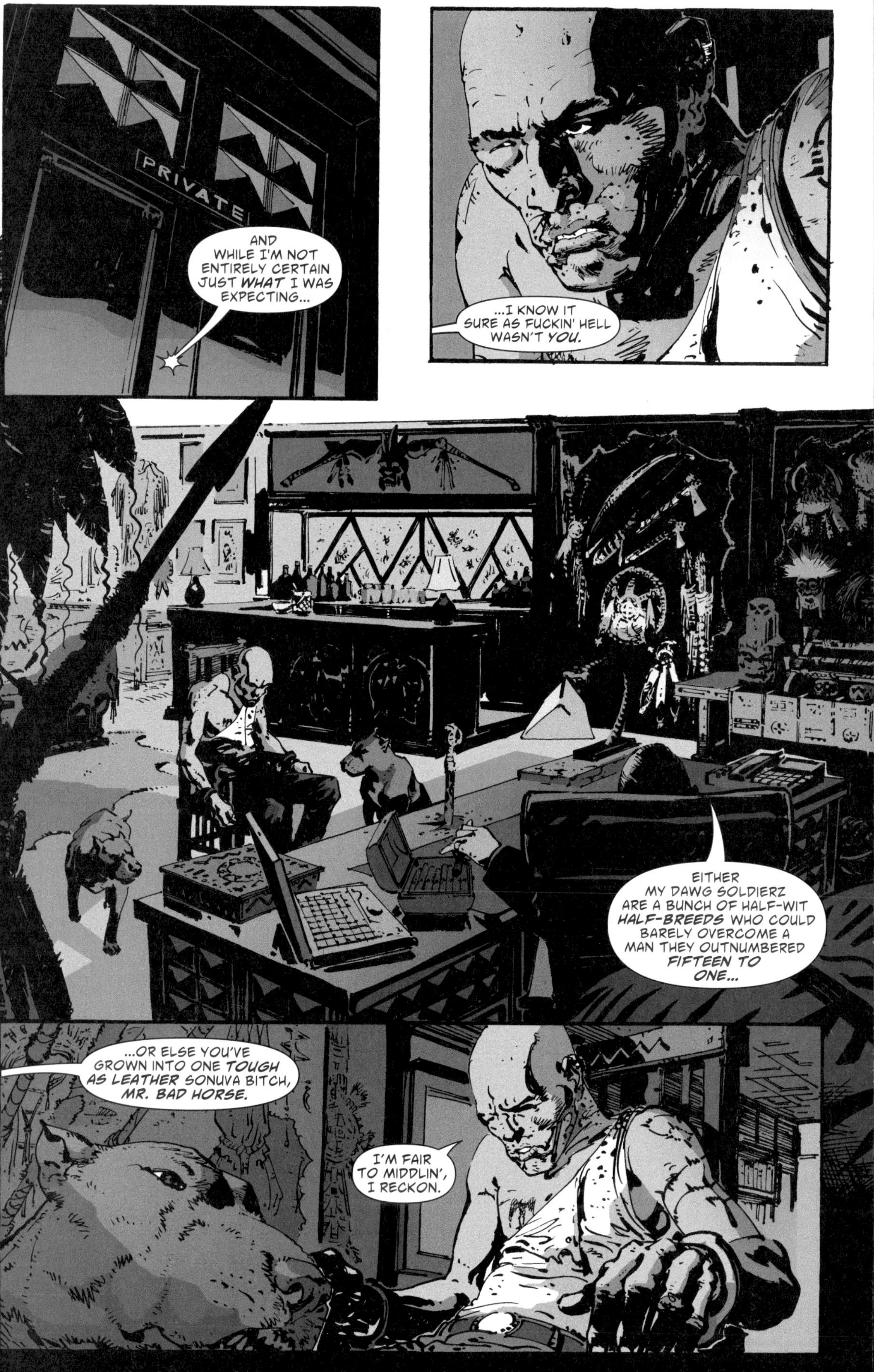
PRIVATE
AND WHILE I'M NOT ENTIRELY CERTAIN JUST WHAT I WAS EXPECTING...
...I KNOW IT SURE AS FUCKIN' HELL WASN'T YOU.
EITHER MY DAWG SOLDIERZ ARE A BUNCH OF HALF-WIT HALF-BREEDS WHO COULD BARELY OVERCOME A MAN THEY OUTNUMBERED FIFTEEN TO ONE...
...OR ELSE YOU'VE GROWN INTO ONE TOUGH AS LEATHER SONUVA BITCH, MR. BAD HORSE.
I'M FAIR TO MIDDLIN', I RECKON.

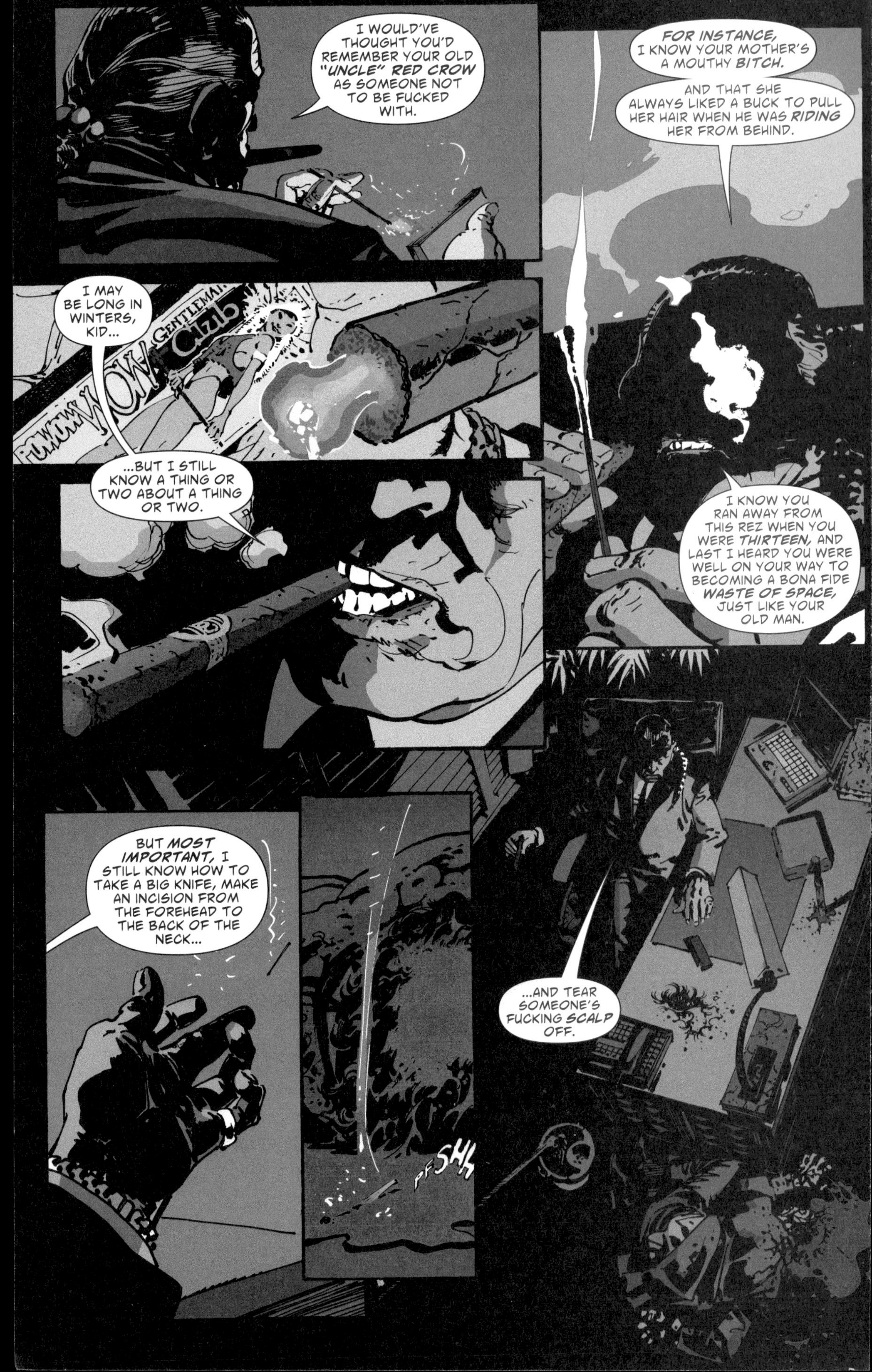
I WOULD'VE THOUGHT YOU'D REMEMBER YOUR OLD "UNCLE" RED CROW AS SOMEONE NOT TO BE FUCKED WITH.
FOR INSTANCE, I KNOW YOUR MOTHER'S A MOUTHY BITCH.
AND THAT SHE ALWAYS LIKED A BUCK TO PULL HER HAIR WHEN HE WAS RIDING HER FROM BEHIND.
I MAY BE LONG IN WINTERS, KID...
...BUT I STILL KNOW A THING OR TWO ABOUT A THING OR TWO.
I KNOW YOU RAN AWAY FROM THIS REZ WHEN YOU WERE THIRTEEN, AND LAST I HEARD YOU WERE WELL ON YOUR WAY TO BECOMING A BONA FIDE WASTE OF SPACE, JUST LIKE YOUR OLD MAN.
BUT MOST IMPORTANT, I STILL KNOW HOW TO TAKE A BIG KNIFE, MAKE AN INCISION FROM THE FOREHEAD TO THE BACK OF THE NECK...
PFSHH
...AND TEAR SOMEONE'S FUCKING SCALP OFF.

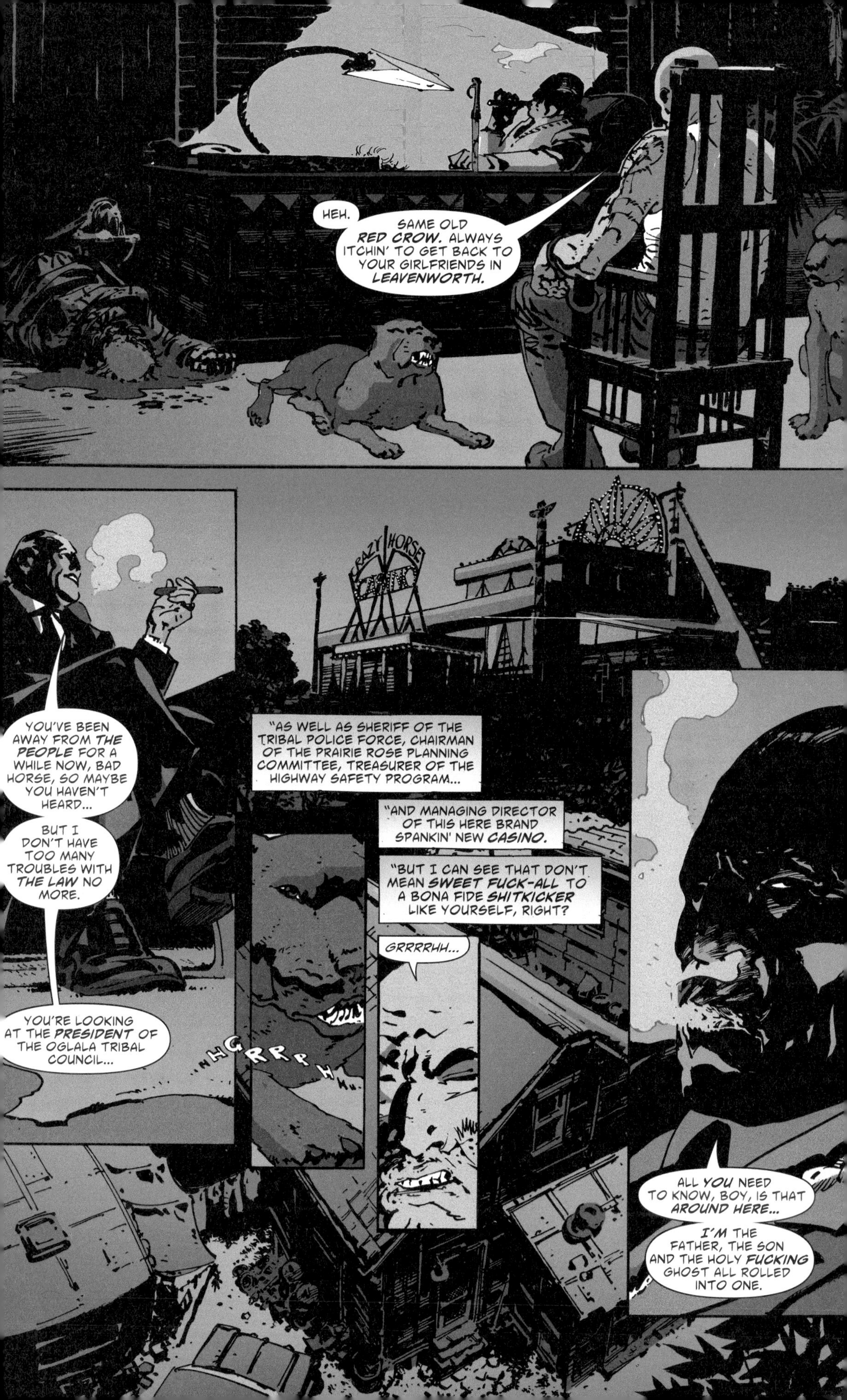
HEH.
SAME OLD RED CROW. ALWAYS ITCHIN' TO GET BACK TO YOUR GIRLFRIENDS IN LEAVENWORTH.
YOU'VE BEEN AWAY FROM THE PEOPLE FOR A WHILE NOW, BAD HORSE, SO MAYBE YOU HAVEN'T HEARD...
BUT I DON'T HAVE TOO MANY TROUBLES WITH THE LAW NO MORE.
YOU'RE LOOKING AT THE PRESIDENT OF THE OGLALA TRIBAL COUNCIL...
CRAZY HORSE
"AS WELL AS SHERIFF OF THE TRIBAL POLICE FORCE, CHAIRMAN OF THE PRAIRIE ROSE PLANNING COMMITTEE, TREASURER OF THE HIGHWAY SAFETY PROGRAM...
"AND MANAGING DIRECTOR OF THIS HERE BRAND SPANKIN' NEW CASINO.
"BUT I CAN SEE THAT DON'T MEAN SWEET FUCK-ALL TO A BONA FIDE SHITKICKER LIKE YOURSELF, RIGHT?
HGRRRPH
GRRRRHH...
ALL YOU NEED TO KNOW, BOY, IS THAT AROUND HERE...
I'M THE FATHER, THE SON AND THE HOLY FUCKING GHOST ALL ROLLED INTO ONE.

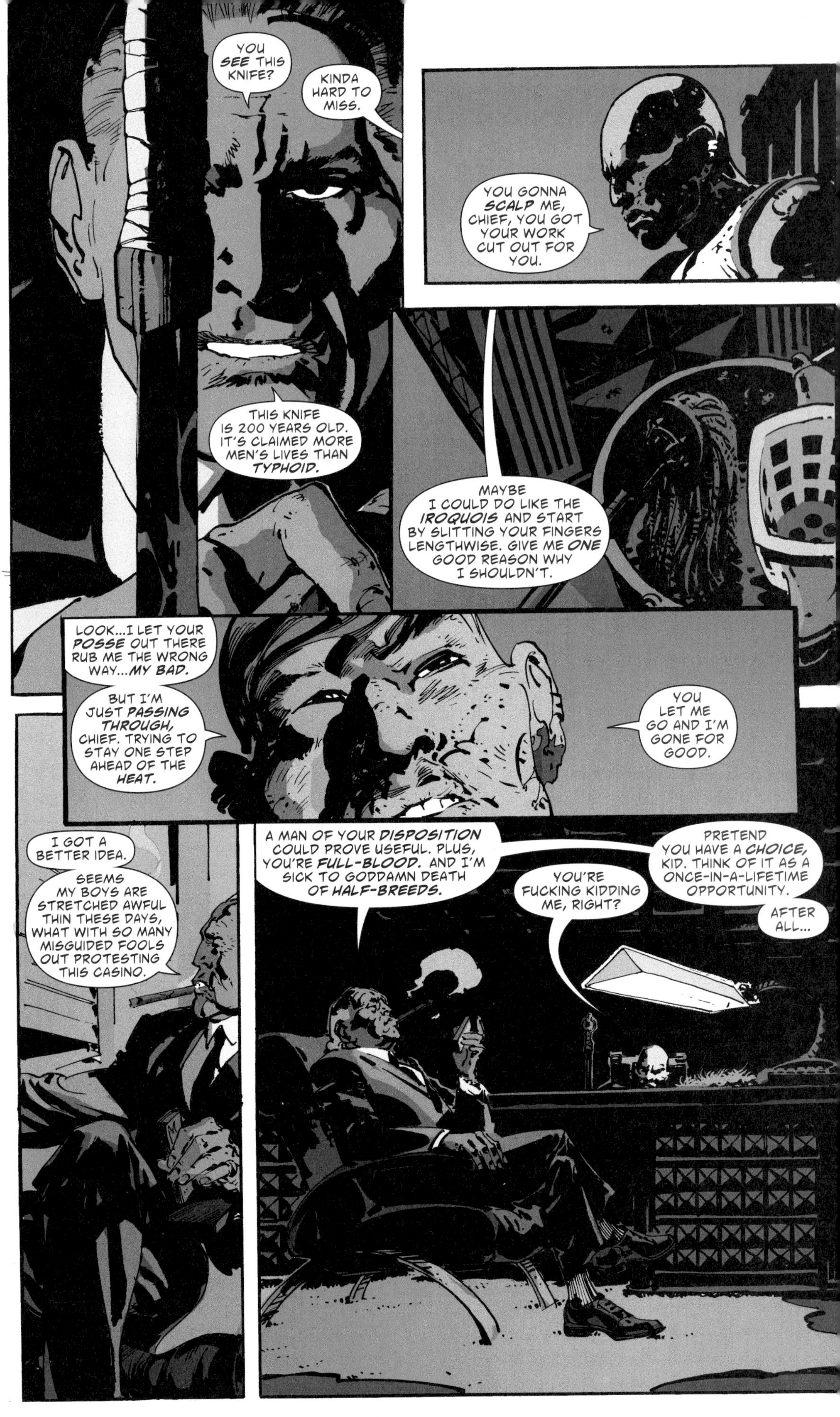

YOU SEE THIS KNIFE?
KINDA HARD TO MISS.
YOU GONNA SCALP ME, CHIEF, YOU GOT YOUR WORK CUT OUT FOR YOU.
THIS KNIFE IS 200 YEARS OLD. IT'S CLAIMED MORE MEN'S LIVES THAN TYPHOID.
MAYBE I COULD DO LIKE THE IROQUOIS AND START BY SLITTING YOUR FINGERS LENGTHWISE. GIVE ME ONE GOOD REASON WHY I SHOULDN'T.
LOOK...I LET YOUR POSSE OUT THERE RUB ME THE WRONG WAY...MY BAD.
BUT I'M JUST PASSING THROUGH, CHIEF. TRYING TO STAY ONE STEP AHEAD OF THE HEAT.
YOU LET ME GO AND I'M GONE FOR GOOD.
I GOT A BETTER IDEA.
SEEMS MY BOYS ARE STRETCHED AWFUL THIN THESE DAYS, WHAT WITH SO MANY MISGUIDED FOOLS OUT PROTESTING THIS CASINO.
A MAN OF YOUR DISPOSITION COULD PROVE USEFUL. PLUS, YOU'RE FULL-BLOOD. AND I'M SICK TO GODDAMN DEATH OF HALF-BREEDS.
YOU'RE FUCKING KIDDING ME, RIGHT?
PRETEND YOU HAVE A CHOICE, KID. THINK OF IT AS A ONCE-IN-A-LIFETIME OPPORTUNITY.
AFTER ALL...

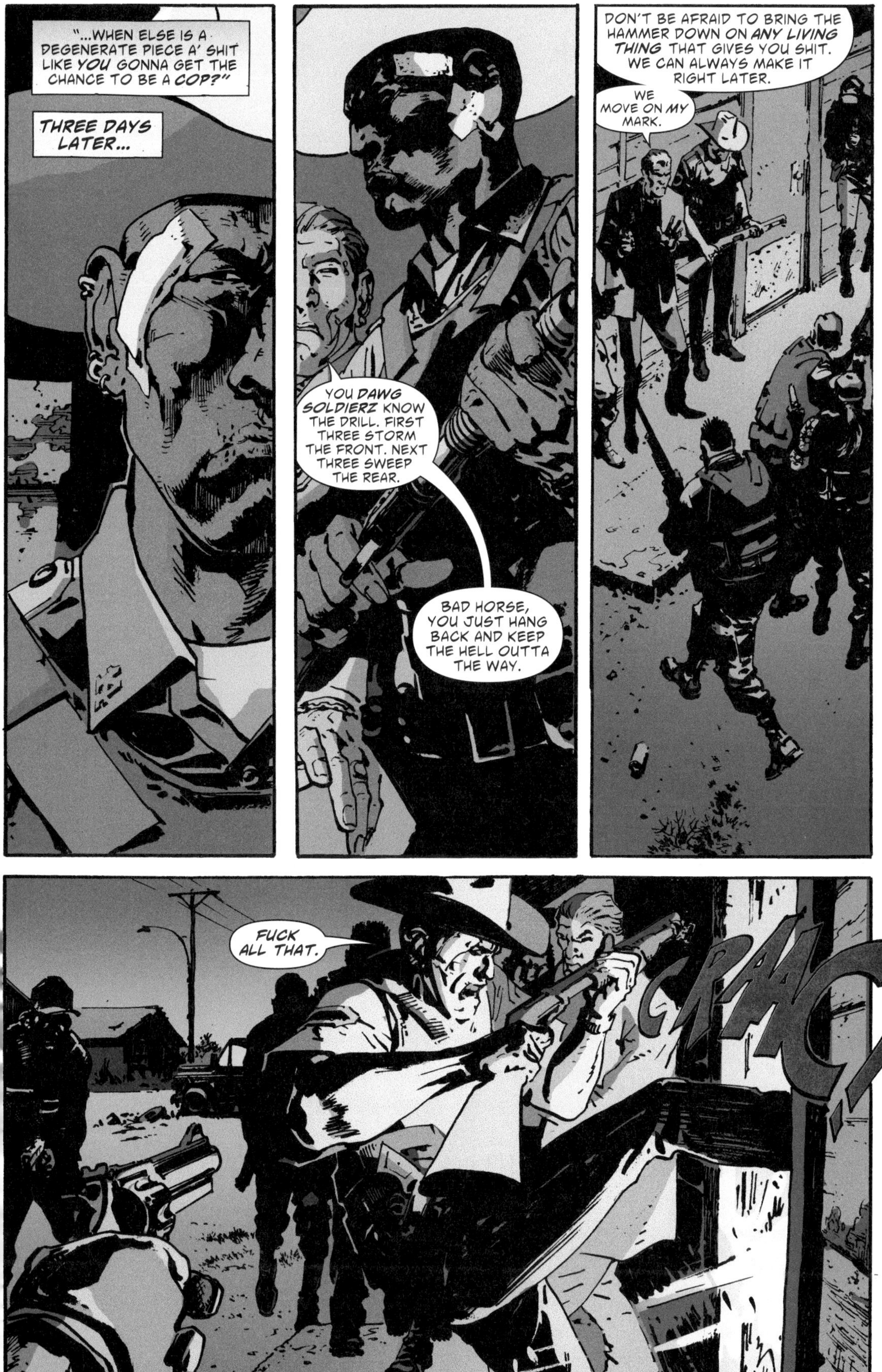
"...WHEN ELSE IS A DEGENERATE PIECE A' SHIT LIKE *YOU* GONNA GET THE CHANCE TO BE A *COP?*"
THREE DAYS LATER...
YOU *DAWG SOLDIERZ* KNOW THE DRILL. FIRST THREE STORM THE FRONT. NEXT THREE SWEEP THE REAR.
BAD HORSE, YOU JUST HANG BACK AND KEEP THE HELL OUTTA THE WAY.
DON'T BE AFRAID TO BRING THE HAMMER DOWN ON *ANY LIVING THING* THAT GIVES YOU SHIT. WE CAN ALWAYS MAKE IT RIGHT LATER.
WE MOVE ON *MY* MARK.
FUCK ALL THAT.
CRAAC!!

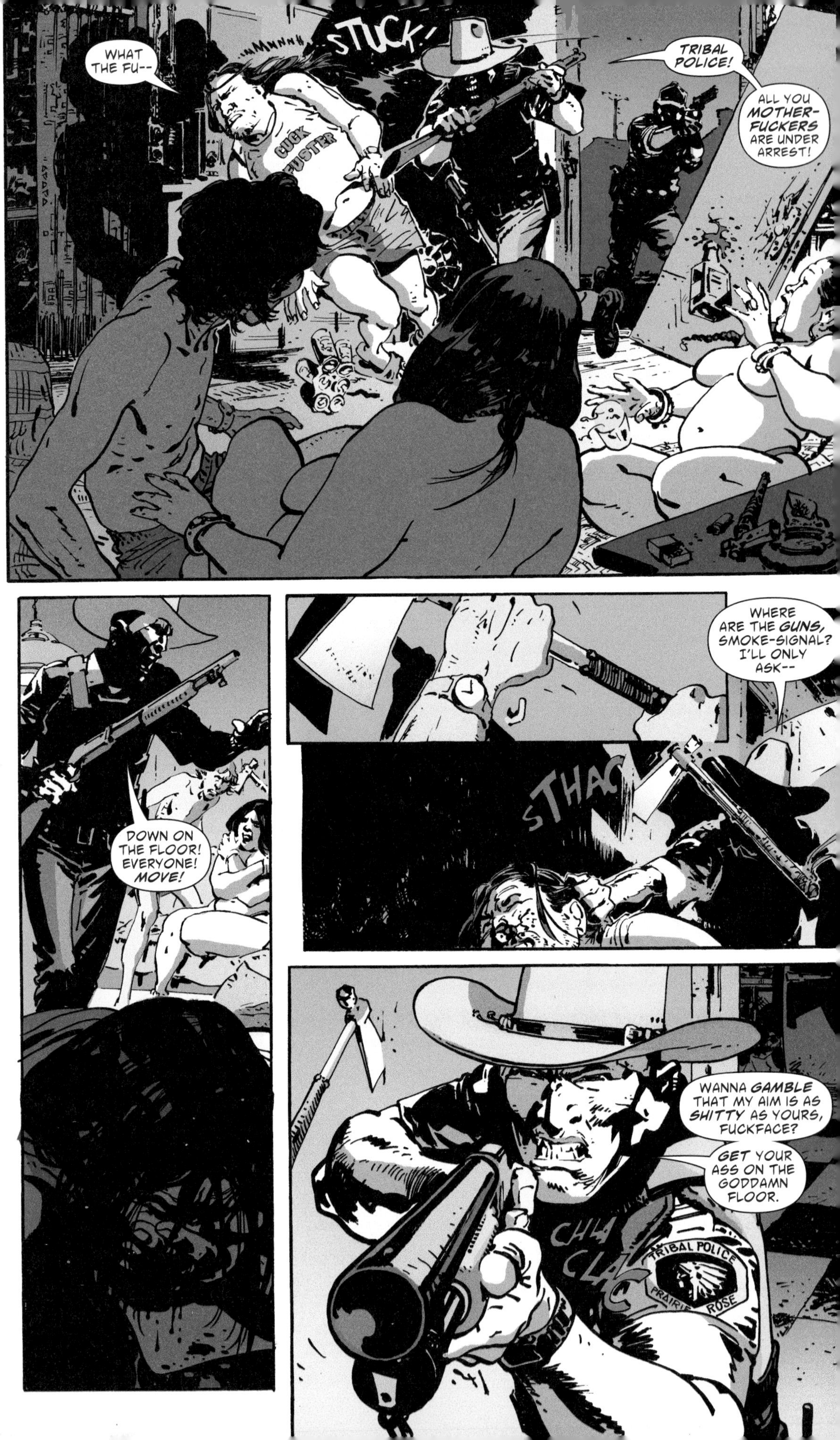

WHAT THE FU--
STUCK!
TRIBAL POLICE!
ALL YOU MOTHER-FUCKERS ARE UNDER ARREST!
DOWN ON THE FLOOR! EVERYONE! MOVE!
WHERE ARE THE GUNS, SMOKE-SIGNAL? I'LL ONLY ASK--
STHAC
WANNA GAMBLE THAT MY AIM IS AS SHITTY AS YOURS, FUCKFACE?
GET YOUR ASS ON THE GODDAMN FLOOR.
CHK CLAC
TRIBAL POLICE
PRAIRIE ROSE

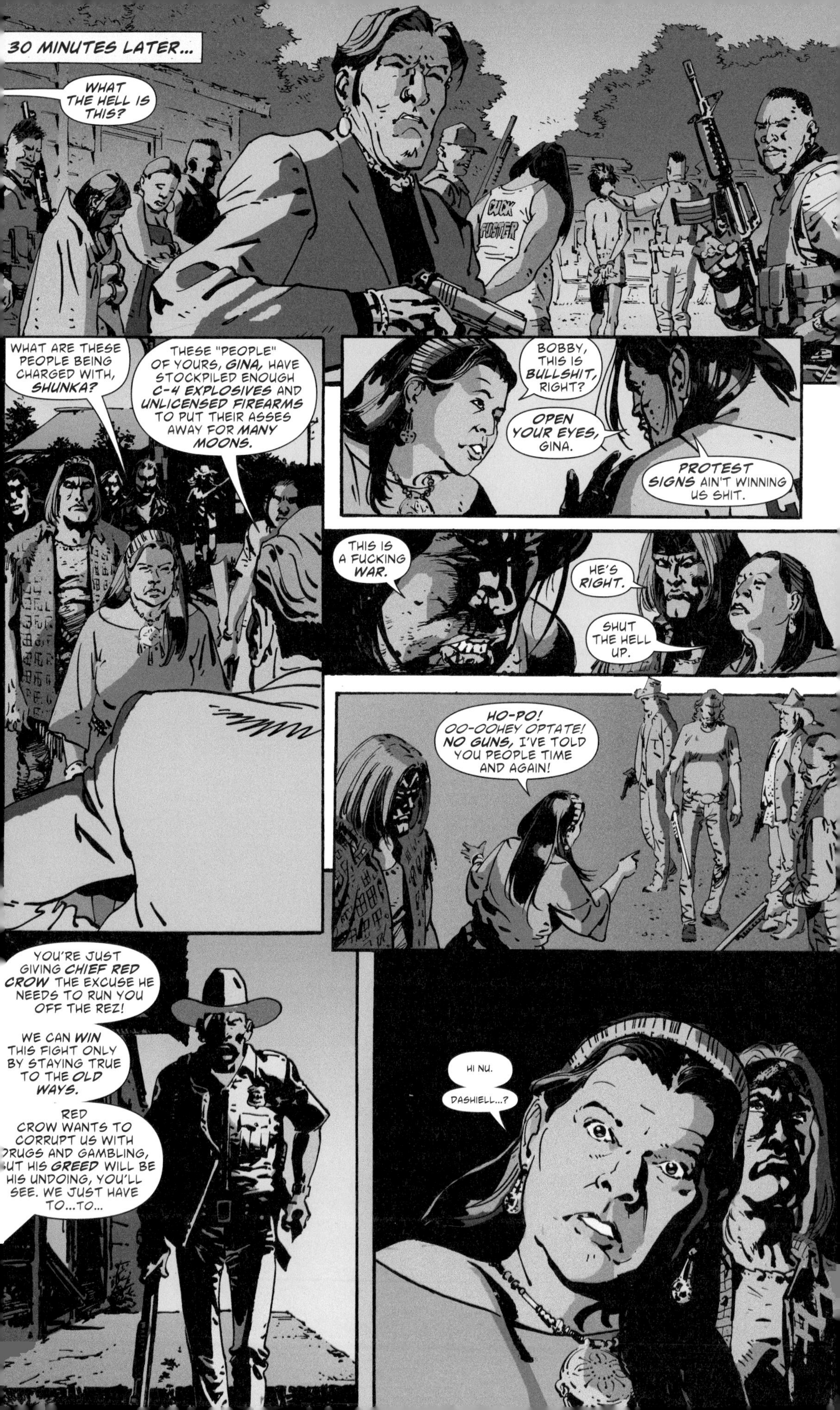
30 MINUTES LATER...
WHAT THE HELL IS THIS?
CUCK FOSTER
WHAT ARE THESE PEOPLE BEING CHARGED WITH, SHUNKA?
THESE "PEOPLE" OF YOURS, GINA, HAVE STOCKPILED ENOUGH C-4 EXPLOSIVES AND UNLICENSED FIREARMS TO PUT THEIR ASSES AWAY FOR MANY MOONS.
BOBBY, THIS IS BULLSHIT, RIGHT?
OPEN YOUR EYES, GINA.
PROTEST SIGNS AIN'T WINNING US SHIT.
THIS IS A FUCKING WAR.
HE'S RIGHT.
SHUT THE HELL UP.
HO-PO! OO-OOHEY OPTATE! NO GUNS, I'VE TOLD YOU PEOPLE TIME AND AGAIN!
YOU'RE JUST GIVING CHIEF RED CROW THE EXCUSE HE NEEDS TO RUN YOU OFF THE REZ!
WE CAN WIN THIS FIGHT ONLY BY STAYING TRUE TO THE OLD WAYS.
RED CROW WANTS TO CORRUPT US WITH DRUGS AND GAMBLING, BUT HIS GREED WILL BE HIS UNDOING, YOU'LL SEE. WE JUST HAVE TO...TO...
HI NU.
DASHIELL...?

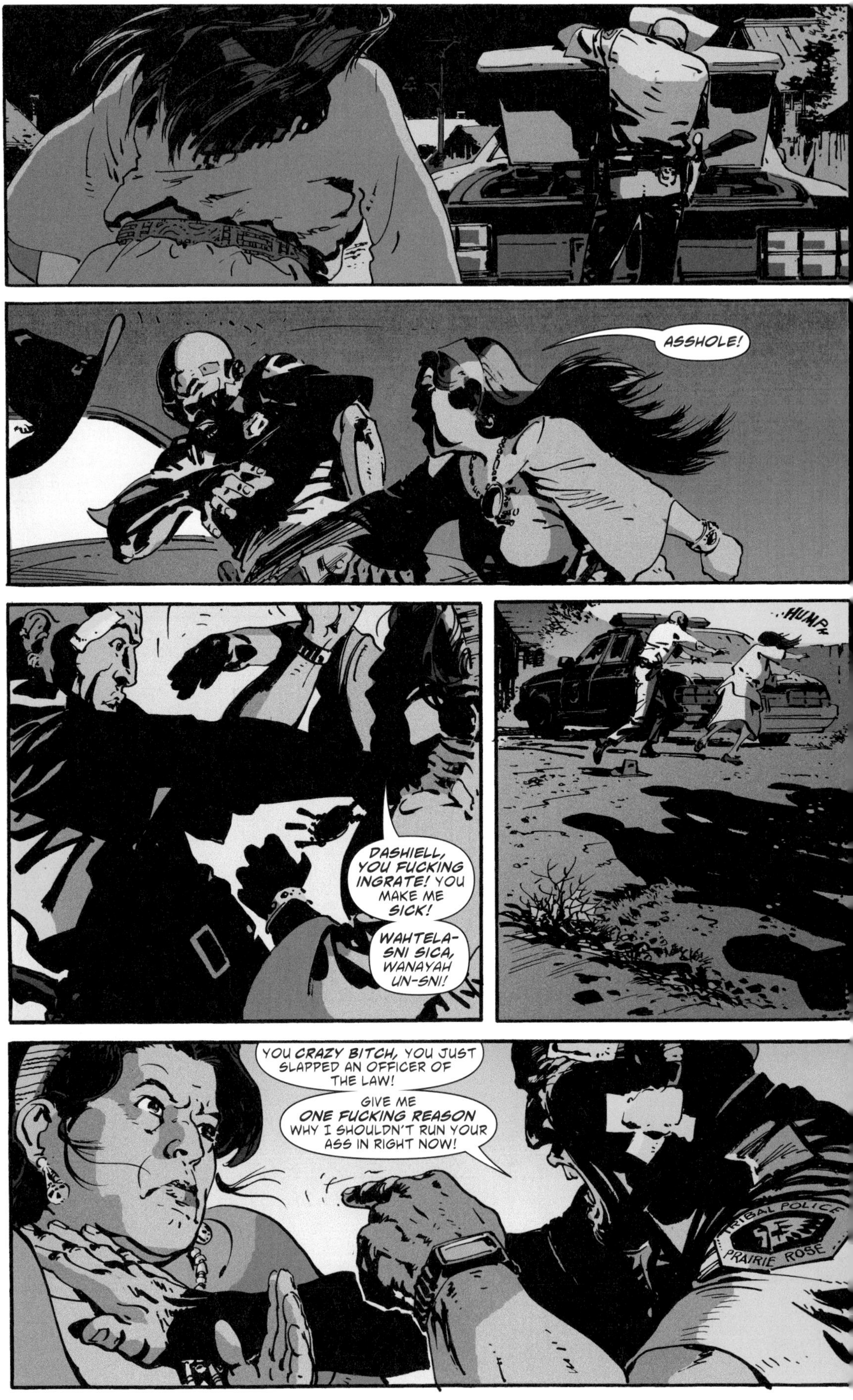
ASSHOLE!
DASHIELL, YOU FUCKING INGRATE! YOU MAKE ME SICK!
WAHTELA-SNI SICA, WANAYAH UN-SNI!
HUMPH
YOU CRAZY BITCH, YOU JUST SLAPPED AN OFFICER OF THE LAW!
GIVE ME ONE FUCKING REASON WHY I SHOULDN'T RUN YOUR ASS IN RIGHT NOW!
TRIBAL POLICE
PRAIRIE ROSE

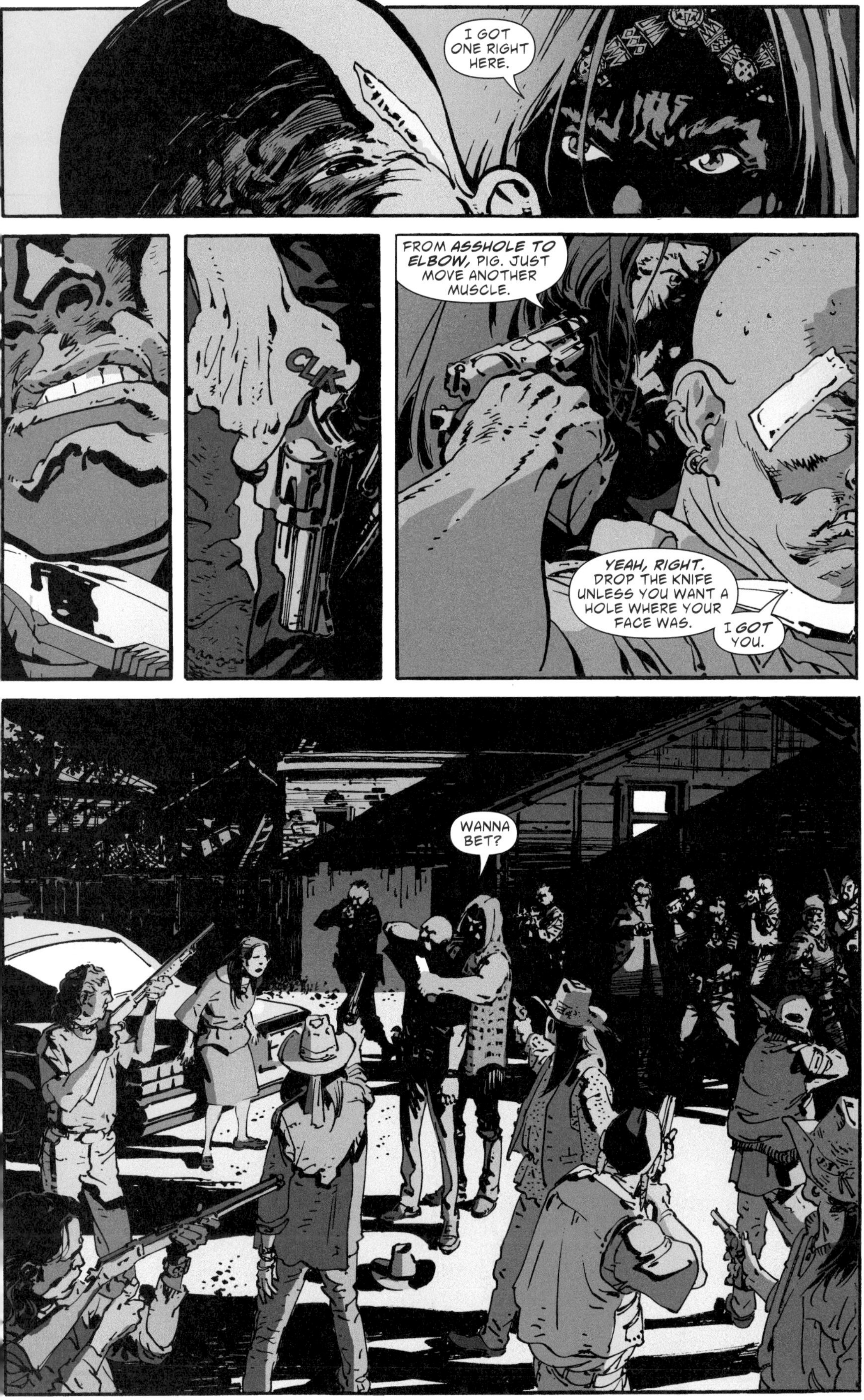
I GOT ONE RIGHT HERE.
CLIK
FROM ASSHOLE TO ELBOW, PIG. JUST MOVE ANOTHER MUSCLE.
YEAH, RIGHT. DROP THE KNIFE UNLESS YOU WANT A HOLE WHERE YOUR FACE WAS.
I GOT YOU.
WANNA BET?

NO! STOP THIS!

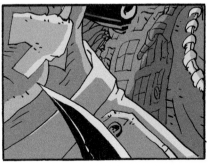

DIESEL, LET IT GO!

THIS *FASCIST PRICK* ISN'T WORTH IT.

HE'S JUST ANOTHER ONE OF RED CROW'S FLUNKIES...

HE'S NOTHING.

THAT THERE'S ONE FIERY-ASS FILLY.

I BET YA THIRTY YEARS AGO SHE COULD REALLY *FUCK* THE *TASTE* OUTTA YOUR MOUTH.

"I DON'T KNOW, SHUNKA...SEEMS LIKE A *COLD-HEARTED BITCH* TO ME.".

"YEAH, BAD HORSE? WELL, *YOU'D* KNOW, I GUESS...".

...SHE'S *YOUR* MOTHER.

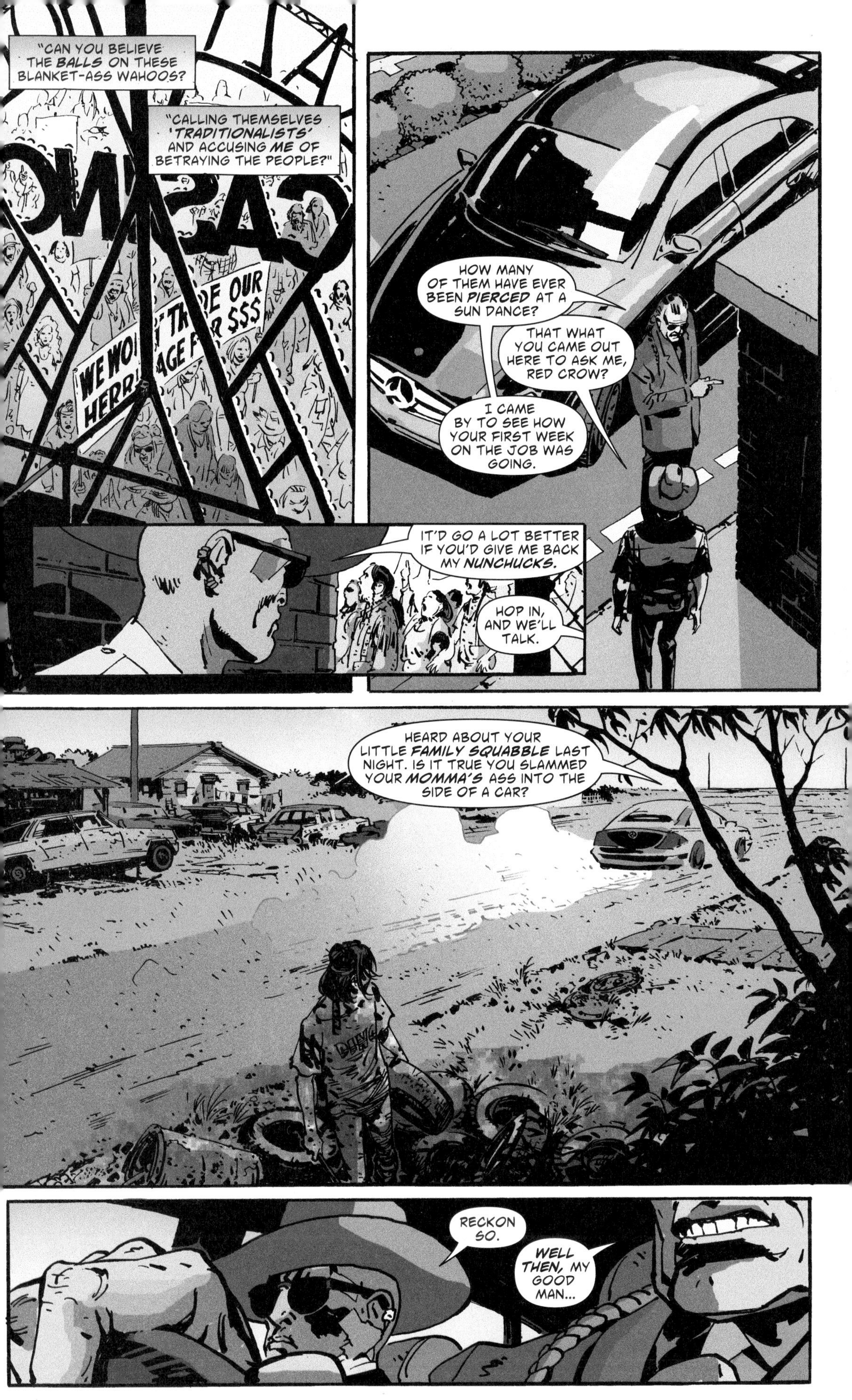
"CAN YOU BELIEVE THE BALLS ON THESE BLANKET-ASS WAHOOS?
"CALLING THEMSELVES 'TRADITIONALISTS' AND ACCUSING ME OF BETRAYING THE PEOPLE?"
HOW MANY OF THEM HAVE EVER BEEN PIERCED AT A SUN DANCE?
THAT WHAT YOU CAME OUT HERE TO ASK ME, RED CROW?
I CAME BY TO SEE HOW YOUR FIRST WEEK ON THE JOB WAS GOING.
IT'D GO A LOT BETTER IF YOU'D GIVE ME BACK MY NUNCHUCKS.
HOP IN, AND WE'LL TALK.
HEARD ABOUT YOUR LITTLE FAMILY SQUABBLE LAST NIGHT. IS IT TRUE YOU SLAMMED YOUR MOMMA'S ASS INTO THE SIDE OF A CAR?
RECKON SO.
WELL THEN, MY GOOD MAN...

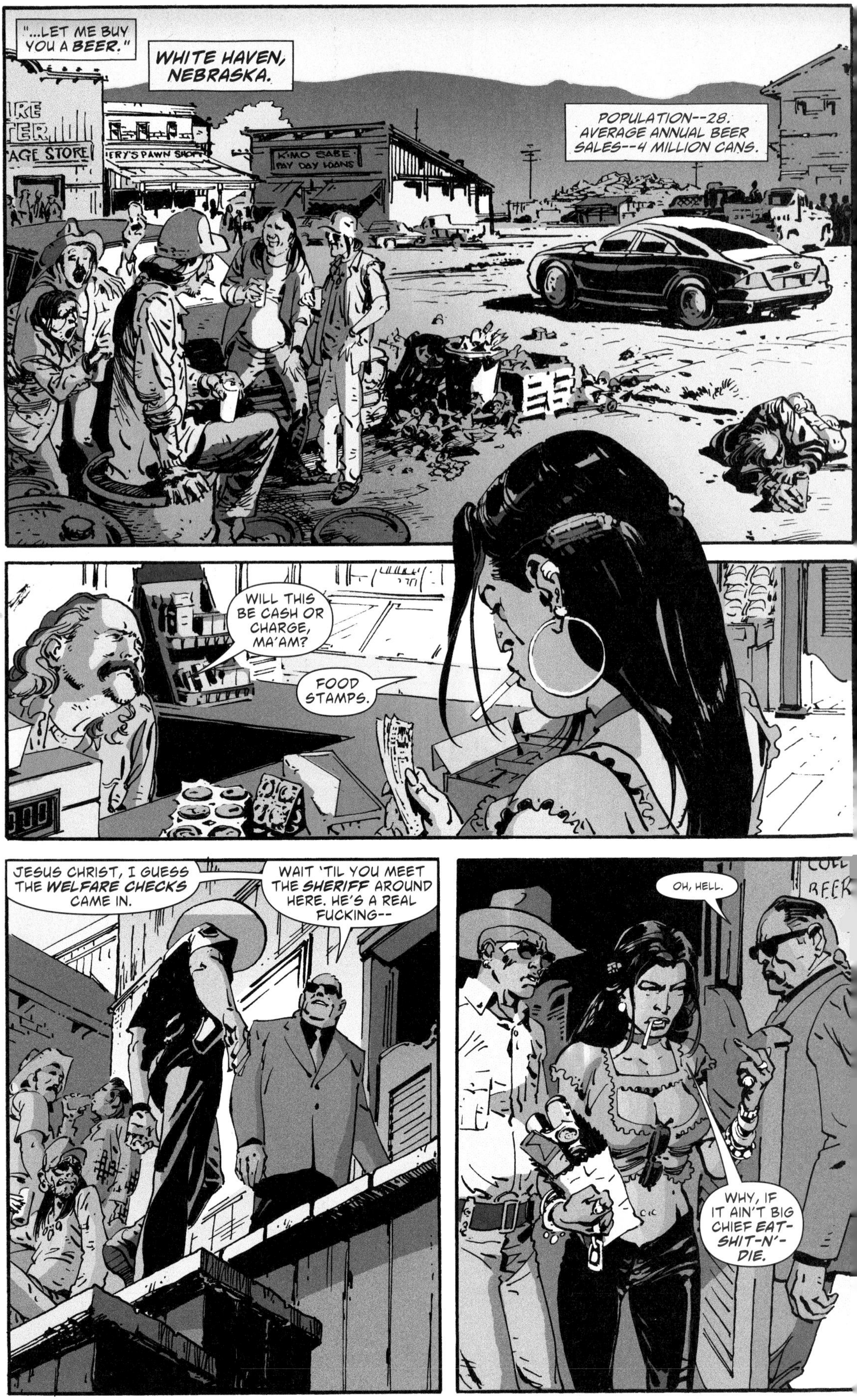
"...LET ME BUY YOU A BEER."
WHITE HAVEN, NEBRASKA.
POPULATION--28. AVERAGE ANNUAL BEER SALES--4 MILLION CANS.
WILL THIS BE CASH OR CHARGE, MA'AM?
FOOD STAMPS.
JESUS CHRIST, I GUESS THE WELFARE CHECKS CAME IN.
WAIT 'TIL YOU MEET THE SHERIFF AROUND HERE. HE'S A REAL FUCKING--
OH, HELL.
WHY, IF IT AIN'T BIG CHIEF EAT-SHIT-N'-DIE.

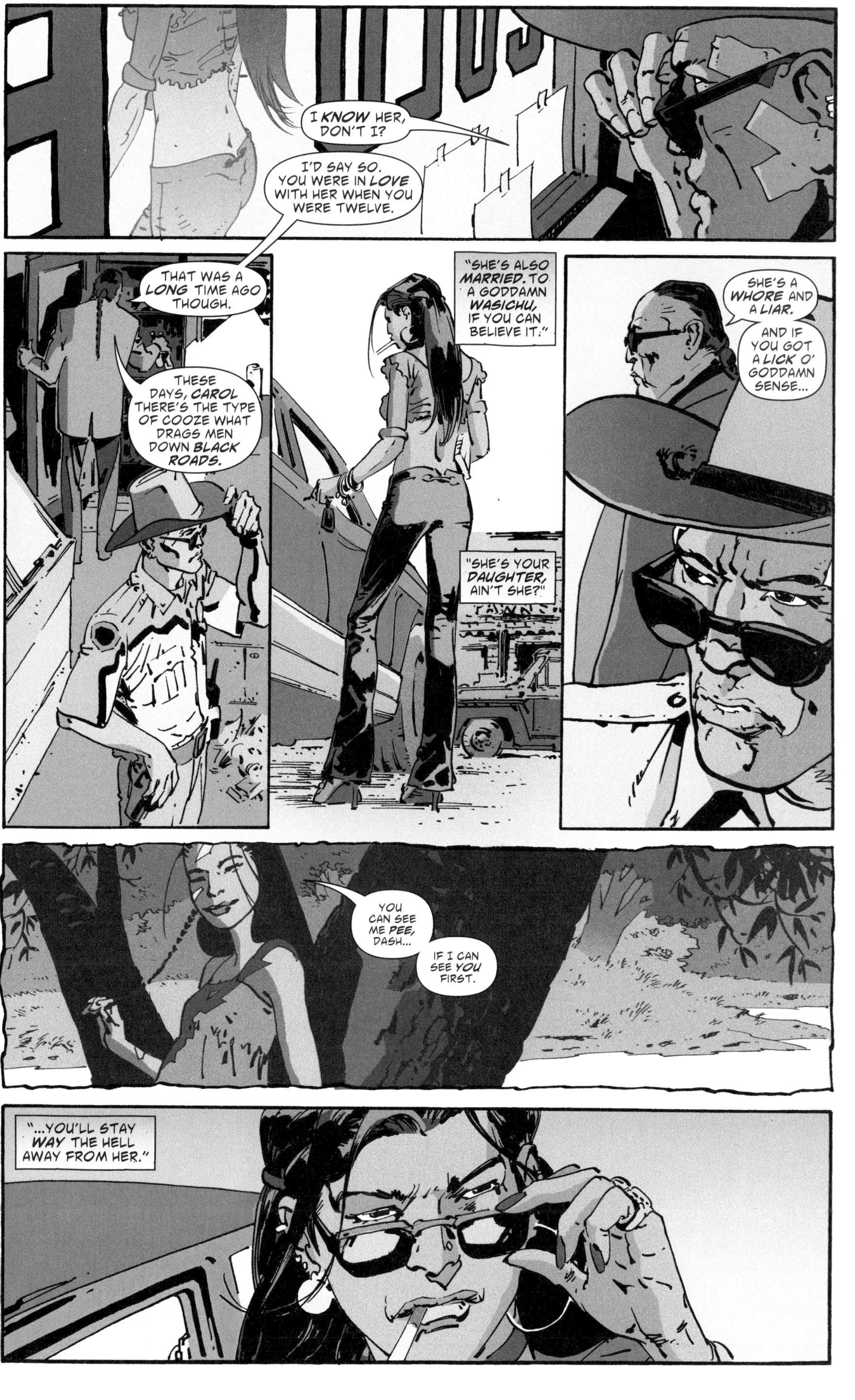

I KNOW HER, DON'T I?
I'D SAY SO. YOU WERE IN LOVE WITH HER WHEN YOU WERE TWELVE.
THAT WAS A LONG TIME AGO THOUGH.
THESE DAYS, CAROL THERE'S THE TYPE OF COOZE WHAT DRAGS MEN DOWN BLACK ROADS.
"SHE'S ALSO MARRIED. TO A GODDAMN WASICHU, IF YOU CAN BELIEVE IT."
"SHE'S YOUR DAUGHTER, AIN'T SHE?"
SHE'S A WHORE AND A LIAR.
AND IF YOU GOT A LICK O' GODDAMN SENSE...
YOU CAN SEE ME PEE, DASH...
IF I CAN SEE YOU FIRST.
"...YOU'LL STAY WAY THE HELL AWAY FROM HER."

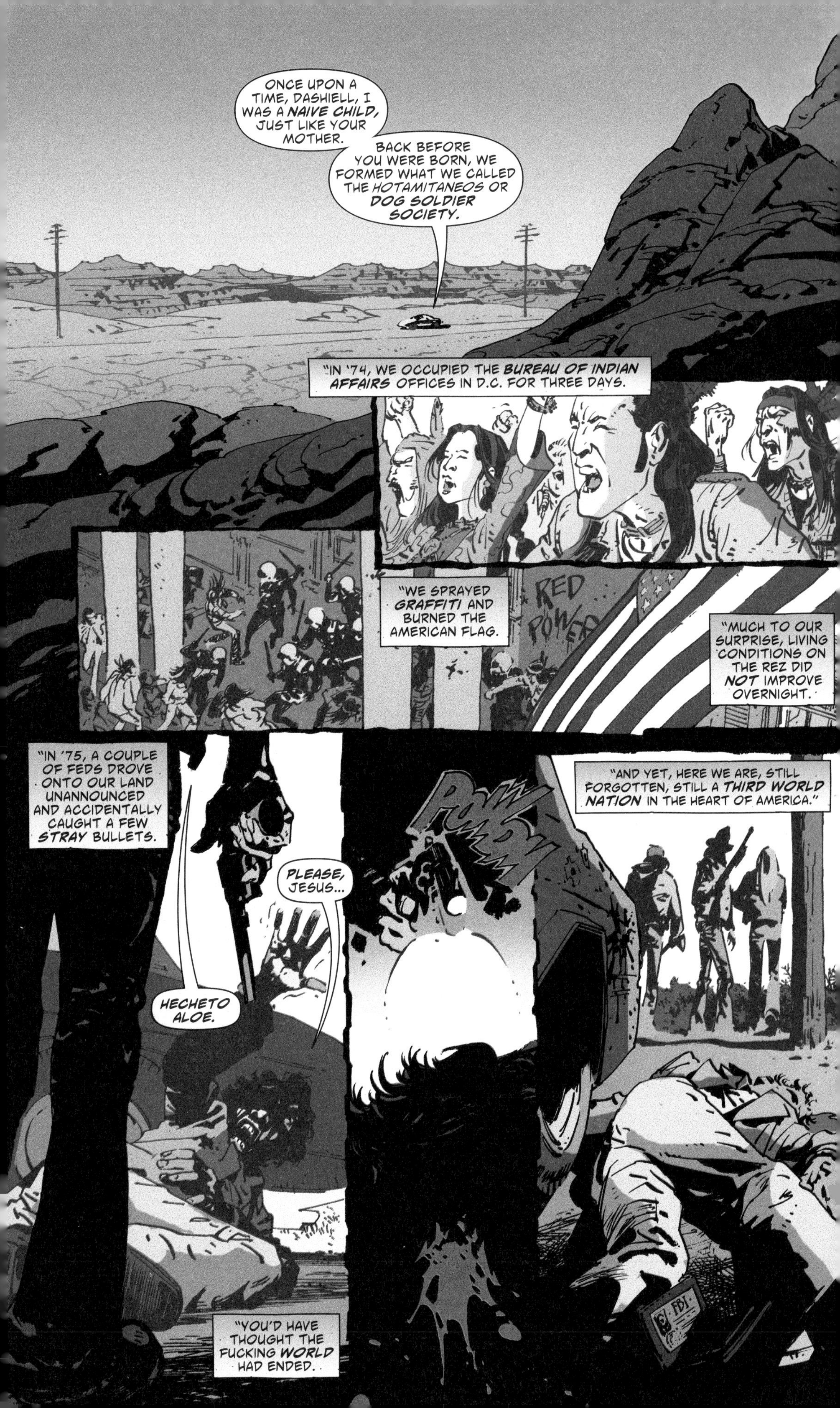

ONCE UPON A TIME, DASHIELL, I WAS A NAIVE CHILD, JUST LIKE YOUR MOTHER.
BACK BEFORE YOU WERE BORN, WE FORMED WHAT WE CALLED THE HOTAMITANEOS OR DOG SOLDIER SOCIETY.
"IN '74, WE OCCUPIED THE BUREAU OF INDIAN AFFAIRS OFFICES IN D.C. FOR THREE DAYS.
"WE SPRAYED GRAFFITI AND BURNED THE AMERICAN FLAG.
RED POWER
"MUCH TO OUR SURPRISE, LIVING CONDITIONS ON THE REZ DID NOT IMPROVE OVERNIGHT.
"IN '75, A COUPLE OF FEDS DROVE ONTO OUR LAND UNANNOUNCED AND ACCIDENTALLY CAUGHT A FEW STRAY BULLETS.
POW
PLEASE, JESUS...
HECHETO ALOE.
"AND YET, HERE WE ARE, STILL FORGOTTEN, STILL A THIRD WORLD NATION IN THE HEART OF AMERICA."
"YOU'D HAVE THOUGHT THE FUCKING WORLD HAD ENDED.
FBI

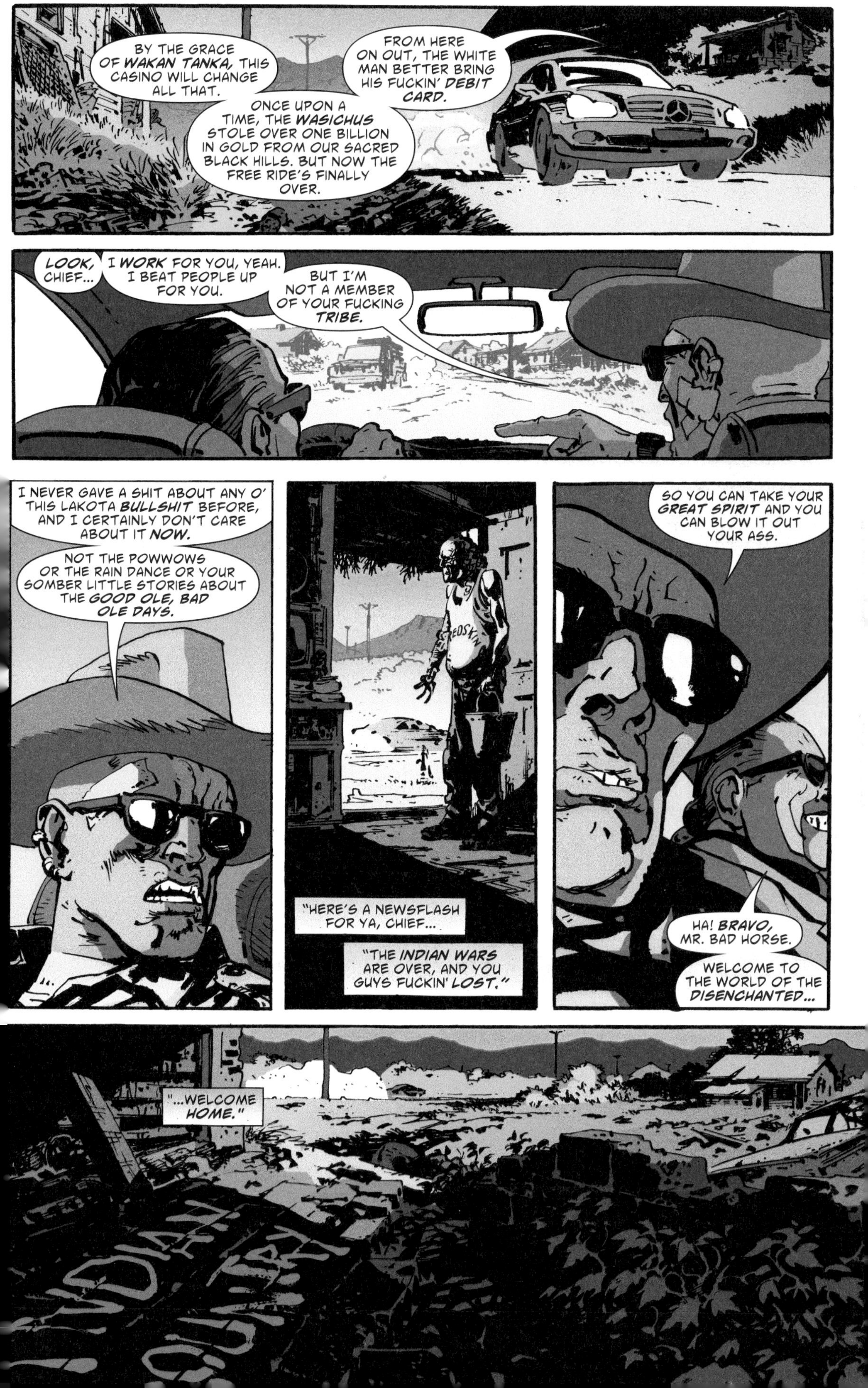
BY THE GRACE OF WAKAN TANKA, THIS CASINO WILL CHANGE ALL THAT.
ONCE UPON A TIME, THE WASICHUS STOLE OVER ONE BILLION IN GOLD FROM OUR SACRED BLACK HILLS. BUT NOW THE FREE RIDE'S FINALLY OVER.
FROM HERE ON OUT, THE WHITE MAN BETTER BRING HIS FUCKIN' DEBIT CARD.
LOOK, CHIEF...
I WORK FOR YOU, YEAH. I BEAT PEOPLE UP FOR YOU.
BUT I'M NOT A MEMBER OF YOUR FUCKING TRIBE.
I NEVER GAVE A SHIT ABOUT ANY O' THIS LAKOTA BULLSHIT BEFORE, AND I CERTAINLY DON'T CARE ABOUT IT NOW.
NOT THE POWWOWS OR THE RAIN DANCE OR YOUR SOMBER LITTLE STORIES ABOUT THE GOOD OLE, BAD OLE DAYS.
"HERE'S A NEWSFLASH FOR YA, CHIEF...
"THE INDIAN WARS ARE OVER, AND YOU GUYS FUCKIN' LOST."
SO YOU CAN TAKE YOUR GREAT SPIRIT AND YOU CAN BLOW IT OUT YOUR ASS.
HA! BRAVO, MR. BAD HORSE.
WELCOME TO THE WORLD OF THE DISENCHANTED...
"...WELCOME HOME."

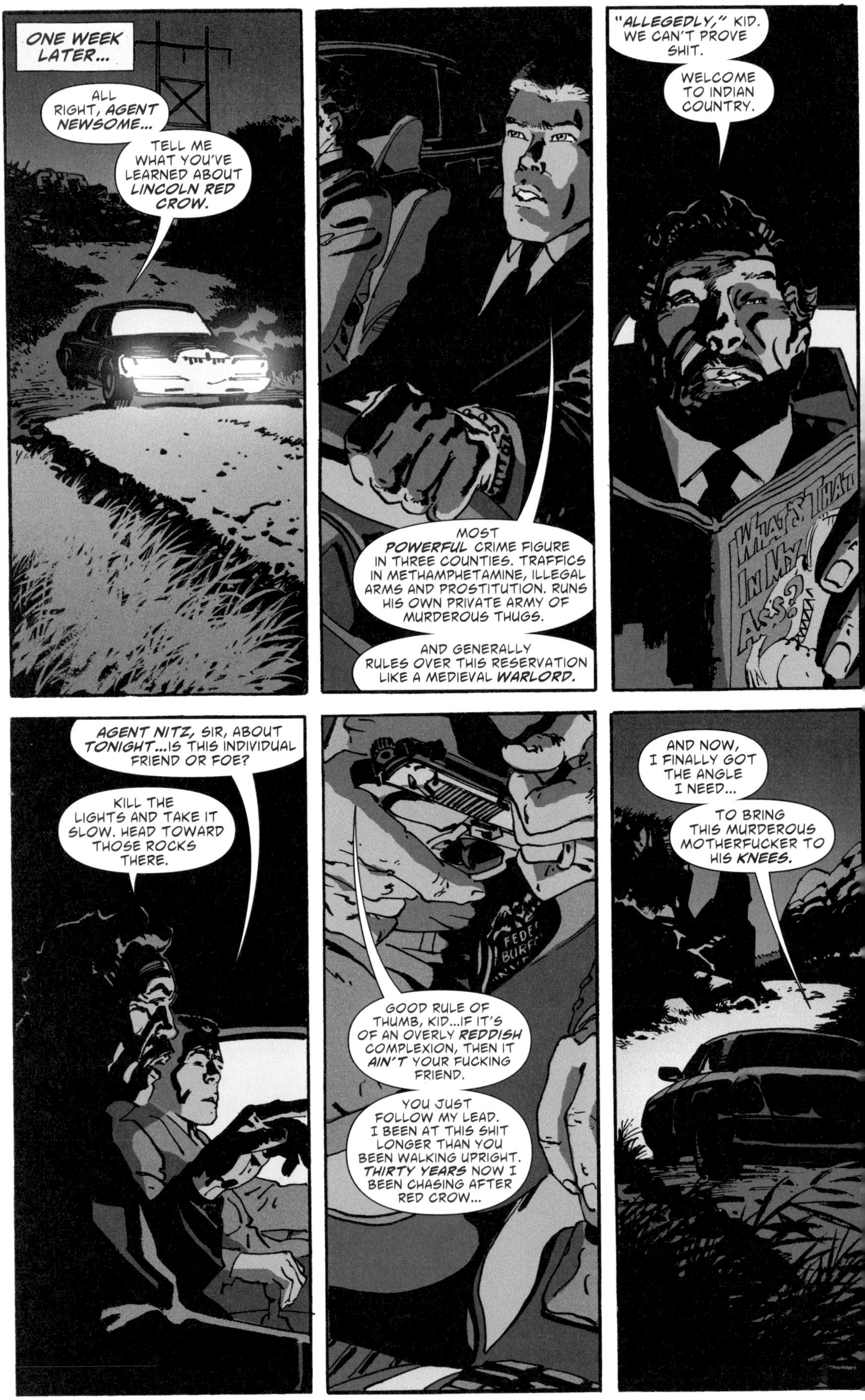
ONE WEEK LATER...
ALL RIGHT, AGENT NEWSOME...
TELL ME WHAT YOU'VE LEARNED ABOUT LINCOLN RED CROW.
MOST POWERFUL CRIME FIGURE IN THREE COUNTIES. TRAFFICS IN METHAMPHETAMINE, ILLEGAL ARMS AND PROSTITUTION. RUNS HIS OWN PRIVATE ARMY OF MURDEROUS THUGS.
AND GENERALLY RULES OVER THIS RESERVATION LIKE A MEDIEVAL WARLORD.
"ALLEGEDLY," KID. WE CAN'T PROVE SHIT.
WELCOME TO INDIAN COUNTRY.
AGENT NITZ, SIR, ABOUT TONIGHT...IS THIS INDIVIDUAL FRIEND OR FOE?
KILL THE LIGHTS AND TAKE IT SLOW. HEAD TOWARD THOSE ROCKS THERE.
GOOD RULE OF THUMB, KID...IF IT'S OF AN OVERLY REDDISH COMPLEXION, THEN IT AIN'T YOUR FUCKING FRIEND.
YOU JUST FOLLOW MY LEAD. I BEEN AT THIS SHIT LONGER THAN YOU BEEN WALKING UPRIGHT. THIRTY YEARS NOW I BEEN CHASING AFTER RED CROW...
AND NOW, I FINALLY GOT THE ANGLE I NEED...
TO BRING THIS MURDEROUS MOTHERFUCKER TO HIS KNEES.

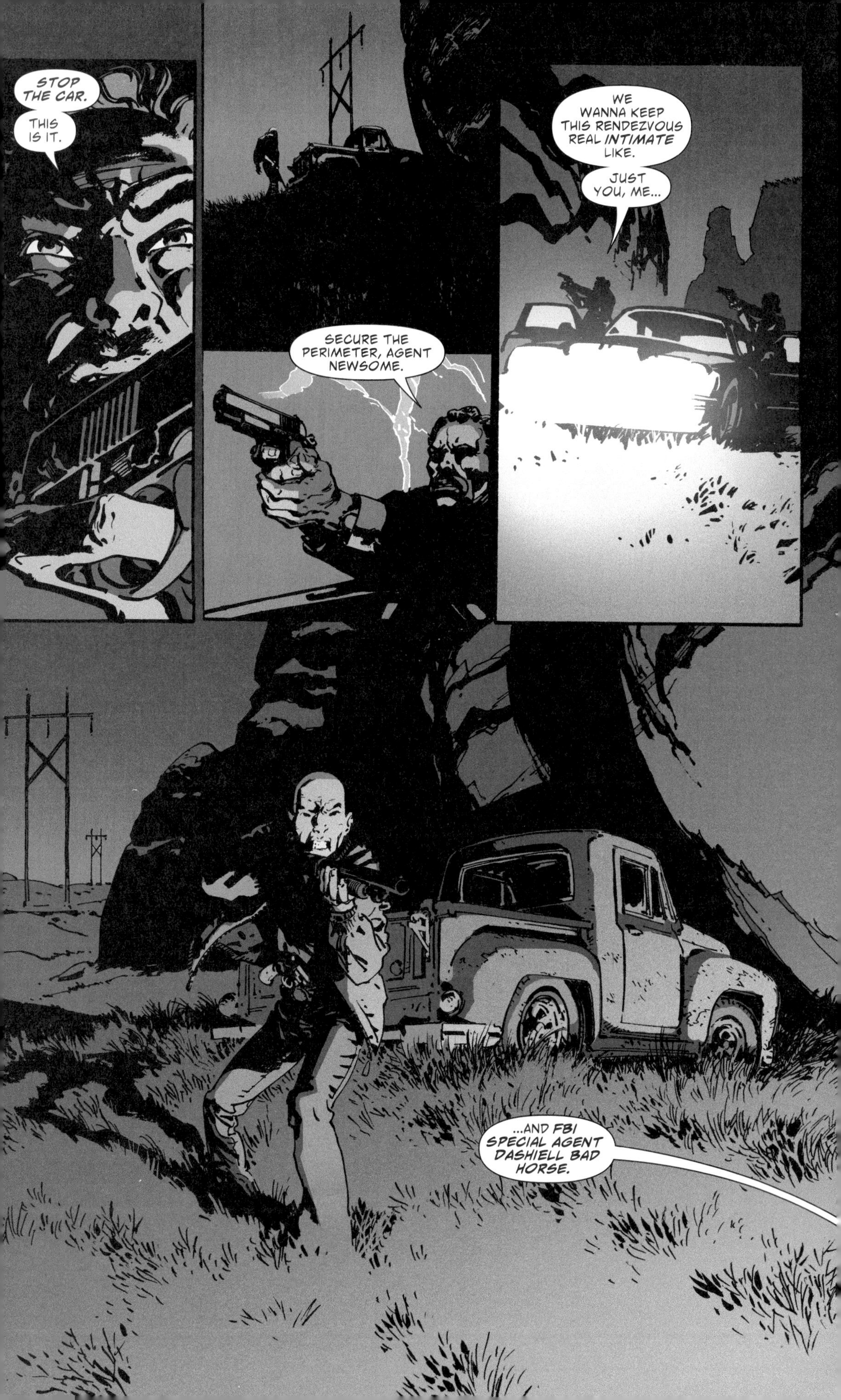
STOP THE CAR.
THIS IS IT.
SECURE THE PERIMETER, AGENT NEWSOME.
WE WANNA KEEP THIS RENDEZVOUS REAL INTIMATE LIKE.
JUST YOU, ME...
...AND FBI SPECIAL AGENT DASHIELL BAD HORSE.

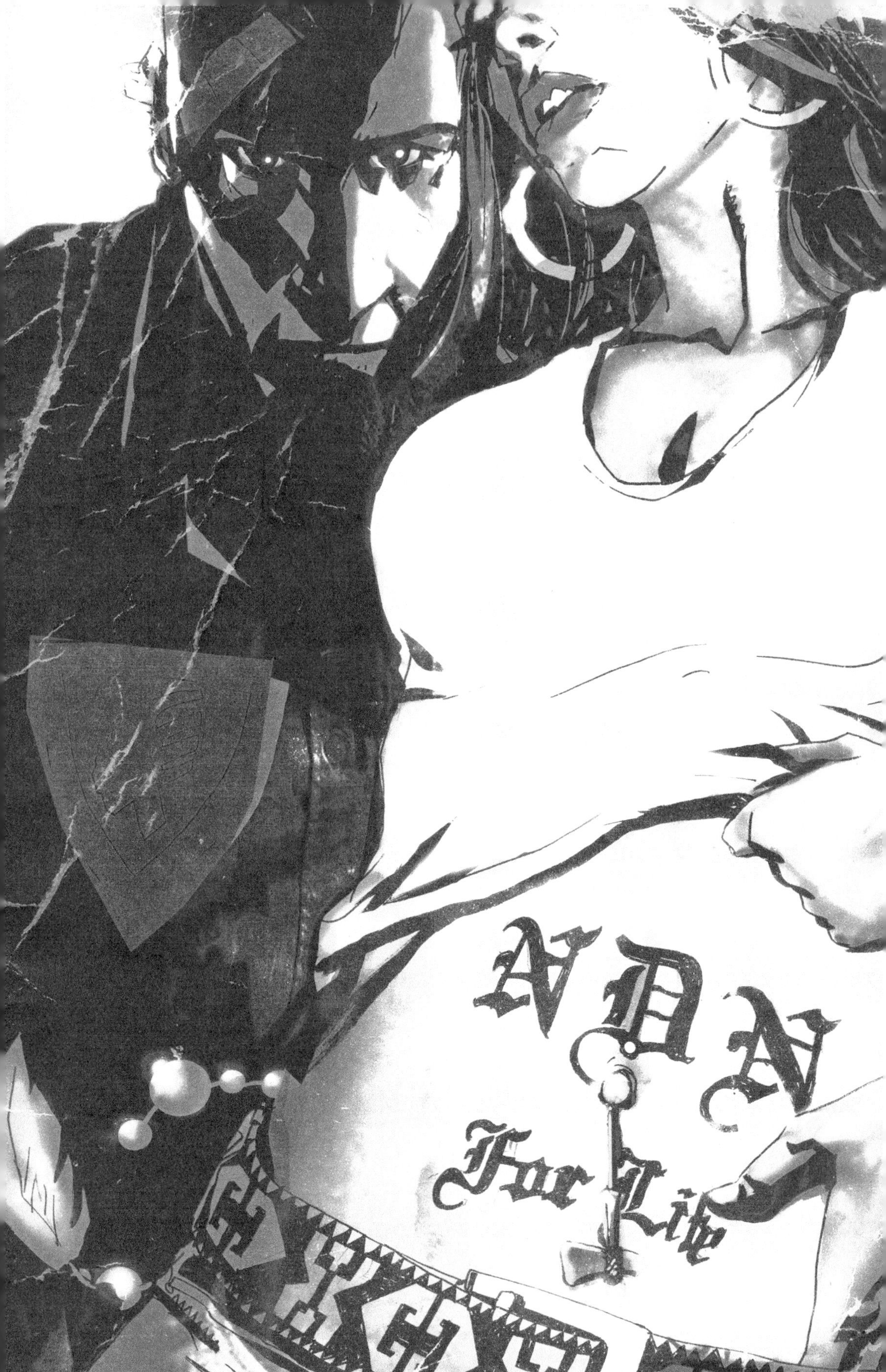
NDN
For Life

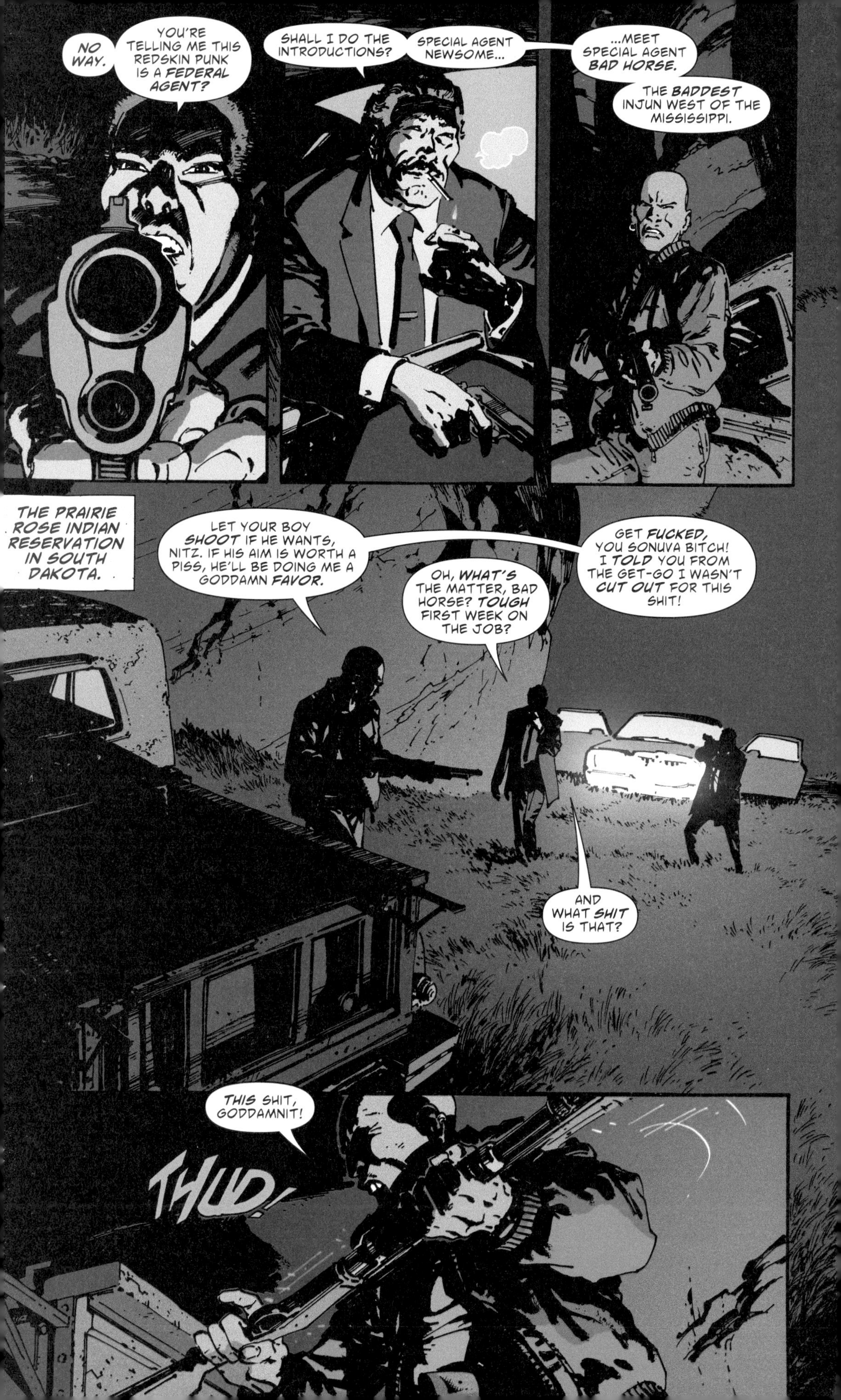
NO WAY.
YOU'RE TELLING ME THIS REDSKIN PUNK IS A FEDERAL AGENT?
SHALL I DO THE INTRODUCTIONS?
SPECIAL AGENT NEWSOME...
...MEET SPECIAL AGENT BAD HORSE.
THE BADDEST INJUN WEST OF THE MISSISSIPPI.
THE PRAIRIE ROSE INDIAN RESERVATION IN SOUTH DAKOTA.
LET YOUR BOY SHOOT IF HE WANTS, NITZ. IF HIS AIM IS WORTH A PISS, HE'LL BE DOING ME A GODDAMN FAVOR.
GET FUCKED, YOU SONUVA BITCH! I TOLD YOU FROM THE GET-GO I WASN'T CUT OUT FOR THIS SHIT!
OH, WHAT'S THE MATTER, BAD HORSE? TOUGH FIRST WEEK ON THE JOB?
AND WHAT SHIT IS THAT?
THIS SHIT, GODDAMNIT!
THUD!

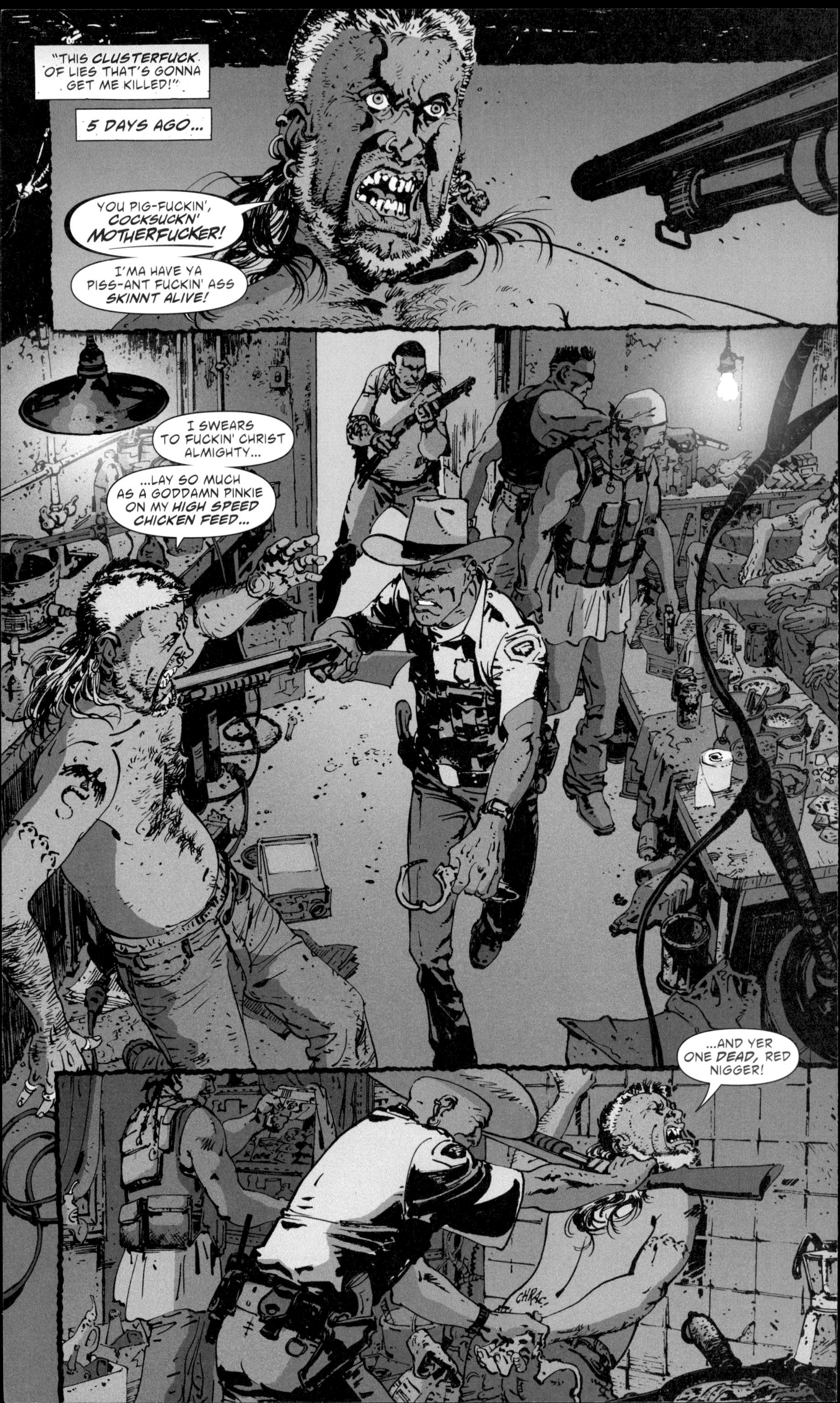

"THIS CLUSTERFUCK OF LIES THAT'S GONNA GET ME KILLED!"
5 DAYS AGO...
YOU PIG-FUCKIN', COCKSUCKN' MOTHERFUCKER!
I'MA HAVE YA PISS-ANT FUCKIN' ASS SKINNT ALIVE!
I SWEARS TO FUCKIN' CHRIST ALMIGHTY...
...LAY SO MUCH AS A GODDAMN PINKIE ON MY HIGH SPEED CHICKEN FEED...
...AND YER ONE DEAD, RED NIGGER!
CHRAC!

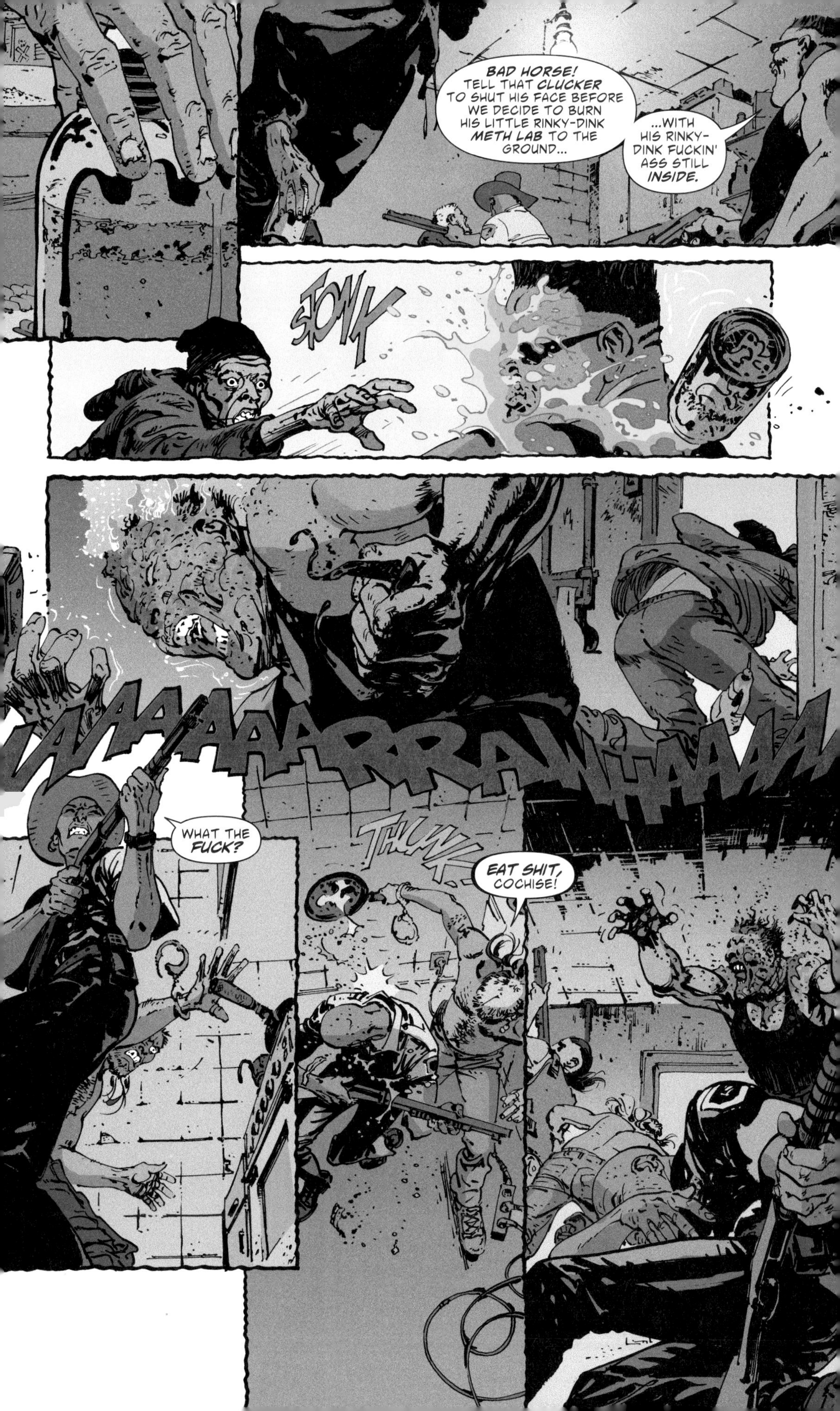
BAD HORSE! TELL THAT CLUCKER TO SHUT HIS FACE BEFORE WE DECIDE TO BURN HIS LITTLE RINKY-DINK METH LAB TO THE GROUND...
...WITH HIS RINKY-DINK FUCKIN' ASS STILL INSIDE.
STONK
AAAAARRRAWHAAAA
WHAT THE FUCK?
THUNK
EAT SHIT, COCHISE!

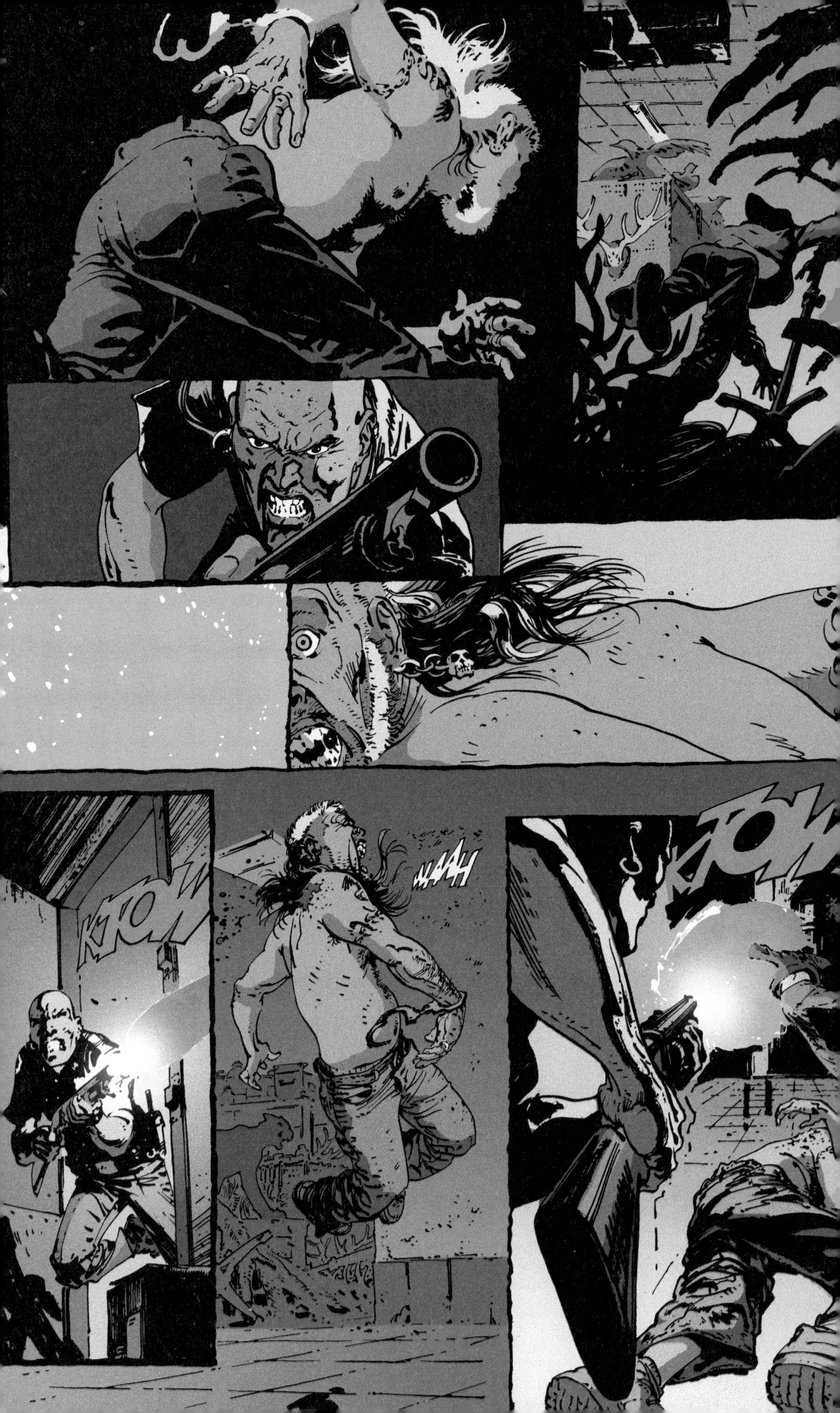
KTOW
AAAH
KTOW

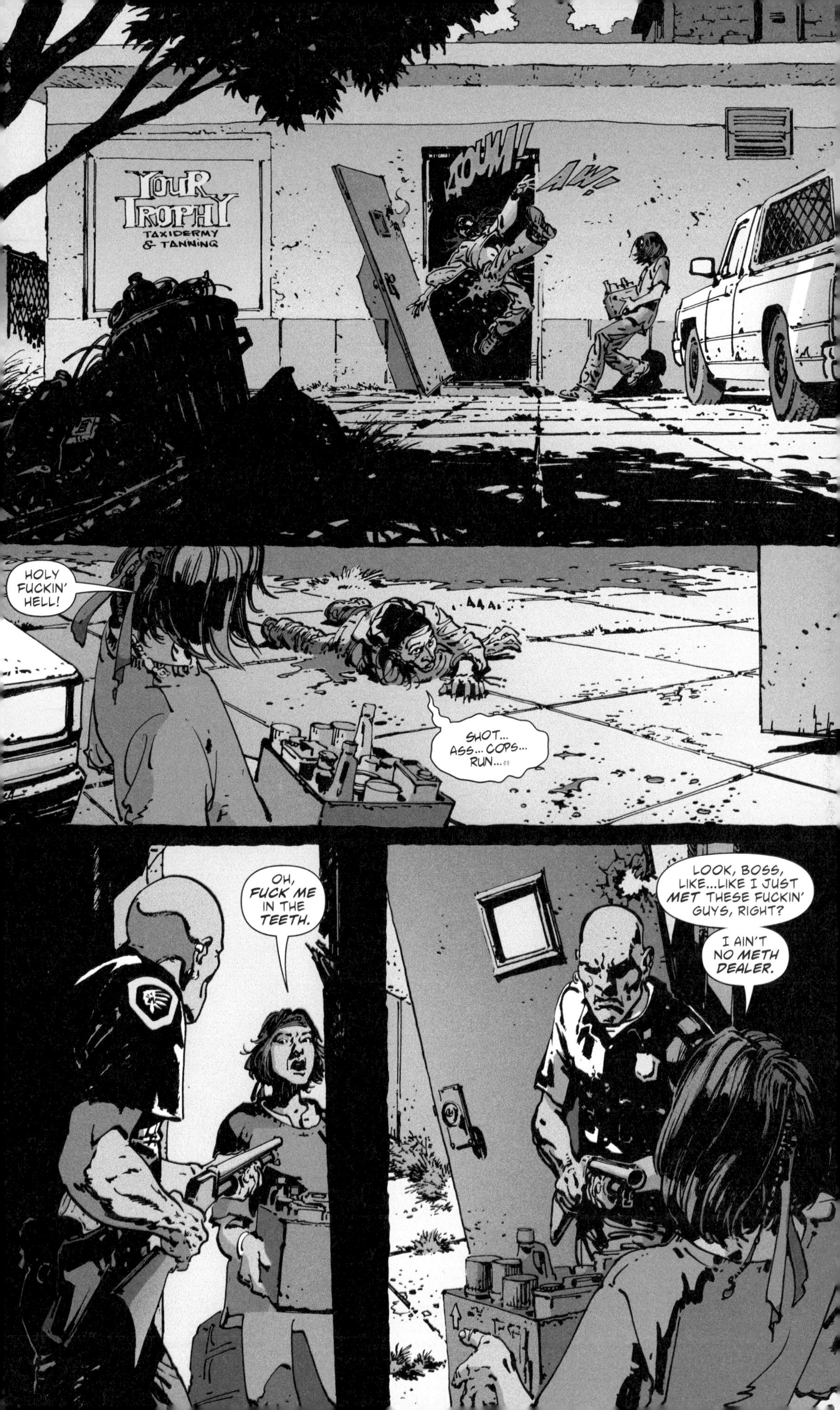
YOUR TROPHY
TAXIDERMY & TANNING
KOOM!!
AH!!
HOLY FUCKIN' HELL!
SHOT... ASS... COPS... RUN...
OH, FUCK ME IN THE TEETH.
LOOK, BOSS, LIKE...LIKE I JUST MET THESE FUCKIN' GUYS, RIGHT?
I AIN'T NO METH DEALER.

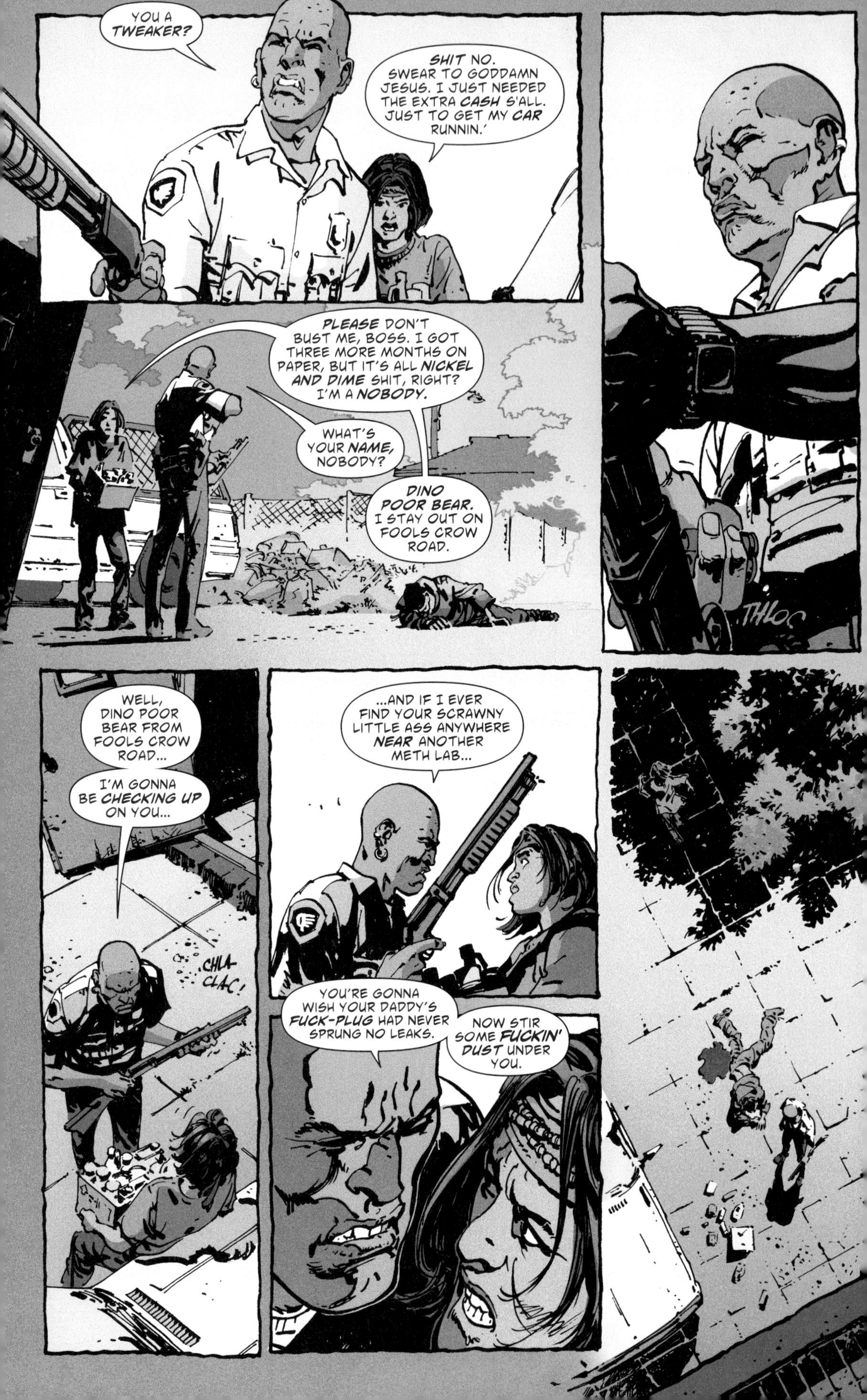

YOU A TWEAKER?
SHIT NO. SWEAR TO GODDAMN JESUS. I JUST NEEDED THE EXTRA CASH S'ALL. JUST TO GET MY CAR RUNNIN.'
PLEASE DON'T BUST ME, BOSS. I GOT THREE MORE MONTHS ON PAPER, BUT IT'S ALL NICKEL AND DIME SHIT, RIGHT? I'M A NOBODY.
WHAT'S YOUR NAME, NOBODY?
DINO POOR BEAR. I STAY OUT ON FOOLS CROW ROAD.
WELL, DINO POOR BEAR FROM FOOLS CROW ROAD...
I'M GONNA BE CHECKING UP ON YOU...
CHLA CLAC!
...AND IF I EVER FIND YOUR SCRAWNY LITTLE ASS ANYWHERE NEAR ANOTHER METH LAB...
YOU'RE GONNA WISH YOUR DADDY'S FUCK-PLUG HAD NEVER SPRUNG NO LEAKS.
NOW STIR SOME FUCKIN' DUST UNDER YOU.

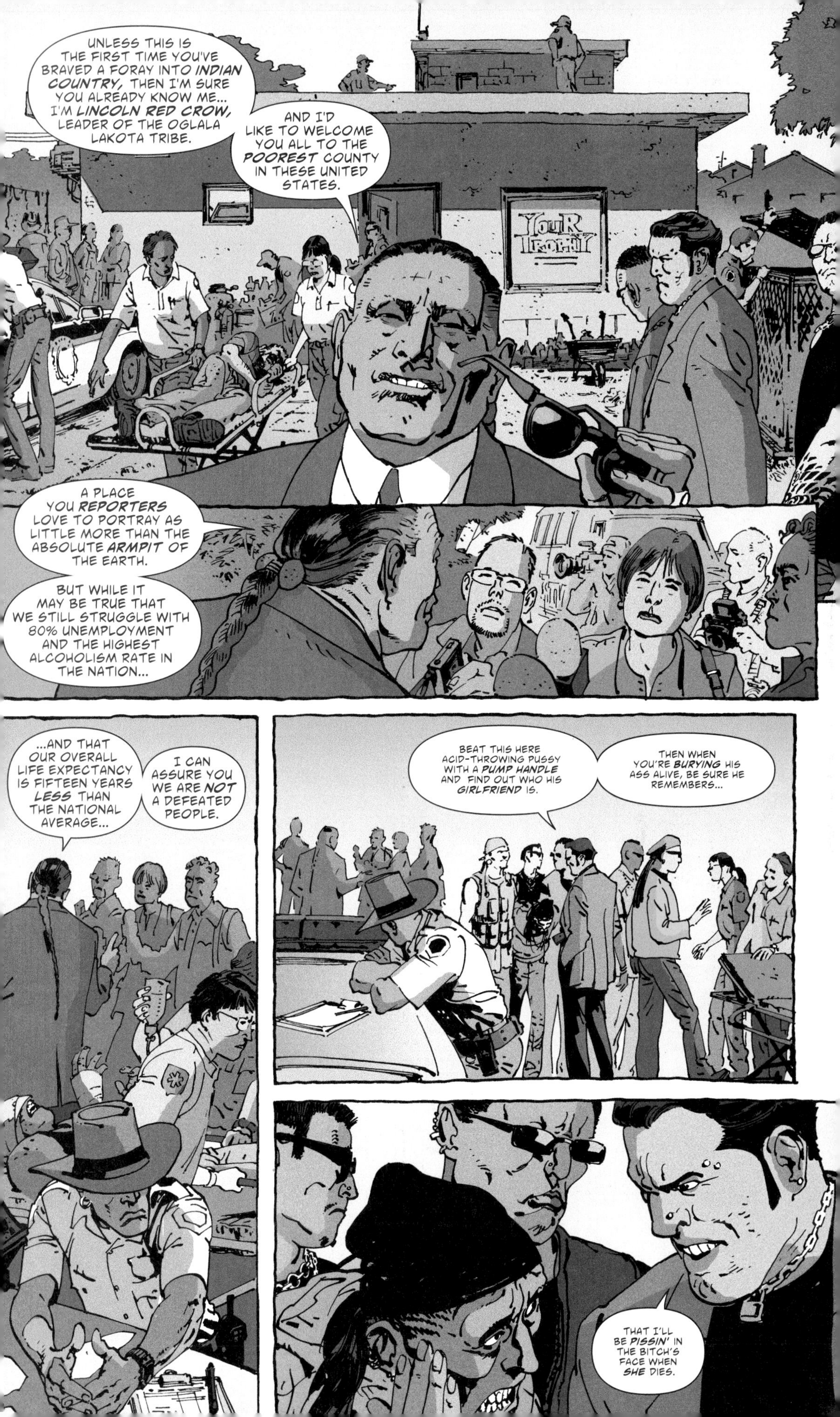
UNLESS THIS IS THE FIRST TIME YOU'VE BRAVED A FORAY INTO INDIAN COUNTRY, THEN I'M SURE YOU ALREADY KNOW ME... I'M LINCOLN RED CROW, LEADER OF THE OGLALA LAKOTA TRIBE.
AND I'D LIKE TO WELCOME YOU ALL TO THE POOREST COUNTY IN THESE UNITED STATES.
YOUR TROPHY
A PLACE YOU REPORTERS LOVE TO PORTRAY AS LITTLE MORE THAN THE ABSOLUTE ARMPIT OF THE EARTH.
BUT WHILE IT MAY BE TRUE THAT WE STILL STRUGGLE WITH 80% UNEMPLOYMENT AND THE HIGHEST ALCOHOLISM RATE IN THE NATION...
...AND THAT OUR OVERALL LIFE EXPECTANCY IS FIFTEEN YEARS LESS THAN THE NATIONAL AVERAGE...
I CAN ASSURE YOU WE ARE NOT A DEFEATED PEOPLE.
BEAT THIS HERE ACID-THROWING PUSSY WITH A PUMP HANDLE AND FIND OUT WHO HIS GIRLFRIEND IS.
THEN WHEN YOU'RE BURYING HIS ASS ALIVE, BE SURE HE REMEMBERS...
THAT I'LL BE PISSIN' IN THE BITCH'S FACE WHEN SHE DIES.

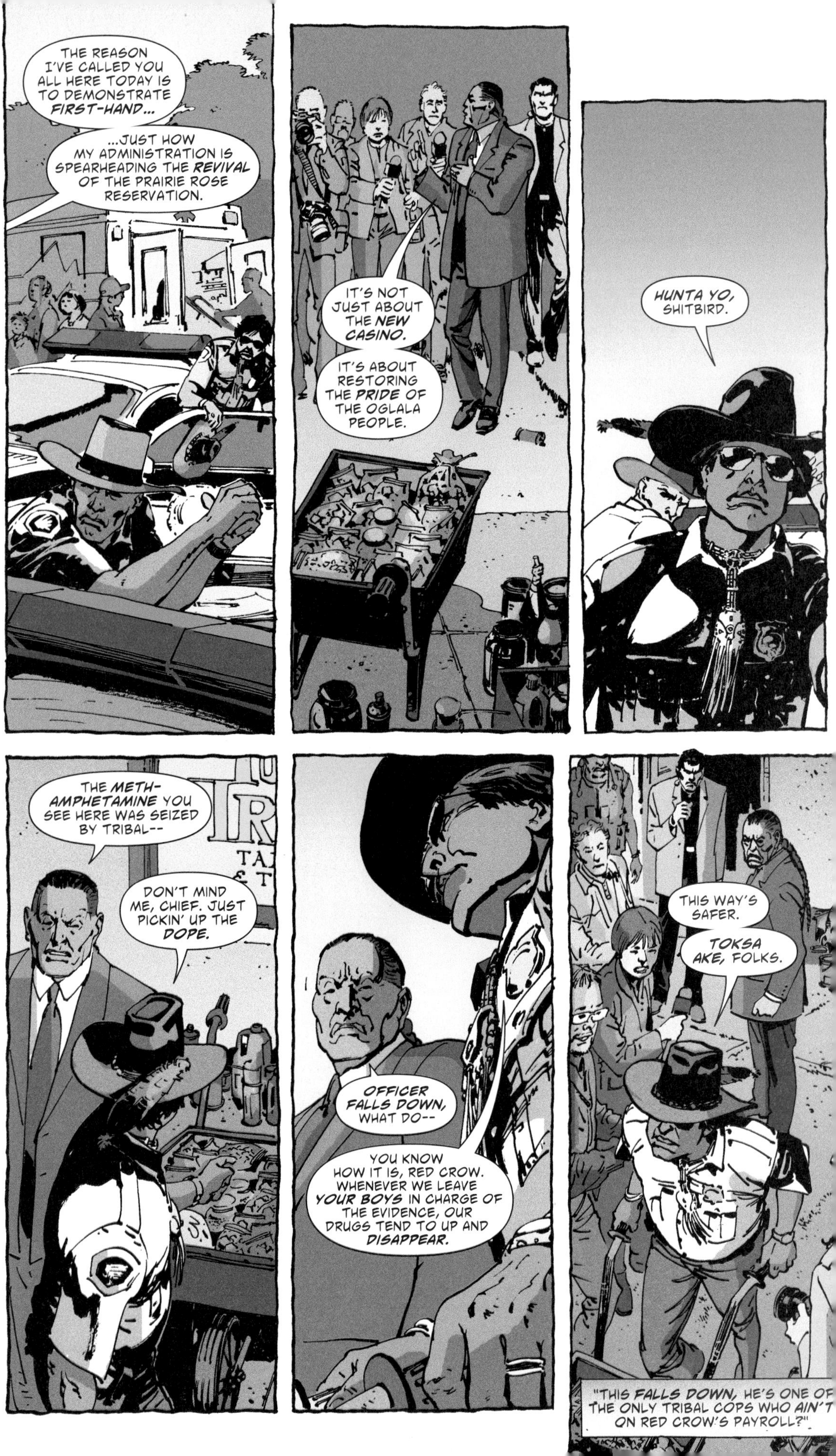
THE REASON I'VE CALLED YOU ALL HERE TODAY IS TO DEMONSTRATE FIRST-HAND...
...JUST HOW MY ADMINISTRATION IS SPEARHEADING THE REVIVAL OF THE PRAIRIE ROSE RESERVATION.
IT'S NOT JUST ABOUT THE NEW CASINO.
IT'S ABOUT RESTORING THE PRIDE OF THE OGLALA PEOPLE.
HUNTA YO, SHITBIRD.
THE METH-AMPHETAMINE YOU SEE HERE WAS SEIZED BY TRIBAL--
DON'T MIND ME, CHIEF. JUST PICKIN' UP THE DOPE.
OFFICER FALLS DOWN, WHAT DO--
YOU KNOW HOW IT IS, RED CROW. WHENEVER WE LEAVE YOUR BOYS IN CHARGE OF THE EVIDENCE, OUR DRUGS TEND TO UP AND DISAPPEAR.
THIS WAY'S SAFER.
TOKSA AKE, FOLKS.
"THIS FALLS DOWN, HE'S ONE OF THE ONLY TRIBAL COPS WHO AIN'T ON RED CROW'S PAYROLL?"

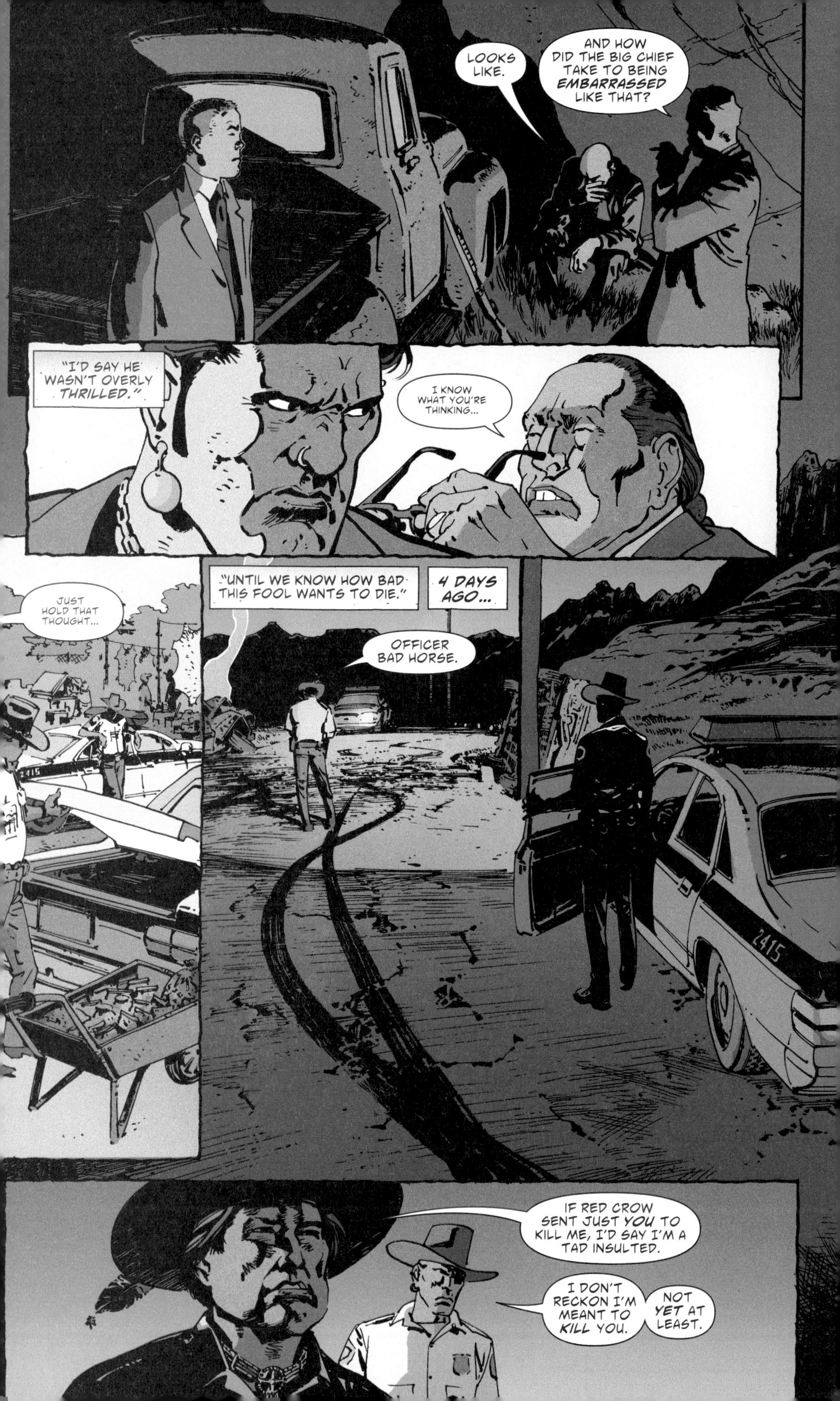
LOOKS LIKE.
AND HOW DID THE BIG CHIEF TAKE TO BEING EMBARRASSED LIKE THAT?
"I'D SAY HE WASN'T OVERLY THRILLED."
I KNOW WHAT YOU'RE THINKING...
JUST HOLD THAT THOUGHT...
"UNTIL WE KNOW HOW BAD THIS FOOL WANTS TO DIE."
4 DAYS AGO...
OFFICER BAD HORSE.
2415
IF RED CROW SENT JUST YOU TO KILL ME, I'D SAY I'M A TAD INSULTED.
I DON'T RECKON I'M MEANT TO KILL YOU.
NOT YET AT LEAST.

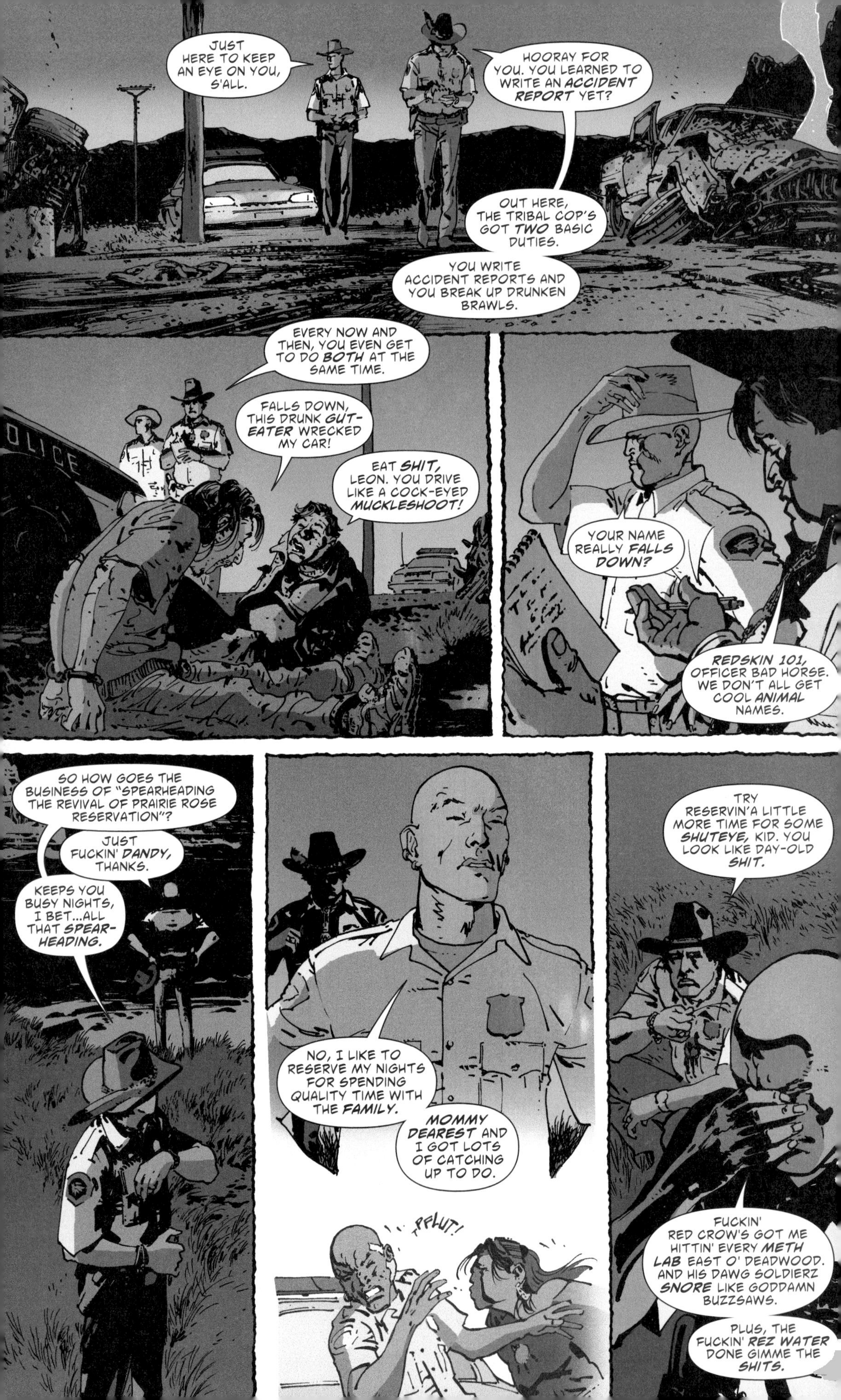
JUST HERE TO KEEP AN EYE ON YOU, S'ALL.
HOORAY FOR YOU. YOU LEARNED TO WRITE AN ACCIDENT REPORT YET?
OUT HERE, THE TRIBAL COP'S GOT TWO BASIC DUTIES.
YOU WRITE ACCIDENT REPORTS AND YOU BREAK UP DRUNKEN BRAWLS.
EVERY NOW AND THEN, YOU EVEN GET TO DO BOTH AT THE SAME TIME.
FALLS DOWN, THIS DRUNK GUT-EATER WRECKED MY CAR!
EAT SHIT, LEON. YOU DRIVE LIKE A COCK-EYED MUCKLESHOOT!
POLICE
YOUR NAME REALLY FALLS DOWN?
REDSKIN 101, OFFICER BAD HORSE. WE DON'T ALL GET COOL ANIMAL NAMES.
SO HOW GOES THE BUSINESS OF "SPEARHEADING THE REVIVAL OF PRAIRIE ROSE RESERVATION"?
JUST FUCKIN' DANDY, THANKS.
KEEPS YOU BUSY NIGHTS, I BET...ALL THAT SPEAR-HEADING.
NO, I LIKE TO RESERVE MY NIGHTS FOR SPENDING QUALITY TIME WITH THE FAMILY.
MOMMY DEAREST AND I GOT LOTS OF CATCHING UP TO DO.
PFLUT!
TRY RESERVIN' A LITTLE MORE TIME FOR SOME SHUTEYE, KID. YOU LOOK LIKE DAY-OLD SHIT.
FUCKIN' RED CROW'S GOT ME HITTIN' EVERY METH LAB EAST O' DEADWOOD. AND HIS DAWG SOLDIERZ SNORE LIKE GODDAMN BUZZSAWS.
PLUS, THE FUCKIN' REZ WATER DONE GIMME THE SHITS.

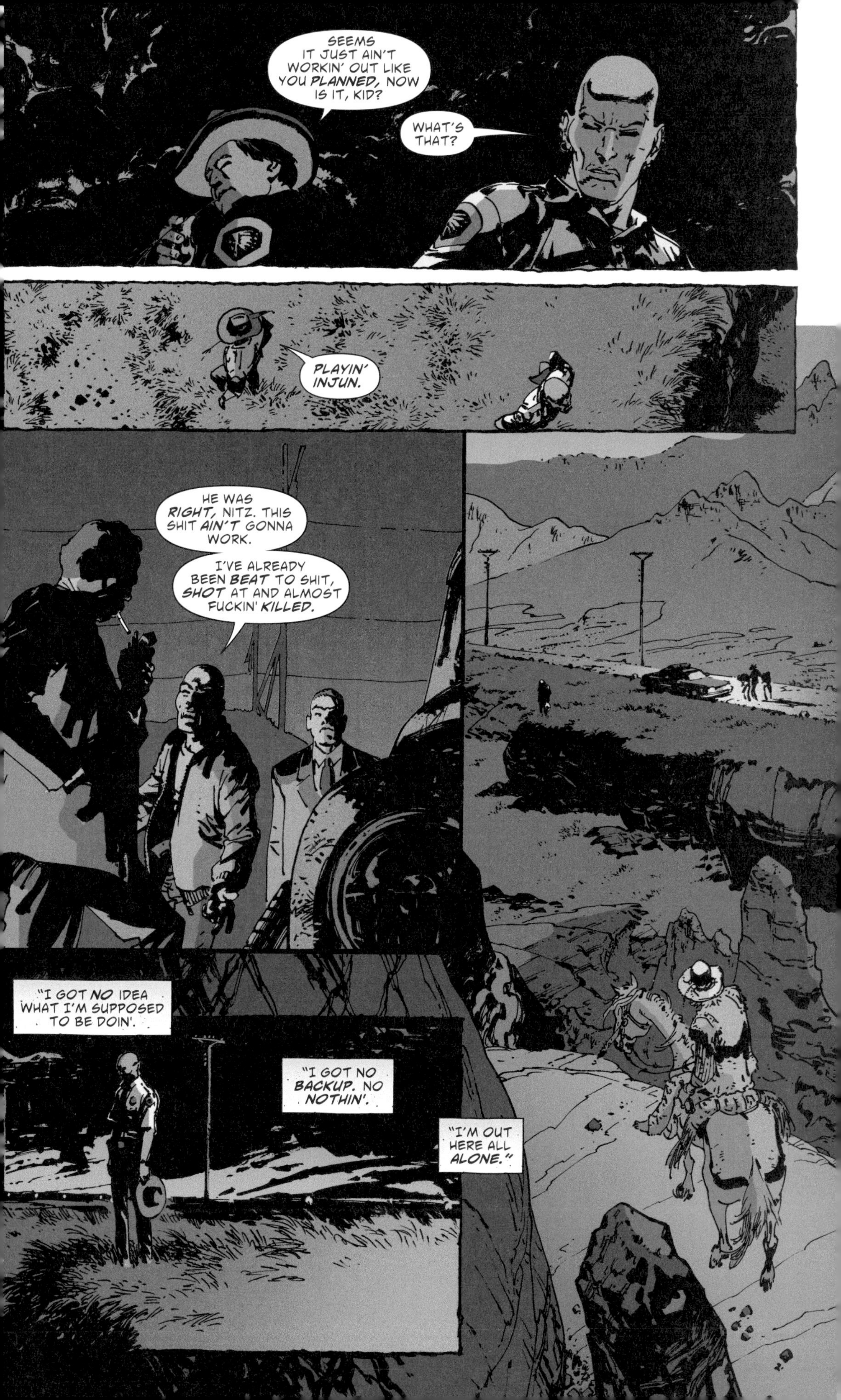

SEEMS IT JUST AIN'T WORKIN' OUT LIKE YOU PLANNED, NOW IS IT, KID?
WHAT'S THAT?
PLAYIN' INJUN.
HE WAS RIGHT, NITZ. THIS SHIT AIN'T GONNA WORK.
I'VE ALREADY BEEN BEAT TO SHIT, SHOT AT AND ALMOST FUCKIN' KILLED.
"I GOT NO IDEA WHAT I'M SUPPOSED TO BE DOIN'.
"I GOT NO BACKUP. NO NOTHIN'.
"I'M OUT HERE ALL ALONE."

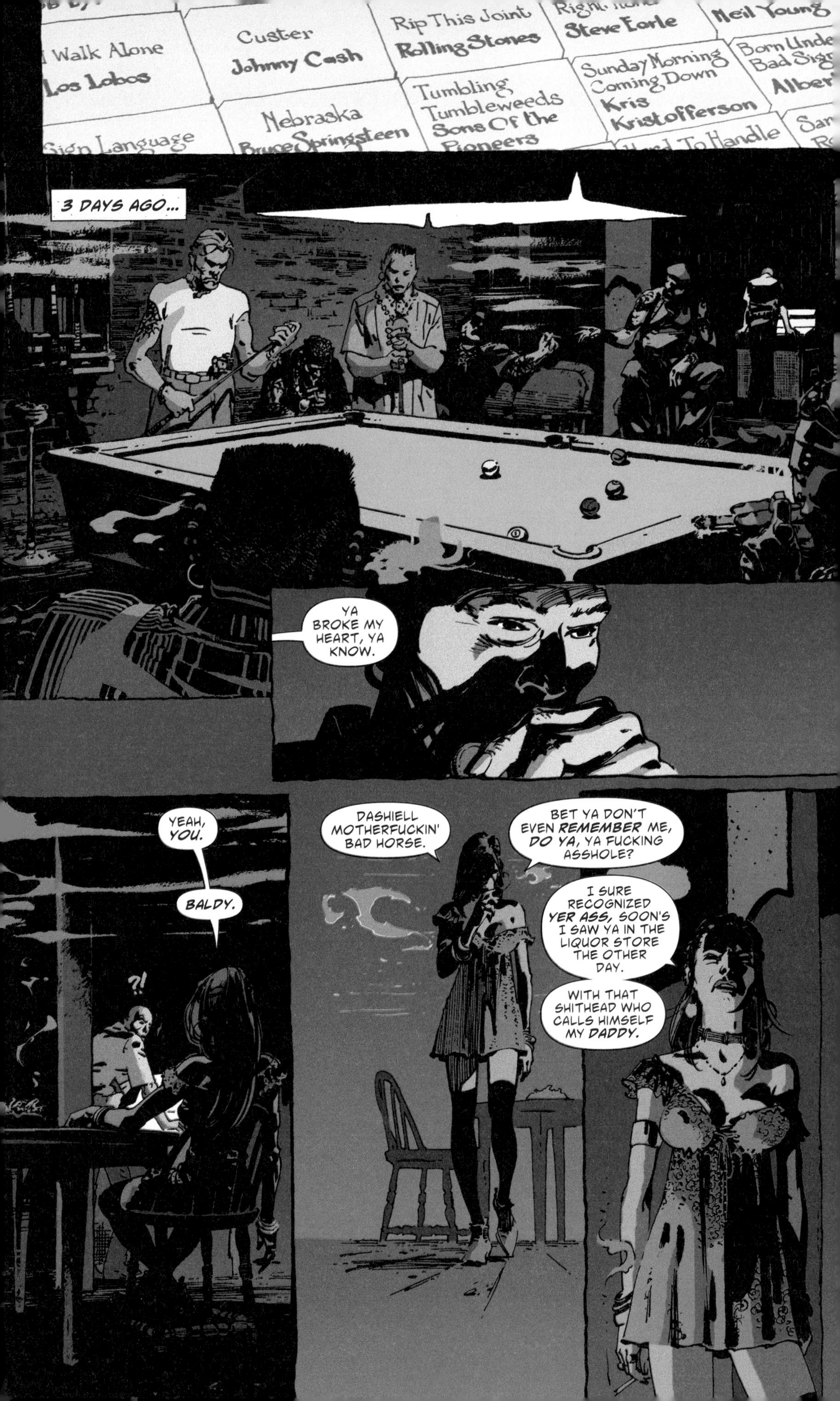

Los Lobos
Custer
Johnny Cash
Rip This Joint
Rolling Stones
Steve Earle
Neil Young
Nebraska
Bruce Springsteen
Tumbling Tumbleweeds
Sons Of the Pioneers
Sunday Morning Coming Down
Kris Kristofferson
3 DAYS AGO...
YA BROKE MY HEART, YA KNOW.
YEAH, *YOU.*
BALDY.
DASHIELL MOTHERFUCKIN' BAD HORSE.
BET YA DON'T EVEN *REMEMBER* ME, *DO YA,* YA FUCKING ASSHOLE?
I SURE RECOGNIZED *YER ASS,* SOON'S I SAW YA IN THE LIQUOR STORE THE OTHER DAY.
WITH THAT SHITHEAD WHO CALLS HIMSELF MY *DADDY.*

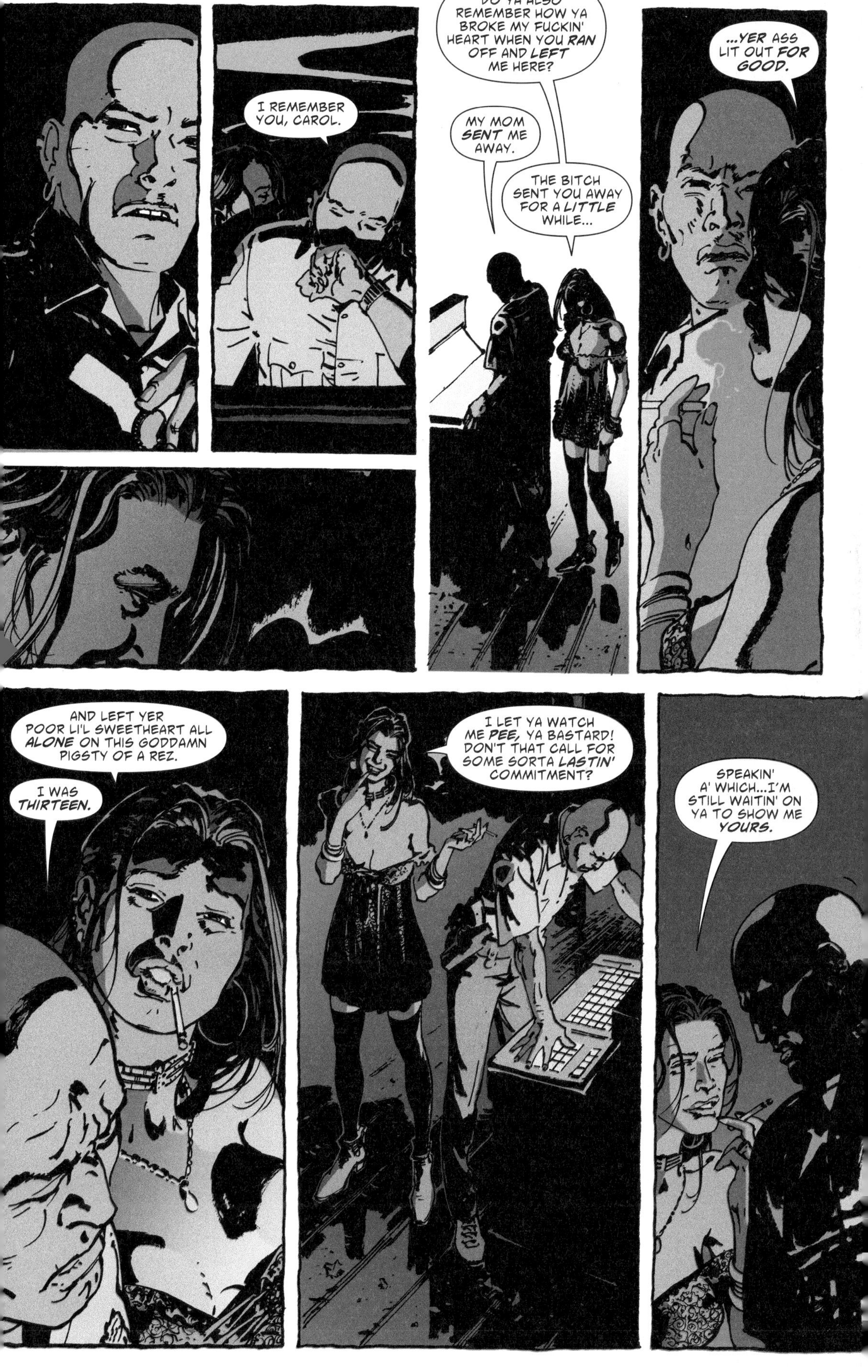
I REMEMBER YOU, CAROL.
YEAH? DO YA ALSO REMEMBER HOW YA BROKE MY FUCKIN' HEART WHEN YOU RAN OFF AND LEFT ME HERE?
MY MOM SENT ME AWAY.
THE BITCH SENT YOU AWAY FOR A LITTLE WHILE...
...YER ASS LIT OUT FOR GOOD.
AND LEFT YER POOR LI'L SWEETHEART ALL ALONE ON THIS GODDAMN PIGSTY OF A REZ.
I WAS THIRTEEN.
I LET YA WATCH ME PEE, YA BASTARD! DON'T THAT CALL FOR SOME SORTA LASTIN' COMMITMENT?
SPEAKIN' A' WHICH...I'M STILL WAITIN' ON YA TO SHOW ME YOURS.

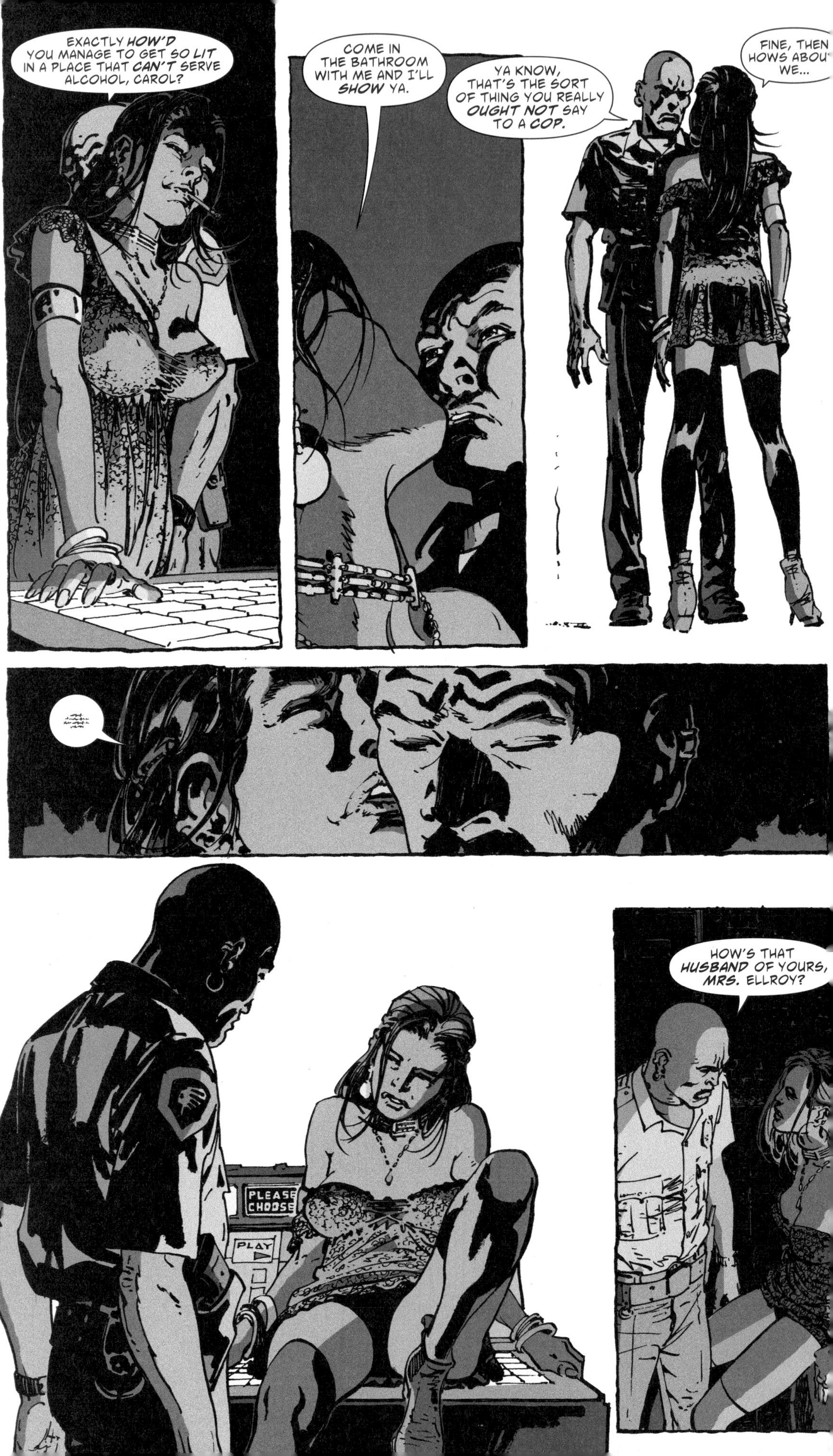
EXACTLY HOW'D YOU MANAGE TO GET SO LIT IN A PLACE THAT CAN'T SERVE ALCOHOL, CAROL?
COME IN THE BATHROOM WITH ME AND I'LL SHOW YA.
YA KNOW, THAT'S THE SORT OF THING YOU REALLY OUGHT NOT SAY TO A COP.
FINE, THEN HOWS ABOUT WE...
PLEASE CHOOSE
PLAY
HOW'S THAT HUSBAND OF YOURS, MRS. ELLROY?

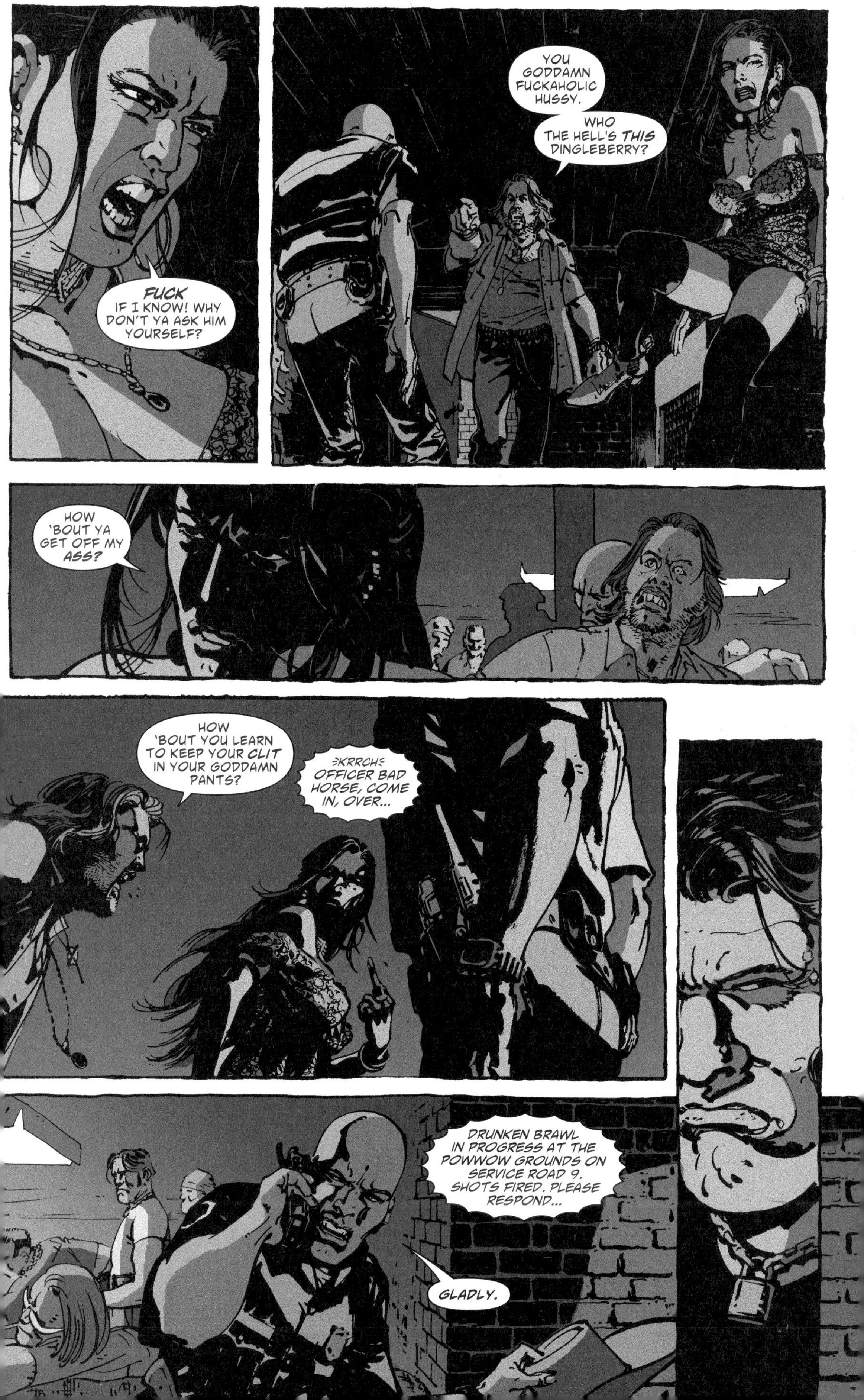
YOU GODDAMN FUCKAHOLIC HUSSY.
WHO THE HELL'S THIS DINGLEBERRY?
FUCK IF I KNOW! WHY DON'T YA ASK HIM YOURSELF?
HOW 'BOUT YA GET OFF MY ASS?
HOW 'BOUT YOU LEARN TO KEEP YOUR CLIT IN YOUR GODDAMN PANTS?
KRRCH OFFICER BAD HORSE, COME IN, OVER...
DRUNKEN BRAWL IN PROGRESS AT THE POWWOW GROUNDS ON SERVICE ROAD 9. SHOTS FIRED. PLEASE RESPOND...
GLADLY.

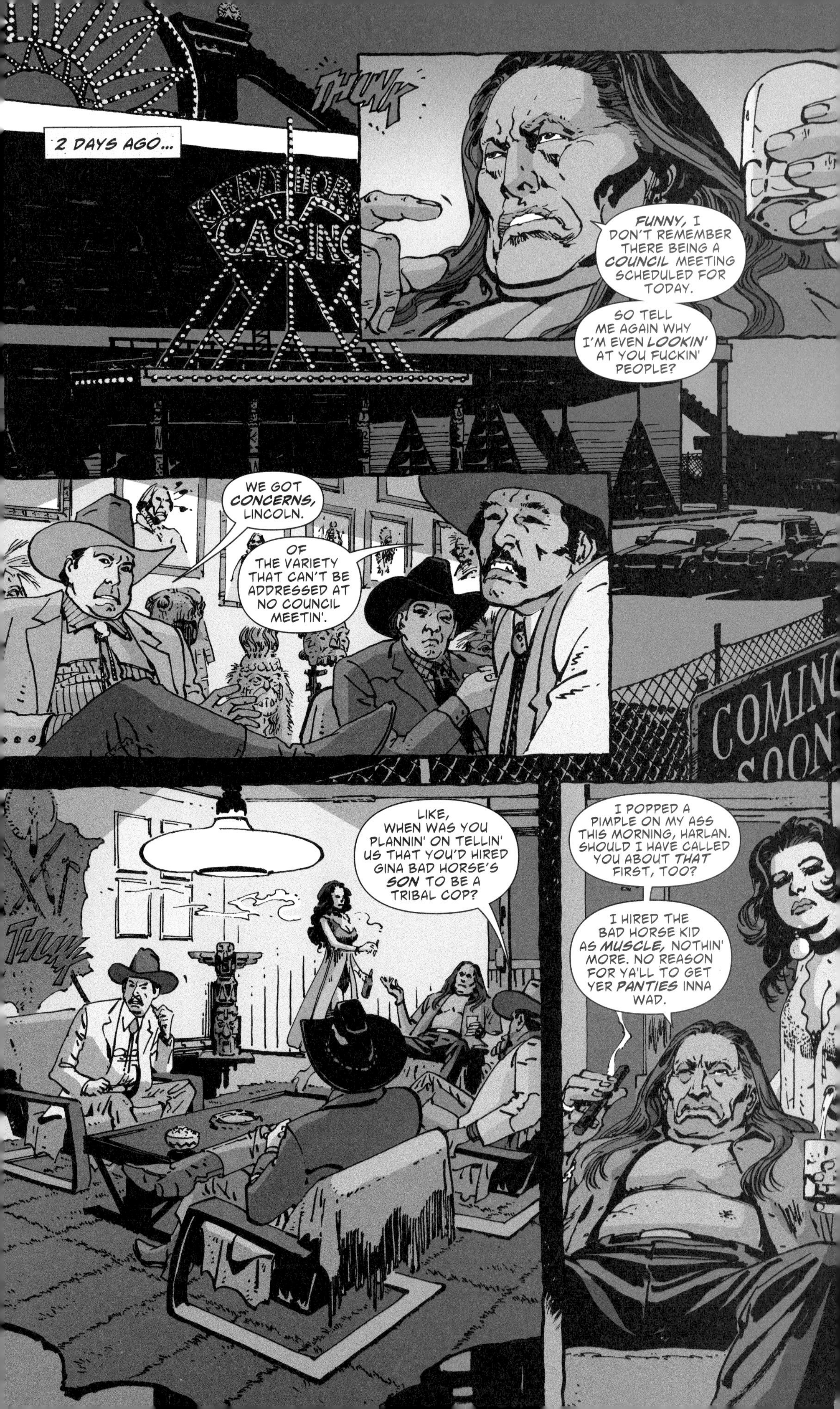
2 DAYS AGO...
THUNK
FUNNY, I DON'T REMEMBER THERE BEING A COUNCIL MEETING SCHEDULED FOR TODAY.
SO TELL ME AGAIN WHY I'M EVEN LOOKIN' AT YOU FUCKIN' PEOPLE?
WE GOT CONCERNS, LINCOLN.
OF THE VARIETY THAT CAN'T BE ADDRESSED AT NO COUNCIL MEETIN'.
COMING SOON
LIKE, WHEN WAS YOU PLANNIN' ON TELLIN' US THAT YOU'D HIRED GINA BAD HORSE'S SON TO BE A TRIBAL COP?
THUNK
I POPPED A PIMPLE ON MY ASS THIS MORNING, HARLAN. SHOULD I HAVE CALLED YOU ABOUT THAT FIRST, TOO?
I HIRED THE BAD HORSE KID AS MUSCLE, NOTHIN' MORE. NO REASON FOR YA'LL TO GET YER PANTIES INNA WAD.

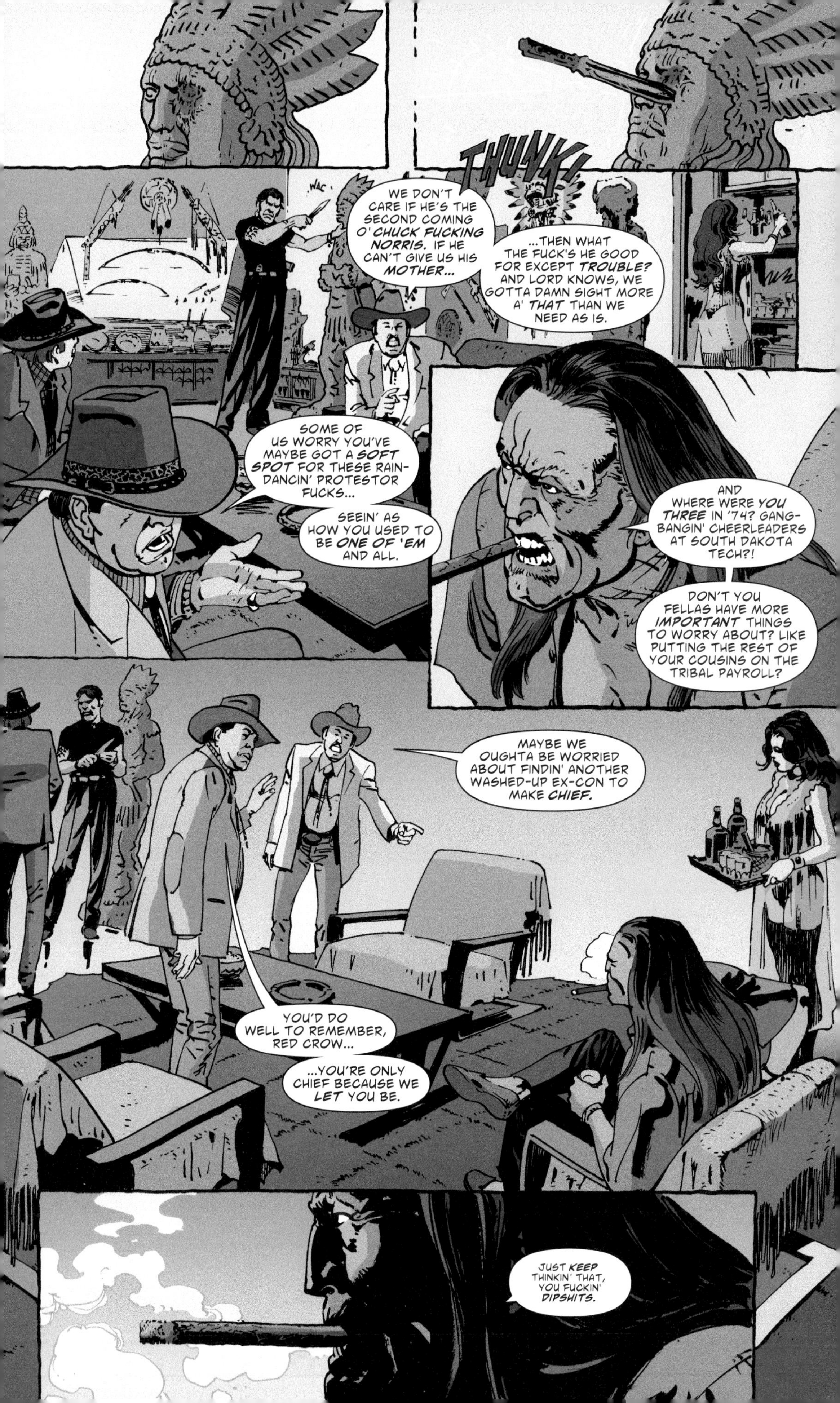
THUNK!
WE DON'T CARE IF HE'S THE SECOND COMING O' CHUCK FUCKING NORRIS. IF HE CAN'T GIVE US HIS MOTHER...
...THEN WHAT THE FUCK'S HE GOOD FOR EXCEPT TROUBLE? AND LORD KNOWS, WE GOTTA DAMN SIGHT MORE A' THAT THAN WE NEED AS IS.
SOME OF US WORRY YOU'VE MAYBE GOT A SOFT SPOT FOR THESE RAIN-DANCIN' PROTESTOR FUCKS...
SEEIN' AS HOW YOU USED TO BE ONE OF 'EM AND ALL.
AND WHERE WERE YOU THREE IN '74? GANG-BANGIN' CHEERLEADERS AT SOUTH DAKOTA TECH?!
DON'T YOU FELLAS HAVE MORE IMPORTANT THINGS TO WORRY ABOUT? LIKE PUTTING THE REST OF YOUR COUSINS ON THE TRIBAL PAYROLL?
MAYBE WE OUGHTA BE WORRIED ABOUT FINDIN' ANOTHER WASHED-UP EX-CON TO MAKE CHIEF.
YOU'D DO WELL TO REMEMBER, RED CROW...
...YOU'RE ONLY CHIEF BECAUSE WE LET YOU BE.
JUST KEEP THINKIN' THAT, YOU FUCKIN' DIPSHITS.

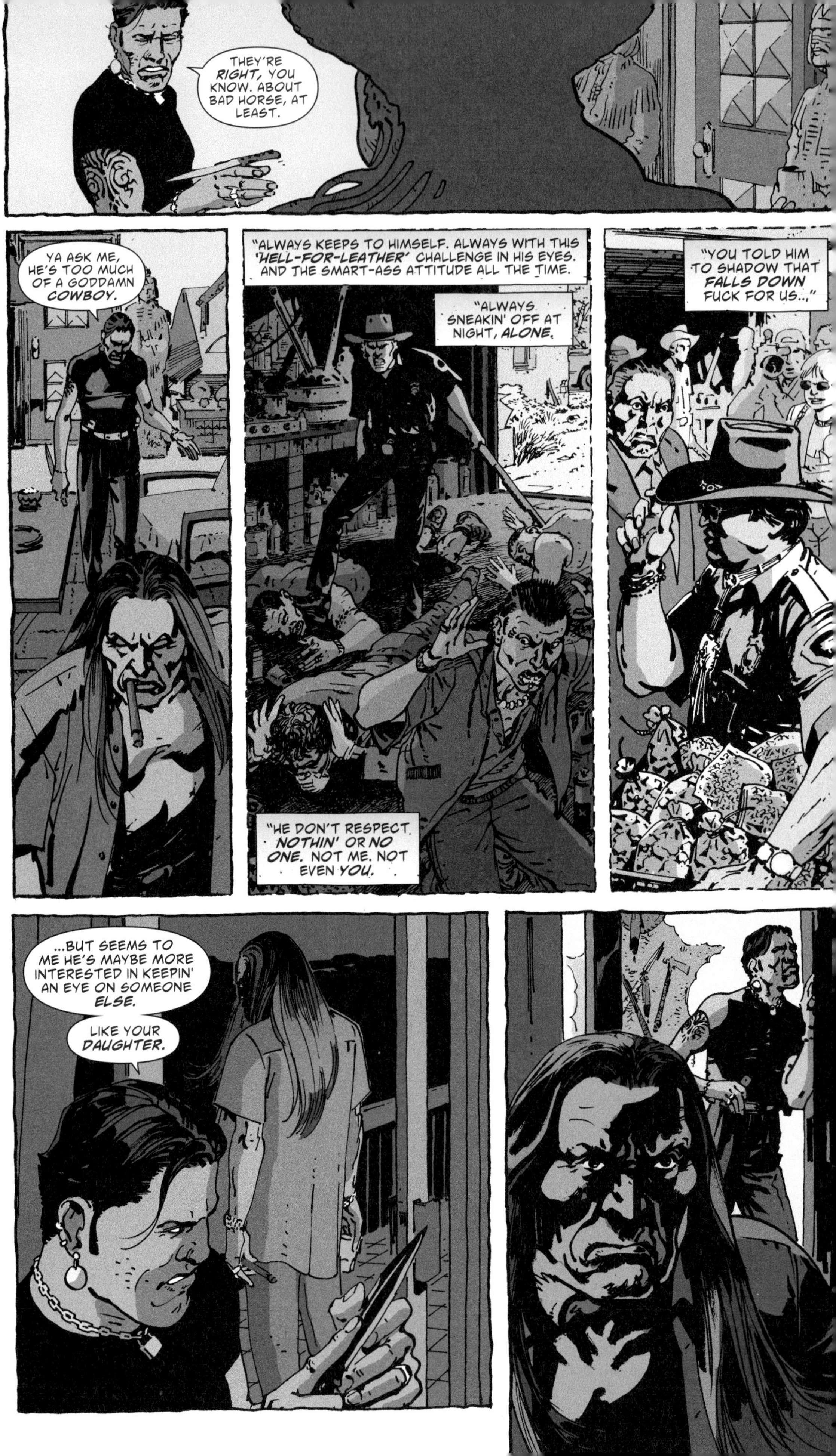
THEY'RE RIGHT, YOU KNOW. ABOUT BAD HORSE, AT LEAST.
YA ASK ME, HE'S TOO MUCH OF A GODDAMN COWBOY.
"ALWAYS KEEPS TO HIMSELF. ALWAYS WITH THIS 'HELL-FOR-LEATHER' CHALLENGE IN HIS EYES. AND THE SMART-ASS ATTITUDE ALL THE TIME.
"ALWAYS SNEAKIN' OFF AT NIGHT, ALONE.
"HE DON'T RESPECT NOTHIN' OR NO ONE. NOT ME. NOT EVEN YOU.
"YOU TOLD HIM TO SHADOW THAT FALLS DOWN FUCK FOR US..."
...BUT SEEMS TO ME HE'S MAYBE MORE INTERESTED IN KEEPIN' AN EYE ON SOMEONE ELSE.
LIKE YOUR DAUGHTER.

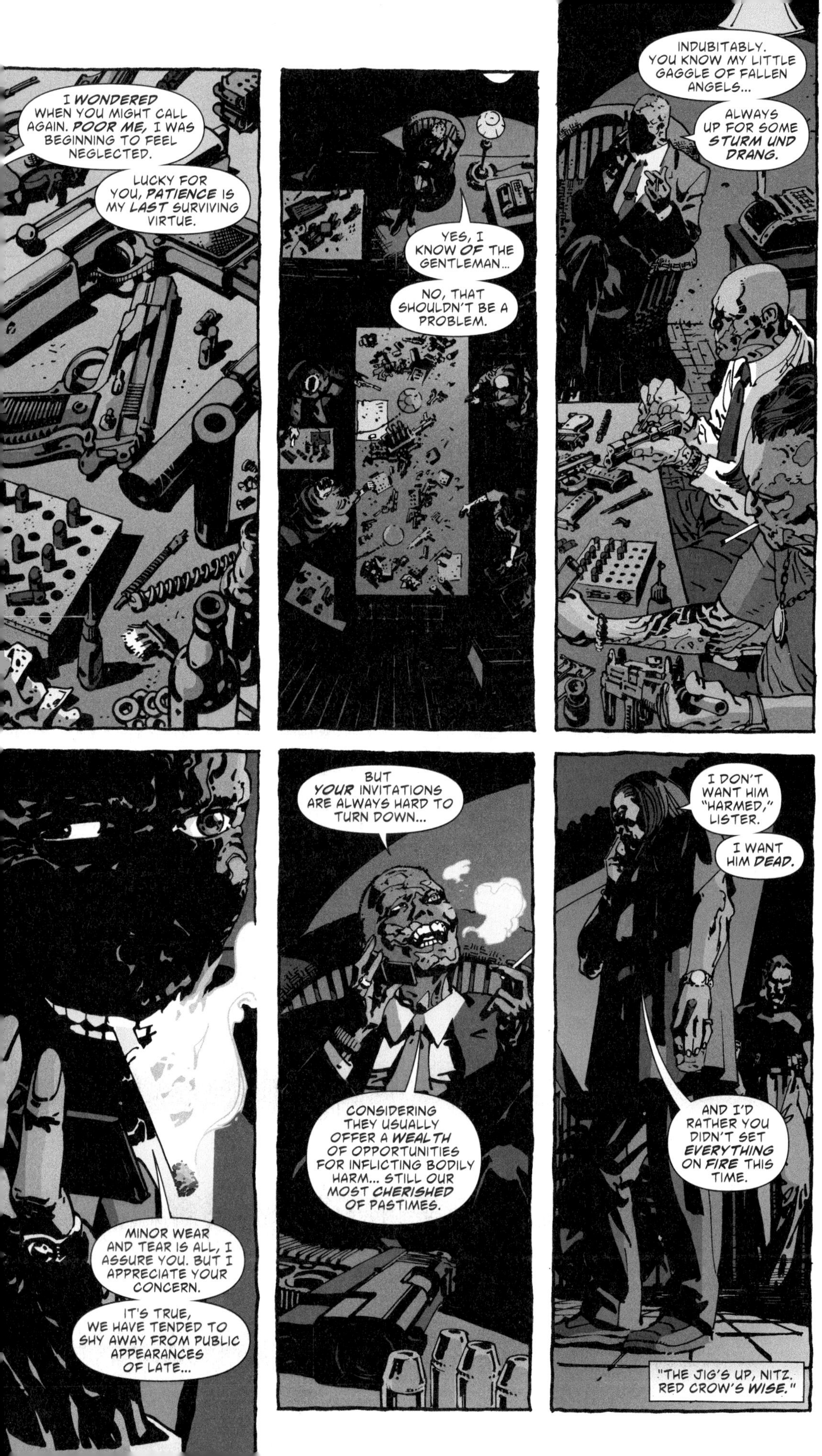
I *WONDERED* WHEN YOU MIGHT CALL AGAIN. *POOR ME,* I WAS BEGINNING TO FEEL NEGLECTED.
LUCKY FOR YOU, *PATIENCE* IS MY *LAST* SURVIVING VIRTUE.
YES, I KNOW *OF* THE GENTLEMAN...
NO, THAT SHOULDN'T BE A PROBLEM.
INDUBITABLY. YOU KNOW MY LITTLE GAGGLE OF FALLEN ANGELS...
ALWAYS UP FOR SOME *STURM UND DRANG.*
MINOR WEAR AND TEAR IS ALL, I ASSURE YOU. BUT I APPRECIATE YOUR CONCERN.
IT'S TRUE, WE HAVE TENDED TO SHY AWAY FROM PUBLIC APPEARANCES OF LATE...
BUT *YOUR* INVITATIONS ARE ALWAYS HARD TO TURN DOWN...
CONSIDERING THEY USUALLY OFFER A *WEALTH* OF OPPORTUNITIES FOR INFLICTING BODILY HARM... STILL OUR MOST *CHERISHED* OF PASTIMES.
I DON'T WANT HIM "HARMED," LISTER.
I WANT HIM *DEAD.*
AND I'D RATHER YOU DIDN'T SET *EVERYTHING* ON *FIRE* THIS TIME.
"THE JIG'S UP, NITZ. RED CROW'S *WISE.*"

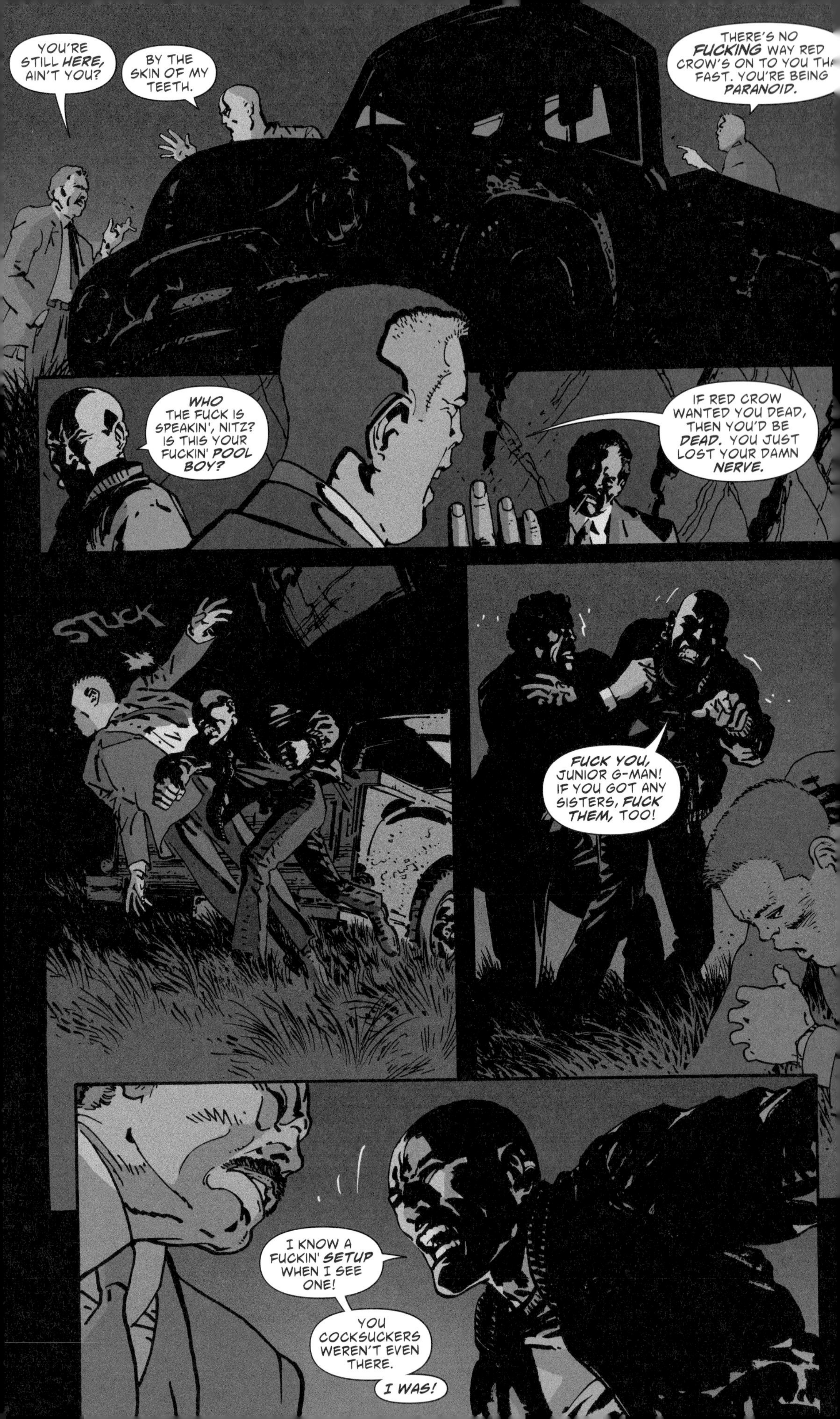
YOU'RE STILL HERE, AIN'T YOU?
BY THE SKIN OF MY TEETH.
THERE'S NO FUCKING WAY RED CROW'S ON TO YOU THA FAST. YOU'RE BEING PARANOID.
WHO THE FUCK IS SPEAKIN', NITZ? IS THIS YOUR FUCKIN' POOL BOY?
IF RED CROW WANTED YOU DEAD, THEN YOU'D BE DEAD. YOU JUST LOST YOUR DAMN NERVE.
STUCK
FUCK YOU, JUNIOR G-MAN! IF YOU GOT ANY SISTERS, FUCK THEM, TOO!
I KNOW A FUCKIN' SETUP WHEN I SEE ONE!
YOU COCKSUCKERS WEREN'T EVEN THERE.
I WAS!

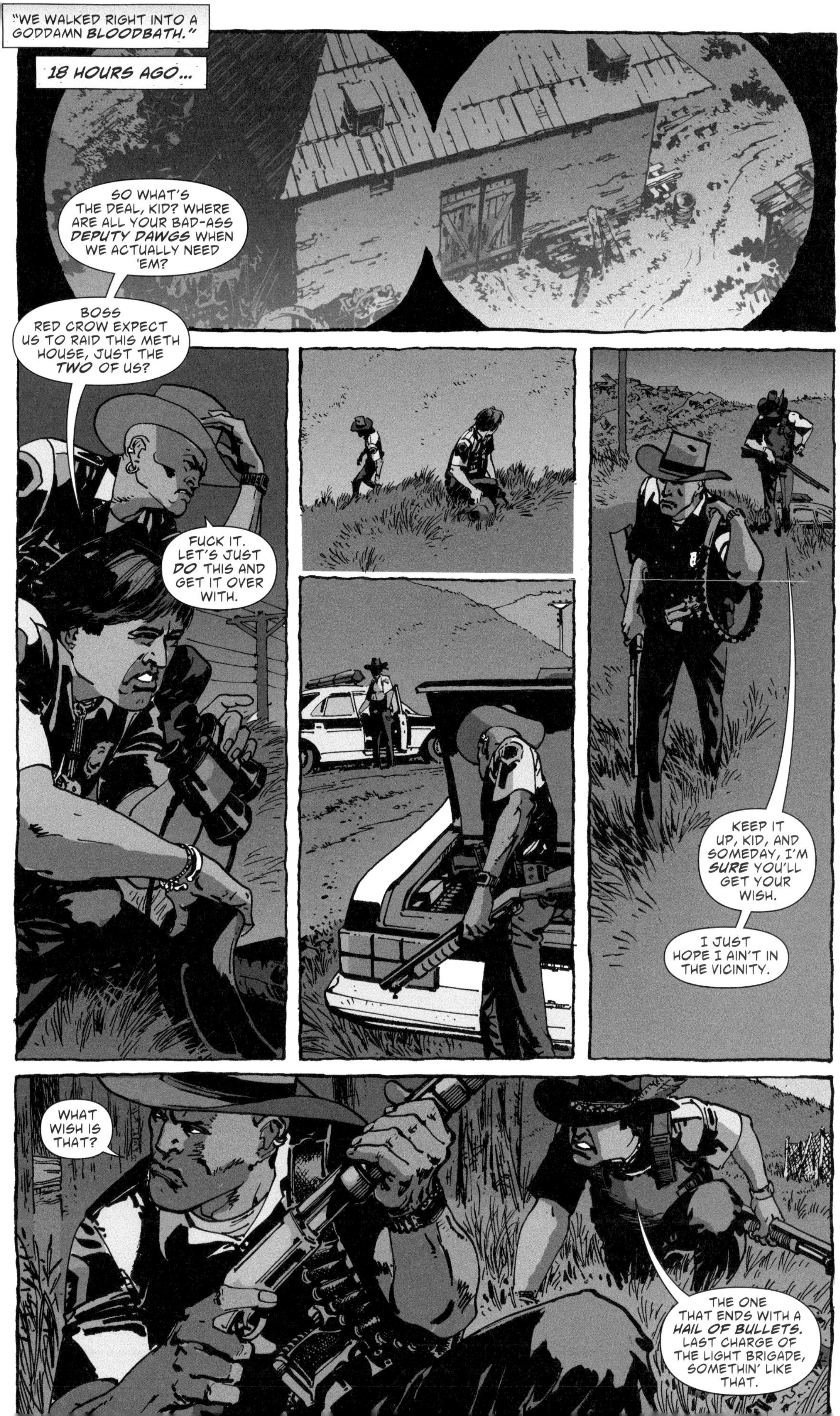
"WE WALKED RIGHT INTO A GODDAMN BLOODBATH."
18 HOURS AGO...
SO WHAT'S THE DEAL, KID? WHERE ARE ALL YOUR BAD-ASS DEPUTY DAWGS WHEN WE ACTUALLY NEED 'EM?
BOSS RED CROW EXPECT US TO RAID THIS METH HOUSE, JUST THE TWO OF US?
FUCK IT. LET'S JUST DO THIS AND GET IT OVER WITH.
KEEP IT UP, KID, AND SOMEDAY, I'M SURE YOU'LL GET YOUR WISH.
I JUST HOPE I AIN'T IN THE VICINITY.
WHAT WISH IS THAT?
THE ONE THAT ENDS WITH A HAIL OF BULLETS. LAST CHARGE OF THE LIGHT BRIGADE, SOMETHIN' LIKE THAT.

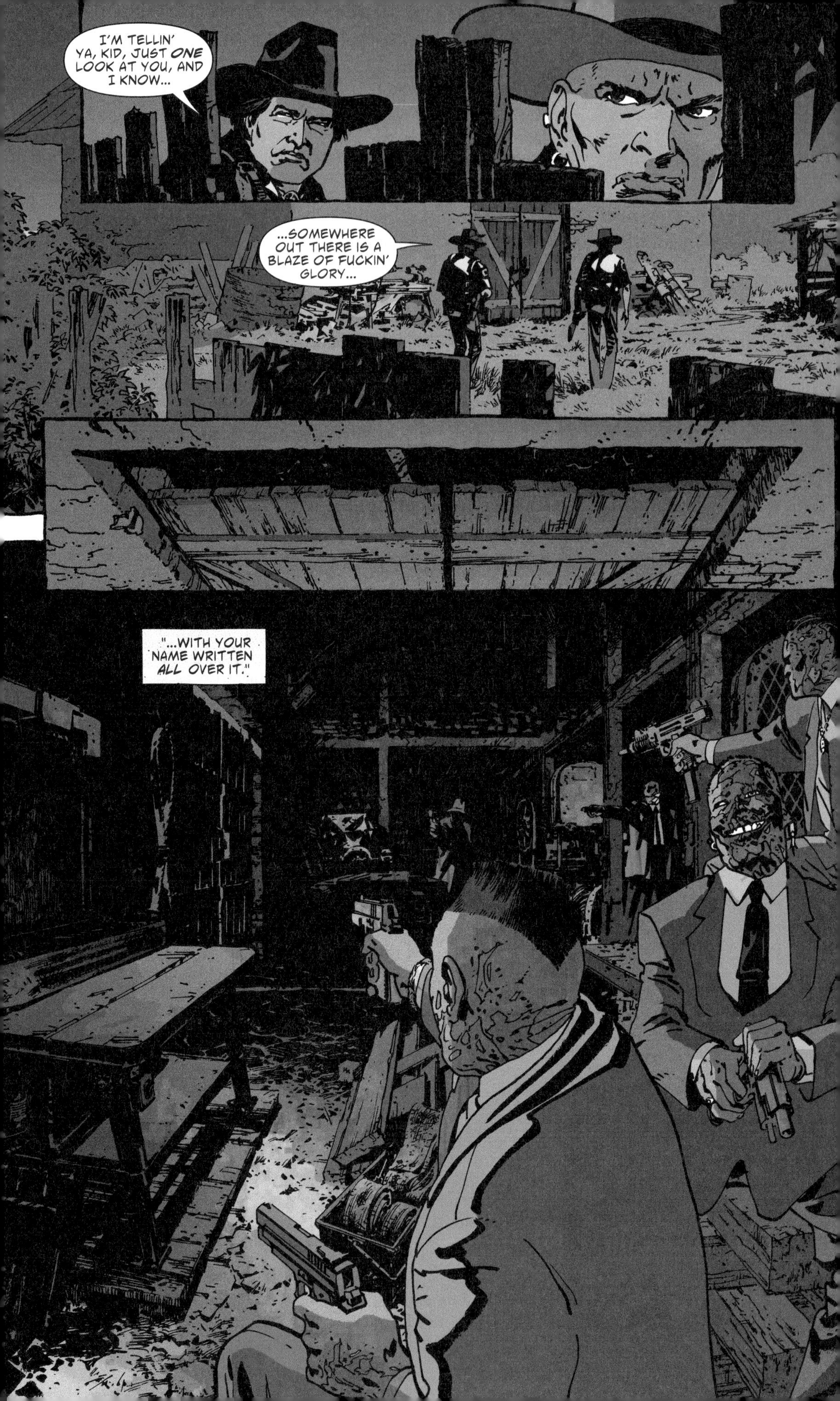
I'M TELLIN' YA, KID, JUST ONE LOOK AT YOU, AND I KNOW...
...SOMEWHERE OUT THERE IS A BLAZE OF FUCKIN' GLORY...
"...WITH YOUR NAME WRITTEN ALL OVER IT."

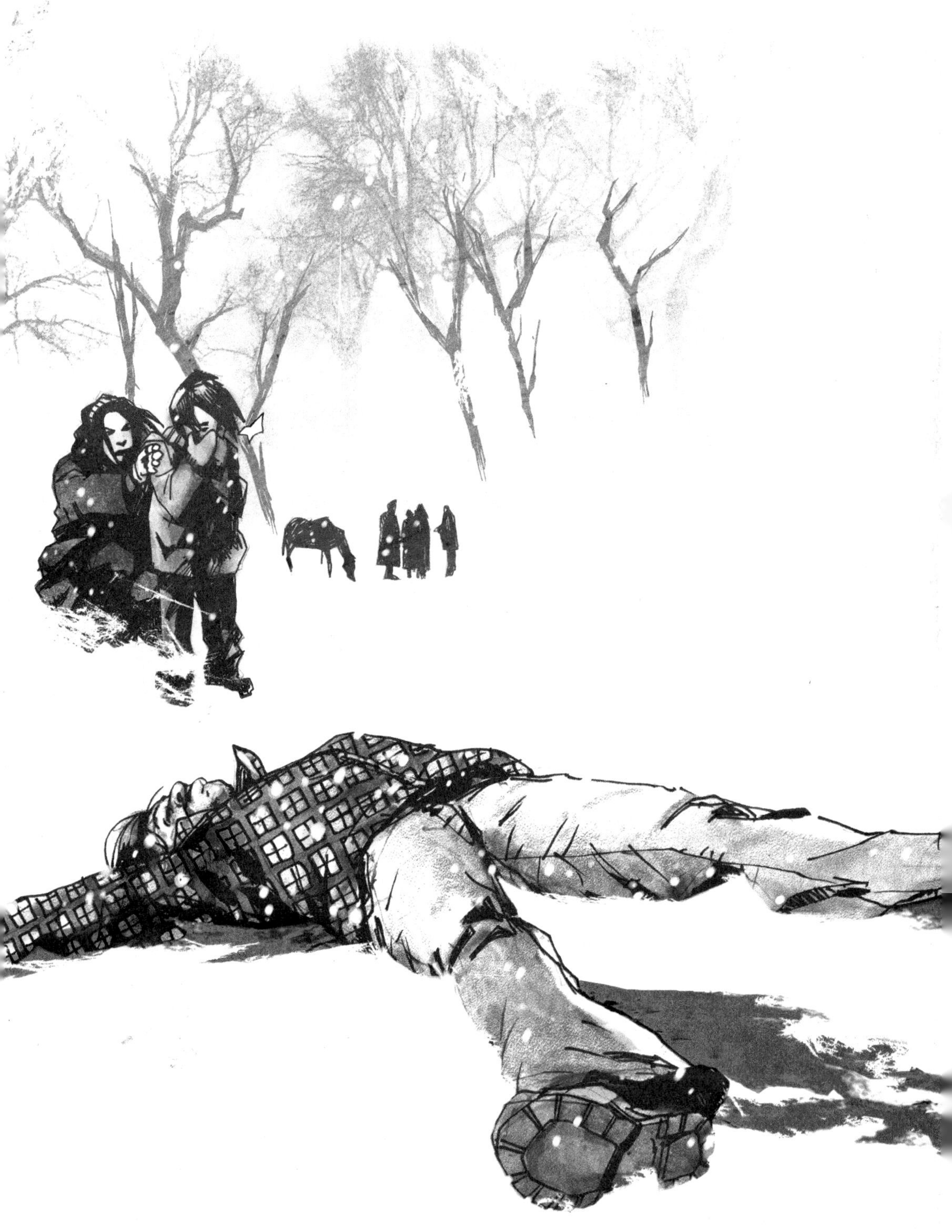

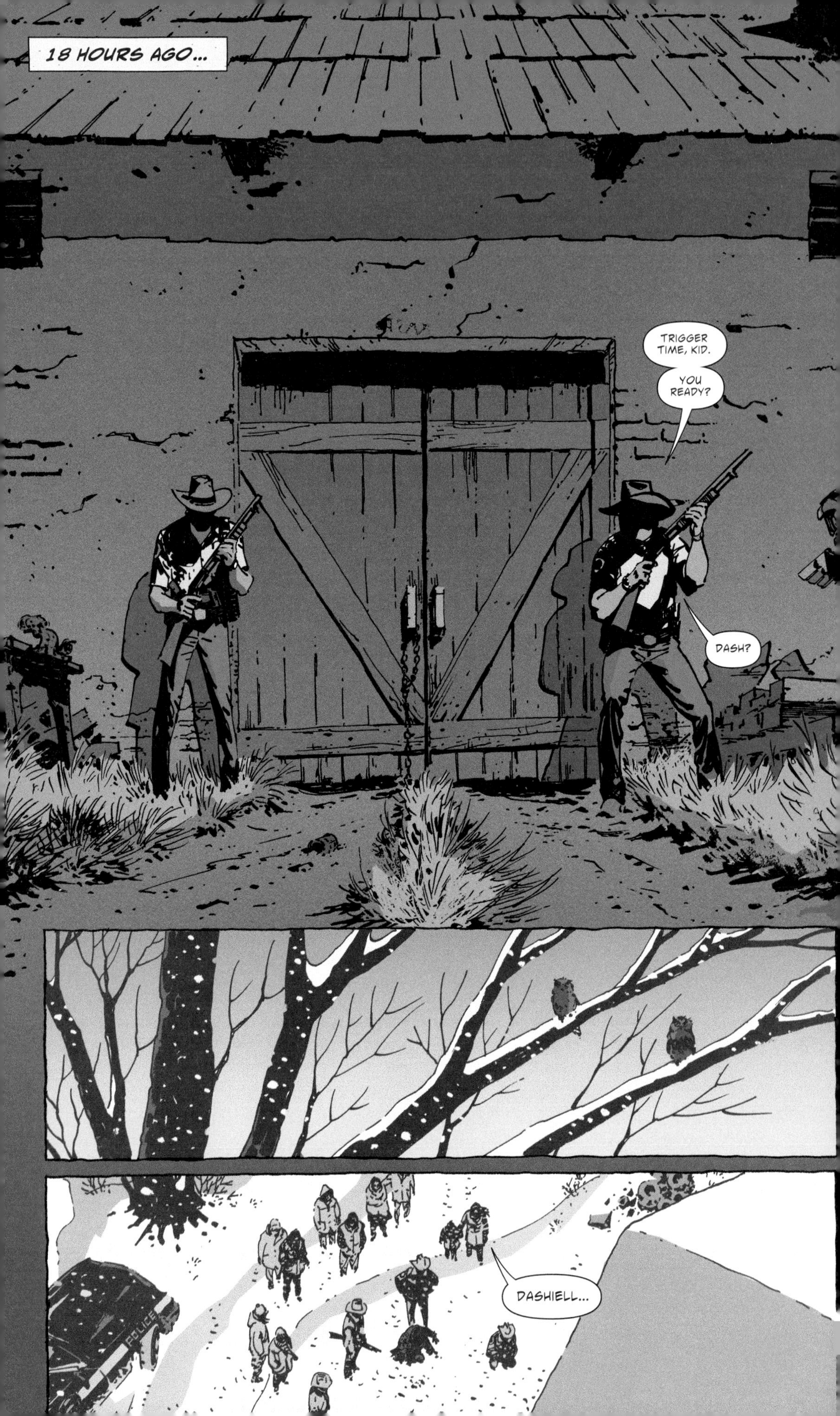
18 HOURS AGO...
TRIGGER TIME, KID.
YOU READY?
DASH?
DASHIELL...

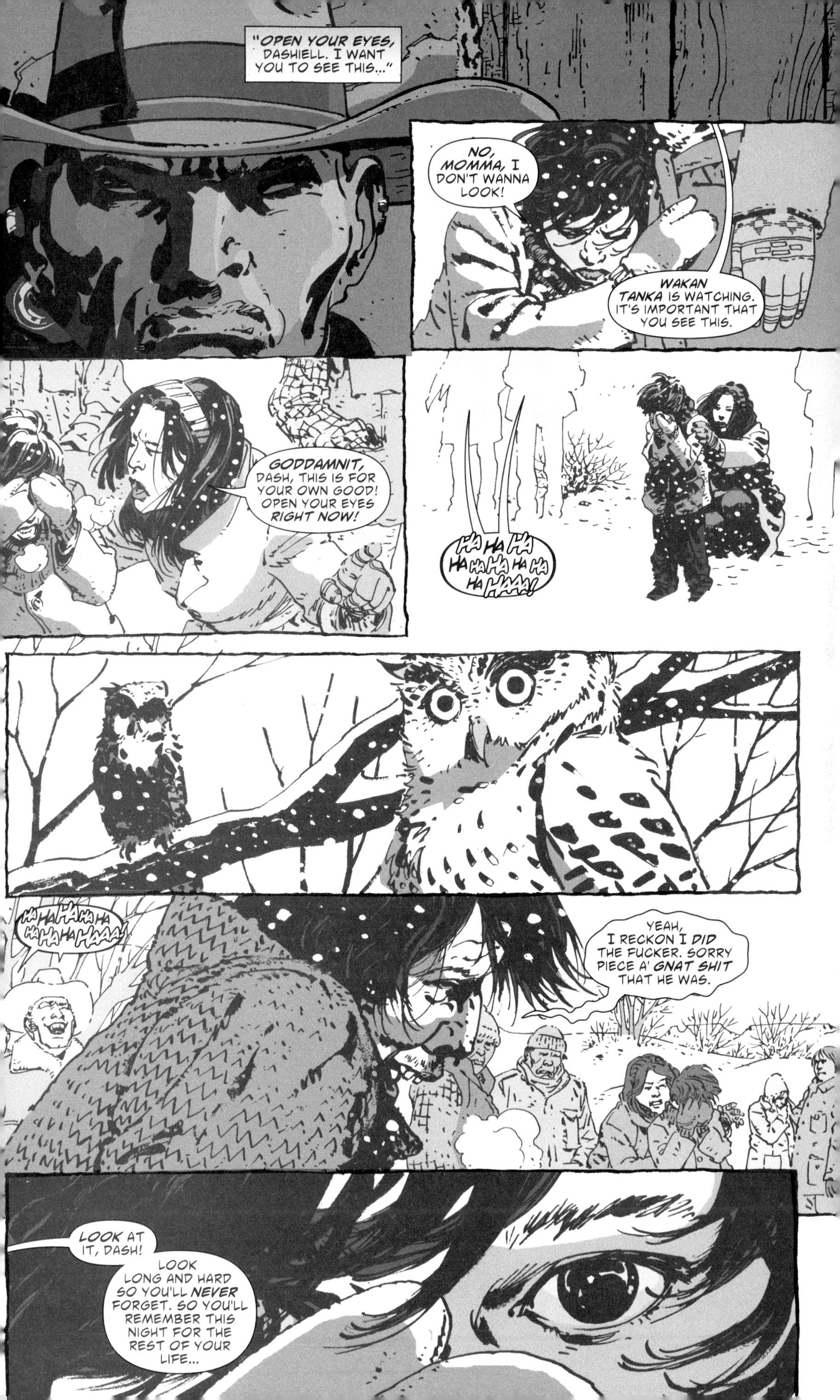
"OPEN YOUR EYES, DASHIELL. I WANT YOU TO SEE THIS..."
NO, MOMMA, I DON'T WANNA LOOK!
WAKAN TANKA IS WATCHING. IT'S IMPORTANT THAT YOU SEE THIS.
GODDAMNIT, DASH, THIS IS FOR YOUR OWN GOOD! OPEN YOUR EYES RIGHT NOW!
HA HA HA HA HA HA HA HA HA HA HAAA!
HA HA HA HA HA HA HA HA HA HAAA!
YEAH, I RECKON I DID THE FUCKER. SORRY PIECE A' GNAT SHIT THAT HE WAS.
LOOK AT IT, DASH!
LOOK LONG AND HARD SO YOU'LL NEVER FORGET. SO YOU'LL REMEMBER THIS NIGHT FOR THE REST OF YOUR LIFE...

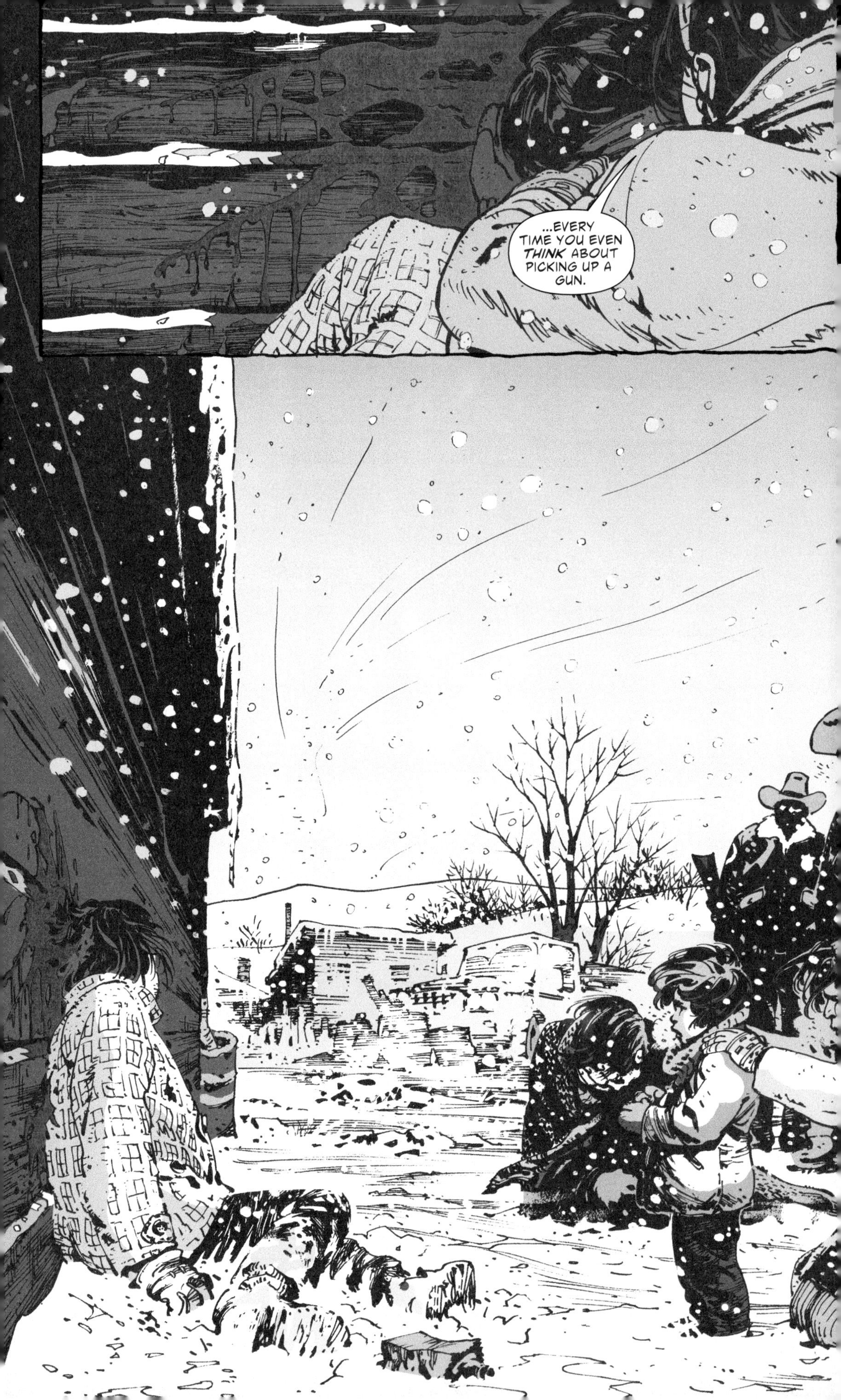
...EVERY TIME YOU EVEN *THINK* ABOUT PICKING UP A GUN.

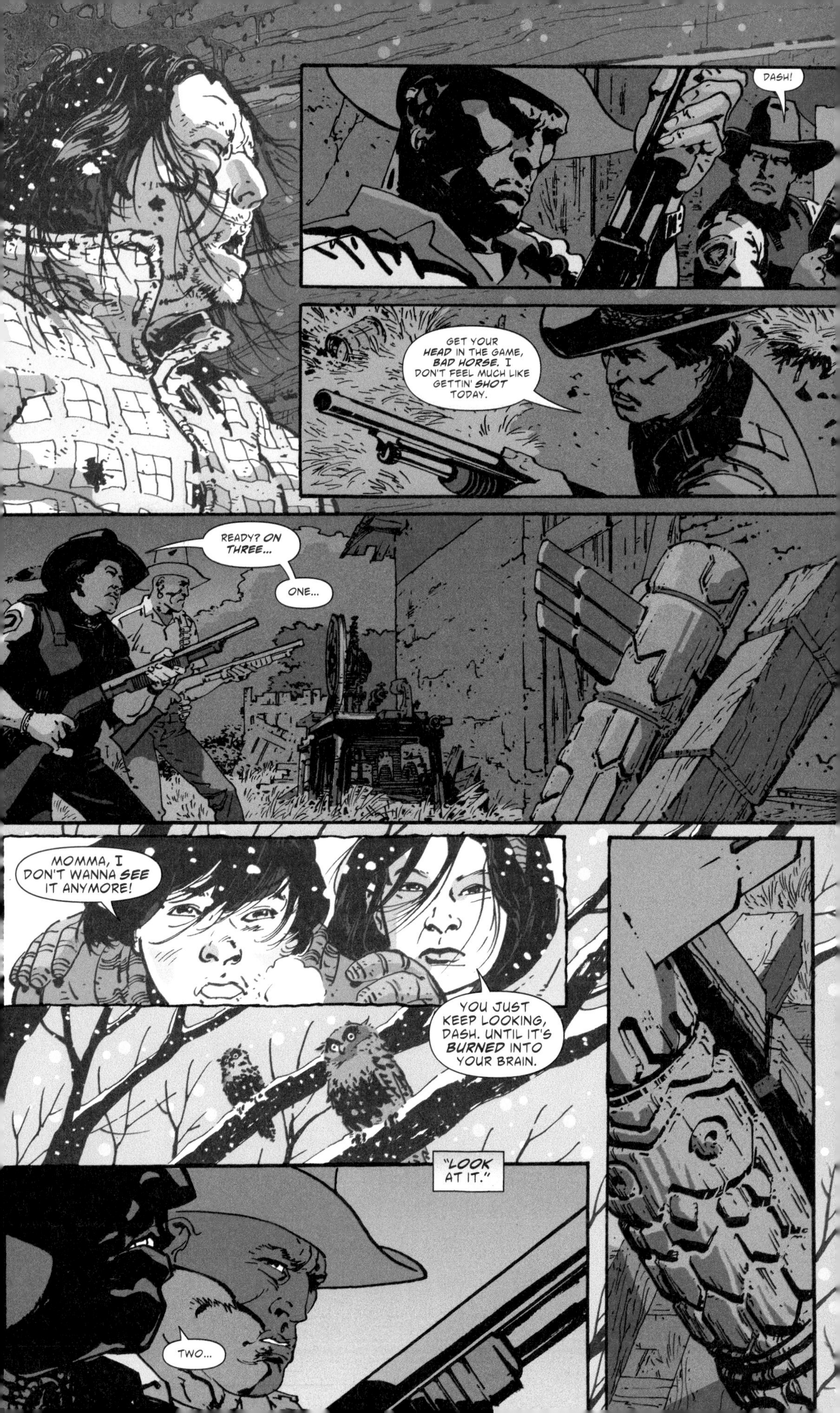
DASH!
GET YOUR HEAD IN THE GAME, BAD HORSE. I DON'T FEEL MUCH LIKE GETTIN' SHOT TODAY.
READY? ON THREE...
ONE...
MOMMA, I DON'T WANNA SEE IT ANYMORE!
YOU JUST KEEP LOOKING, DASH. UNTIL IT'S BURNED INTO YOUR BRAIN.
"LOOK AT IT."
TWO...

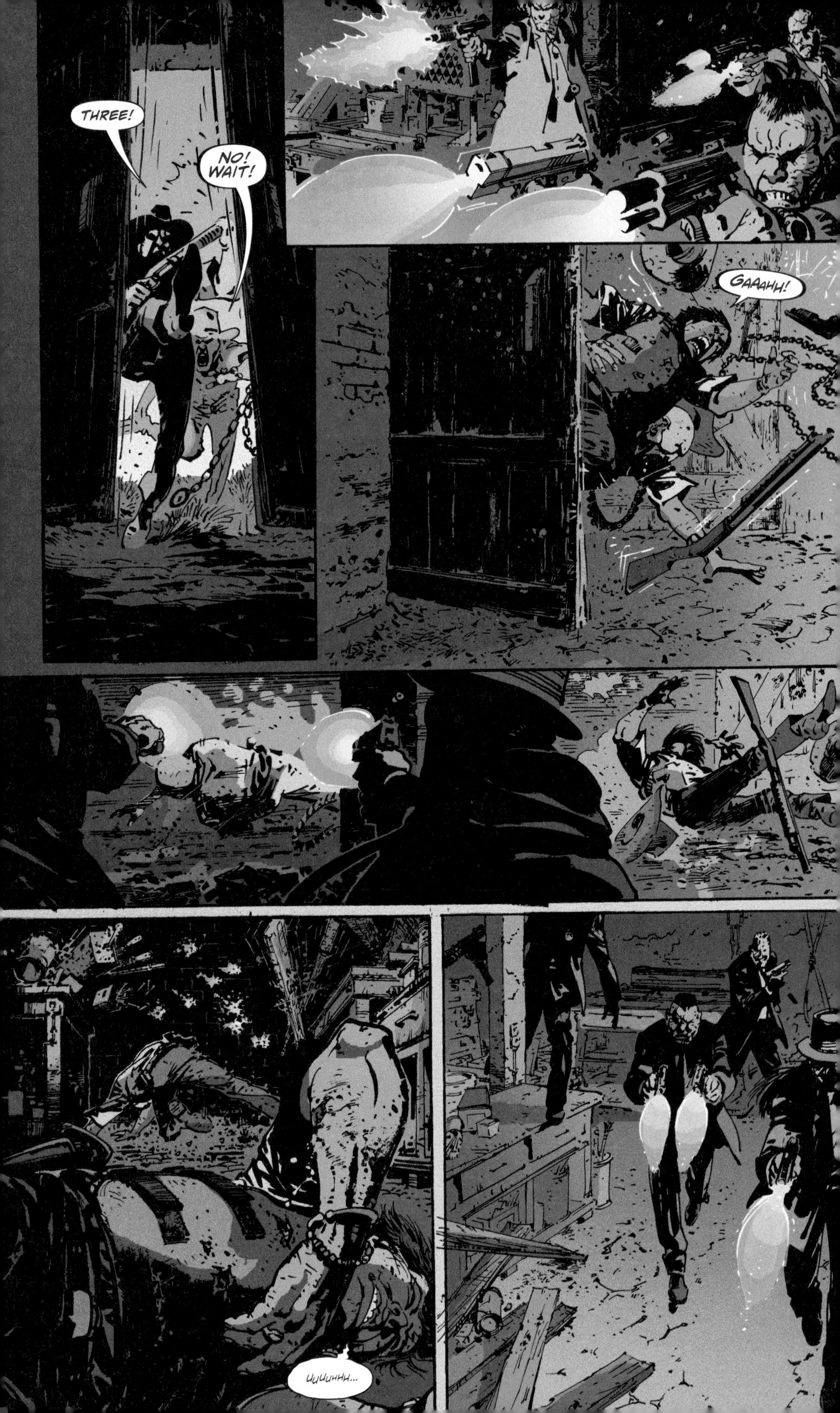
THREE!
NO! WAIT!
GAAAHH!
UUUUHHH...

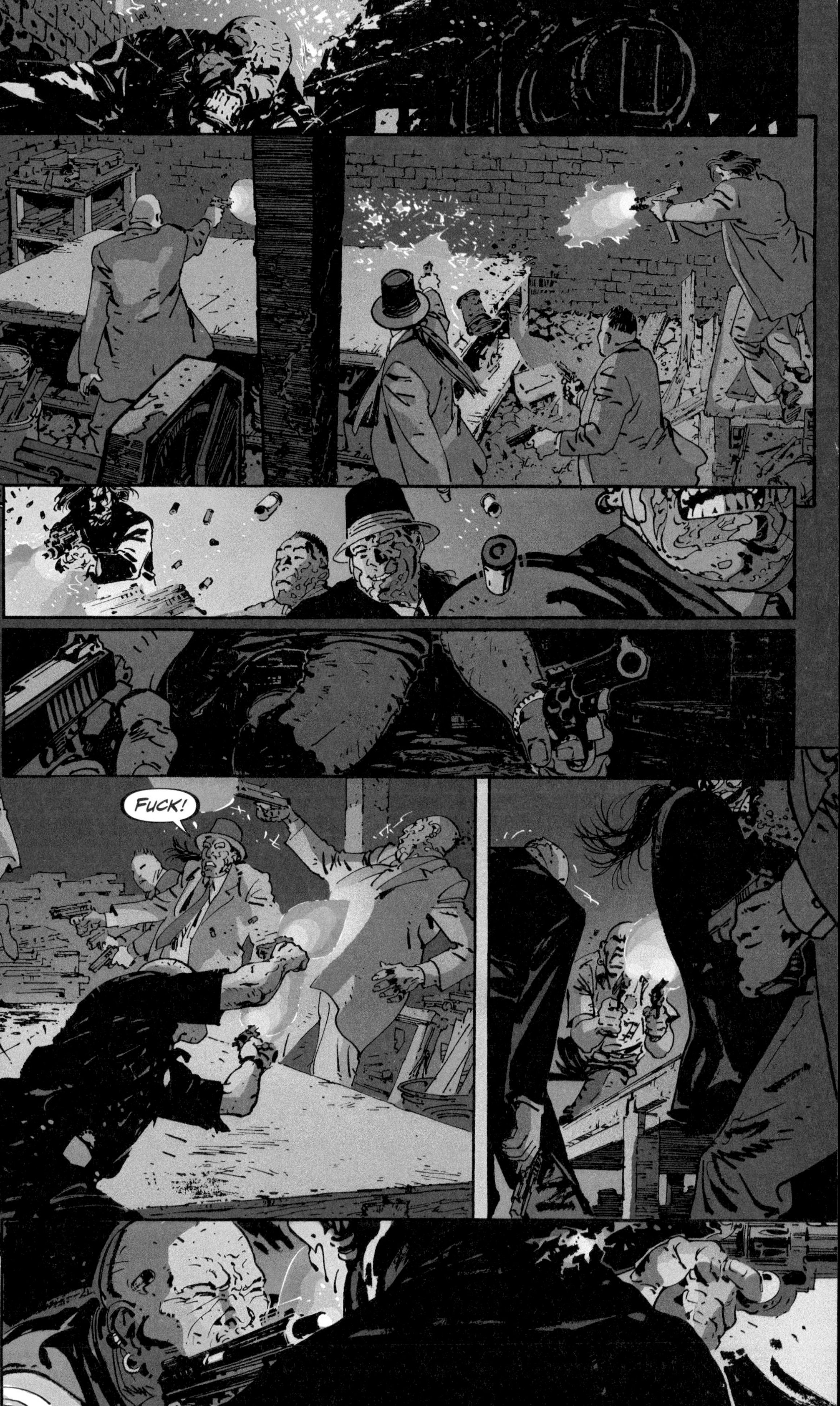
FUCK!

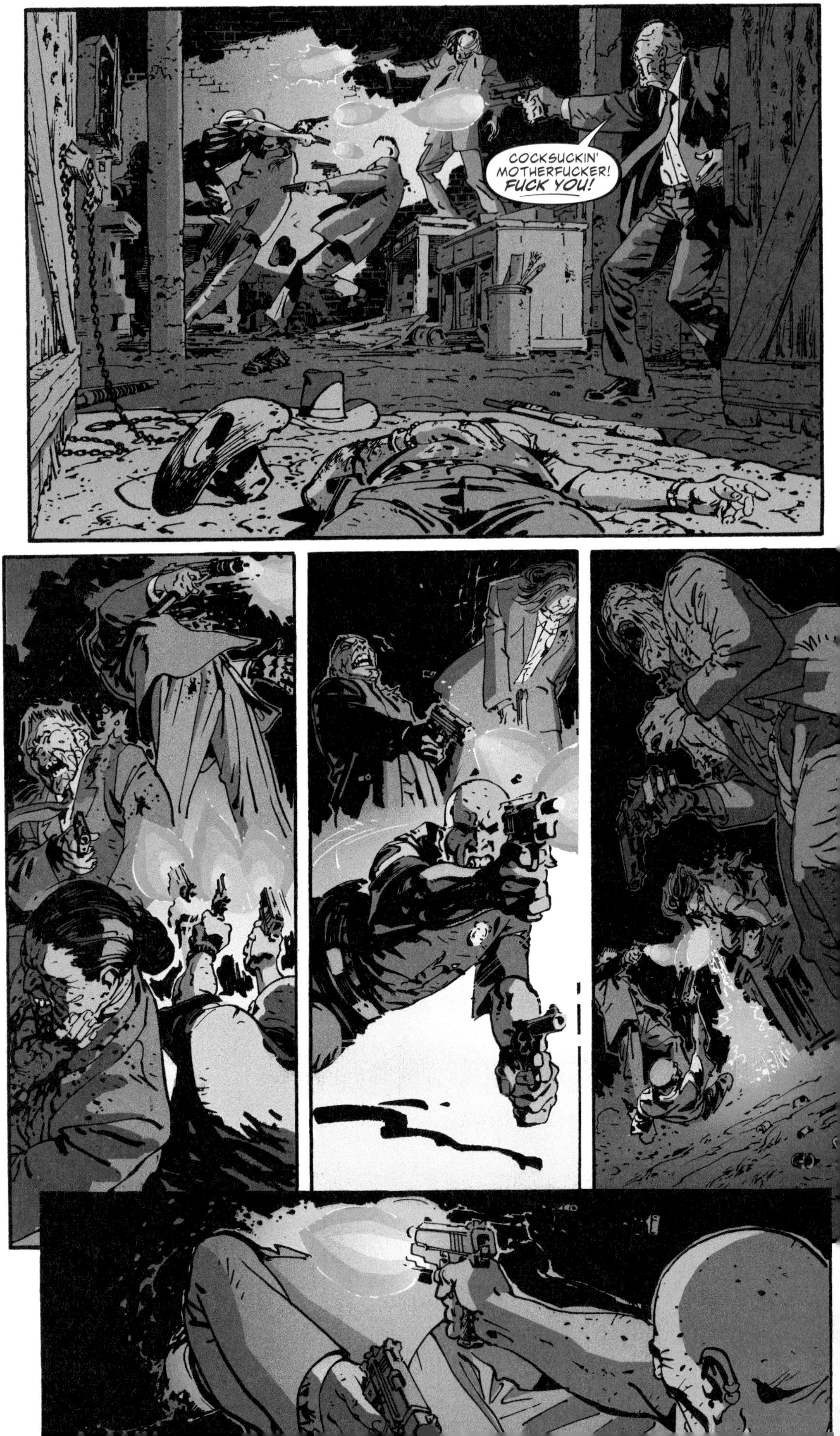
COCKSUCKIN' MOTHERFUCKER! FUCK YOU!

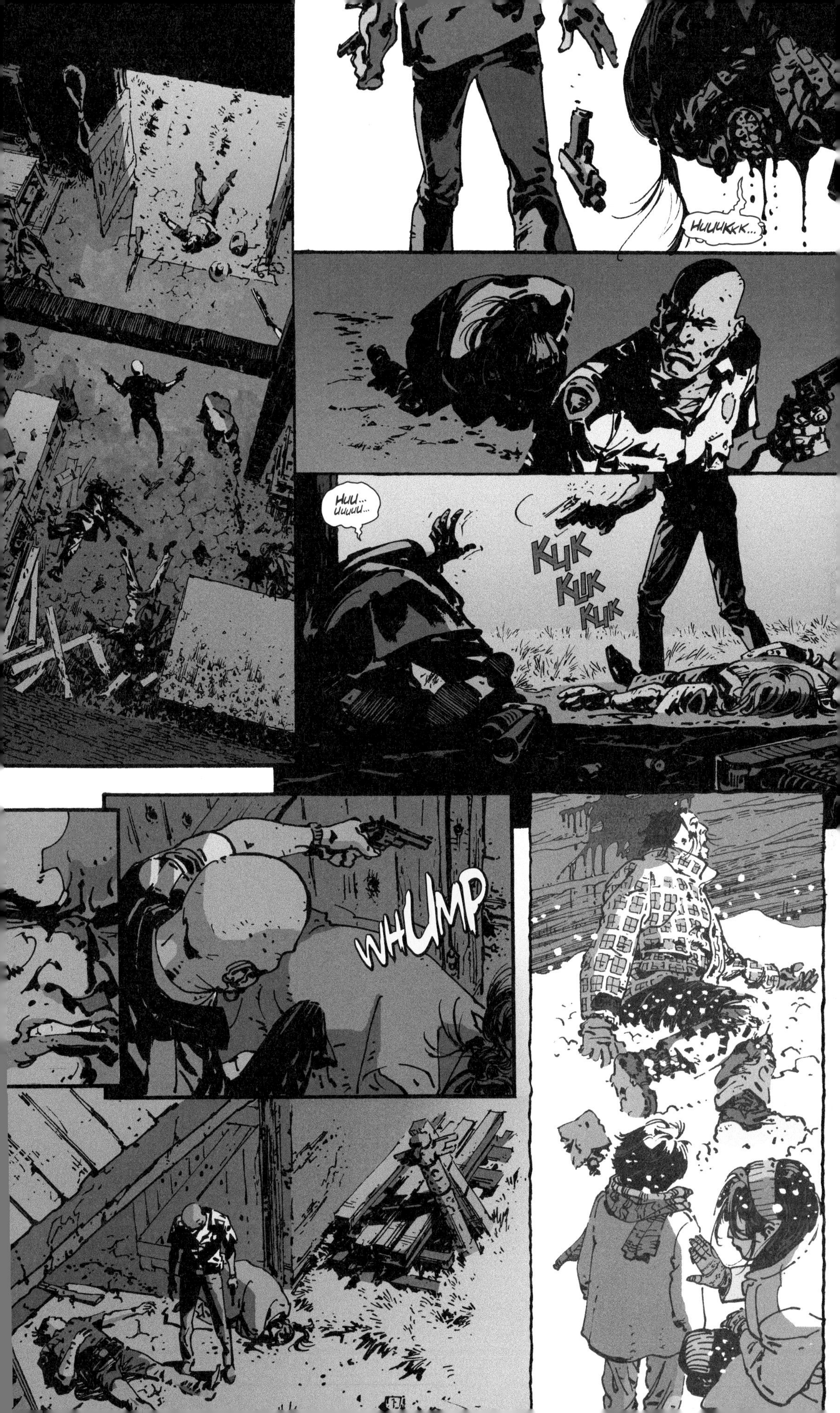
HUUUKKK...
HUU...
UUUUU...
KUK
KUK
KUK
WHUMP

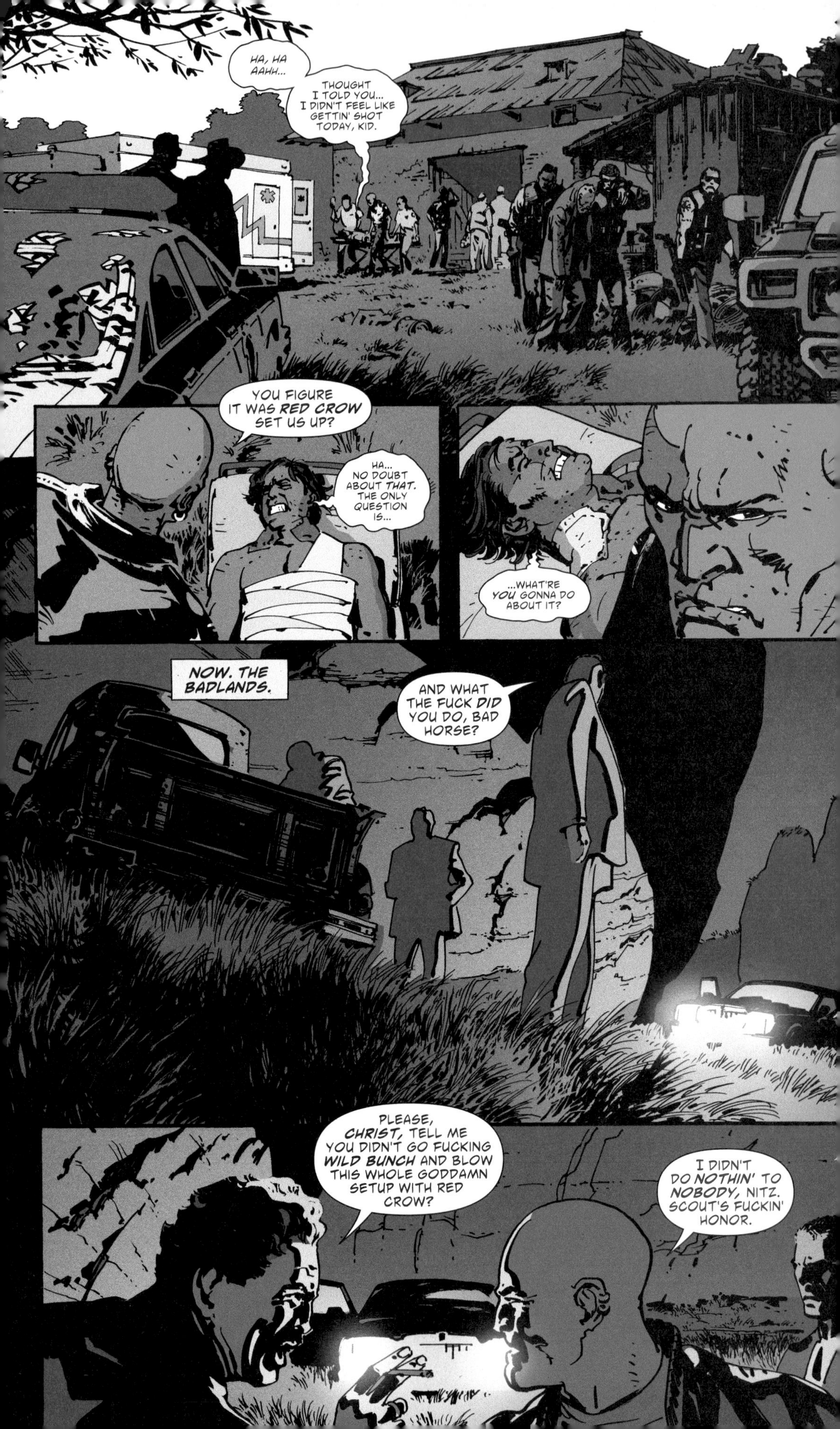
HA, HA AAHH...
THOUGHT I TOLD YOU... I DIDN'T FEEL LIKE GETTIN' SHOT TODAY, KID.
YOU FIGURE IT WAS RED CROW SET US UP?
HA... NO DOUBT ABOUT THAT. THE ONLY QUESTION IS...
...WHAT'RE YOU GONNA DO ABOUT IT?
NOW. THE BADLANDS.
AND WHAT THE FUCK DID YOU DO, BAD HORSE?
PLEASE, CHRIST, TELL ME YOU DIDN'T GO FUCKING WILD BUNCH AND BLOW THIS WHOLE GODDAMN SETUP WITH RED CROW?
I DIDN'T DO NOTHIN' TO NOBODY, NITZ. SCOUT'S FUCKIN' HONOR.

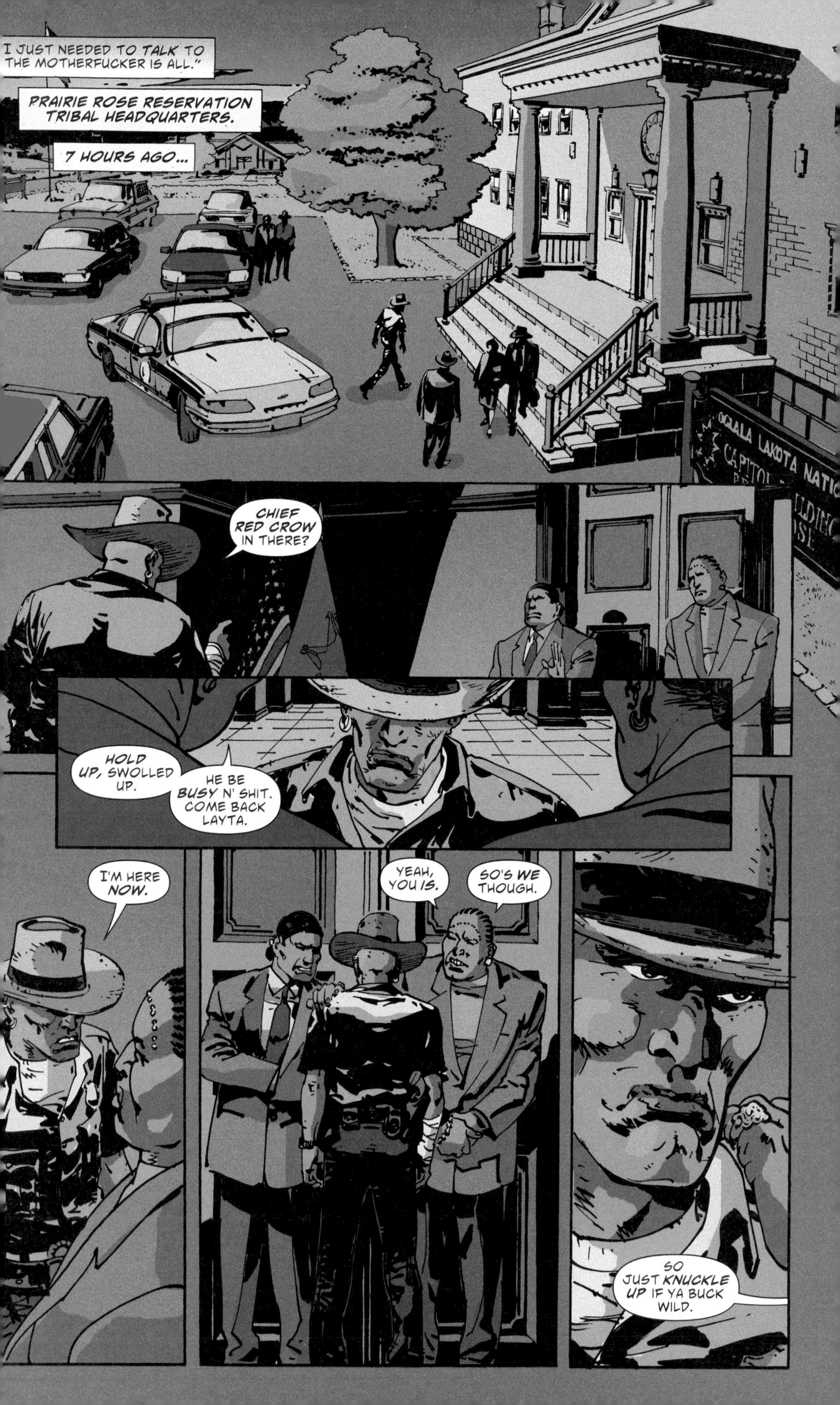
I JUST NEEDED TO TALK TO THE MOTHERFUCKER IS ALL."
PRAIRIE ROSE RESERVATION TRIBAL HEADQUARTERS.
7 HOURS AGO...
OGLALA LAKOTA NATIC
CAPITOL
CHIEF RED CROW IN THERE?
HOLD UP, SWOLLED UP.
HE BE BUSY N' SHIT. COME BACK LAYTA.
I'M HERE NOW.
YEAH, YOU IS.
SO'S WE THOUGH.
SO JUST KNUCKLE UP IF YA BUCK WILD.

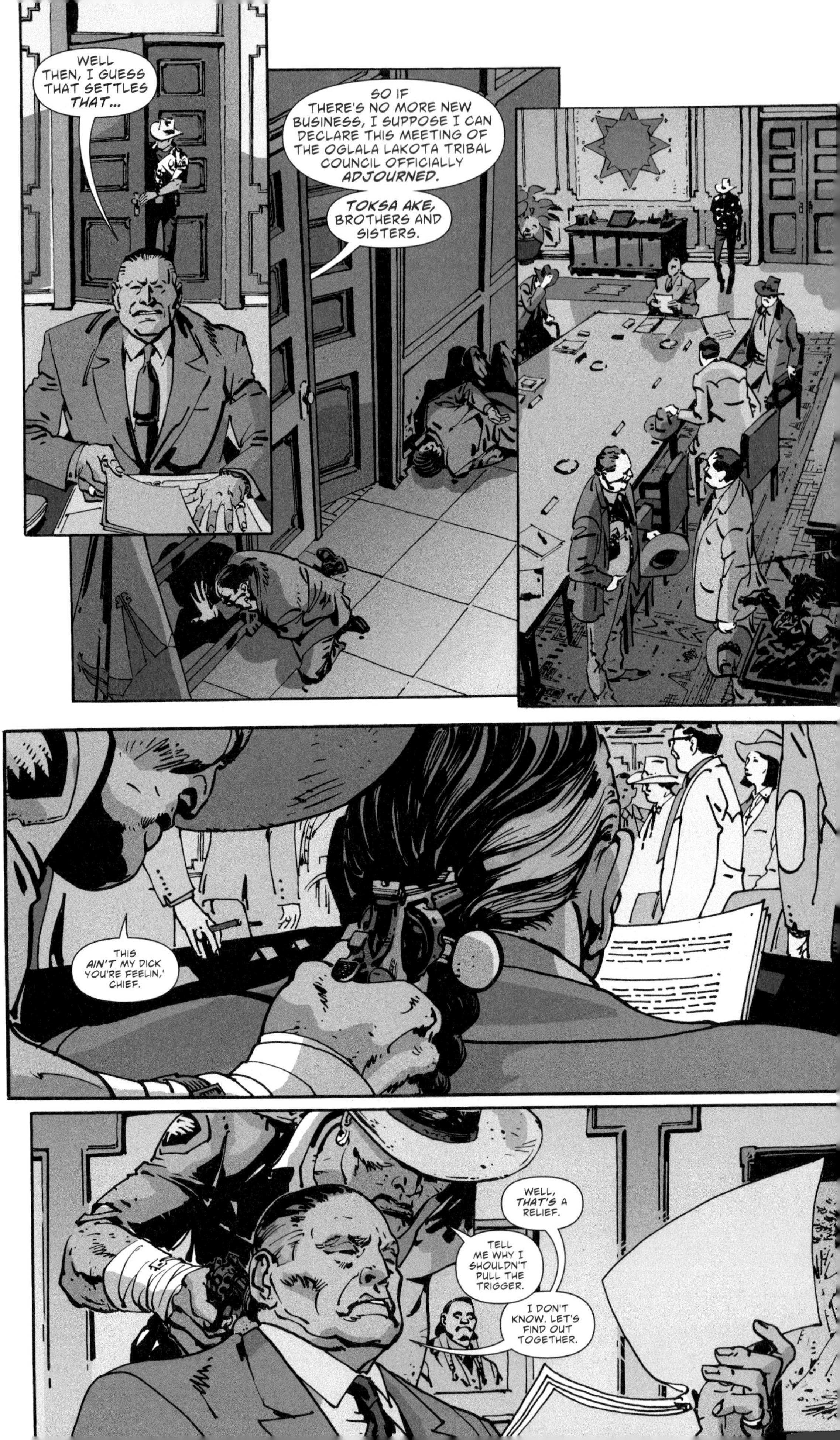
WELL THEN, I GUESS THAT SETTLES *THAT...*
SO IF THERE'S NO MORE NEW BUSINESS, I SUPPOSE I CAN DECLARE THIS MEETING OF THE OGLALA LAKOTA TRIBAL COUNCIL OFFICIALLY *ADJOURNED.*
TOKSA AKE, BROTHERS AND SISTERS.
THIS *AIN'T* MY DICK YOU'RE FEELIN,' CHIEF.
WELL, *THAT'S* A RELIEF.
TELL ME WHY I SHOULDN'T PULL THE TRIGGER.
I DON'T KNOW. LET'S FIND OUT TOGETHER.

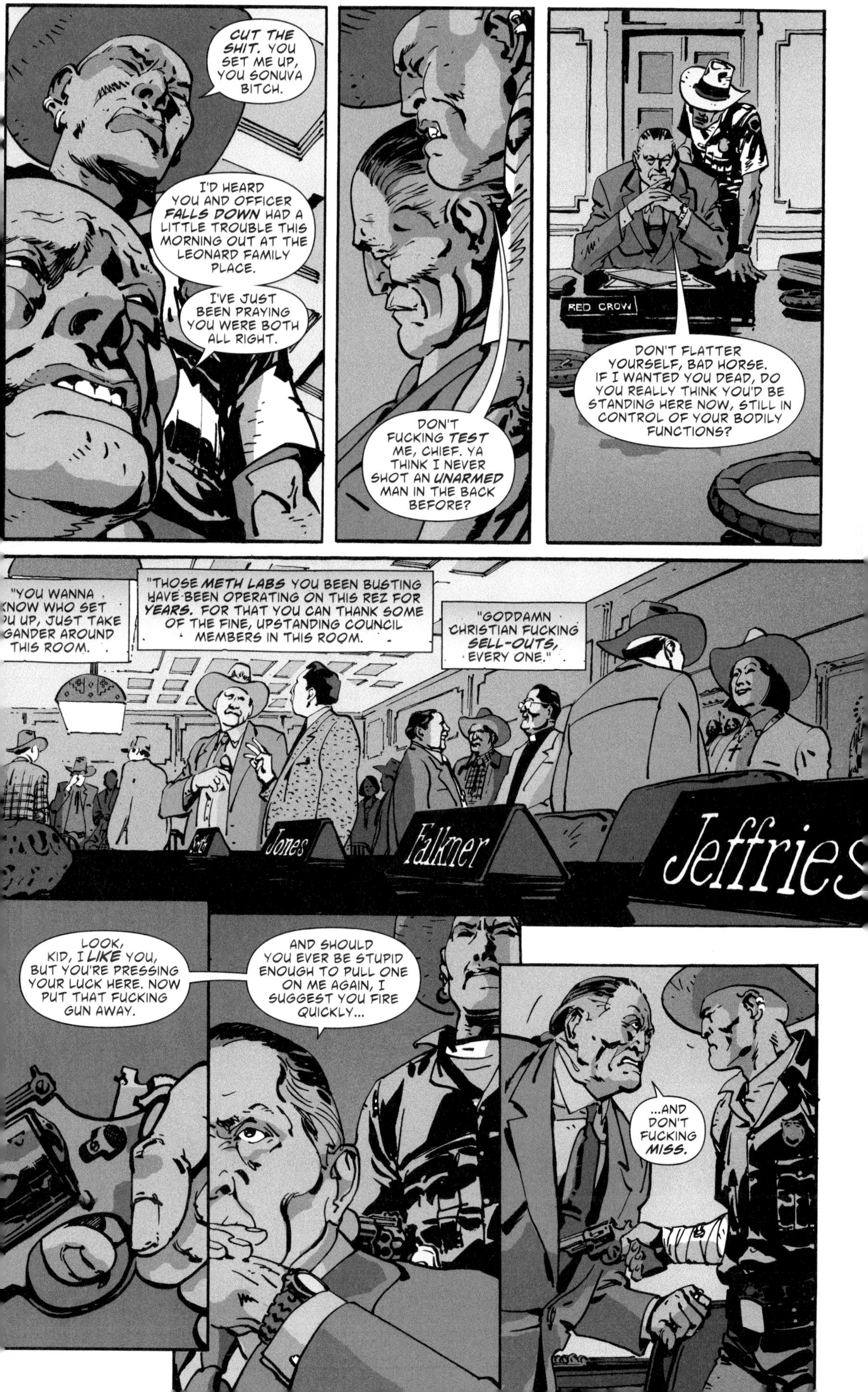
CUT THE SHIT. YOU SET ME UP, YOU SONUVA BITCH.
I'D HEARD YOU AND OFFICER FALLS DOWN HAD A LITTLE TROUBLE THIS MORNING OUT AT THE LEONARD FAMILY PLACE.
I'VE JUST BEEN PRAYING YOU WERE BOTH ALL RIGHT.
DON'T FUCKING TEST ME, CHIEF. YA THINK I NEVER SHOT AN UNARMED MAN IN THE BACK BEFORE?
RED CROW
DON'T FLATTER YOURSELF, BAD HORSE. IF I WANTED YOU DEAD, DO YOU REALLY THINK YOU'D BE STANDING HERE NOW, STILL IN CONTROL OF YOUR BODILY FUNCTIONS?
"YOU WANNA KNOW WHO SET OU UP, JUST TAKE GANDER AROUND THIS ROOM.
"THOSE METH LABS YOU BEEN BUSTING HAVE BEEN OPERATING ON THIS REZ FOR YEARS. FOR THAT YOU CAN THANK SOME OF THE FINE, UPSTANDING COUNCIL MEMBERS IN THIS ROOM.
"GODDAMN CHRISTIAN FUCKING SELL-OUTS, EVERY ONE."
Jones
Falkner
Jeffries
LOOK, KID, I LIKE YOU, BUT YOU'RE PRESSING YOUR LUCK HERE. NOW PUT THAT FUCKING GUN AWAY.
AND SHOULD YOU EVER BE STUPID ENOUGH TO PULL ONE ON ME AGAIN, I SUGGEST YOU FIRE QUICKLY...
...AND DON'T FUCKING MISS.

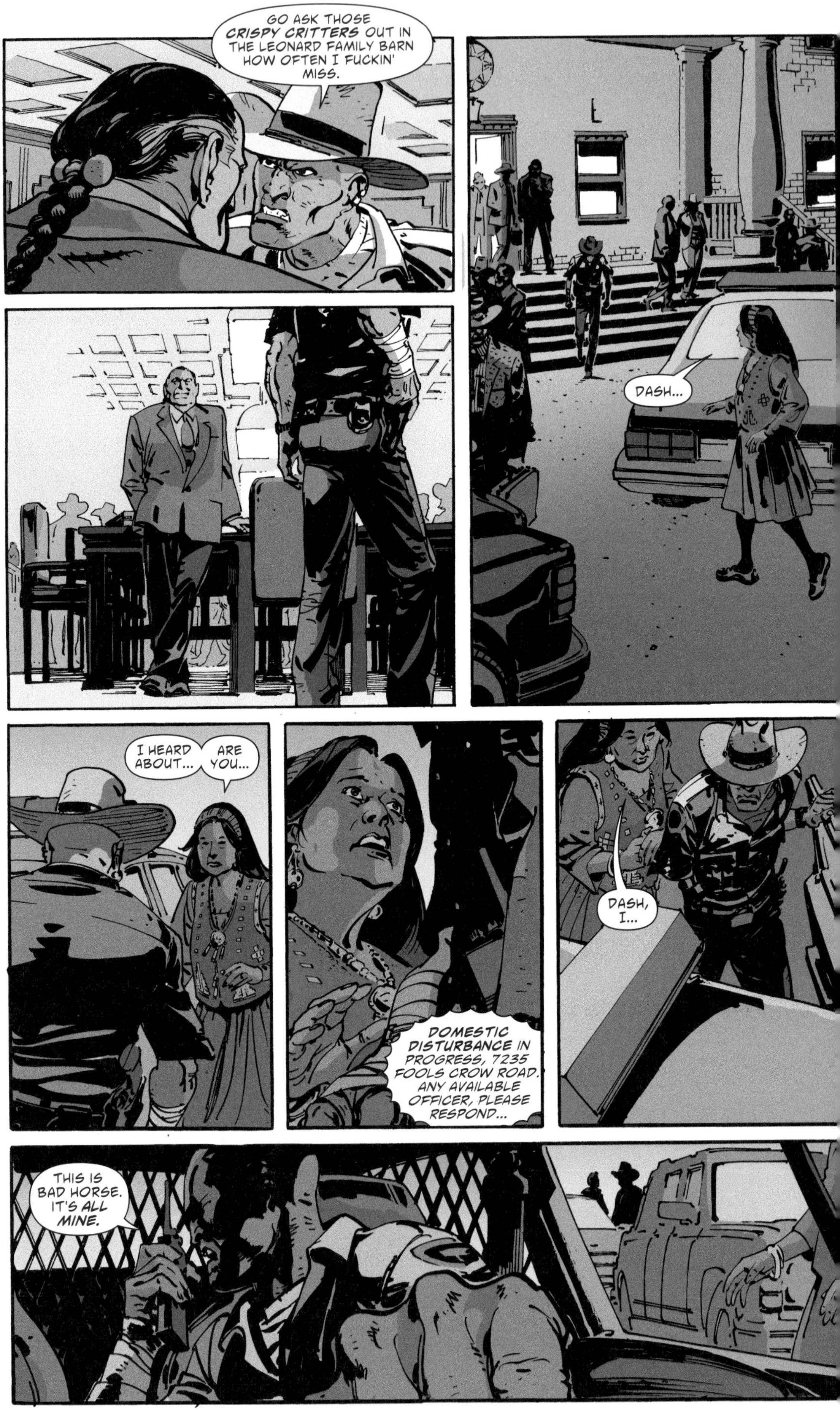

GO ASK THOSE CRISPY CRITTERS OUT IN THE LEONARD FAMILY BARN HOW OFTEN I FUCKIN' MISS.
DASH...
I HEARD ABOUT...
ARE YOU...
DOMESTIC DISTURBANCE IN PROGRESS, 7235 FOOLS CROW ROAD. ANY AVAILABLE OFFICER, PLEASE RESPOND...
DASH, I...
THIS IS BAD HORSE. IT'S ALL MINE.

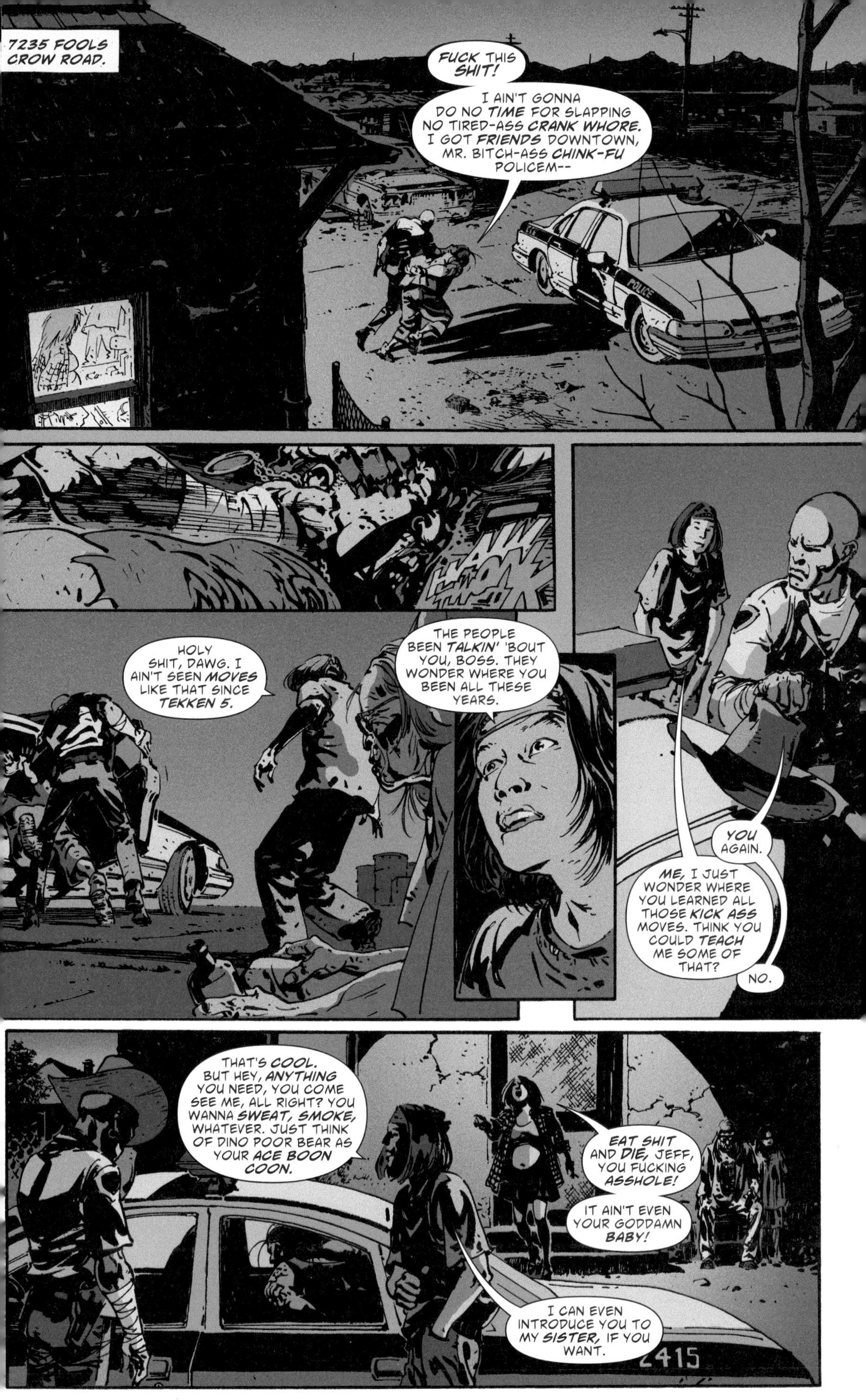
7235 FOOLS CROW ROAD.
FUCK THIS SHIT!
I AIN'T GONNA DO NO TIME FOR SLAPPING NO TIRED-ASS CRANK WHORE. I GOT FRIENDS DOWNTOWN, MR. BITCH-ASS CHINK-FU POLICEM--
POLICE
HOLY SHIT, DAWG. I AIN'T SEEN MOVES LIKE THAT SINCE TEKKEN 5.
THE PEOPLE BEEN TALKIN' 'BOUT YOU, BOSS. THEY WONDER WHERE YOU BEEN ALL THESE YEARS.
YOU AGAIN.
ME, I JUST WONDER WHERE YOU LEARNED ALL THOSE KICK ASS MOVES. THINK YOU COULD TEACH ME SOME OF THAT?
NO.
THAT'S COOL. BUT HEY, ANYTHING YOU NEED, YOU COME SEE ME, ALL RIGHT? YOU WANNA SWEAT, SMOKE, WHATEVER. JUST THINK OF DINO POOR BEAR AS YOUR ACE BOON COON.
EAT SHIT AND DIE, JEFF, YOU FUCKING ASSHOLE!
IT AIN'T EVEN YOUR GODDAMN BABY!
I CAN EVEN INTRODUCE YOU TO MY SISTER, IF YOU WANT.
2415

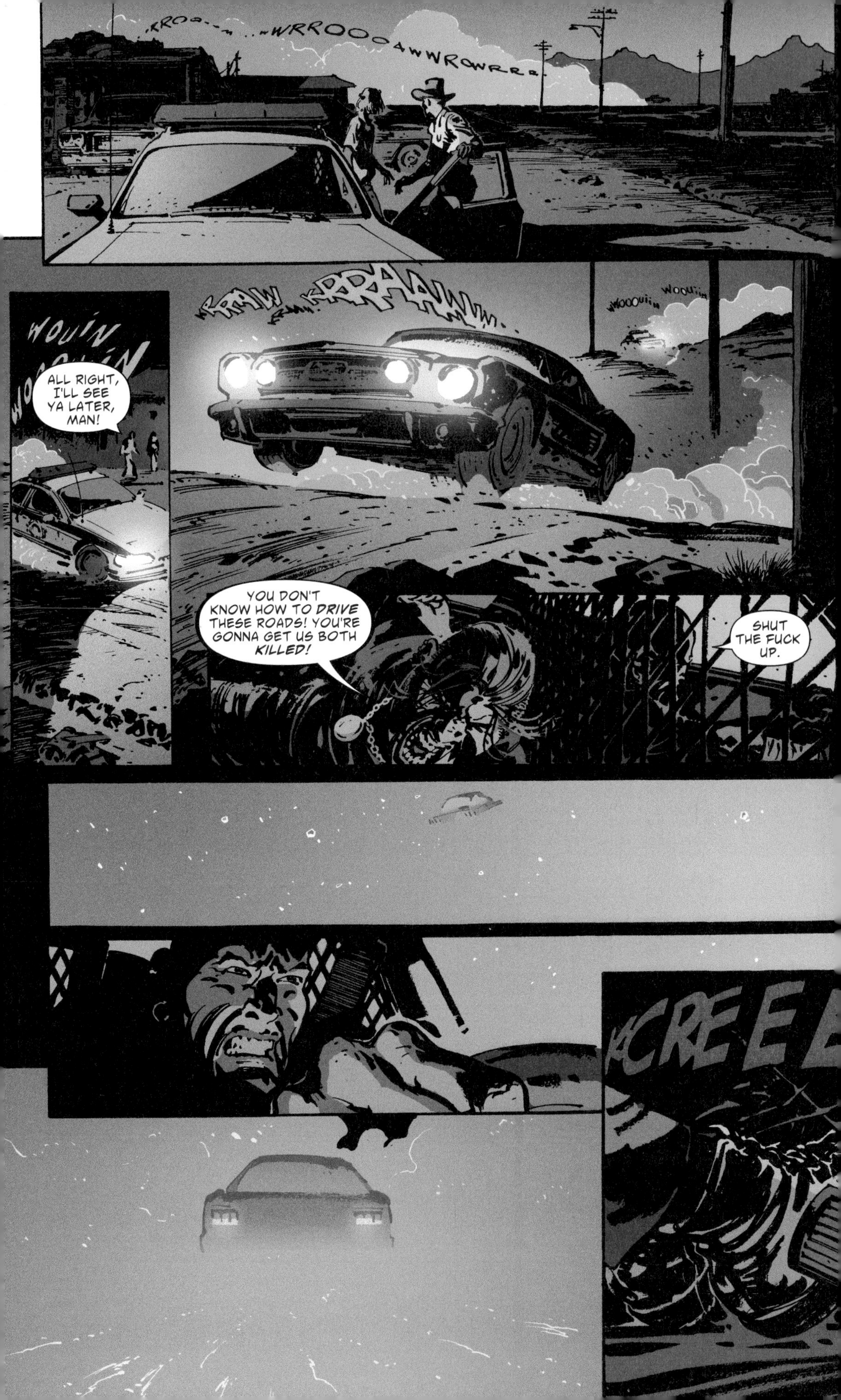

KROO---M ...MWRROOOAWWRAWRRRR.
WOUIN
ALL RIGHT, I'LL SEE YA LATER, MAN!
RAW KRRAAWW
WOOOUII WOOUIIN
YOU DON'T KNOW HOW TO DRIVE THESE ROADS! YOU'RE GONNA GET US BOTH KILLED!
SHUT THE FUCK UP.
CREE

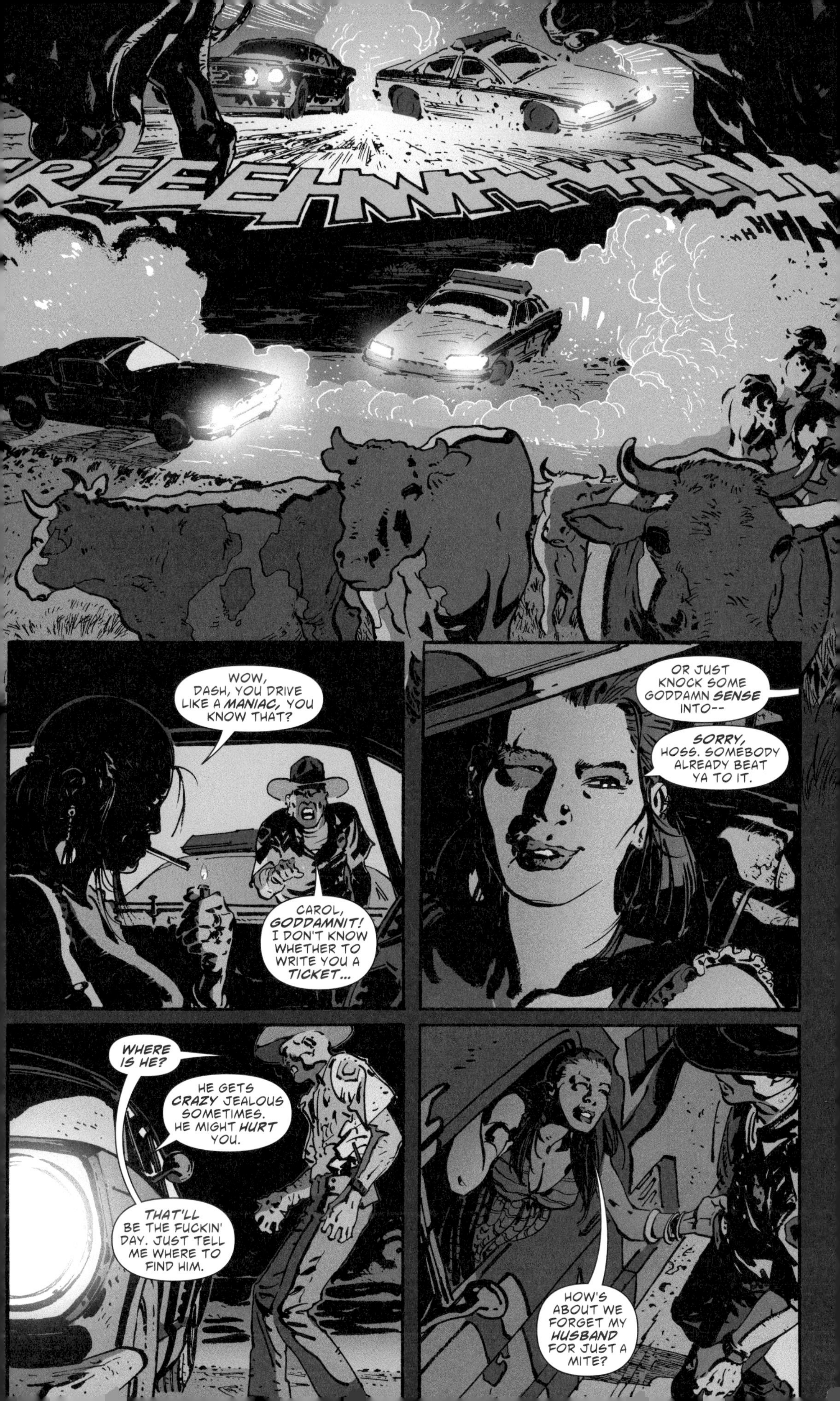
REEEHNNNHHH
WOW, DASH, YOU DRIVE LIKE A MANIAC, YOU KNOW THAT?
CAROL, GODDAMNIT! I DON'T KNOW WHETHER TO WRITE YOU A TICKET...
OR JUST KNOCK SOME GODDAMN SENSE INTO--
SORRY, HOSS. SOMEBODY ALREADY BEAT YA TO IT.
WHERE IS HE?
HE GETS CRAZY JEALOUS SOMETIMES. HE MIGHT HURT YOU.
THAT'LL BE THE FUCKIN' DAY. JUST TELL ME WHERE TO FIND HIM.
HOW'S ABOUT WE FORGET MY HUSBAND FOR JUST A MITE?

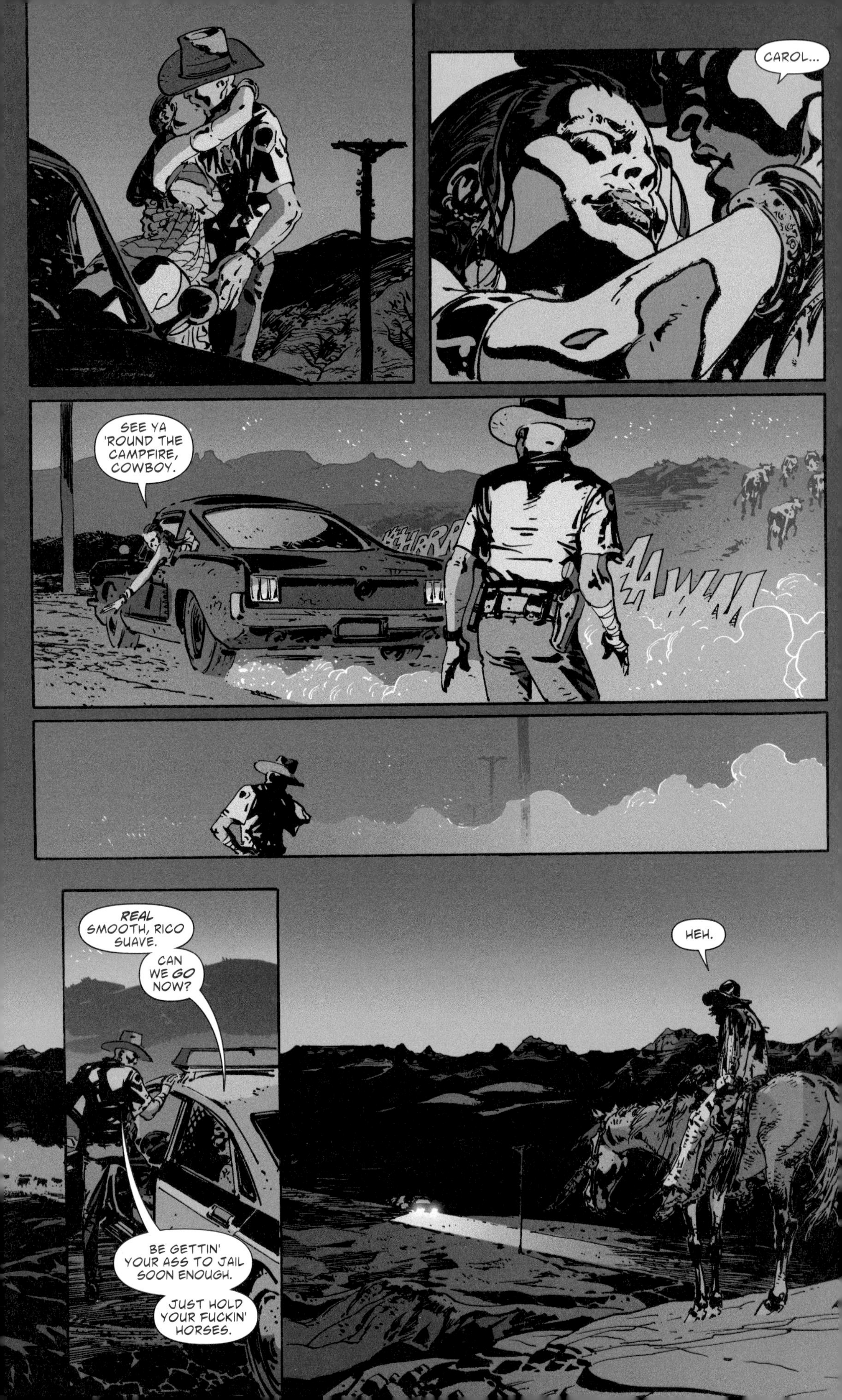
CAROL...
SEE YA 'ROUND THE CAMPFIRE, COWBOY.
SKREEE
REAL SMOOTH, RICO SUAVE.
CAN WE GO NOW?
BE GETTIN' YOUR ASS TO JAIL SOON ENOUGH.
JUST HOLD YOUR FUCKIN' HORSES.
HEH.

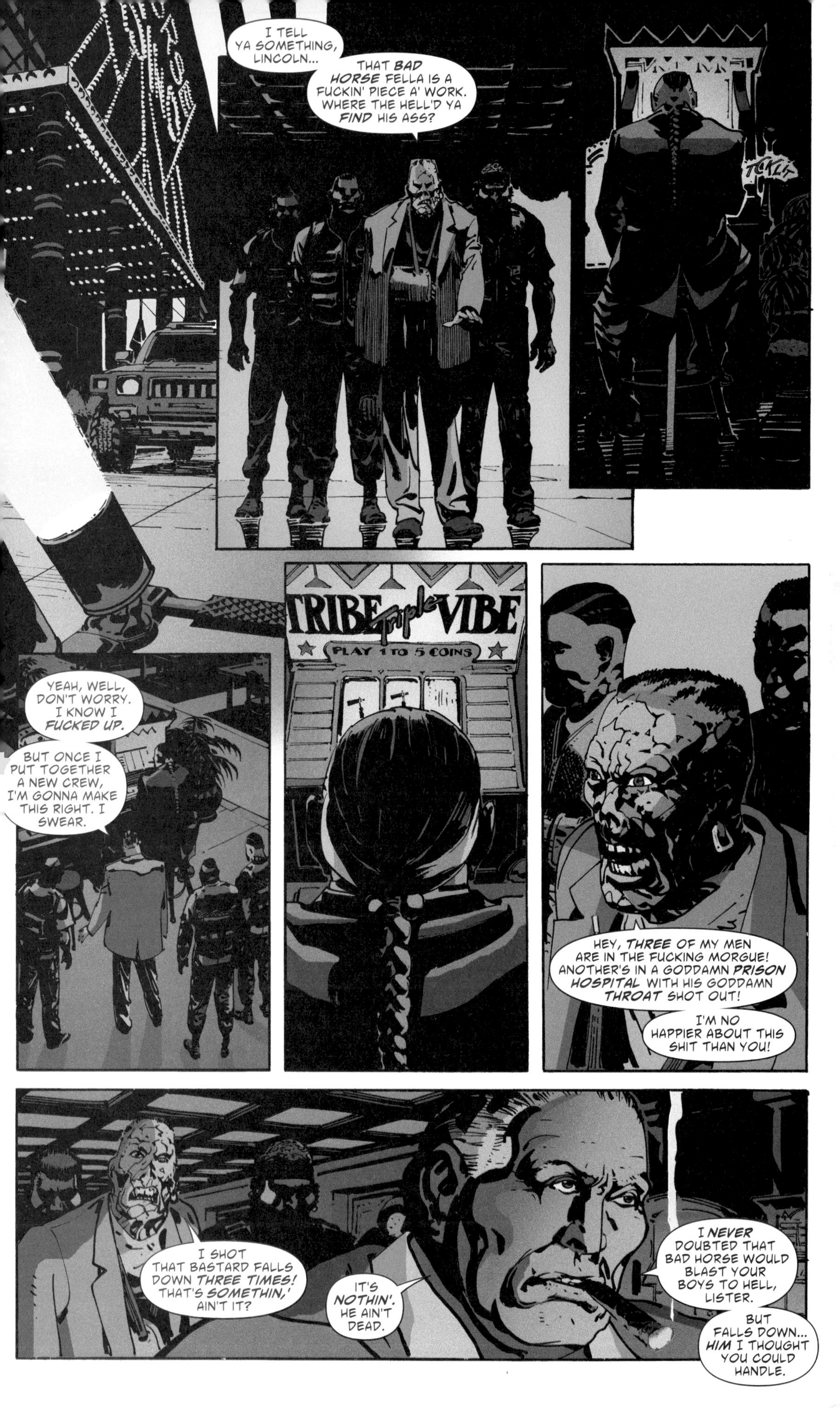
I TELL YA SOMETHING, LINCOLN...
THAT BAD HORSE FELLA IS A FUCKIN' PIECE A' WORK. WHERE THE HELL'D YA FIND HIS ASS?
YEAH, WELL, DON'T WORRY. I KNOW I FUCKED UP.
BUT ONCE I PUT TOGETHER A NEW CREW, I'M GONNA MAKE THIS RIGHT. I SWEAR.
TRIBE Triple VIBE
PLAY 1 TO 5 COINS
HEY, THREE OF MY MEN ARE IN THE FUCKING MORGUE! ANOTHER'S IN A GODDAMN PRISON HOSPITAL WITH HIS GODDAMN THROAT SHOT OUT!
I'M NO HAPPIER ABOUT THIS SHIT THAN YOU!
I SHOT THAT BASTARD FALLS DOWN THREE TIMES! THAT'S SOMETHIN,' AIN'T IT?
IT'S NOTHIN'. HE AIN'T DEAD.
I NEVER DOUBTED THAT BAD HORSE WOULD BLAST YOUR BOYS TO HELL, LISTER.
BUT FALLS DOWN... HIM I THOUGHT YOU COULD HANDLE.

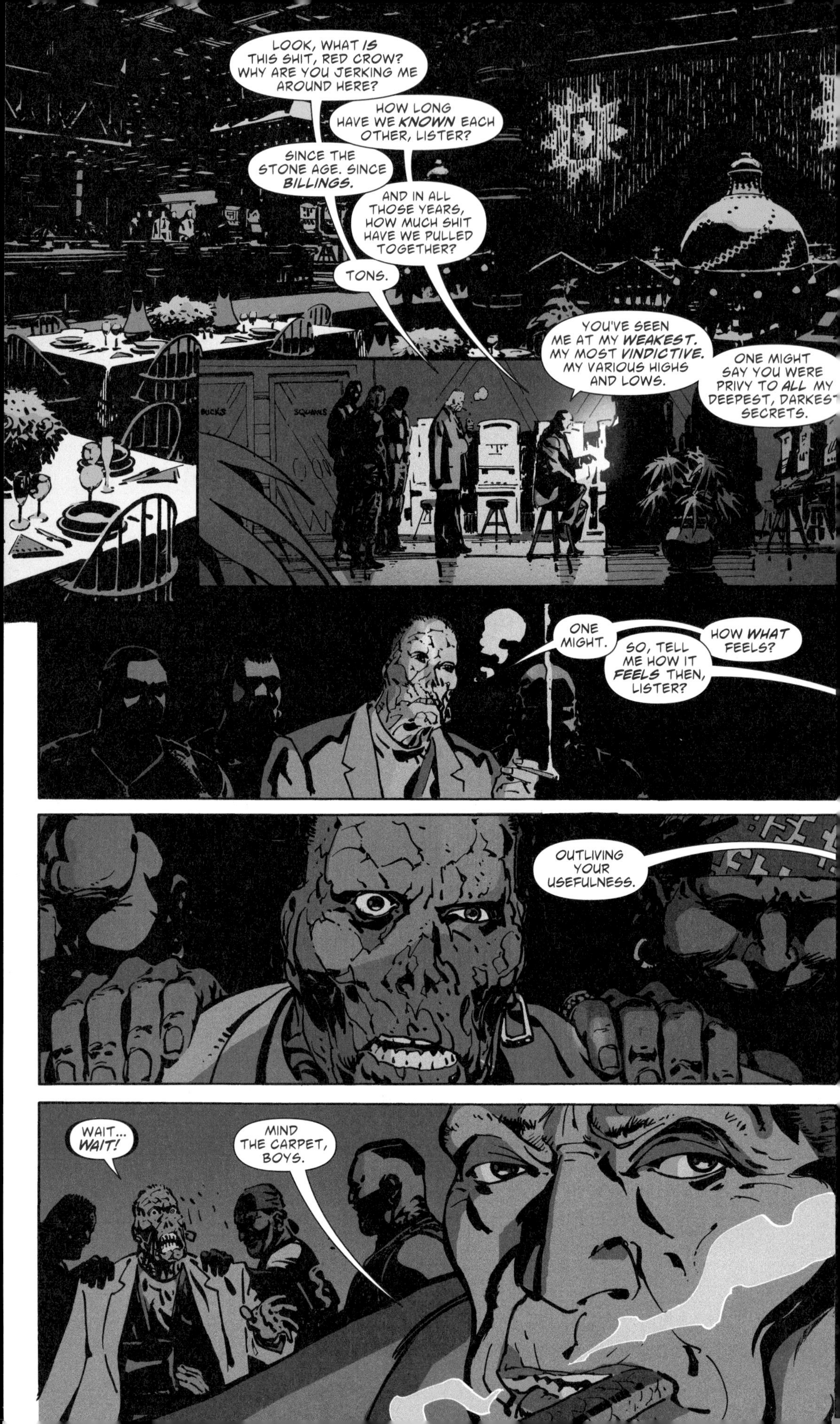
LOOK, WHAT *IS* THIS SHIT, RED CROW? WHY ARE YOU JERKING ME AROUND HERE?
HOW LONG HAVE WE *KNOWN* EACH OTHER, LISTER?
SINCE THE STONE AGE. SINCE *BILLINGS.*
AND IN ALL THOSE YEARS, HOW MUCH SHIT HAVE WE PULLED TOGETHER?
TONS.
YOU'VE SEEN ME AT MY *WEAKEST.* MY MOST *VINDICTIVE.* MY VARIOUS HIGHS AND LOWS.
ONE MIGHT SAY YOU WERE PRIVY TO *ALL* MY DEEPEST, DARKEST SECRETS.
ONE MIGHT.
SO, TELL ME HOW IT *FEELS* THEN, LISTER?
HOW *WHAT* FEELS?
OUTLIVING YOUR USEFULNESS.
WAIT... *WAIT!*
MIND THE CARPET, BOYS.

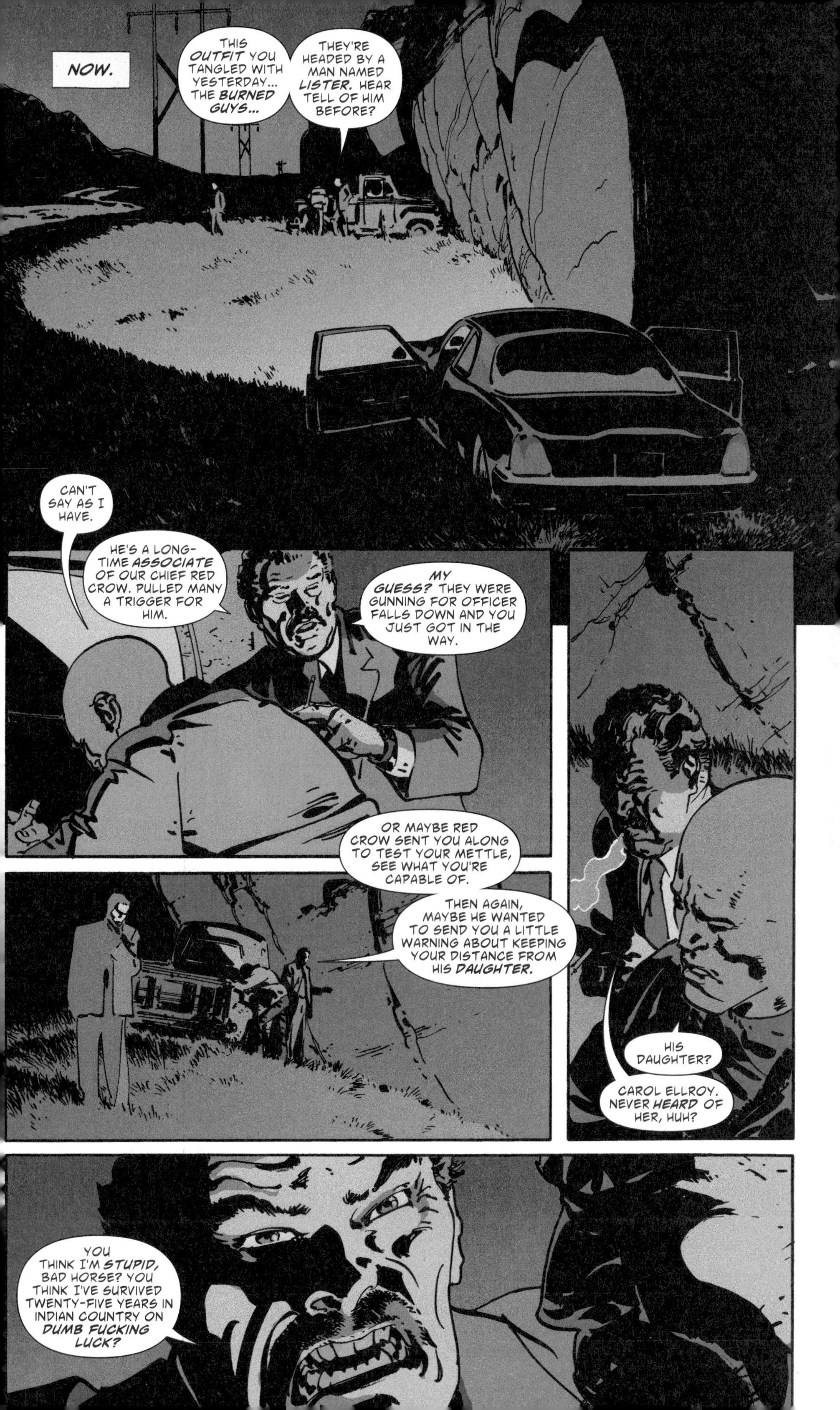
NOW.
THIS OUTFIT YOU TANGLED WITH YESTERDAY... THE BURNED GUYS...
THEY'RE HEADED BY A MAN NAMED LISTER. HEAR TELL OF HIM BEFORE?
CAN'T SAY AS I HAVE.
HE'S A LONG-TIME ASSOCIATE OF OUR CHIEF RED CROW. PULLED MANY A TRIGGER FOR HIM.
MY GUESS? THEY WERE GUNNING FOR OFFICER FALLS DOWN AND YOU JUST GOT IN THE WAY.
OR MAYBE RED CROW SENT YOU ALONG TO TEST YOUR METTLE, SEE WHAT YOU'RE CAPABLE OF.
THEN AGAIN, MAYBE HE WANTED TO SEND YOU A LITTLE WARNING ABOUT KEEPING YOUR DISTANCE FROM HIS DAUGHTER.
HIS DAUGHTER?
CAROL ELLROY. NEVER HEARD OF HER, HUH?
YOU THINK I'M STUPID, BAD HORSE? YOU THINK I'VE SURVIVED TWENTY-FIVE YEARS IN INDIAN COUNTRY ON DUMB FUCKING LUCK?

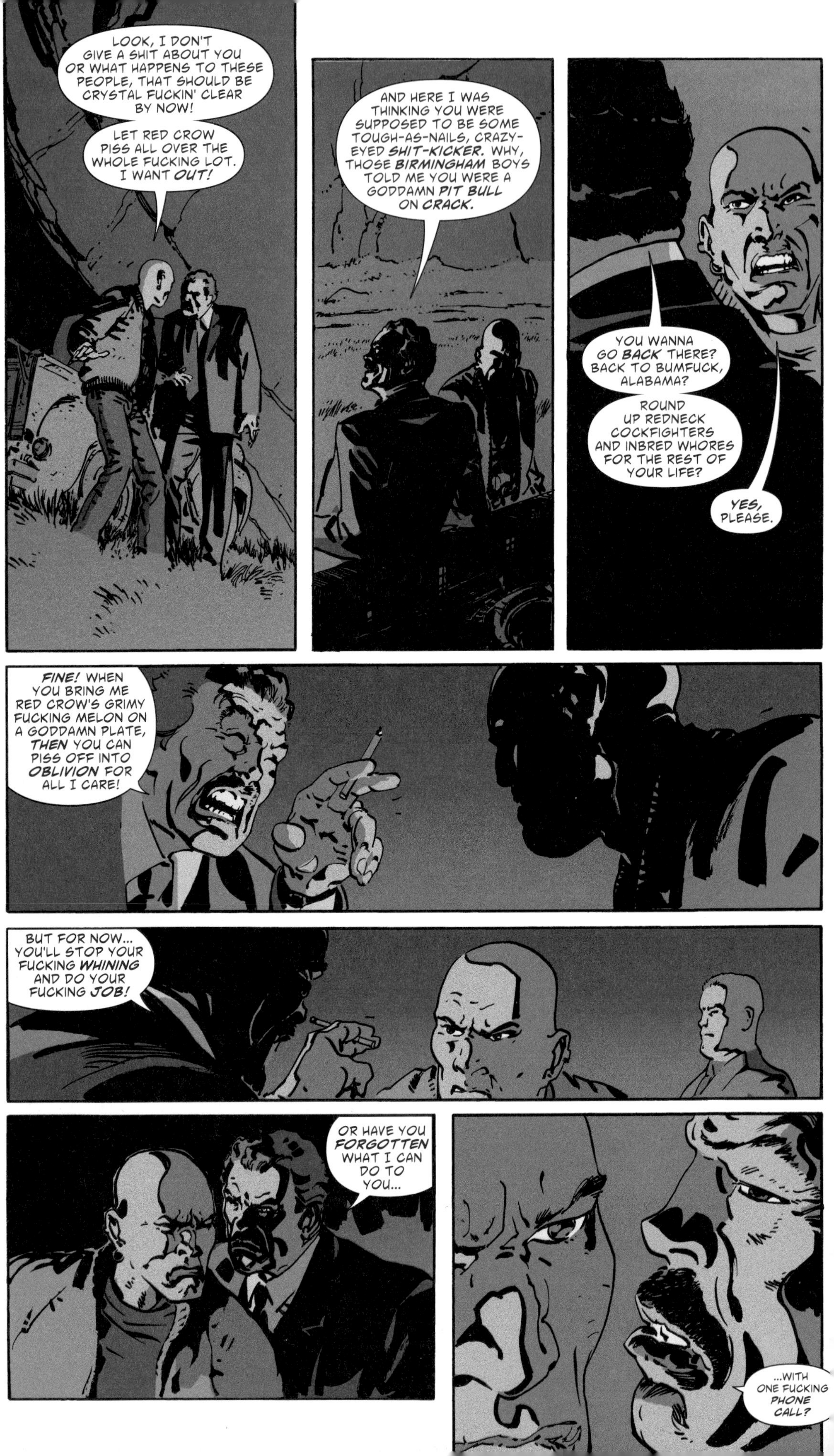
LOOK, I DON'T GIVE A SHIT ABOUT YOU OR WHAT HAPPENS TO THESE PEOPLE, THAT SHOULD BE CRYSTAL FUCKIN' CLEAR BY NOW!
LET RED CROW PISS ALL OVER THE WHOLE FUCKING LOT. I WANT OUT!
AND HERE I WAS THINKING YOU WERE SUPPOSED TO BE SOME TOUGH-AS-NAILS, CRAZY-EYED SHIT-KICKER. WHY, THOSE BIRMINGHAM BOYS TOLD ME YOU WERE A GODDAMN PIT BULL ON CRACK.
YOU WANNA GO BACK THERE? BACK TO BUMFUCK, ALABAMA?
ROUND UP REDNECK COCKFIGHTERS AND INBRED WHORES FOR THE REST OF YOUR LIFE?
YES, PLEASE.
FINE! WHEN YOU BRING ME RED CROW'S GRIMY FUCKING MELON ON A GODDAMN PLATE, THEN YOU CAN PISS OFF INTO OBLIVION FOR ALL I CARE!
BUT FOR NOW... YOU'LL STOP YOUR FUCKING WHINING AND DO YOUR FUCKING JOB!
OR HAVE YOU FORGOTTEN WHAT I CAN DO TO YOU...
...WITH ONE FUCKING PHONE CALL?

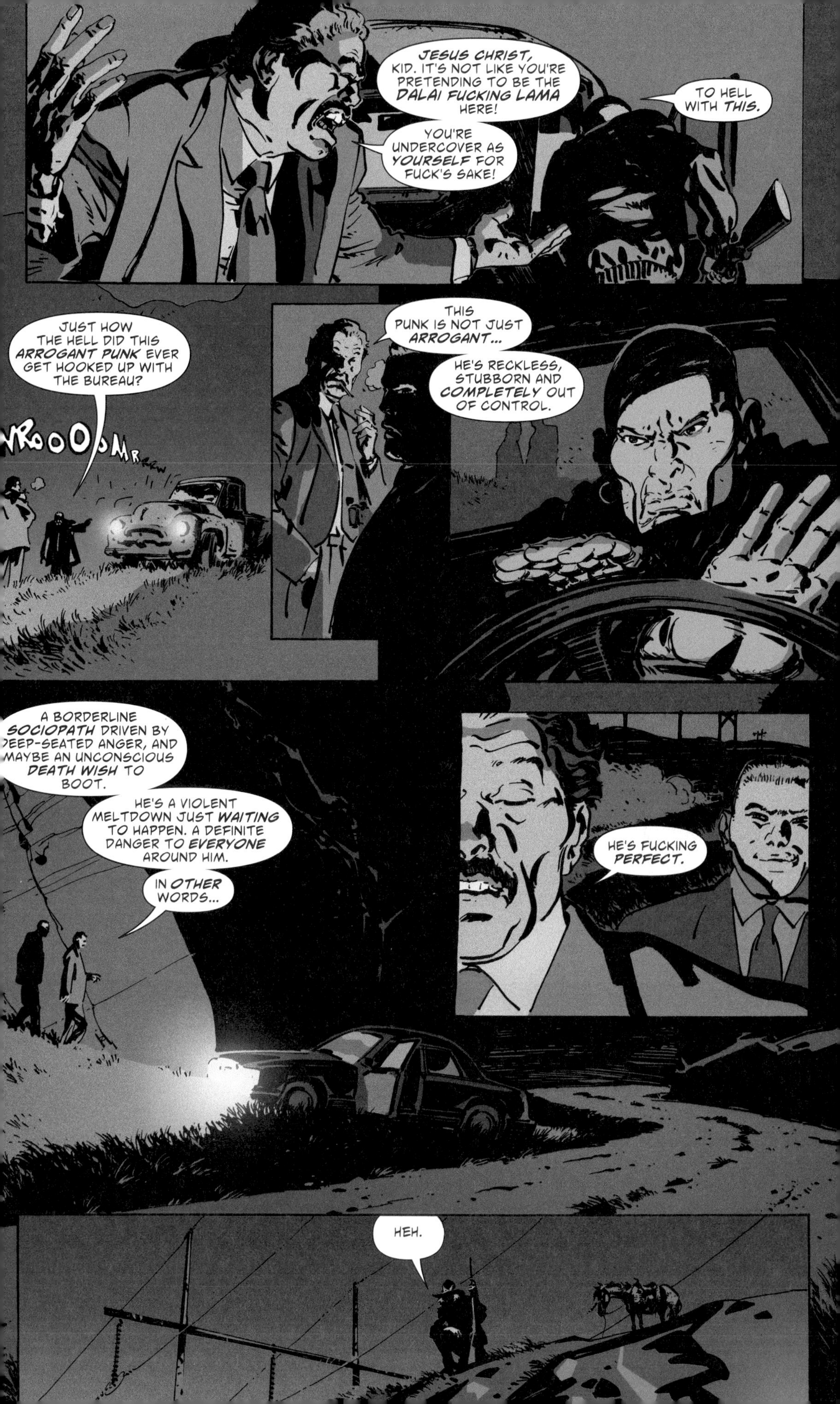
JESUS CHRIST, KID. IT'S NOT LIKE YOU'RE PRETENDING TO BE THE DALAI FUCKING LAMA HERE!
YOU'RE UNDERCOVER AS YOURSELF FOR FUCK'S SAKE!
TO HELL WITH THIS.
JUST HOW THE HELL DID THIS ARROGANT PUNK EVER GET HOOKED UP WITH THE BUREAU?
VROOOOMR
THIS PUNK IS NOT JUST ARROGANT...
HE'S RECKLESS, STUBBORN AND COMPLETELY OUT OF CONTROL.
A BORDERLINE SOCIOPATH DRIVEN BY DEEP-SEATED ANGER, AND MAYBE AN UNCONSCIOUS DEATH WISH TO BOOT.
HE'S A VIOLENT MELTDOWN JUST WAITING TO HAPPEN. A DEFINITE DANGER TO EVERYONE AROUND HIM.
IN OTHER WORDS...
HE'S FUCKING PERFECT.
HEH.

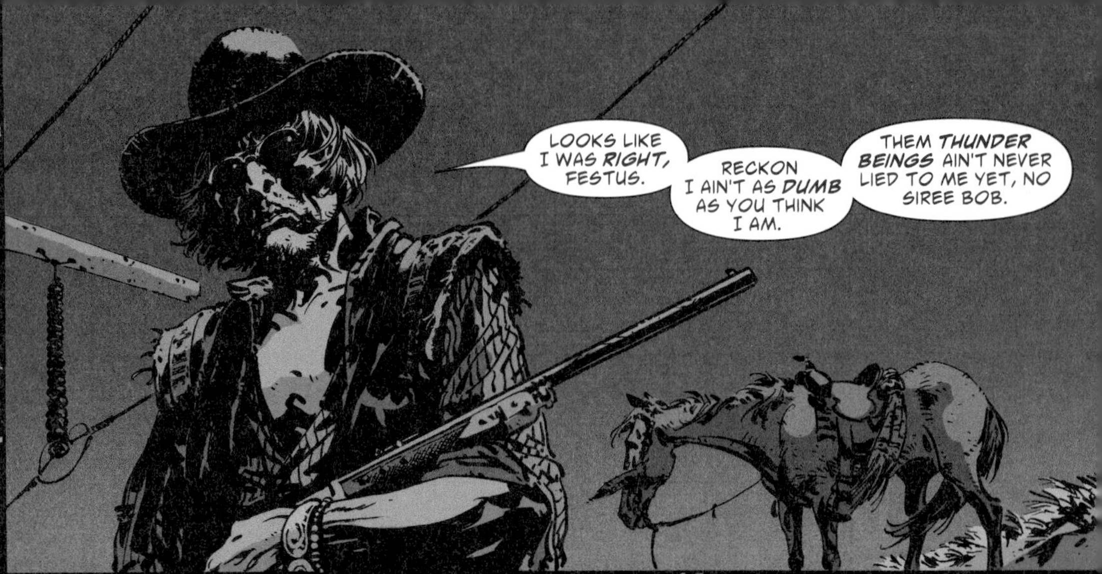
LOOKS LIKE I WAS RIGHT, FESTUS.
RECKON I AIN'T AS DUMB AS YOU THINK I AM.
THEM THUNDER BEINGS AIN'T NEVER LIED TO ME YET, NO SIREE BOB.

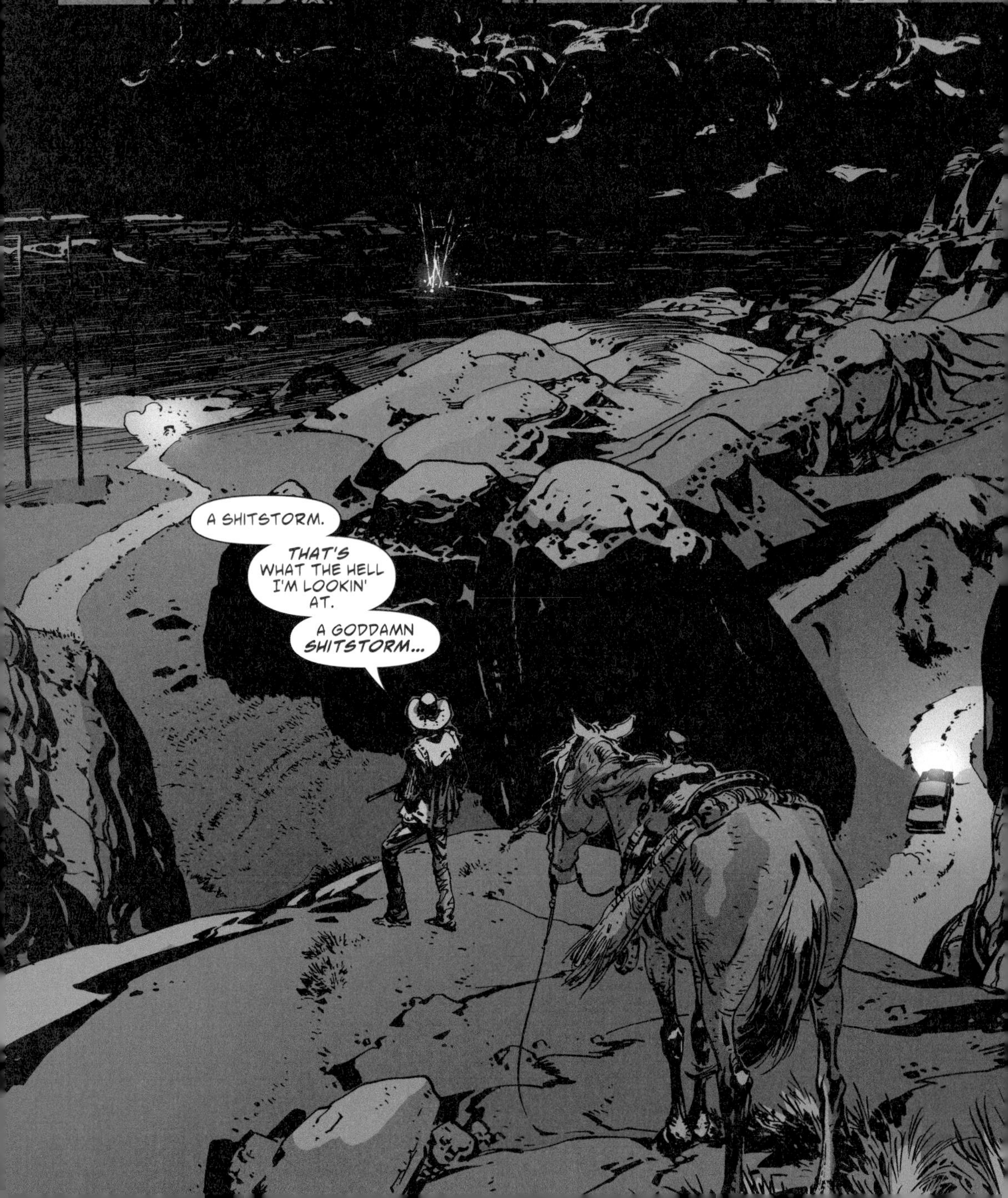
A SHITSTORM.
THAT'S WHAT THE HELL I'M LOOKIN' AT.
A GODDAMN SHITSTORM...

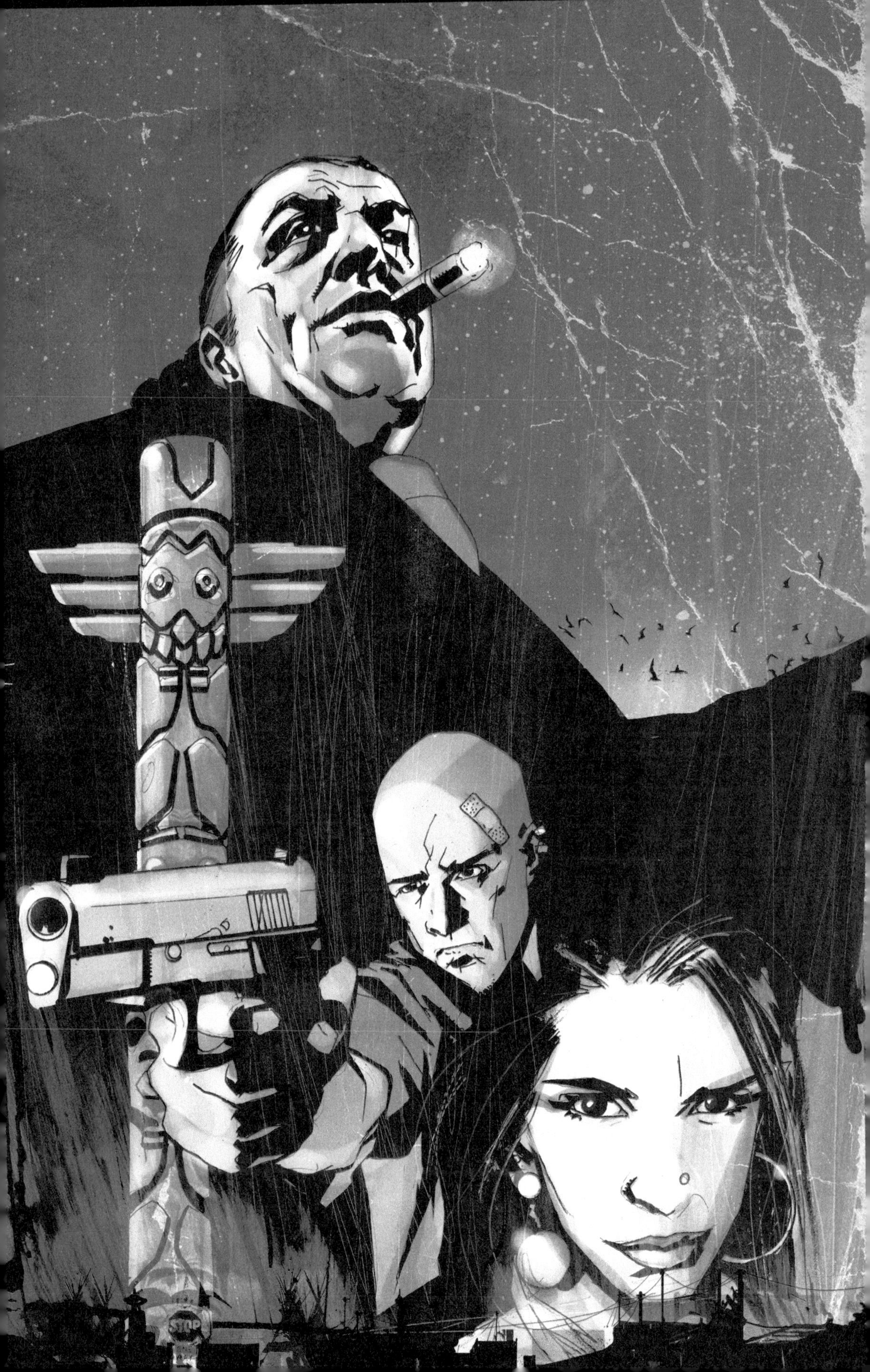
STOP

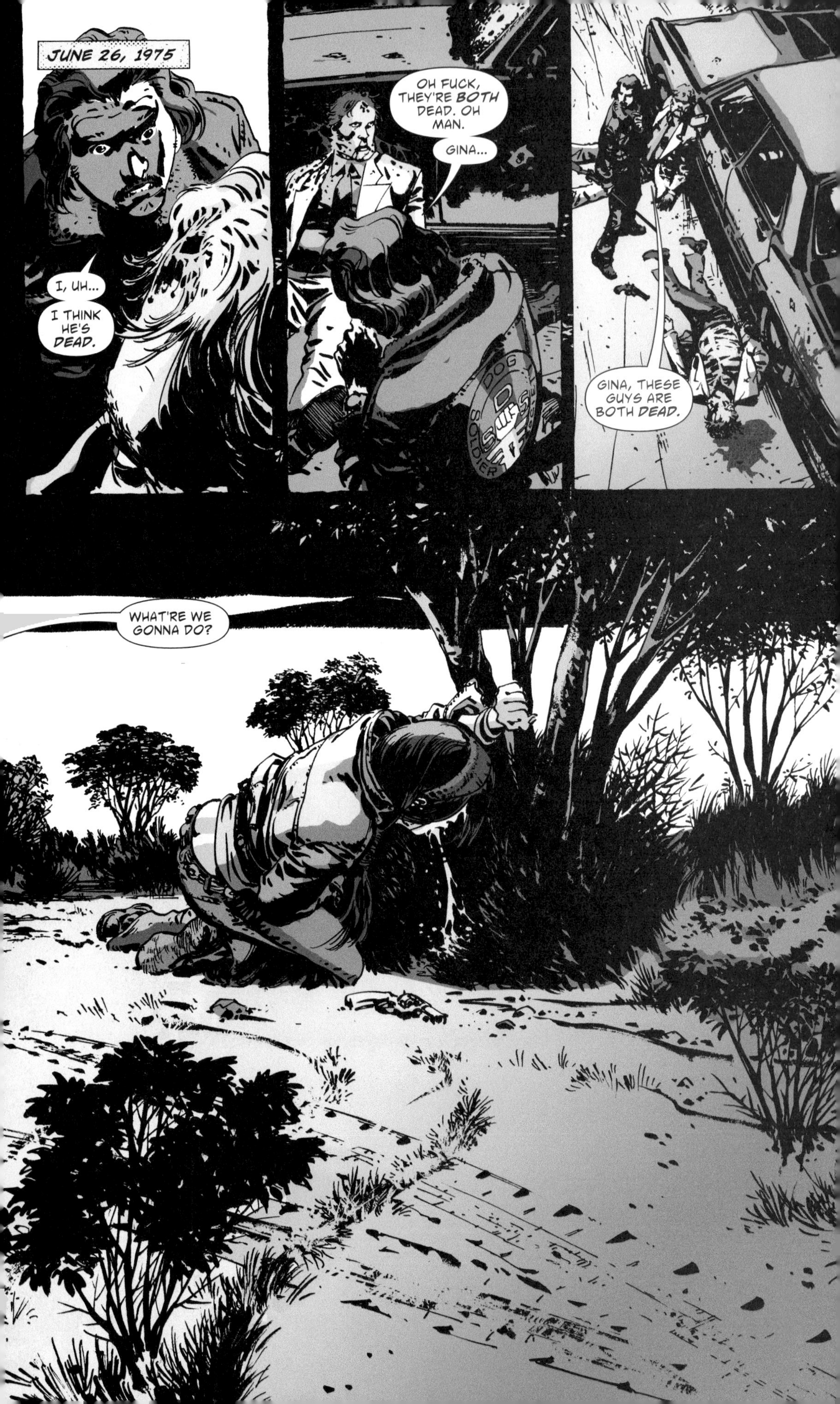
JUNE 26, 1975
I, UH...
I THINK HE'S DEAD.
OH FUCK, THEY'RE BOTH DEAD. OH MAN.
GINA...
GINA, THESE GUYS ARE BOTH DEAD.
WHAT'RE WE GONNA DO?

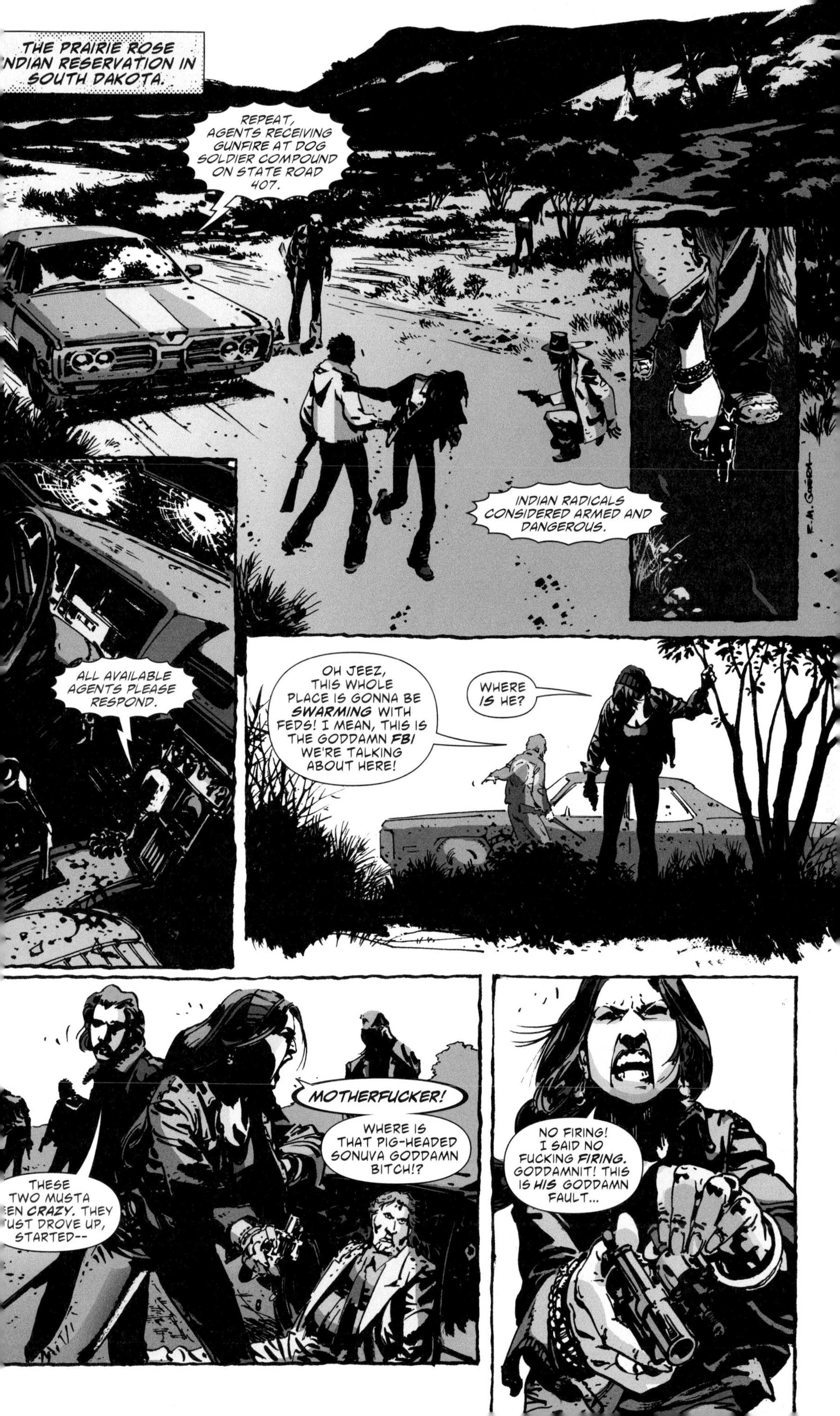
THE PRAIRIE ROSE INDIAN RESERVATION IN SOUTH DAKOTA.
REPEAT, AGENTS RECEIVING GUNFIRE AT DOG SOLDIER COMPOUND ON STATE ROAD 407.
INDIAN RADICALS CONSIDERED ARMED AND DANGEROUS.
ALL AVAILABLE AGENTS PLEASE RESPOND.
OH JEEZ, THIS WHOLE PLACE IS GONNA BE SWARMING WITH FEDS! I MEAN, THIS IS THE GODDAMN FBI WE'RE TALKING ABOUT HERE!
WHERE IS HE?
THESE TWO MUSTA BEEN CRAZY. THEY JUST DROVE UP, STARTED--
MOTHERFUCKER!
WHERE IS THAT PIG-HEADED SONUVA GODDAMN BITCH!?
NO FIRING! I SAID NO FUCKING FIRING. GODDAMNIT! THIS IS HIS GODDAMN FAULT...

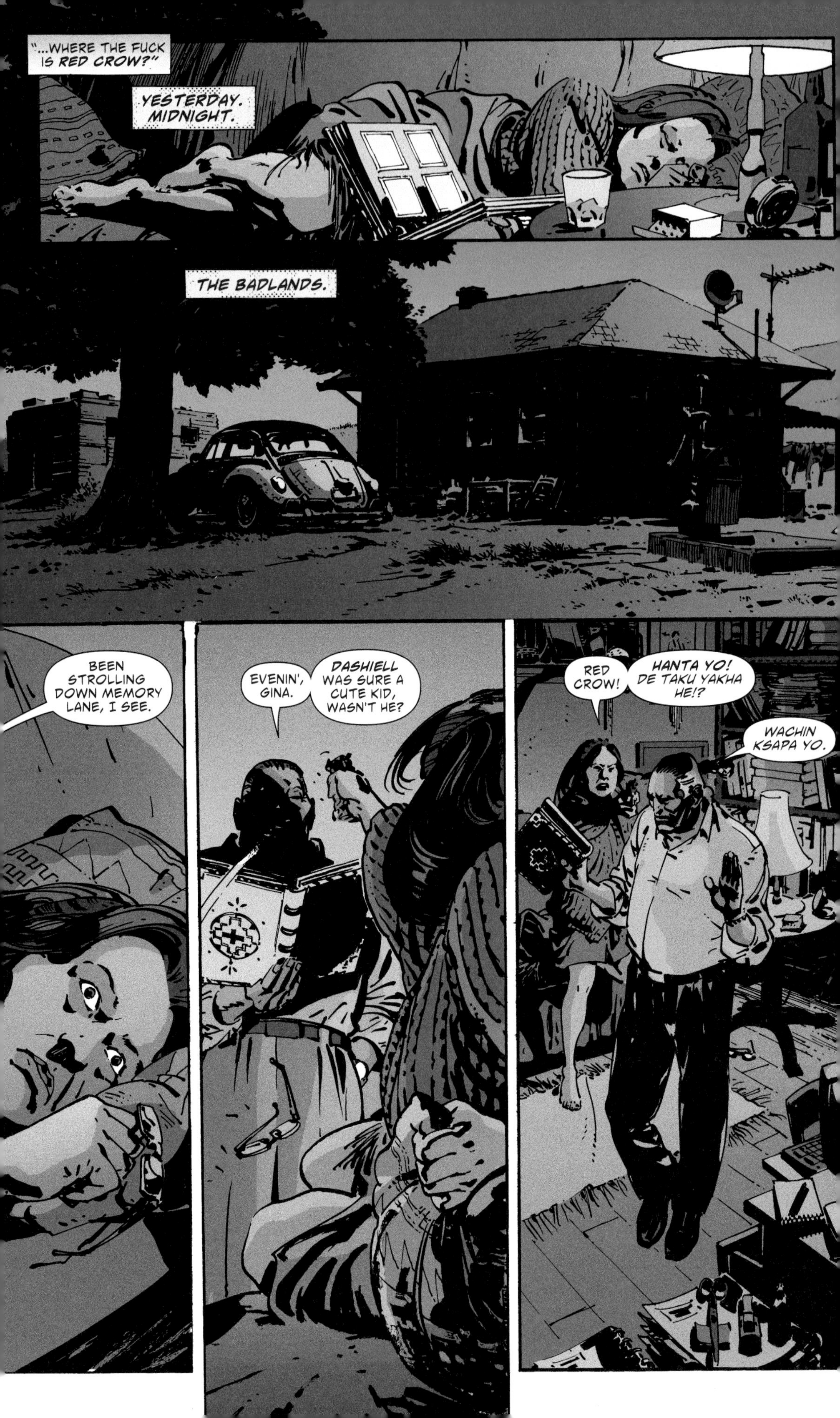
"...WHERE THE FUCK IS RED CROW?"
YESTERDAY. MIDNIGHT.
THE BADLANDS.
BEEN STROLLING DOWN MEMORY LANE, I SEE.
EVENIN', GINA.
DASHIELL WAS SURE A CUTE KID, WASN'T HE?
RED CROW!
HANTA YO! DE TAKU YAKHA HE!?
WACHIN KSAPA YO.

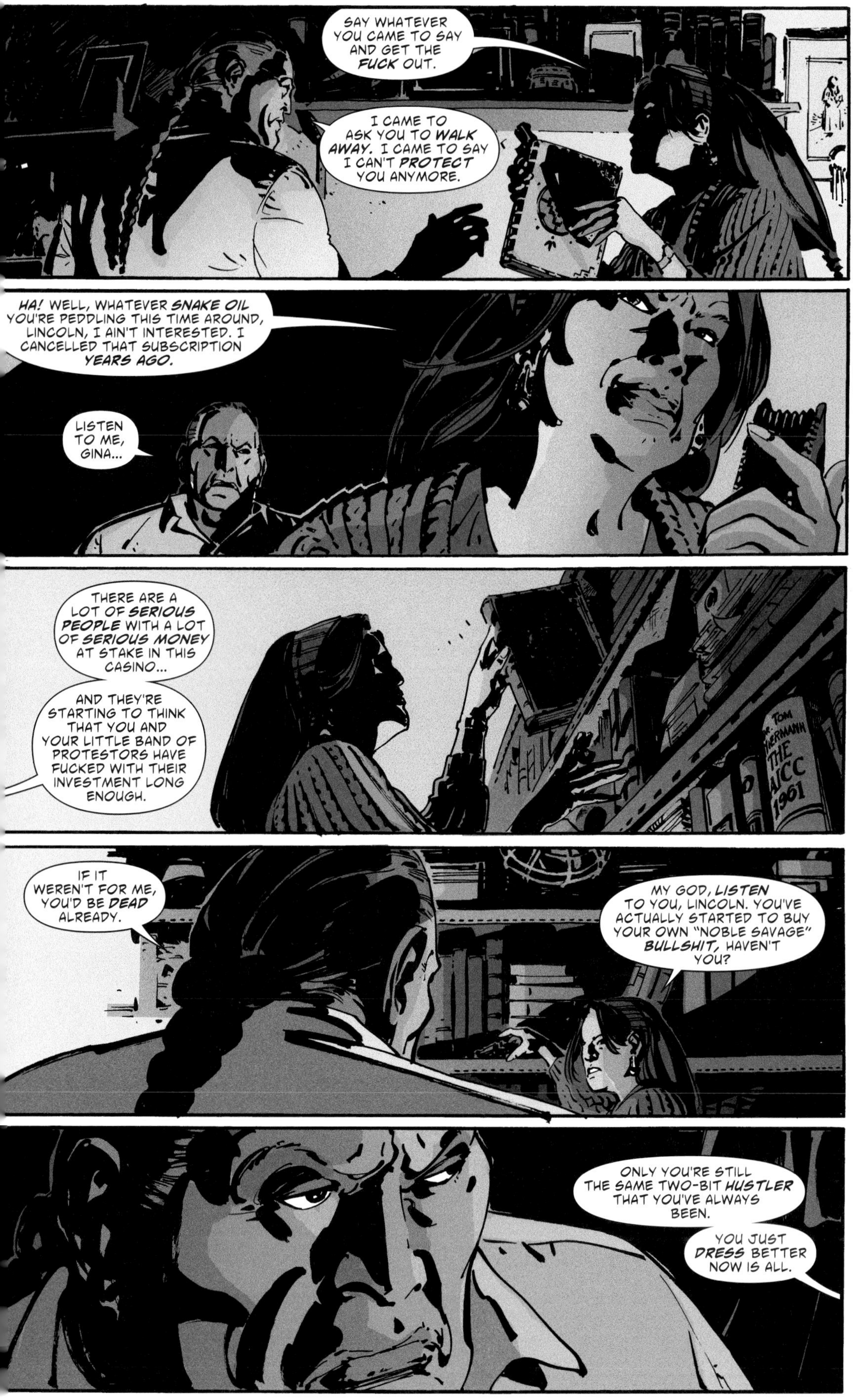
SAY WHATEVER YOU CAME TO SAY AND GET THE FUCK OUT.
I CAME TO ASK YOU TO WALK AWAY. I CAME TO SAY I CAN'T PROTECT YOU ANYMORE.
HA! WELL, WHATEVER SNAKE OIL YOU'RE PEDDLING THIS TIME AROUND, LINCOLN, I AIN'T INTERESTED. I CANCELLED THAT SUBSCRIPTION YEARS AGO.
LISTEN TO ME, GINA...
THERE ARE A LOT OF SERIOUS PEOPLE WITH A LOT OF SERIOUS MONEY AT STAKE IN THIS CASINO...
AND THEY'RE STARTING TO THINK THAT YOU AND YOUR LITTLE BAND OF PROTESTORS HAVE FUCKED WITH THEIR INVESTMENT LONG ENOUGH.
IF IT WEREN'T FOR ME, YOU'D BE DEAD ALREADY.
MY GOD, LISTEN TO YOU, LINCOLN. YOU'VE ACTUALLY STARTED TO BUY YOUR OWN "NOBLE SAVAGE" BULLSHIT, HAVEN'T YOU?
ONLY YOU'RE STILL THE SAME TWO-BIT HUSTLER THAT YOU'VE ALWAYS BEEN.
YOU JUST DRESS BETTER NOW IS ALL.

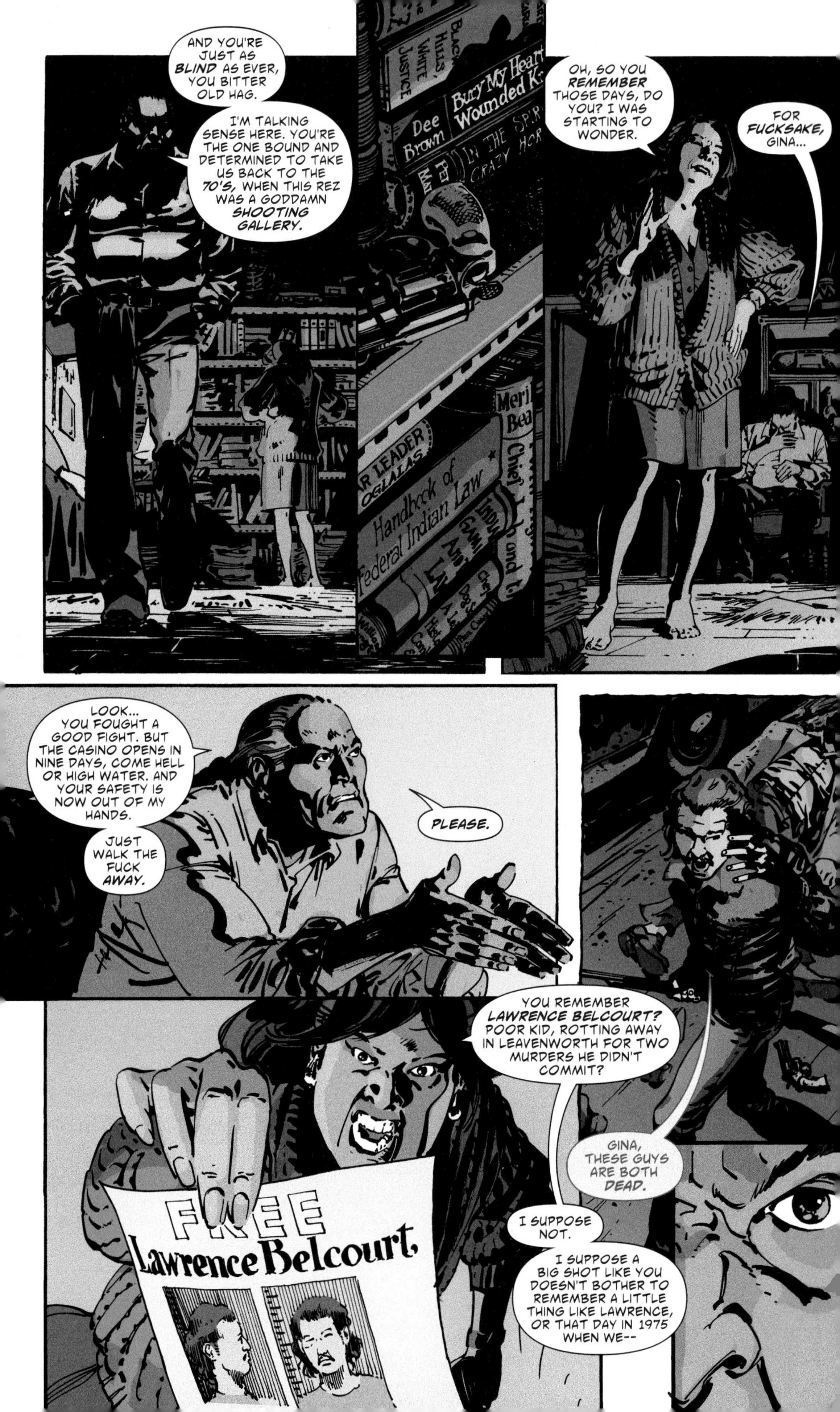

AND YOU'RE JUST AS BLIND AS EVER, YOU BITTER OLD HAG.
I'M TALKING SENSE HERE. YOU'RE THE ONE BOUND AND DETERMINED TO TAKE US BACK TO THE 70'S, WHEN THIS REZ WAS A GODDAMN SHOOTING GALLERY.
Black Hills White Justice
Dee Brown
Bury My Heart at Wounded Knee
In the Spirit of Crazy Horse
OH, SO YOU REMEMBER THOSE DAYS, DO YOU? I WAS STARTING TO WONDER.
FOR FUCKSAKE, GINA...
Handbook of Federal Indian Law
Oglalas
LOOK... YOU FOUGHT A GOOD FIGHT. BUT THE CASINO OPENS IN NINE DAYS, COME HELL OR HIGH WATER. AND YOUR SAFETY IS NOW OUT OF MY HANDS.
JUST WALK THE FUCK AWAY.
PLEASE.
YOU REMEMBER LAWRENCE BELCOURT? POOR KID, ROTTING AWAY IN LEAVENWORTH FOR TWO MURDERS HE DIDN'T COMMIT?
GINA, THESE GUYS ARE BOTH DEAD.
I SUPPOSE NOT.
I SUPPOSE A BIG SHOT LIKE YOU DOESN'T BOTHER TO REMEMBER A LITTLE THING LIKE LAWRENCE, OR THAT DAY IN 1975 WHEN WE--
FREE Lawrence Belcourt,

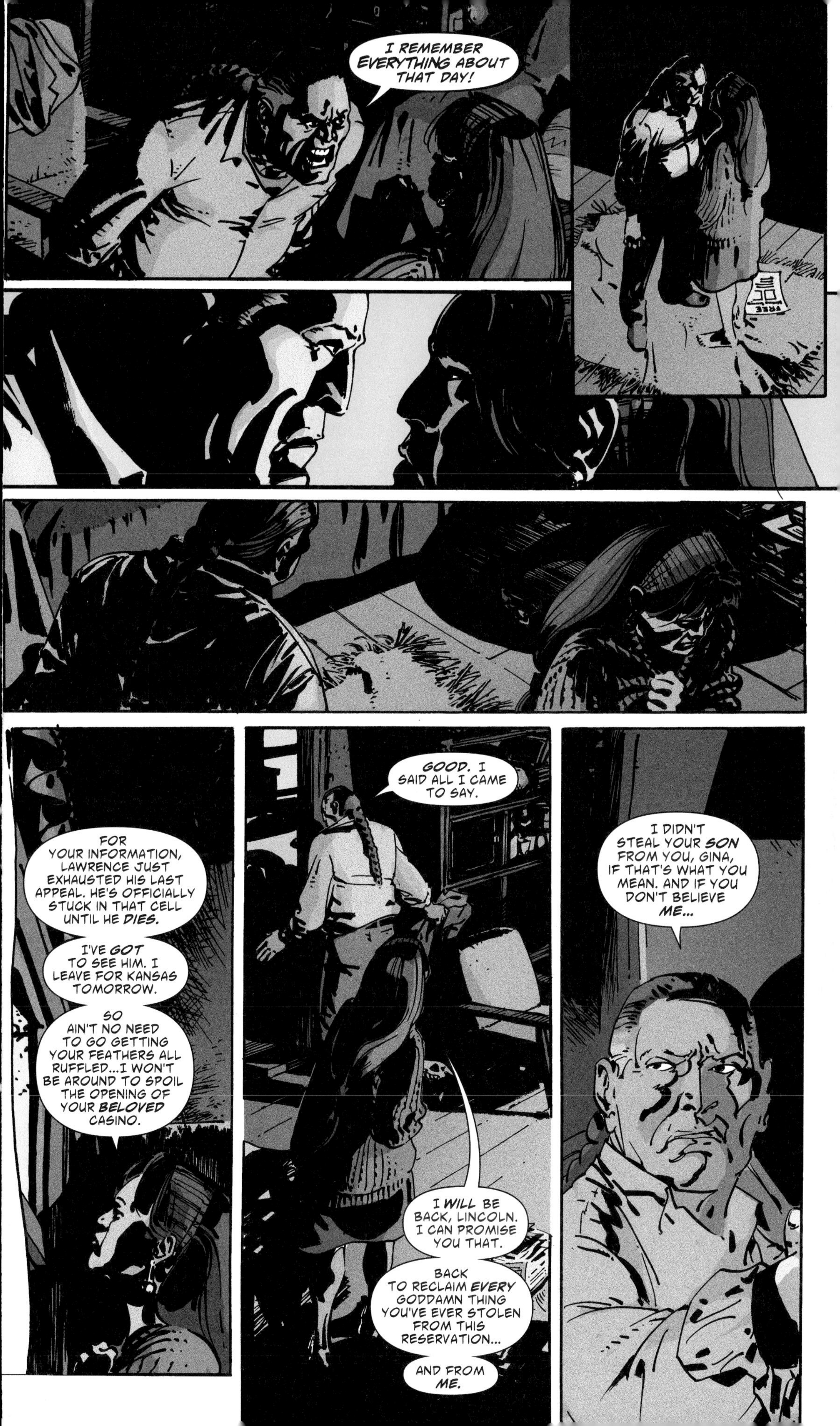
I REMEMBER EVERYTHING ABOUT THAT DAY!
FOR YOUR INFORMATION, LAWRENCE JUST EXHAUSTED HIS LAST APPEAL. HE'S OFFICIALLY STUCK IN THAT CELL UNTIL HE DIES.
I'VE GOT TO SEE HIM. I LEAVE FOR KANSAS TOMORROW.
SO AIN'T NO NEED TO GO GETTING YOUR FEATHERS ALL RUFFLED...I WON'T BE AROUND TO SPOIL THE OPENING OF YOUR BELOVED CASINO.
GOOD. I SAID ALL I CAME TO SAY.
I WILL BE BACK, LINCOLN. I CAN PROMISE YOU THAT.
BACK TO RECLAIM EVERY GODDAMN THING YOU'VE EVER STOLEN FROM THIS RESERVATION...
AND FROM ME.
I DIDN'T STEAL YOUR SON FROM YOU, GINA, IF THAT'S WHAT YOU MEAN. AND IF YOU DON'T BELIEVE ME...

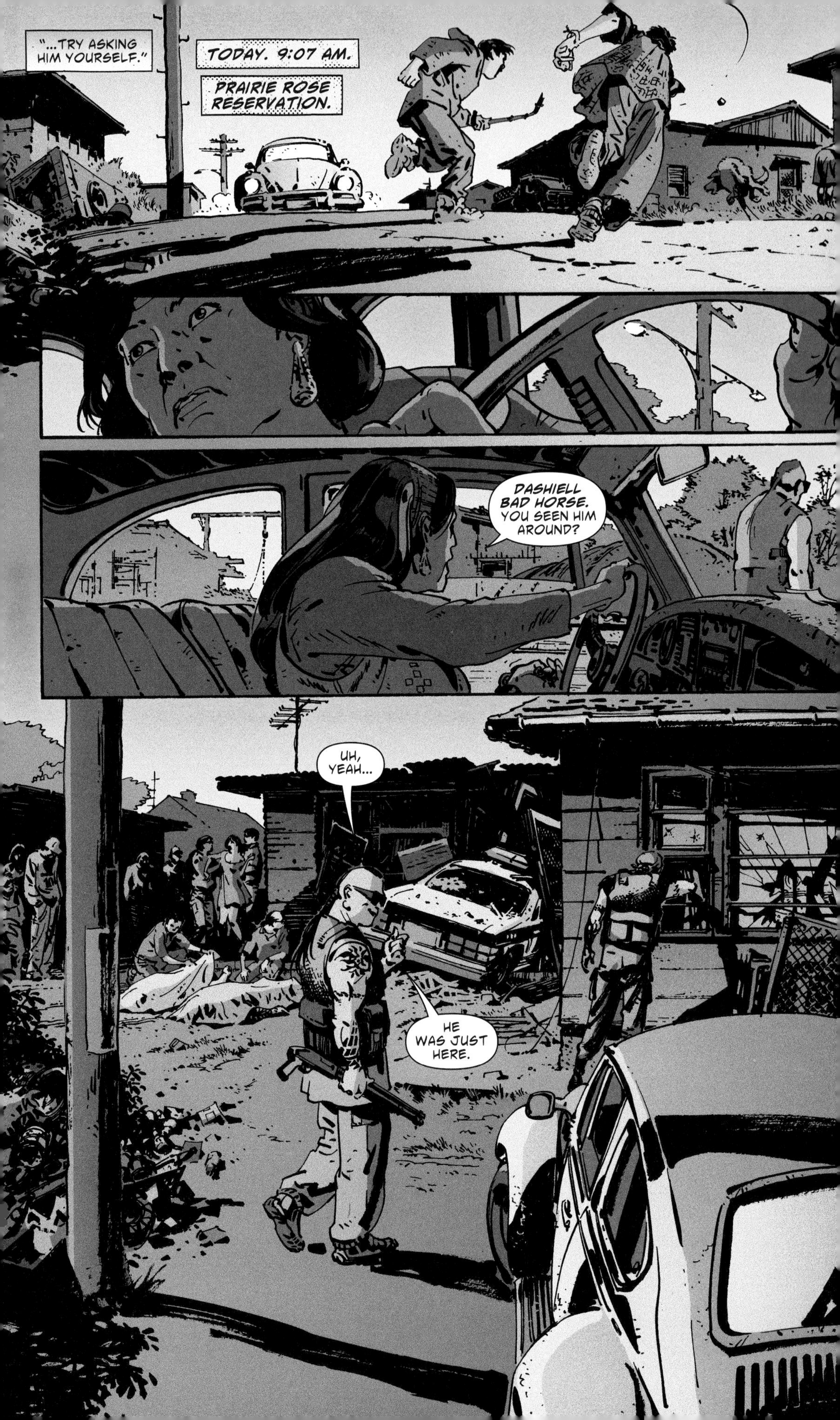
"...TRY ASKING HIM YOURSELF."
TODAY. 9:07 AM.
PRAIRIE ROSE RESERVATION.
DASHIELL BAD HORSE. YOU SEEN HIM AROUND?
UH, YEAH...
HE WAS JUST HERE.

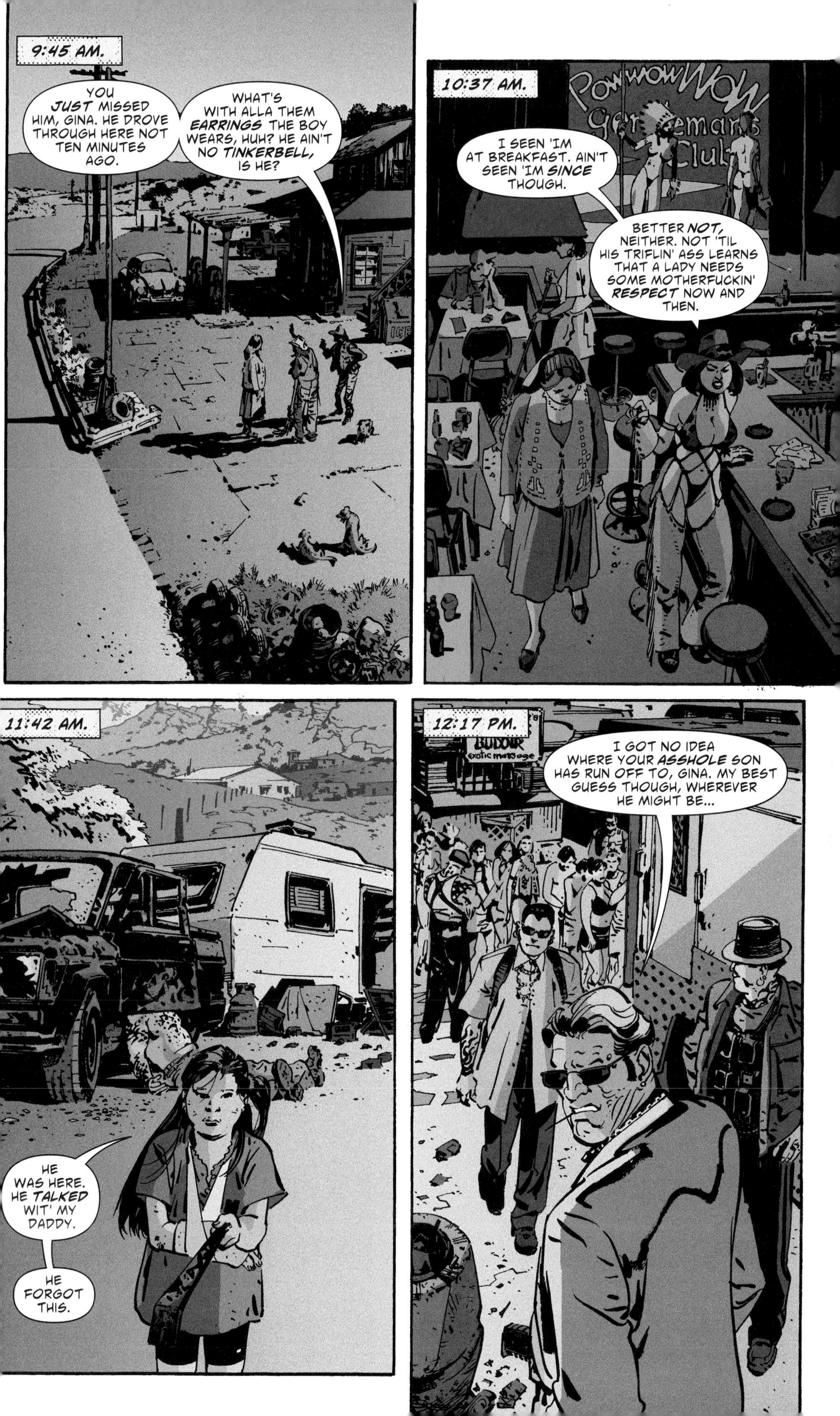
9:45 AM.
YOU JUST MISSED HIM, GINA. HE DROVE THROUGH HERE NOT TEN MINUTES AGO.
WHAT'S WITH ALLA THEM EARRINGS THE BOY WEARS, HUH? HE AIN'T NO TINKERBELL, IS HE?
10:37 AM.
I SEEN 'IM AT BREAKFAST. AIN'T SEEN 'IM SINCE THOUGH.
BETTER NOT, NEITHER. NOT 'TIL HIS TRIFLIN' ASS LEARNS THAT A LADY NEEDS SOME MOTHERFUCKIN' RESPECT NOW AND THEN.
11:42 AM.
HE WAS HERE. HE TALKED WIT' MY DADDY.
HE FORGOT THIS.
12:17 PM.
I GOT NO IDEA WHERE YOUR ASSHOLE SON HAS RUN OFF TO, GINA. MY BEST GUESS THOUGH, WHEREVER HE MIGHT BE...

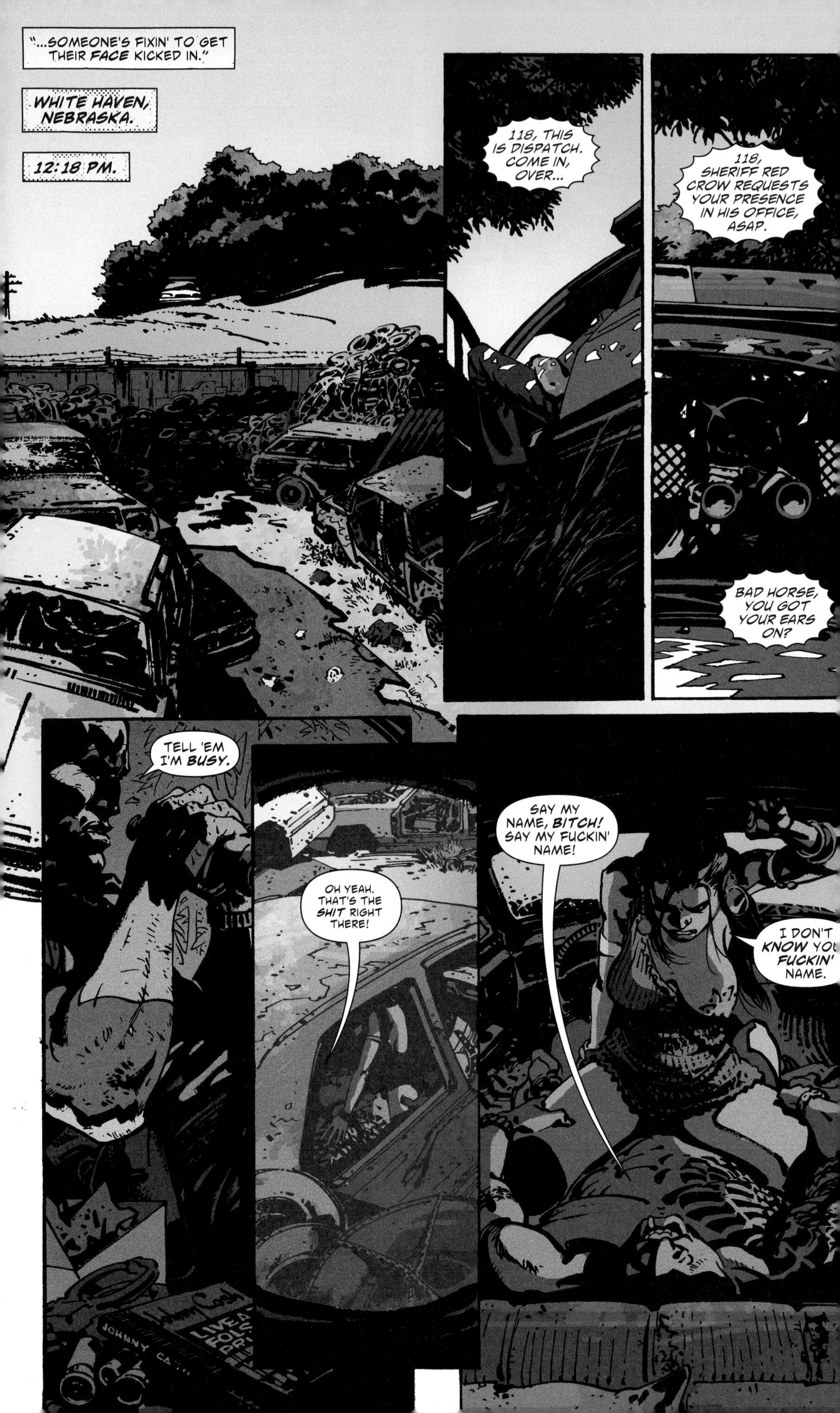
"...SOMEONE'S FIXIN' TO GET THEIR FACE KICKED IN."
WHITE HAVEN, NEBRASKA.
12:18 PM.
118, THIS IS DISPATCH. COME IN, OVER...
118, SHERIFF RED CROW REQUESTS YOUR PRESENCE IN HIS OFFICE, ASAP.
BAD HORSE, YOU GOT YOUR EARS ON?
TELL 'EM I'M BUSY.
OH YEAH. THAT'S THE SHIT RIGHT THERE!
SAY MY NAME, BITCH! SAY MY FUCKIN' NAME!
I DON'T KNOW YO FUCKIN' NAME.

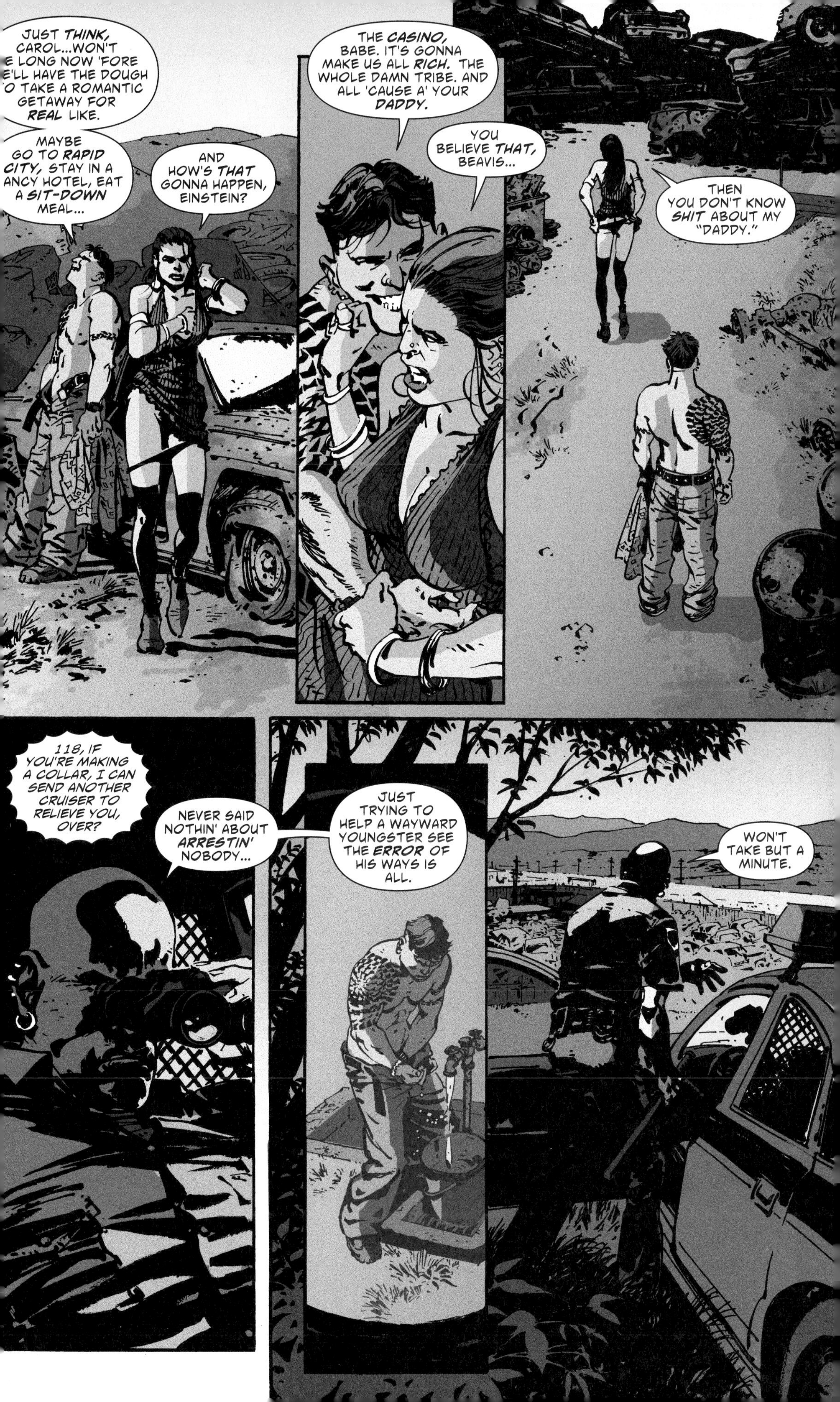

JUST THINK, CAROL...WON'T E LONG NOW 'FORE E'LL HAVE THE DOUGH 'O TAKE A ROMANTIC GETAWAY FOR REAL LIKE.
MAYBE GO TO RAPID CITY, STAY IN A ANCY HOTEL, EAT A SIT-DOWN MEAL...
AND HOW'S THAT GONNA HAPPEN, EINSTEIN?
THE CASINO, BABE. IT'S GONNA MAKE US ALL RICH. THE WHOLE DAMN TRIBE. AND ALL 'CAUSE A' YOUR DADDY.
YOU BELIEVE THAT, BEAVIS...
THEN YOU DON'T KNOW SHIT ABOUT MY "DADDY."
118, IF YOU'RE MAKING A COLLAR, I CAN SEND ANOTHER CRUISER TO RELIEVE YOU, OVER?
NEVER SAID NOTHIN' ABOUT ARRESTIN' NOBODY...
JUST TRYING TO HELP A WAYWARD YOUNGSTER SEE THE ERROR OF HIS WAYS IS ALL.
WON'T TAKE BUT A MINUTE.

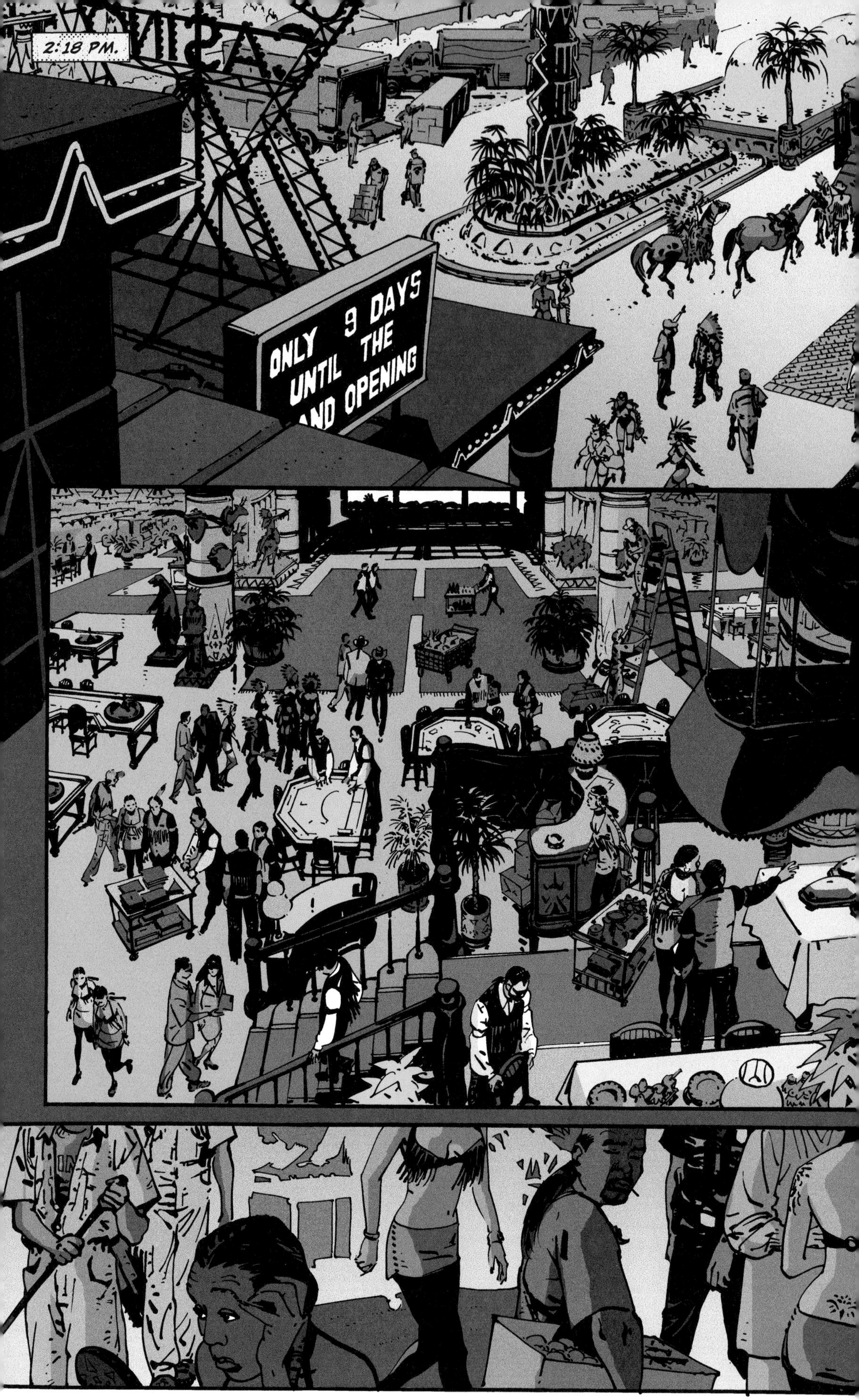
2:18 PM.
ONLY 9 DAYS
UNTIL THE
AND OPENING

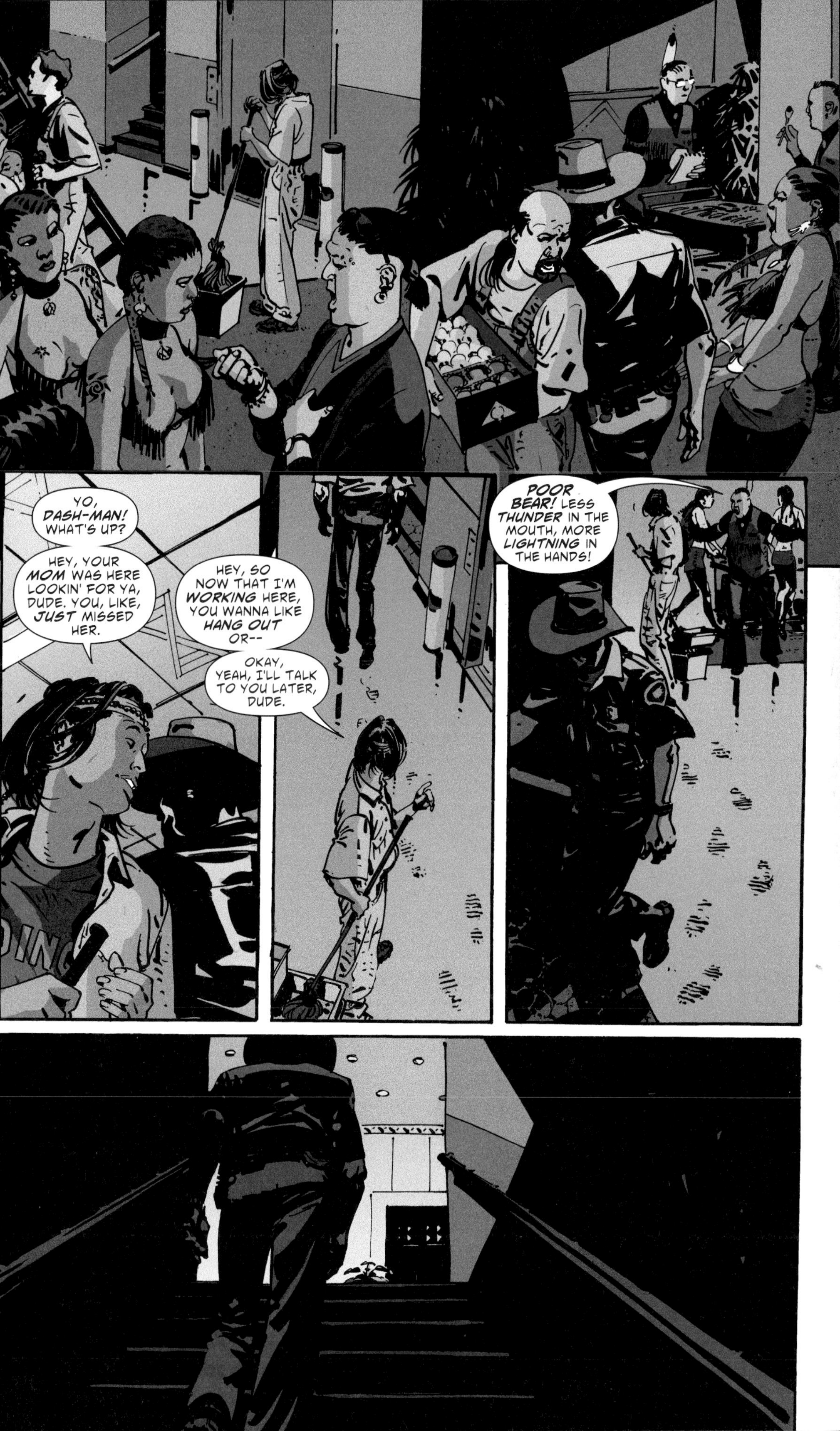
YO, DASH-MAN! WHAT'S UP?
HEY, YOUR MOM WAS HERE LOOKIN' FOR YA, DUDE. YOU, LIKE, JUST MISSED HER.
HEY, SO NOW THAT I'M WORKING HERE, YOU WANNA LIKE HANG OUT OR--
OKAY, YEAH, I'LL TALK TO YOU LATER, DUDE.
POOR BEAR! LESS THUNDER IN THE MOUTH, MORE LIGHTNING IN THE HANDS!

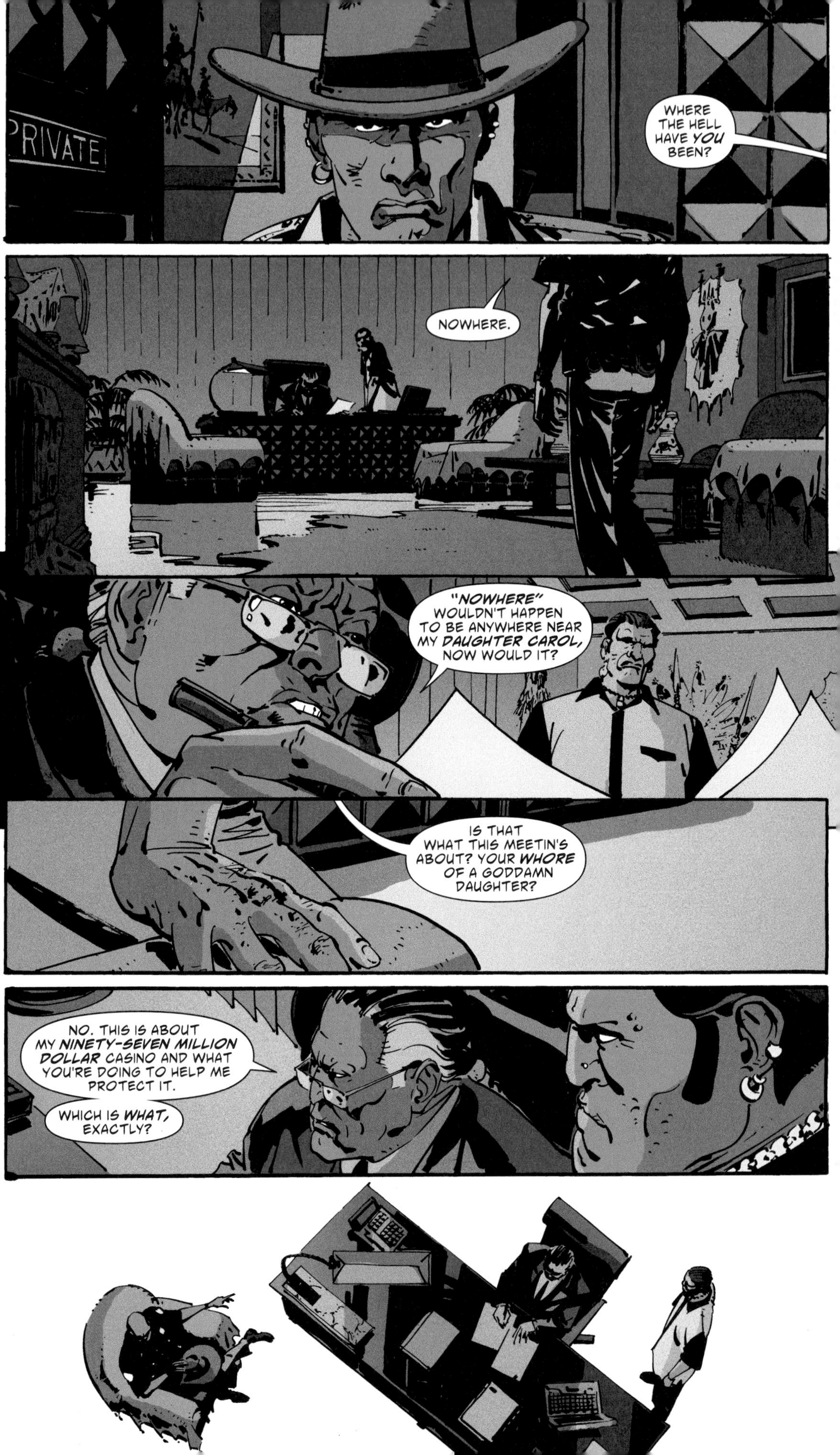
PRIVATE
WHERE THE HELL HAVE YOU BEEN?
NOWHERE.
"NOWHERE" WOULDN'T HAPPEN TO BE ANYWHERE NEAR MY DAUGHTER CAROL, NOW WOULD IT?
IS THAT WHAT THIS MEETIN'S ABOUT? YOUR WHORE OF A GODDAMN DAUGHTER?
NO. THIS IS ABOUT MY NINETY-SEVEN MILLION DOLLAR CASINO AND WHAT YOU'RE DOING TO HELP ME PROTECT IT.
WHICH IS WHAT, EXACTLY?

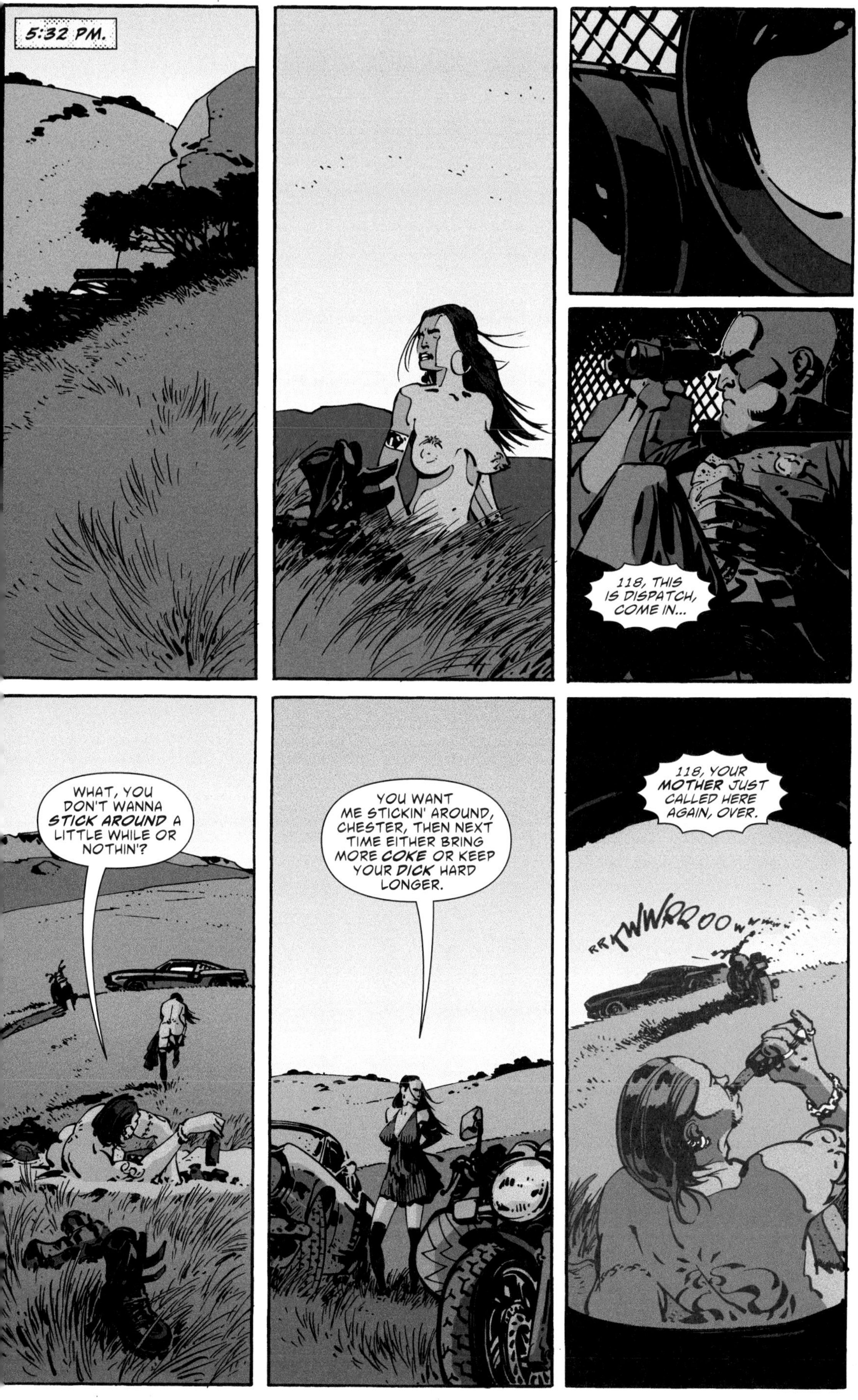
5:32 PM.
118, THIS IS DISPATCH, COME IN...
WHAT, YOU DON'T WANNA STICK AROUND A LITTLE WHILE OR NOTHIN'?
YOU WANT ME STICKIN' AROUND, CHESTER, THEN NEXT TIME EITHER BRING MORE COKE OR KEEP YOUR DICK HARD LONGER.
118, YOUR MOTHER JUST CALLED HERE AGAIN, OVER.
RRKWWRROOOWWW

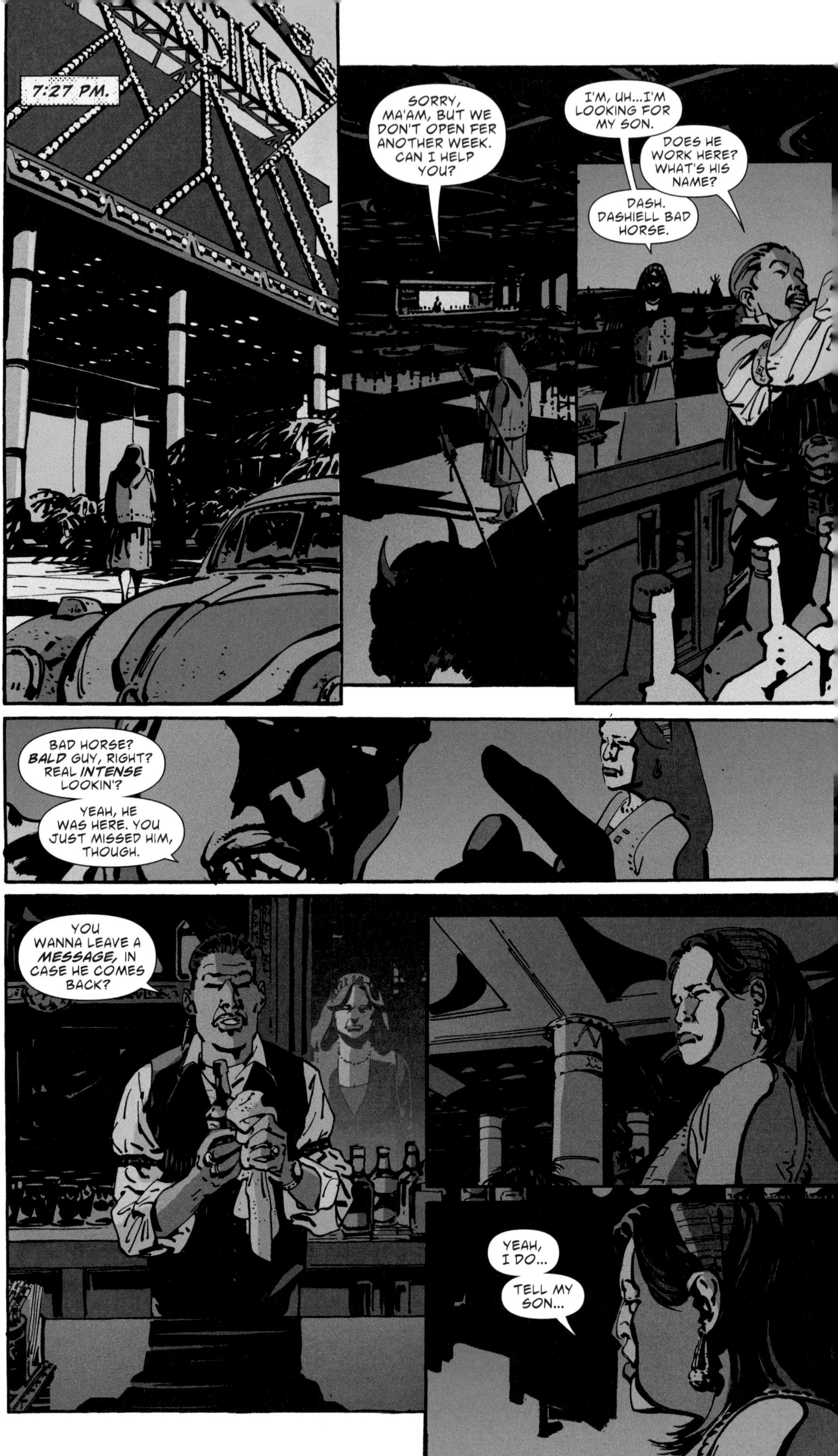
7:27 PM.
SORRY, MA'AM, BUT WE DON'T OPEN FER ANOTHER WEEK. CAN I HELP YOU?
I'M, UH...I'M LOOKING FOR MY SON.
DOES HE WORK HERE? WHAT'S HIS NAME?
DASH. DASHIELL BAD HORSE.
BAD HORSE? BALD GUY, RIGHT? REAL INTENSE LOOKIN'?
YEAH, HE WAS HERE. YOU JUST MISSED HIM, THOUGH.
YOU WANNA LEAVE A MESSAGE, IN CASE HE COMES BACK?
YEAH, I DO...
TELL MY SON...

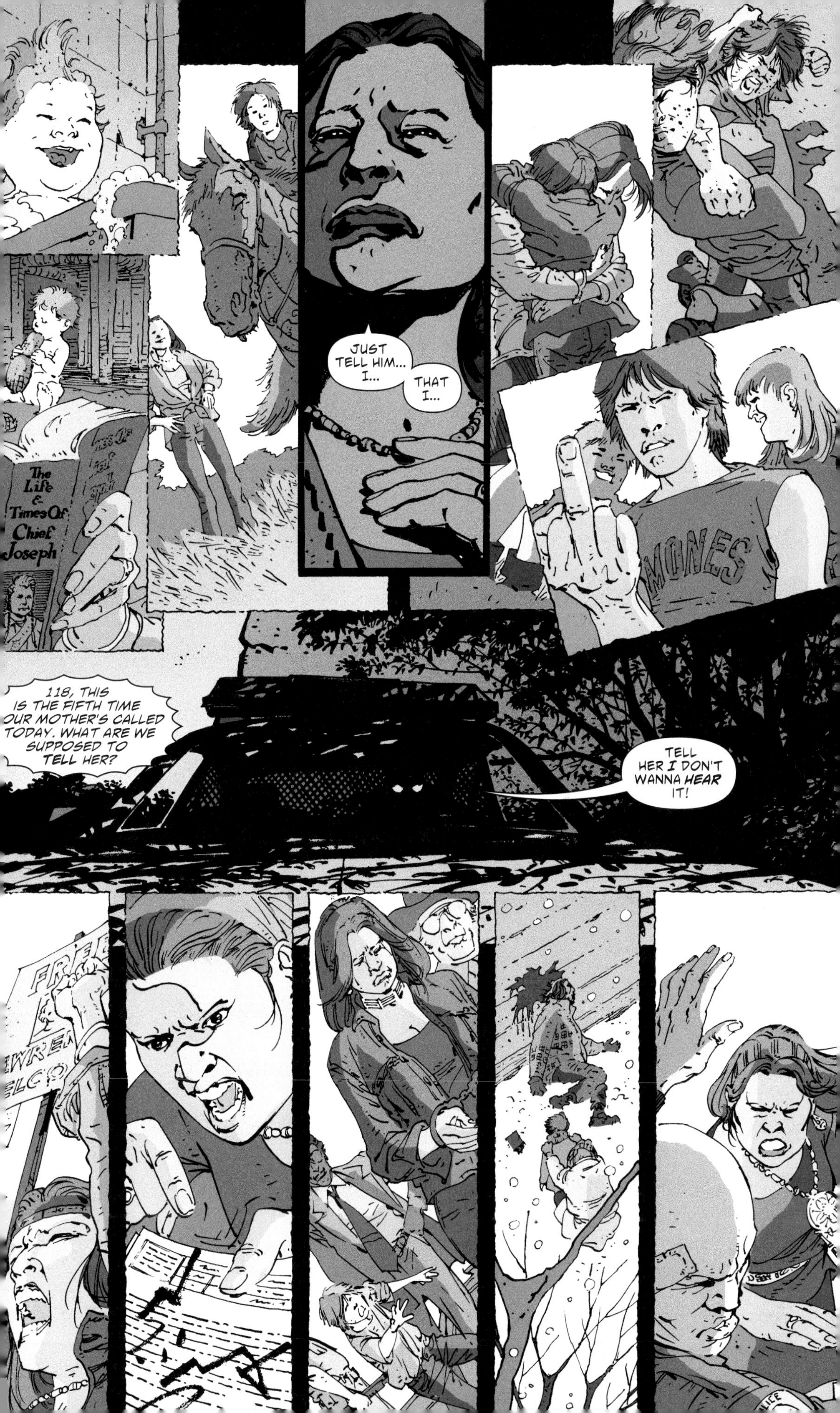
The Life & Times Of Chief Joseph
JUST TELL HIM... I...
THAT I...
MONES
118, THIS IS THE FIFTH TIME OUR MOTHER'S CALLED TODAY. WHAT ARE WE SUPPOSED TO TELL HER?
TELL HER I DON'T WANNA HEAR IT!

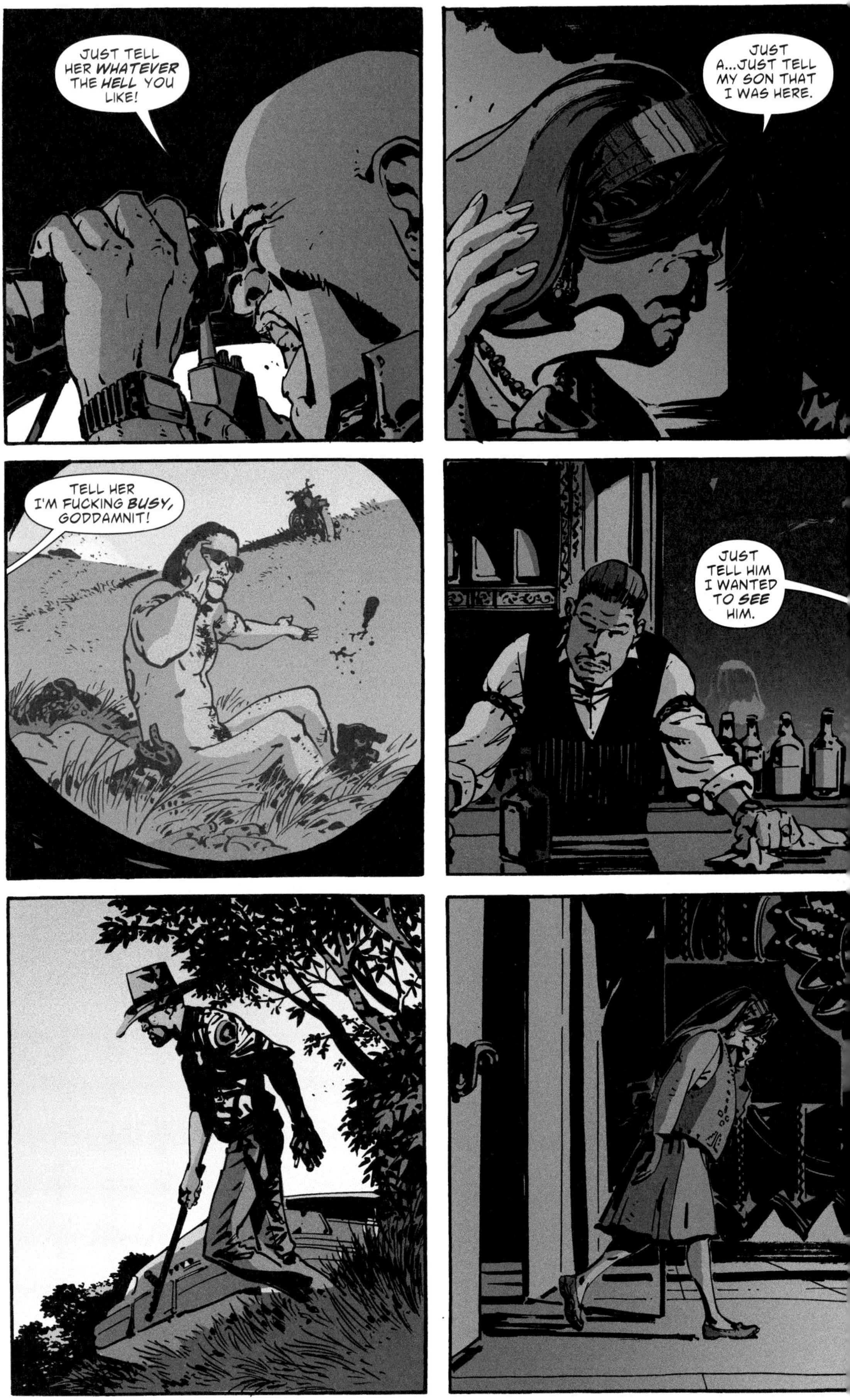
JUST TELL HER WHATEVER THE HELL YOU LIKE!
JUST A...JUST TELL MY SON THAT I WAS HERE.
TELL HER I'M FUCKING BUSY, GODDAMNIT!
JUST TELL HIM I WANTED TO SEE HIM.

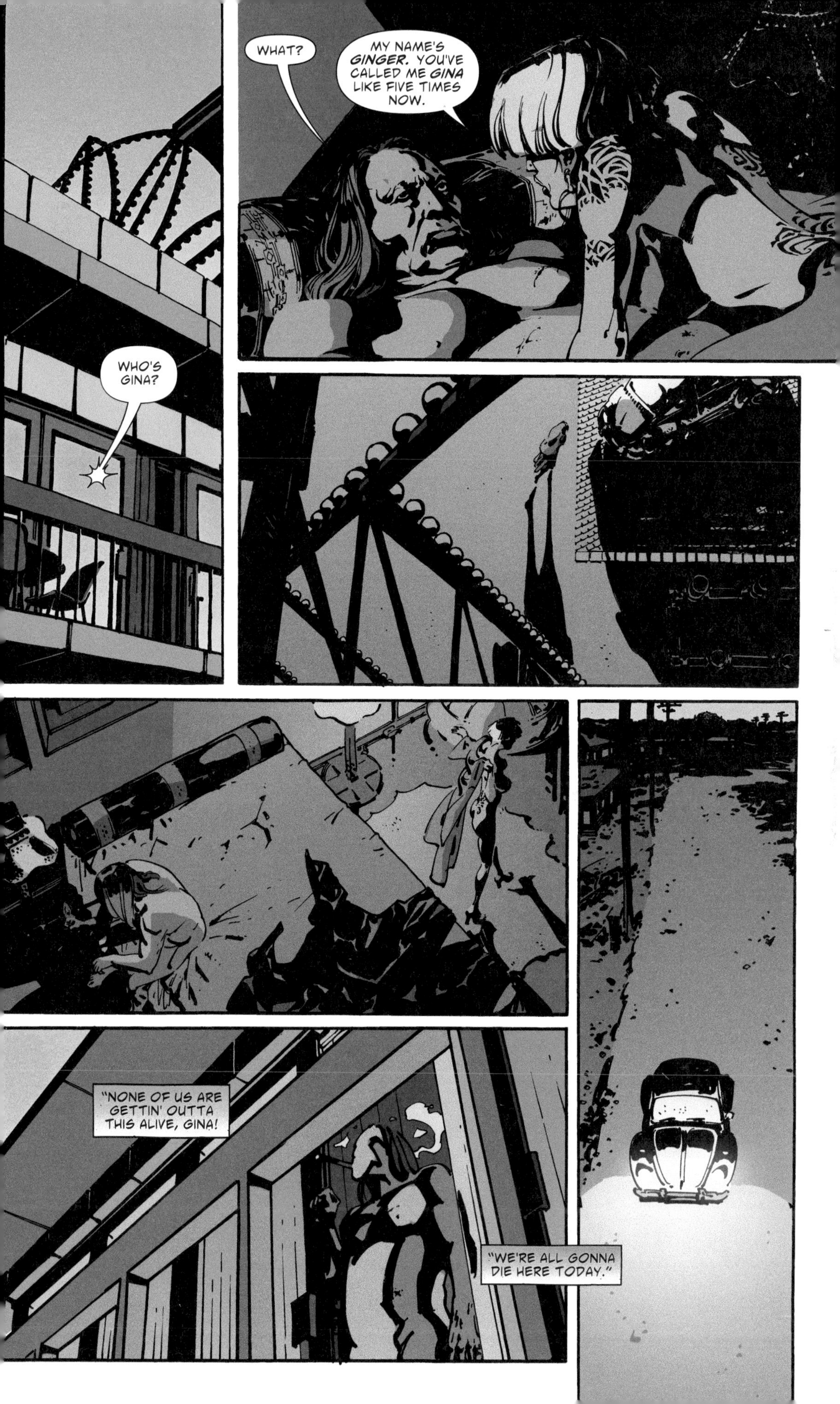
WHO'S GINA?
WHAT?
MY NAME'S GINGER. YOU'VE CALLED ME GINA LIKE FIVE TIMES NOW.
"NONE OF US ARE GETTIN' OUTTA THIS ALIVE, GINA!
"WE'RE ALL GONNA DIE HERE TODAY."

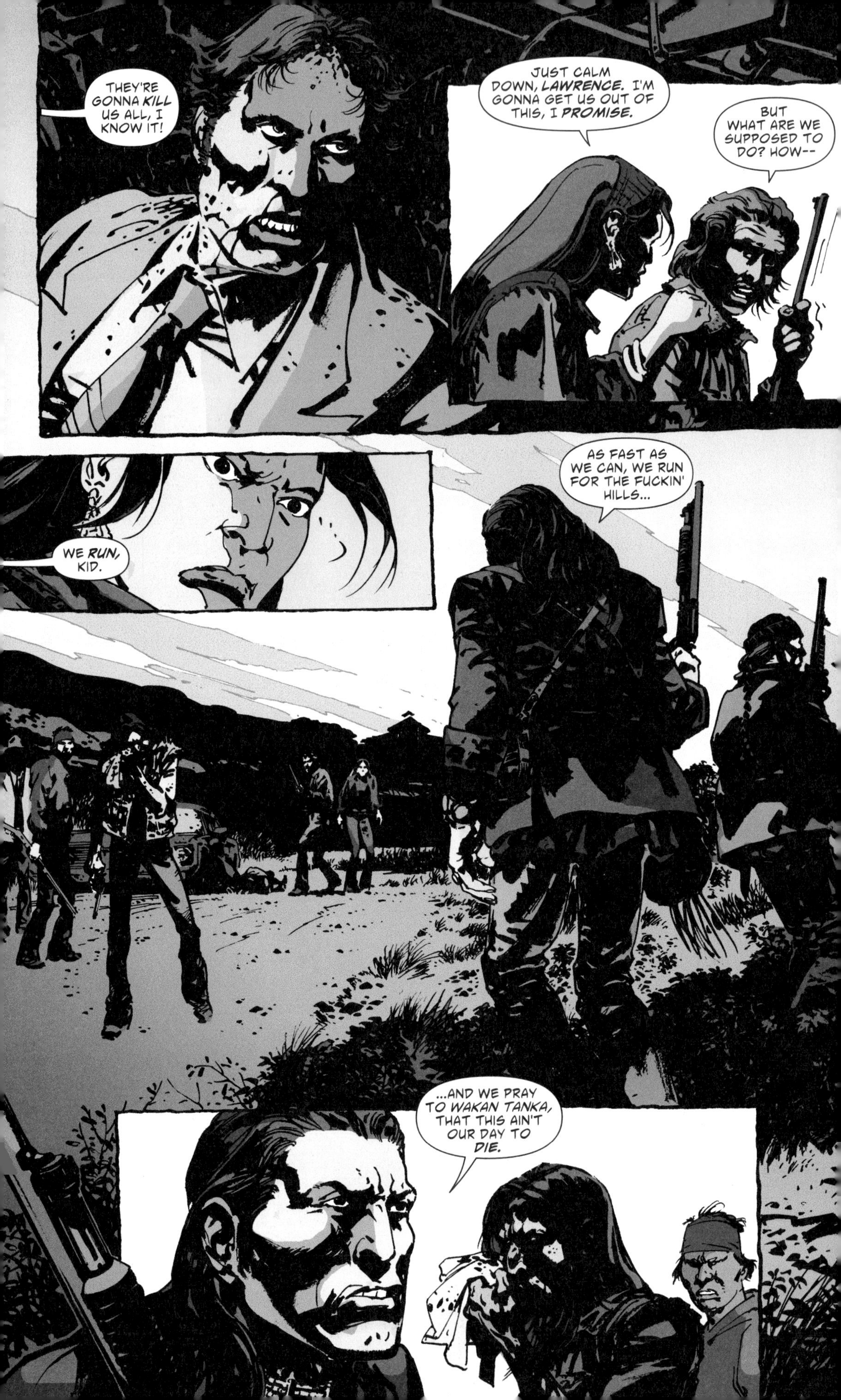
THEY'RE GONNA KILL US ALL, I KNOW IT!
JUST CALM DOWN, LAWRENCE. I'M GONNA GET US OUT OF THIS, I PROMISE.
BUT WHAT ARE WE SUPPOSED TO DO? HOW--
WE RUN, KID.
AS FAST AS WE CAN, WE RUN FOR THE FUCKIN' HILLS...
...AND WE PRAY TO WAKAN TANKA, THAT THIS AIN'T OUR DAY TO DIE.

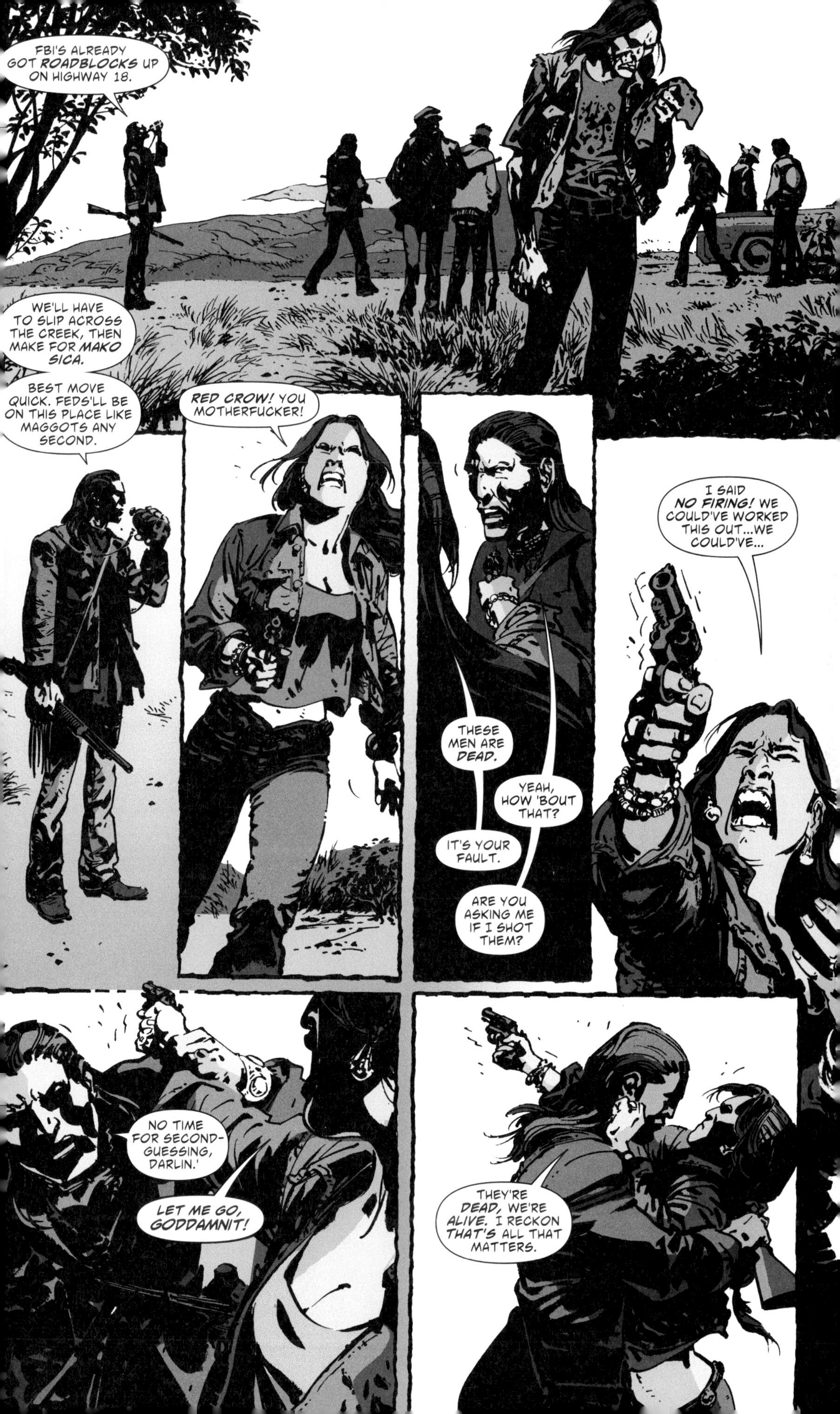
FBI'S ALREADY GOT ROADBLOCKS UP ON HIGHWAY 18.
WE'LL HAVE TO SLIP ACROSS THE CREEK, THEN MAKE FOR MAKO SICA.
BEST MOVE QUICK. FEDS'LL BE ON THIS PLACE LIKE MAGGOTS ANY SECOND.
RED CROW! YOU MOTHERFUCKER!
THESE MEN ARE DEAD.
IT'S YOUR FAULT.
YEAH, HOW 'BOUT THAT?
ARE YOU ASKING ME IF I SHOT THEM?
I SAID NO FIRING! WE COULD'VE WORKED THIS OUT...WE COULD'VE...
NO TIME FOR SECOND-GUESSING, DARLIN.'
LET ME GO, GODDAMNIT!
THEY'RE DEAD, WE'RE ALIVE. I RECKON THAT'S ALL THAT MATTERS.

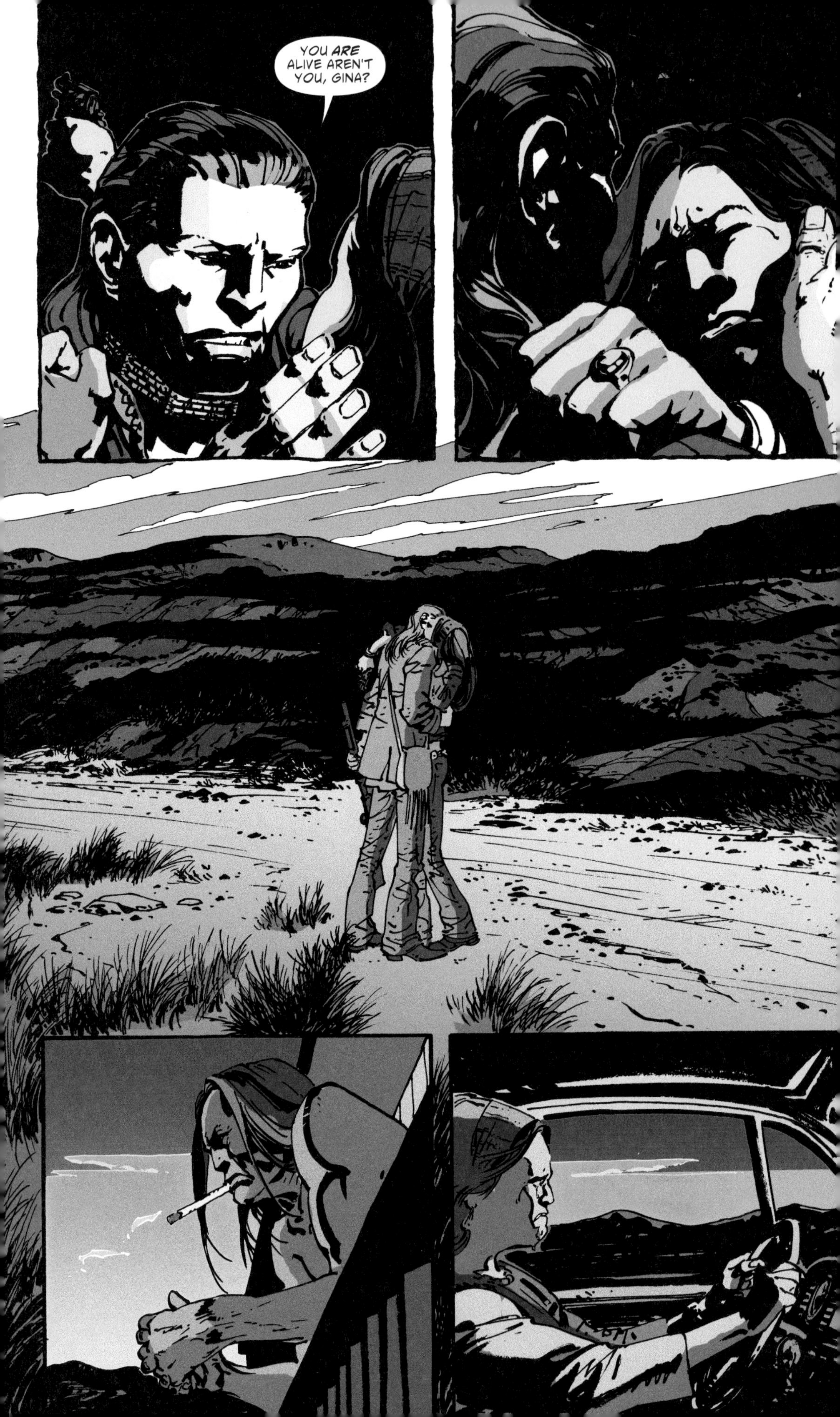
YOU ARE ALIVE AREN'T YOU, GINA?

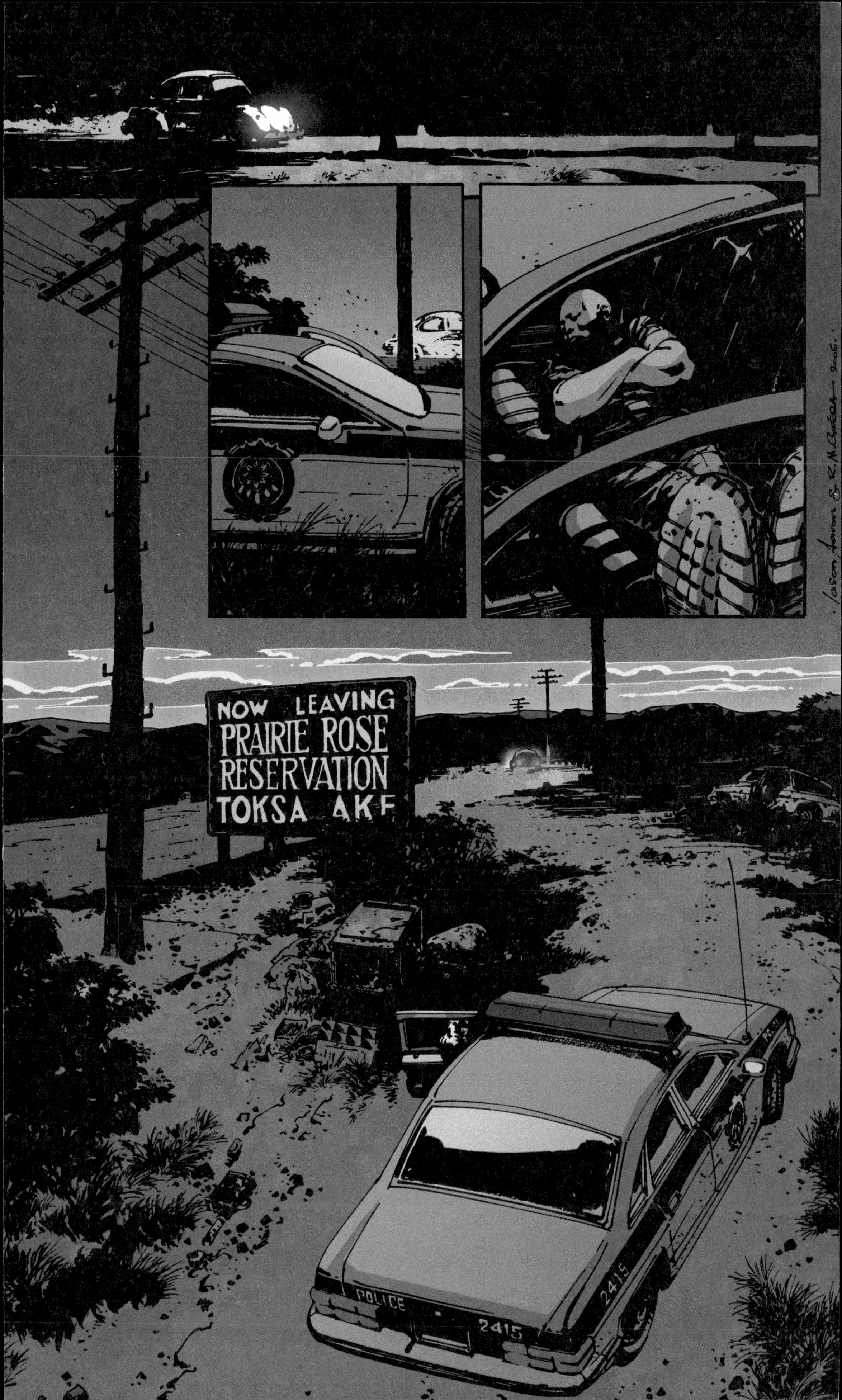
NOW LEAVING
PRAIRIE ROSE
RESERVATION
TOKSA AKE
POLICE
2415
2415

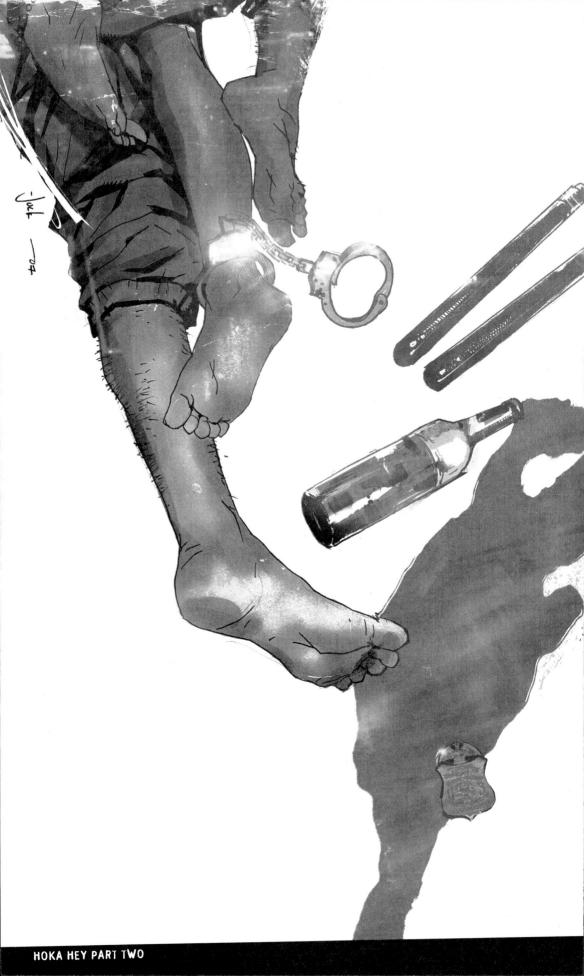

HOKA HEY PART TWO

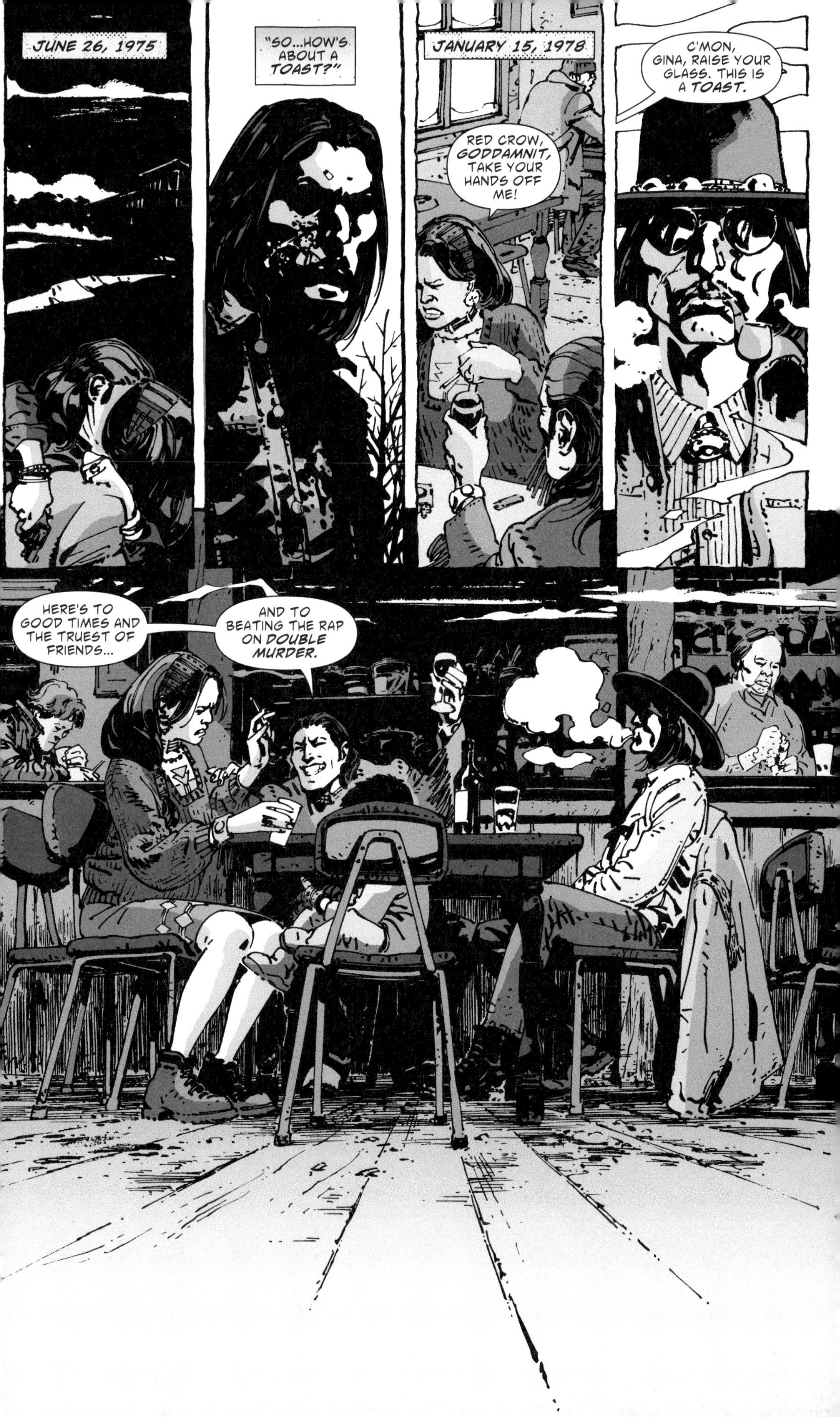
JUNE 26, 1975
"SO...HOW'S ABOUT A TOAST?"
JANUARY 15, 1978
RED CROW, GODDAMNIT, TAKE YOUR HANDS OFF ME!
C'MON, GINA, RAISE YOUR GLASS. THIS IS A TOAST.
HERE'S TO GOOD TIMES AND THE TRUEST OF FRIENDS...
AND TO BEATING THE RAP ON DOUBLE MURDER.

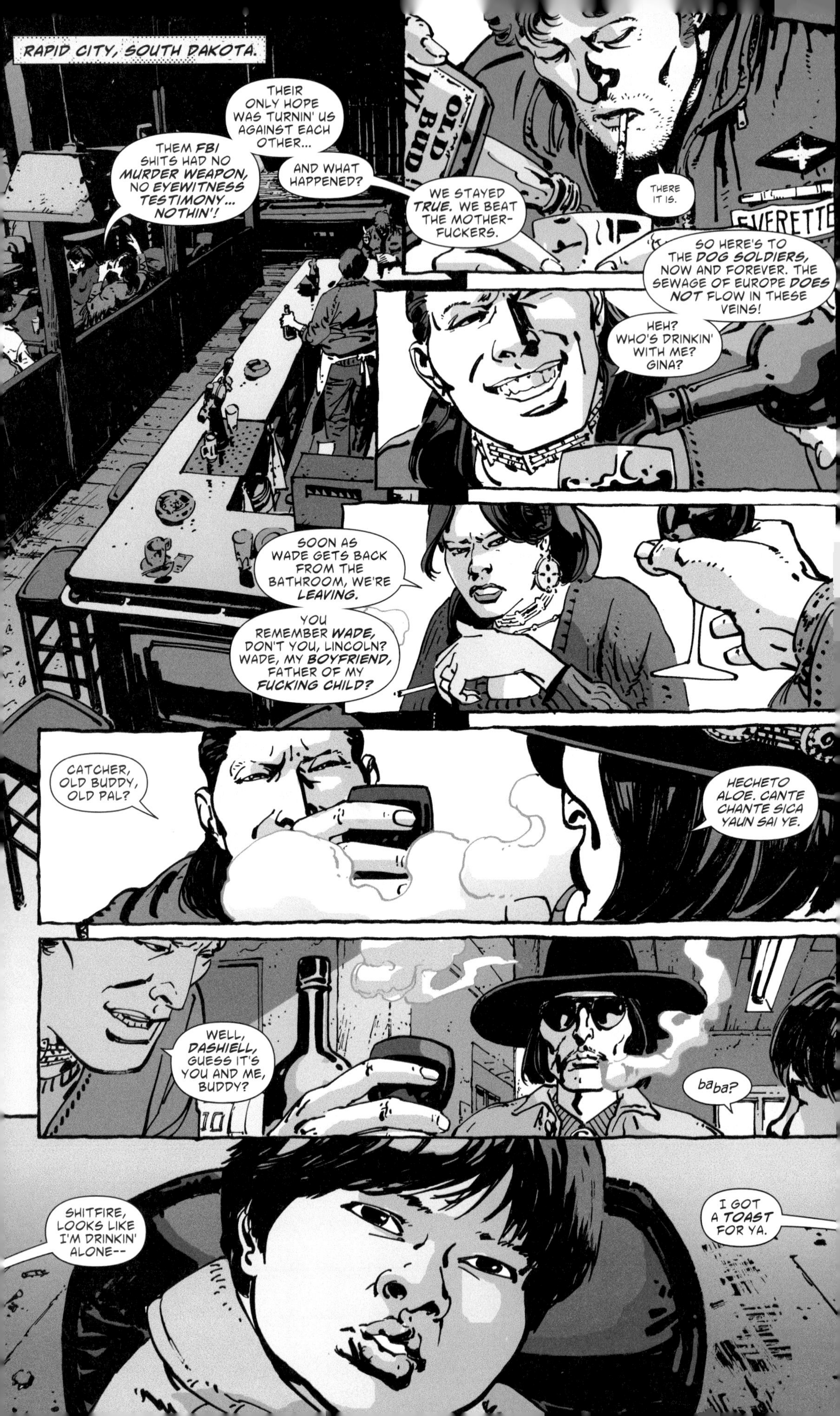

RAPID CITY, SOUTH DAKOTA.
THEM FBI SHITS HAD NO MURDER WEAPON, NO EYEWITNESS TESTIMONY... NOTHIN'!
THEIR ONLY HOPE WAS TURNIN' US AGAINST EACH OTHER...
AND WHAT HAPPENED?
WE STAYED TRUE. WE BEAT THE MOTHER-FUCKERS.
OLD BUD
THERE IT IS.
EVERETTE
SO HERE'S TO THE DOG SOLDIERS, NOW AND FOREVER. THE SEWAGE OF EUROPE DOES NOT FLOW IN THESE VEINS!
HEH? WHO'S DRINKIN' WITH ME? GINA?
SOON AS WADE GETS BACK FROM THE BATHROOM, WE'RE LEAVING.
YOU REMEMBER WADE, DON'T YOU, LINCOLN? WADE, MY BOYFRIEND, FATHER OF MY FUCKING CHILD?
CATCHER, OLD BUDDY, OLD PAL?
HECHETO ALOE. CANTE CHANTE SICA YAUN SAI YE.
WELL, DASHIELL, GUESS IT'S YOU AND ME, BUDDY?
baba?
SHITFIRE, LOOKS LIKE I'M DRINKIN' ALONE--
I GOT A TOAST FOR YA.

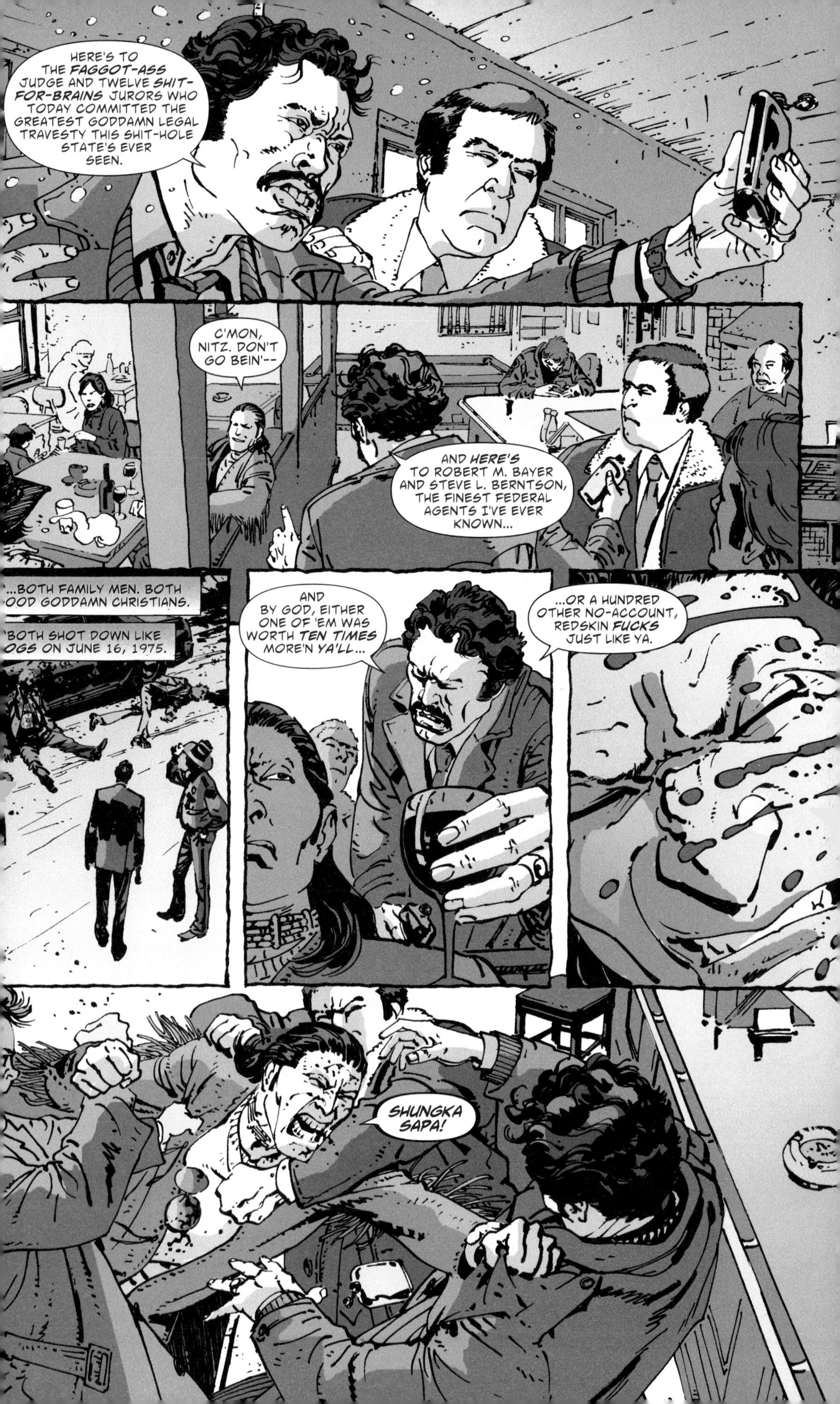
HERE'S TO THE FAGGOT-ASS JUDGE AND TWELVE SHIT-FOR-BRAINS JURORS WHO TODAY COMMITTED THE GREATEST GODDAMN LEGAL TRAVESTY THIS SHIT-HOLE STATE'S EVER SEEN.
C'MON, NITZ. DON'T GO BEIN'--
AND HERE'S TO ROBERT M. BAYER AND STEVE L. BERNTSON, THE FINEST FEDERAL AGENTS I'VE EVER KNOWN...
...BOTH FAMILY MEN. BOTH OOD GODDAMN CHRISTIANS.
BOTH SHOT DOWN LIKE OGS ON JUNE 16, 1975.
AND BY GOD, EITHER ONE OF 'EM WAS WORTH TEN TIMES MORE'N YA'LL...
...OR A HUNDRED OTHER NO-ACCOUNT, REDSKIN FUCKS JUST LIKE YA.
SHUNGKA SAPA!

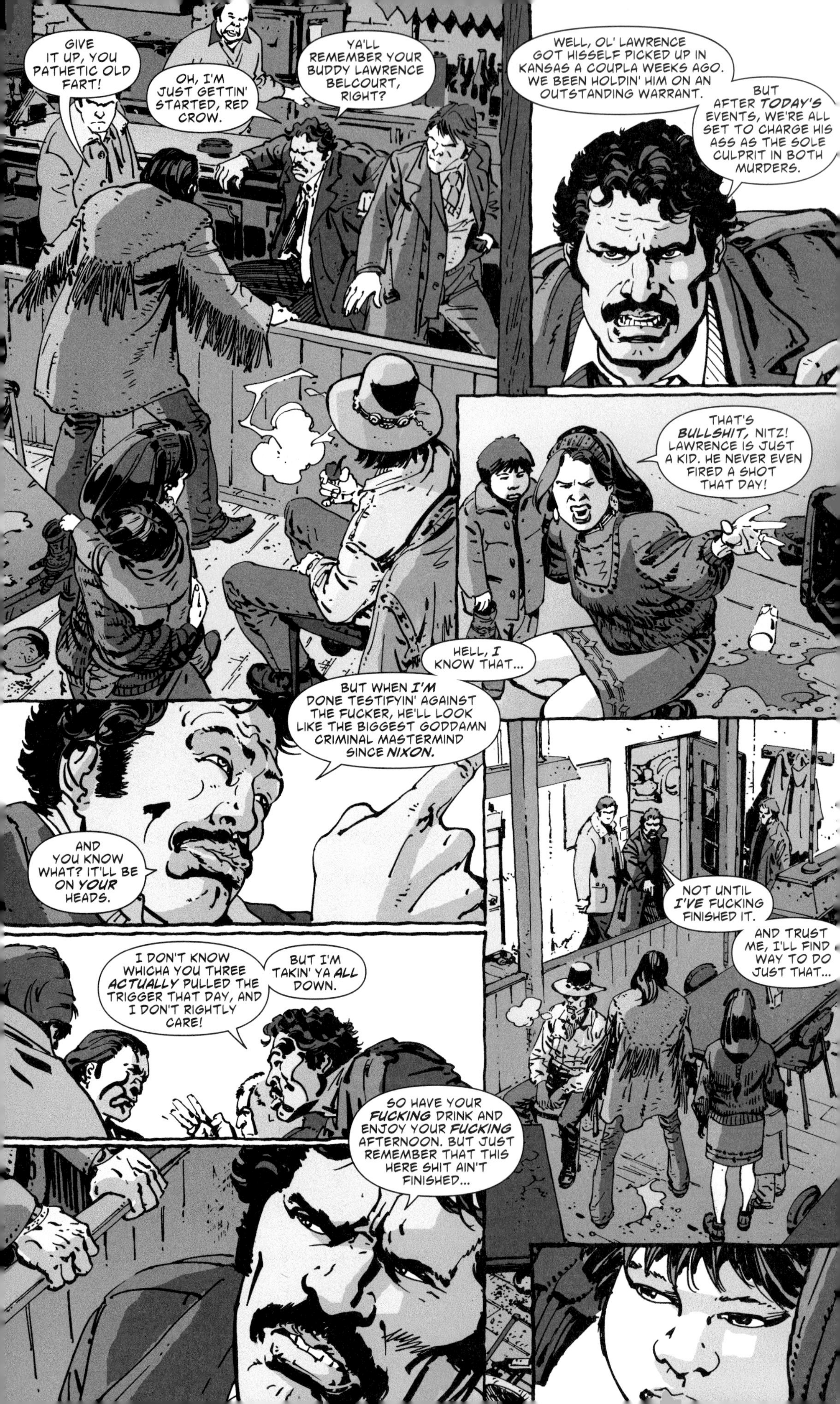
GIVE IT UP, YOU PATHETIC OLD FART!
OH, I'M JUST GETTIN' STARTED, RED CROW.
YA'LL REMEMBER YOUR BUDDY LAWRENCE BELCOURT, RIGHT?
WELL, OL' LAWRENCE GOT HISSELF PICKED UP IN KANSAS A COUPLA WEEKS AGO. WE BEEN HOLDIN' HIM ON AN OUTSTANDING WARRANT.
BUT AFTER TODAY'S EVENTS, WE'RE ALL SET TO CHARGE HIS ASS AS THE SOLE CULPRIT IN BOTH MURDERS.
THAT'S BULLSHIT, NITZ! LAWRENCE IS JUST A KID. HE NEVER EVEN FIRED A SHOT THAT DAY!
HELL, I KNOW THAT...
BUT WHEN I'M DONE TESTIFYIN' AGAINST THE FUCKER, HE'LL LOOK LIKE THE BIGGEST GODDAMN CRIMINAL MASTERMIND SINCE NIXON.
AND YOU KNOW WHAT? IT'LL BE ON YOUR HEADS.
I DON'T KNOW WHICHA YOU THREE ACTUALLY PULLED THE TRIGGER THAT DAY, AND I DON'T RIGHTLY CARE!
BUT I'M TAKIN' YA ALL DOWN.
SO HAVE YOUR FUCKING DRINK AND ENJOY YOUR FUCKING AFTERNOON. BUT JUST REMEMBER THAT THIS HERE SHIT AIN'T FINISHED...
NOT UNTIL I'VE FUCKING FINISHED IT.
AND TRUST ME, I'LL FIND WAY TO DO JUST THAT...

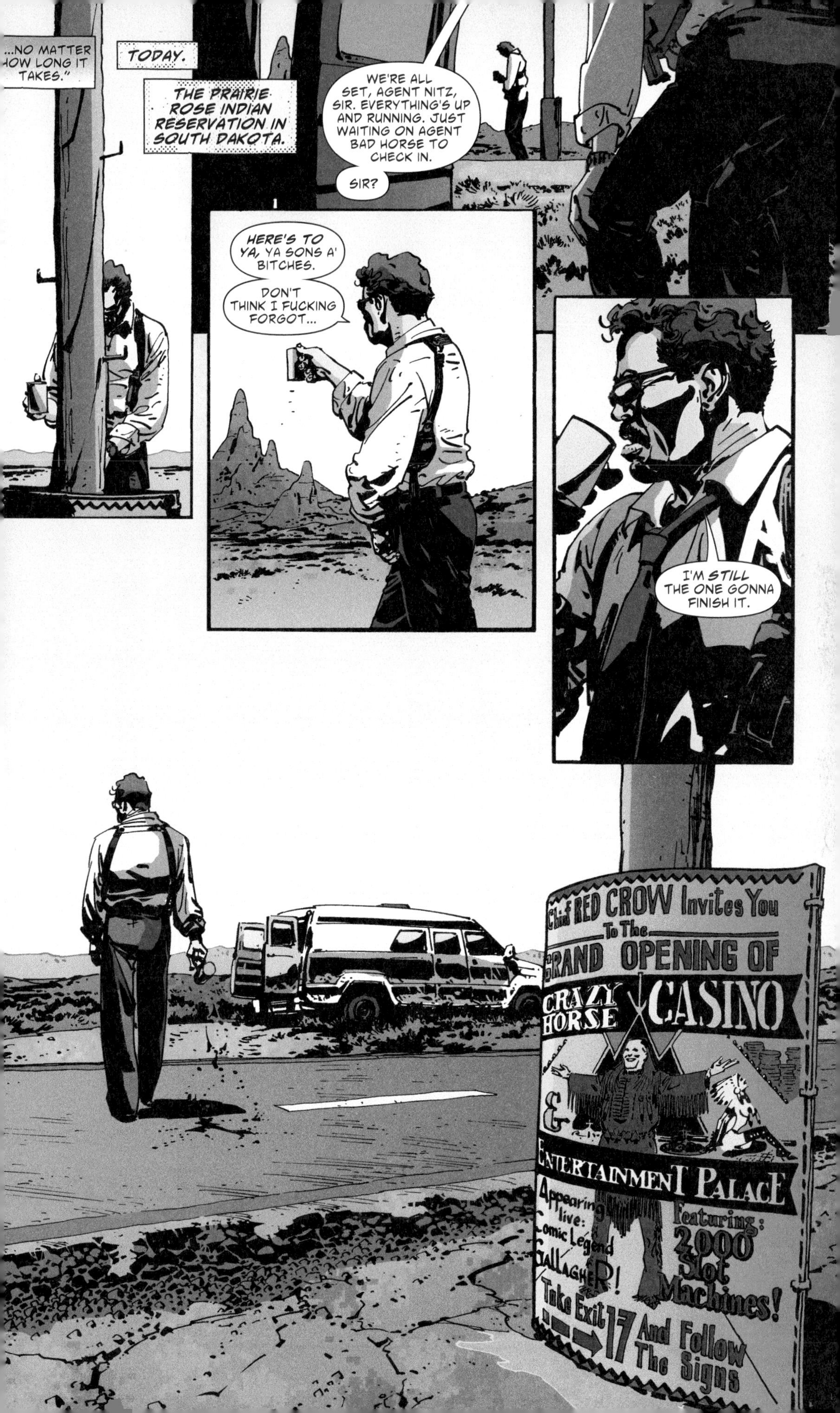
...NO MATTER HOW LONG IT TAKES."
TODAY.
THE PRAIRIE ROSE INDIAN RESERVATION IN SOUTH DAKOTA.
WE'RE ALL SET, AGENT NITZ, SIR. EVERYTHING'S UP AND RUNNING. JUST WAITING ON AGENT BAD HORSE TO CHECK IN.
SIR?
HERE'S TO YA, YA SONS A' BITCHES.
DON'T THINK I FUCKING FORGOT...
I'M STILL THE ONE GONNA FINISH IT.
Chief RED CROW Invites You To The GRAND OPENING OF
CRAZY HORSE CASINO
& ENTERTAINMENT PALACE
Appearing live: Comic Legend GALLAGHER!
Featuring: 2000 Slot Machines!
Take Exit 17 And Follow The Signs

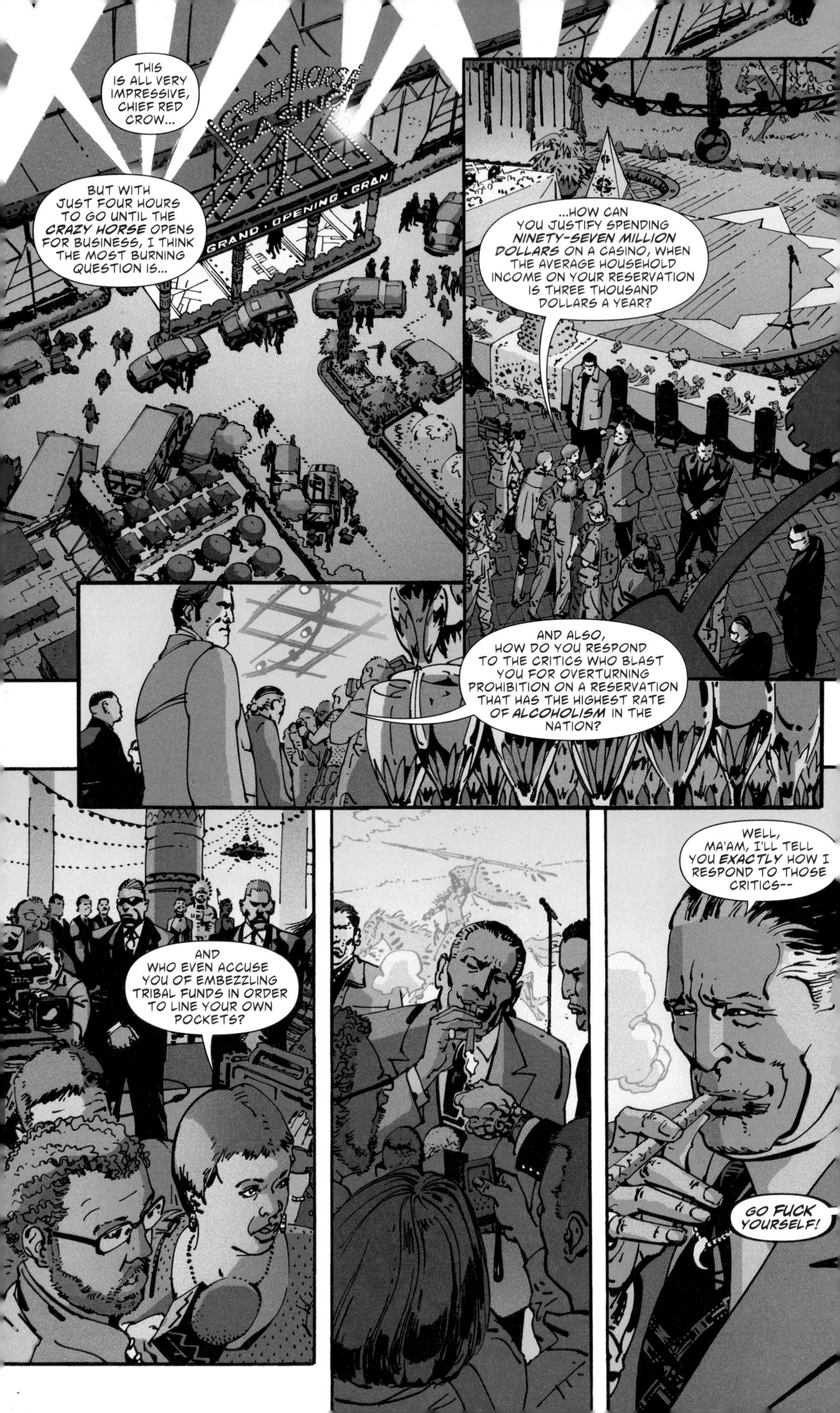
CRAZY HORSE CASINO
GRAND · OPENING · GRAN
THIS IS ALL VERY IMPRESSIVE, CHIEF RED CROW...
BUT WITH JUST FOUR HOURS TO GO UNTIL THE CRAZY HORSE OPENS FOR BUSINESS, I THINK THE MOST BURNING QUESTION IS...
...HOW CAN YOU JUSTIFY SPENDING NINETY-SEVEN MILLION DOLLARS ON A CASINO, WHEN THE AVERAGE HOUSEHOLD INCOME ON YOUR RESERVATION IS THREE THOUSAND DOLLARS A YEAR?
AND ALSO, HOW DO YOU RESPOND TO THE CRITICS WHO BLAST YOU FOR OVERTURNING PROHIBITION ON A RESERVATION THAT HAS THE HIGHEST RATE OF ALCOHOLISM IN THE NATION?
AND WHO EVEN ACCUSE YOU OF EMBEZZLING TRIBAL FUNDS IN ORDER TO LINE YOUR OWN POCKETS?
WELL, MA'AM, I'LL TELL YOU EXACTLY HOW I RESPOND TO THOSE CRITICS--
GO FUCK YOURSELF!

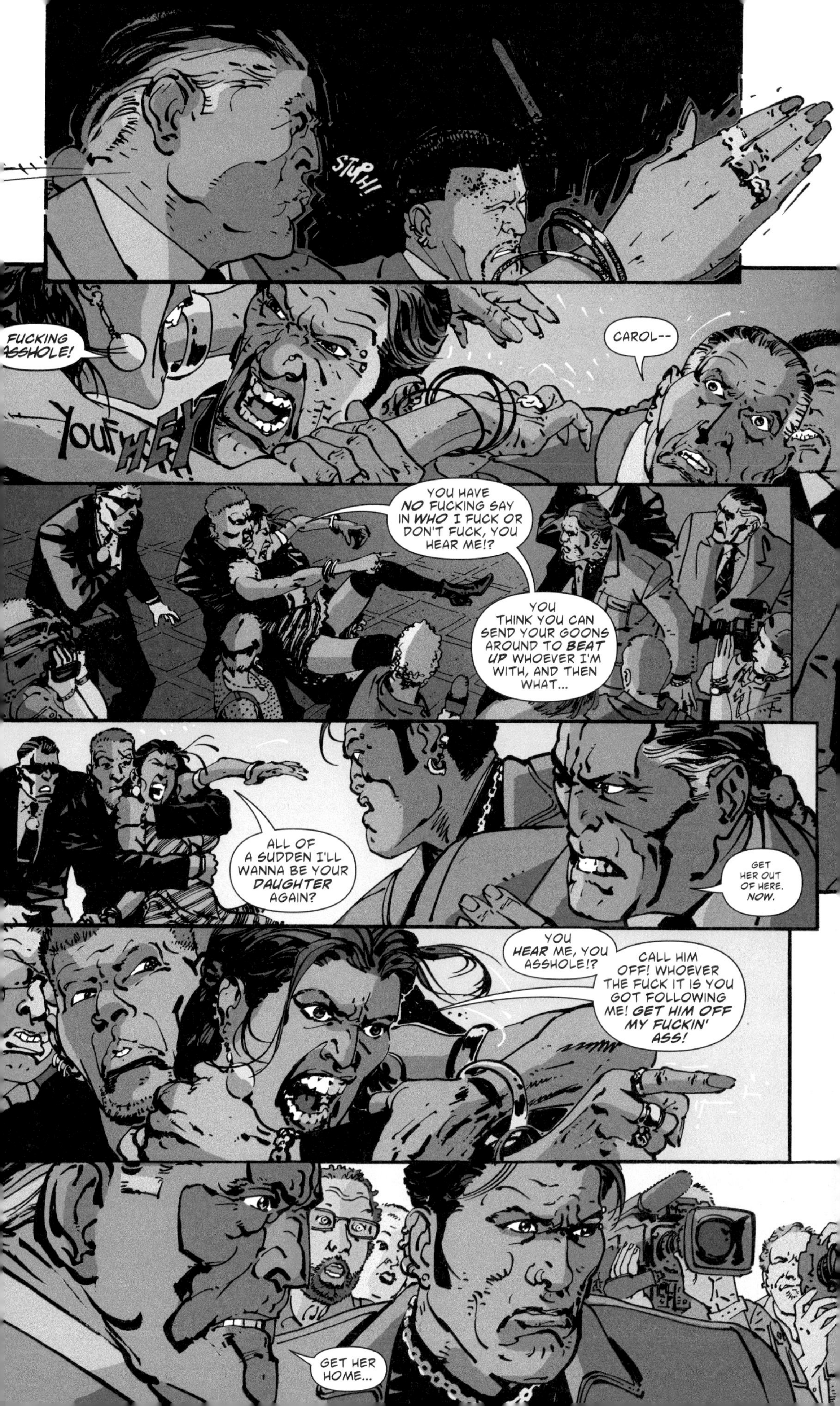
STUPH!
FUCKING ASSHOLE!
YOUF
HEY
CAROL--
YOU HAVE NO FUCKING SAY IN WHO I FUCK OR DON'T FUCK, YOU HEAR ME!?
YOU THINK YOU CAN SEND YOUR GOONS AROUND TO BEAT UP WHOEVER I'M WITH, AND THEN WHAT...
ALL OF A SUDDEN I'LL WANNA BE YOUR DAUGHTER AGAIN?
GET HER OUT OF HERE. NOW.
YOU HEAR ME, YOU ASSHOLE!?
CALL HIM OFF! WHOEVER THE FUCK IT IS YOU GOT FOLLOWING ME! GET HIM OFF MY FUCKIN' ASS!
GET HER HOME...

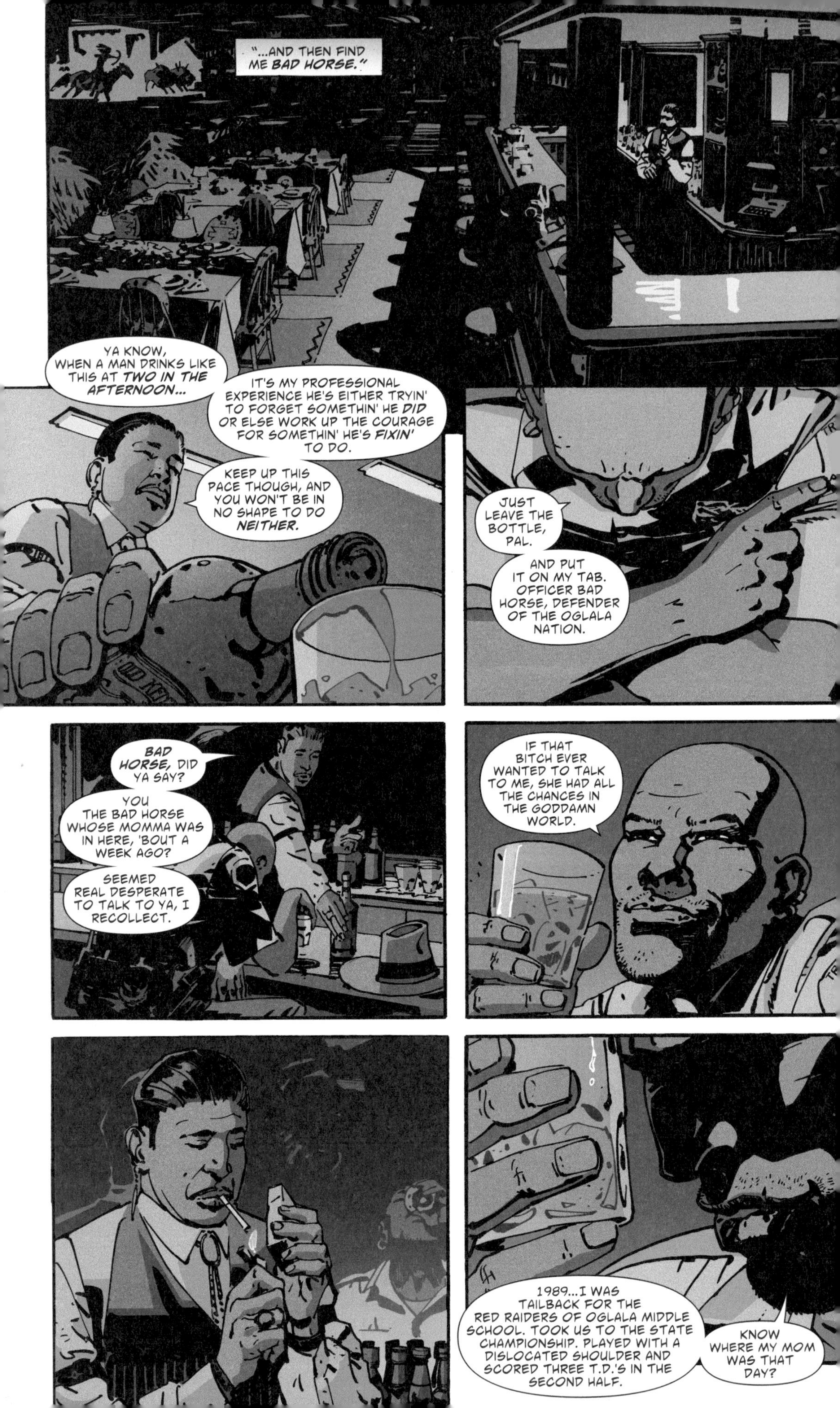

"...AND THEN FIND ME BAD HORSE."
YA KNOW, WHEN A MAN DRINKS LIKE THIS AT TWO IN THE AFTERNOON...
IT'S MY PROFESSIONAL EXPERIENCE HE'S EITHER TRYIN' TO FORGET SOMETHIN' HE DID OR ELSE WORK UP THE COURAGE FOR SOMETHIN' HE'S FIXIN' TO DO.
KEEP UP THIS PACE THOUGH, AND YOU WON'T BE IN NO SHAPE TO DO NEITHER.
JUST LEAVE THE BOTTLE, PAL.
AND PUT IT ON MY TAB. OFFICER BAD HORSE, DEFENDER OF THE OGLALA NATION.
BAD HORSE, DID YA SAY?
YOU THE BAD HORSE WHOSE MOMMA WAS IN HERE, 'BOUT A WEEK AGO?
SEEMED REAL DESPERATE TO TALK TO YA, I RECOLLECT.
IF THAT BITCH EVER WANTED TO TALK TO ME, SHE HAD ALL THE CHANCES IN THE GODDAMN WORLD.
1989...I WAS TAILBACK FOR THE RED RAIDERS OF OGLALA MIDDLE SCHOOL. TOOK US TO THE STATE CHAMPIONSHIP. PLAYED WITH A DISLOCATED SHOULDER AND SCORED THREE T.D.'S IN THE SECOND HALF.
KNOW WHERE MY MOM WAS THAT DAY?

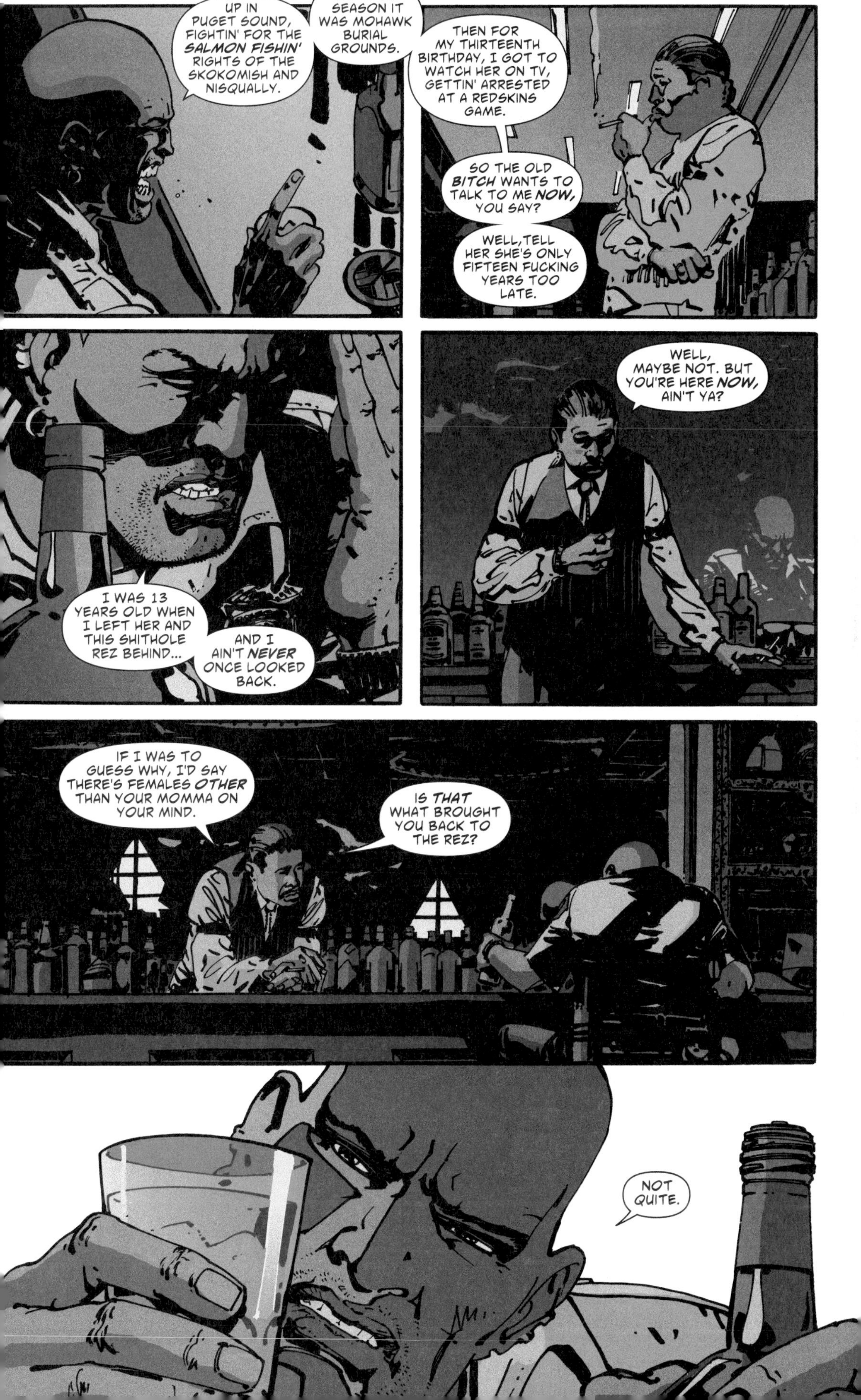
UP IN PUGET SOUND, FIGHTIN' FOR THE SALMON FISHIN' RIGHTS OF THE SKOKOMISH AND NISQUALLY.
THE NEXT SEASON IT WAS MOHAWK BURIAL GROUNDS.
THEN FOR MY THIRTEENTH BIRTHDAY, I GOT TO WATCH HER ON TV, GETTIN' ARRESTED AT A REDSKINS GAME.
SO THE OLD BITCH WANTS TO TALK TO ME NOW, YOU SAY?
WELL, TELL HER SHE'S ONLY FIFTEEN FUCKING YEARS TOO LATE.
I WAS 13 YEARS OLD WHEN I LEFT HER AND THIS SHITHOLE REZ BEHIND...
AND I AIN'T NEVER ONCE LOOKED BACK.
WELL, MAYBE NOT. BUT YOU'RE HERE NOW, AIN'T YA?
IF I WAS TO GUESS WHY, I'D SAY THERE'S FEMALES OTHER THAN YOUR MOMMA ON YOUR MIND.
IS THAT WHAT BROUGHT YOU BACK TO THE REZ?
NOT QUITE.

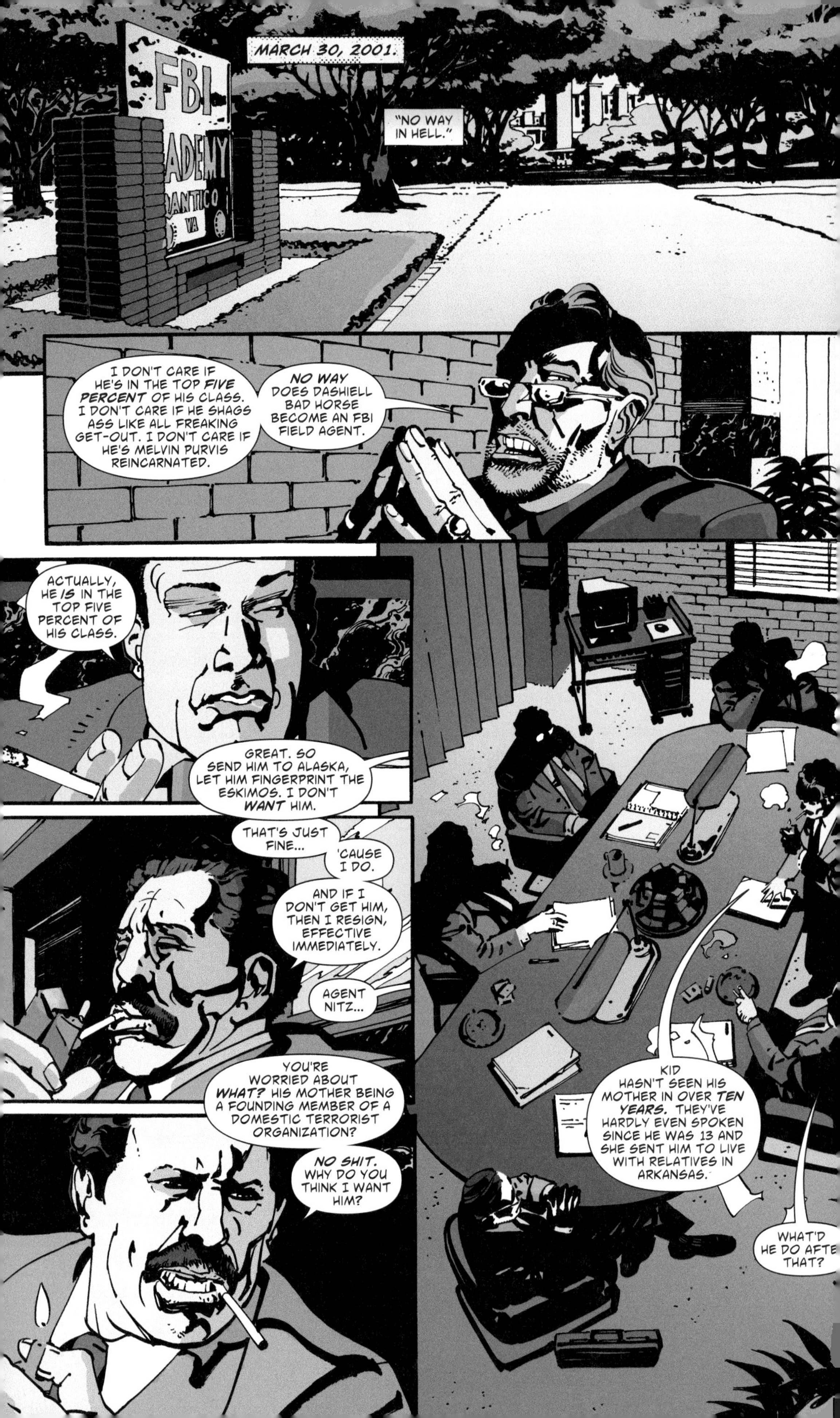
MARCH 30, 2001.
FBI ACADEMY QUANTICO VA
"NO WAY IN HELL."
I DON'T CARE IF HE'S IN THE TOP FIVE PERCENT OF HIS CLASS. I DON'T CARE IF HE SHAGS ASS LIKE ALL FREAKING GET-OUT. I DON'T CARE IF HE'S MELVIN PURVIS REINCARNATED.
NO WAY DOES DASHIELL BAD HORSE BECOME AN FBI FIELD AGENT.
ACTUALLY, HE IS IN THE TOP FIVE PERCENT OF HIS CLASS.
GREAT. SO SEND HIM TO ALASKA, LET HIM FINGERPRINT THE ESKIMOS. I DON'T WANT HIM.
THAT'S JUST FINE...
'CAUSE I DO.
AND IF I DON'T GET HIM, THEN I RESIGN, EFFECTIVE IMMEDIATELY.
AGENT NITZ...
YOU'RE WORRIED ABOUT WHAT? HIS MOTHER BEING A FOUNDING MEMBER OF A DOMESTIC TERRORIST ORGANIZATION?
NO SHIT. WHY DO YOU THINK I WANT HIM?
KID HASN'T SEEN HIS MOTHER IN OVER TEN YEARS. THEY'VE HARDLY EVEN SPOKEN SINCE HE WAS 13 AND SHE SENT HIM TO LIVE WITH RELATIVES IN ARKANSAS.
WHAT'D HE DO AFTE THAT?

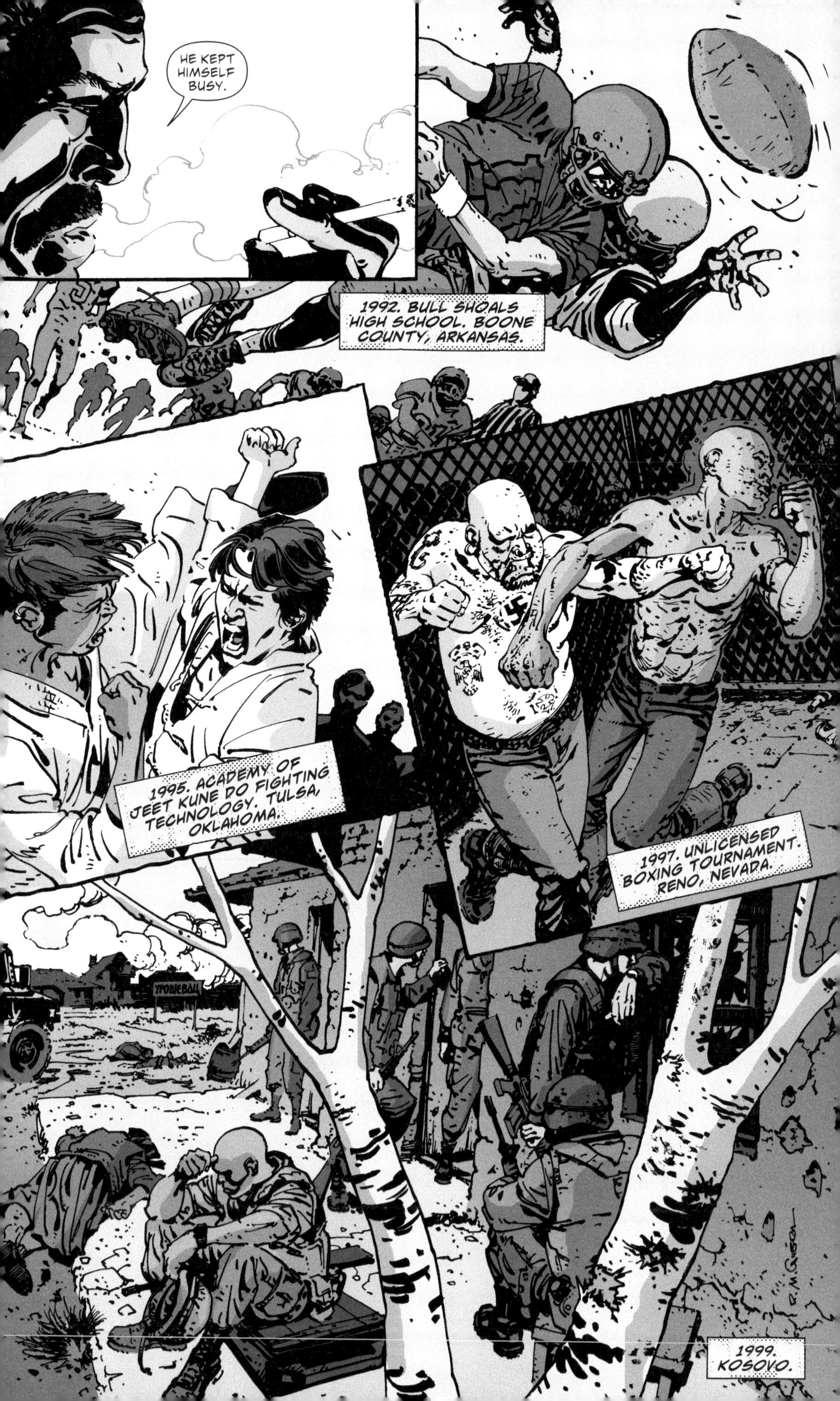

HE KEPT HIMSELF BUSY.
1992. BULL SHOALS HIGH SCHOOL. BOONE COUNTY, ARKANSAS.
1995. ACADEMY OF JEET KUNE DO FIGHTING TECHNOLOGY. TULSA, OKLAHOMA.
1997. UNLICENSED BOXING TOURNAMENT. RENO, NEVADA.
1999. KOSOVO.

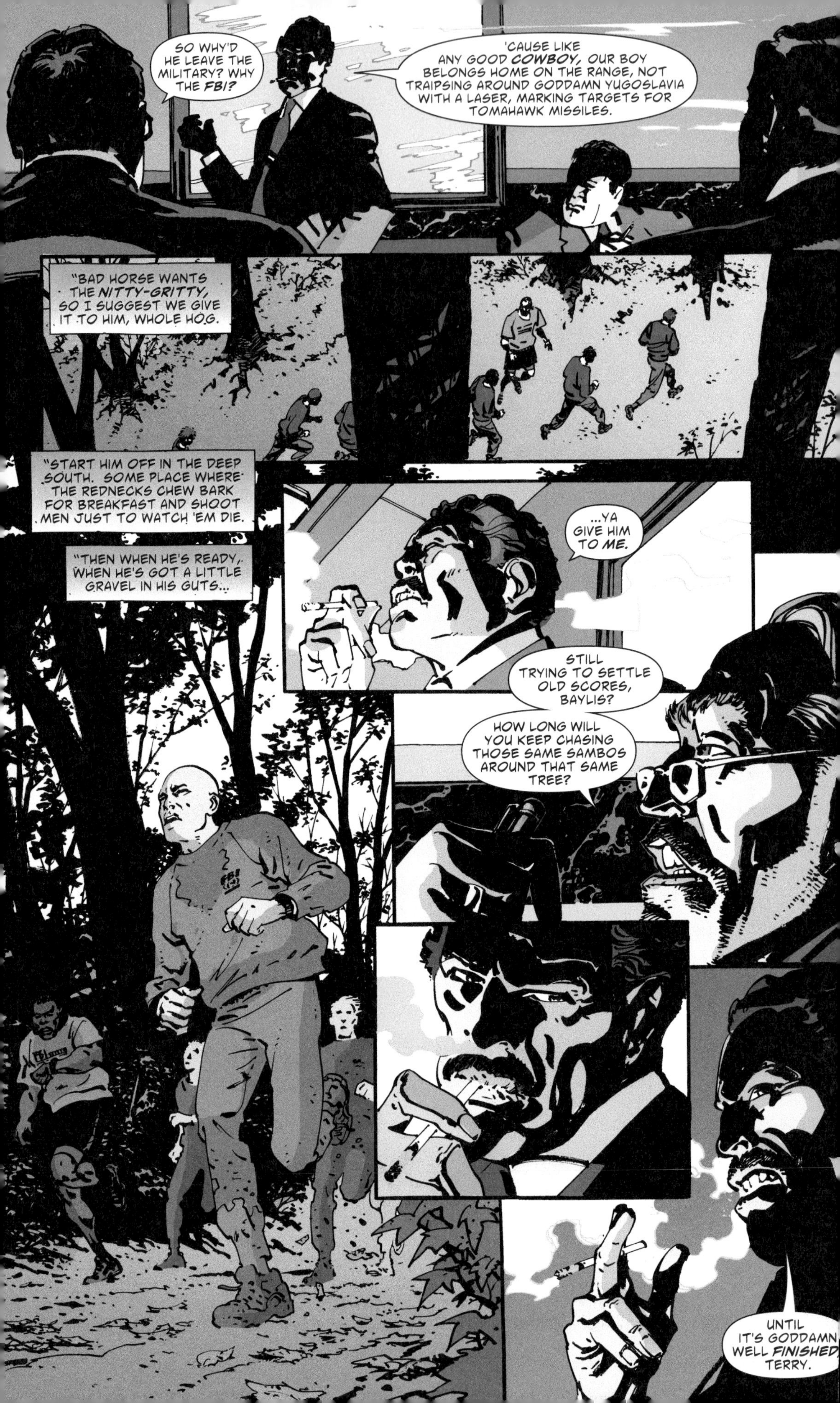

SO WHY'D HE LEAVE THE MILITARY? WHY THE FBI?
'CAUSE LIKE ANY GOOD COWBOY, OUR BOY BELONGS HOME ON THE RANGE, NOT TRAIPSING AROUND GODDAMN YUGOSLAVIA WITH A LASER, MARKING TARGETS FOR TOMAHAWK MISSILES.
"BAD HORSE WANTS THE NITTY-GRITTY, SO I SUGGEST WE GIVE IT TO HIM, WHOLE HOG.
"START HIM OFF IN THE DEEP SOUTH. SOME PLACE WHERE THE REDNECKS CHEW BARK FOR BREAKFAST AND SHOOT MEN JUST TO WATCH 'EM DIE.
"THEN WHEN HE'S READY, WHEN HE'S GOT A LITTLE GRAVEL IN HIS GUTS...
...YA GIVE HIM TO ME.
STILL TRYING TO SETTLE OLD SCORES, BAYLIS?
HOW LONG WILL YOU KEEP CHASING THOSE SAME SAMBOS AROUND THAT SAME TREE?
UNTIL IT'S GODDAMN WELL FINISHED, TERRY.

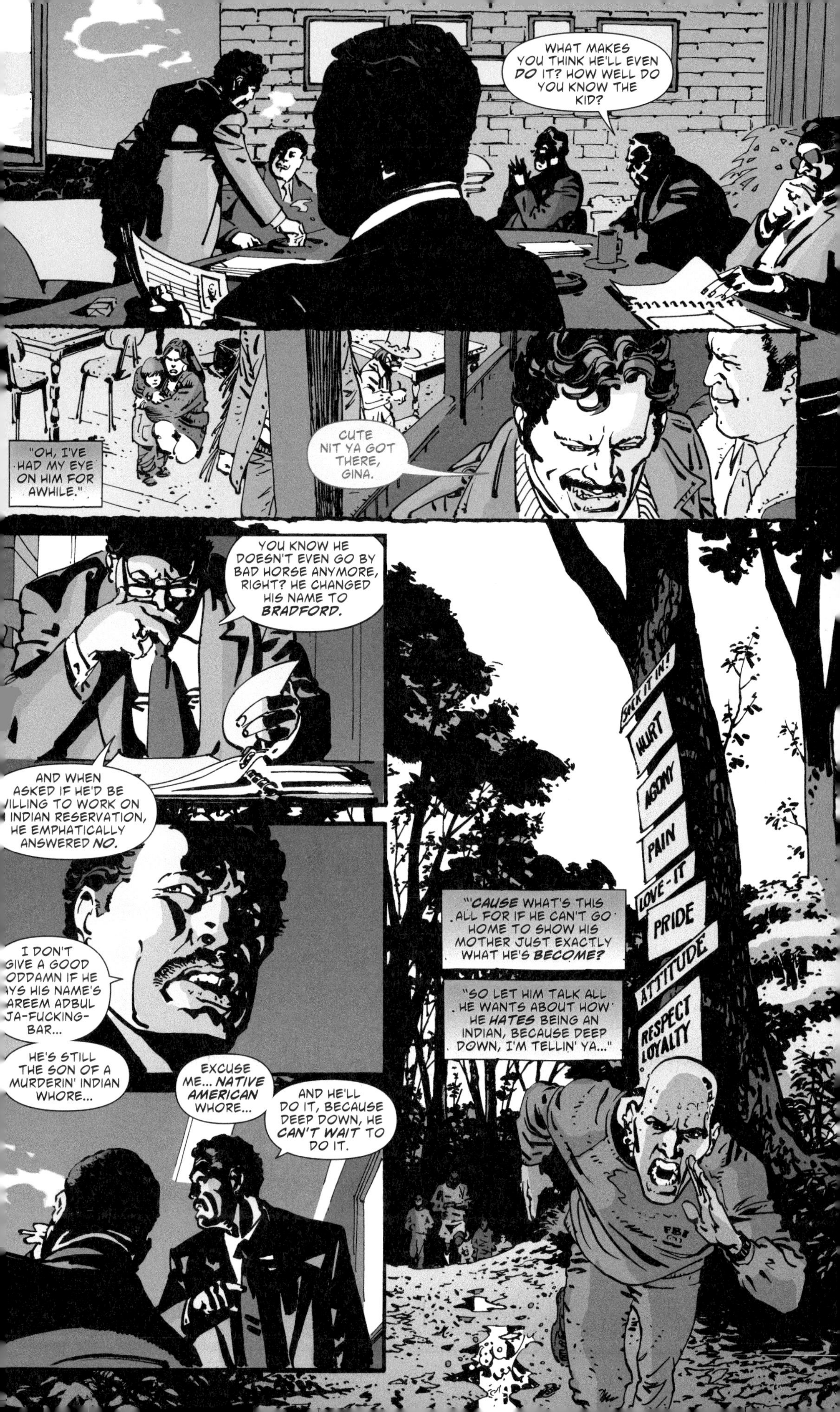
WHAT MAKES YOU THINK HE'LL EVEN DO IT? HOW WELL DO YOU KNOW THE KID?
"OH, I'VE HAD MY EYE ON HIM FOR AWHILE."
CUTE NIT YA GOT THERE, GINA.
YOU KNOW HE DOESN'T EVEN GO BY BAD HORSE ANYMORE, RIGHT? HE CHANGED HIS NAME TO BRADFORD.
AND WHEN ASKED IF HE'D BE WILLING TO WORK ON INDIAN RESERVATION, HE EMPHATICALLY ANSWERED NO.
I DON'T GIVE A GOOD ODDAMN IF HE AYS HIS NAME'S AREEM ADBUL JA-FUCKING-BAR...
HE'S STILL THE SON OF A MURDERIN' INDIAN WHORE...
EXCUSE ME... NATIVE AMERICAN WHORE...
AND HE'LL DO IT, BECAUSE DEEP DOWN, HE CAN'T WAIT TO DO IT.
SUCK IT IN!
HURT
AGONY
PAIN
LOVE-IT
PRIDE
ATTITUDE
RESPECT
LOYALTY
"'CAUSE WHAT'S THIS ALL FOR IF HE CAN'T GO HOME TO SHOW HIS MOTHER JUST EXACTLY WHAT HE'S BECOME?
"SO LET HIM TALK ALL HE WANTS ABOUT HOW HE HATES BEING AN INDIAN, BECAUSE DEEP DOWN, I'M TELLIN' YA..."
FBI

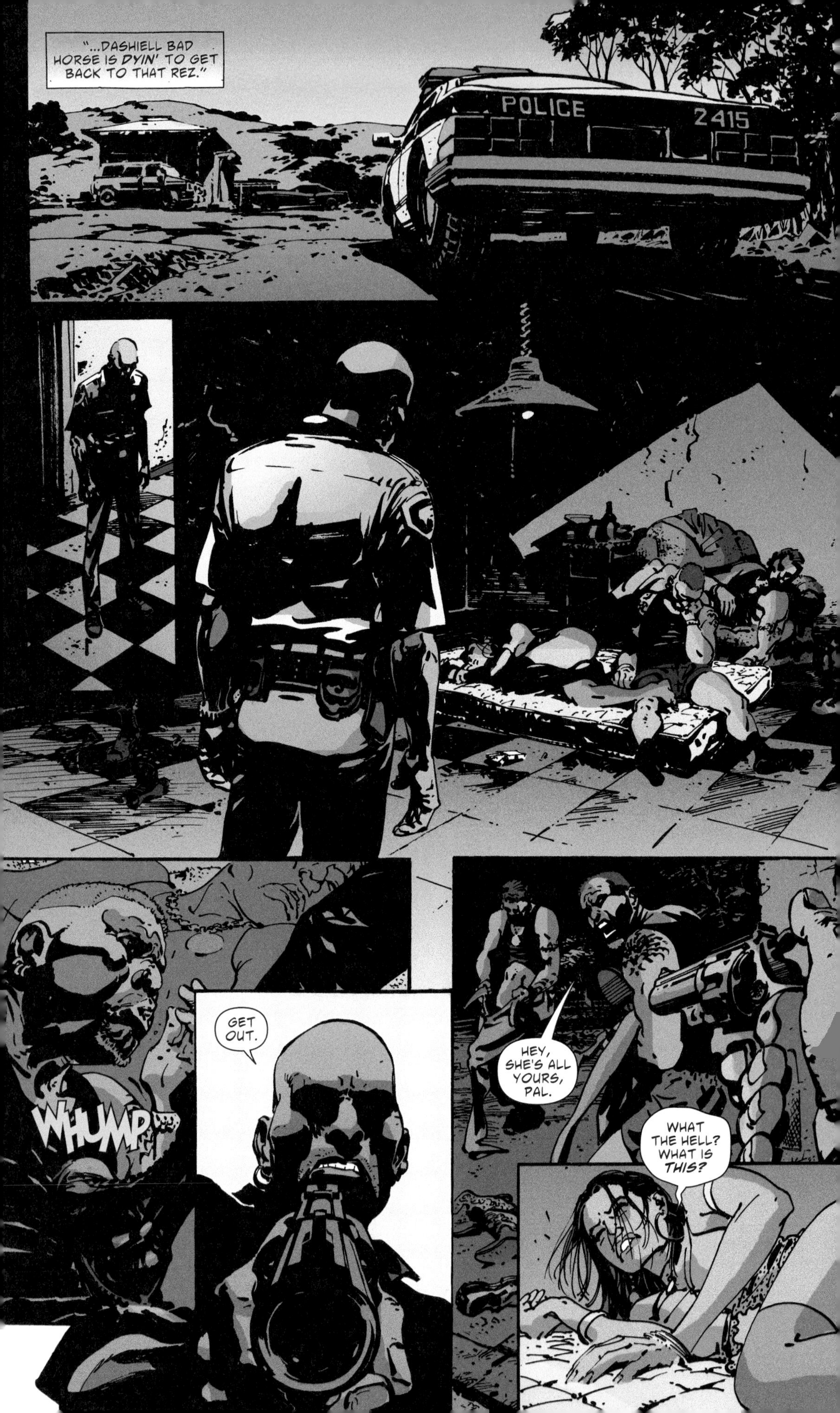
"...DASHIELL BAD HORSE IS DYIN' TO GET BACK TO THAT REZ."
POLICE
2415
WHUMP
GET OUT.
HEY, SHE'S ALL YOURS, PAL.
WHAT THE HELL? WHAT IS THIS?

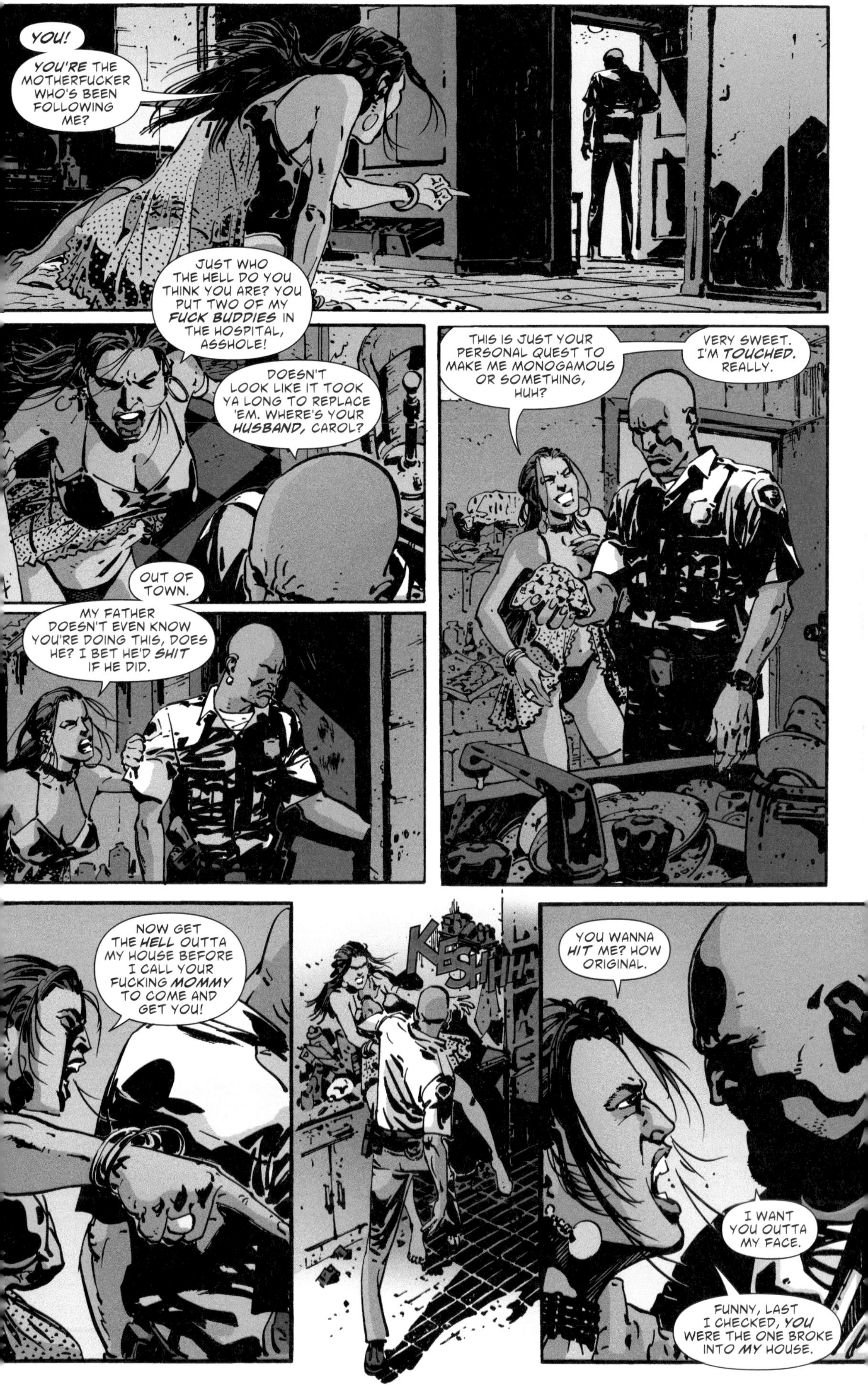
YOU!
YOU'RE THE MOTHERFUCKER WHO'S BEEN FOLLOWING ME?
JUST WHO THE HELL DO YOU THINK YOU ARE? YOU PUT TWO OF MY FUCK BUDDIES IN THE HOSPITAL, ASSHOLE!
DOESN'T LOOK LIKE IT TOOK YA LONG TO REPLACE 'EM. WHERE'S YOUR HUSBAND, CAROL?
OUT OF TOWN.
MY FATHER DOESN'T EVEN KNOW YOU'RE DOING THIS, DOES HE? I BET HE'D SHIT IF HE DID.
THIS IS JUST YOUR PERSONAL QUEST TO MAKE ME MONOGAMOUS OR SOMETHING, HUH?
VERY SWEET. I'M TOUCHED. REALLY.
NOW GET THE HELL OUTTA MY HOUSE BEFORE I CALL YOUR FUCKING MOMMY TO COME AND GET YOU!
KSHHH
YOU WANNA HIT ME? HOW ORIGINAL.
I WANT YOU OUTTA MY FACE.
FUNNY, LAST I CHECKED, YOU WERE THE ONE BROKE INTO MY HOUSE.

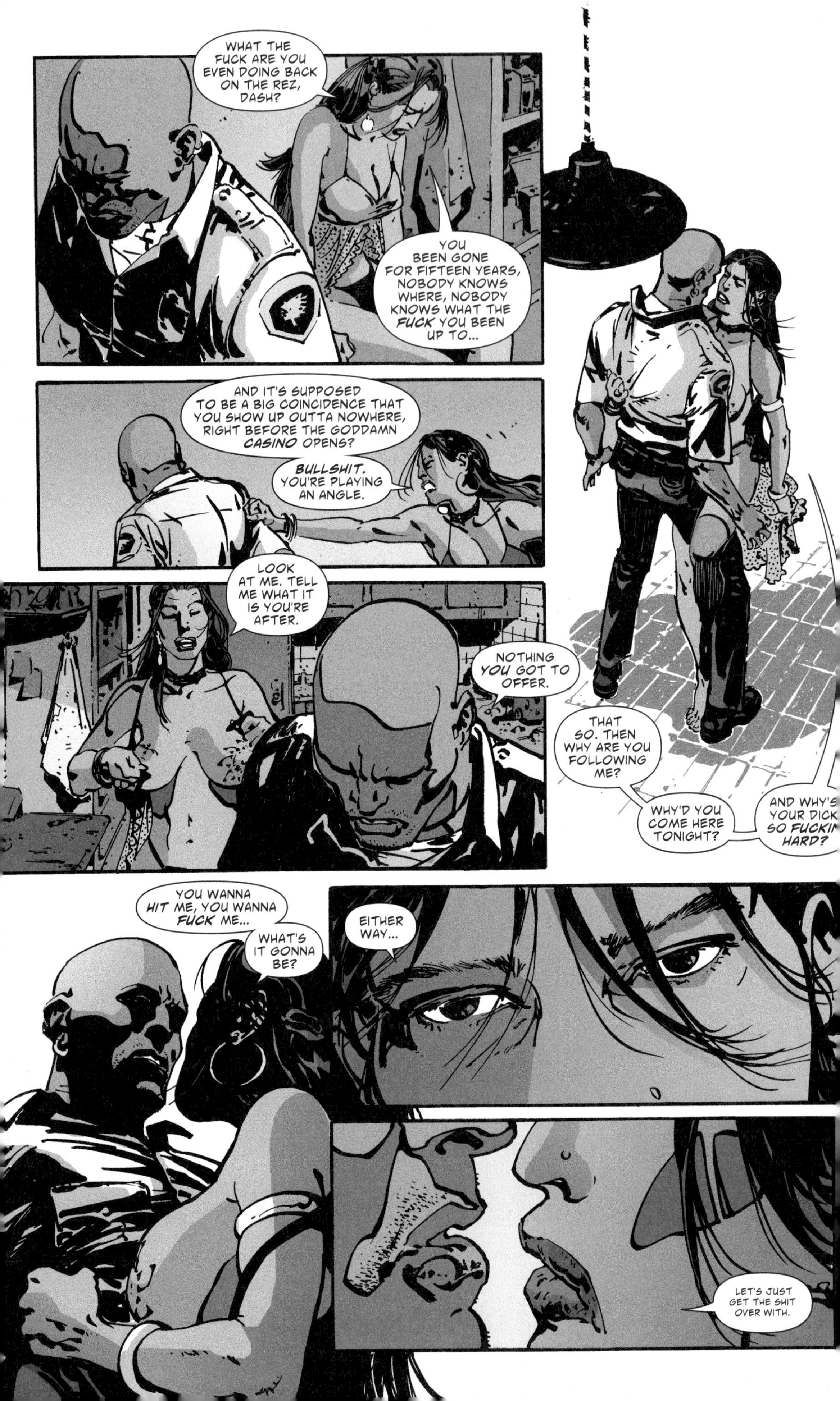

WHAT THE FUCK ARE YOU EVEN DOING BACK ON THE REZ, DASH?
YOU BEEN GONE FOR FIFTEEN YEARS, NOBODY KNOWS WHERE, NOBODY KNOWS WHAT THE FUCK YOU BEEN UP TO...
AND IT'S SUPPOSED TO BE A BIG COINCIDENCE THAT YOU SHOW UP OUTTA NOWHERE, RIGHT BEFORE THE GODDAMN CASINO OPENS?
BULLSHIT. YOU'RE PLAYING AN ANGLE.
LOOK AT ME. TELL ME WHAT IT IS YOU'RE AFTER.
NOTHING YOU GOT TO OFFER.
THAT SO. THEN WHY ARE YOU FOLLOWING ME?
WHY'D YOU COME HERE TONIGHT?
AND WHY'S YOUR DICK SO FUCKI HARD?
YOU WANNA HIT ME, YOU WANNA FUCK ME...
WHAT'S IT GONNA BE?
EITHER WAY...
LET'S JUST GET THE SHIT OVER WITH.

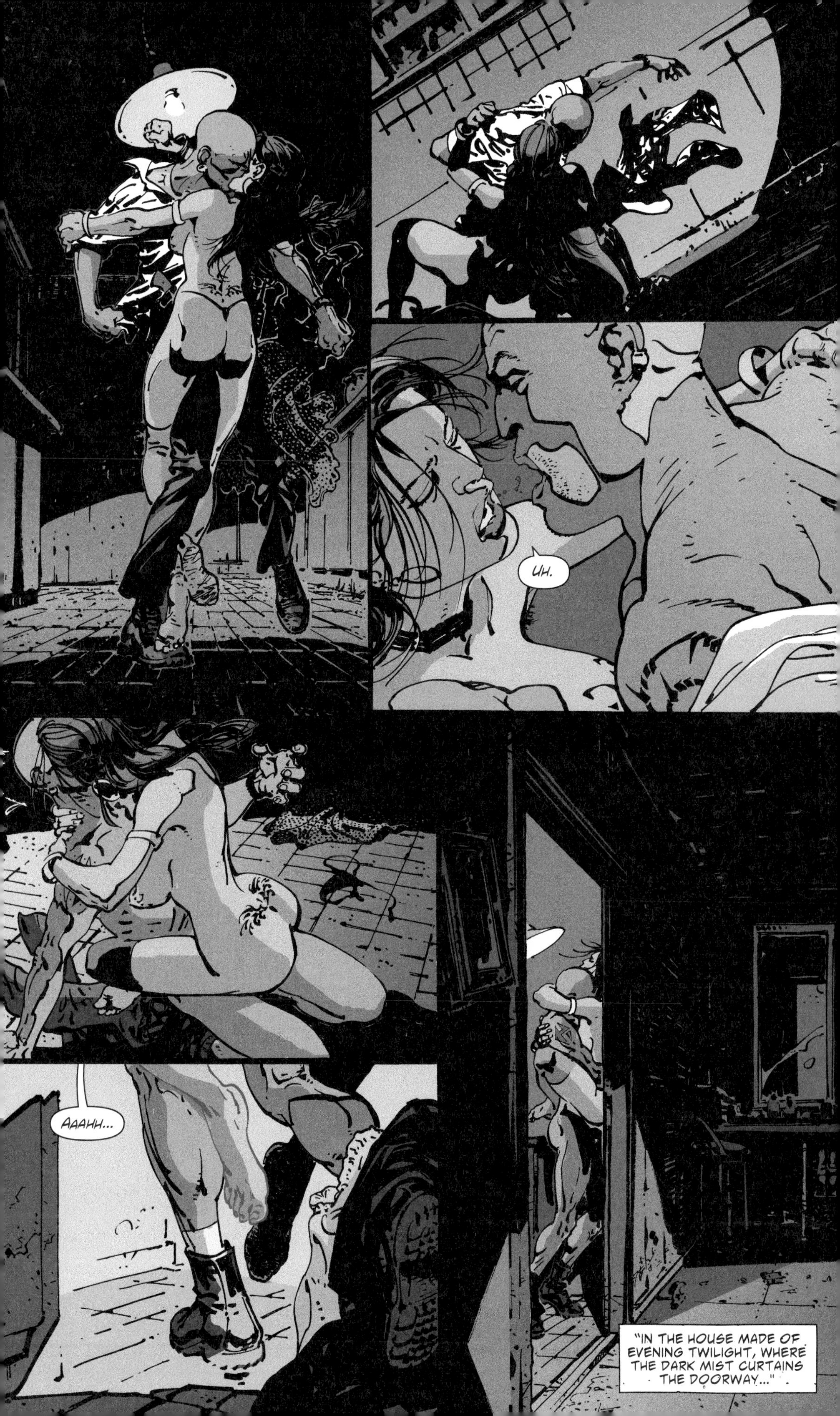
UH.
AAAHH...
"IN THE HOUSE MADE OF EVENING TWILIGHT, WHERE THE DARK MIST CURTAINS THE DOORWAY..."

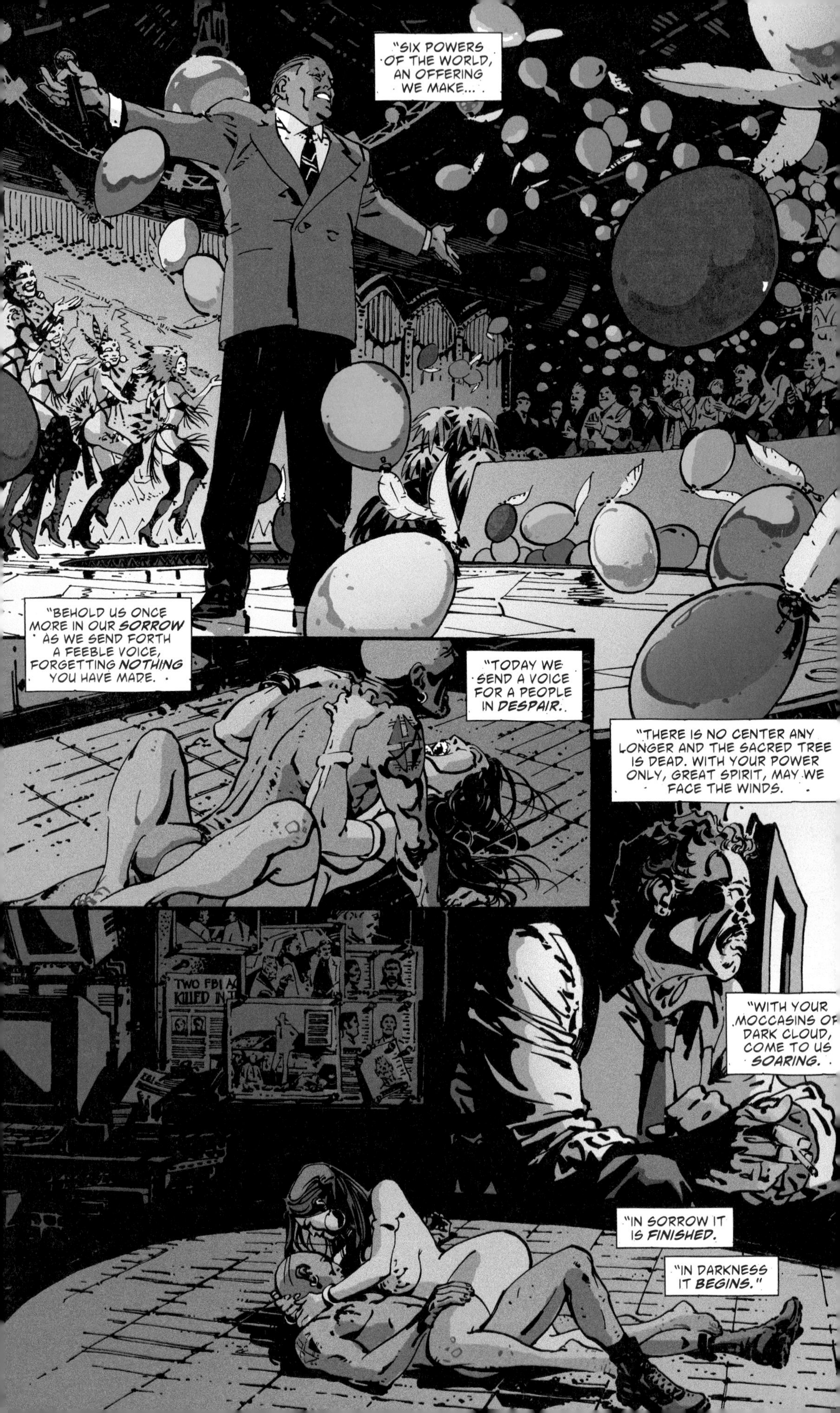
"SIX POWERS OF THE WORLD, AN OFFERING WE MAKE...
"BEHOLD US ONCE MORE IN OUR SORROW AS WE SEND FORTH A FEEBLE VOICE, FORGETTING NOTHING YOU HAVE MADE.
"TODAY WE SEND A VOICE FOR A PEOPLE IN DESPAIR.
"THERE IS NO CENTER ANY LONGER AND THE SACRED TREE IS DEAD. WITH YOUR POWER ONLY, GREAT SPIRIT, MAY WE FACE THE WINDS.
TWO FBI A
KILLED IN
"WITH YOUR MOCCASINS OF DARK CLOUD, COME TO US SOARING.
"IN SORROW IT IS FINISHED.
"IN DARKNESS IT BEGINS."

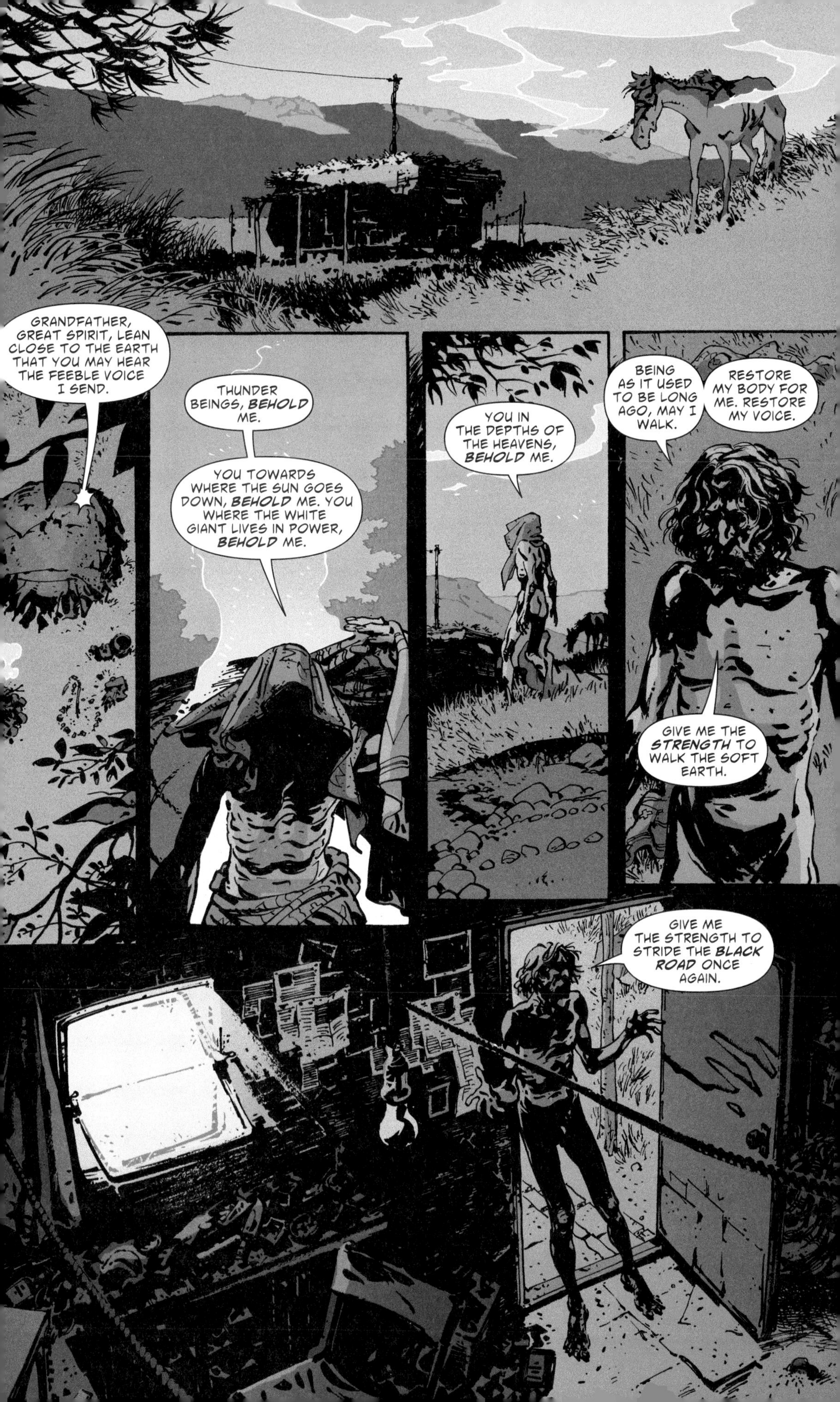
GRANDFATHER, GREAT SPIRIT, LEAN CLOSE TO THE EARTH THAT YOU MAY HEAR THE FEEBLE VOICE I SEND.
THUNDER BEINGS, BEHOLD ME.
YOU TOWARDS WHERE THE SUN GOES DOWN, BEHOLD ME. YOU WHERE THE WHITE GIANT LIVES IN POWER, BEHOLD ME.
YOU IN THE DEPTHS OF THE HEAVENS, BEHOLD ME.
BEING AS IT USED TO BE LONG AGO, MAY I WALK.
RESTORE MY BODY FOR ME. RESTORE MY VOICE.
GIVE ME THE STRENGTH TO WALK THE SOFT EARTH.
GIVE ME THE STRENGTH TO STRIDE THE BLACK ROAD ONCE AGAIN.

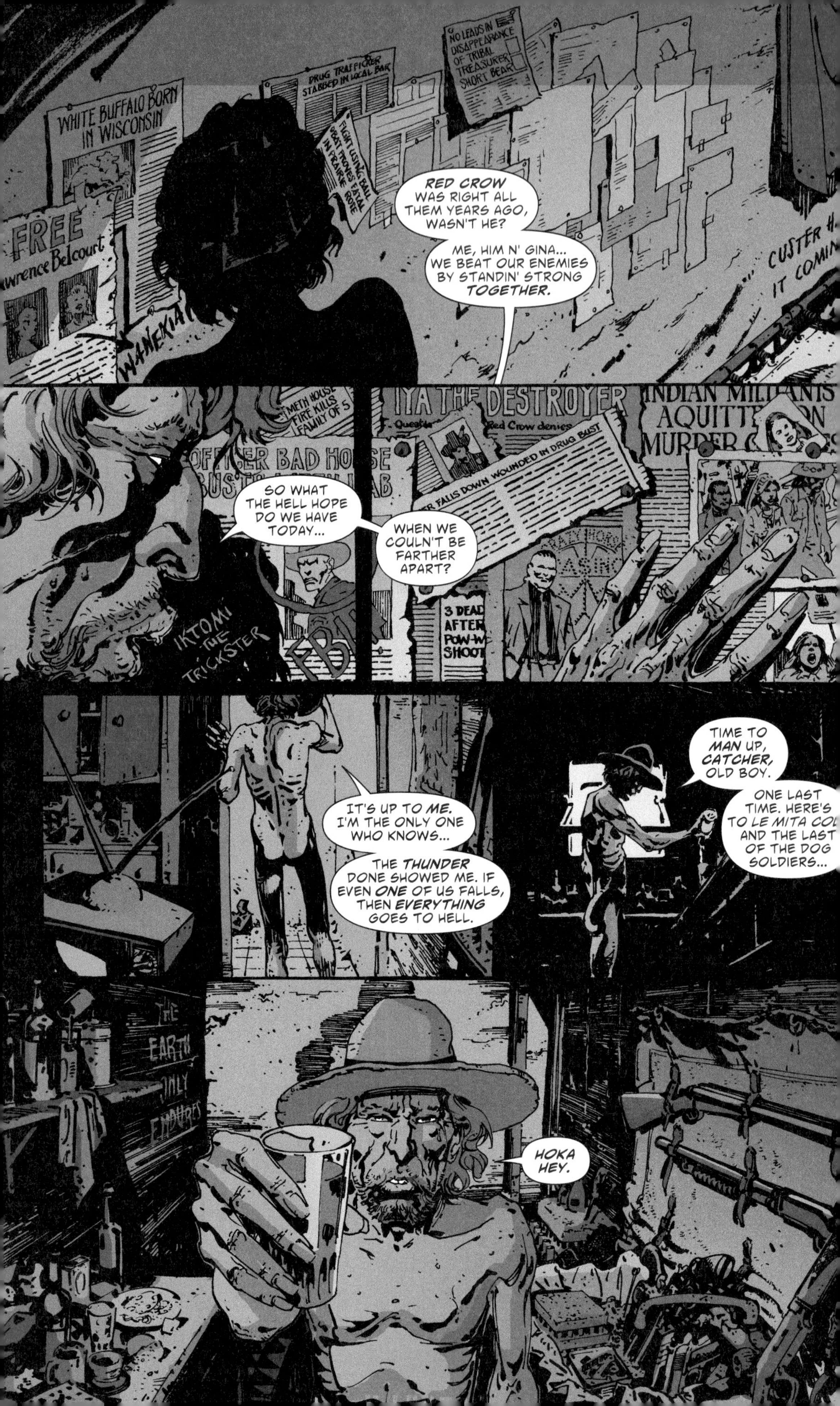

WHITE BUFFALO BORN IN WISCONSIN
DRUG TRAFFICKER STABBED IN LOCAL BAR
NO LEADS IN DISAPPEARANCE OF TRIBAL TREASURER SHORT BEAR
FREE
RED CROW WAS RIGHT ALL THEM YEARS AGO, WASN'T HE?
ME, HIM N' GINA... WE BEAT OUR ENEMIES BY STANDIN' STRONG TOGETHER.
IYA THE DESTROYER
INDIAN MILITANTS AQUITTED ON MURDER CHARGES
METH HOUSE FIRE KILLS FAMILY OF 5
SO WHAT THE HELL HOPE DO WE HAVE TODAY...
WHEN WE COULN'T BE FARTHER APART?
IKTOMI THE TRICKSTER
IT'S UP TO ME. I'M THE ONLY ONE WHO KNOWS...
THE THUNDER DONE SHOWED ME. IF EVEN ONE OF US FALLS, THEN EVERYTHING GOES TO HELL.
TIME TO MAN UP, CATCHER, OLD BOY.
ONE LAST TIME. HERE'S TO LE MITA COL AND THE LAST OF THE DOG SOLDIERS...
THE EARTH ONLY ENDURES
HOKA HEY.

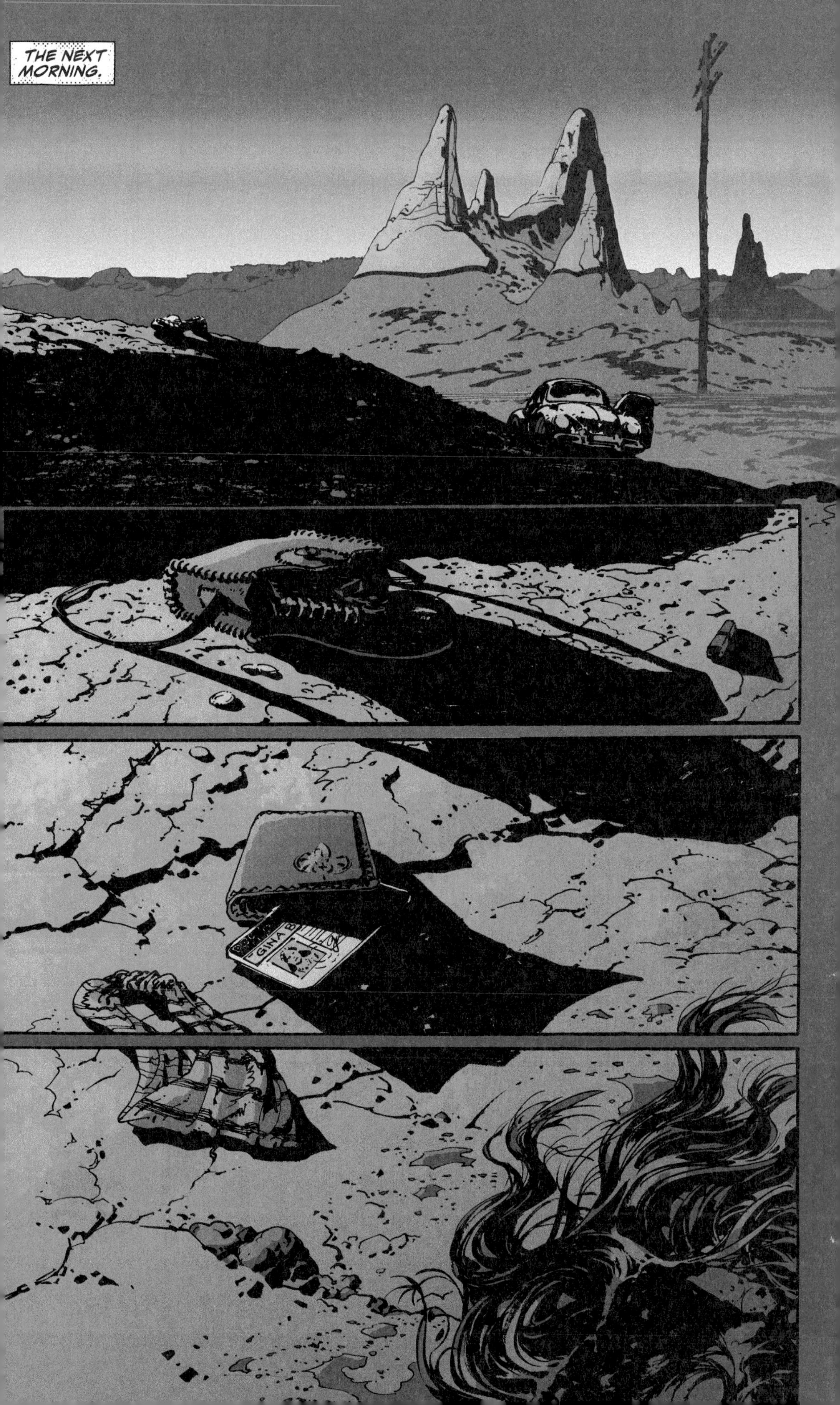
THE NEXT MORNING.
GINA B

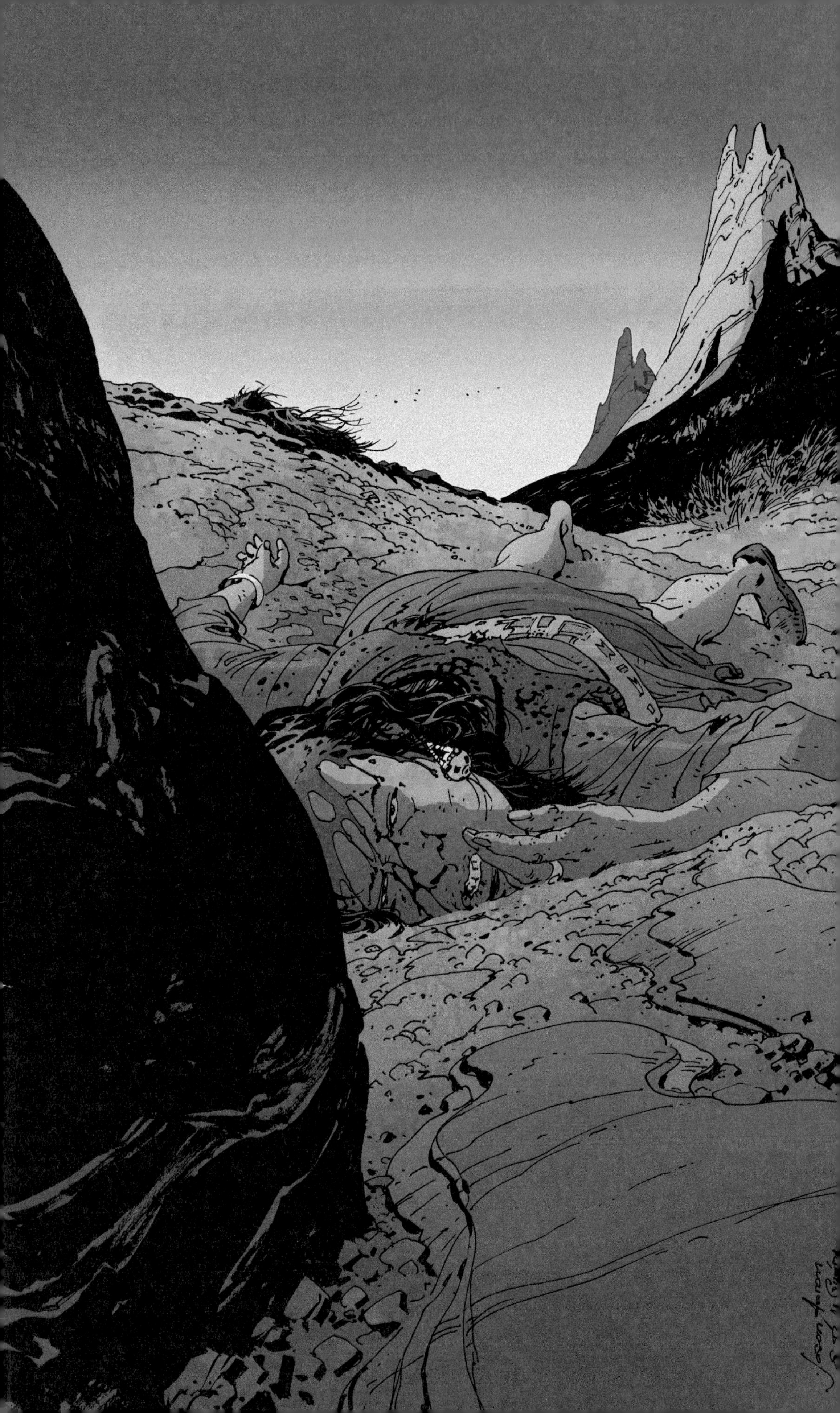

CASINO BOOGIE PART ONE: THE MAN WHO FIGHTS THE BULL

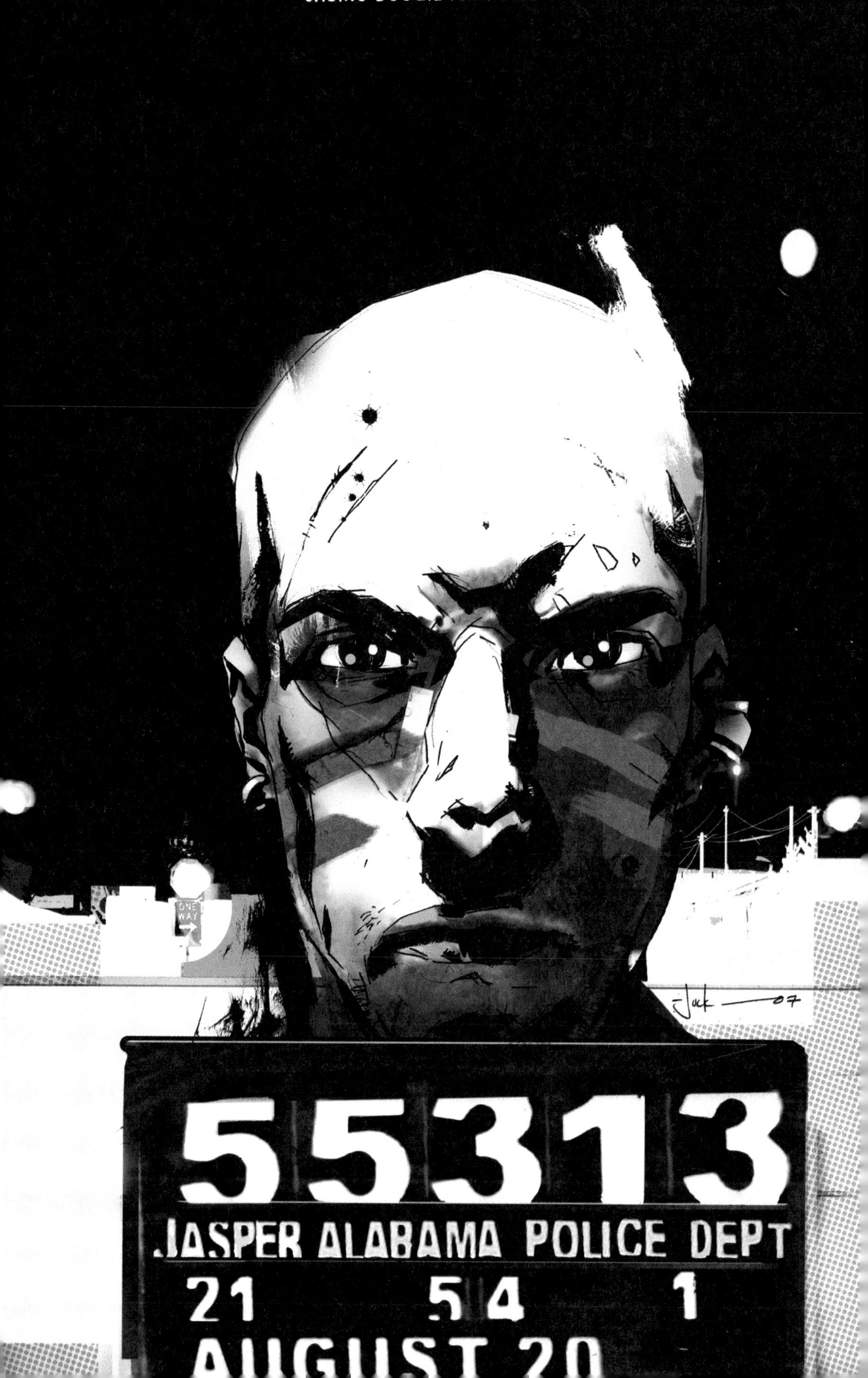
ONE WAY
55313
JASPER ALABAMA POLICE DEPT
21 54 1
AUGUST 20

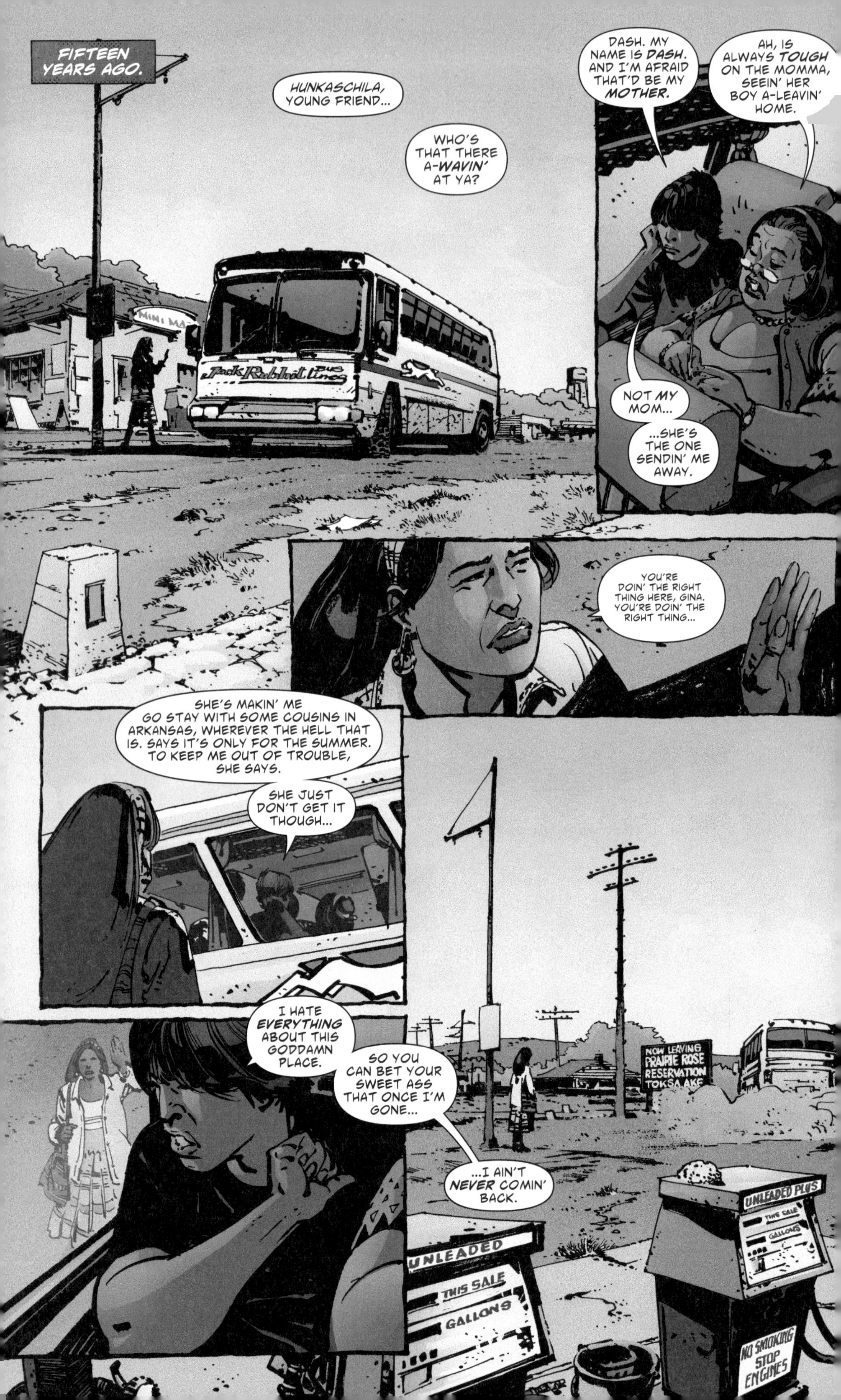
FIFTEEN YEARS AGO.
HUNKASCHILA, YOUNG FRIEND...
WHO'S THAT THERE A-WAVIN' AT YA?
MINI MA
Jack Rabbit Bus Lines
DASH. MY NAME IS DASH. AND I'M AFRAID THAT'D BE MY MOTHER.
AH, IS ALWAYS TOUGH ON THE MOMMA, SEEIN' HER BOY A-LEAVIN' HOME.
NOT MY MOM...
...SHE'S THE ONE SENDIN' ME AWAY.
YOU'RE DOIN' THE RIGHT THING HERE, GINA. YOU'RE DOIN' THE RIGHT THING...
SHE'S MAKIN' ME GO STAY WITH SOME COUSINS IN ARKANSAS, WHEREVER THE HELL THAT IS. SAYS IT'S ONLY FOR THE SUMMER. TO KEEP ME OUT OF TROUBLE, SHE SAYS.
SHE JUST DON'T GET IT THOUGH...
I HATE EVERYTHING ABOUT THIS GODDAMN PLACE.
SO YOU CAN BET YOUR SWEET ASS THAT ONCE I'M GONE...
...I AIN'T NEVER COMIN' BACK.
NOW LEAVING PRAIRIE ROSE RESERVATION TOKSA AKE
UNLEADED PLUS
THIS SALE
GALLONS
UNLEADED
THIS SALE
GALLONS
NO SMOKING STOP ENGINES

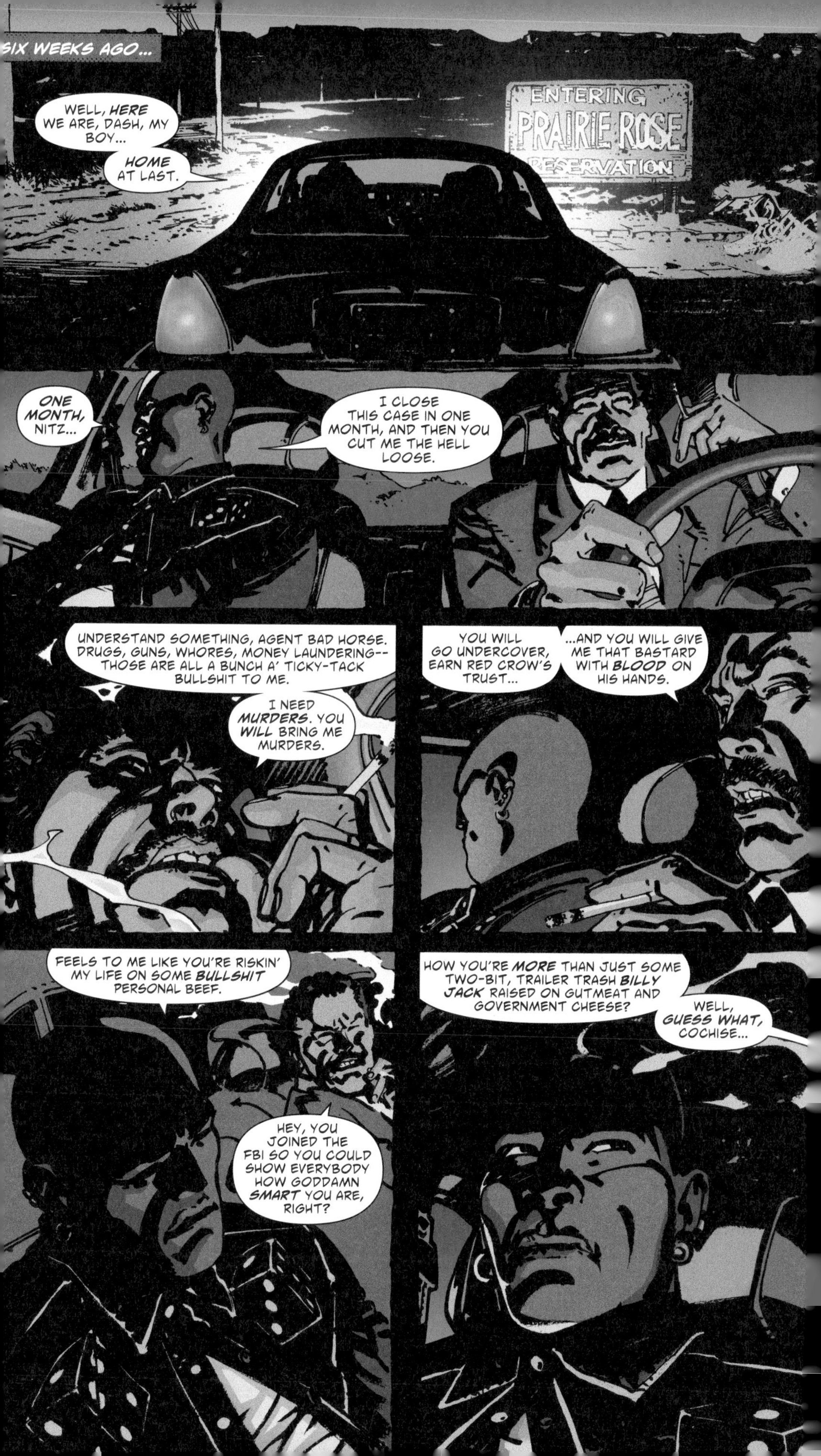
SIX WEEKS AGO...
ENTERING PRAIRIE ROSE RESERVATION
WELL, HERE WE ARE, DASH, MY BOY...
HOME AT LAST.
ONE MONTH, NITZ...
I CLOSE THIS CASE IN ONE MONTH, AND THEN YOU CUT ME THE HELL LOOSE.
UNDERSTAND SOMETHING, AGENT BAD HORSE. DRUGS, GUNS, WHORES, MONEY LAUNDERING-- THOSE ARE ALL A BUNCH A' TICKY-TACK BULLSHIT TO ME.
I NEED MURDERS. YOU WILL BRING ME MURDERS.
YOU WILL GO UNDERCOVER, EARN RED CROW'S TRUST...
...AND YOU WILL GIVE ME THAT BASTARD WITH BLOOD ON HIS HANDS.
FEELS TO ME LIKE YOU'RE RISKIN' MY LIFE ON SOME BULLSHIT PERSONAL BEEF.
HEY, YOU JOINED THE FBI SO YOU COULD SHOW EVERYBODY HOW GODDAMN SMART YOU ARE, RIGHT?
HOW YOU'RE MORE THAN JUST SOME TWO-BIT, TRAILER TRASH BILLY JACK RAISED ON GUTMEAT AND GOVERNMENT CHEESE?
WELL, GUESS WHAT, COCHISE...

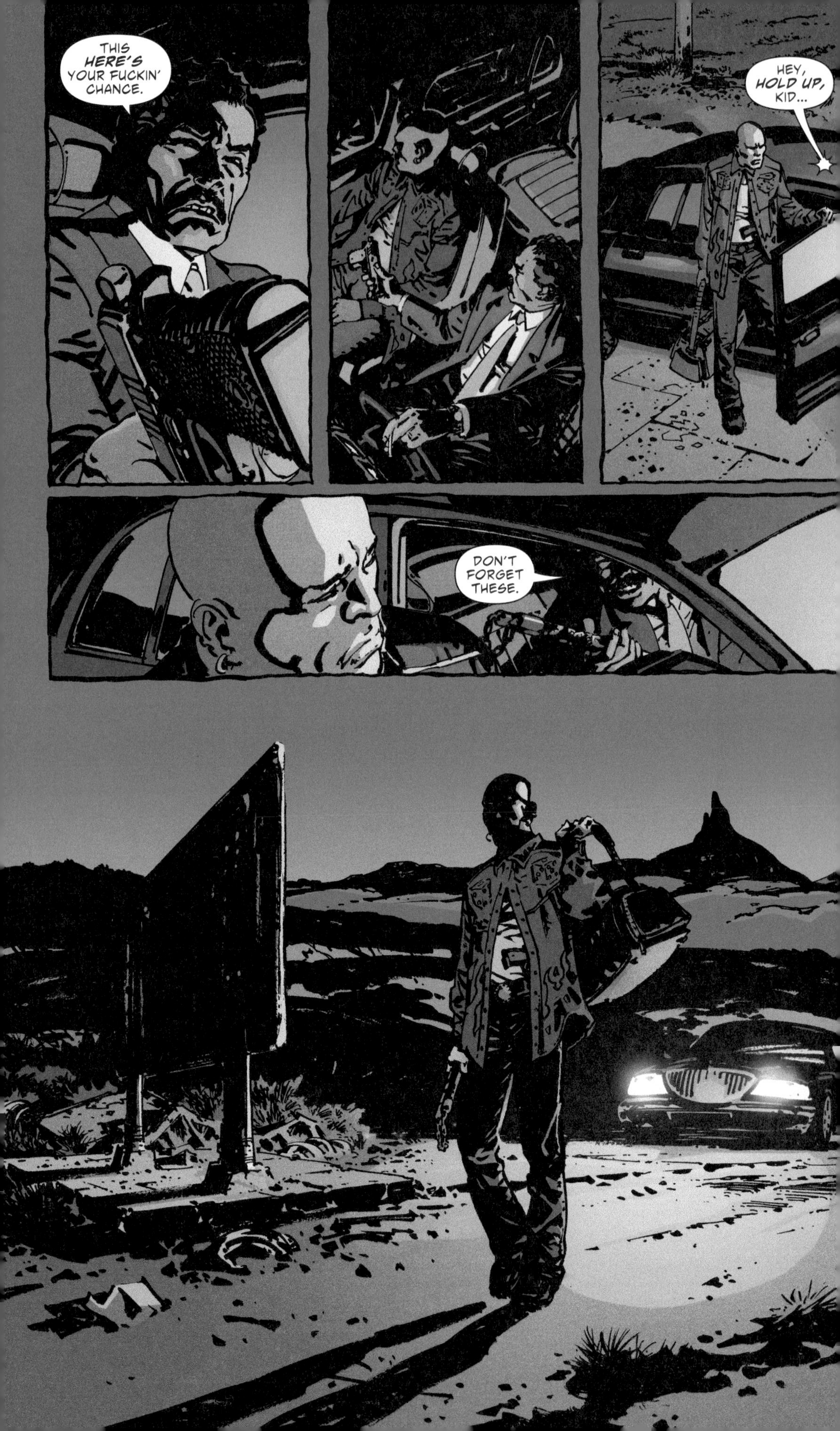
THIS HERE'S YOUR FUCKIN' CHANCE.
HEY, HOLD UP, KID...
DON'T FORGET THESE.

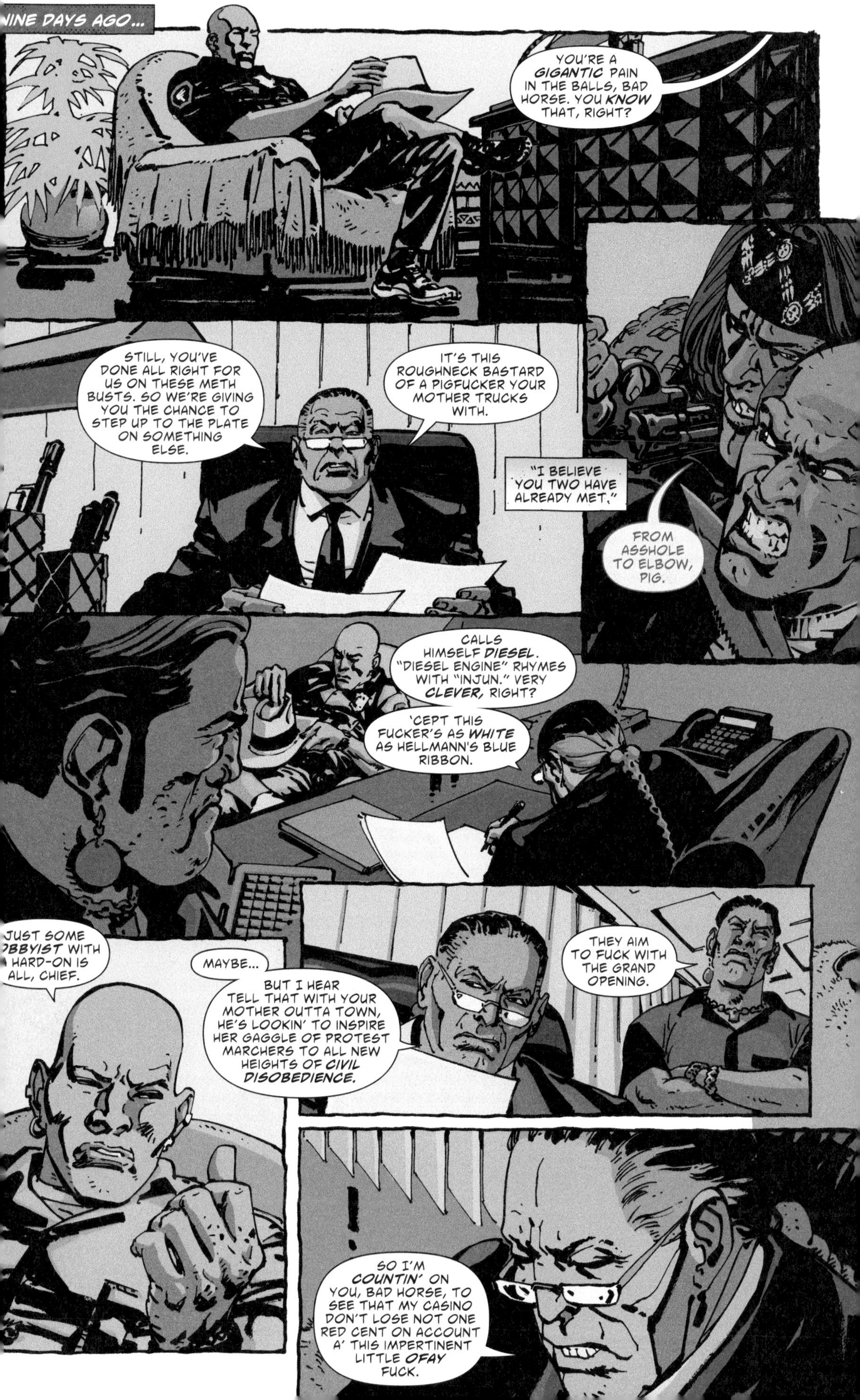
NINE DAYS AGO...
YOU'RE A GIGANTIC PAIN IN THE BALLS, BAD HORSE. YOU KNOW THAT, RIGHT?
STILL, YOU'VE DONE ALL RIGHT FOR US ON THESE METH BUSTS. SO WE'RE GIVING YOU THE CHANCE TO STEP UP TO THE PLATE ON SOMETHING ELSE.
IT'S THIS ROUGHNECK BASTARD OF A PIGFUCKER YOUR MOTHER TRUCKS WITH.
"I BELIEVE YOU TWO HAVE ALREADY MET."
FROM ASSHOLE TO ELBOW, PIG.
CALLS HIMSELF DIESEL. "DIESEL ENGINE" RHYMES WITH "INJUN." VERY CLEVER, RIGHT?
'CEPT THIS FUCKER'S AS WHITE AS HELLMANN'S BLUE RIBBON.
JUST SOME OBBYIST WITH HARD-ON IS ALL, CHIEF.
MAYBE...
BUT I HEAR TELL THAT WITH YOUR MOTHER OUTTA TOWN, HE'S LOOKIN' TO INSPIRE HER GAGGLE OF PROTEST MARCHERS TO ALL NEW HEIGHTS OF CIVIL DISOBEDIENCE.
THEY AIM TO FUCK WITH THE GRAND OPENING.
SO I'M COUNTIN' ON YOU, BAD HORSE, TO SEE THAT MY CASINO DON'T LOSE NOT ONE RED CENT ON ACCOUNT A' THIS IMPERTINENT LITTLE OFAY FUCK.

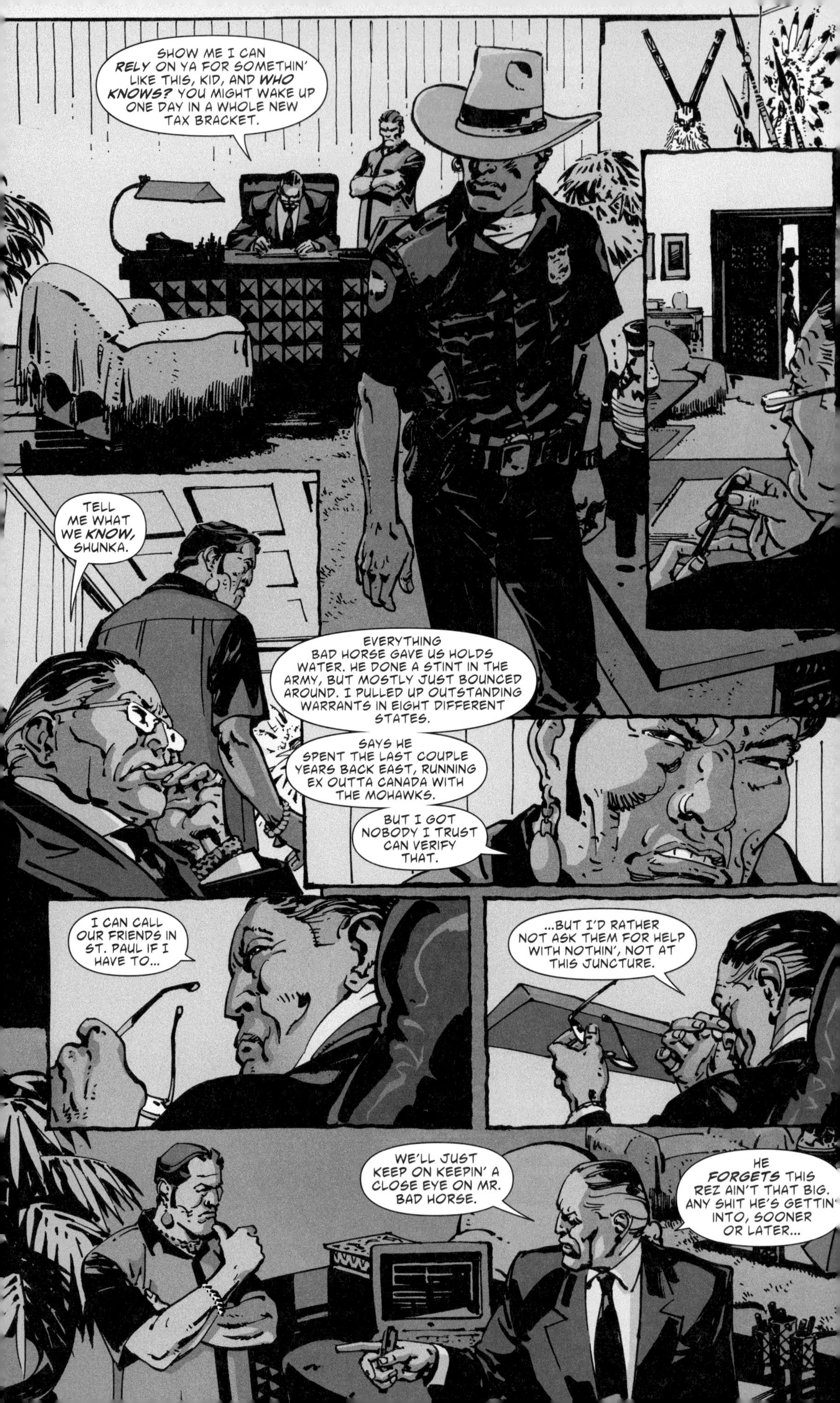
SHOW ME I CAN RELY ON YA FOR SOMETHIN' LIKE THIS, KID, AND WHO KNOWS? YOU MIGHT WAKE UP ONE DAY IN A WHOLE NEW TAX BRACKET.
TELL ME WHAT WE KNOW, SHUNKA.
EVERYTHING BAD HORSE GAVE US HOLDS WATER. HE DONE A STINT IN THE ARMY, BUT MOSTLY JUST BOUNCED AROUND. I PULLED UP OUTSTANDING WARRANTS IN EIGHT DIFFERENT STATES.
SAYS HE SPENT THE LAST COUPLE YEARS BACK EAST, RUNNING EX OUTTA CANADA WITH THE MOHAWKS.
BUT I GOT NOBODY I TRUST CAN VERIFY THAT.
I CAN CALL OUR FRIENDS IN ST. PAUL IF I HAVE TO...
...BUT I'D RATHER NOT ASK THEM FOR HELP WITH NOTHIN', NOT AT THIS JUNCTURE.
WE'LL JUST KEEP ON KEEPIN' A CLOSE EYE ON MR. BAD HORSE.
HE FORGETS THIS REZ AIN'T THAT BIG. ANY SHIT HE'S GETTIN' INTO, SOONER OR LATER...

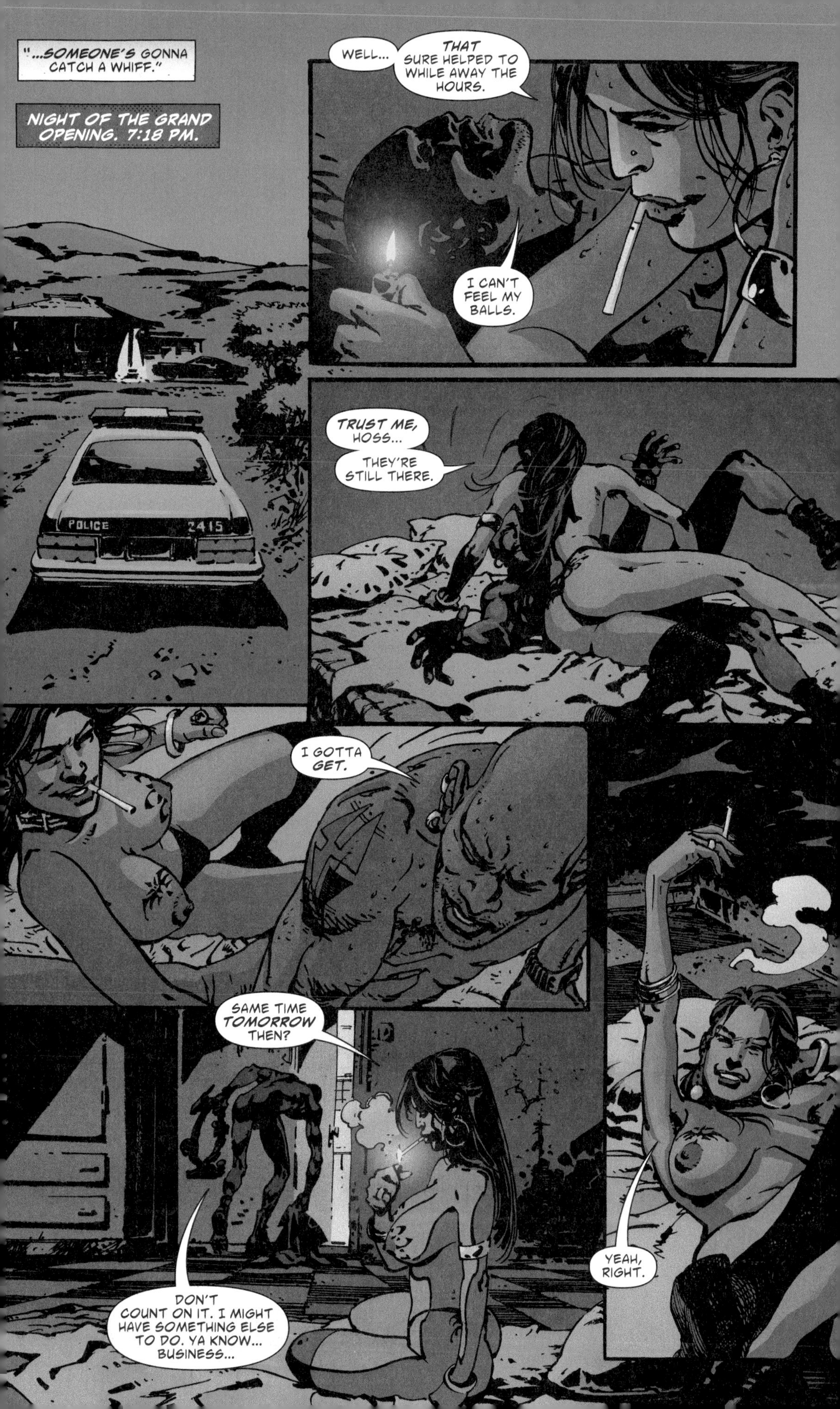

"...SOMEONE'S GONNA CATCH A WHIFF."
NIGHT OF THE GRAND OPENING. 7:18 PM.
POLICE 2415
WELL...
THAT SURE HELPED TO WHILE AWAY THE HOURS.
I CAN'T FEEL MY BALLS.
TRUST ME, HOSS...
THEY'RE STILL THERE.
I GOTTA GET.
SAME TIME TOMORROW THEN?
DON'T COUNT ON IT. I MIGHT HAVE SOMETHING ELSE TO DO. YA KNOW... BUSINESS...
YEAH, RIGHT.

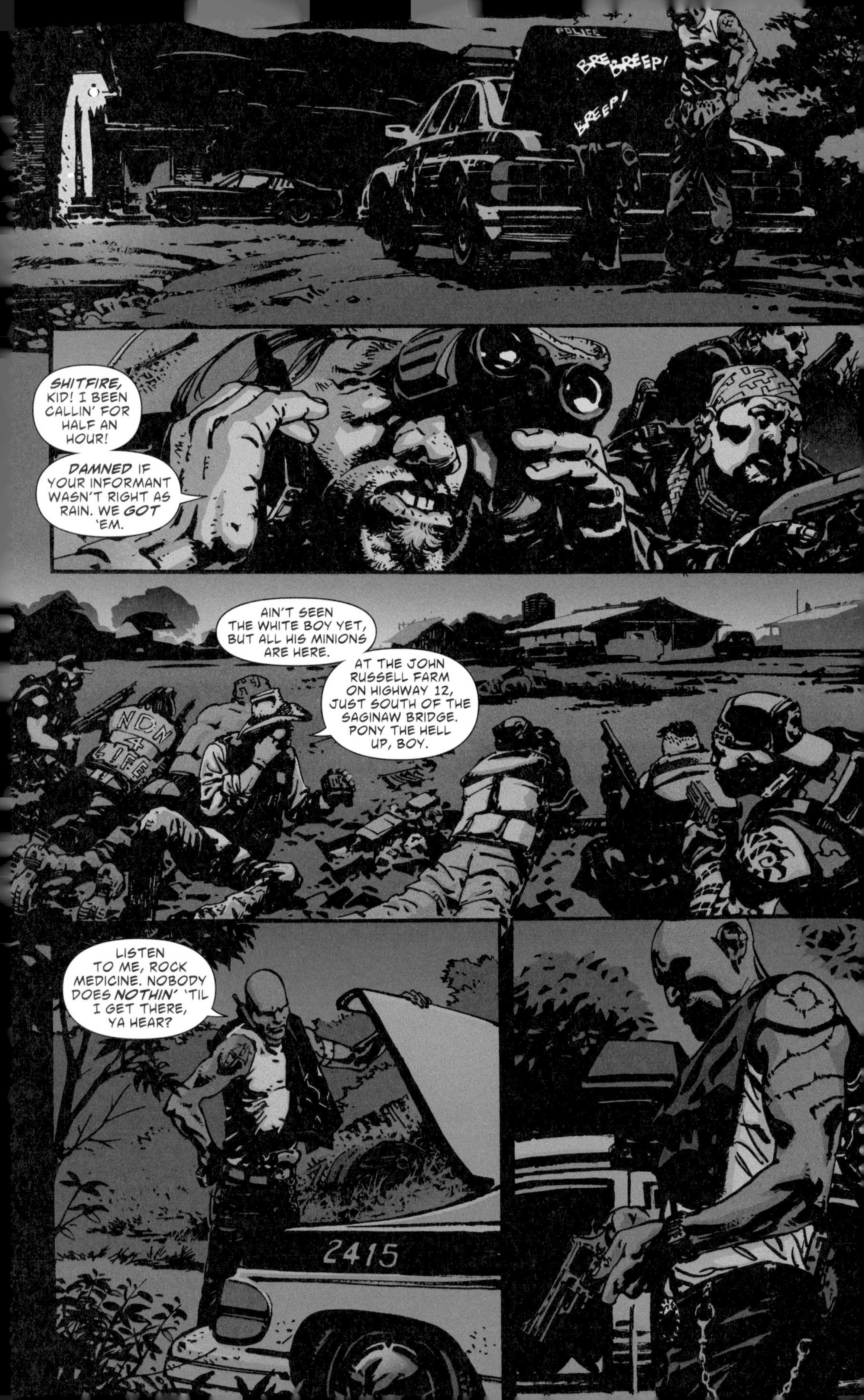
POLICE
BRE BREEP!
BREEP!
SHITFIRE, KID! I BEEN CALLIN' FOR HALF AN HOUR!
DAMNED IF YOUR INFORMANT WASN'T RIGHT AS RAIN. WE GOT 'EM.
AIN'T SEEN THE WHITE BOY YET, BUT ALL HIS MINIONS ARE HERE.
AT THE JOHN RUSSELL FARM ON HIGHWAY 12, JUST SOUTH OF THE SAGINAW BRIDGE. PONY THE HELL UP, BOY.
NDN 4 LIFE
LISTEN TO ME, ROCK MEDICINE. NOBODY DOES NOTHIN' 'TIL I GET THERE, YA HEAR?
2415

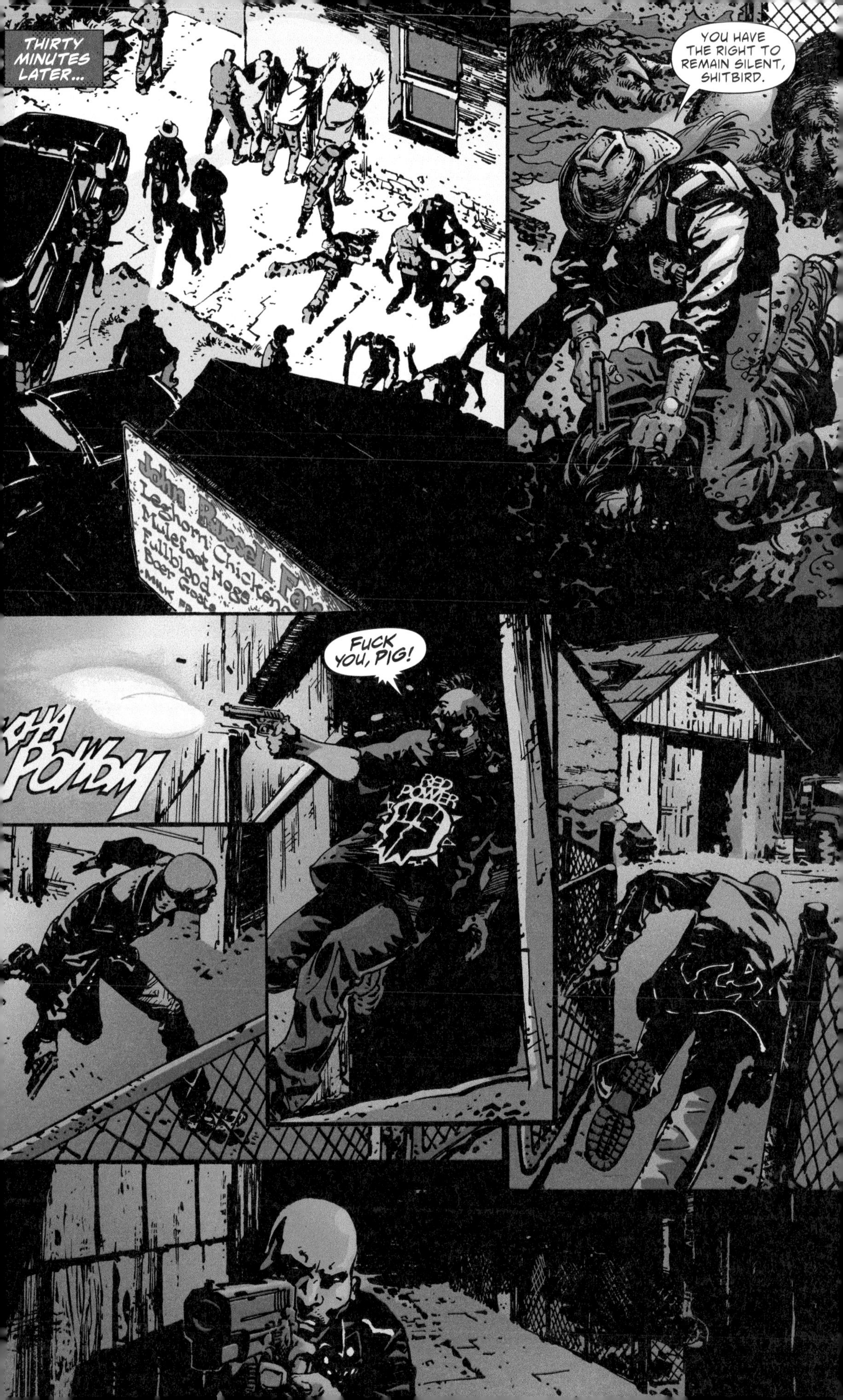
THIRTY MINUTES LATER...
Leghorn Chickens
Mulefoot Hogs
Fullblood
Boer Goats
YOU HAVE THE RIGHT TO REMAIN SILENT, SHITBIRD.
FUCK YOU, PIG!
RED POWER

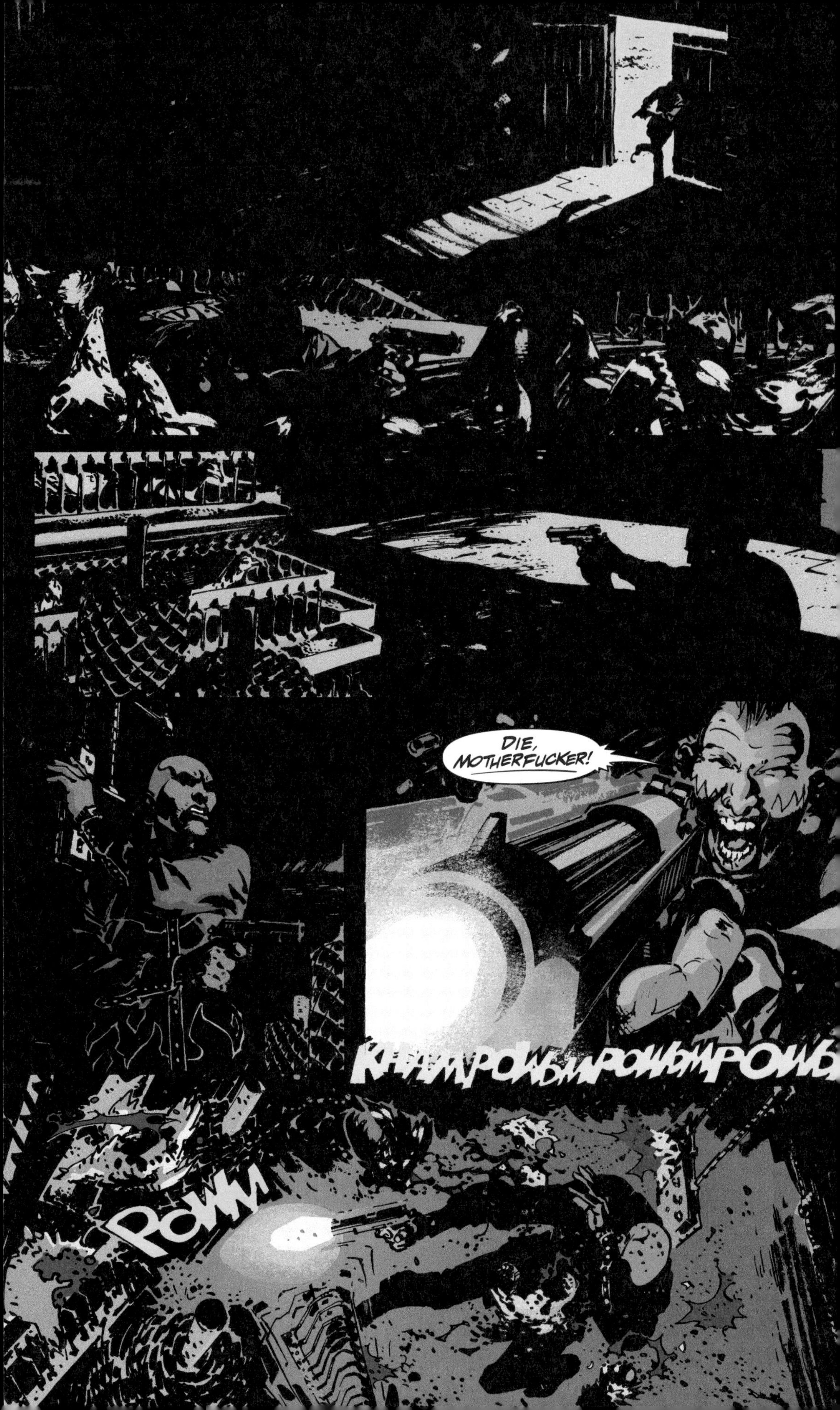
DIE, MOTHERFUCKER!
KHAMPOWDMPOWDMPOW
POW

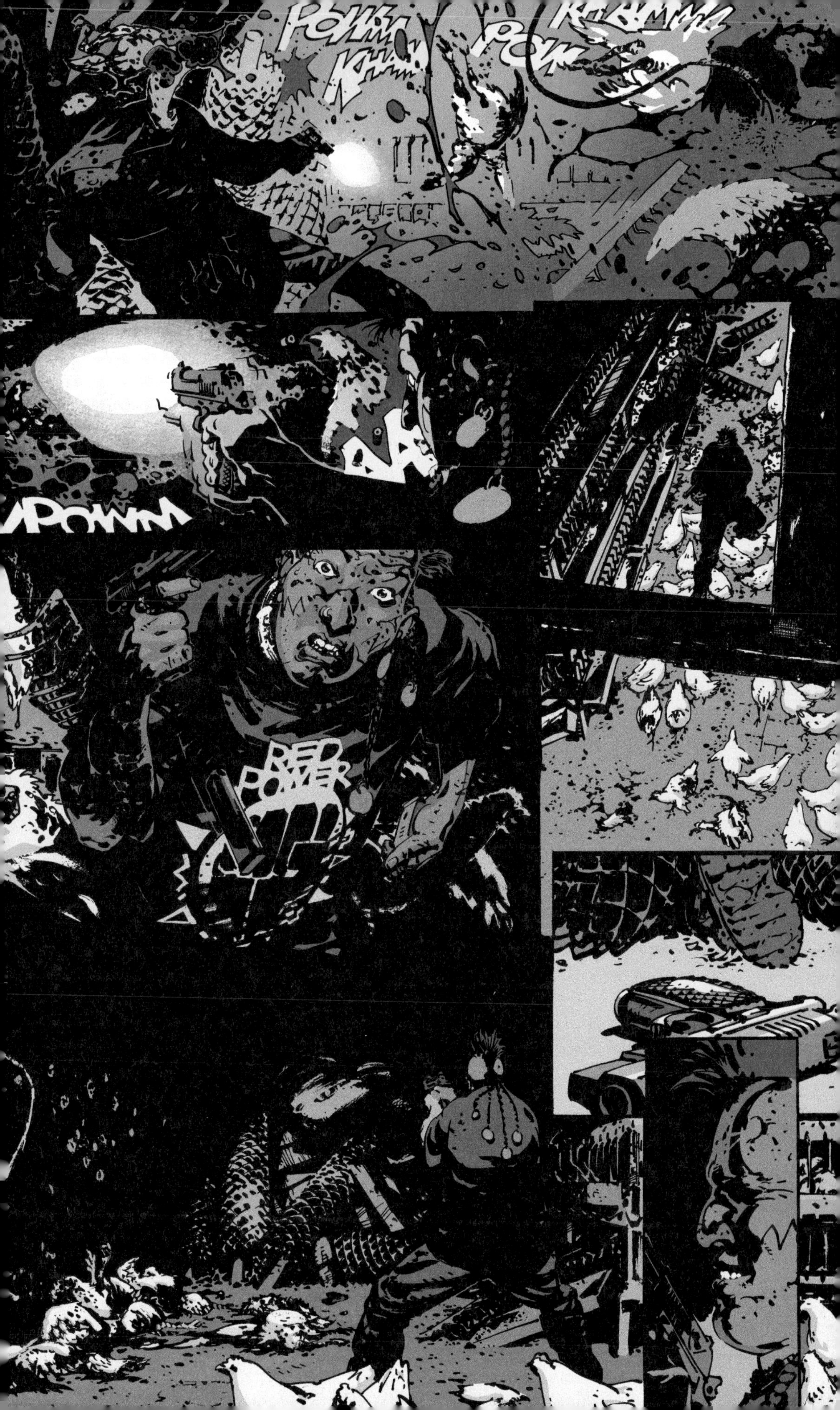
RED POWER

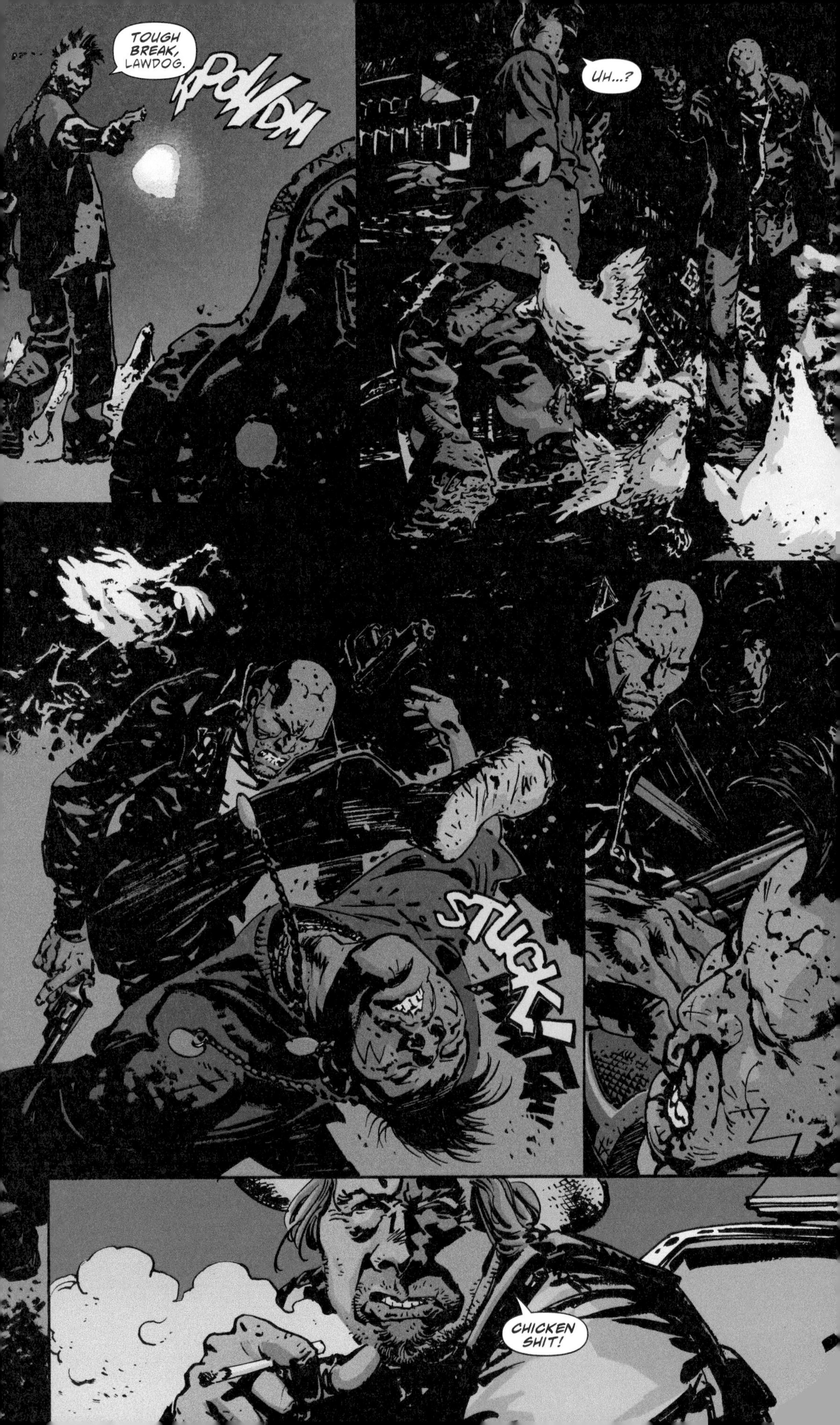
TOUGH BREAK, LAWDOG.
KPOWDH
UH...?
STUCK!
CHICKEN SHIT!

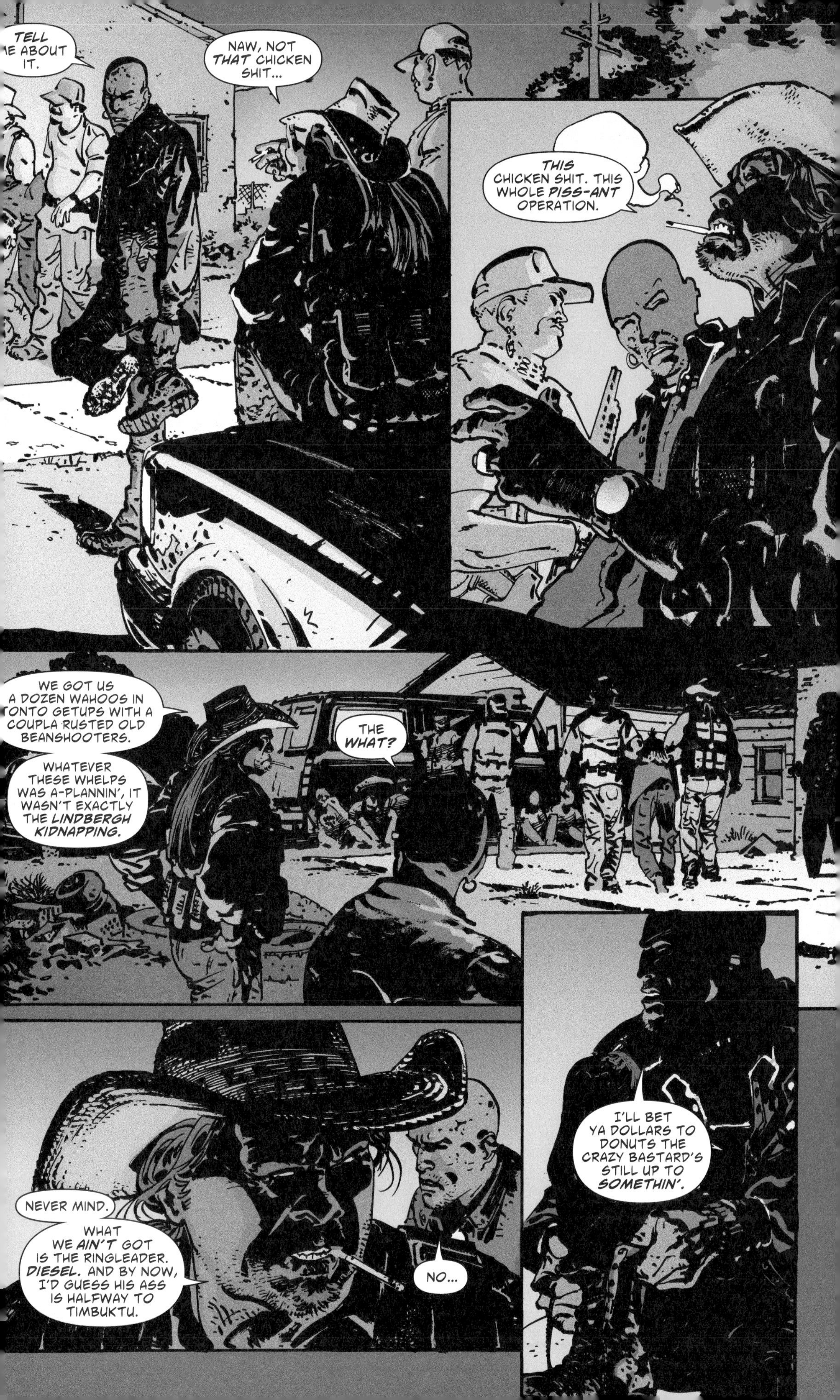

TELL ME ABOUT IT.
NAW, NOT THAT CHICKEN SHIT...
THIS CHICKEN SHIT. THIS WHOLE PISS-ANT OPERATION.
WE GOT US A DOZEN WAHOOS IN TONTO GETUPS WITH A COUPLA RUSTED OLD BEANSHOOTERS.
WHATEVER THESE WHELPS WAS A-PLANNIN', IT WASN'T EXACTLY THE LINDBERGH KIDNAPPING.
THE WHAT?
NEVER MIND.
WHAT WE AIN'T GOT IS THE RINGLEADER. DIESEL. AND BY NOW, I'D GUESS HIS ASS IS HALFWAY TO TIMBUKTU.
NO...
I'LL BET YA DOLLARS TO DONUTS THE CRAZY BASTARD'S STILL UP TO SOMETHIN'.

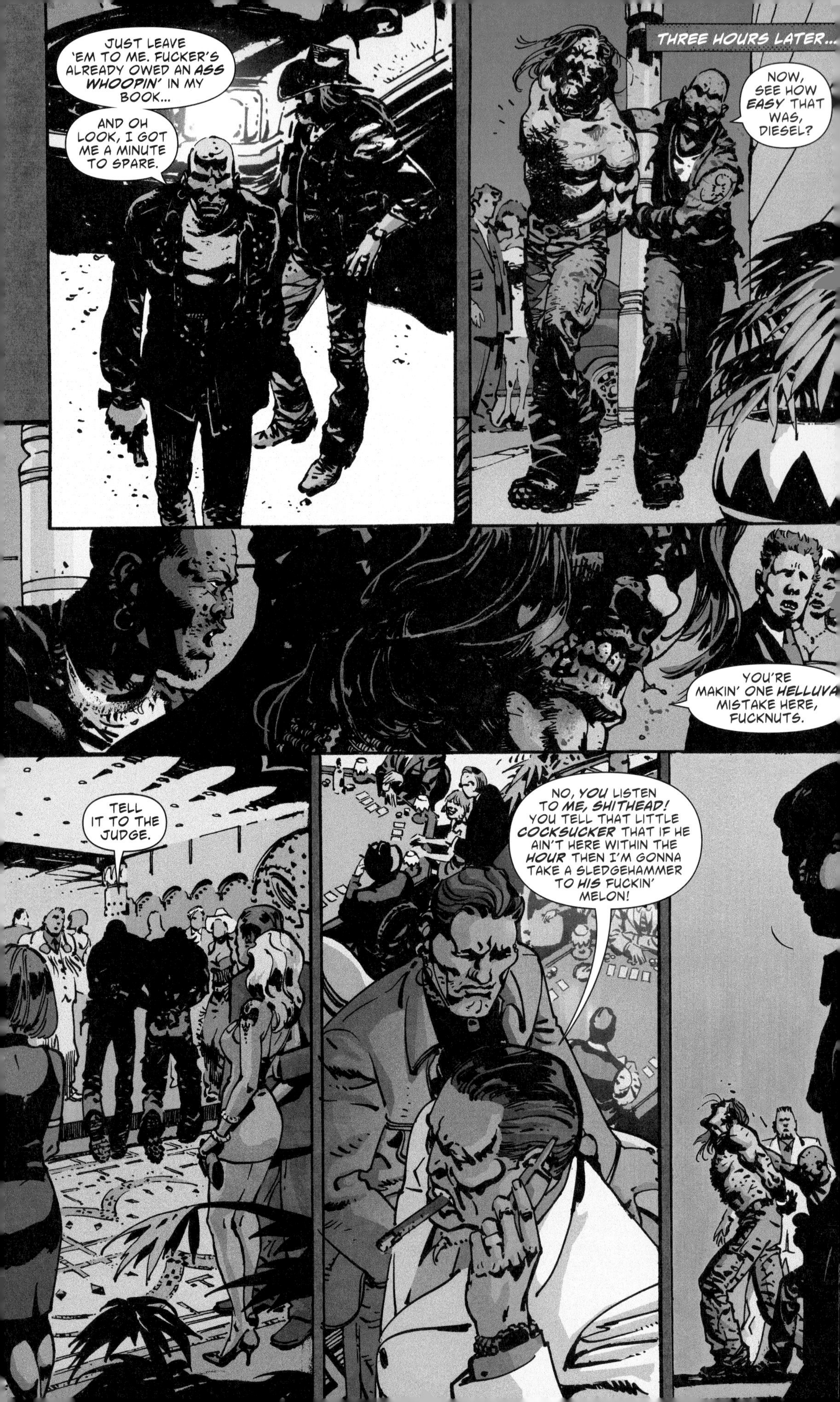
JUST LEAVE 'EM TO ME. FUCKER'S ALREADY OWED AN ASS WHOOPIN' IN MY BOOK...
AND OH LOOK, I GOT ME A MINUTE TO SPARE.
THREE HOURS LATER...
NOW, SEE HOW EASY THAT WAS, DIESEL?
YOU'RE MAKIN' ONE HELLUVA MISTAKE HERE, FUCKNUTS.
TELL IT TO THE JUDGE.
NO, YOU LISTEN TO ME, SHITHEAD! YOU TELL THAT LITTLE COCKSUCKER THAT IF HE AIN'T HERE WITHIN THE HOUR THEN I'M GONNA TAKE A SLEDGEHAMMER TO HIS FUCKIN' MELON!

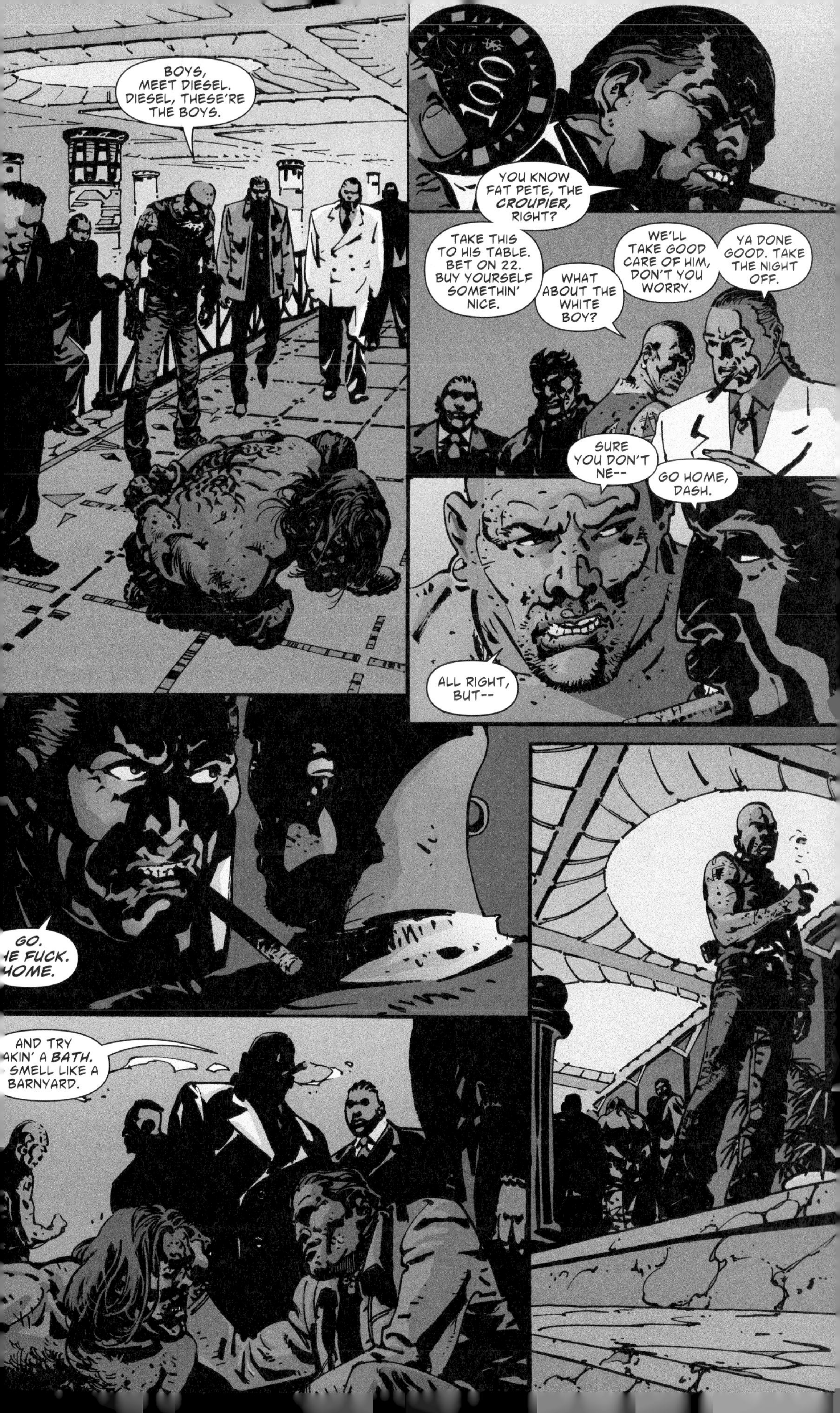
BOYS, MEET DIESEL. DIESEL, THESE'RE THE BOYS.
YOU KNOW FAT PETE, THE *CROUPIER,* RIGHT?
TAKE THIS TO HIS TABLE. BET ON 22. BUY YOURSELF SOMETHIN' NICE.
WHAT ABOUT THE WHITE BOY?
WE'LL TAKE GOOD CARE OF HIM, DON'T YOU WORRY.
YA DONE GOOD. TAKE THE NIGHT OFF.
SURE YOU DON'T NE--
GO HOME, DASH.
ALL RIGHT, BUT--
GO.
HE FUCK.
HOME.
AND TRY
AKIN' A *BATH.*
SMELL LIKE A
BARNYARD.

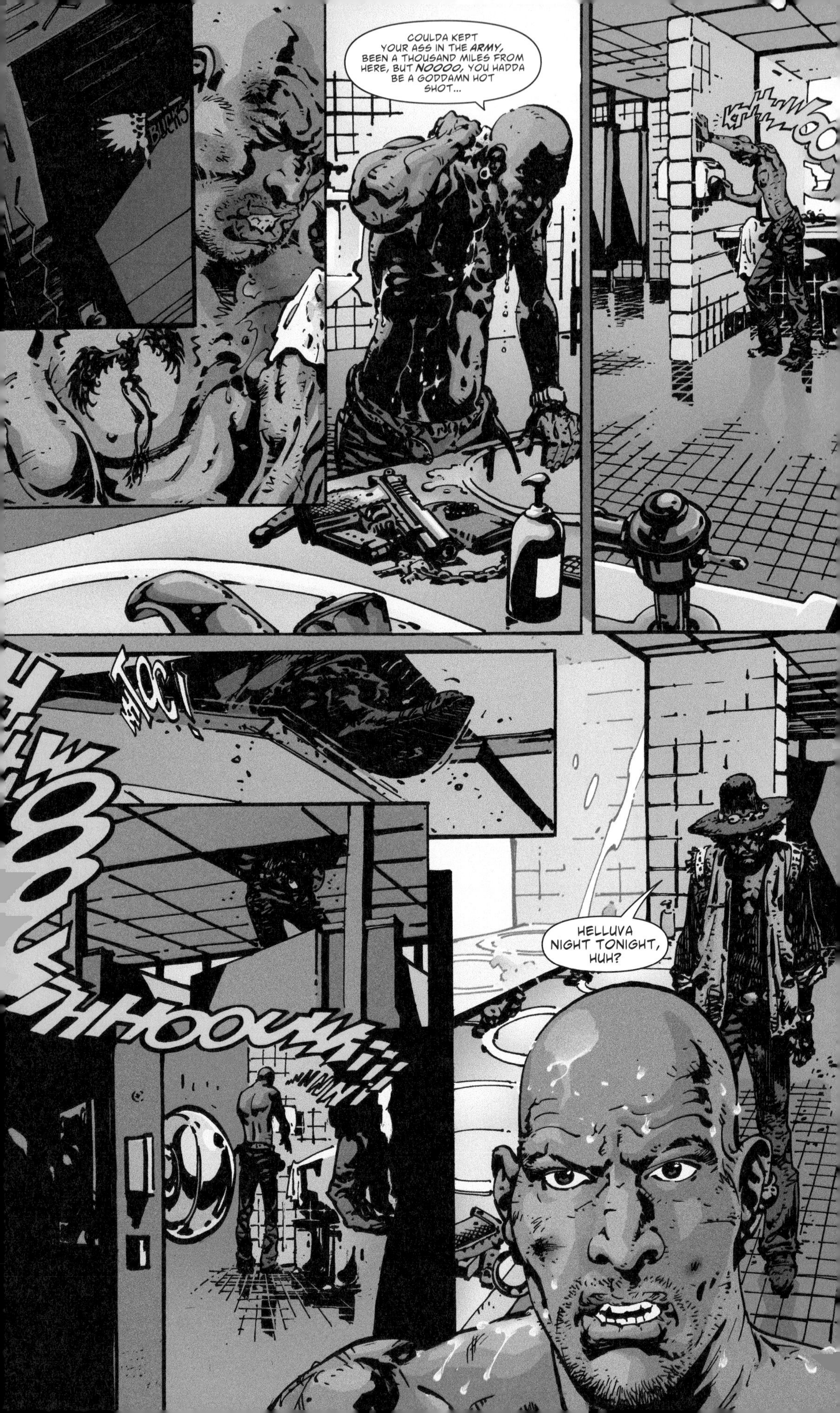
BUCKS
COULDA KEPT YOUR ASS IN THE ARMY, BEEN A THOUSAND MILES FROM HERE, BUT NOOOO, YOU HADDA BE A GODDAMN HOT SHOT...
TOCC!
HELLUVA NIGHT TONIGHT, HUH?

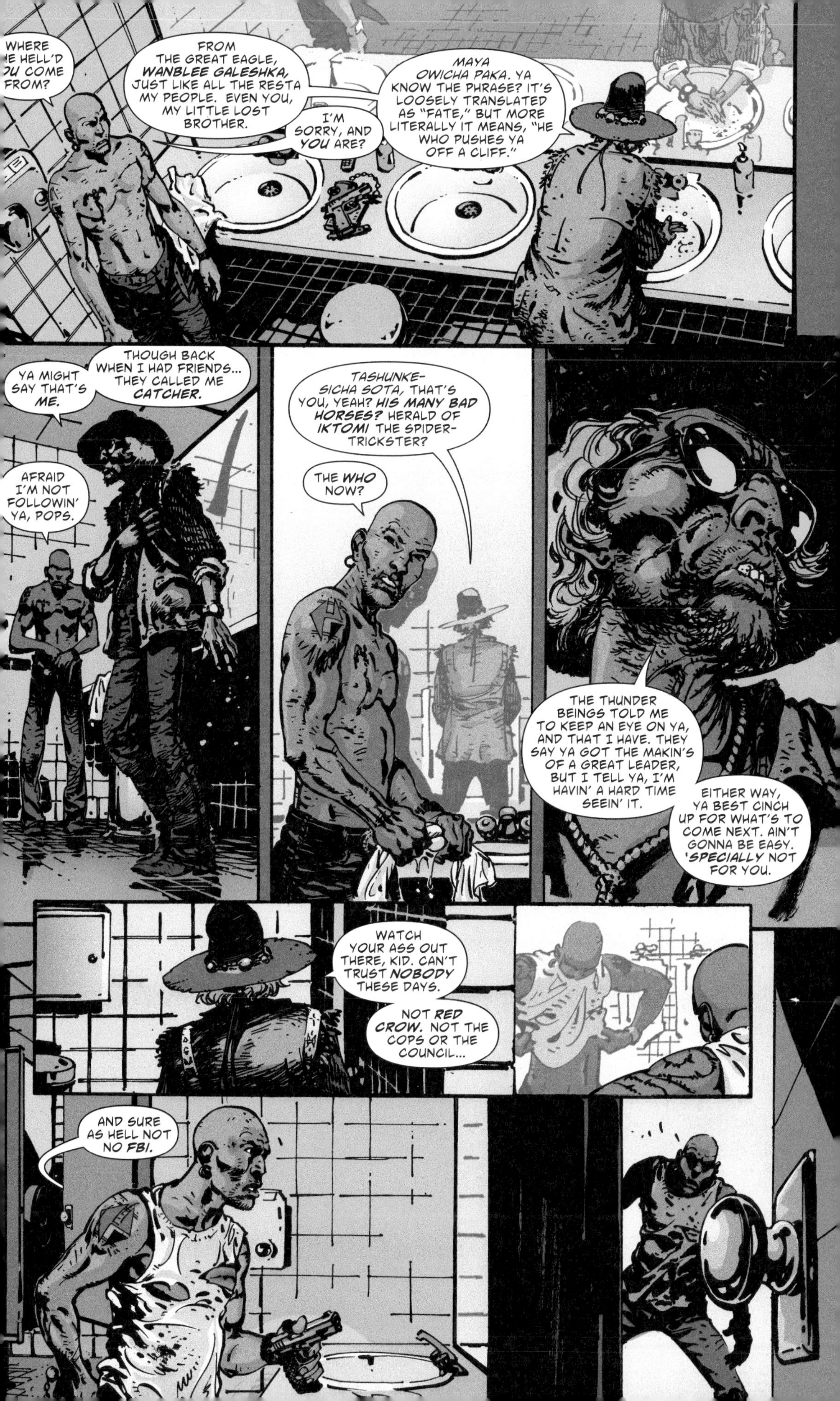

WHERE
E HELL'D
OU COME
FROM?
FROM THE GREAT EAGLE, WANBLEE GALESHKA, JUST LIKE ALL THE RESTA MY PEOPLE. EVEN YOU, MY LITTLE LOST BROTHER.
I'M SORRY, AND YOU ARE?
MAYA OWICHA PAKA. YA KNOW THE PHRASE? IT'S LOOSELY TRANSLATED AS "FATE," BUT MORE LITERALLY IT MEANS, "HE WHO PUSHES YA OFF A CLIFF."
YA MIGHT SAY THAT'S ME.
THOUGH BACK WHEN I HAD FRIENDS... THEY CALLED ME CATCHER.
AFRAID I'M NOT FOLLOWIN' YA, POPS.
TASHUNKE-SICHA SOTA, THAT'S YOU, YEAH? HIS MANY BAD HORSES? HERALD OF IKTOMI THE SPIDER-TRICKSTER?
THE WHO NOW?
THE THUNDER BEINGS TOLD ME TO KEEP AN EYE ON YA, AND THAT I HAVE. THEY SAY YA GOT THE MAKIN'S OF A GREAT LEADER, BUT I TELL YA, I'M HAVIN' A HARD TIME SEEIN' IT.
EITHER WAY, YA BEST CINCH UP FOR WHAT'S TO COME NEXT. AIN'T GONNA BE EASY. 'SPECIALLY NOT FOR YOU.
WATCH YOUR ASS OUT THERE, KID. CAN'T TRUST NOBODY THESE DAYS.
NOT RED CROW. NOT THE COPS OR THE COUNCIL...
AND SURE AS HELL NOT NO FBI.

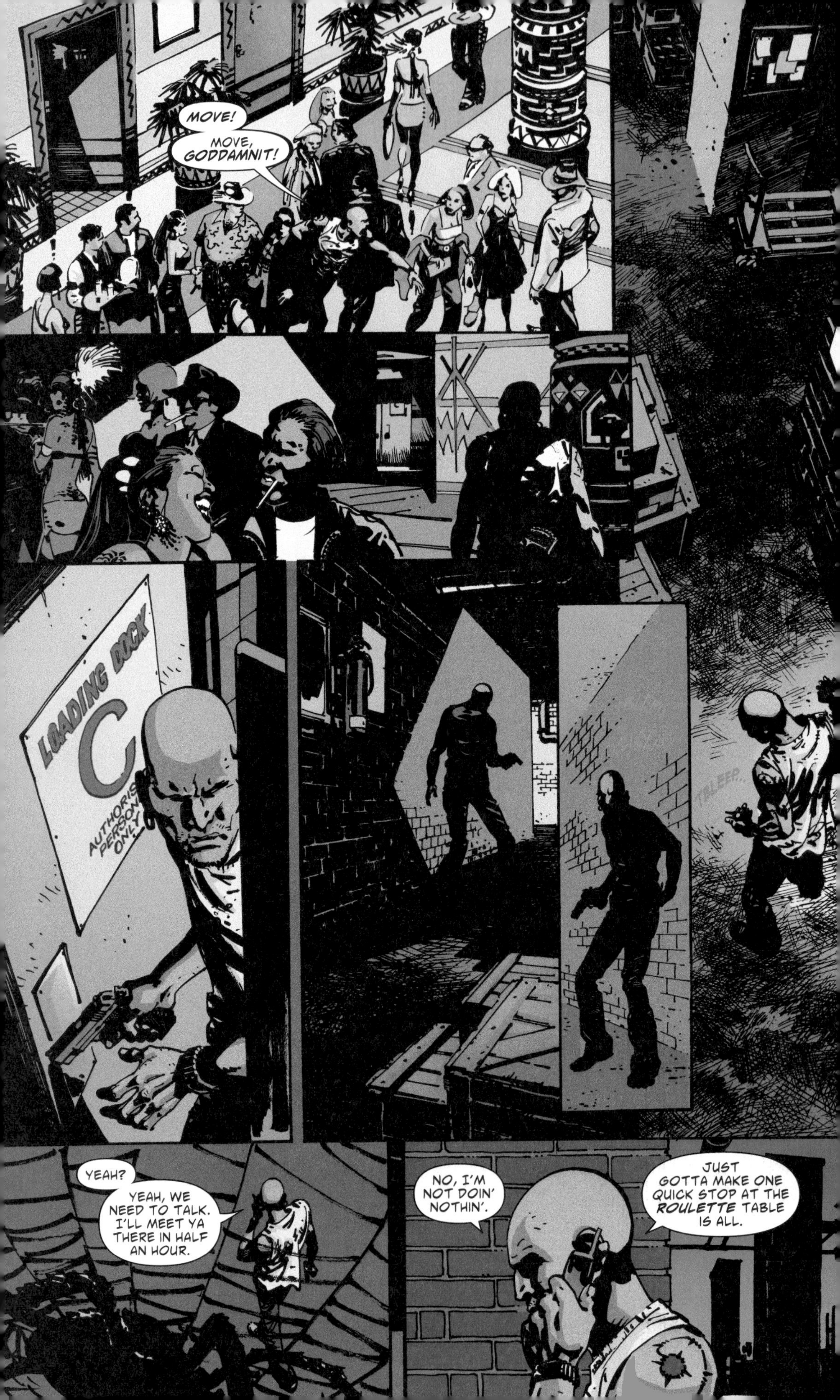
MOVE!
MOVE, GODDAMNIT!
LOADING DOCK C
AUTHORIS PERSON ONLY
TBLEEP...
YEAH?
YEAH, WE NEED TO TALK. I'LL MEET YA THERE IN HALF AN HOUR.
NO, I'M NOT DOIN' NOTHIN'.
JUST GOTTA MAKE ONE QUICK STOP AT THE *ROULETTE* TABLE IS ALL.

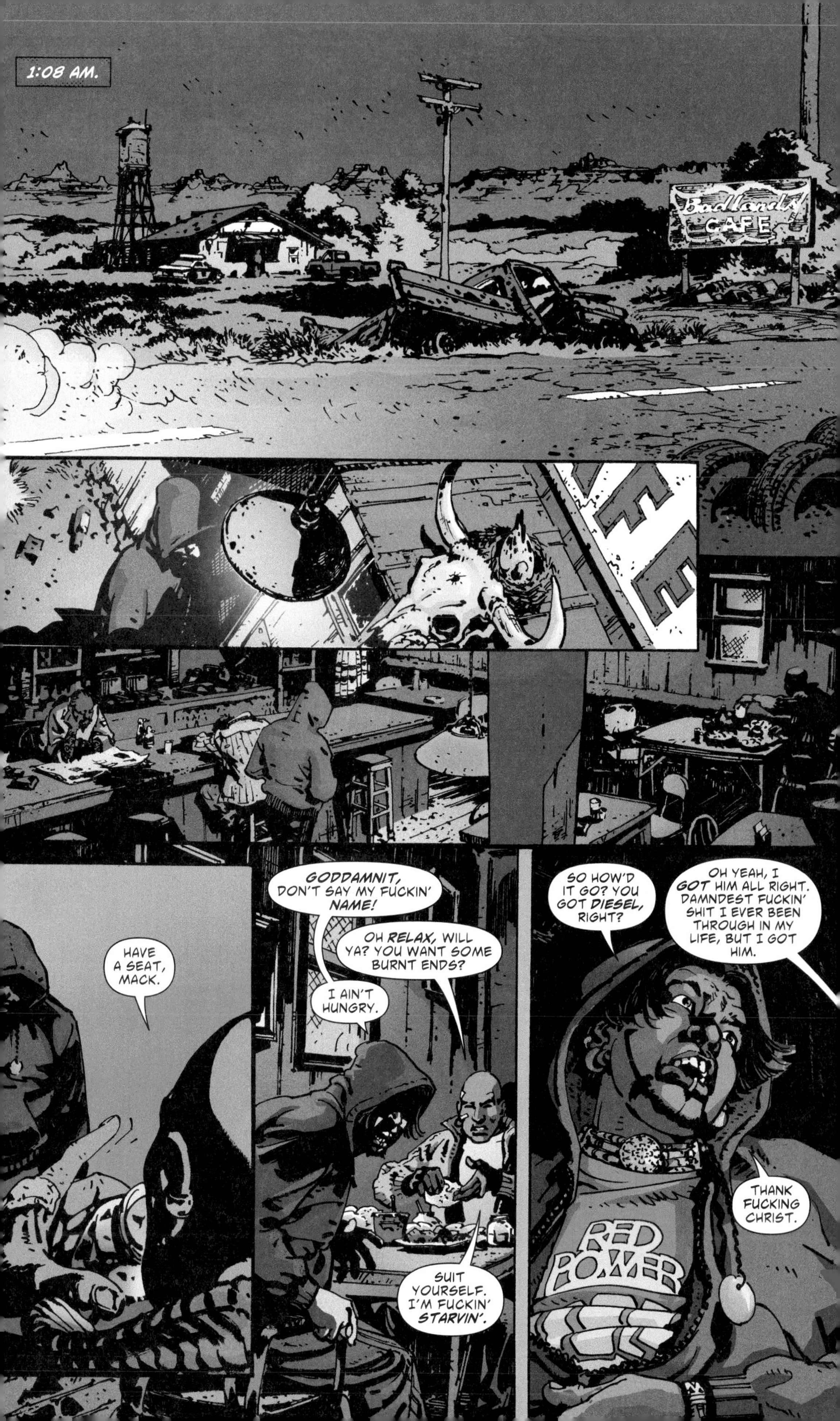

1:08 AM.
Badlands CAFE
HAVE A SEAT, MACK.
GODDAMNIT, DON'T SAY MY FUCKIN' NAME!
OH RELAX, WILL YA? YOU WANT SOME BURNT ENDS?
I AIN'T HUNGRY.
SUIT YOURSELF. I'M FUCKIN' STARVIN'.
SO HOW'D IT GO? YOU GOT DIESEL, RIGHT?
OH YEAH, I GOT HIM ALL RIGHT. DAMNDEST FUCKIN' SHIT I EVER BEEN THROUGH IN MY LIFE, BUT I GOT HIM.
THANK FUCKING CHRIST.
RED POWER

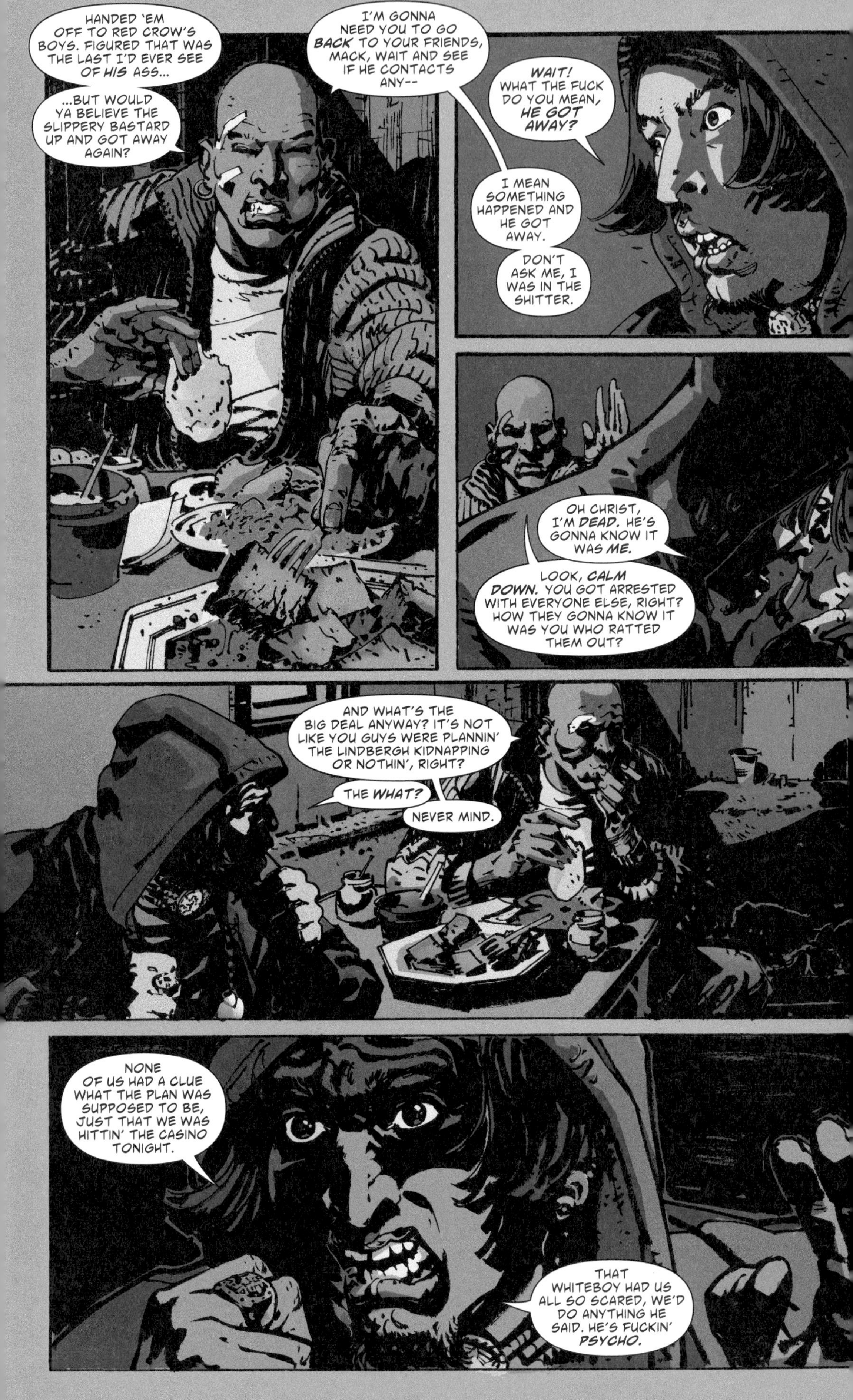
HANDED 'EM OFF TO RED CROW'S BOYS. FIGURED THAT WAS THE LAST I'D EVER SEE OF HIS ASS...
...BUT WOULD YA BELIEVE THE SLIPPERY BASTARD UP AND GOT AWAY AGAIN?
I'M GONNA NEED YOU TO GO BACK TO YOUR FRIENDS, MACK, WAIT AND SEE IF HE CONTACTS ANY--
WAIT! WHAT THE FUCK DO YOU MEAN, HE GOT AWAY?
I MEAN SOMETHING HAPPENED AND HE GOT AWAY.
DON'T ASK ME, I WAS IN THE SHITTER.
OH CHRIST, I'M DEAD. HE'S GONNA KNOW IT WAS ME.
LOOK, CALM DOWN. YOU GOT ARRESTED WITH EVERYONE ELSE, RIGHT? HOW THEY GONNA KNOW IT WAS YOU WHO RATTED THEM OUT?
AND WHAT'S THE BIG DEAL ANYWAY? IT'S NOT LIKE YOU GUYS WERE PLANNIN' THE LINDBERGH KIDNAPPING OR NOTHIN', RIGHT?
THE WHAT?
NEVER MIND.
NONE OF US HAD A CLUE WHAT THE PLAN WAS SUPPOSED TO BE, JUST THAT WE WAS HITTIN' THE CASINO TONIGHT.
THAT WHITEBOY HAD US ALL SO SCARED, WE'D DO ANYTHING HE SAID. HE'S FUCKIN' PSYCHO.

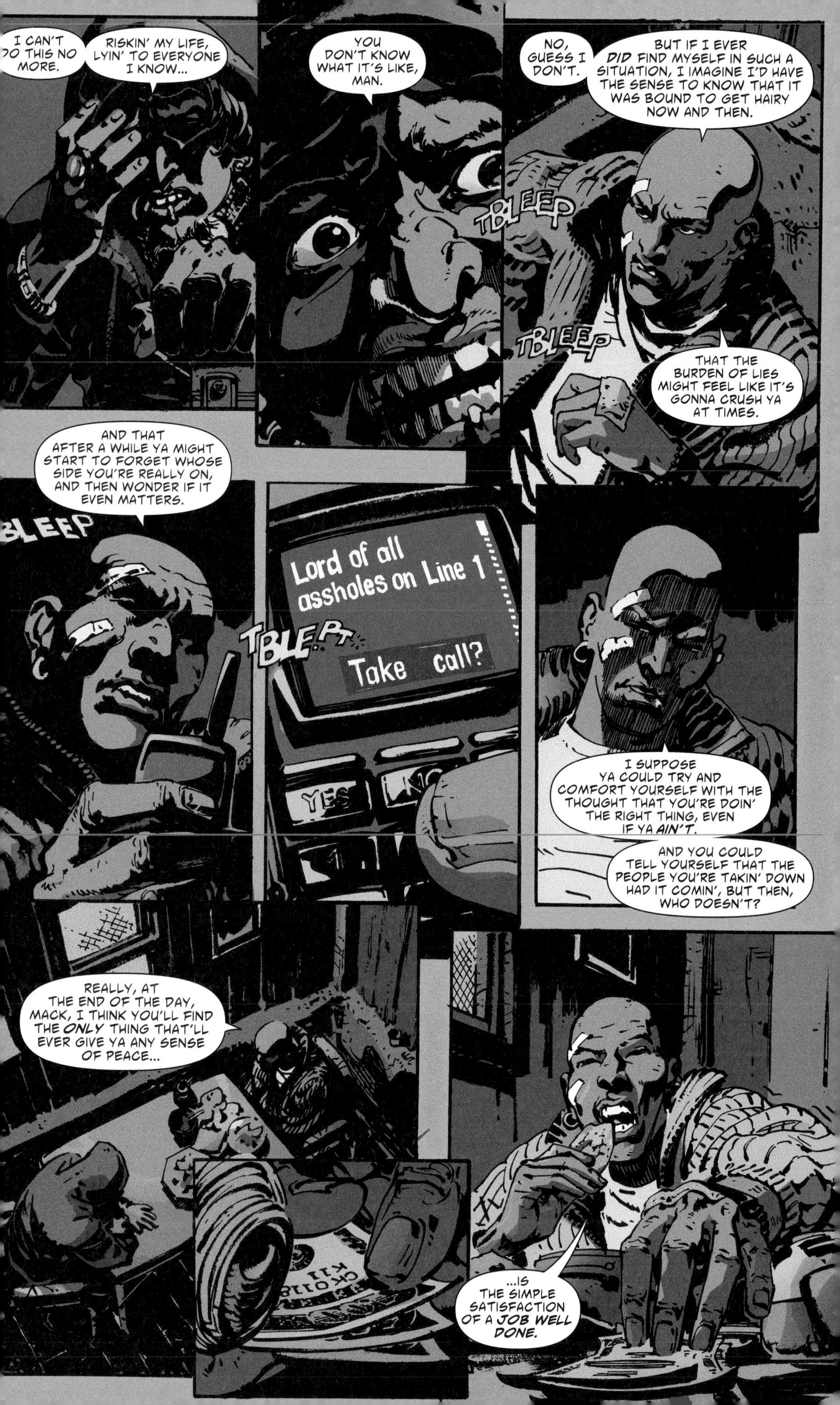

I CAN'T DO THIS NO MORE.
RISKIN' MY LIFE, LYIN' TO EVERYONE I KNOW...
YOU DON'T KNOW WHAT IT'S LIKE, MAN.
NO, GUESS I DON'T.
BUT IF I EVER DID FIND MYSELF IN SUCH A SITUATION, I IMAGINE I'D HAVE THE SENSE TO KNOW THAT IT WAS BOUND TO GET HAIRY NOW AND THEN.
TBLEEP
TBLEEP
THAT THE BURDEN OF LIES MIGHT FEEL LIKE IT'S GONNA CRUSH YA AT TIMES.
AND THAT AFTER A WHILE YA MIGHT START TO FORGET WHOSE SIDE YOU'RE REALLY ON, AND THEN WONDER IF IT EVEN MATTERS.
BLEEP
Lord of all assholes on Line 1
TBLEEPT
Take call?
YES
I SUPPOSE YA COULD TRY AND COMFORT YOURSELF WITH THE THOUGHT THAT YOU'RE DOIN' THE RIGHT THING, EVEN IF YA AIN'T.
AND YOU COULD TELL YOURSELF THAT THE PEOPLE YOU'RE TAKIN' DOWN HAD IT COMIN', BUT THEN, WHO DOESN'T?
REALLY, AT THE END OF THE DAY, MACK, I THINK YOU'LL FIND THE ONLY THING THAT'LL EVER GIVE YA ANY SENSE OF PEACE...
...IS THE SIMPLE SATISFACTION OF A JOB WELL DONE.

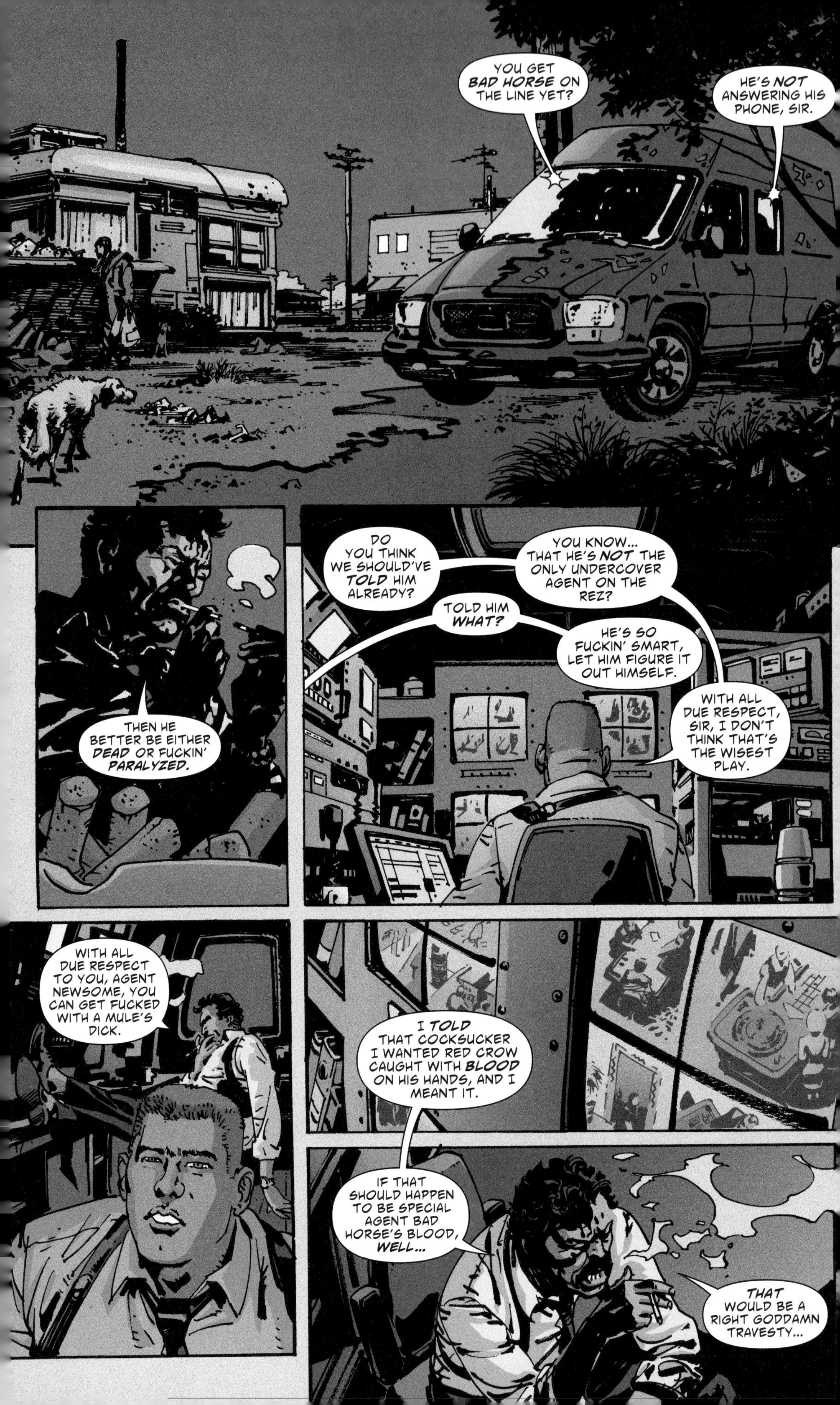
YOU GET BAD HORSE ON THE LINE YET?
HE'S NOT ANSWERING HIS PHONE, SIR.
THEN HE BETTER BE EITHER DEAD OR FUCKIN' PARALYZED.
DO YOU THINK WE SHOULD'VE TOLD HIM ALREADY?
YOU KNOW... THAT HE'S NOT THE ONLY UNDERCOVER AGENT ON THE REZ?
TOLD HIM WHAT?
HE'S SO FUCKIN' SMART, LET HIM FIGURE IT OUT HIMSELF.
WITH ALL DUE RESPECT, SIR, I DON'T THINK THAT'S THE WISEST PLAY.
WITH ALL DUE RESPECT TO YOU, AGENT NEWSOME, YOU CAN GET FUCKED WITH A MULE'S DICK.
I TOLD THAT COCKSUCKER I WANTED RED CROW CAUGHT WITH BLOOD ON HIS HANDS, AND I MEANT IT.
IF THAT SHOULD HAPPEN TO BE SPECIAL AGENT BAD HORSE'S BLOOD, WELL...
THAT WOULD BE A RIGHT GODDAMN TRAVESTY...

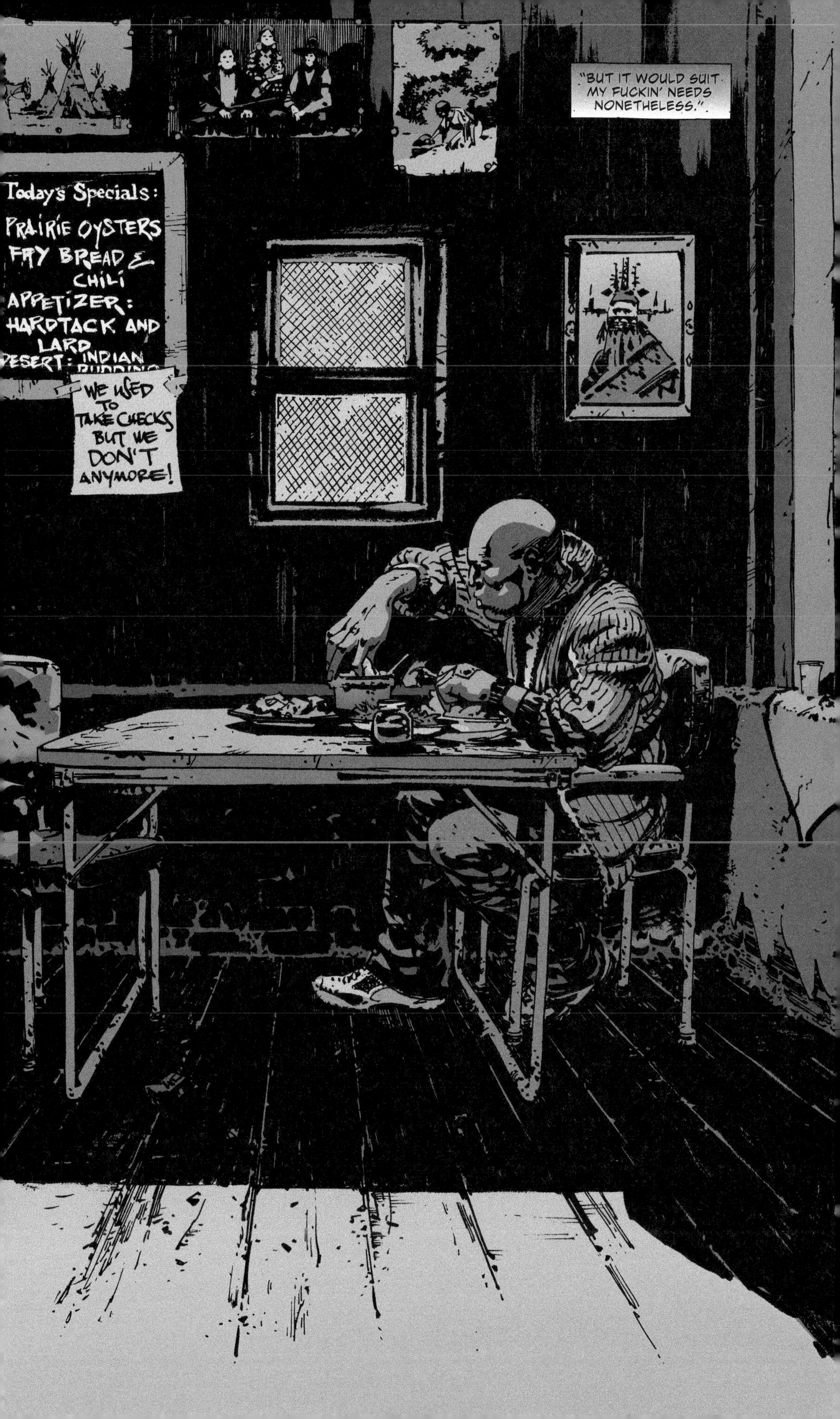
"BUT IT WOULD SUIT MY FUCKIN' NEEDS NONETHELESS."
Today's Specials:
PRAIRIE OYSTERS
FRY BREAD & CHILI
APPETIZER:
HARDTACK AND LARD
DESERT: INDIAN
WE USED TO TAKE CHECKS BUT WE DON'T ANYMORE!

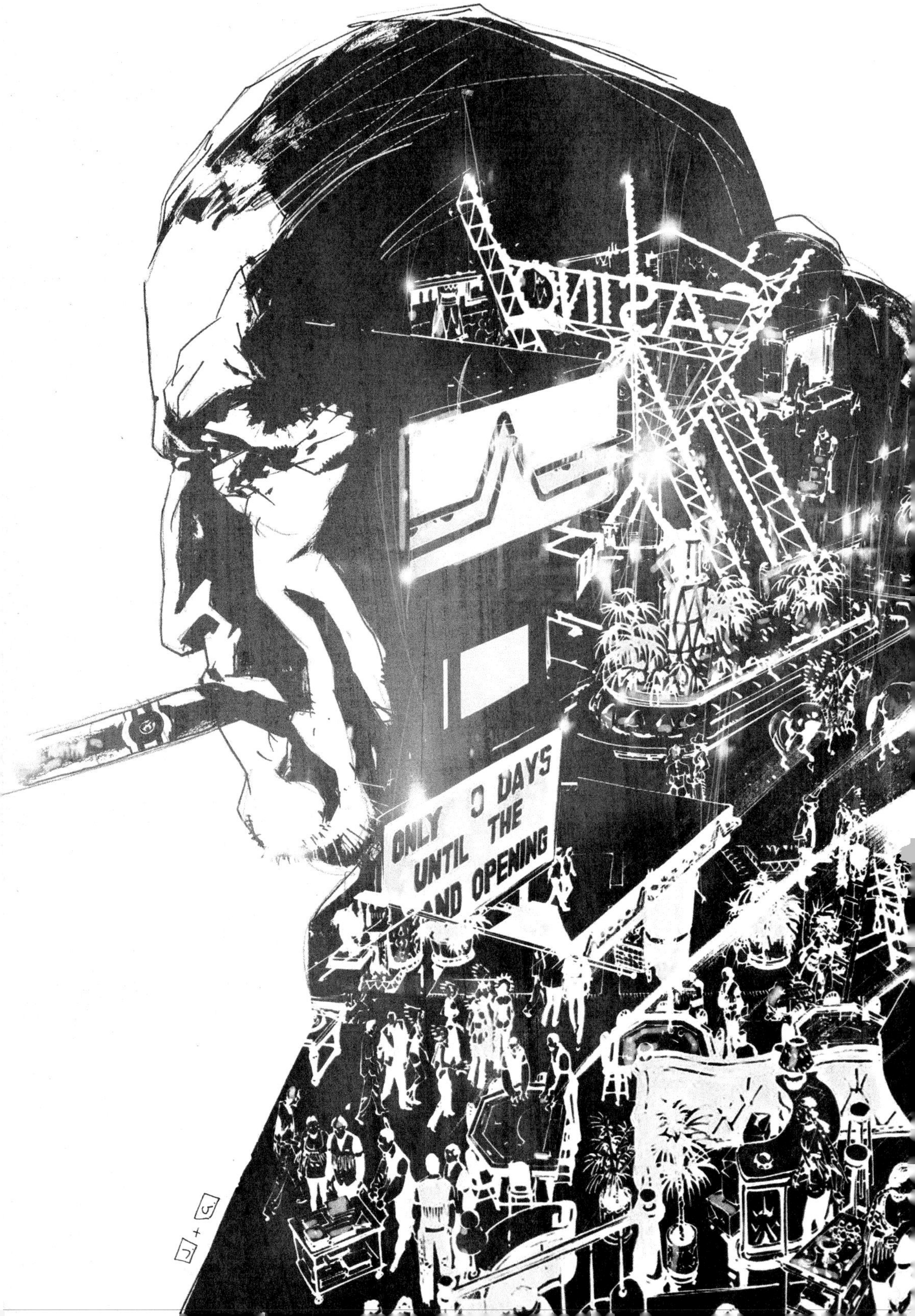
ONLY 0 DAYS
UNTIL THE
AND OPENING

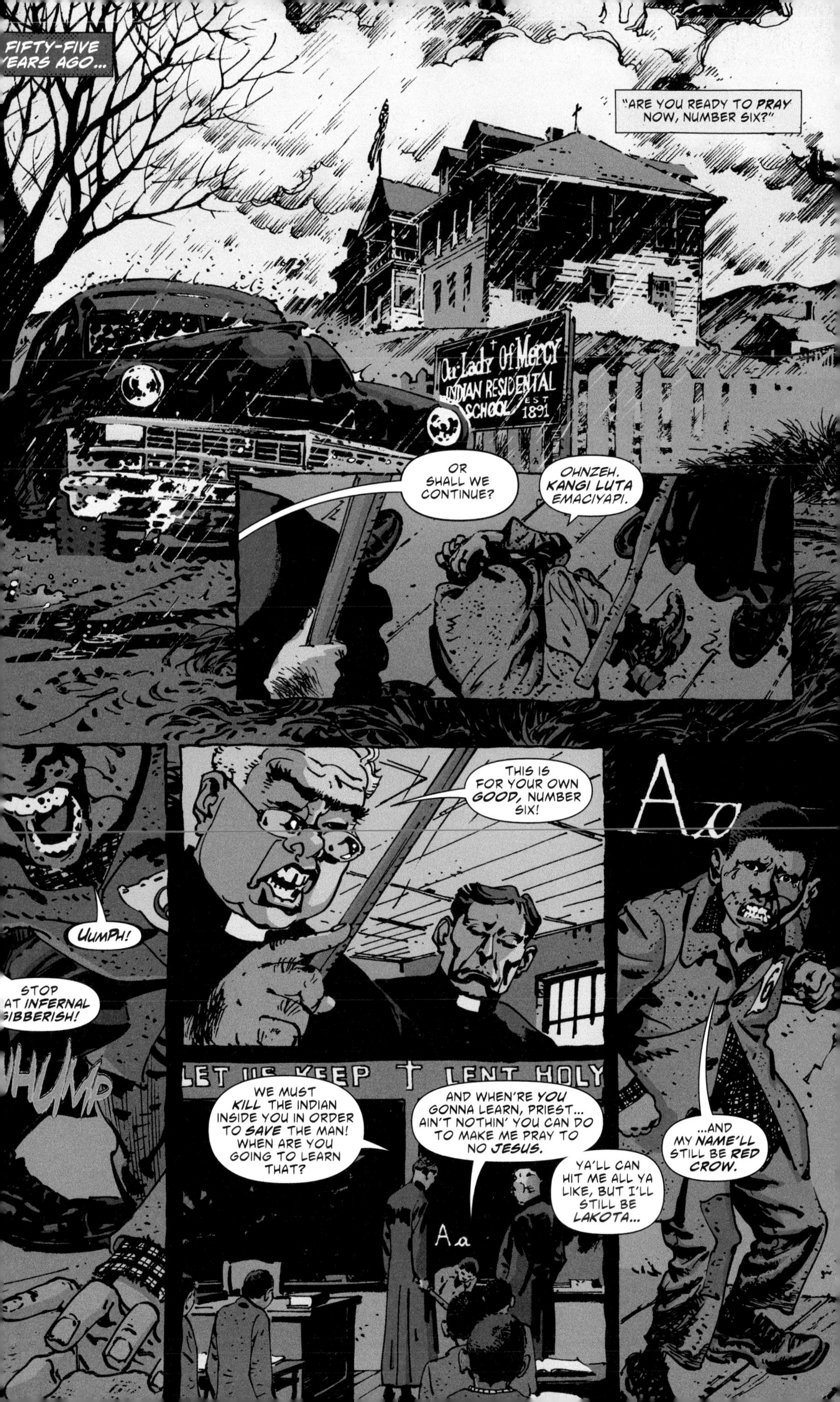
FIFTY-FIVE YEARS AGO...
"ARE YOU READY TO PRAY NOW, NUMBER SIX?"
Our Lady Of Mercy INDIAN RESIDENTIAL SCHOOL EST 1891
OR SHALL WE CONTINUE?
OHNZEH. KANGI LUTA EMACIYAPI.
THIS IS FOR YOUR OWN GOOD, NUMBER SIX!
UUMPH!
STOP AT INFERNAL GIBBERISH!
THUMP
LET US KEEP LENT HOLY
WE MUST KILL THE INDIAN INSIDE YOU IN ORDER TO SAVE THE MAN! WHEN ARE YOU GOING TO LEARN THAT?
AND WHEN'RE YOU GONNA LEARN, PRIEST... AIN'T NOTHIN' YOU CAN DO TO MAKE ME PRAY TO NO JESUS.
YA'LL CAN HIT ME ALL YA LIKE, BUT I'LL STILL BE LAKOTA...
...AND MY NAME'LL STILL BE RED CROW.

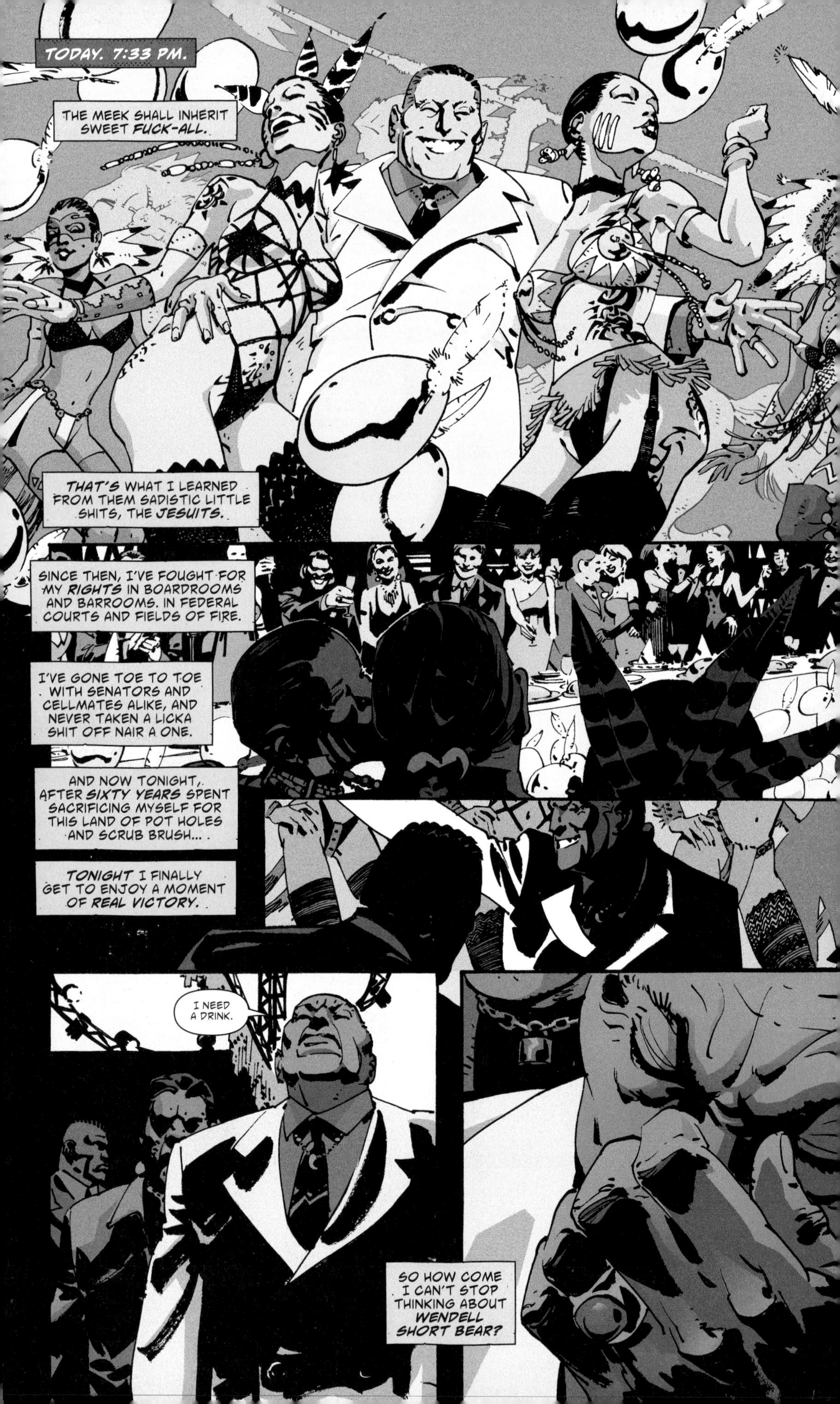
TODAY. 7:33 PM.
THE MEEK SHALL INHERIT SWEET FUCK-ALL.
THAT'S WHAT I LEARNED FROM THEM SADISTIC LITTLE SHITS, THE JESUITS.
SINCE THEN, I'VE FOUGHT FOR MY RIGHTS IN BOARDROOMS AND BARROOMS. IN FEDERAL COURTS AND FIELDS OF FIRE.
I'VE GONE TOE TO TOE WITH SENATORS AND CELLMATES ALIKE, AND NEVER TAKEN A LICKA SHIT OFF NAIR A ONE.
AND NOW TONIGHT, AFTER SIXTY YEARS SPENT SACRIFICING MYSELF FOR THIS LAND OF POT HOLES AND SCRUB BRUSH...
TONIGHT I FINALLY GET TO ENJOY A MOMENT OF REAL VICTORY.
I NEED A DRINK.
SO HOW COME I CAN'T STOP THINKING ABOUT WENDELL SHORT BEAR?

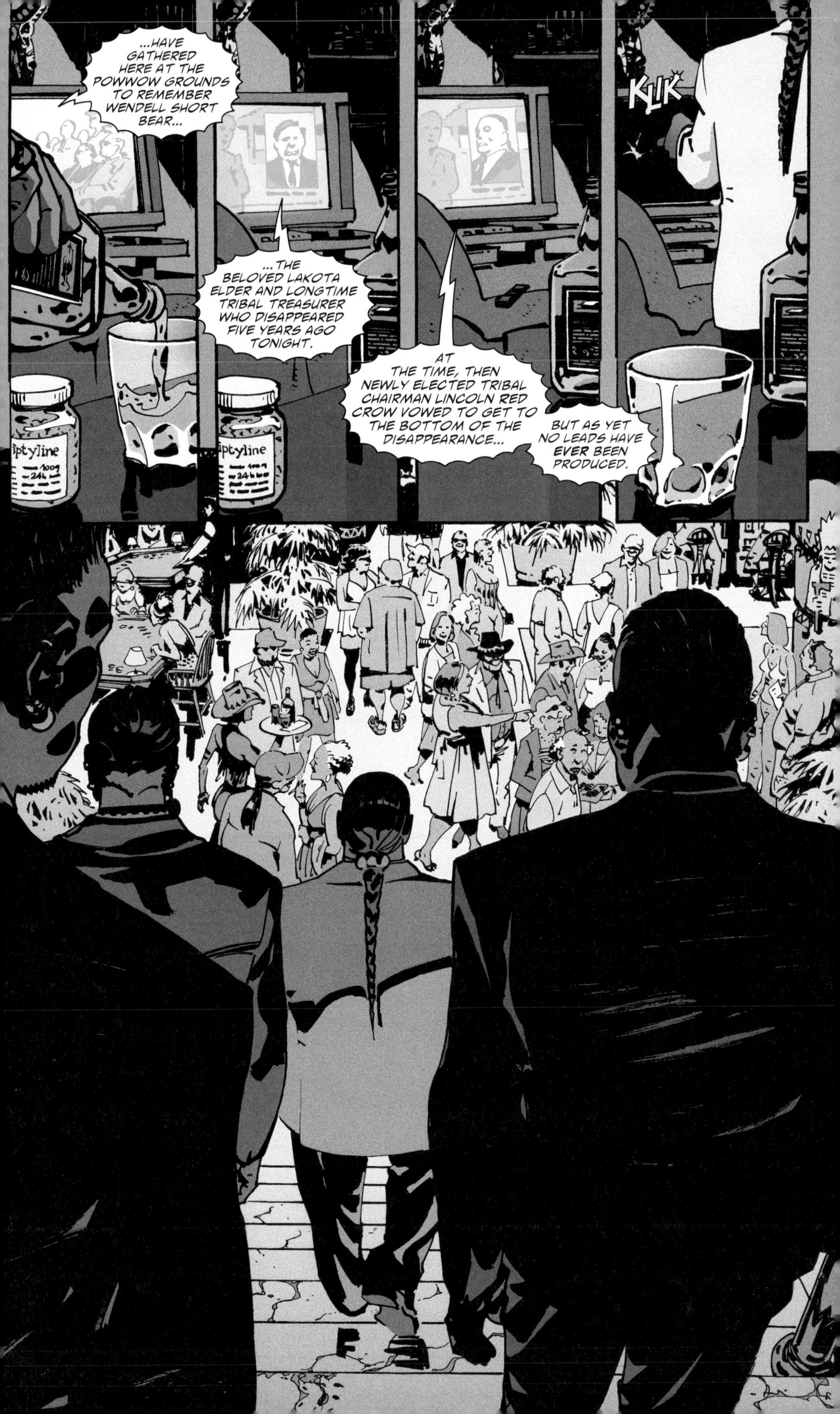
...HAVE GATHERED HERE AT THE POWWOW GROUNDS TO REMEMBER WENDELL SHORT BEAR...
...THE BELOVED LAKOTA ELDER AND LONGTIME TRIBAL TREASURER WHO DISAPPEARED FIVE YEARS AGO TONIGHT.
AT THE TIME, THEN NEWLY ELECTED TRIBAL CHAIRMAN LINCOLN RED CROW VOWED TO GET TO THE BOTTOM OF THE DISAPPEARANCE...
BUT AS YET NO LEADS HAVE EVER BEEN PRODUCED.
KLIK
iptyline

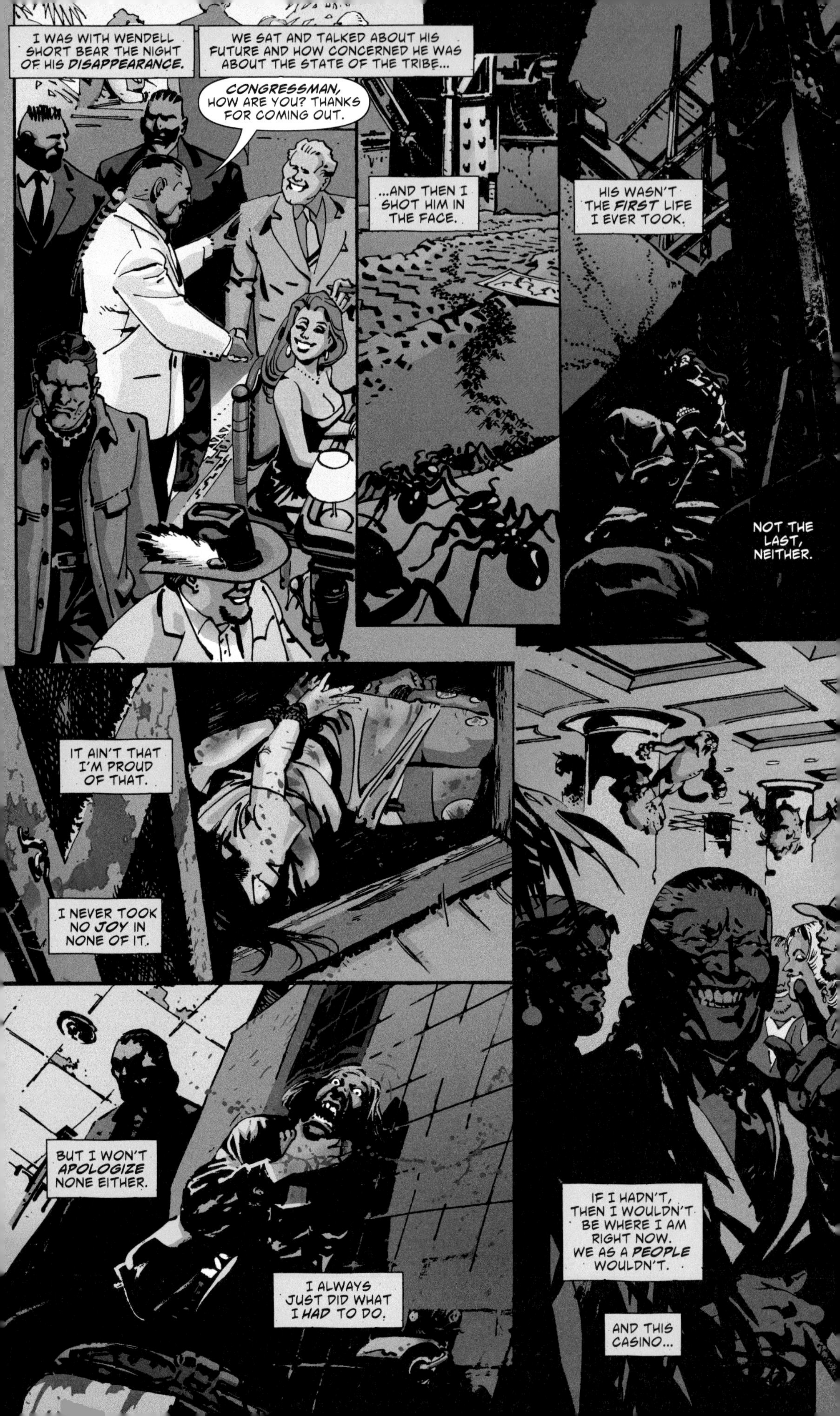
I WAS WITH WENDELL SHORT BEAR THE NIGHT OF HIS *DISAPPEARANCE.*
WE SAT AND TALKED ABOUT HIS FUTURE AND HOW CONCERNED HE WAS ABOUT THE STATE OF THE TRIBE...
CONGRESSMAN, HOW ARE YOU? THANKS FOR COMING OUT.
...AND THEN I SHOT HIM IN THE FACE.
HIS WASN'T THE *FIRST* LIFE I EVER TOOK.
NOT THE LAST, NEITHER.
IT AIN'T THAT I'M PROUD OF THAT.
I NEVER TOOK NO *JOY* IN NONE OF IT.
BUT I WON'T *APOLOGIZE* NONE EITHER.
I ALWAYS JUST DID WHAT I *HAD* TO DO.
IF I HADN'T, THEN I WOULDN'T BE WHERE I AM RIGHT NOW. WE AS A *PEOPLE* WOULDN'T.
AND THIS CASINO...

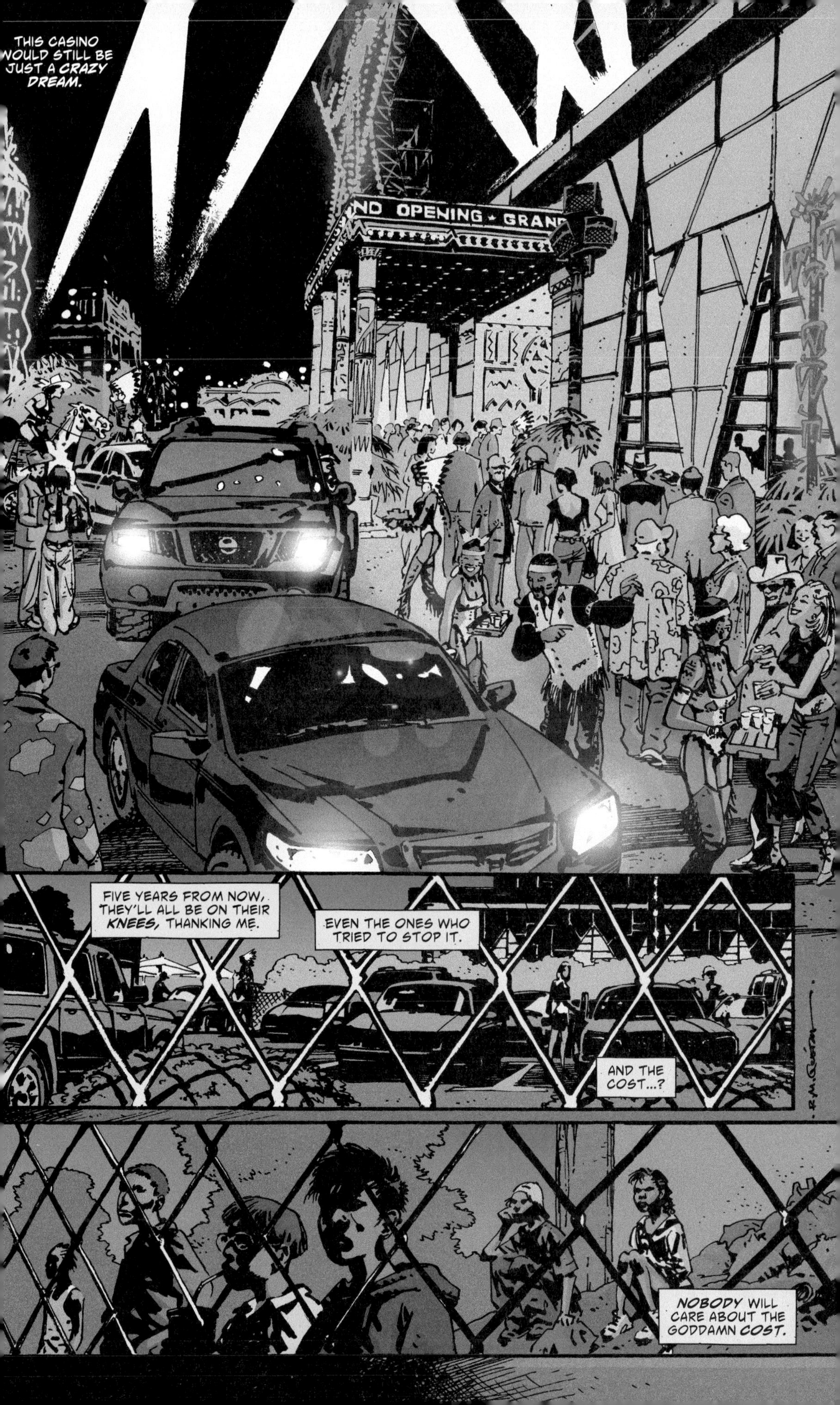
THIS CASINO WOULD STILL BE JUST A CRAZY DREAM.
ND OPENING • GRAND
FIVE YEARS FROM NOW, THEY'LL ALL BE ON THEIR KNEES, THANKING ME.
EVEN THE ONES WHO TRIED TO STOP IT.
AND THE COST...?
NOBODY WILL CARE ABOUT THE GODDAMN COST.

8:27 P.M.

197... 198...

199... 200.

FIFTEEN YEARS AFTER HE SURVIVED THE MASSACRE AT *WOUNDED KNEE*, MY GREAT GRANDFATHER WAS *SHOT DEAD* BY HIS BEST FRIEND, DURING AN ARGUMENT OVER SOME COWBOY BOOTS.

NEEDLESS TO SAY, THERE WAS *WHISKEY* INVOLVED.

MY GRANDFATHER SURVIVED THE TRENCHES O THE WESTERN FRONT ONLY TO DIE IN A *DITCH* IN LOOM NEBRASKA, SO SHIT-FACED DRUNK HE *DROWNED* IN THR INCHES OF MUDDY WATER.

MY DADDY DRANK THUNDERBIRD *EVER DAY* I EVER KNEW H INCLUDING THE *LAS*

ALL THAT, EVEN THOUGH ALCOHOL SALES HAVE BEEN *ILLEGAL* ON THIS REZ FOR 115 YEARS.

THEY'RE ALL THERE, SIR. JUST SIGN RIGHT HERE.

I WONDE WHAT THO ANCESTO OF MINE WOULD SA

...IF THEY WERE ALL HERE RIGHT NOW.

PREMIUM Lager

CLASSIC BITTER

SOUR MASH WHISKEY

ALE

Wheat Bear

Natural Draft

BARLEY WINE

London Dry Gin

Picka Bouka

Tennessee Whiskey

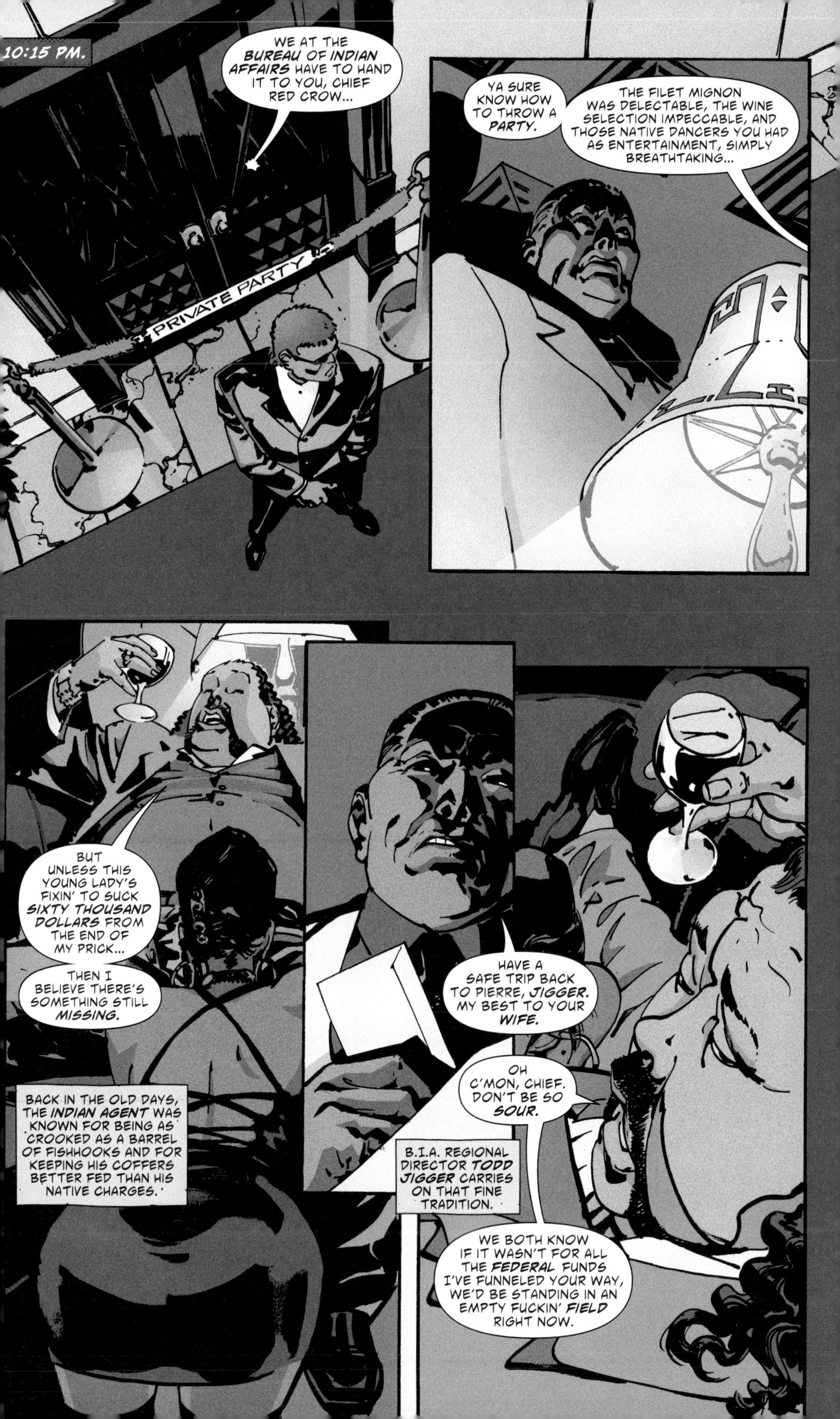
10:15 PM.
WE AT THE BUREAU OF INDIAN AFFAIRS HAVE TO HAND IT TO YOU, CHIEF RED CROW...
PRIVATE PARTY
YA SURE KNOW HOW TO THROW A PARTY.
THE FILET MIGNON WAS DELECTABLE, THE WINE SELECTION IMPECCABLE, AND THOSE NATIVE DANCERS YOU HAD AS ENTERTAINMENT, SIMPLY BREATHTAKING...
BUT UNLESS THIS YOUNG LADY'S FIXIN' TO SUCK SIXTY THOUSAND DOLLARS FROM THE END OF MY PRICK...
THEN I BELIEVE THERE'S SOMETHING STILL MISSING.
BACK IN THE OLD DAYS, THE INDIAN AGENT WAS KNOWN FOR BEING AS CROOKED AS A BARREL OF FISHHOOKS AND FOR KEEPING HIS COFFERS BETTER FED THAN HIS NATIVE CHARGES.
HAVE A SAFE TRIP BACK TO PIERRE, JIGGER. MY BEST TO YOUR WIFE.
B.I.A. REGIONAL DIRECTOR TODD JIGGER CARRIES ON THAT FINE TRADITION.
OH C'MON, CHIEF. DON'T BE SO SOUR.
WE BOTH KNOW IF IT WASN'T FOR ALL THE FEDERAL FUNDS I'VE FUNNELED YOUR WAY, WE'D BE STANDING IN AN EMPTY FUCKIN' FIELD RIGHT NOW.

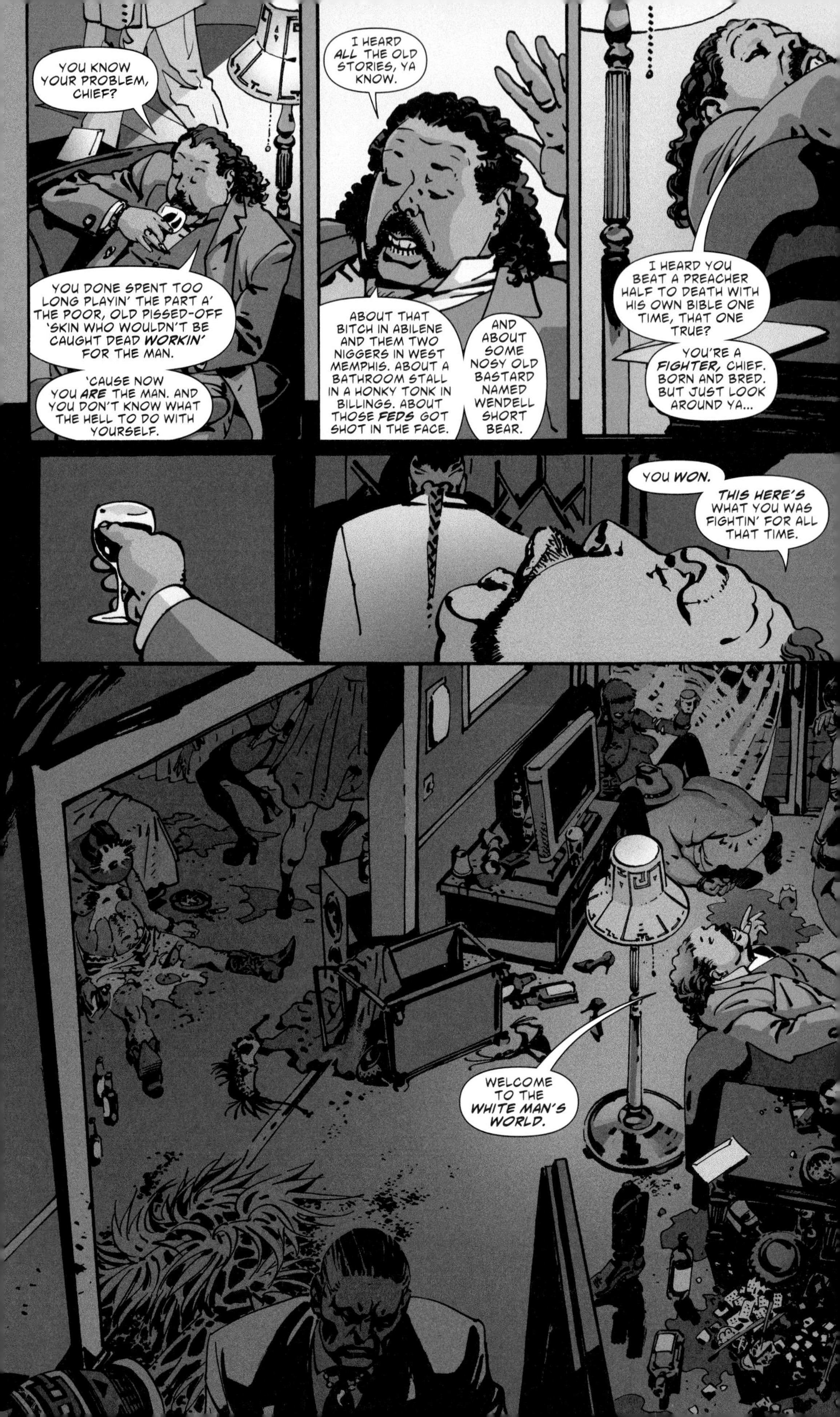

YOU KNOW YOUR PROBLEM, CHIEF?
YOU DONE SPENT TOO LONG PLAYIN' THE PART A' THE POOR, OLD PISSED-OFF 'SKIN WHO WOULDN'T BE CAUGHT DEAD WORKIN' FOR THE MAN.
'CAUSE NOW YOU ARE THE MAN. AND YOU DON'T KNOW WHAT THE HELL TO DO WITH YOURSELF.
I HEARD ALL THE OLD STORIES, YA KNOW.
ABOUT THAT BITCH IN ABILENE AND THEM TWO NIGGERS IN WEST MEMPHIS. ABOUT A BATHROOM STALL IN A HONKY TONK IN BILLINGS. ABOUT THOSE FEDS GOT SHOT IN THE FACE.
AND ABOUT SOME NOSY OLD BASTARD NAMED WENDELL SHORT BEAR.
I HEARD YOU BEAT A PREACHER HALF TO DEATH WITH HIS OWN BIBLE ONE TIME, THAT ONE TRUE?
YOU'RE A FIGHTER, CHIEF. BORN AND BRED. BUT JUST LOOK AROUND YA...
YOU WON.
THIS HERE'S WHAT YOU WAS FIGHTIN' FOR ALL THAT TIME.
WELCOME TO THE WHITE MAN'S WORLD.

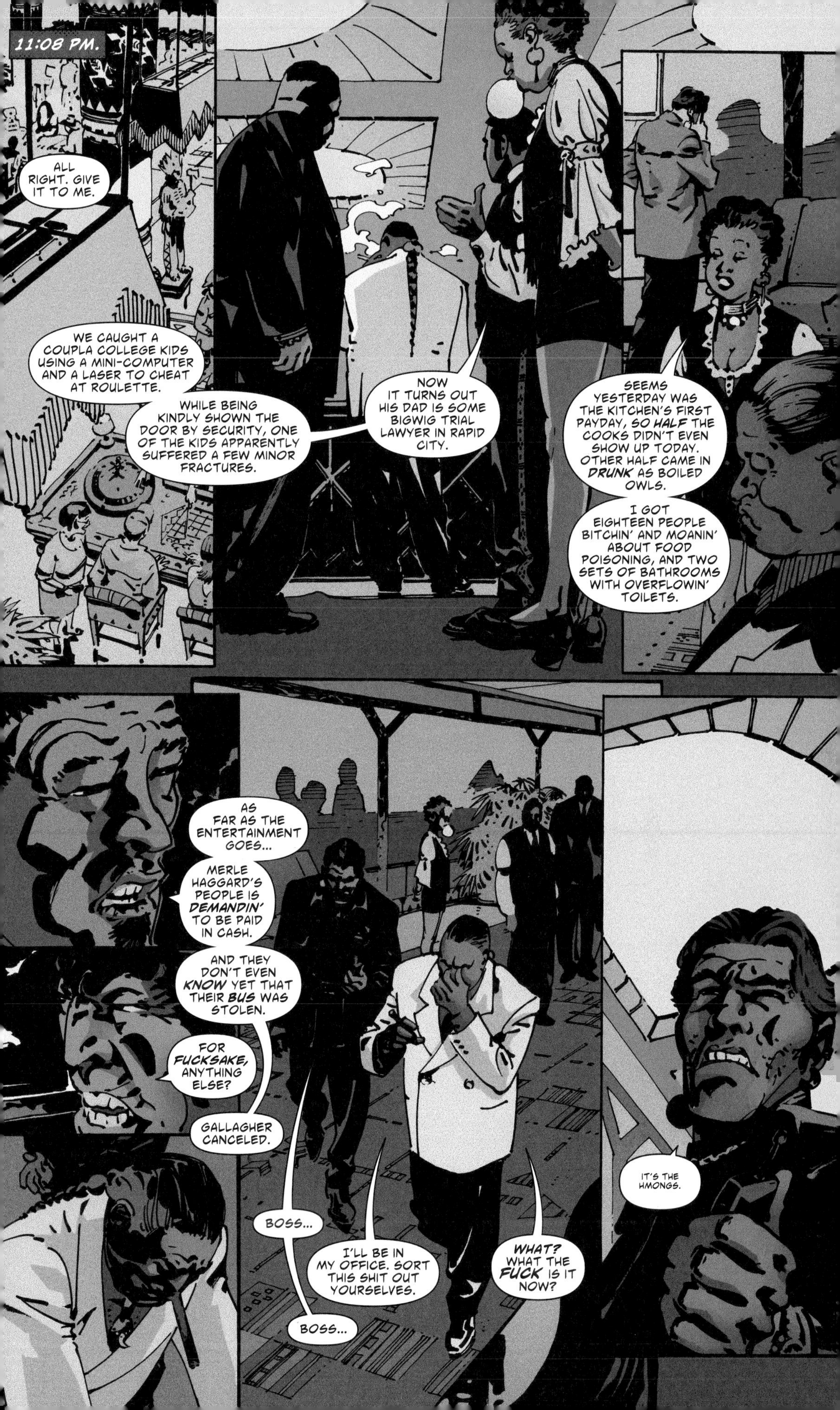
11:08 PM.
ALL RIGHT. GIVE IT TO ME.
WE CAUGHT A COUPLA COLLEGE KIDS USING A MINI-COMPUTER AND A LASER TO CHEAT AT ROULETTE.
WHILE BEING KINDLY SHOWN THE DOOR BY SECURITY, ONE OF THE KIDS APPARENTLY SUFFERED A FEW MINOR FRACTURES.
NOW IT TURNS OUT HIS DAD IS SOME BIGWIG TRIAL LAWYER IN RAPID CITY.
SEEMS YESTERDAY WAS THE KITCHEN'S FIRST PAYDAY, SO HALF THE COOKS DIDN'T EVEN SHOW UP TODAY. OTHER HALF CAME IN DRUNK AS BOILED OWLS.
I GOT EIGHTEEN PEOPLE BITCHIN' AND MOANIN' ABOUT FOOD POISONING, AND TWO SETS OF BATHROOMS WITH OVERFLOWIN' TOILETS.
AS FAR AS THE ENTERTAINMENT GOES...
MERLE HAGGARD'S PEOPLE IS DEMANDIN' TO BE PAID IN CASH.
AND THEY DON'T EVEN KNOW YET THAT THEIR BUS WAS STOLEN.
FOR FUCKSAKE, ANYTHING ELSE?
GALLAGHER CANCELED.
BOSS...
I'LL BE IN MY OFFICE. SORT THIS SHIT OUT YOURSELVES.
BOSS...
WHAT? WHAT THE FUCK IS IT NOW?
IT'S THE HMONGS.

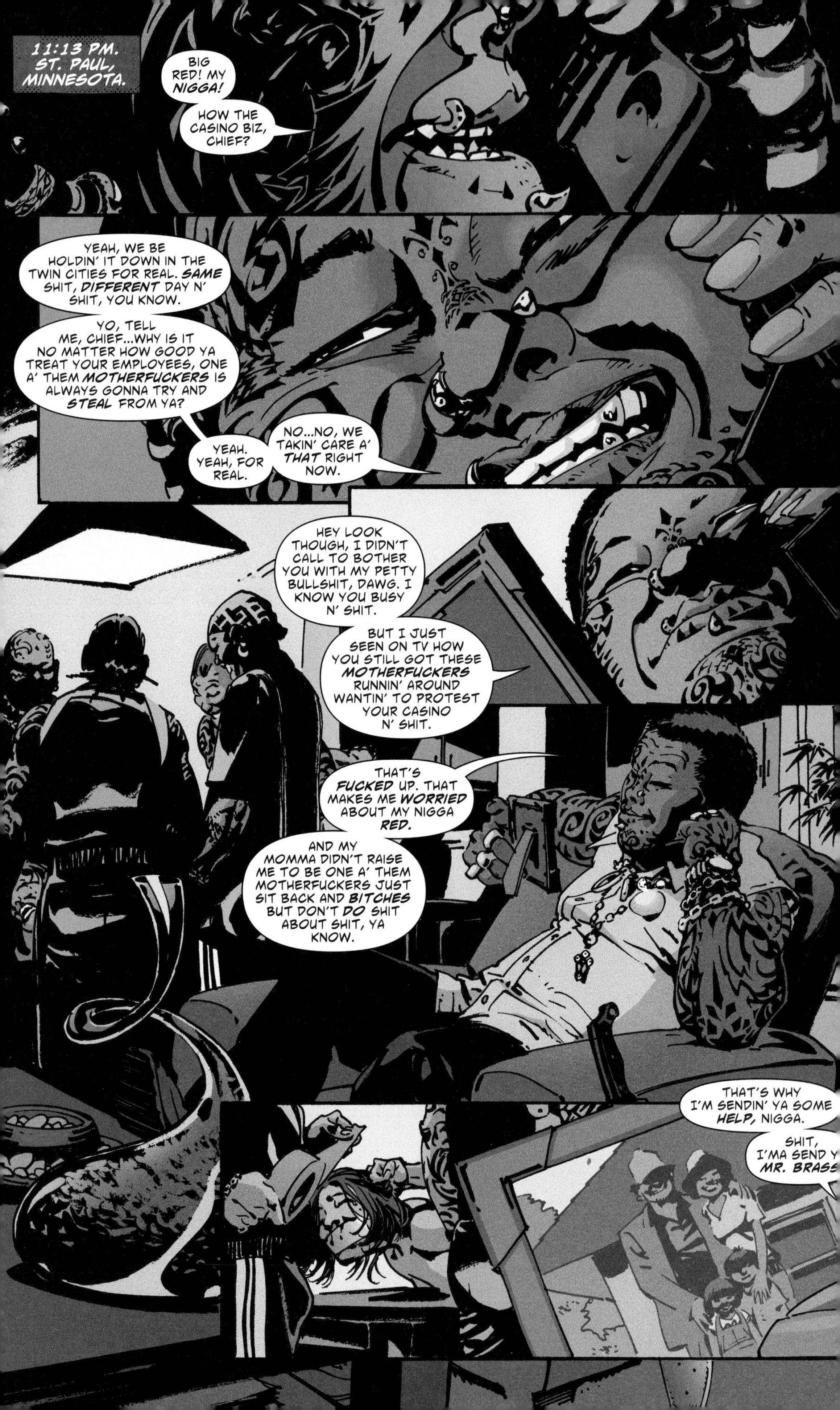

11:13 PM. ST. PAUL, MINNESOTA.
BIG RED! MY NIGGA!
HOW THE CASINO BIZ, CHIEF?
YEAH, WE BE HOLDIN' IT DOWN IN THE TWIN CITIES FOR REAL. SAME SHIT, DIFFERENT DAY N' SHIT, YOU KNOW.
YO, TELL ME, CHIEF...WHY IS IT NO MATTER HOW GOOD YA TREAT YOUR EMPLOYEES, ONE A' THEM MOTHERFUCKERS IS ALWAYS GONNA TRY AND STEAL FROM YA?
YEAH. YEAH, FOR REAL.
NO...NO, WE TAKIN' CARE A' THAT RIGHT NOW.
HEY LOOK THOUGH, I DIDN'T CALL TO BOTHER YOU WITH MY PETTY BULLSHIT, DAWG. I KNOW YOU BUSY N' SHIT.
BUT I JUST SEEN ON TV HOW YOU STILL GOT THESE MOTHERFUCKERS RUNNIN' AROUND WANTIN' TO PROTEST YOUR CASINO N' SHIT.
THAT'S FUCKED UP. THAT MAKES ME WORRIED ABOUT MY NIGGA RED.
AND MY MOMMA DIDN'T RAISE ME TO BE ONE A' THEM MOTHERFUCKERS JUST SIT BACK AND BITCHES BUT DON'T DO SHIT ABOUT SHIT, YA KNOW.
THAT'S WHY I'M SENDIN' YA SOME HELP, NIGGA.
SHIT, I'MA SEND Y MR. BRASS

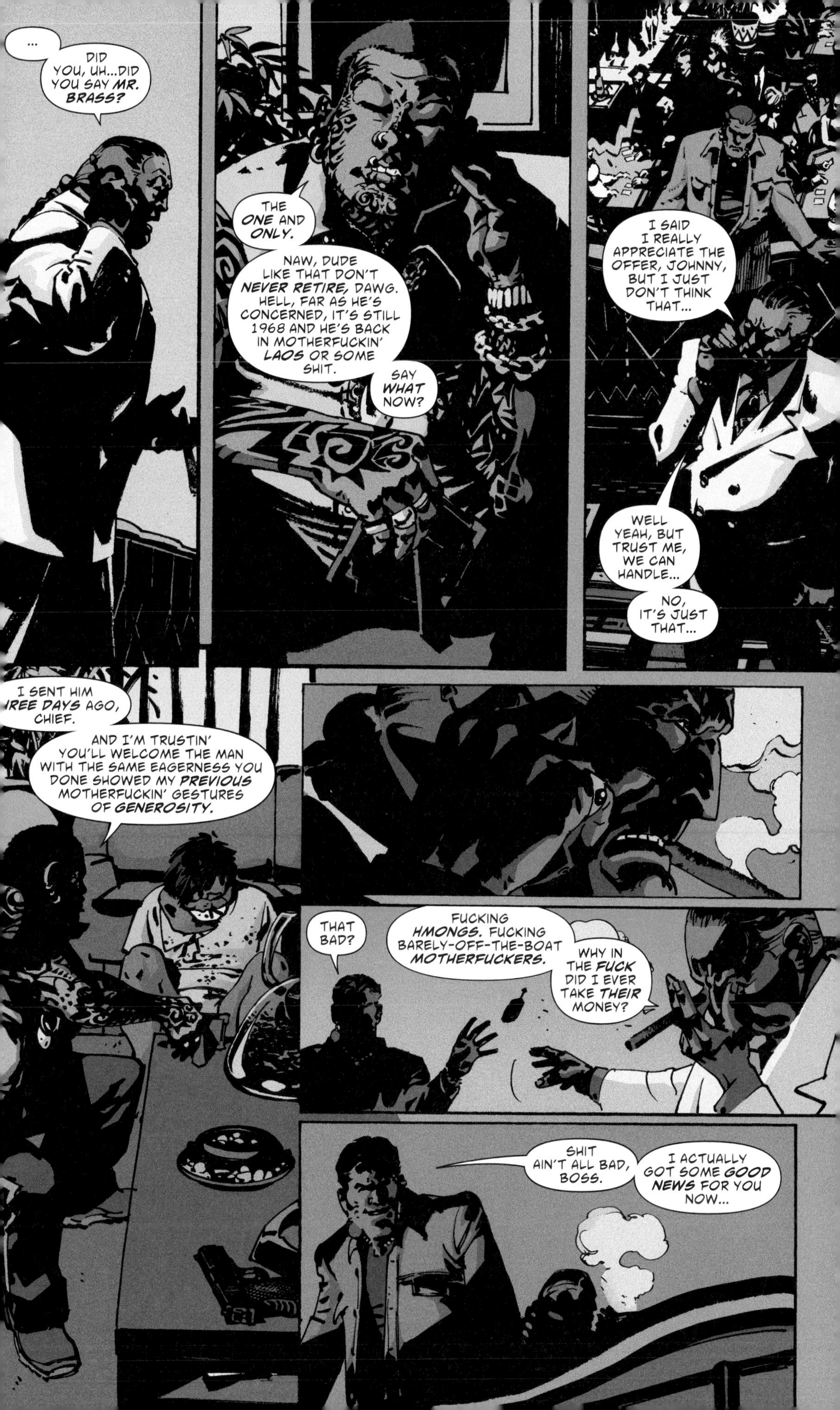
...
DID YOU, UH...DID YOU SAY MR. BRASS?
THE ONE AND ONLY.
NAW, DUDE LIKE THAT DON'T NEVER RETIRE, DAWG. HELL, FAR AS HE'S CONCERNED, IT'S STILL 1968 AND HE'S BACK IN MOTHERFUCKIN' LAOS OR SOME SHIT.
SAY WHAT NOW?
I SAID I REALLY APPRECIATE THE OFFER, JOHNNY, BUT I JUST DON'T THINK THAT...
WELL YEAH, BUT TRUST ME, WE CAN HANDLE...
NO, IT'S JUST THAT...
I SENT HIM REE DAYS AGO, CHIEF.
AND I'M TRUSTIN' YOU'LL WELCOME THE MAN WITH THE SAME EAGERNESS YOU DONE SHOWED MY PREVIOUS MOTHERFUCKIN' GESTURES OF GENEROSITY.
THAT BAD?
FUCKING HMONGS. FUCKING BARELY-OFF-THE-BOAT MOTHERFUCKERS.
WHY IN THE FUCK DID I EVER TAKE THEIR MONEY?
SHIT AIN'T ALL BAD, BOSS.
I ACTUALLY GOT SOME GOOD NEWS FOR YOU NOW...

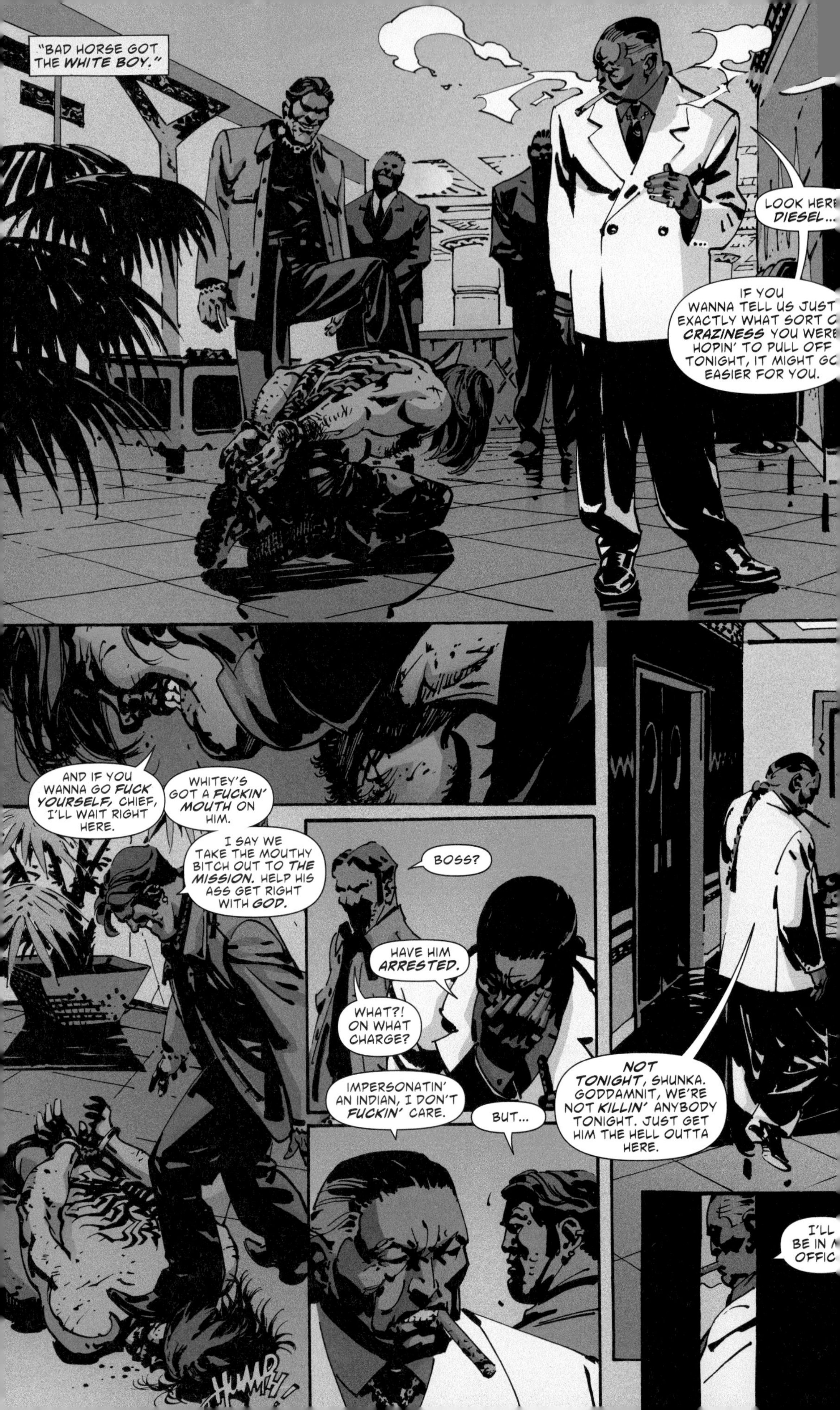
"BAD HORSE GOT THE WHITE BOY."
LOOK HERE DIESEL...
IF YOU WANNA TELL US JUST EXACTLY WHAT SORT O CRAZINESS YOU WERE HOPIN' TO PULL OFF TONIGHT, IT MIGHT GO EASIER FOR YOU.
AND IF YOU WANNA GO FUCK YOURSELF, CHIEF, I'LL WAIT RIGHT HERE.
WHITEY'S GOT A FUCKIN' MOUTH ON HIM.
I SAY WE TAKE THE MOUTHY BITCH OUT TO THE MISSION. HELP HIS ASS GET RIGHT WITH GOD.
BOSS?
HAVE HIM ARRESTED.
WHAT?! ON WHAT CHARGE?
IMPERSONATIN' AN INDIAN, I DON'T FUCKIN' CARE.
BUT...
NOT TONIGHT, SHUNKA. GODDAMNIT, WE'RE NOT KILLIN' ANYBODY TONIGHT. JUST GET HIM THE HELL OUTTA HERE.
HUMPH!
I'LL BE IN M OFFIC

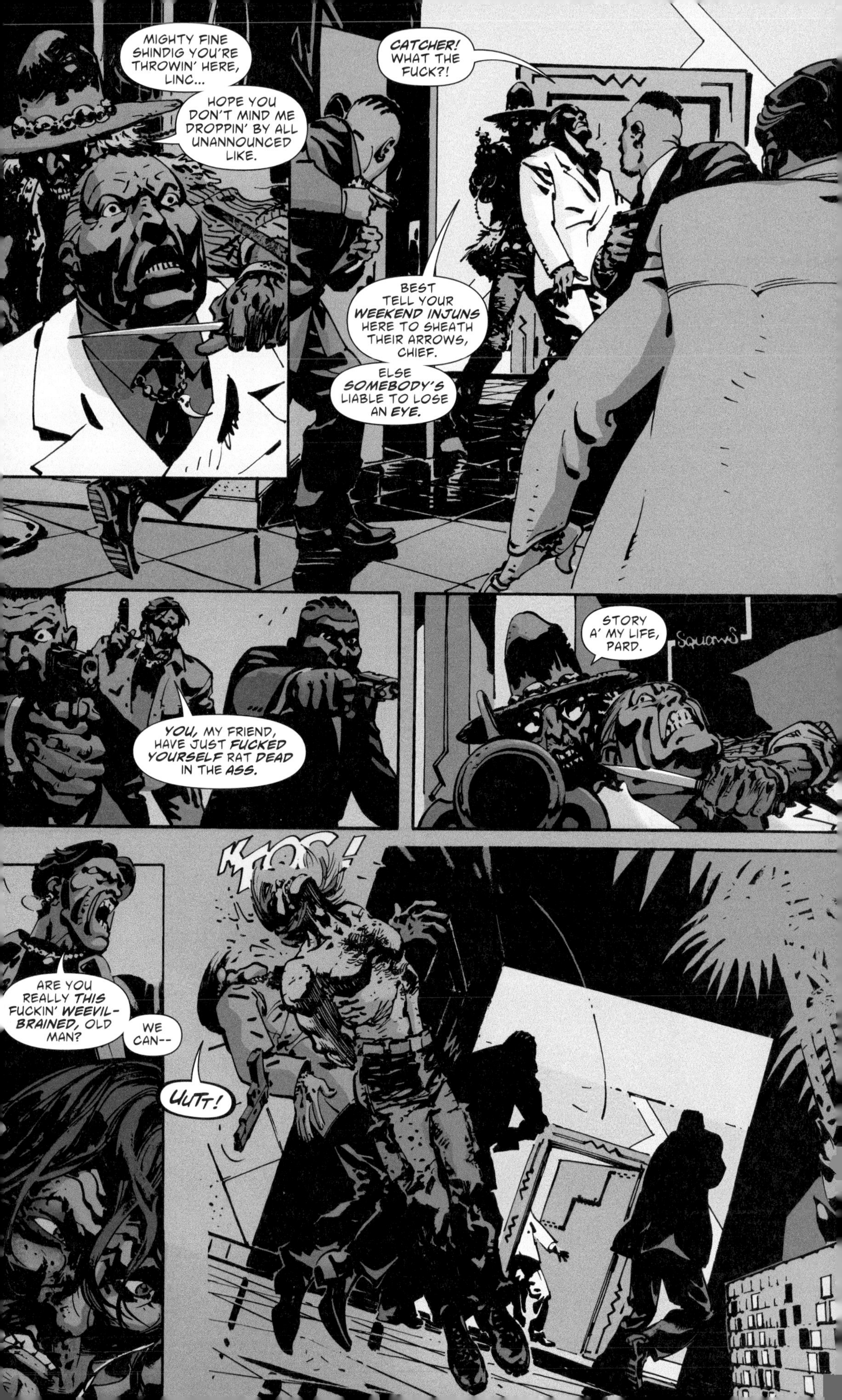
MIGHTY FINE SHINDIG YOU'RE THROWIN' HERE, LINC...
HOPE YOU DON'T MIND ME DROPPIN' BY ALL UNANNOUNCED LIKE.
CATCHER! WHAT THE FUCK?!
BEST TELL YOUR WEEKEND INJUNS HERE TO SHEATH THEIR ARROWS, CHIEF.
ELSE SOMEBODY'S LIABLE TO LOSE AN EYE.
YOU, MY FRIEND, HAVE JUST FUCKED YOURSELF RAT DEAD IN THE ASS.
STORY A' MY LIFE, PARD.
SQUAWS
KTOOF!
ARE YOU REALLY THIS FUCKIN' WEEVIL-BRAINED, OLD MAN?
WE CAN--
UUTT!

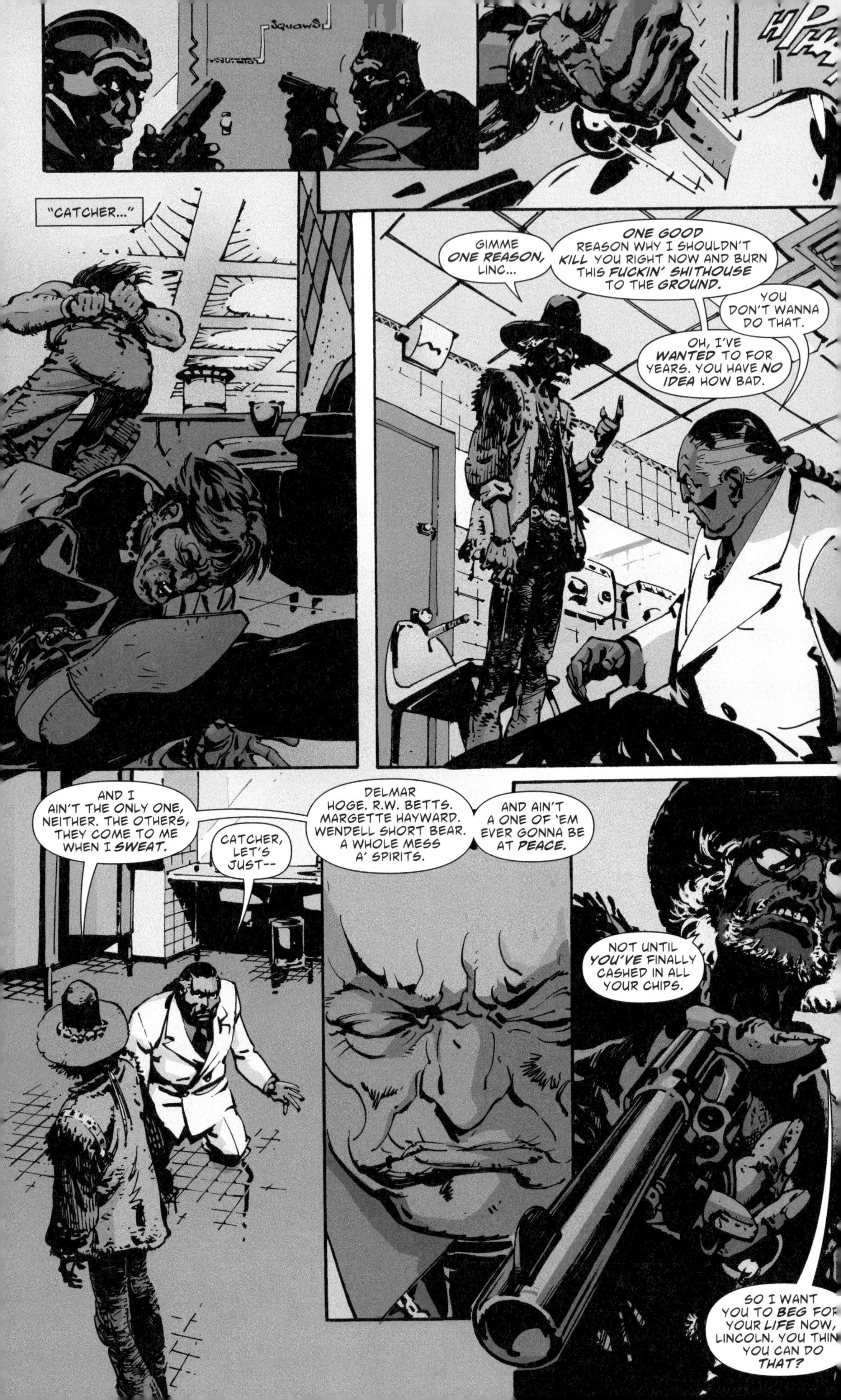

SQUAWS
"CATCHER..."
GIMME ONE REASON, LINC...
ONE GOOD REASON WHY I SHOULDN'T KILL YOU RIGHT NOW AND BURN THIS FUCKIN' SHITHOUSE TO THE GROUND.
YOU DON'T WANNA DO THAT.
OH, I'VE WANTED TO FOR YEARS. YOU HAVE NO IDEA HOW BAD.
AND I AIN'T THE ONLY ONE, NEITHER. THE OTHERS, THEY COME TO ME WHEN I SWEAT.
CATCHER, LET'S JUST--
DELMAR HOGE. R.W. BETTS. MARGETTE HAYWARD. WENDELL SHORT BEAR. A WHOLE MESS A' SPIRITS.
AND AIN'T A ONE OF 'EM EVER GONNA BE AT PEACE.
NOT UNTIL YOU'VE FINALLY CASHED IN ALL YOUR CHIPS.
SO I WANT YOU TO BEG FOR YOUR LIFE NOW, LINCOLN. YOU THIN YOU CAN DO THAT?

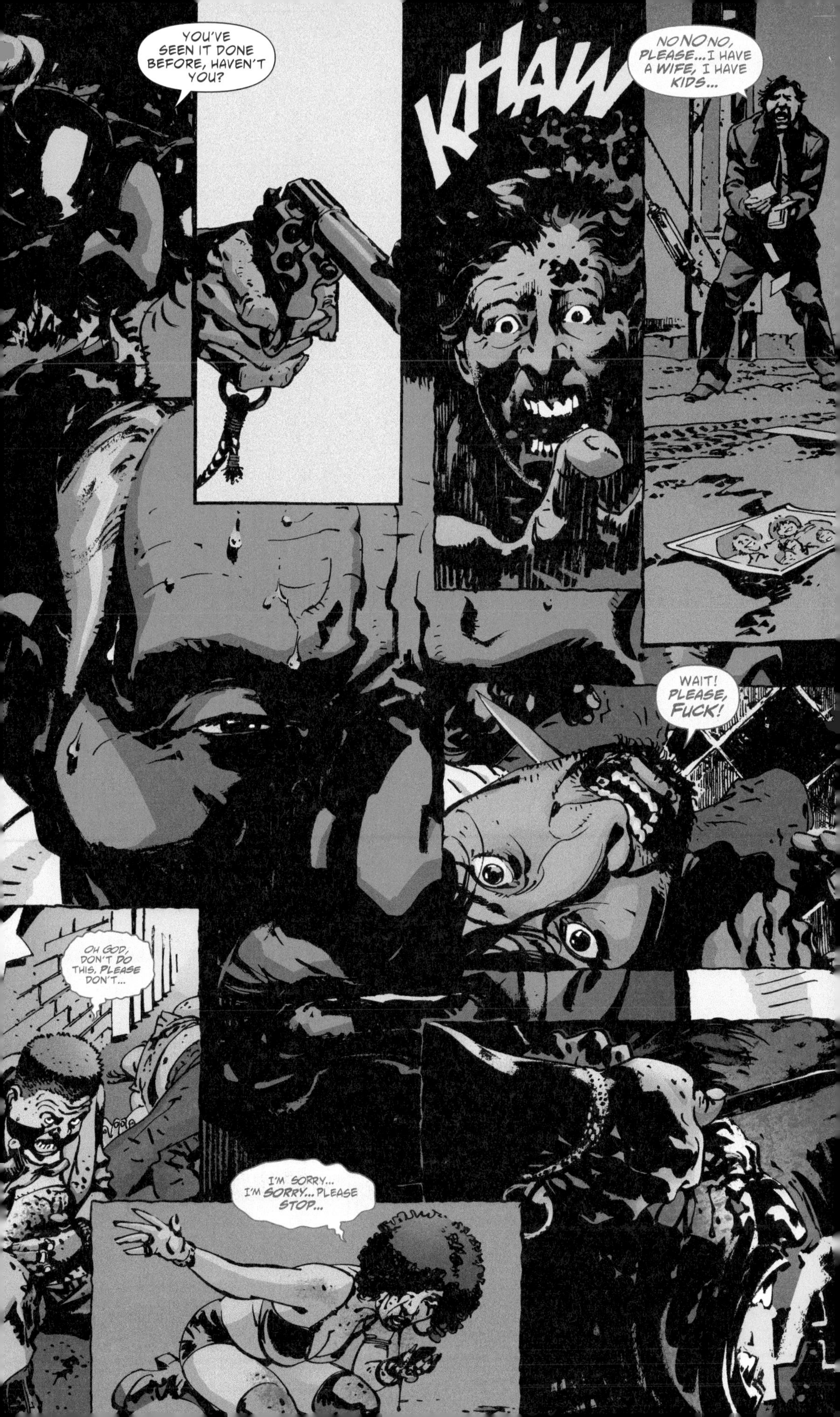
YOU'VE SEEN IT DONE BEFORE, HAVEN'T YOU?
KTHAW
NO NO NO, PLEASE...I HAVE A WIFE, I HAVE KIDS...
WAIT! PLEASE, FUCK!
OH GOD, DON'T DO THIS, PLEASE DON'T...
I'M SORRY... I'M SORRY... PLEASE STOP...

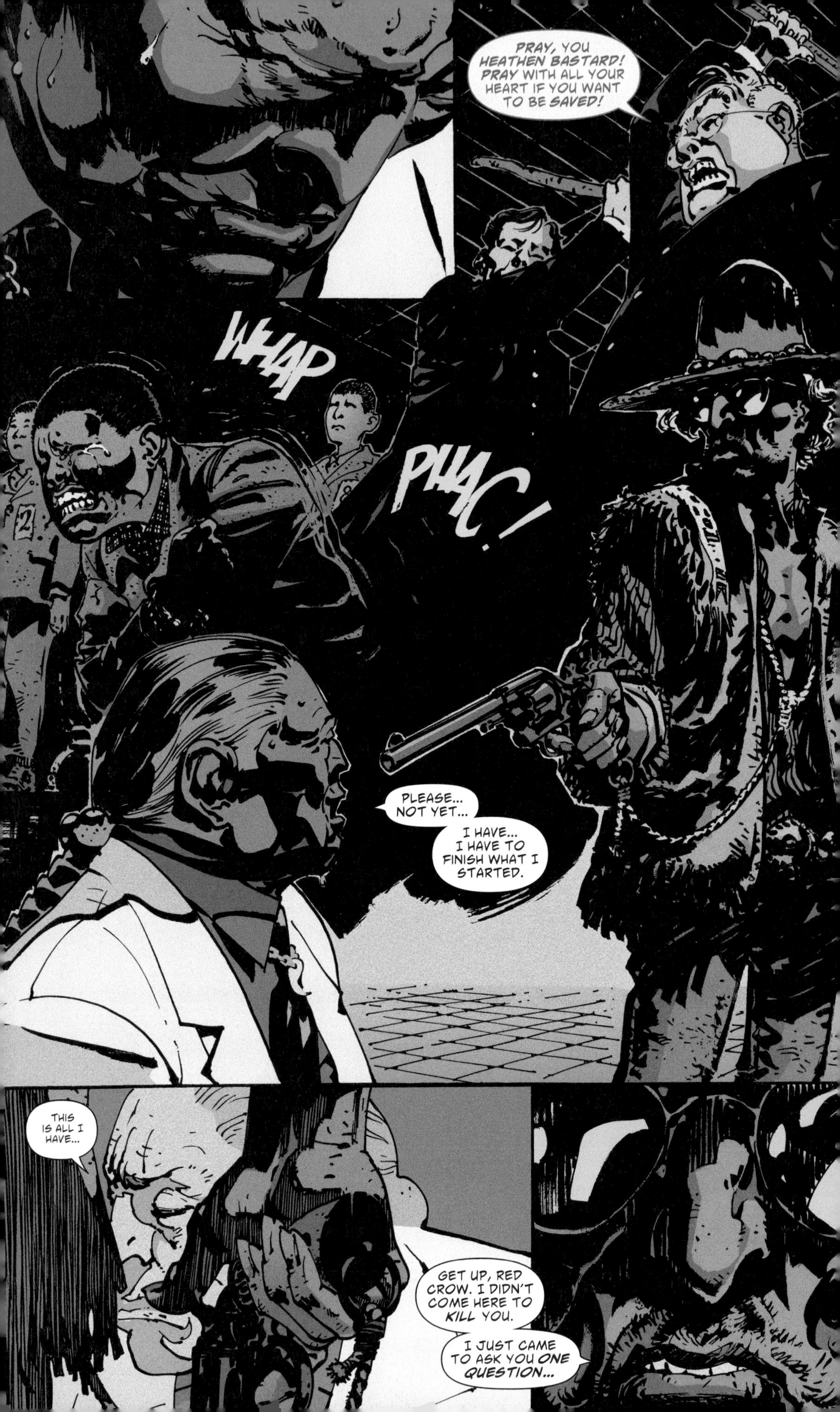
PRAY, YOU HEATHEN BASTARD! PRAY WITH ALL YOUR HEART IF YOU WANT TO BE SAVED!
WHAP
PHAC!
PLEASE... NOT YET...
I HAVE... I HAVE TO FINISH WHAT I STARTED.
THIS IS ALL I HAVE...
GET UP, RED CROW. I DIDN'T COME HERE TO KILL YOU.
I JUST CAME TO ASK YOU ONE QUESTION...

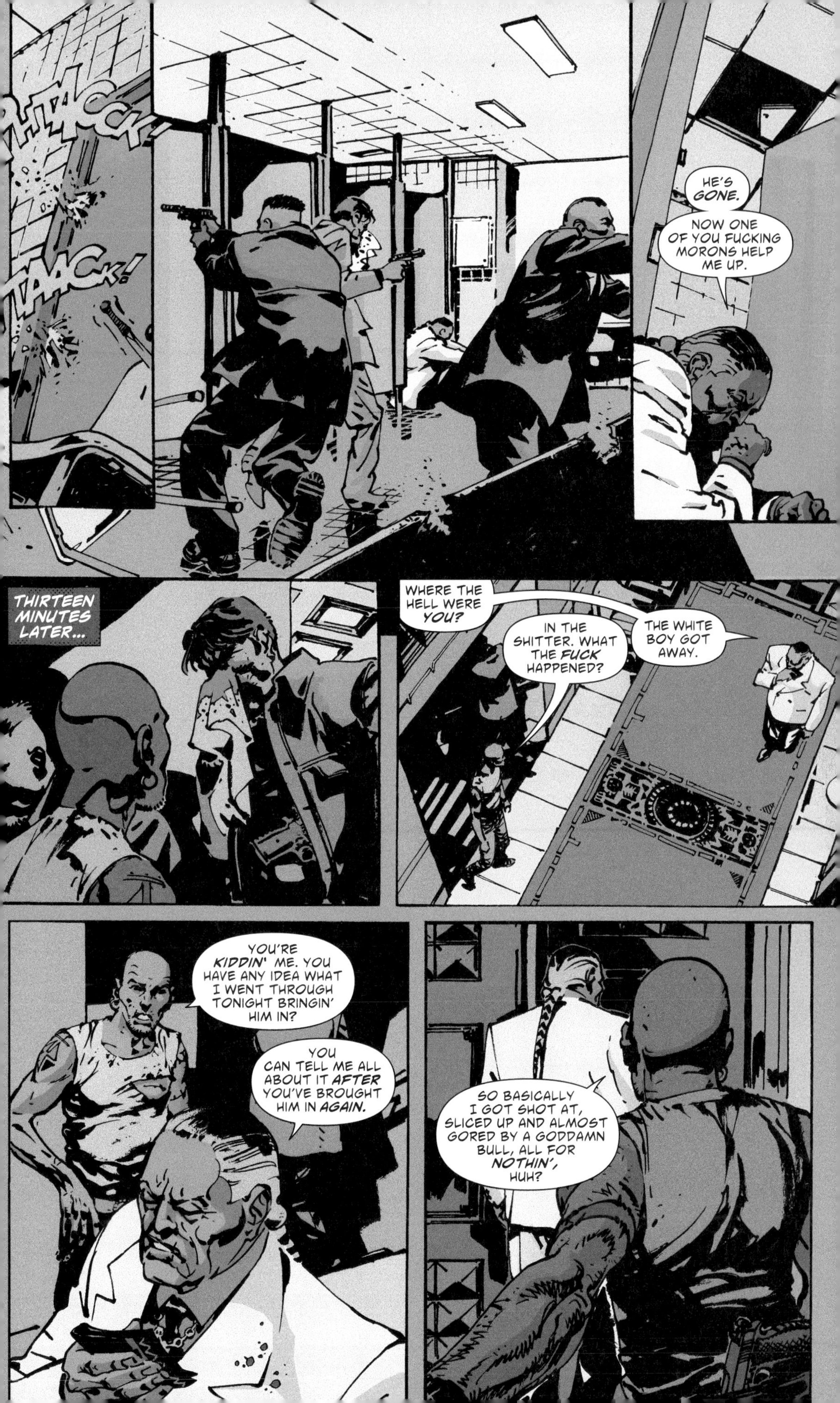

THACK!
TAACK!
HE'S GONE.
NOW ONE OF YOU FUCKING MORONS HELP ME UP.
THIRTEEN MINUTES LATER...
WHERE THE HELL WERE YOU?
IN THE SHITTER. WHAT THE FUCK HAPPENED?
THE WHITE BOY GOT AWAY.
YOU'RE KIDDIN' ME. YOU HAVE ANY IDEA WHAT I WENT THROUGH TONIGHT BRINGIN' HIM IN?
YOU CAN TELL ME ALL ABOUT IT AFTER YOU'VE BROUGHT HIM IN AGAIN.
SO BASICALLY I GOT SHOT AT, SLICED UP AND ALMOST GORED BY A GODDAMN BULL, ALL FOR NOTHIN', HUH?

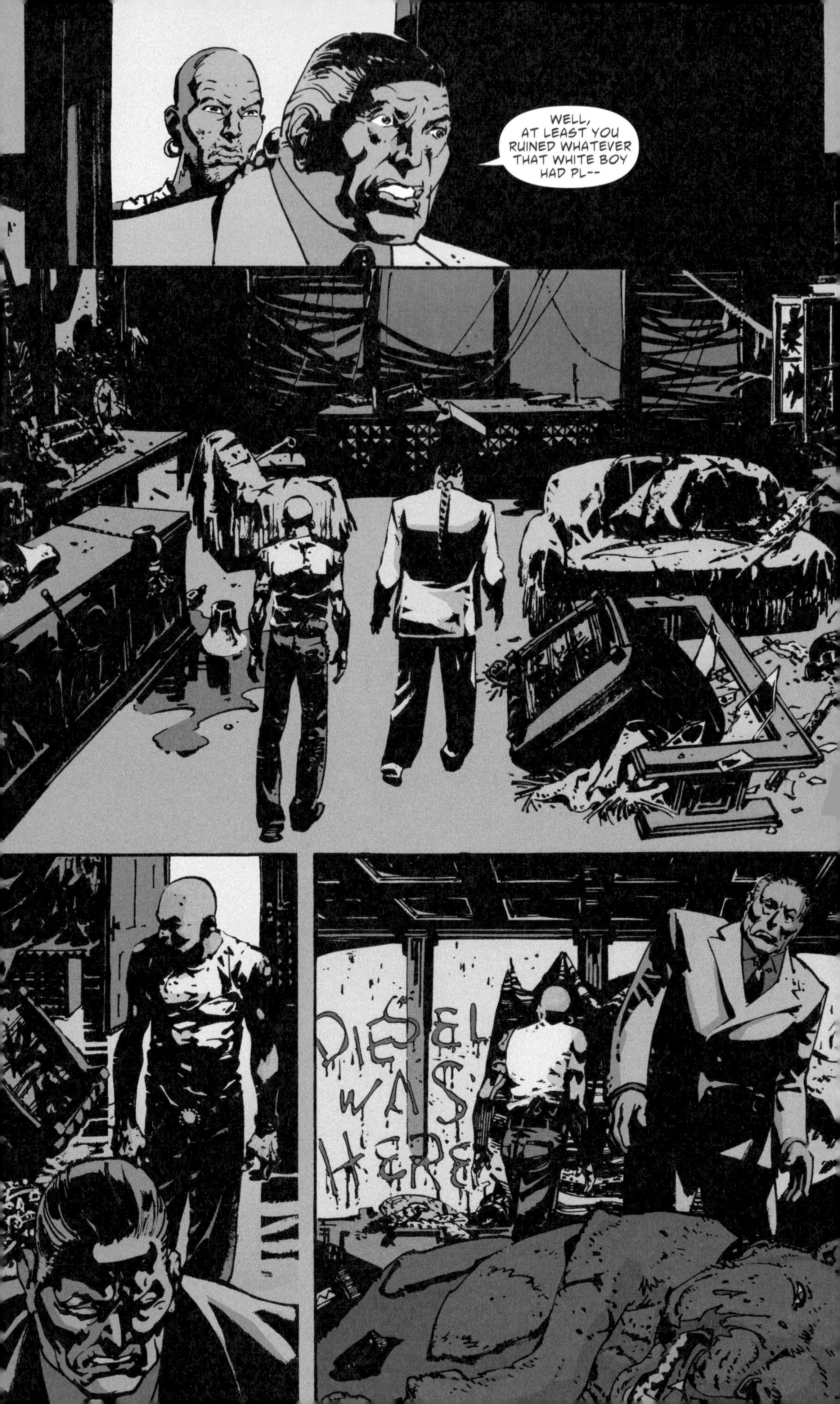

WELL, AT LEAST YOU RUINED WHATEVER THAT WHITE BOY HAD PL--
DIESEL WAS HERE

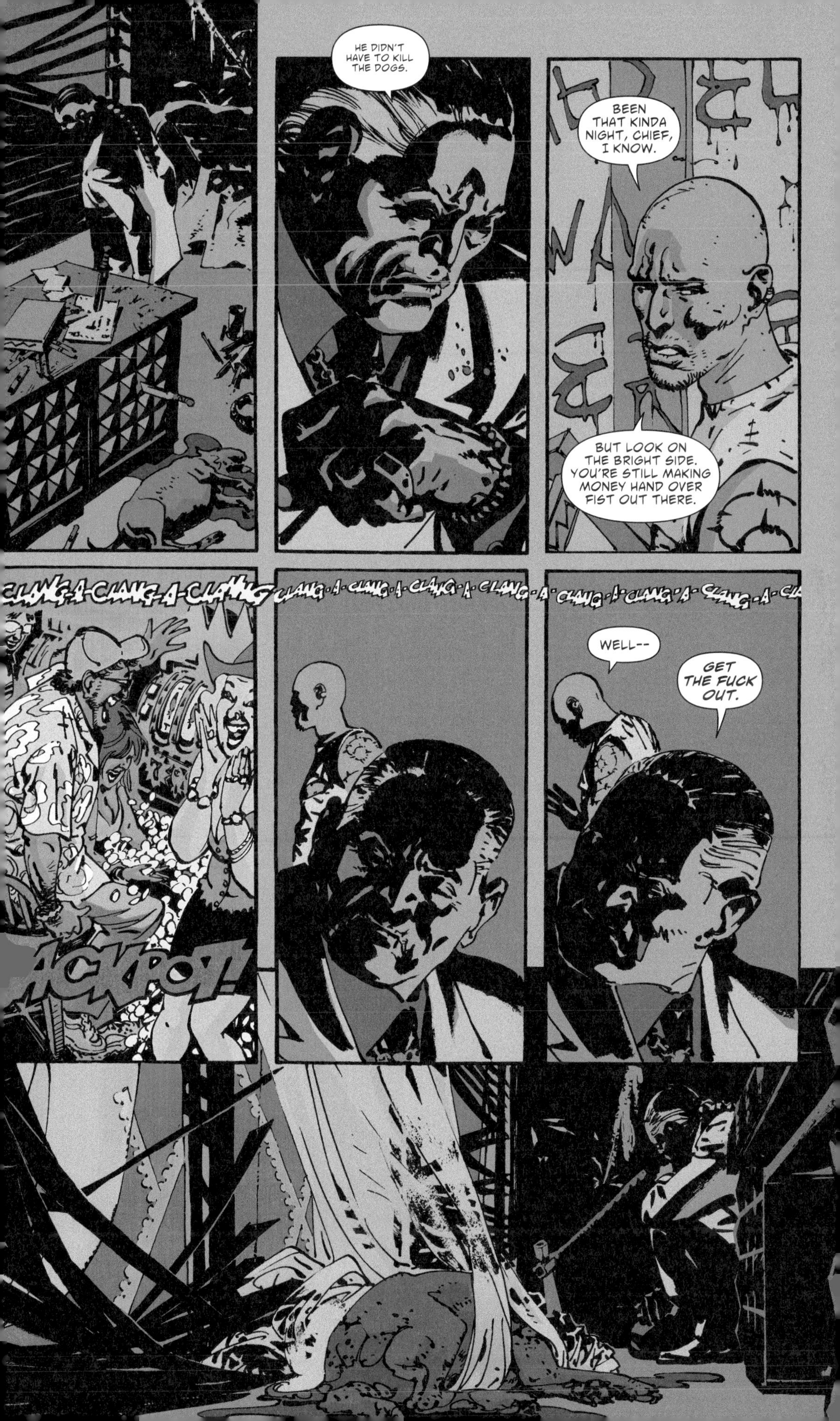
HE DIDN'T HAVE TO KILL THE DOGS.
BEEN THAT KINDA NIGHT, CHIEF, I KNOW.
BUT LOOK ON THE BRIGHT SIDE. YOU'RE STILL MAKING MONEY HAND OVER FIST OUT THERE.
CLANG-A-CLANG-A-CLANG
CLANG-A-CLANG-A-CLANG-A-CLANG-A-CLANG-A-CLANG-A-CLANG-A-CL
WELL--
GET THE FUCK OUT.

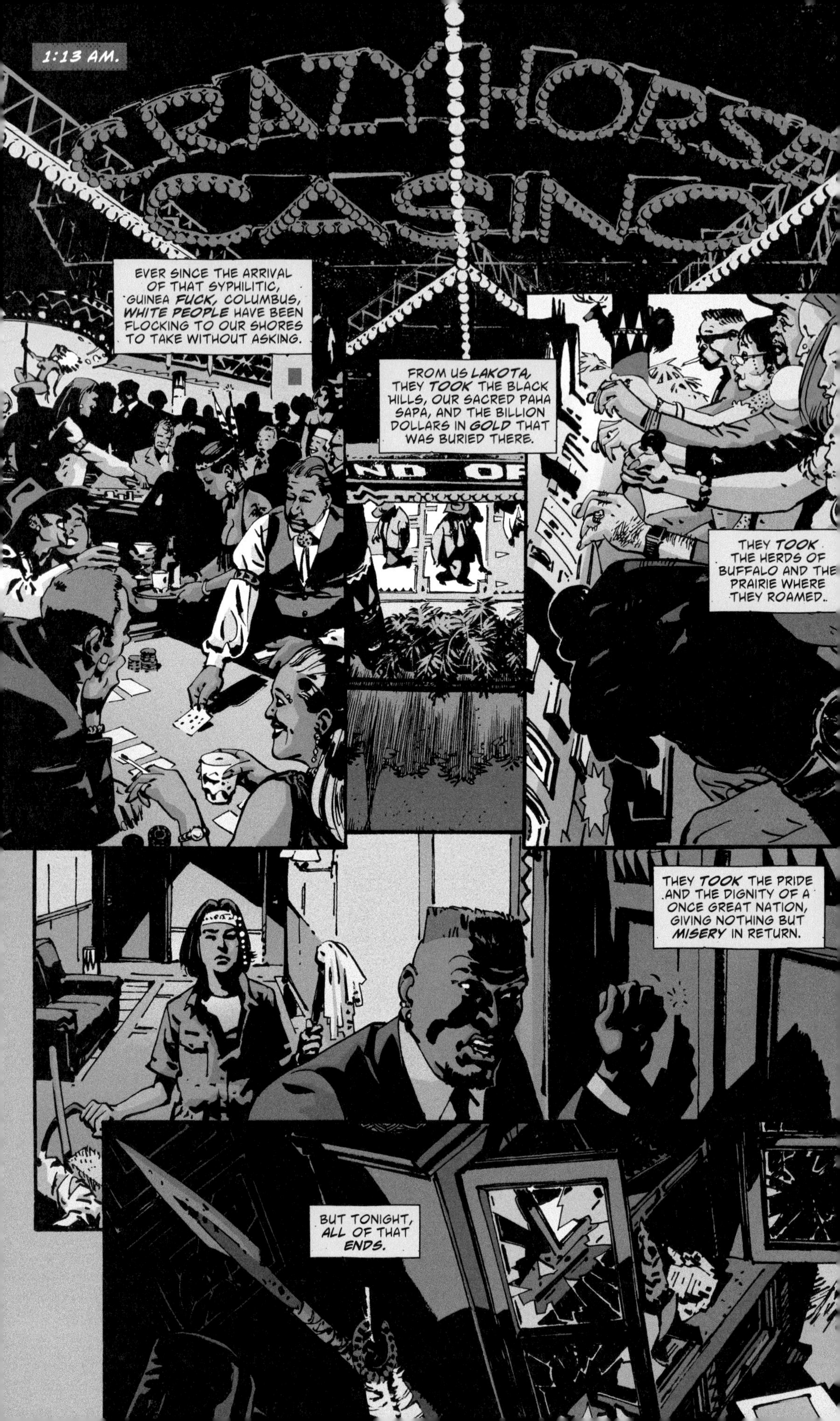
1:13 AM.
EVER SINCE THE ARRIVAL OF THAT SYPHILITIC, GUINEA FUCK, COLUMBUS, WHITE PEOPLE HAVE BEEN FLOCKING TO OUR SHORES TO TAKE WITHOUT ASKING.
FROM US LAKOTA, THEY TOOK THE BLACK HILLS, OUR SACRED PAHA SAPA, AND THE BILLION DOLLARS IN GOLD THAT WAS BURIED THERE.
THEY TOOK THE HERDS OF BUFFALO AND THE PRAIRIE WHERE THEY ROAMED..
THEY TOOK THE PRIDE AND THE DIGNITY OF A ONCE GREAT NATION, GIVING NOTHING BUT MISERY IN RETURN.
BUT TONIGHT, ALL OF THAT ENDS.

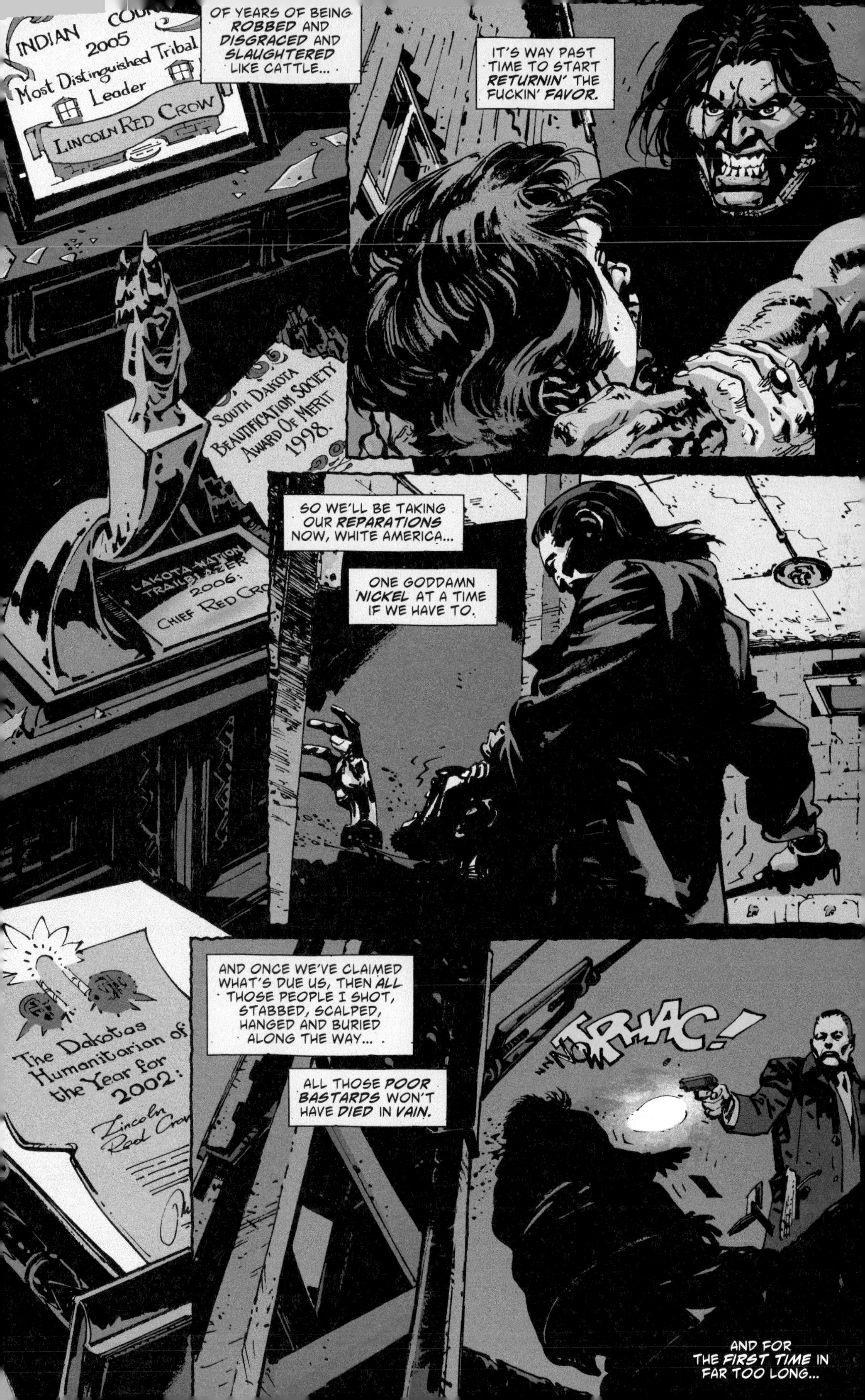
INDIAN COU
2005
Most Distinguished Tribal Leader
LINCOLN RED CROW
OF YEARS OF BEING ROBBED AND DISGRACED AND SLAUGHTERED LIKE CATTLE...
IT'S WAY PAST TIME TO START RETURNIN' THE FUCKIN' FAVOR.
SOUTH DAKOTA BEAUTIFICATION SOCIETY AWARD OF MERIT 1998.
LAKOTA NATION TRAILBLAZER 2006: CHIEF RED CRO
SO WE'LL BE TAKING OUR REPARATIONS NOW, WHITE AMERICA...
ONE GODDAMN NICKEL AT A TIME IF WE HAVE TO.
The Dakotas Humanitarian of the Year for 2002:
Lincoln Red Crow
AND ONCE WE'VE CLAIMED WHAT'S DUE US, THEN ALL THOSE PEOPLE I SHOT, STABBED, SCALPED, HANGED AND BURIED ALONG THE WAY...
ALL THOSE POOR BASTARDS WON'T HAVE DIED IN VAIN.
...NOW
THRAC!
AND FOR THE FIRST TIME IN FAR TOO LONG...

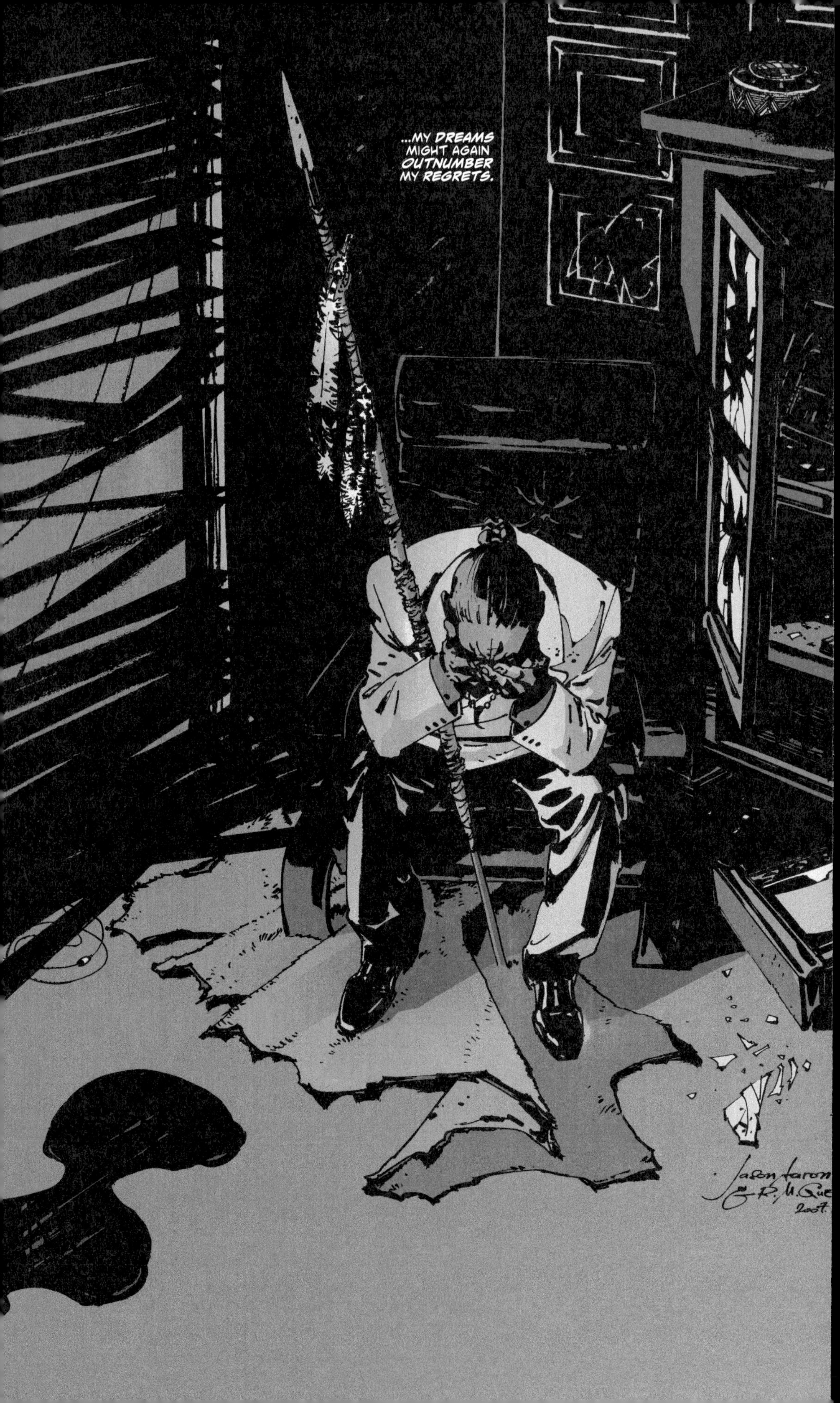
...MY DREAMS MIGHT AGAIN OUTNUMBER MY REGRETS.
Jason Aaron
R.M. Guéra 2007

CASINO BOOGIE PART THREE: THE WAY OF THE INTERCEPTING FIST

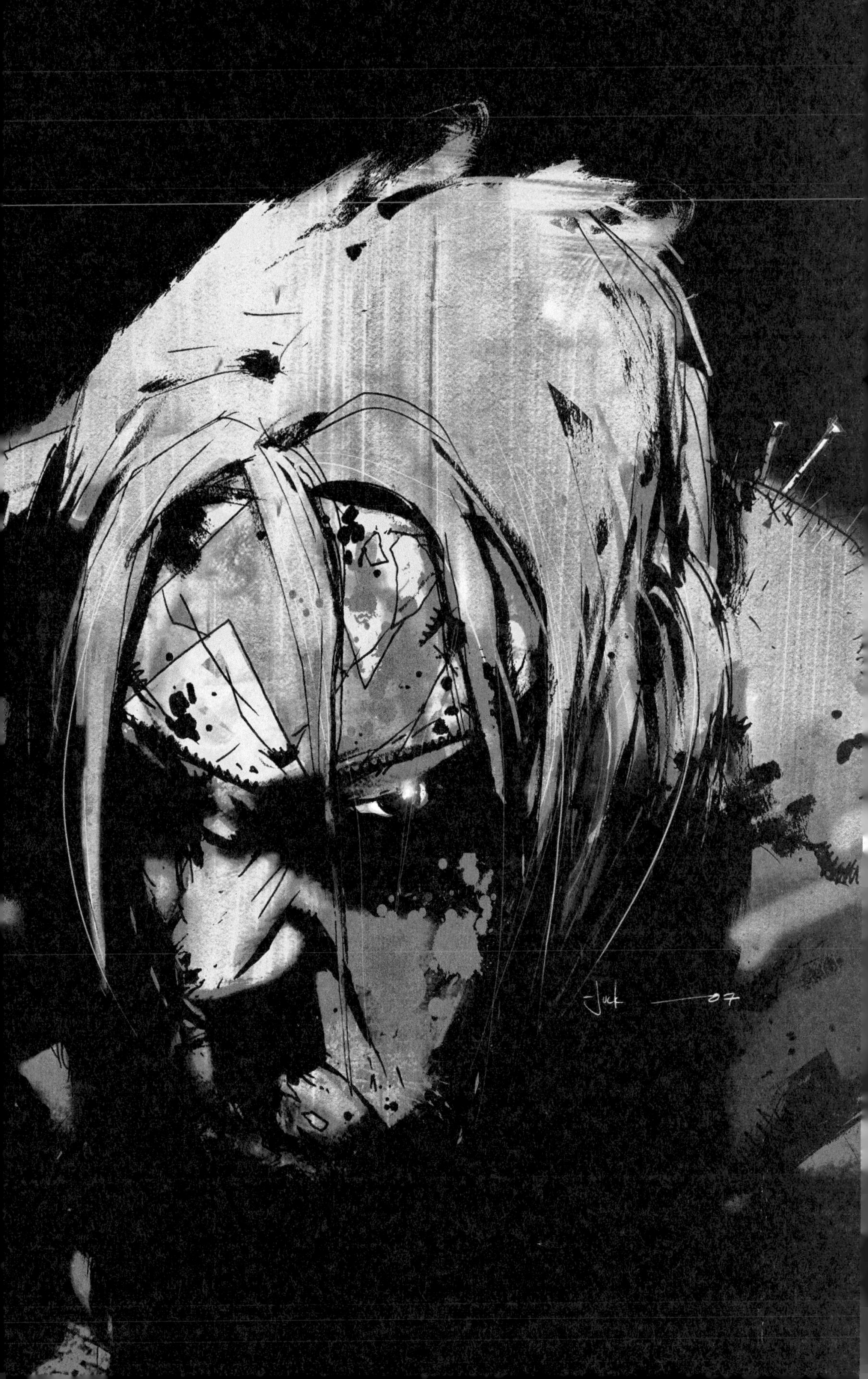

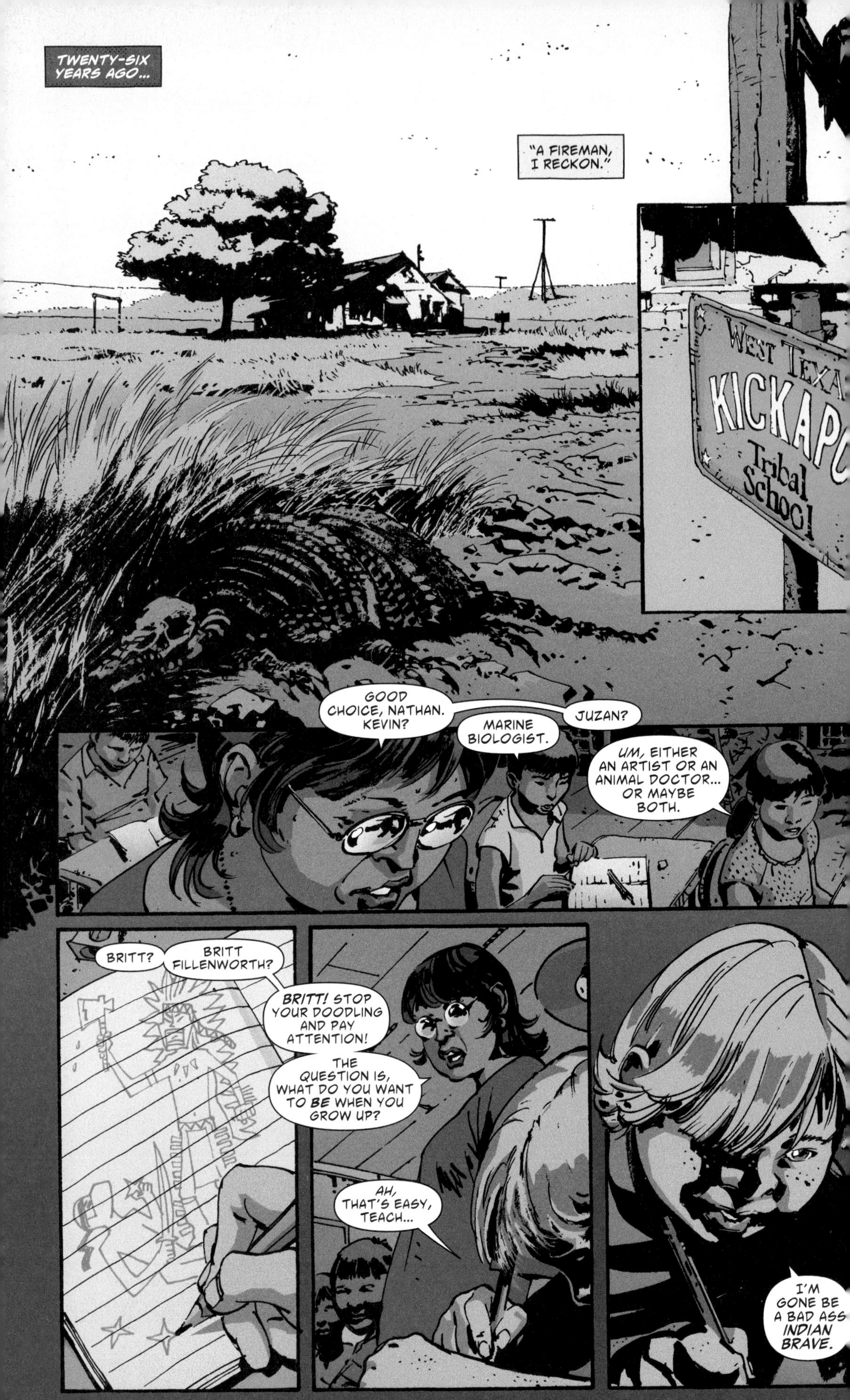
TWENTY-SIX YEARS AGO...
"A FIREMAN, I RECKON."
WEST TEXA
KICKAPU
Tribal School
GOOD CHOICE, NATHAN. KEVIN?
MARINE BIOLOGIST.
JUZAN?
UM, EITHER AN ARTIST OR AN ANIMAL DOCTOR... OR MAYBE BOTH.
BRITT?
BRITT FILLENWORTH?
BRITT! STOP YOUR DOODLING AND PAY ATTENTION!
THE QUESTION IS, WHAT DO YOU WANT TO BE WHEN YOU GROW UP?
AH, THAT'S EASY, TEACH...
I'M GONE BE A BAD ASS INDIAN BRAVE.

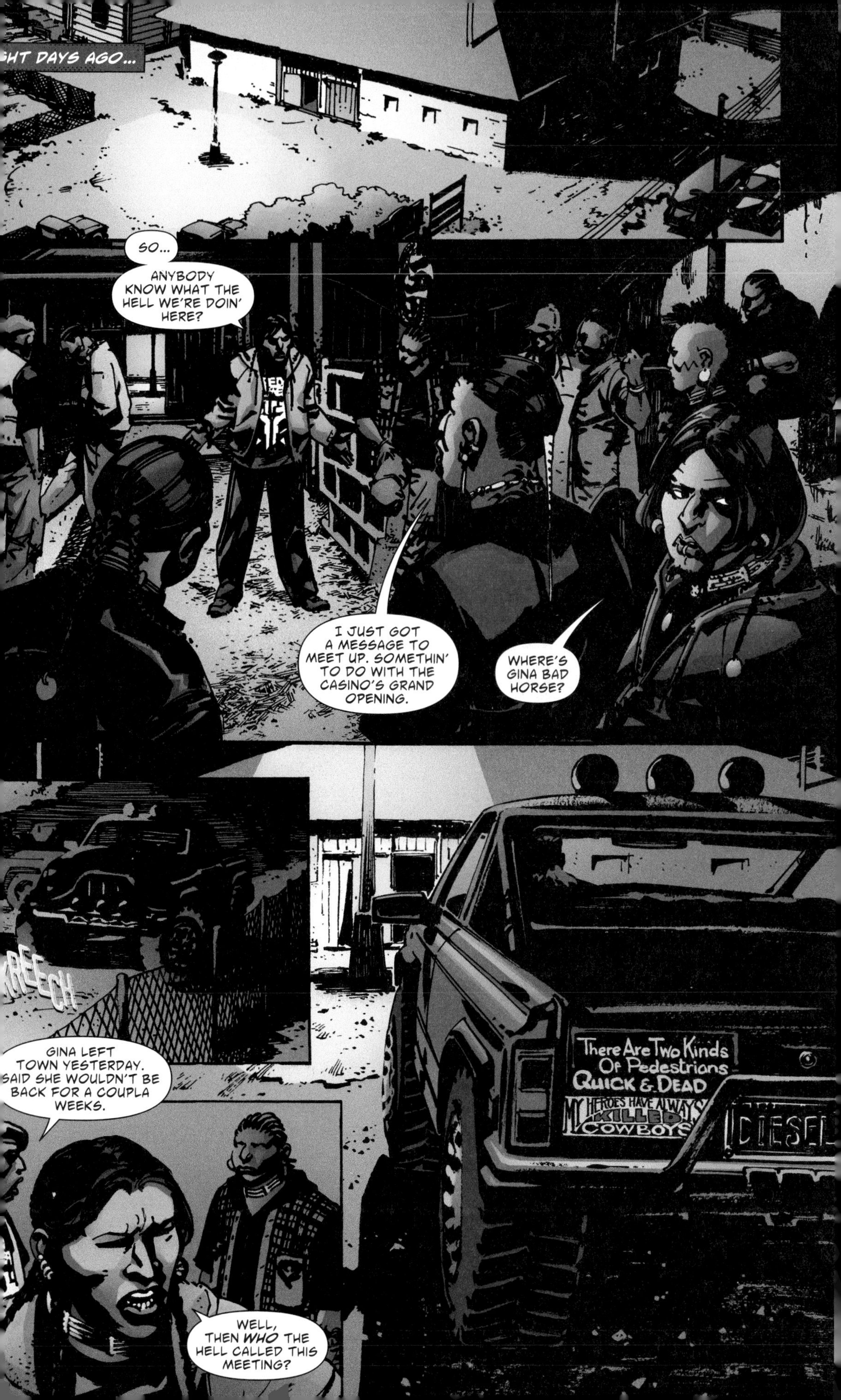

...GHT DAYS AGO...
SO...
ANYBODY KNOW WHAT THE HELL WE'RE DOIN' HERE?
I JUST GOT A MESSAGE TO MEET UP. SOMETHIN' TO DO WITH THE CASINO'S GRAND OPENING.
WHERE'S GINA BAD HORSE?
...REECH
GINA LEFT TOWN YESTERDAY. ...SAID SHE WOULDN'T BE BACK FOR A COUPLA WEEKS.
There Are Two Kinds Of Pedestrians QUICK & DEAD
MY HEROES HAVE ALWAYS KILLED COWBOYS
DIESEL
WELL, THEN *WHO* THE HELL CALLED THIS MEETING?

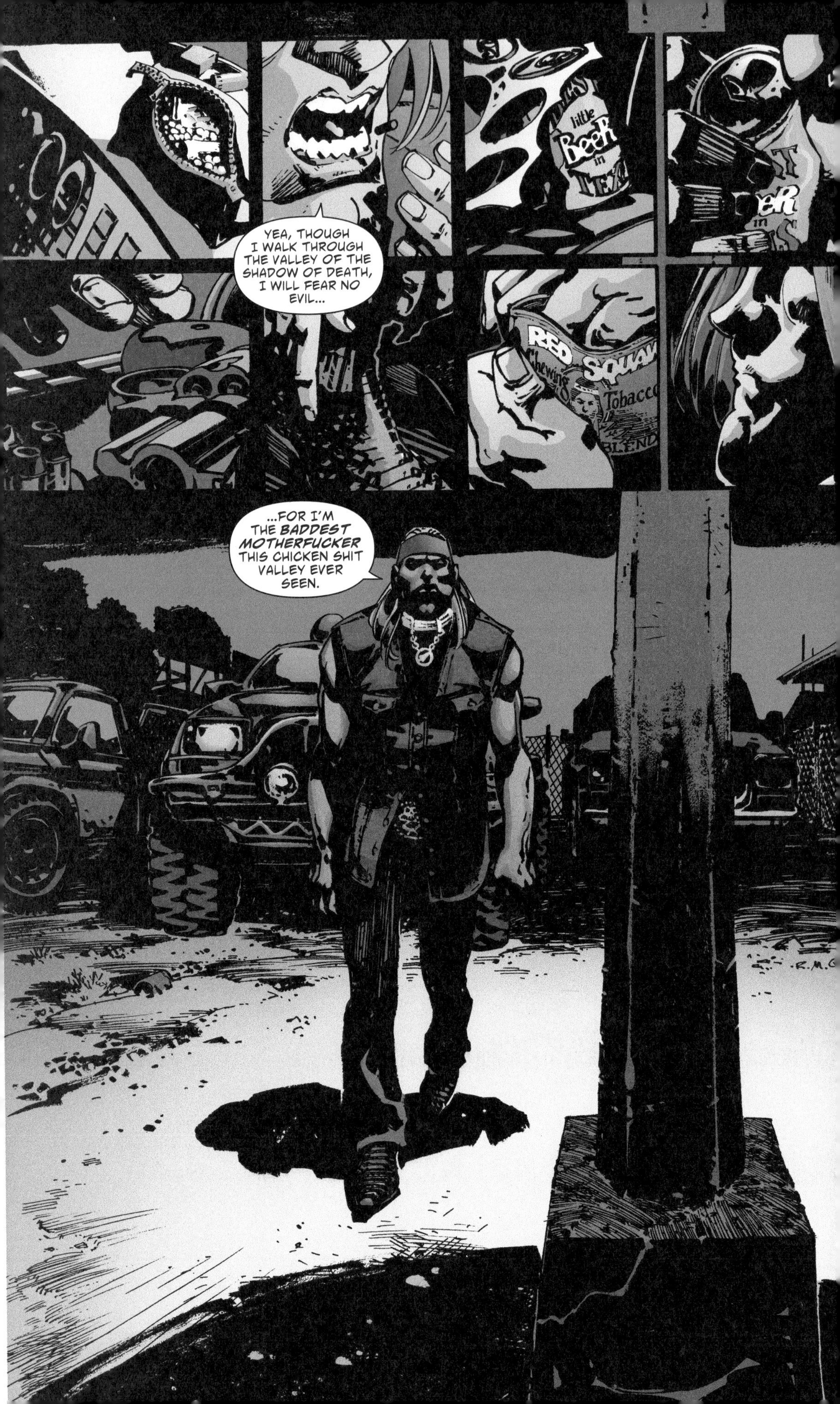

YEA, THOUGH I WALK THROUGH THE VALLEY OF THE SHADOW OF DEATH, I WILL FEAR NO EVIL...
little BeeR in TEXAS
RED SQUAW Chewing Tobacco BLEND
...FOR I'M THE *BADDEST MOTHERFUCKER* THIS CHICKEN SHIT VALLEY EVER SEEN.
R.M.G

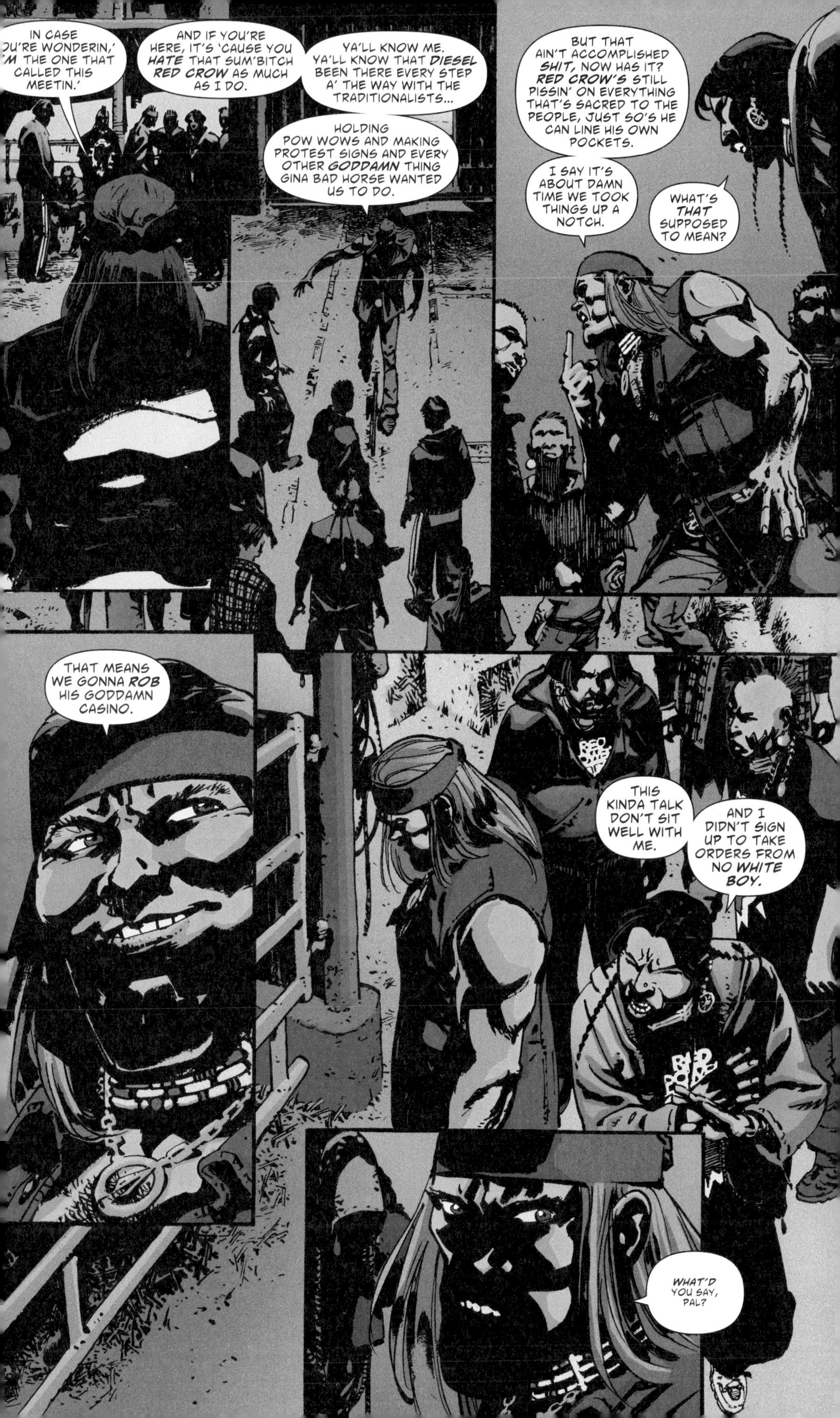
IN CASE YOU'RE WONDERIN,' I'M THE ONE THAT CALLED THIS MEETIN.'
AND IF YOU'RE HERE, IT'S 'CAUSE YOU HATE THAT SUM'BITCH RED CROW AS MUCH AS I DO.
YA'LL KNOW ME. YA'LL KNOW THAT DIESEL BEEN THERE EVERY STEP A' THE WAY WITH THE TRADITIONALISTS...
HOLDING POW WOWS AND MAKING PROTEST SIGNS AND EVERY OTHER GODDAMN THING GINA BAD HORSE WANTED US TO DO.
BUT THAT AIN'T ACCOMPLISHED SHIT, NOW HAS IT? RED CROW'S STILL PISSIN' ON EVERYTHING THAT'S SACRED TO THE PEOPLE, JUST SO'S HE CAN LINE HIS OWN POCKETS.
I SAY IT'S ABOUT DAMN TIME WE TOOK THINGS UP A NOTCH.
WHAT'S THAT SUPPOSED TO MEAN?
THAT MEANS WE GONNA ROB HIS GODDAMN CASINO.
THIS KINDA TALK DON'T SIT WELL WITH ME.
AND I DIDN'T SIGN UP TO TAKE ORDERS FROM NO WHITE BOY.
WHAT'D YOU SAY, PAL?

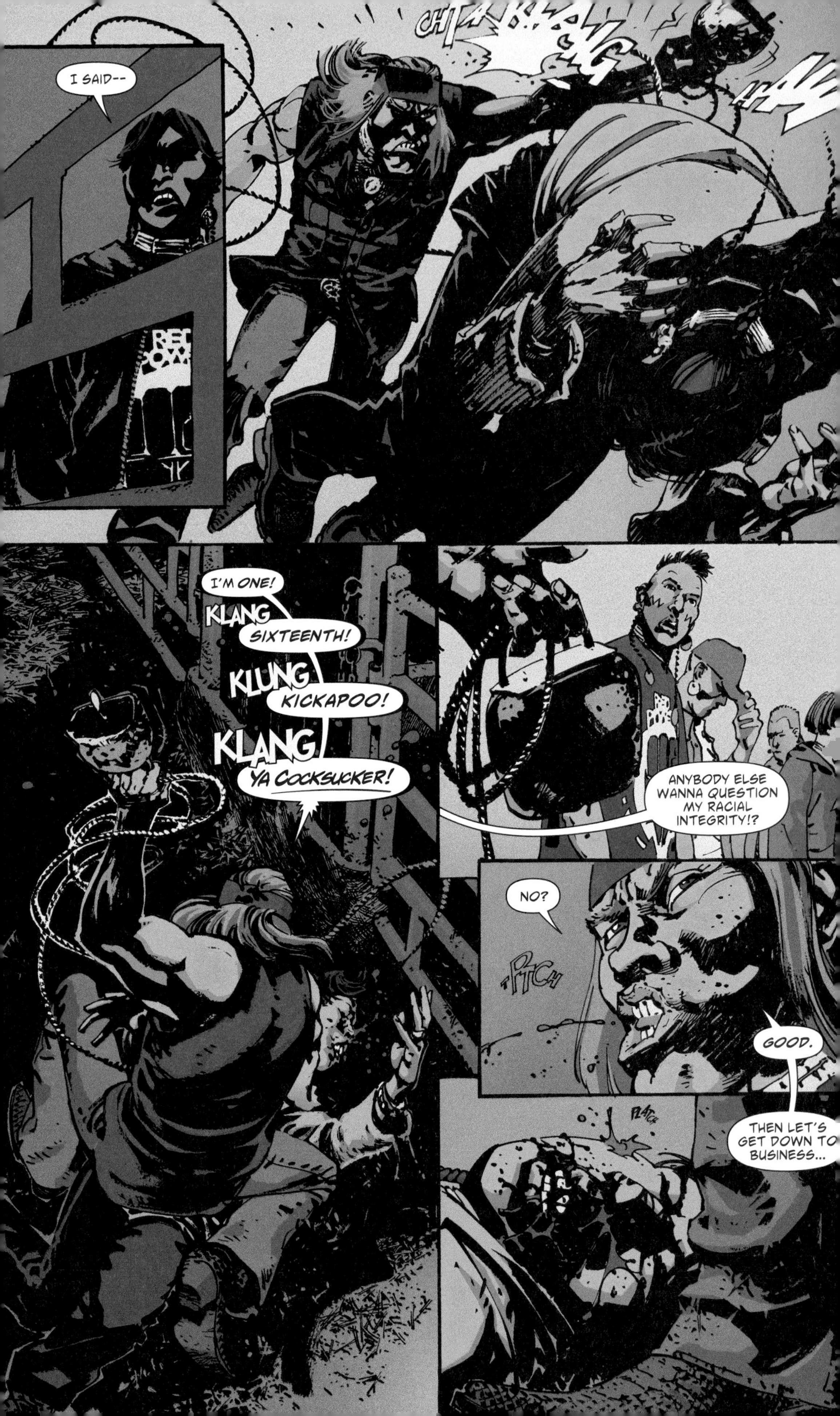
I SAID--
CHTANGWANG
I'M ONE!
KLANG
SIXTEENTH!
KLUNG
KICKAPOO!
KLANG
YA COCKSUCKER!
ANYBODY ELSE WANNA QUESTION MY RACIAL INTEGRITY!?
NO?
TPTCH
GOOD.
THEN LET'S GET DOWN TO BUSINESS...

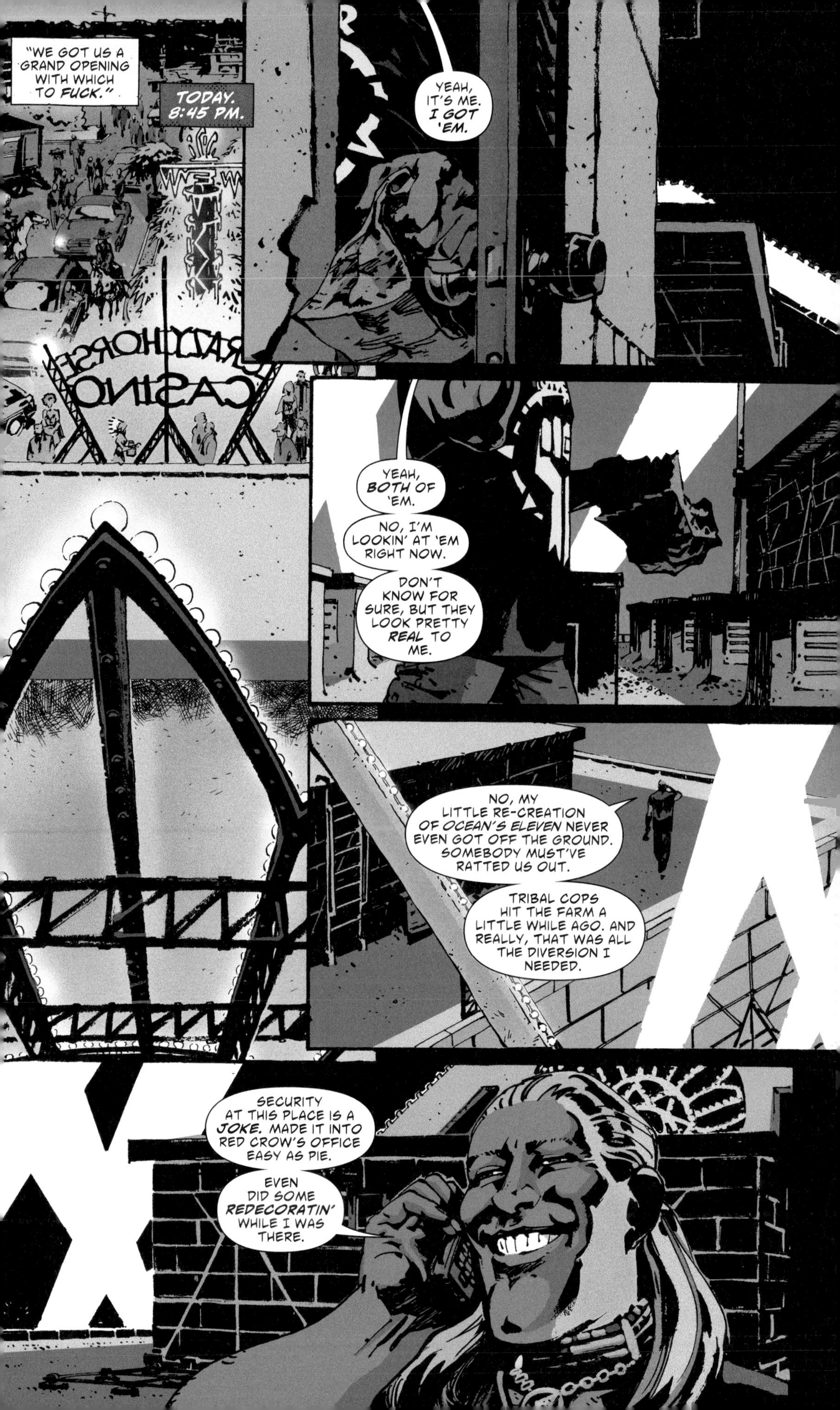
"WE GOT US A GRAND OPENING WITH WHICH TO FUCK."
TODAY. 8:45 PM.
CRAZY HORSE CASINO
YEAH, IT'S ME. I GOT 'EM.
YEAH, BOTH OF 'EM.
NO, I'M LOOKIN' AT 'EM RIGHT NOW.
DON'T KNOW FOR SURE, BUT THEY LOOK PRETTY REAL TO ME.
NO, MY LITTLE RE-CREATION OF OCEAN'S ELEVEN NEVER EVEN GOT OFF THE GROUND. SOMEBODY MUST'VE RATTED US OUT.
TRIBAL COPS HIT THE FARM A LITTLE WHILE AGO. AND REALLY, THAT WAS ALL THE DIVERSION I NEEDED.
SECURITY AT THIS PLACE IS A JOKE. MADE IT INTO RED CROW'S OFFICE EASY AS PIE.
EVEN DID SOME REDECORATIN' WHILE I WAS THERE.

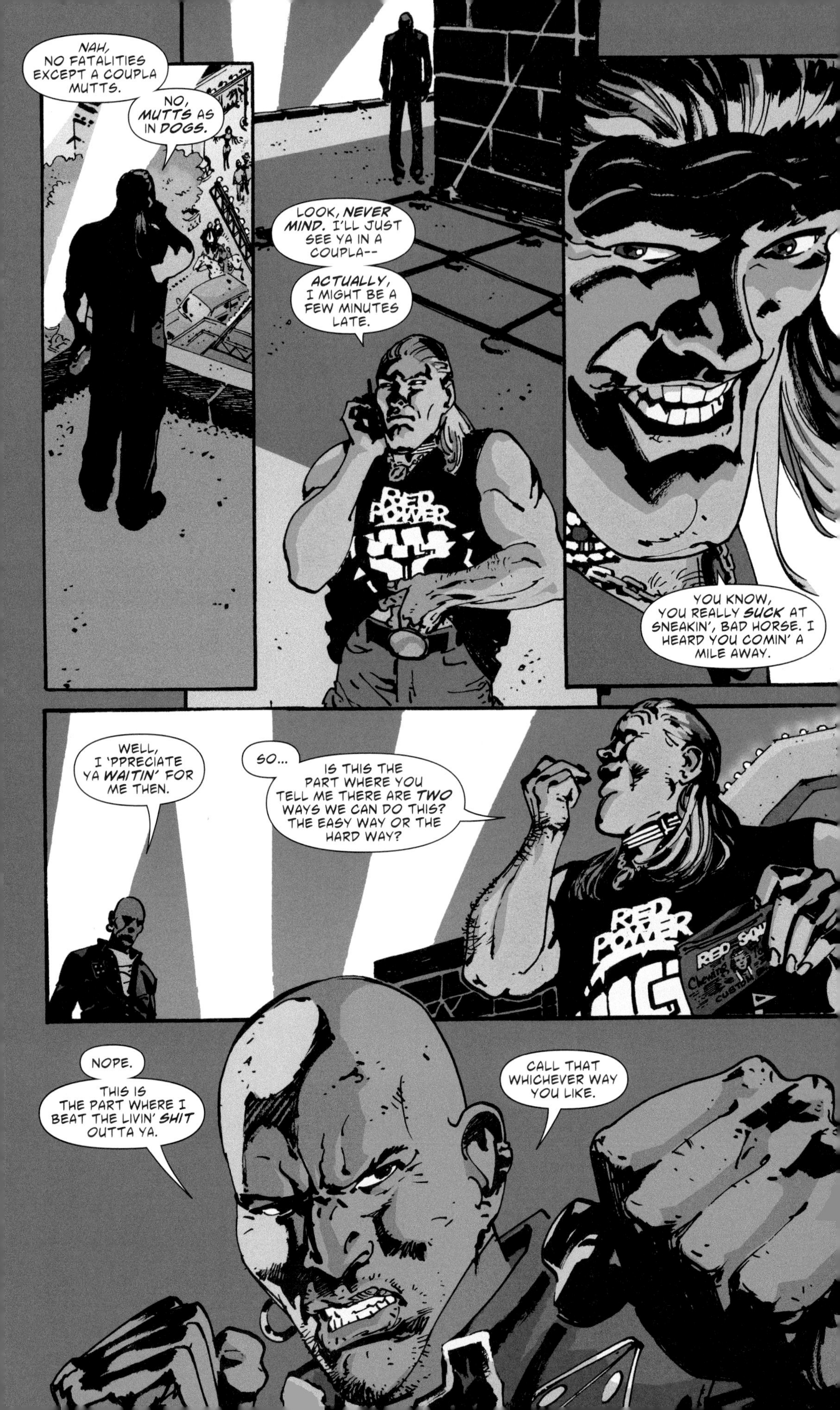
NAH, NO FATALITIES EXCEPT A COUPLA MUTTS.
NO, MUTTS AS IN DOGS.
LOOK, NEVER MIND. I'LL JUST SEE YA IN A COUPLA--
ACTUALLY, I MIGHT BE A FEW MINUTES LATE.
YOU KNOW, YOU REALLY SUCK AT SNEAKIN', BAD HORSE. I HEARD YOU COMIN' A MILE AWAY.
RED POWER
WELL, I 'PPRECIATE YA WAITIN' FOR ME THEN.
SO...
IS THIS THE PART WHERE YOU TELL ME THERE ARE TWO WAYS WE CAN DO THIS? THE EASY WAY OR THE HARD WAY?
RED POWER
NOPE.
THIS IS THE PART WHERE I BEAT THE LIVIN' SHIT OUTTA YA.
CALL THAT WHICHEVER WAY YOU LIKE.

OU'VE BLOWN OUT
UR *KNEE* BEFORE,
HAVEN'T YOU?

YEARS AGO.
FOOTBALL, I'D
GUESS.

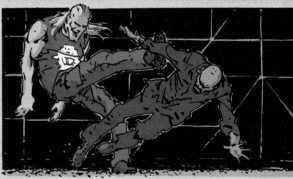

WHERE'D YOU
LEARN KARATE? A
CORRESPONDENCE
COURSE?

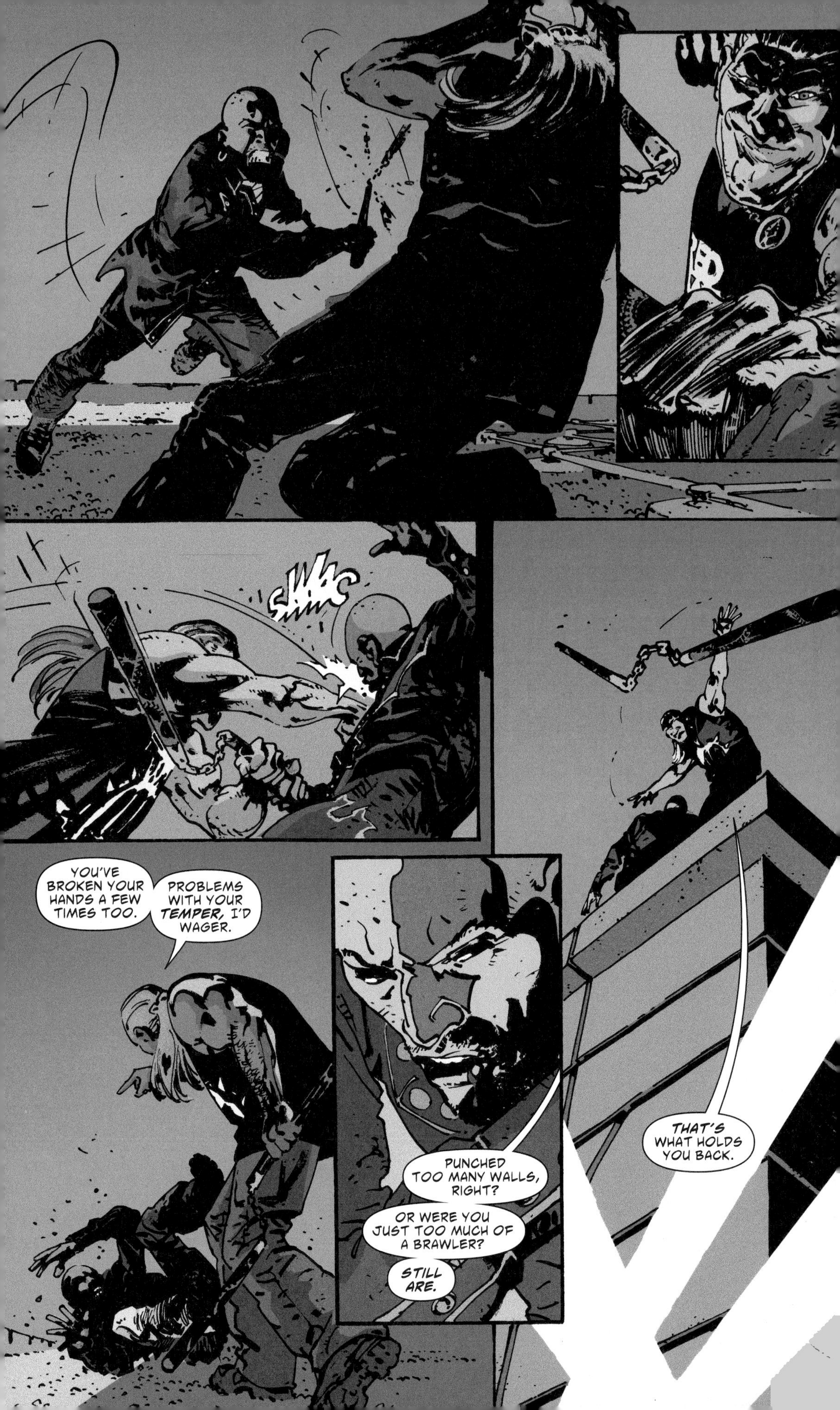
SHHAC
YOU'VE BROKEN YOUR HANDS A FEW TIMES TOO.
PROBLEMS WITH YOUR *TEMPER*, I'D WAGER.
PUNCHED TOO MANY WALLS, RIGHT?
OR WERE YOU JUST TOO MUCH OF A BRAWLER?
STILL ARE.
THAT'S WHAT HOLDS YOU BACK.

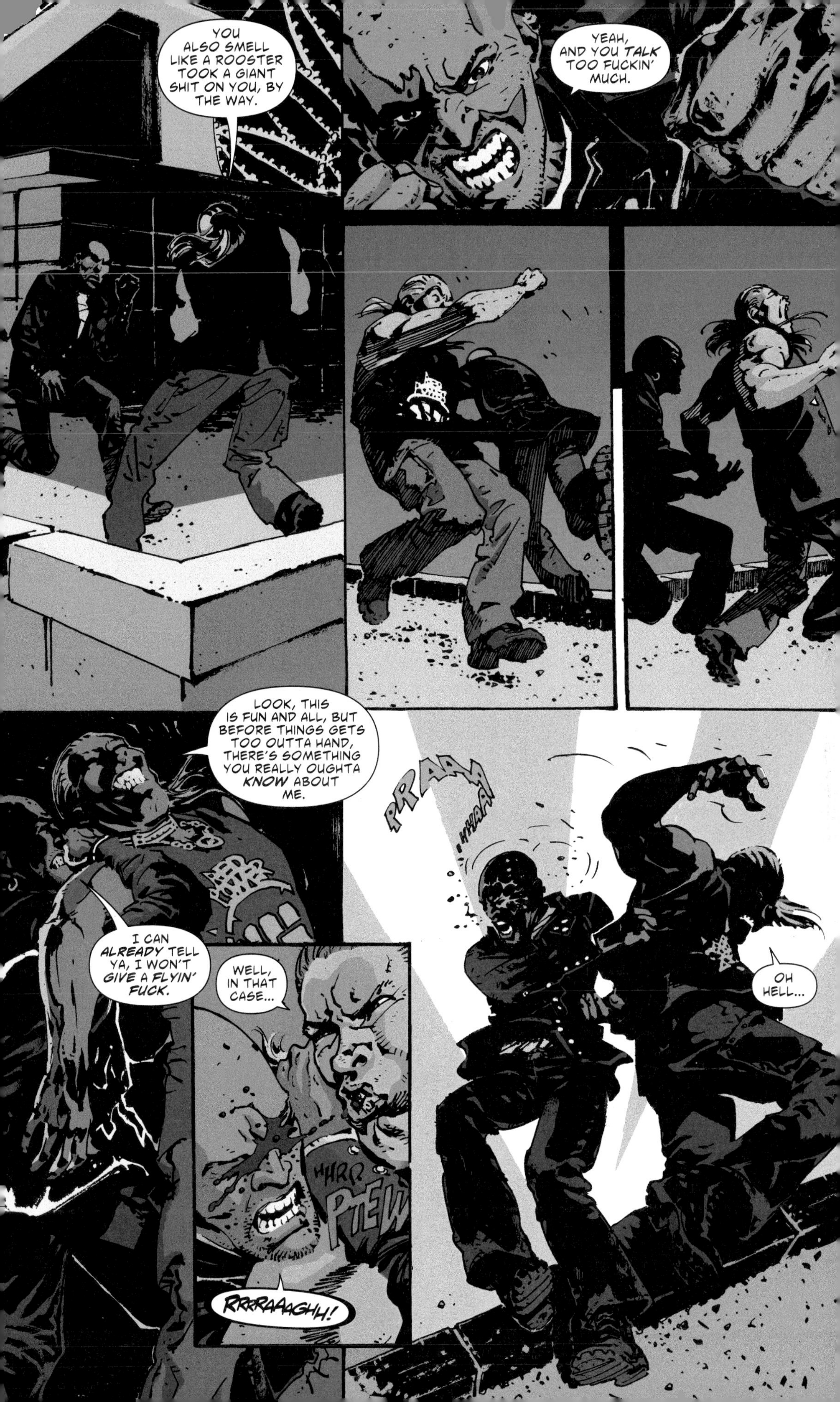

YOU ALSO SMELL LIKE A ROOSTER TOOK A GIANT SHIT ON YOU, BY THE WAY.
YEAH, AND YOU TALK TOO FUCKIN' MUCH.
LOOK, THIS IS FUN AND ALL, BUT BEFORE THINGS GETS TOO OUTTA HAND, THERE'S SOMETHING YOU REALLY OUGHTA KNOW ABOUT ME.
I CAN ALREADY TELL YA, I WON'T GIVE A FLYIN' FUCK.
WELL, IN THAT CASE...
PTEW
RRRRAAAGHH!
RRAAAA
OH HELL...

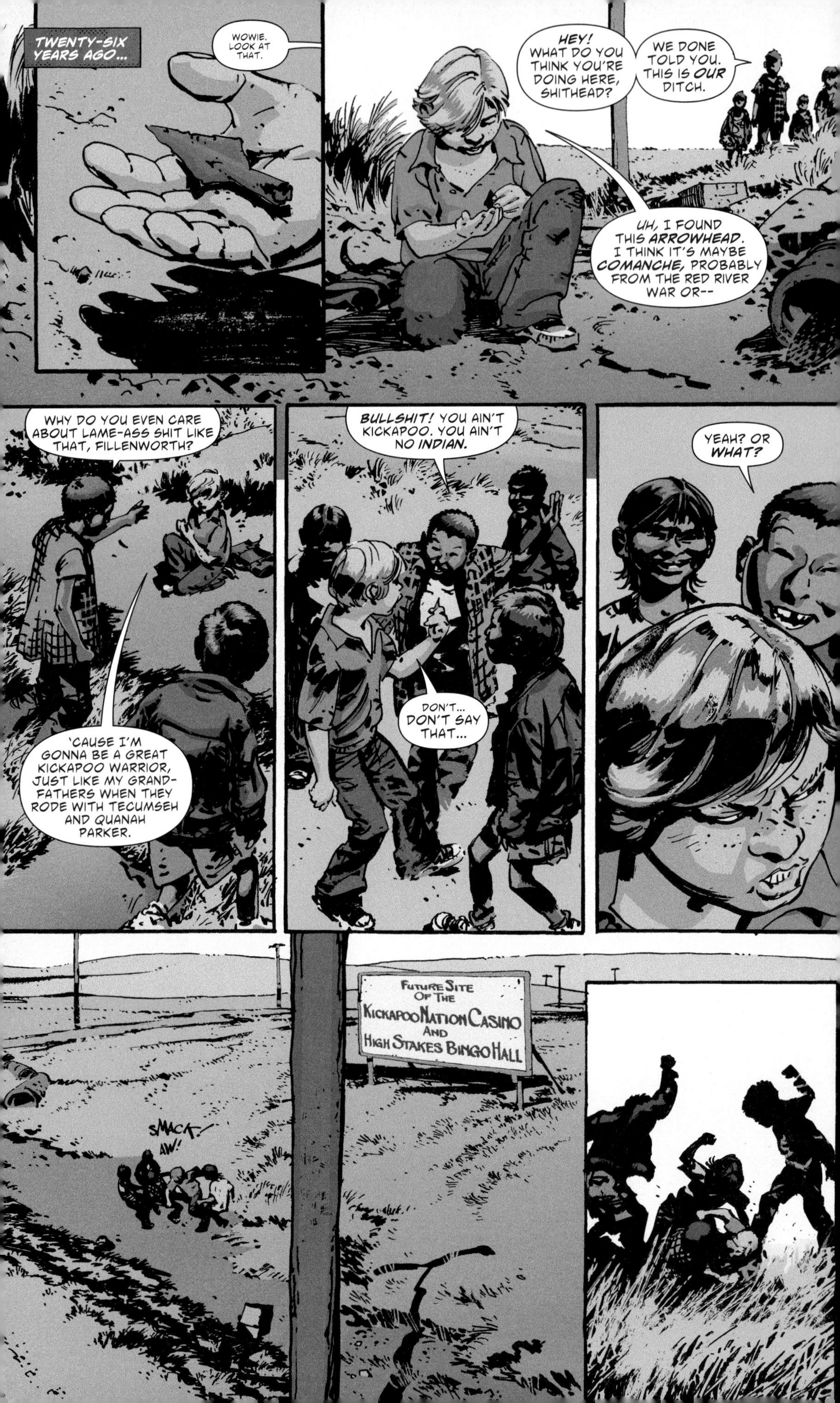
TWENTY-SIX YEARS AGO...
WOWIE. LOOK AT THAT.
HEY! WHAT DO YOU THINK YOU'RE DOING HERE, SHITHEAD?
WE DONE TOLD YOU. THIS IS OUR DITCH.
UH, I FOUND THIS ARROWHEAD. I THINK IT'S MAYBE COMANCHE, PROBABLY FROM THE RED RIVER WAR OR--
WHY DO YOU EVEN CARE ABOUT LAME-ASS SHIT LIKE THAT, FILLENWORTH?
'CAUSE I'M GONNA BE A GREAT KICKAPOO WARRIOR, JUST LIKE MY GRANDFATHERS WHEN THEY RODE WITH TECUMSEH AND QUANAH PARKER.
BULLSHIT! YOU AIN'T KICKAPOO. YOU AIN'T NO INDIAN.
DON'T... DON'T SAY THAT...
YEAH? OR WHAT?
FUTURE SITE OF THE KICKAPOO NATION CASINO AND HIGH STAKES BINGO HALL
SMACK!
AW!

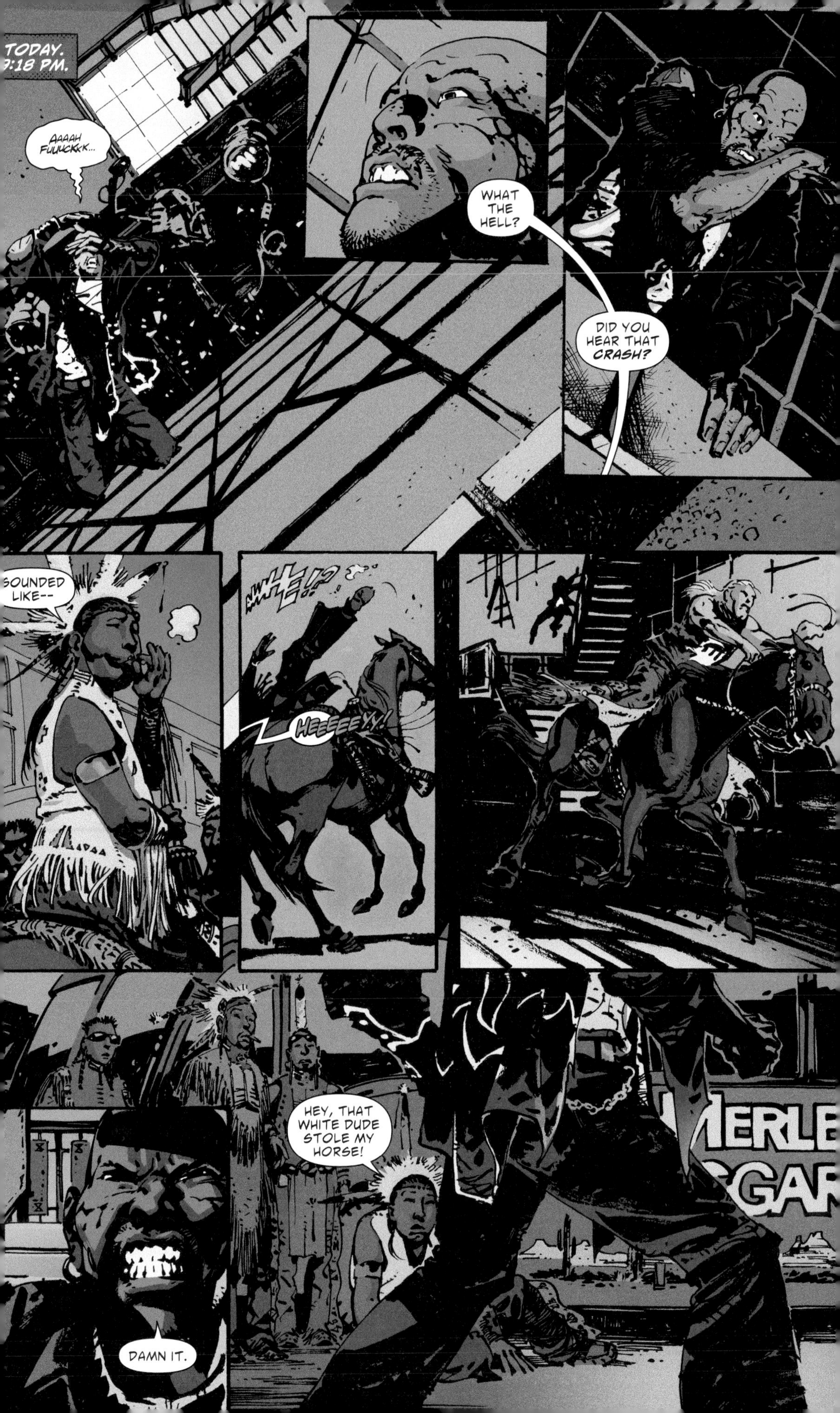
TODAY.
7:18 PM.
AAAAH FUUUCKKK...
WHAT THE HELL?
DID YOU HEAR THAT CRASH?
SOUNDED LIKE--
HEEEEEYY!
HEY, THAT WHITE DUDE STOLE MY HORSE!
DAMN IT.
MERLE
GAR

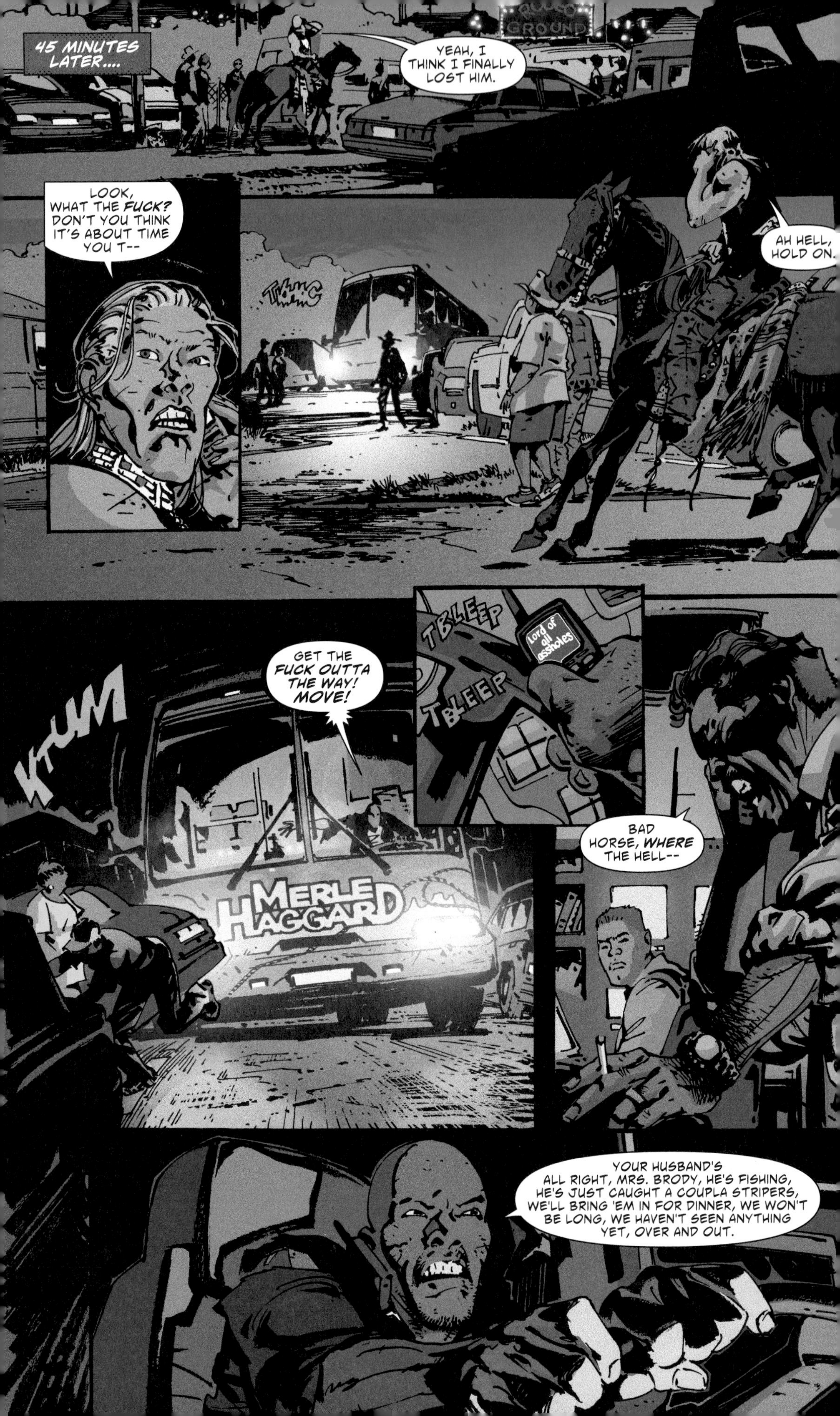
45 MINUTES LATER....
YEAH, I THINK I FINALLY LOST HIM.
LOOK, WHAT THE FUCK? DON'T YOU THINK IT'S ABOUT TIME YOU T--
TWANC
AH HELL, HOLD ON.
KTUM
GET THE FUCK OUTTA THE WAY! MOVE!
MERLE HAGGARD
TBLEEP
TBLEEP
Lord of all assholes
BAD HORSE, WHERE THE HELL--
YOUR HUSBAND'S ALL RIGHT, MRS. BRODY, HE'S FISHING, HE'S JUST CAUGHT A COUPLA STRIPERS, WE'LL BRING 'EM IN FOR DINNER, WE WON'T BE LONG, WE HAVEN'T SEEN ANYTHING YET, OVER AND OUT.

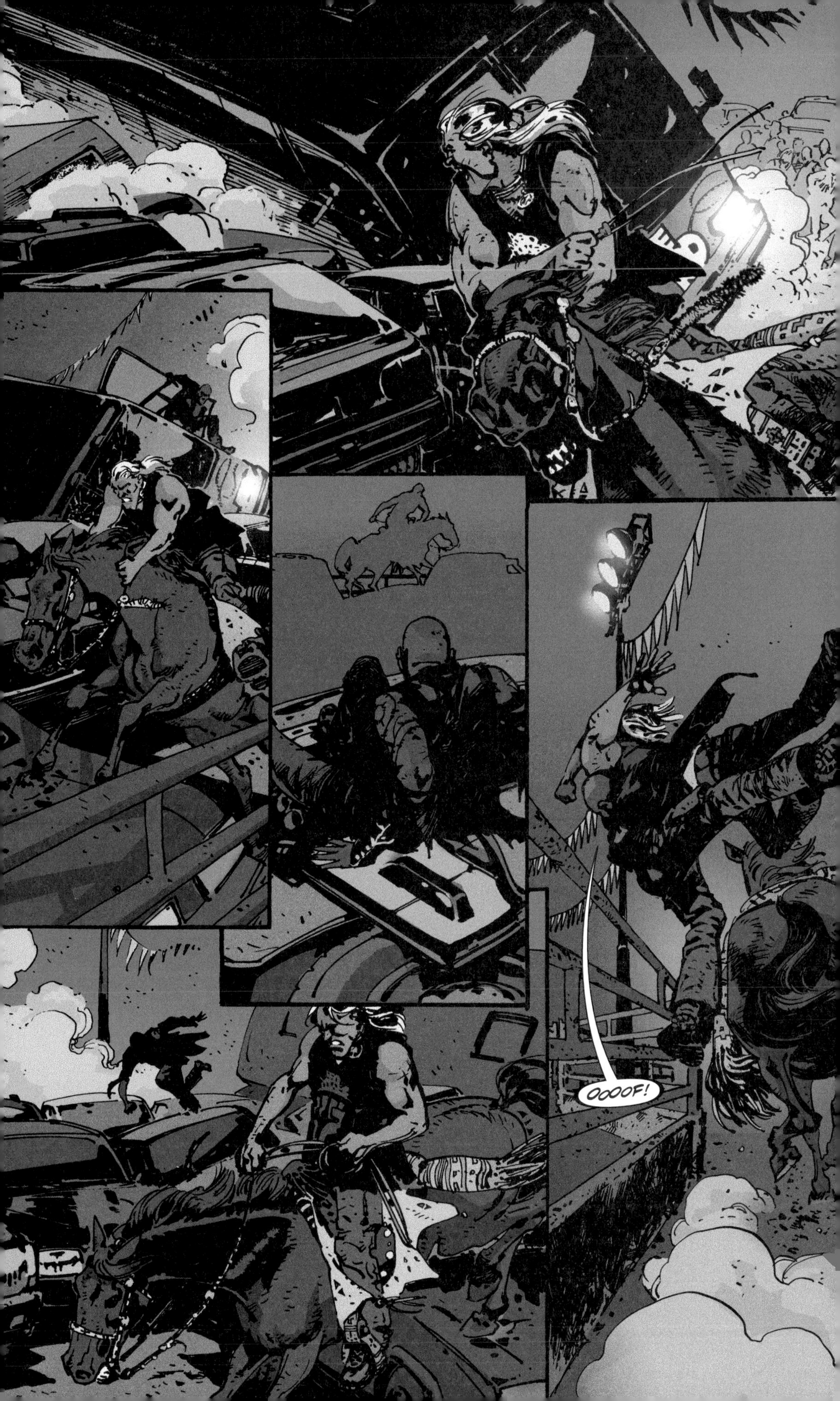
OOOOF!

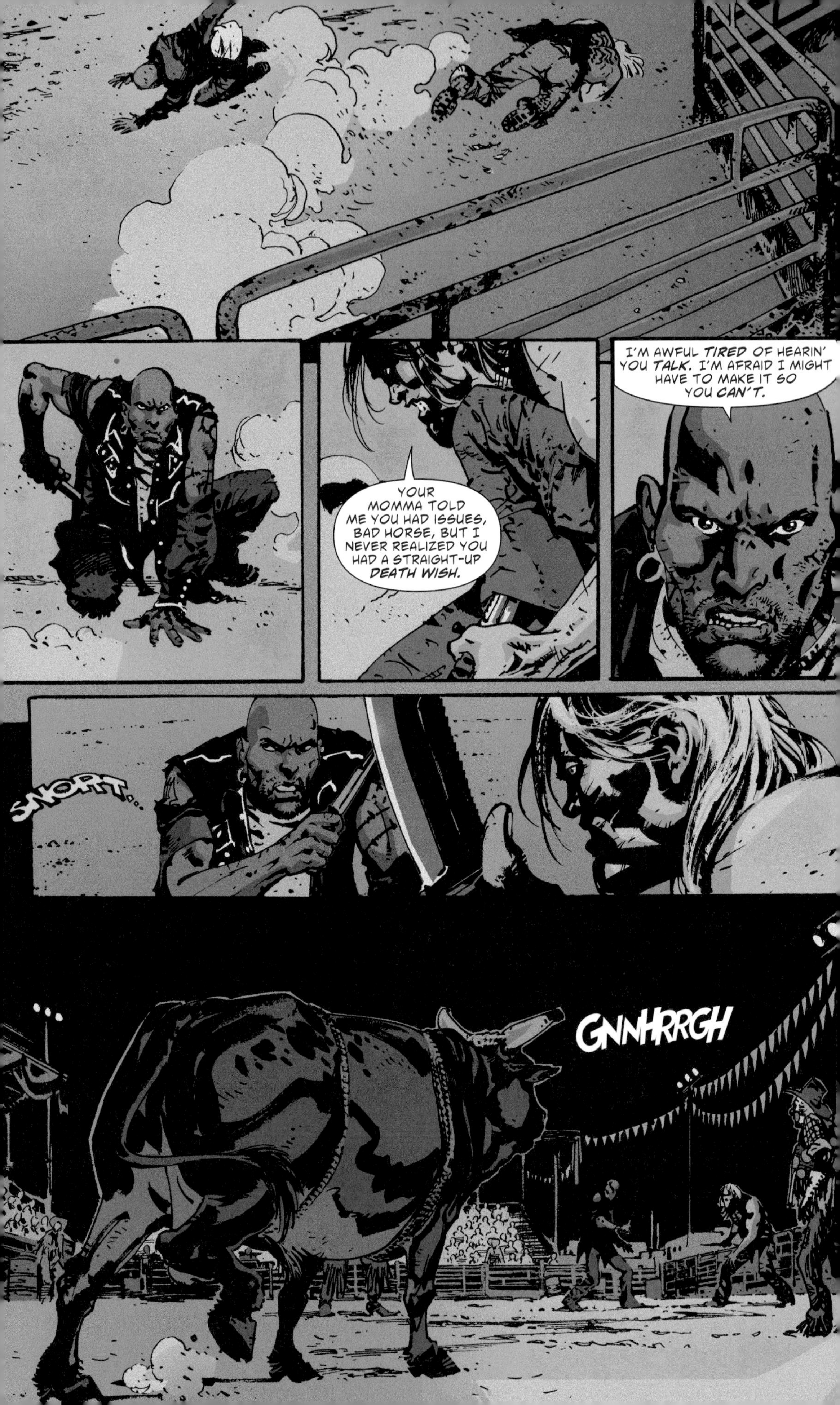
YOUR MOMMA TOLD ME YOU HAD ISSUES, BAD HORSE, BUT I NEVER REALIZED YOU HAD A STRAIGHT-UP DEATH WISH.
I'M AWFUL TIRED OF HEARIN' YOU TALK. I'M AFRAID I MIGHT HAVE TO MAKE IT SO YOU CAN'T.
SNORT...
GNNHRRGH

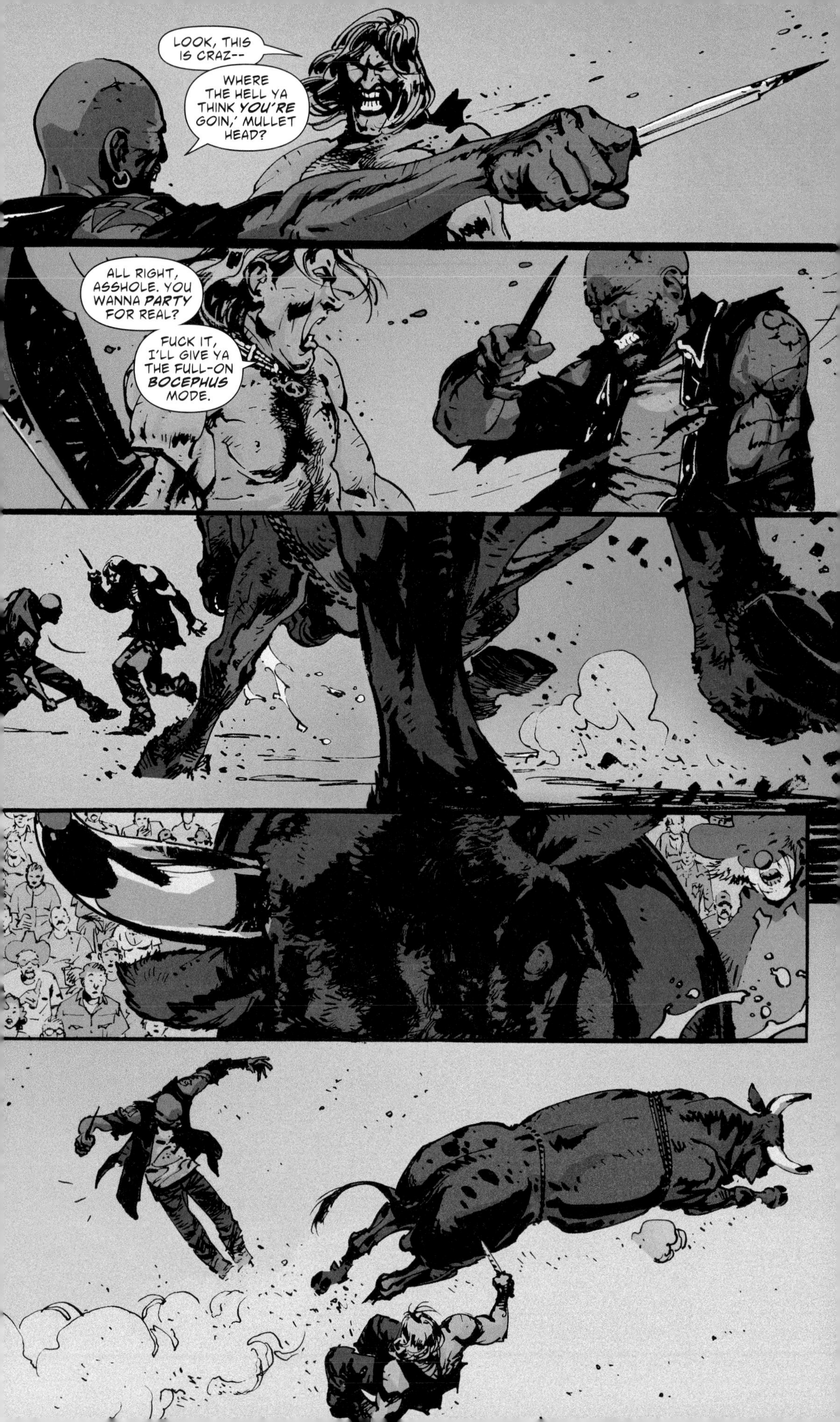
LOOK, THIS IS CRAZ--
WHERE THE HELL YA THINK YOU'RE GOIN,' MULLET HEAD?
ALL RIGHT, ASSHOLE. YOU WANNA PARTY FOR REAL?
FUCK IT, I'LL GIVE YA THE FULL-ON BOCEPHUS MODE.

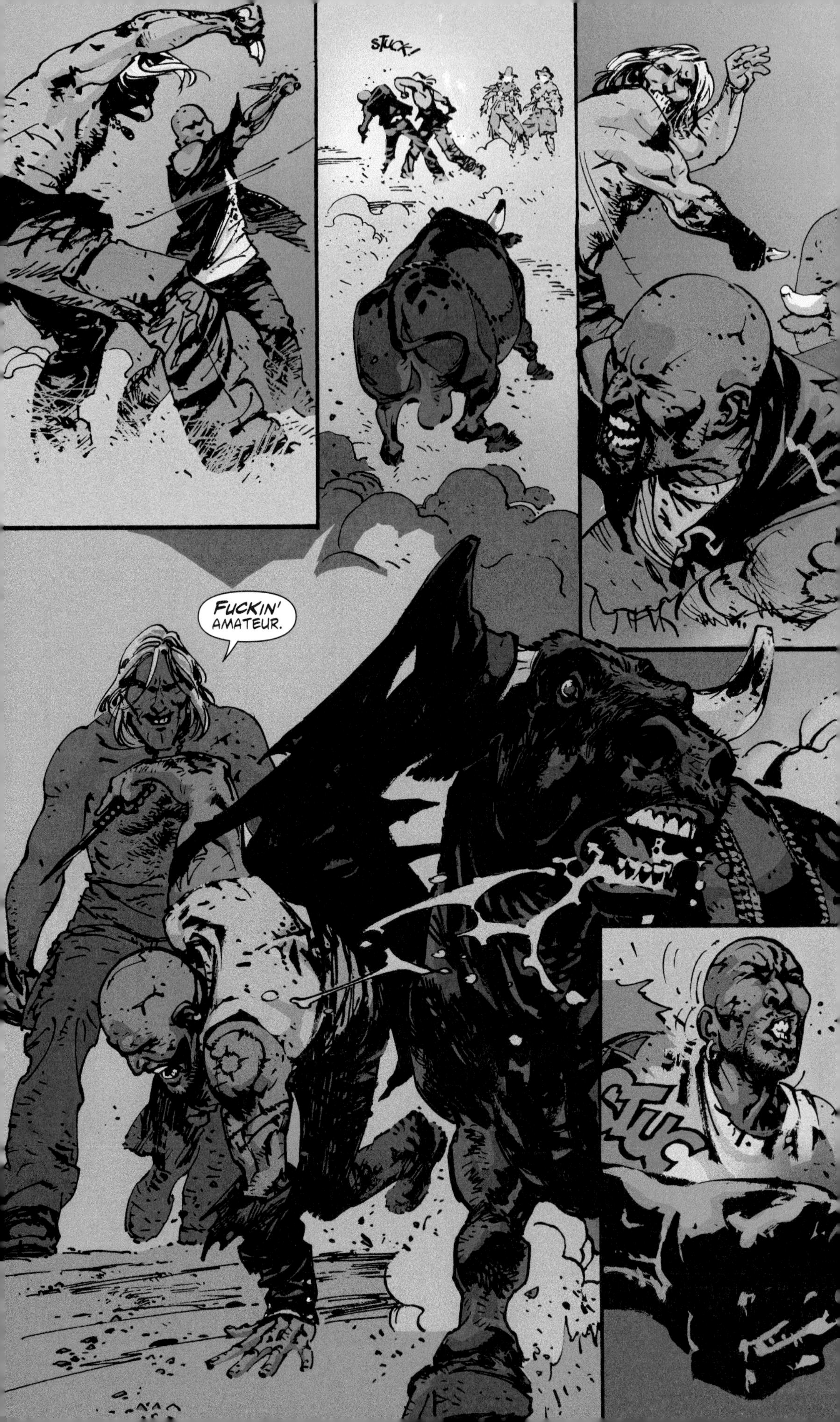
STUCK!
FUCKIN' AMATEUR.

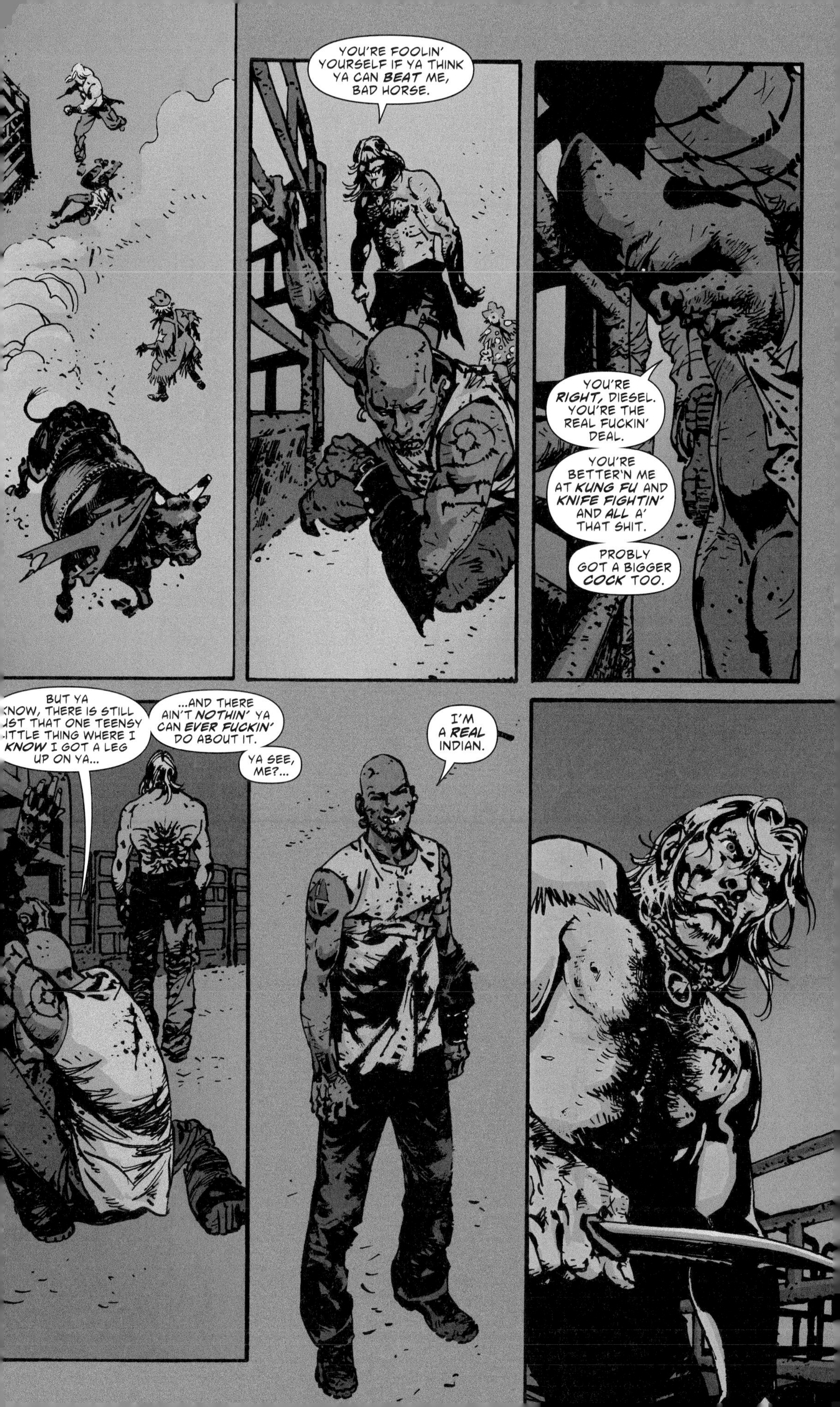
YOU'RE FOOLIN' YOURSELF IF YA THINK YA CAN BEAT ME, BAD HORSE.
YOU'RE RIGHT, DIESEL. YOU'RE THE REAL FUCKIN' DEAL.
YOU'RE BETTER'N ME AT KUNG FU AND KNIFE FIGHTIN' AND ALL A' THAT SHIT.
PROBLY GOT A BIGGER COCK TOO.
BUT YA KNOW, THERE IS STILL ST THAT ONE TEENSY ITTLE THING WHERE I KNOW I GOT A LEG UP ON YA...
...AND THERE AIN'T NOTHIN' YA CAN EVER FUCKIN' DO ABOUT IT.
YA SEE, ME?...
I'M A REAL INDIAN.

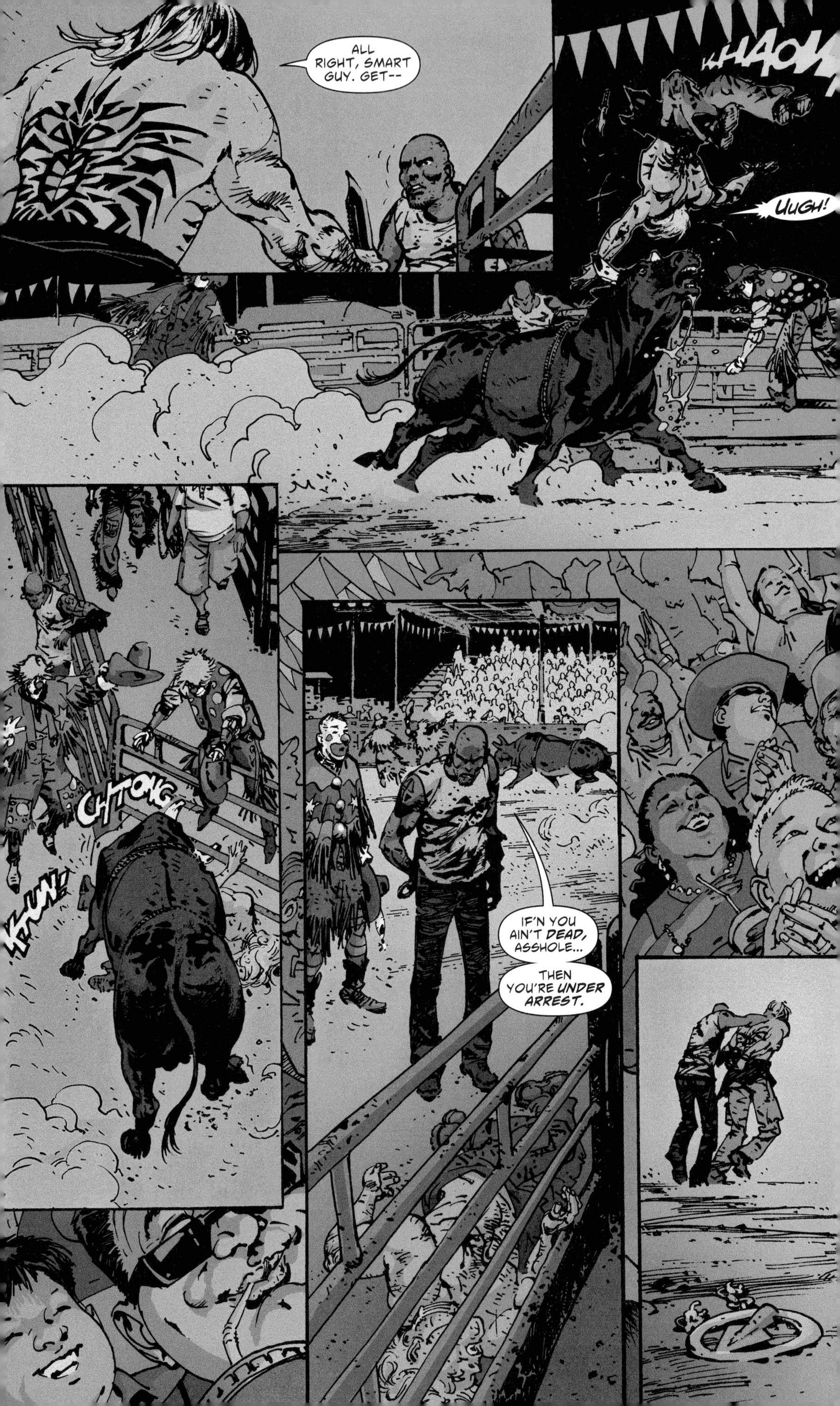
ALL RIGHT, SMART GUY. GET--
KHAOW
UUGH!
CHTONG
KRUN!
IF'N YOU AIN'T DEAD, ASSHOLE...
THEN YOU'RE UNDER ARREST.

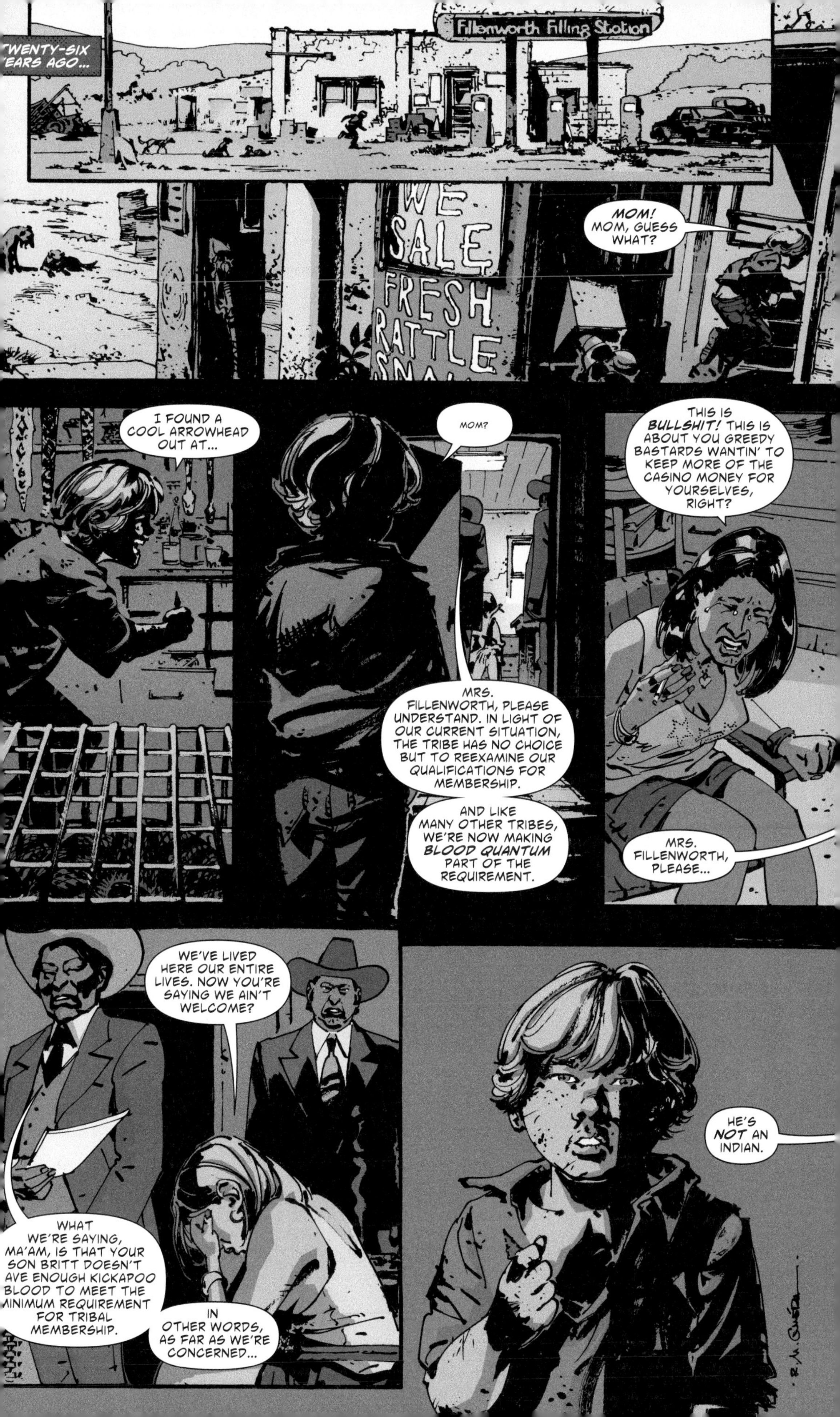

TWENTY-SIX YEARS AGO...
Fillenworth Filling Station
WE SALE FRESH RATTLE SNA...
MOM! MOM, GUESS WHAT?
I FOUND A COOL ARROWHEAD OUT AT...
MOM?
MRS. FILLENWORTH, PLEASE UNDERSTAND. IN LIGHT OF OUR CURRENT SITUATION, THE TRIBE HAS NO CHOICE BUT TO REEXAMINE OUR QUALIFICATIONS FOR MEMBERSHIP.
AND LIKE MANY OTHER TRIBES, WE'RE NOW MAKING BLOOD QUANTUM PART OF THE REQUIREMENT.
THIS IS BULLSHIT! THIS IS ABOUT YOU GREEDY BASTARDS WANTIN' TO KEEP MORE OF THE CASINO MONEY FOR YOURSELVES, RIGHT?
MRS. FILLENWORTH, PLEASE...
WE'VE LIVED HERE OUR ENTIRE LIVES. NOW YOU'RE SAYING WE AIN'T WELCOME?
WHAT WE'RE SAYING, MA'AM, IS THAT YOUR SON BRITT DOESN'T HAVE ENOUGH KICKAPOO BLOOD TO MEET THE MINIMUM REQUIREMENT FOR TRIBAL MEMBERSHIP.
IN OTHER WORDS, AS FAR AS WE'RE CONCERNED...
HE'S NOT AN INDIAN.

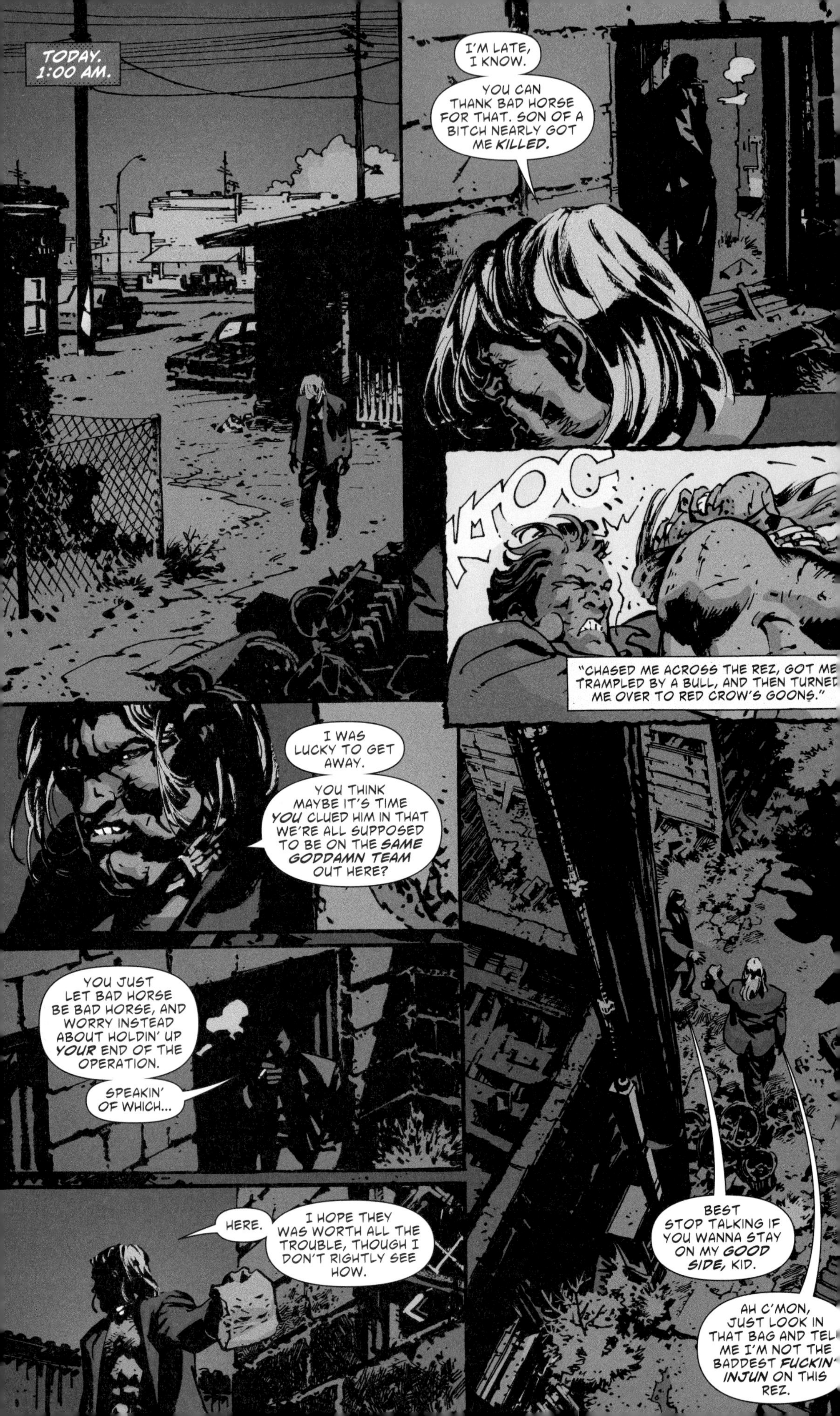
TODAY. 1:00 AM.
I'M LATE, I KNOW.
YOU CAN THANK BAD HORSE FOR THAT. SON OF A BITCH NEARLY GOT ME KILLED.
KTOOG
"CHASED ME ACROSS THE REZ, GOT ME TRAMPLED BY A BULL, AND THEN TURNED ME OVER TO RED CROW'S GOONS."
I WAS LUCKY TO GET AWAY.
YOU THINK MAYBE IT'S TIME YOU CLUED HIM IN THAT WE'RE ALL SUPPOSED TO BE ON THE SAME GODDAMN TEAM OUT HERE?
YOU JUST LET BAD HORSE BE BAD HORSE, AND WORRY INSTEAD ABOUT HOLDIN' UP YOUR END OF THE OPERATION.
SPEAKIN' OF WHICH...
HERE.
I HOPE THEY WAS WORTH ALL THE TROUBLE, THOUGH I DON'T RIGHTLY SEE HOW.
BEST STOP TALKING IF YOU WANNA STAY ON MY GOOD SIDE, KID.
AH C'MON, JUST LOOK IN THAT BAG AND TELL ME I'M NOT THE BADDEST FUCKIN' INJUN ON THIS REZ.

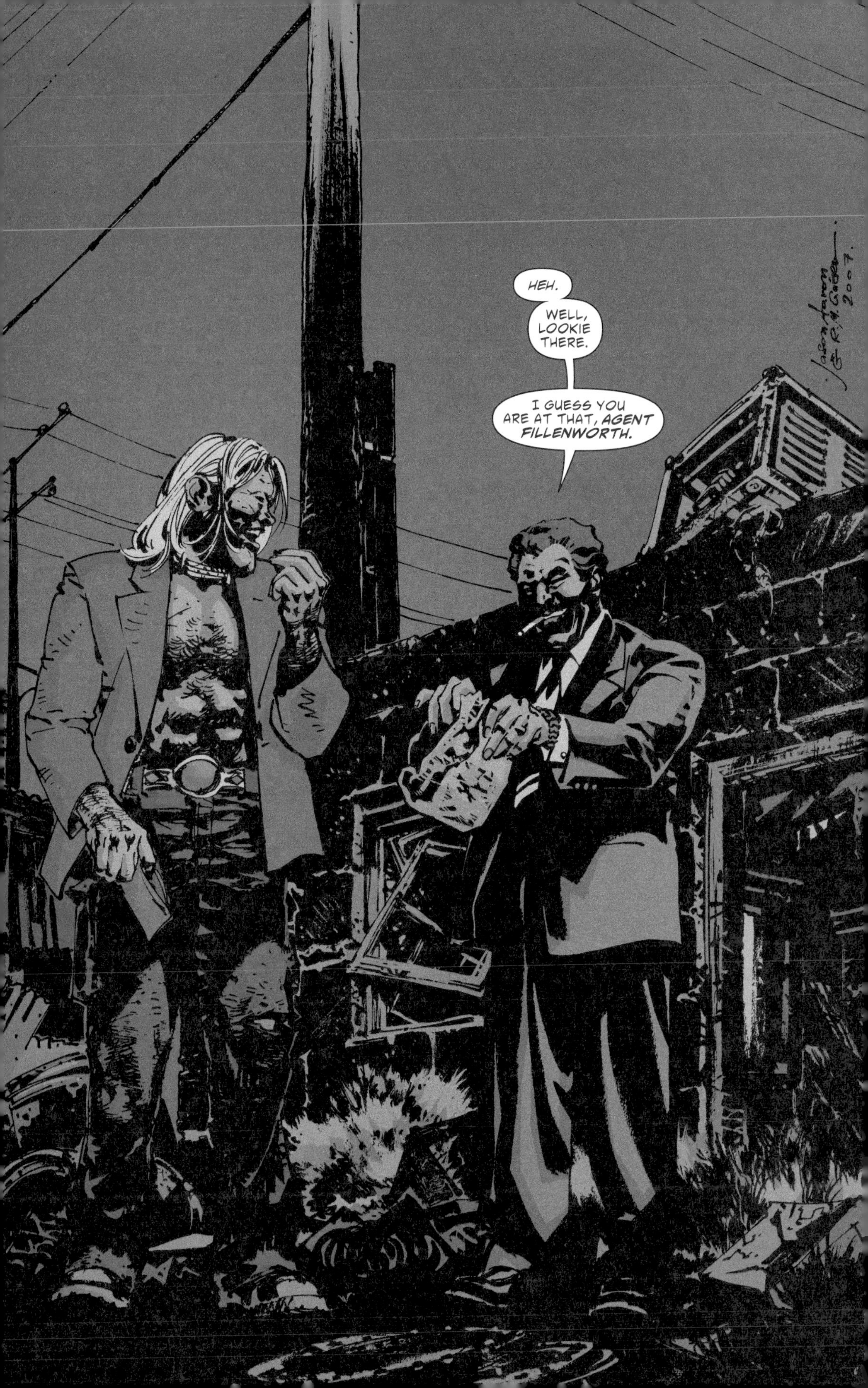
HEH.
WELL, LOOKIE THERE.
I GUESS YOU ARE AT THAT, AGENT FILLENWORTH.

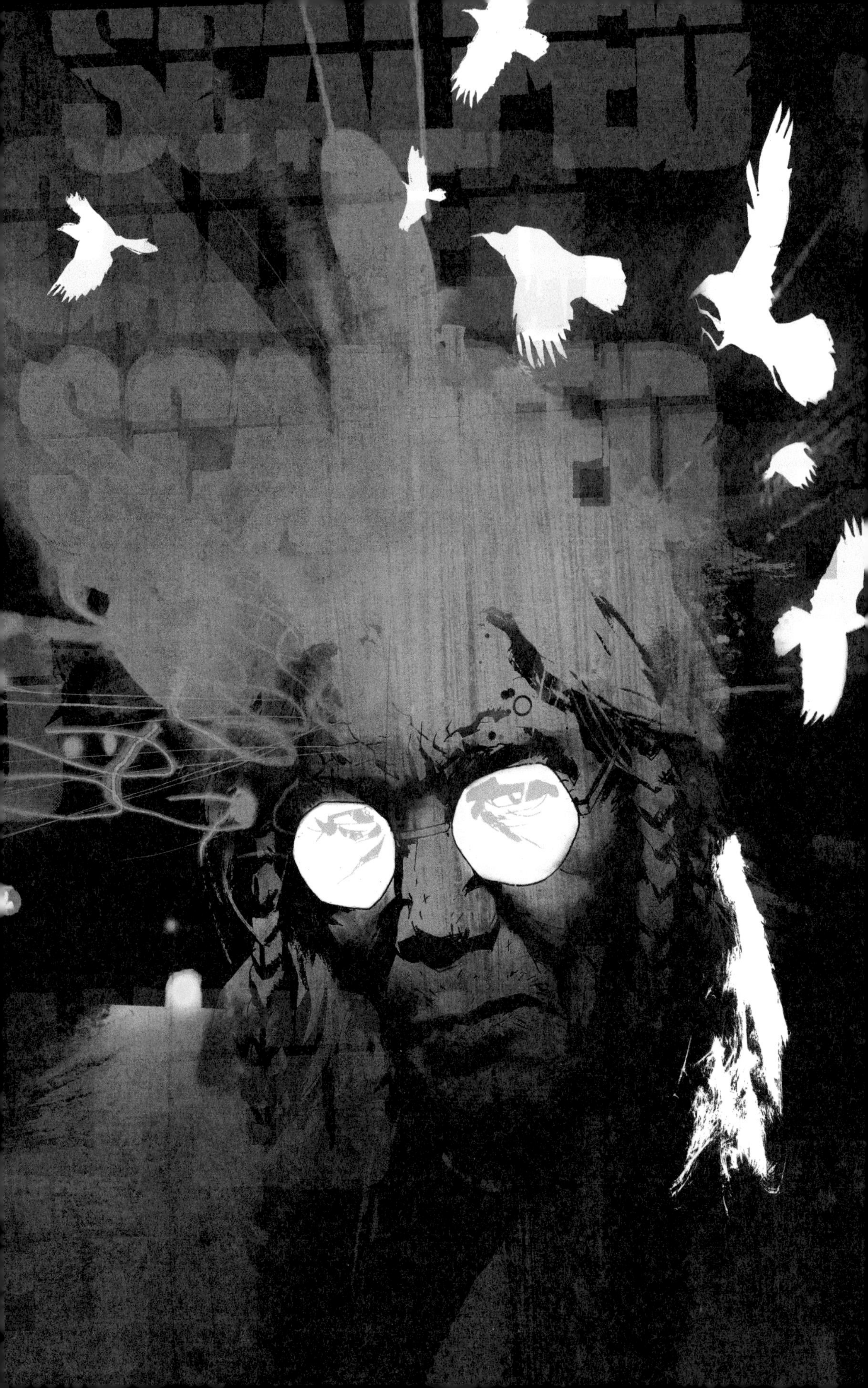

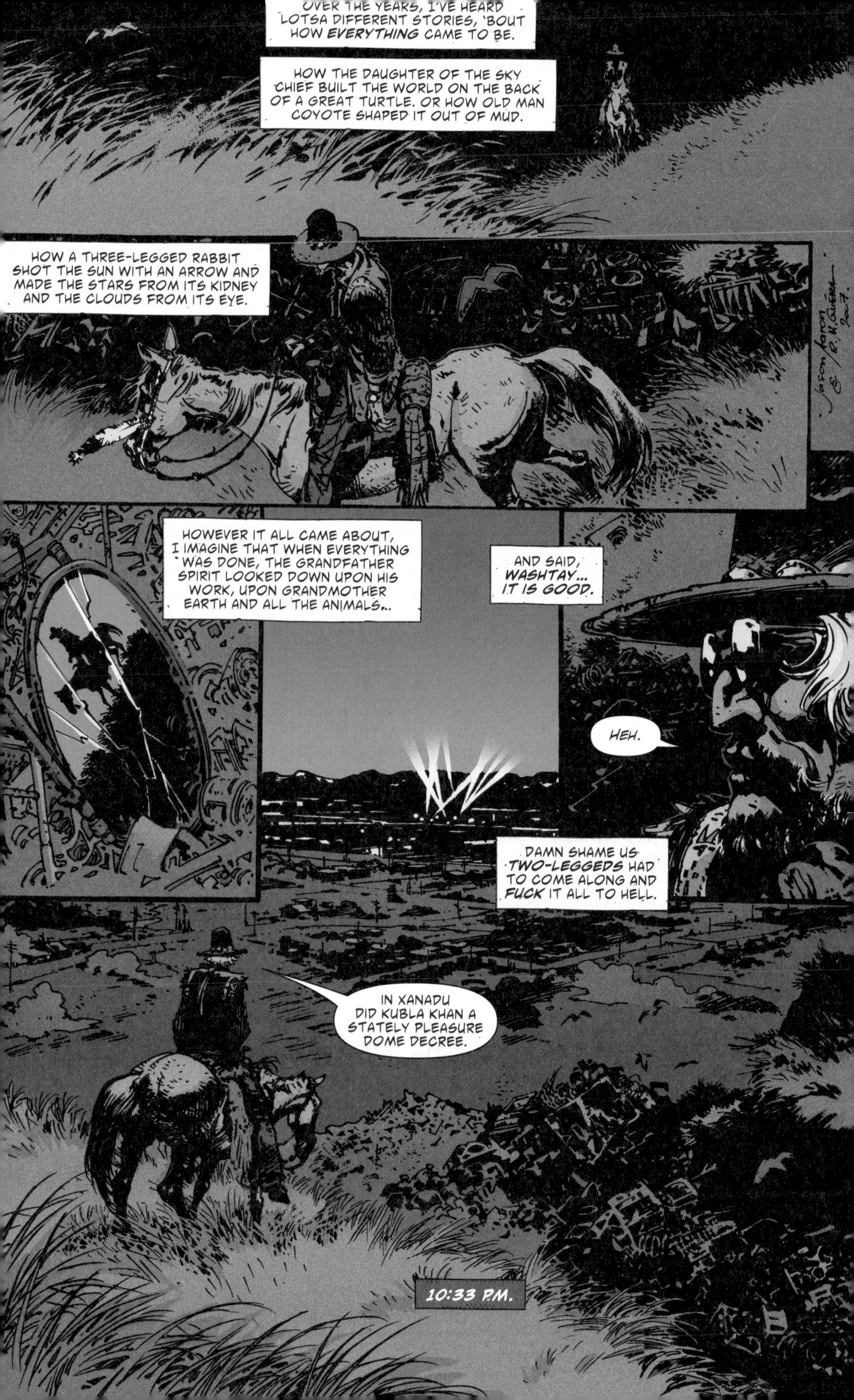
OVER THE YEARS, I'VE HEARD LOTSA DIFFERENT STORIES, 'BOUT HOW EVERYTHING CAME TO BE.
HOW THE DAUGHTER OF THE SKY CHIEF BUILT THE WORLD ON THE BACK OF A GREAT TURTLE. OR HOW OLD MAN COYOTE SHAPED IT OUT OF MUD.
HOW A THREE-LEGGED RABBIT SHOT THE SUN WITH AN ARROW AND MADE THE STARS FROM ITS KIDNEY AND THE CLOUDS FROM ITS EYE.
HOWEVER IT ALL CAME ABOUT, I IMAGINE THAT WHEN EVERYTHING WAS DONE, THE GRANDFATHER SPIRIT LOOKED DOWN UPON HIS WORK, UPON GRANDMOTHER EARTH AND ALL THE ANIMALS...
AND SAID, WASHTAY... IT IS GOOD.
HEH.
DAMN SHAME US TWO-LEGGEDS HAD TO COME ALONG AND FUCK IT ALL TO HELL.
IN XANADU DID KUBLA KHAN A STATELY PLEASURE DOME DECREE.
10:33 P.M.

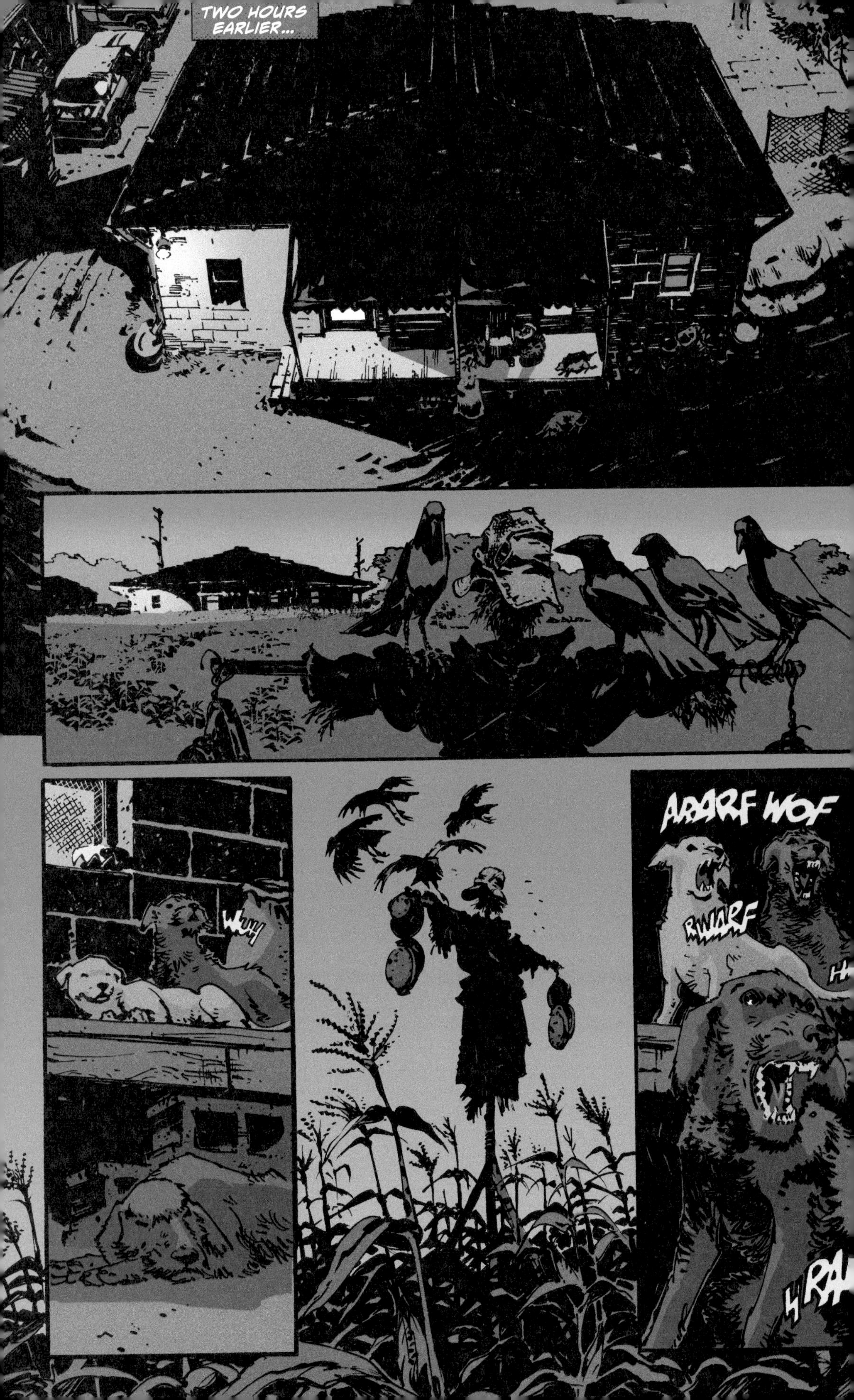
TWO HOURS
EARLIER...
WUH
ARARF WOF
RWARF

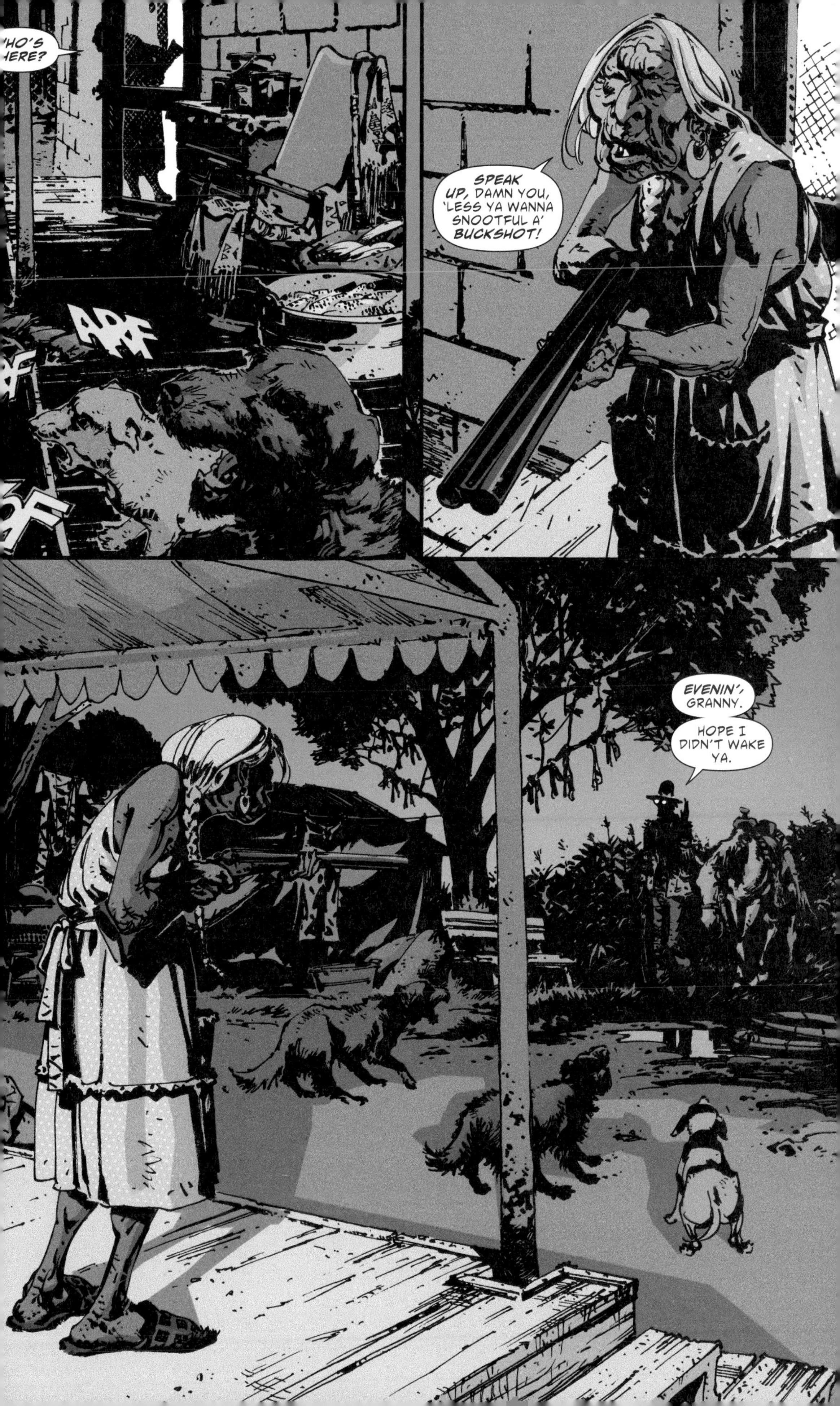

'HO'S
HERE?
ARF
SPEAK UP, DAMN YOU, 'LESS YA WANNA SNOOTFUL A' BUCKSHOT!
EVENIN', GRANNY.
HOPE I DIDN'T WAKE YA.

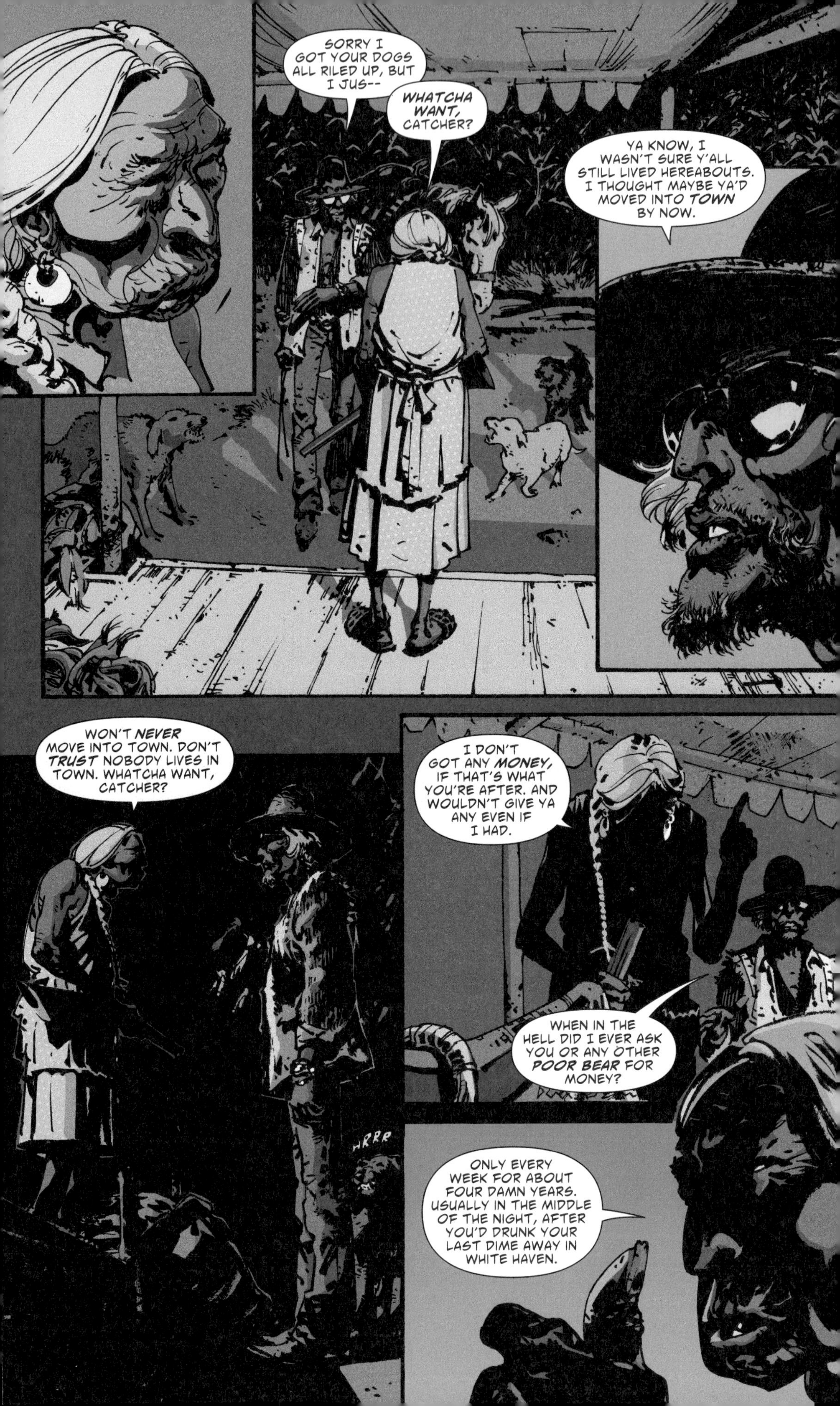
SORRY I GOT YOUR DOGS ALL RILED UP, BUT I JUS--
WHATCHA WANT, CATCHER?
YA KNOW, I WASN'T SURE Y'ALL STILL LIVED HEREABOUTS. I THOUGHT MAYBE YA'D MOVED INTO TOWN BY NOW.
WON'T NEVER MOVE INTO TOWN. DON'T TRUST NOBODY LIVES IN TOWN. WHATCHA WANT, CATCHER?
HRRR
I DON'T GOT ANY MONEY, IF THAT'S WHAT YOU'RE AFTER. AND WOULDN'T GIVE YA ANY EVEN IF I HAD.
WHEN IN THE HELL DID I EVER ASK YOU OR ANY OTHER POOR BEAR FOR MONEY?
ONLY EVERY WEEK FOR ABOUT FOUR DAMN YEARS. USUALLY IN THE MIDDLE OF THE NIGHT, AFTER YOU'D DRUNK YOUR LAST DIME AWAY IN WHITE HAVEN.

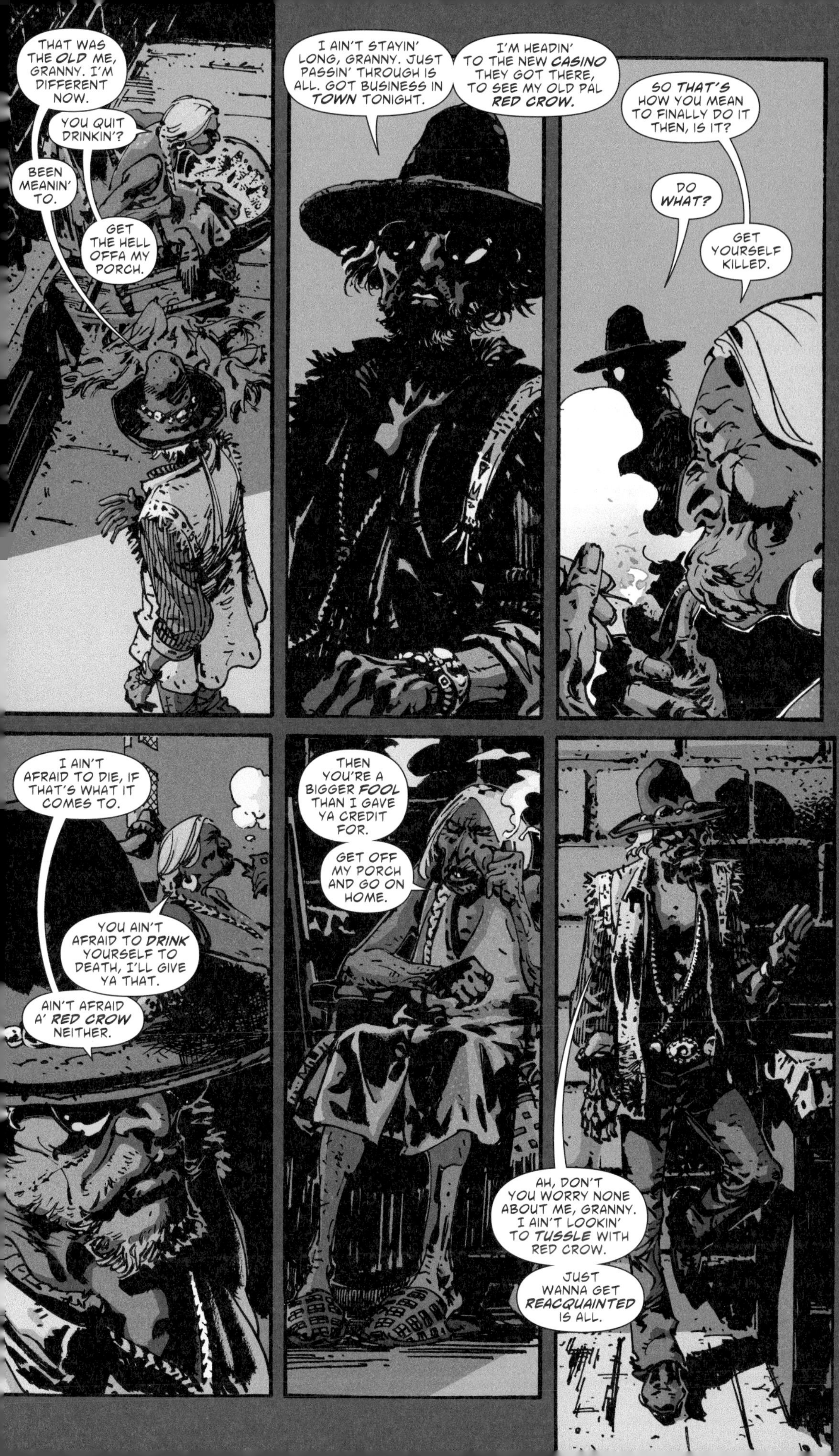
THAT WAS THE OLD ME, GRANNY. I'M DIFFERENT NOW.
YOU QUIT DRINKIN'?
BEEN MEANIN' TO.
GET THE HELL OFFA MY PORCH.
I AIN'T STAYIN' LONG, GRANNY. JUST PASSIN' THROUGH IS ALL. GOT BUSINESS IN TOWN TONIGHT.
I'M HEADIN' TO THE NEW CASINO THEY GOT THERE, TO SEE MY OLD PAL RED CROW.
SO THAT'S HOW YOU MEAN TO FINALLY DO IT THEN, IS IT?
DO WHAT?
GET YOURSELF KILLED.
I AIN'T AFRAID TO DIE, IF THAT'S WHAT IT COMES TO.
YOU AIN'T AFRAID TO DRINK YOURSELF TO DEATH, I'LL GIVE YA THAT.
AIN'T AFRAID A' RED CROW NEITHER.
THEN YOU'RE A BIGGER FOOL THAN I GAVE YA CREDIT FOR.
GET OFF MY PORCH AND GO ON HOME.
AH, DON'T YOU WORRY NONE ABOUT ME, GRANNY. I AIN'T LOOKIN' TO TUSSLE WITH RED CROW.
JUST WANNA GET REACQUAINTED IS ALL.

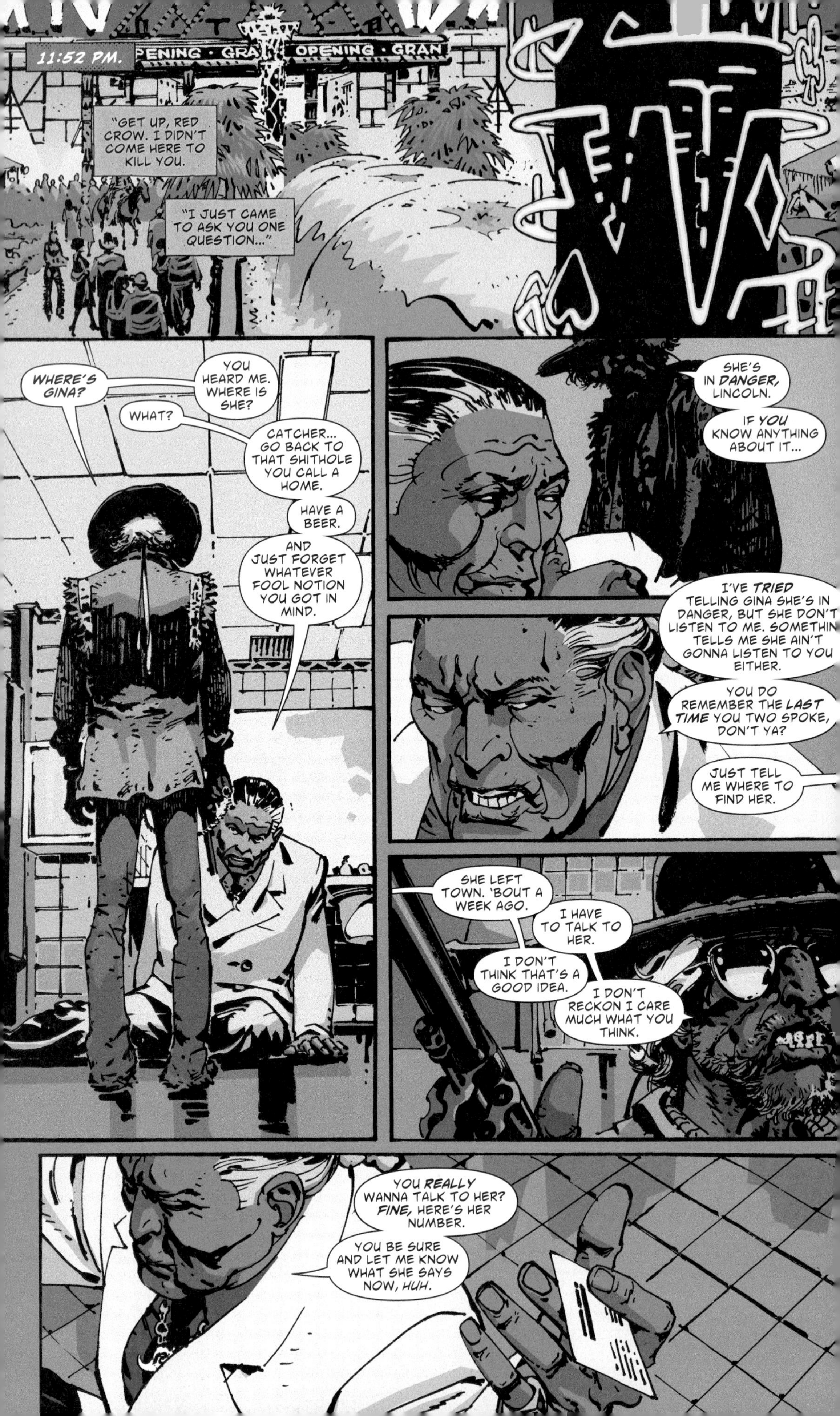
11:52 PM.
OPENING · GRAN
OPENING · GRAN
"GET UP, RED CROW. I DIDN'T COME HERE TO KILL YOU.
"I JUST CAME TO ASK YOU ONE QUESTION..."
WHERE'S GINA?
WHAT?
YOU HEARD ME. WHERE IS SHE?
CATCHER... GO BACK TO THAT SHITHOLE YOU CALL A HOME.
HAVE A BEER.
AND JUST FORGET WHATEVER FOOL NOTION YOU GOT IN MIND.
SHE'S IN DANGER, LINCOLN.
IF YOU KNOW ANYTHING ABOUT IT...
I'VE TRIED TELLING GINA SHE'S IN DANGER, BUT SHE DON'T LISTEN TO ME. SOMETHIN TELLS ME SHE AIN'T GONNA LISTEN TO YOU EITHER.
YOU DO REMEMBER THE LAST TIME YOU TWO SPOKE, DON'T YA?
JUST TELL ME WHERE TO FIND HER.
SHE LEFT TOWN. 'BOUT A WEEK AGO.
I HAVE TO TALK TO HER.
I DON'T THINK THAT'S A GOOD IDEA.
I DON'T RECKON I CARE MUCH WHAT YOU THINK.
YOU REALLY WANNA TALK TO HER? FINE, HERE'S HER NUMBER.
YOU BE SURE AND LET ME KNOW WHAT SHE SAYS NOW, HUH.

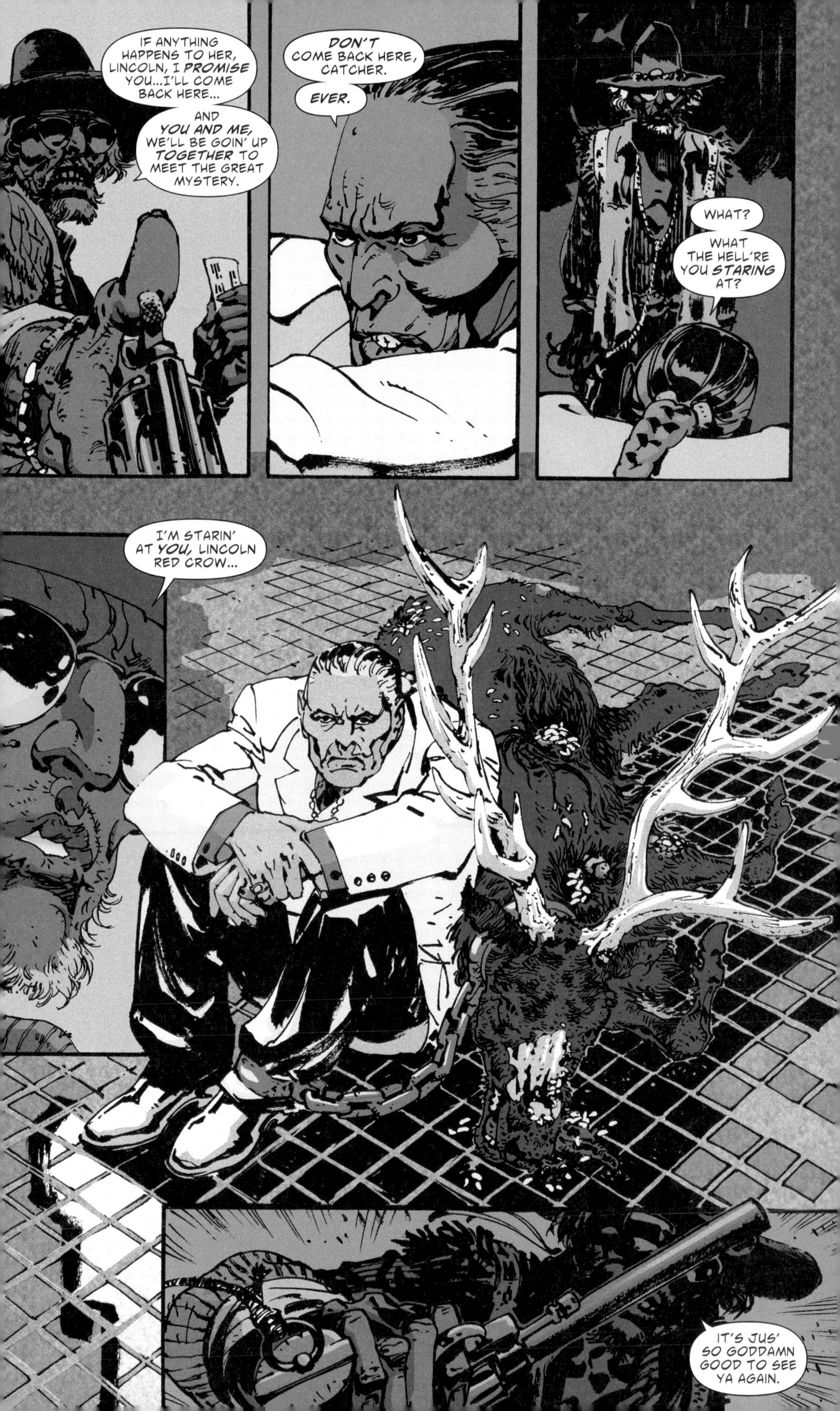
IF ANYTHING HAPPENS TO HER, LINCOLN, I *PROMISE* YOU...I'LL COME BACK HERE...
AND *YOU AND ME,* WE'LL BE GOIN' UP *TOGETHER* TO MEET THE GREAT MYSTERY.
DON'T COME BACK HERE, CATCHER.
EVER.
WHAT?
WHAT THE HELL'RE YOU *STARING* AT?
I'M STARIN' AT *YOU,* LINCOLN RED CROW...
IT'S JUS' SO GODDAMN GOOD TO SEE YA AGAIN.

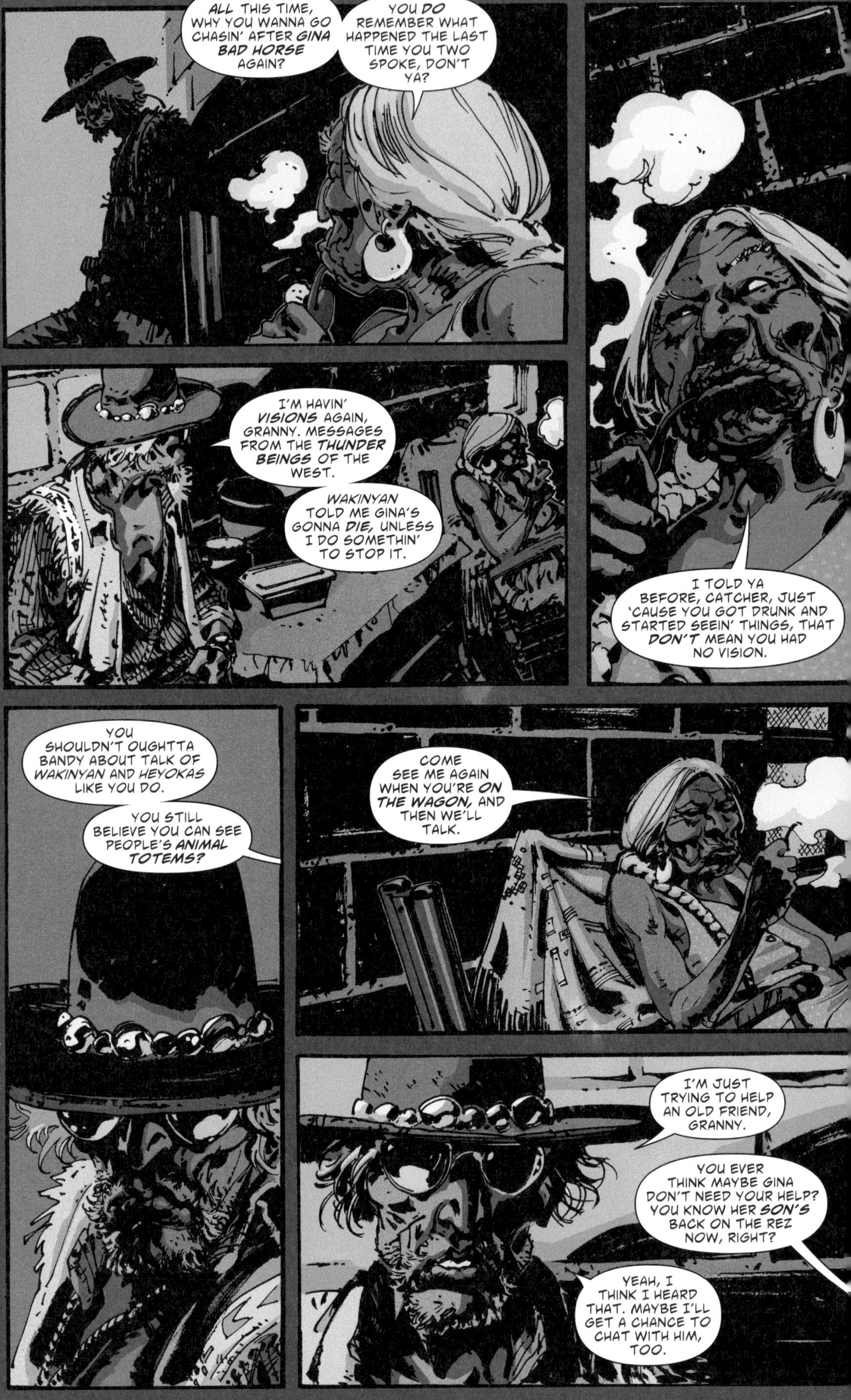
AFTER ALL THIS TIME, WHY YOU WANNA GO CHASIN' AFTER GINA BAD HORSE AGAIN?
YOU DO REMEMBER WHAT HAPPENED THE LAST TIME YOU TWO SPOKE, DON'T YA?
I'M HAVIN' VISIONS AGAIN, GRANNY. MESSAGES FROM THE THUNDER BEINGS OF THE WEST.
WAKINYAN TOLD ME GINA'S GONNA DIE, UNLESS I DO SOMETHIN' TO STOP IT.
I TOLD YA BEFORE, CATCHER, JUST 'CAUSE YOU GOT DRUNK AND STARTED SEEIN' THINGS, THAT DON'T MEAN YOU HAD NO VISION.
YOU SHOULDN'T OUGHTTA BANDY ABOUT TALK OF WAKINYAN AND HEYOKAS LIKE YOU DO.
YOU STILL BELIEVE YOU CAN SEE PEOPLE'S ANIMAL TOTEMS?
COME SEE ME AGAIN WHEN YOU'RE ON THE WAGON, AND THEN WE'LL TALK.
I'M JUST TRYING TO HELP AN OLD FRIEND, GRANNY.
YOU EVER THINK MAYBE GINA DON'T NEED YOUR HELP? YOU KNOW HER SON'S BACK ON THE REZ NOW, RIGHT?
YEAH, I THINK I HEARD THAT. MAYBE I'LL GET A CHANCE TO CHAT WITH HIM, TOO.

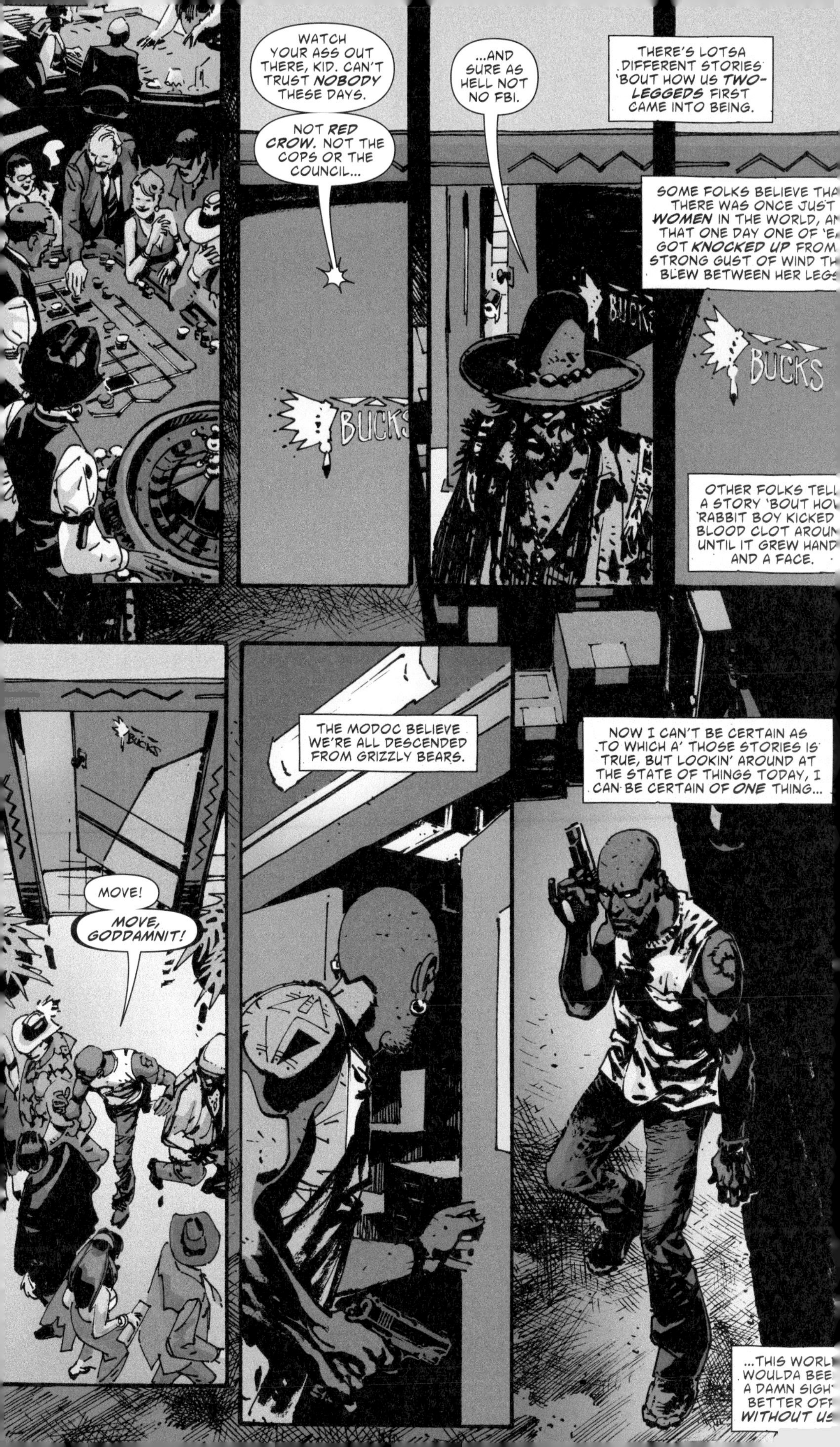
WATCH YOUR ASS OUT THERE, KID. CAN'T TRUST *NOBODY* THESE DAYS.
NOT *RED CROW.* NOT THE COPS OR THE COUNCIL...
...AND SURE AS HELL NOT NO FBI.
THERE'S LOTSA DIFFERENT STORIES 'BOUT HOW US *TWO-LEGGEDS* FIRST CAME INTO BEING.
SOME FOLKS BELIEVE THA THERE WAS ONCE JUST *WOMEN* IN THE WORLD, AN THAT ONE DAY ONE OF 'EA GOT *KNOCKED UP* FROM STRONG GUST OF WIND TH BLEW BETWEEN HER LEGS
BUCKS
OTHER FOLKS TELL A STORY 'BOUT HOW RABBIT BOY KICKED BLOOD CLOT AROUN UNTIL IT GREW HAND AND A FACE.
MOVE!
MOVE, GODDAMNIT!
THE MODOC BELIEVE WE'RE ALL DESCENDED FROM GRIZZLY BEARS.
NOW I CAN'T BE CERTAIN AS TO WHICH A' THOSE STORIES IS TRUE, BUT LOOKIN' AROUND AT THE STATE OF THINGS TODAY, I CAN BE CERTAIN OF *ONE* THING...
...THIS WORL WOULDA BEE A DAMN SIGH BETTER OFF *WITHOUT US*

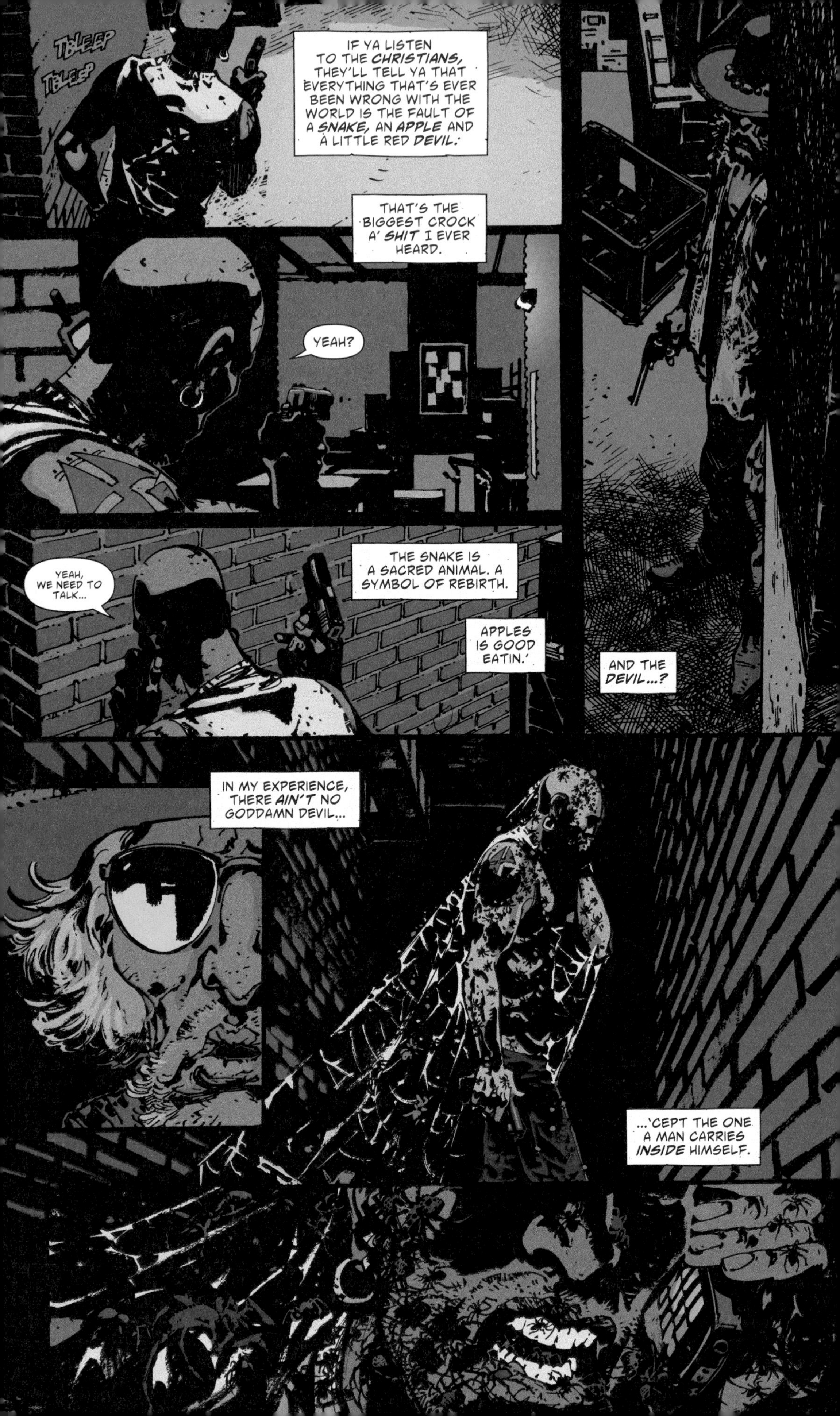
TBLEEP
TBLEEP
IF YA LISTEN TO THE CHRISTIANS, THEY'LL TELL YA THAT EVERYTHING THAT'S EVER BEEN WRONG WITH THE WORLD IS THE FAULT OF A SNAKE, AN APPLE AND A LITTLE RED DEVIL.
THAT'S THE BIGGEST CROCK A' SHIT I EVER HEARD.
YEAH?
YEAH, WE NEED TO TALK...
THE SNAKE IS A SACRED ANIMAL. A SYMBOL OF REBIRTH.
APPLES IS GOOD EATIN.'
AND THE DEVIL...?
IN MY EXPERIENCE, THERE AIN'T NO GODDAMN DEVIL...
...'CEPT THE ONE A MAN CARRIES INSIDE HIMSELF.

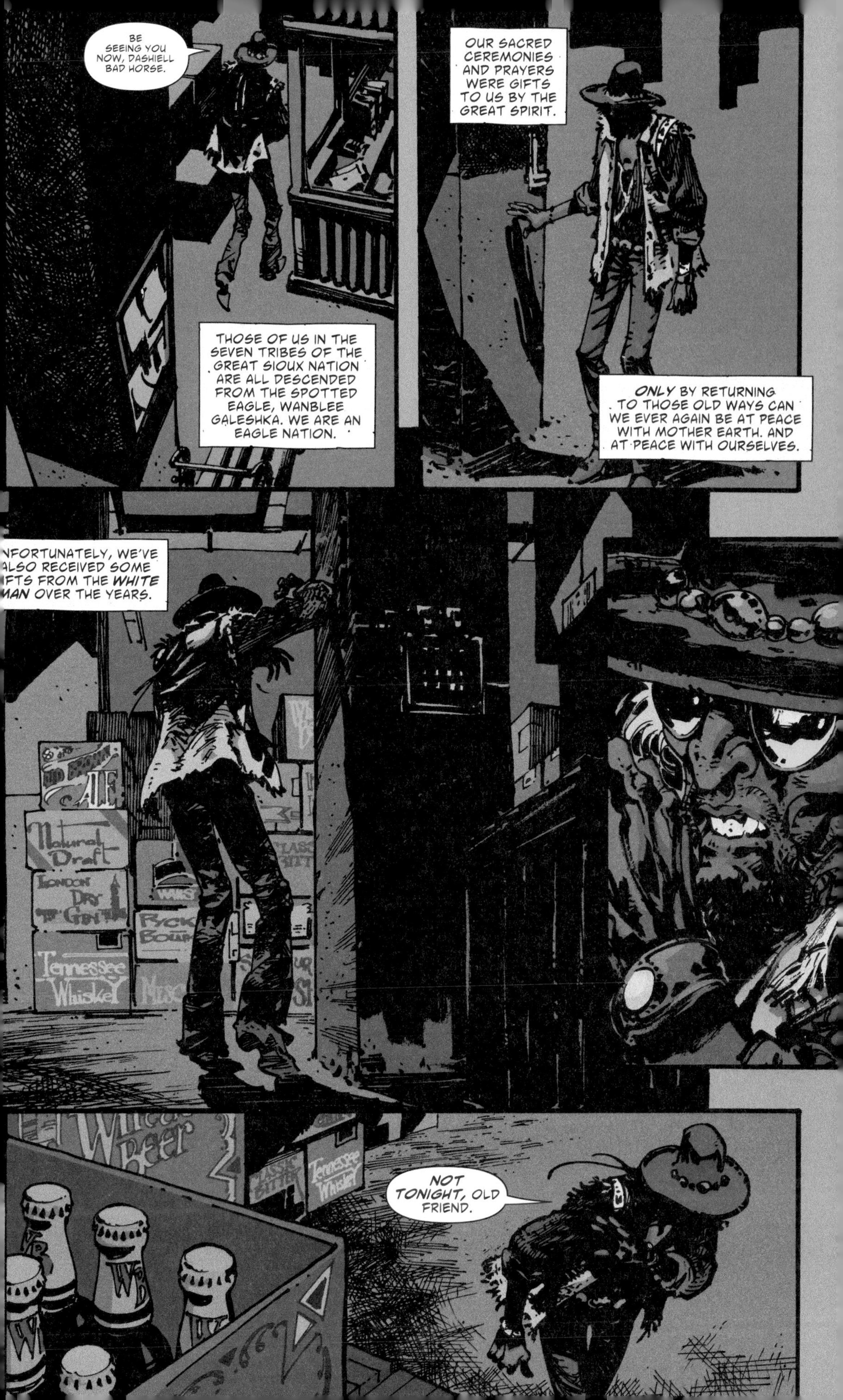
BE SEEING YOU NOW, DASHIELL BAD HORSE.
THOSE OF US IN THE SEVEN TRIBES OF THE GREAT SIOUX NATION ARE ALL DESCENDED FROM THE SPOTTED EAGLE, WANBLEE GALESHKA. WE ARE AN EAGLE NATION.
OUR SACRED CEREMONIES AND PRAYERS WERE GIFTS TO US BY THE GREAT SPIRIT.
ONLY BY RETURNING TO THOSE OLD WAYS CAN WE EVER AGAIN BE AT PEACE WITH MOTHER EARTH. AND AT PEACE WITH OURSELVES.
NFORTUNATELY, WE'VE ALSO RECEIVED SOME FTS FROM THE ***WHITE MAN*** OVER THE YEARS.
ALE
Natural Draft
London Dry Gin
Tennessee Whiskey
Tennessee Whiskey
NOT TONIGHT, OLD FRIEND.

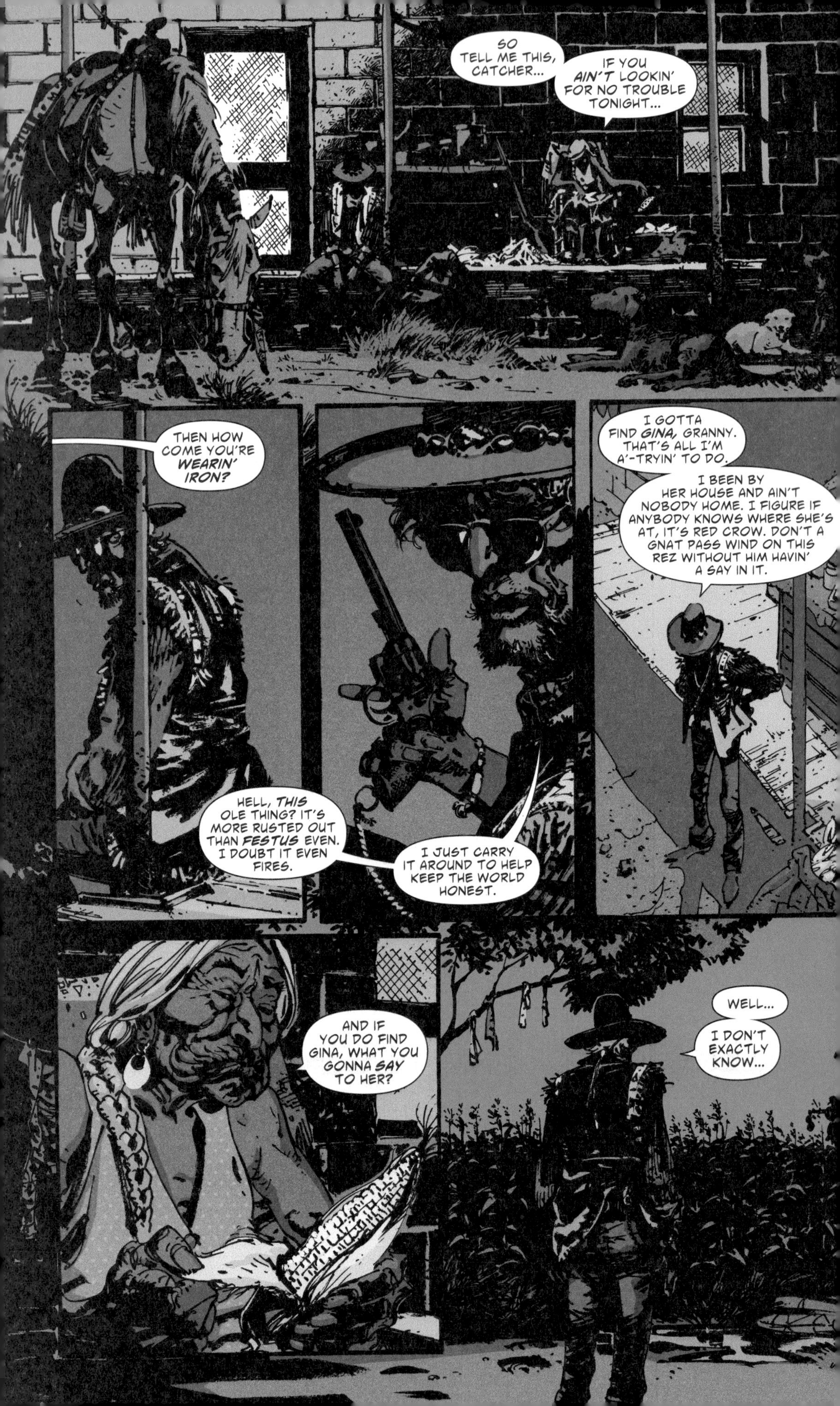
SO TELL ME THIS, CATCHER...
IF YOU AIN'T LOOKIN' FOR NO TROUBLE TONIGHT...
THEN HOW COME YOU'RE WEARIN' IRON?
HELL, THIS OLE THING? IT'S MORE RUSTED OUT THAN FESTUS EVEN. I DOUBT IT EVEN FIRES.
I JUST CARRY IT AROUND TO HELP KEEP THE WORLD HONEST.
I GOTTA FIND GINA, GRANNY. THAT'S ALL I'M A'-TRYIN' TO DO.
I BEEN BY HER HOUSE AND AIN'T NOBODY HOME. I FIGURE IF ANYBODY KNOWS WHERE SHE'S AT, IT'S RED CROW. DON'T A GNAT PASS WIND ON THIS REZ WITHOUT HIM HAVIN' A SAY IN IT.
AND IF YOU DO FIND GINA, WHAT YOU GONNA SAY TO HER?
WELL...
I DON'T EXACTLY KNOW...

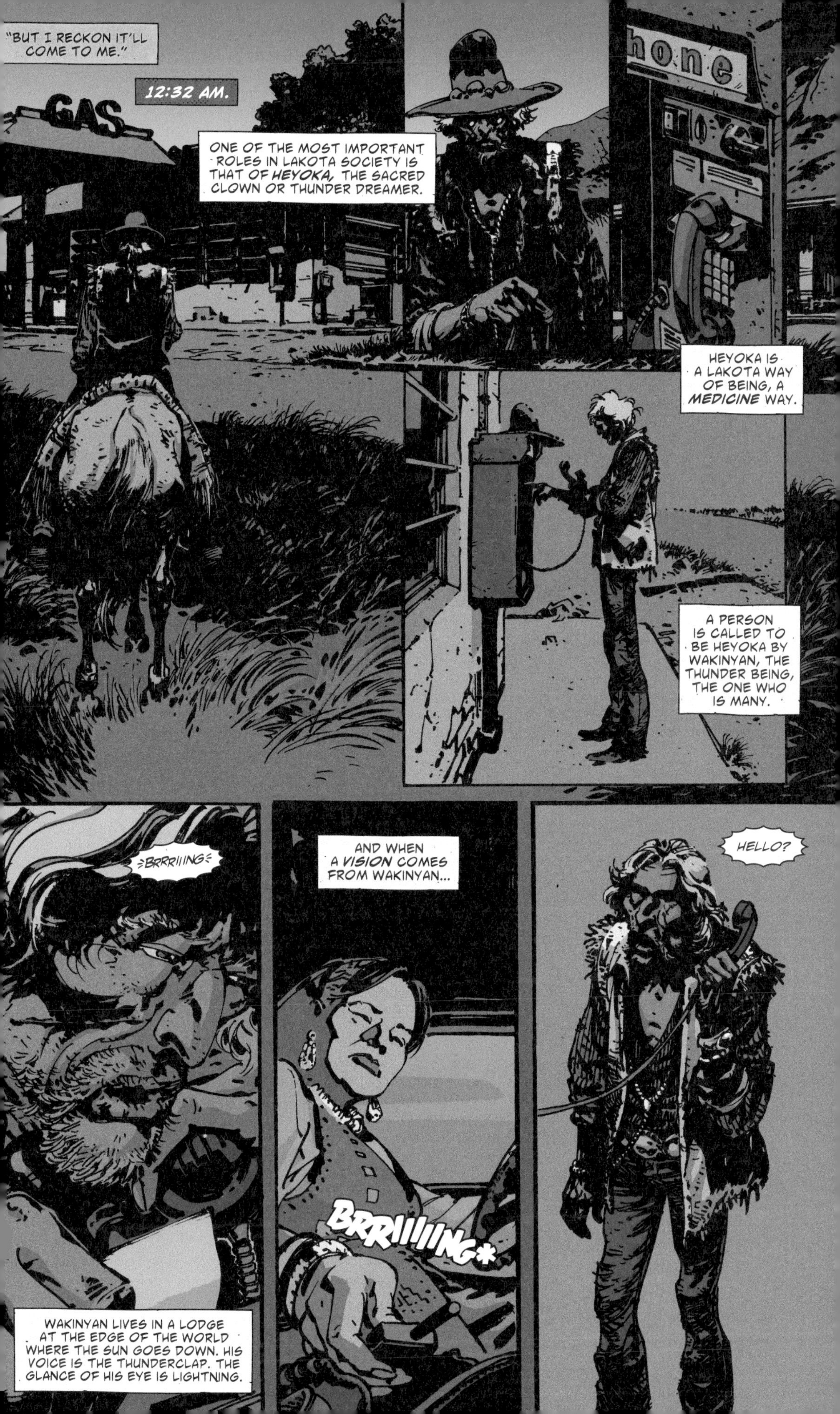

"BUT I RECKON IT'LL COME TO ME."
12:32 AM.
GAS
ONE OF THE MOST IMPORTANT ROLES IN LAKOTA SOCIETY IS THAT OF *HEYOKA,* THE SACRED CLOWN OR THUNDER DREAMER.
hone
HEYOKA IS A LAKOTA WAY OF BEING, A *MEDICINE* WAY.
A PERSON IS CALLED TO BE HEYOKA BY WAKINYAN, THE THUNDER BEING, THE ONE WHO IS MANY.
BRRRIIING
WAKINYAN LIVES IN A LODGE AT THE EDGE OF THE WORLD WHERE THE SUN GOES DOWN. HIS VOICE IS THE THUNDERCLAP. THE GLANCE OF HIS EYE IS LIGHTNING.
AND WHEN A *VISION* COMES FROM WAKINYAN...
BRRIIIIING*
HELLO?

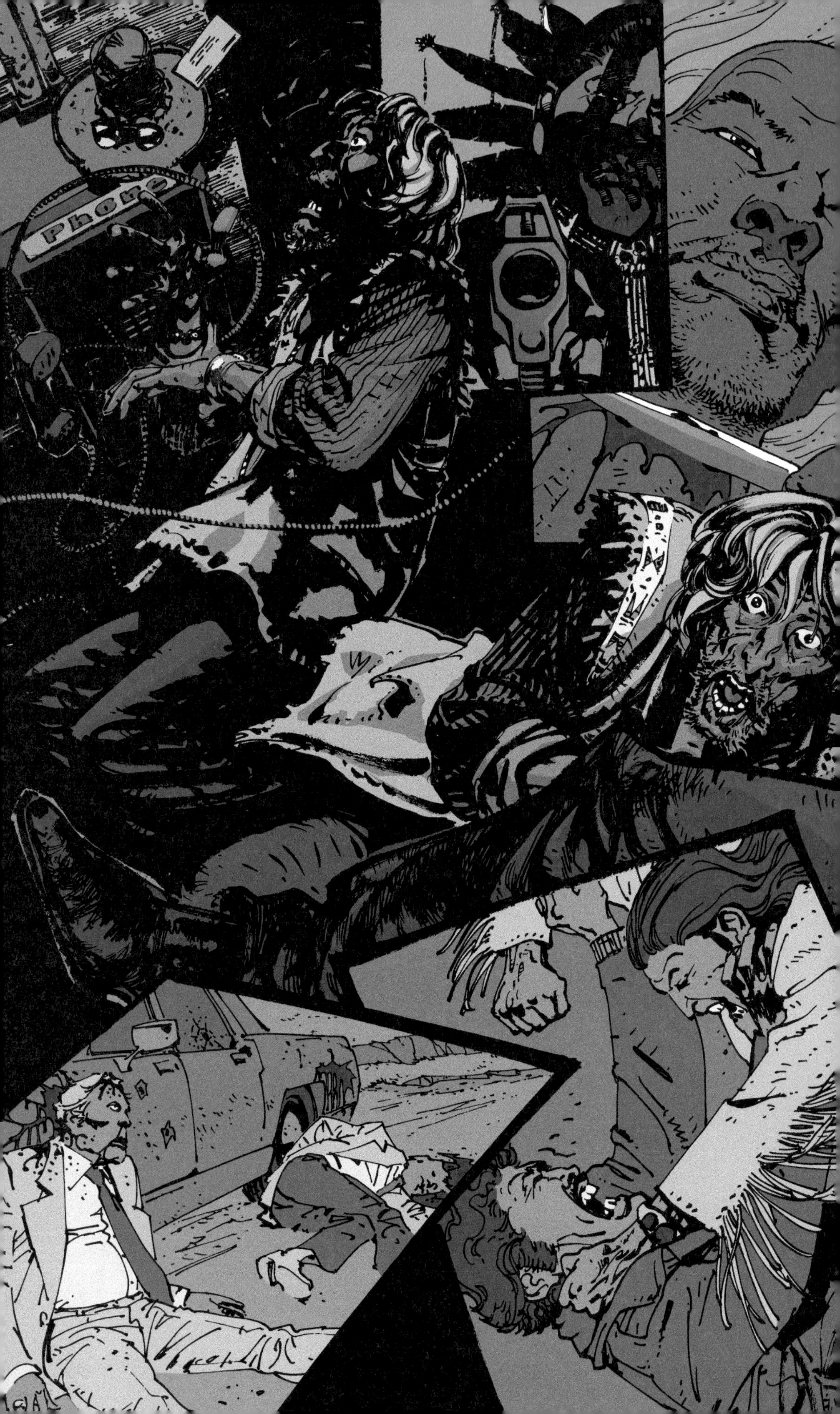
Phone

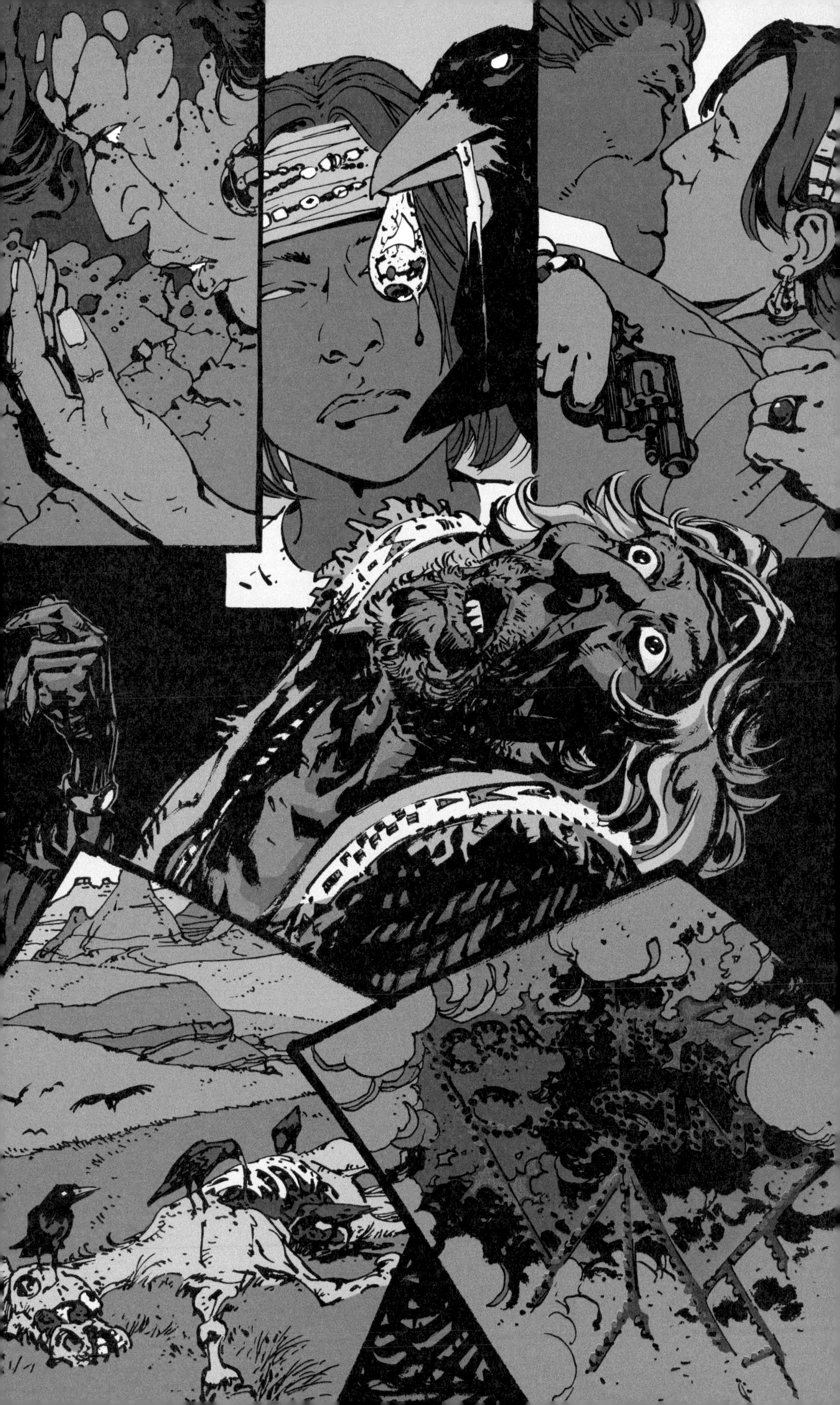

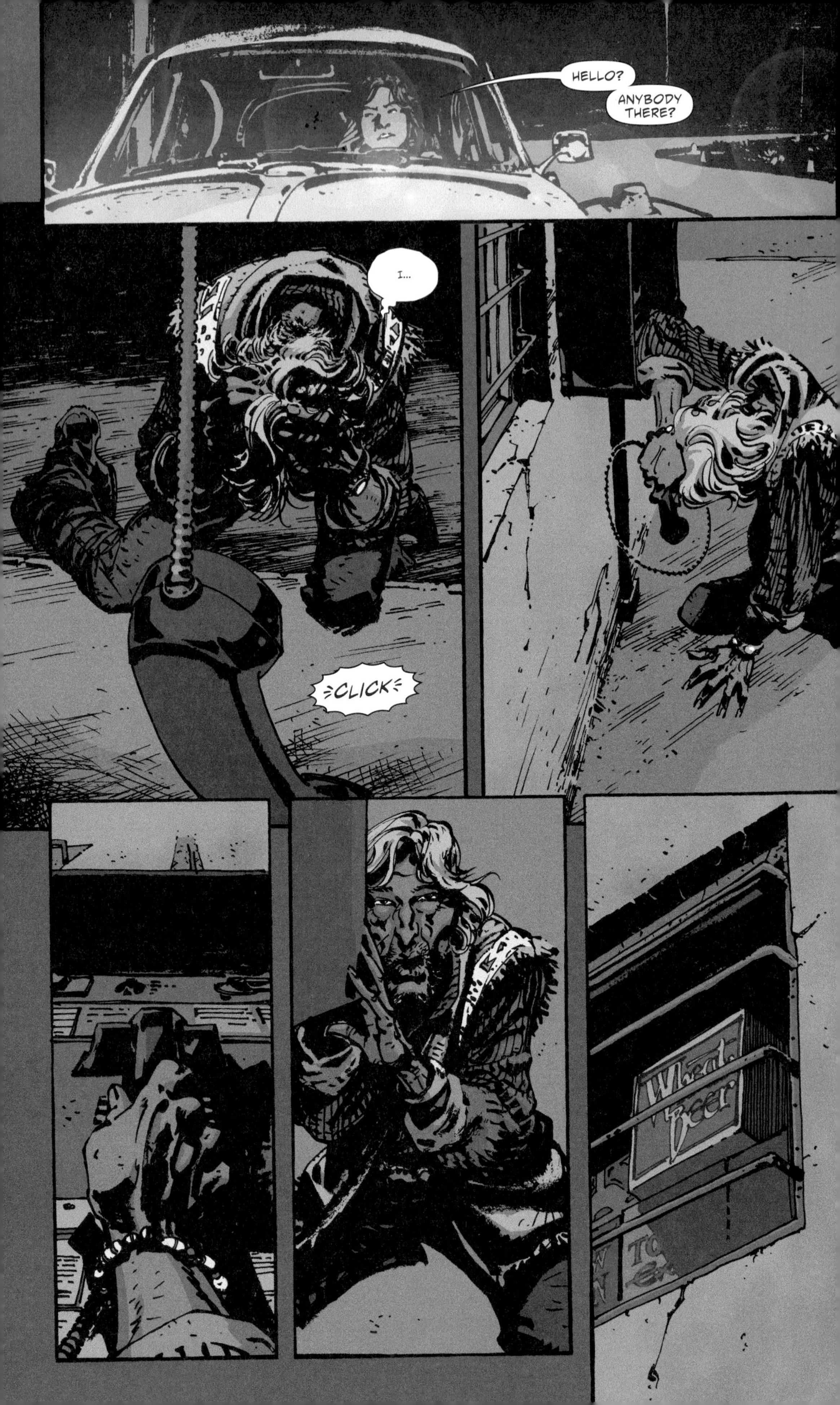
HELLO?
ANYBODY THERE?
I...
CLICK
Wheat Beer

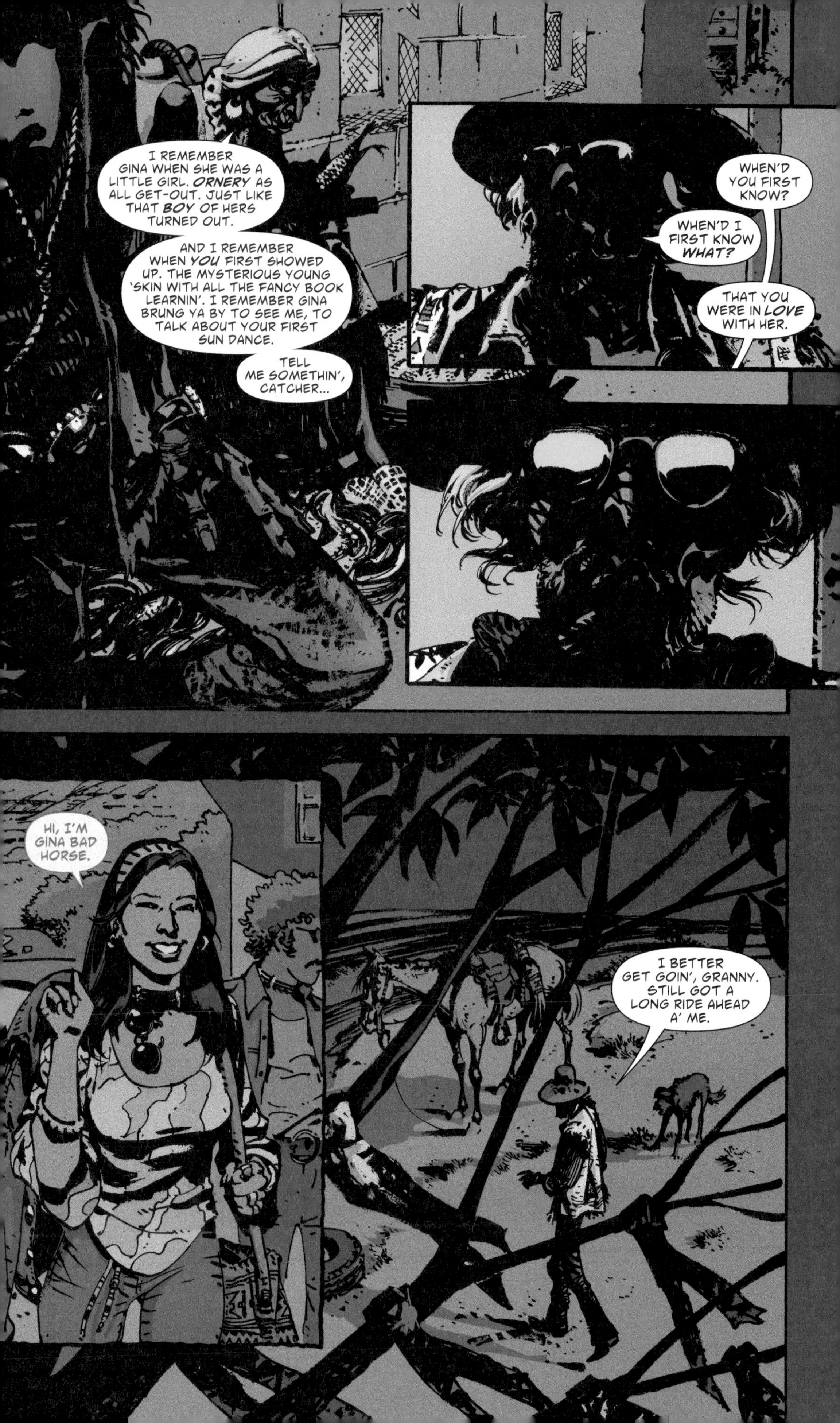
I REMEMBER GINA WHEN SHE WAS A LITTLE GIRL. *ORNERY* AS ALL GET-OUT. JUST LIKE THAT *BOY* OF HERS TURNED OUT.
AND I REMEMBER WHEN *YOU* FIRST SHOWED UP. THE MYSTERIOUS YOUNG 'SKIN WITH ALL THE FANCY BOOK LEARNIN'. I REMEMBER GINA BRUNG YA BY TO SEE ME, TO TALK ABOUT YOUR FIRST SUN DANCE.
TELL ME SOMETHIN', CATCHER...
WHEN'D YOU FIRST KNOW?
WHEN'D I FIRST KNOW *WHAT?*
THAT YOU WERE IN *LOVE* WITH HER.
HI, I'M GINA BAD HORSE.
I BETTER GET GOIN', GRANNY. STILL GOT A LONG RIDE AHEAD A' ME.

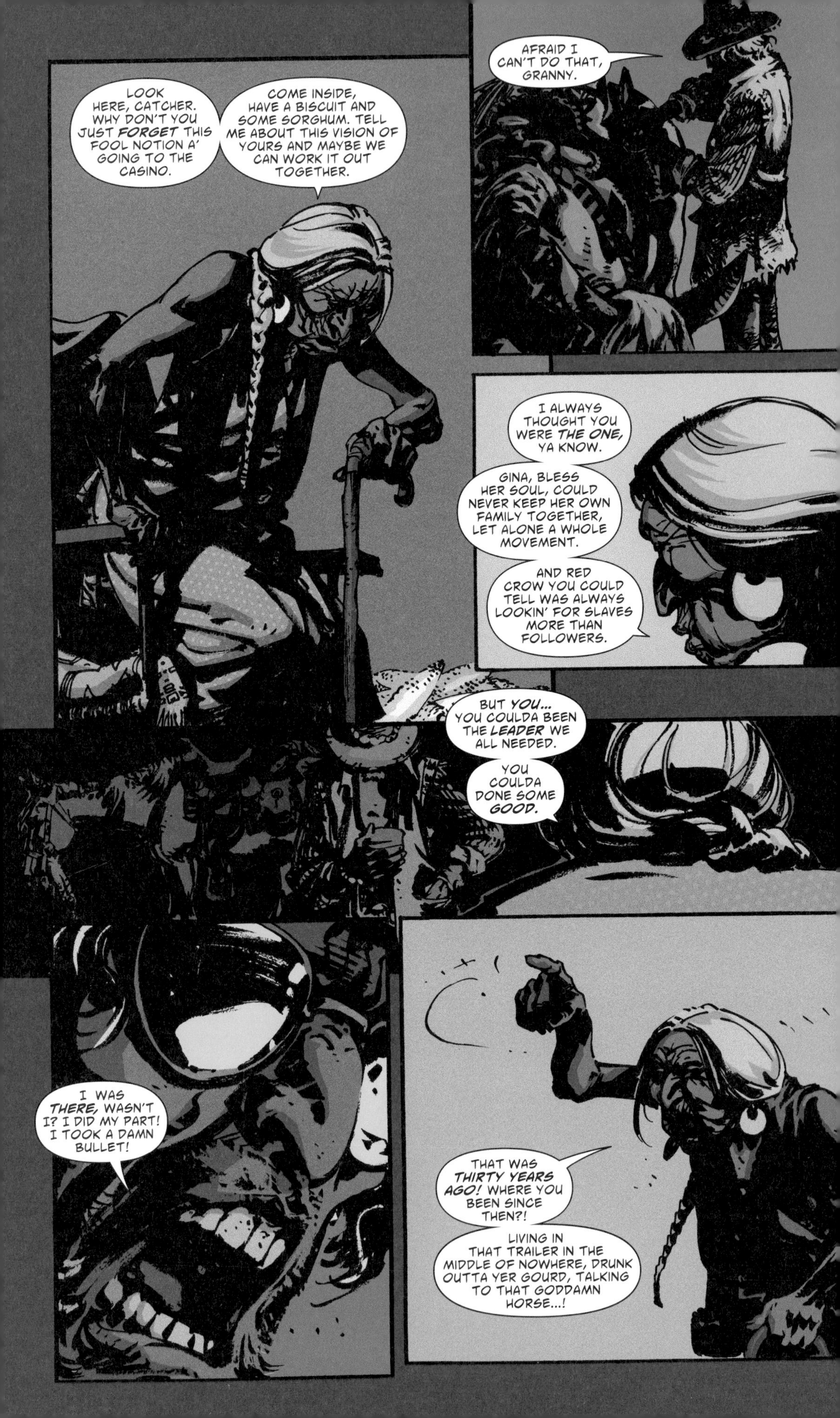
LOOK HERE, CATCHER. WHY DON'T YOU JUST FORGET THIS FOOL NOTION A' GOING TO THE CASINO.
COME INSIDE, HAVE A BISCUIT AND SOME SORGHUM. TELL ME ABOUT THIS VISION OF YOURS AND MAYBE WE CAN WORK IT OUT TOGETHER.
AFRAID I CAN'T DO THAT, GRANNY.
I ALWAYS THOUGHT YOU WERE THE ONE, YA KNOW.
GINA, BLESS HER SOUL, COULD NEVER KEEP HER OWN FAMILY TOGETHER, LET ALONE A WHOLE MOVEMENT.
AND RED CROW YOU COULD TELL WAS ALWAYS LOOKIN' FOR SLAVES MORE THAN FOLLOWERS.
BUT YOU... YOU COULDA BEEN THE LEADER WE ALL NEEDED.
YOU COULDA DONE SOME GOOD.
I WAS THERE, WASN'T I? I DID MY PART! I TOOK A DAMN BULLET!
THAT WAS THIRTY YEARS AGO! WHERE YOU BEEN SINCE THEN?!
LIVING IN THAT TRAILER IN THE MIDDLE OF NOWHERE, DRUNK OUTTA YER GOURD, TALKING TO THAT GODDAMN HORSE...!

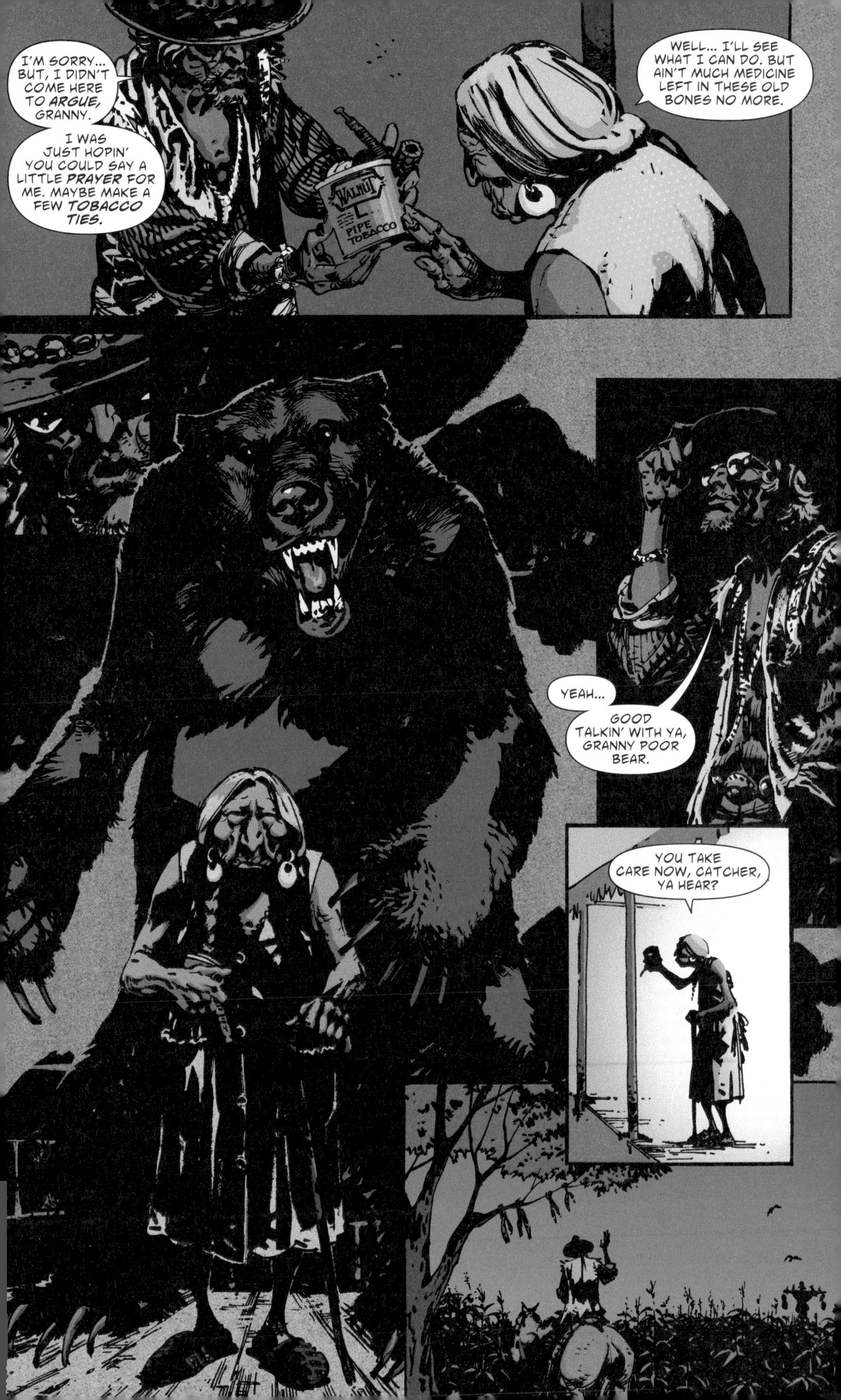

I'M SORRY... BUT, I DIDN'T COME HERE TO ARGUE, GRANNY.
I WAS JUST HOPIN' YOU COULD SAY A LITTLE PRAYER FOR ME. MAYBE MAKE A FEW TOBACCO TIES.
WALNUT
PIPE TOBACCO
WELL... I'LL SEE WHAT I CAN DO. BUT AIN'T MUCH MEDICINE LEFT IN THESE OLD BONES NO MORE.
YEAH...
GOOD TALKIN' WITH YA, GRANNY POOR BEAR.
YOU TAKE CARE NOW, CATCHER, YA HEAR?

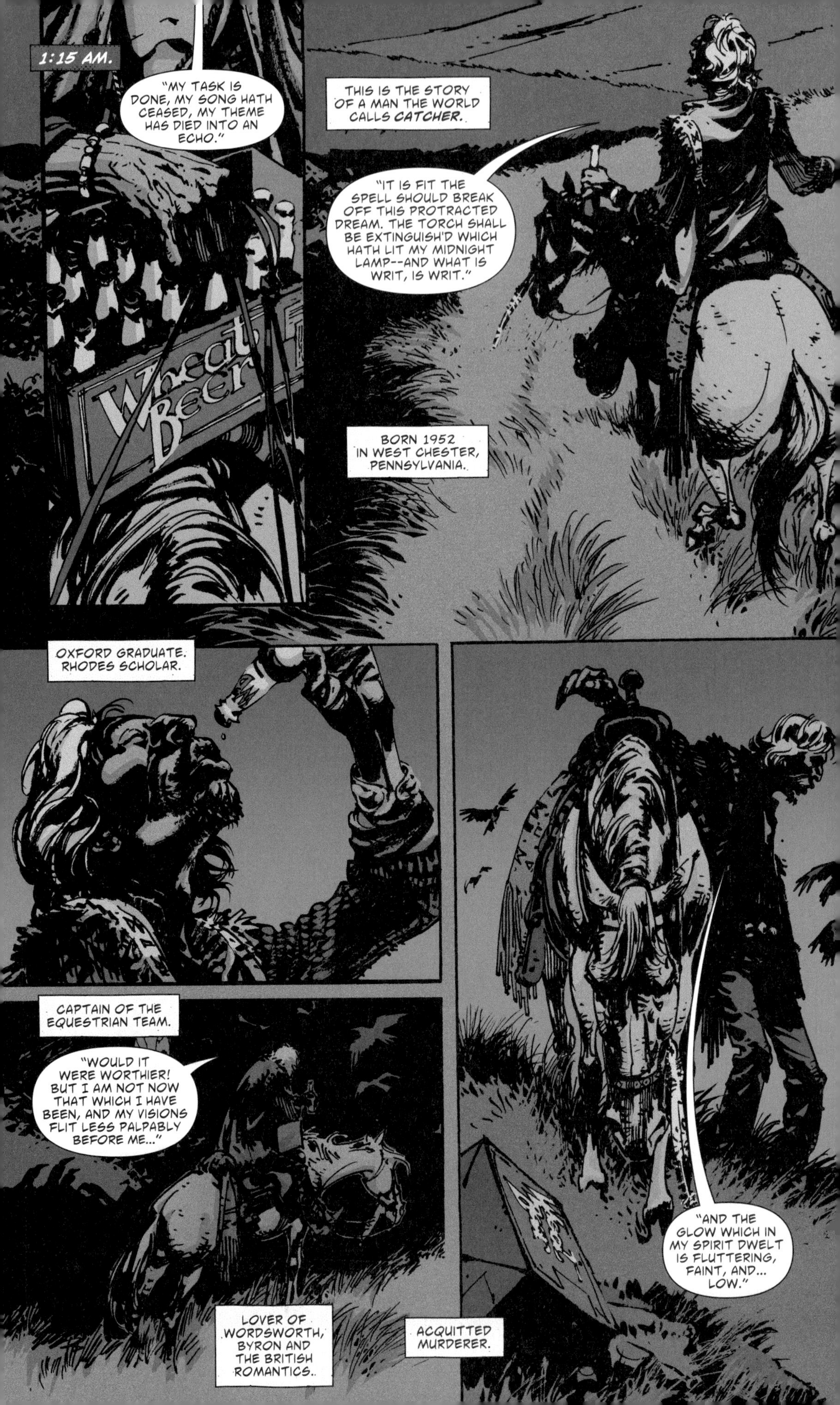
1:15 AM.
"MY TASK IS DONE, MY SONG HATH CEASED, MY THEME HAS DIED INTO AN ECHO."
THIS IS THE STORY OF A MAN THE WORLD CALLS CATCHER.
"IT IS FIT THE SPELL SHOULD BREAK OFF THIS PROTRACTED DREAM. THE TORCH SHALL BE EXTINGUISH'D WHICH HATH LIT MY MIDNIGHT LAMP--AND WHAT IS WRIT, IS WRIT."
Wheat Beer
BORN 1952 IN WEST CHESTER, PENNSYLVANIA.
OXFORD GRADUATE. RHODES SCHOLAR.
CAPTAIN OF THE EQUESTRIAN TEAM.
"WOULD IT WERE WORTHIER! BUT I AM NOT NOW THAT WHICH I HAVE BEEN, AND MY VISIONS FLIT LESS PALPABLY BEFORE ME..."
"AND THE GLOW WHICH IN MY SPIRIT DWELT IS FLUTTERING, FAINT, AND... LOW."
LOVER OF WORDSWORTH, BYRON AND THE BRITISH ROMANTICS.
ACQUITTED MURDERER.

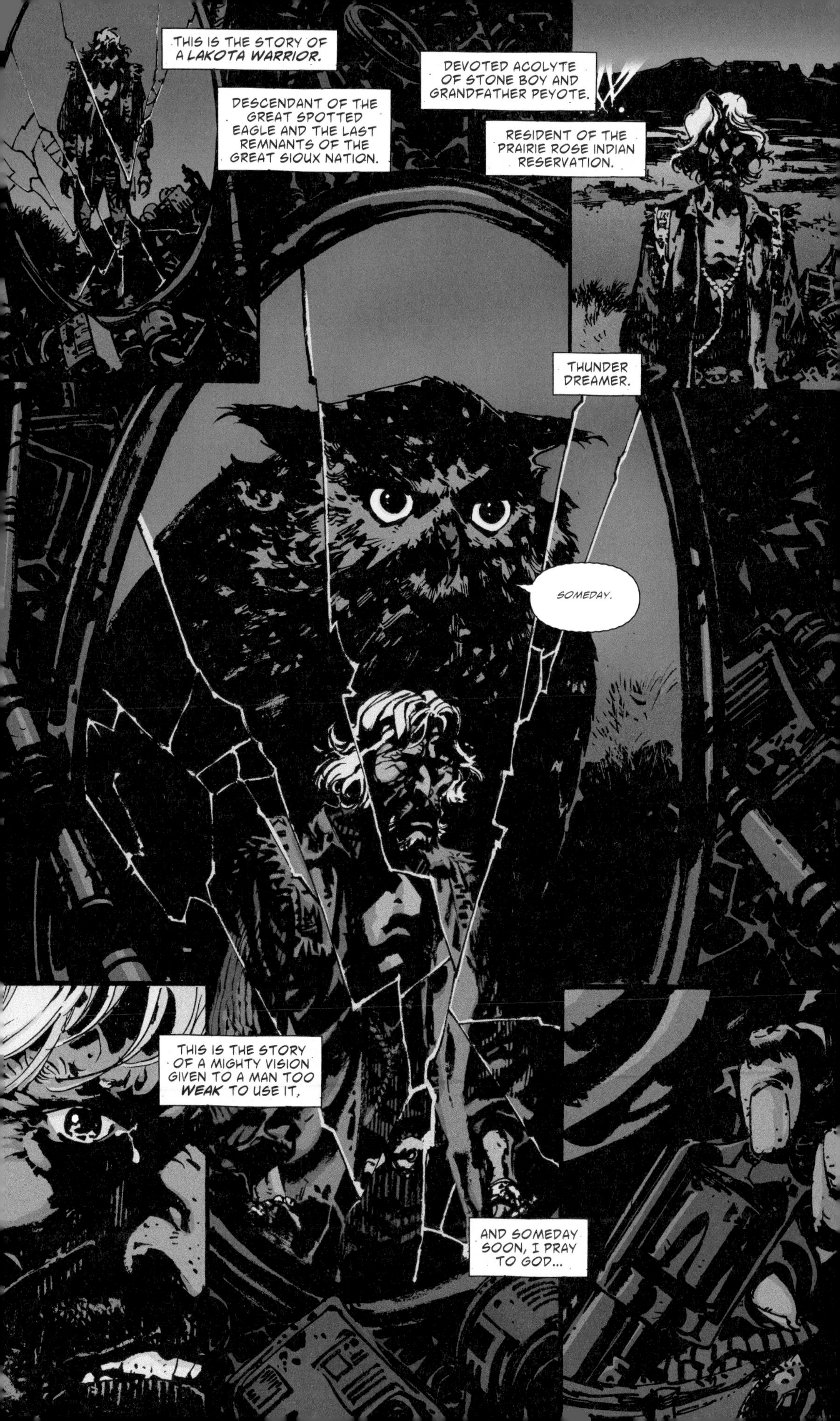
THIS IS THE STORY OF A LAKOTA WARRIOR.
DESCENDANT OF THE GREAT SPOTTED EAGLE AND THE LAST REMNANTS OF THE GREAT SIOUX NATION.
DEVOTED ACOLYTE OF STONE BOY AND GRANDFATHER PEYOTE.
RESIDENT OF THE PRAIRIE ROSE INDIAN RESERVATION.
THUNDER DREAMER.
SOMEDAY.
THIS IS THE STORY OF A MIGHTY VISION GIVEN TO A MAN TOO WEAK TO USE IT.
AND SOMEDAY SOON, I PRAY TO GOD...

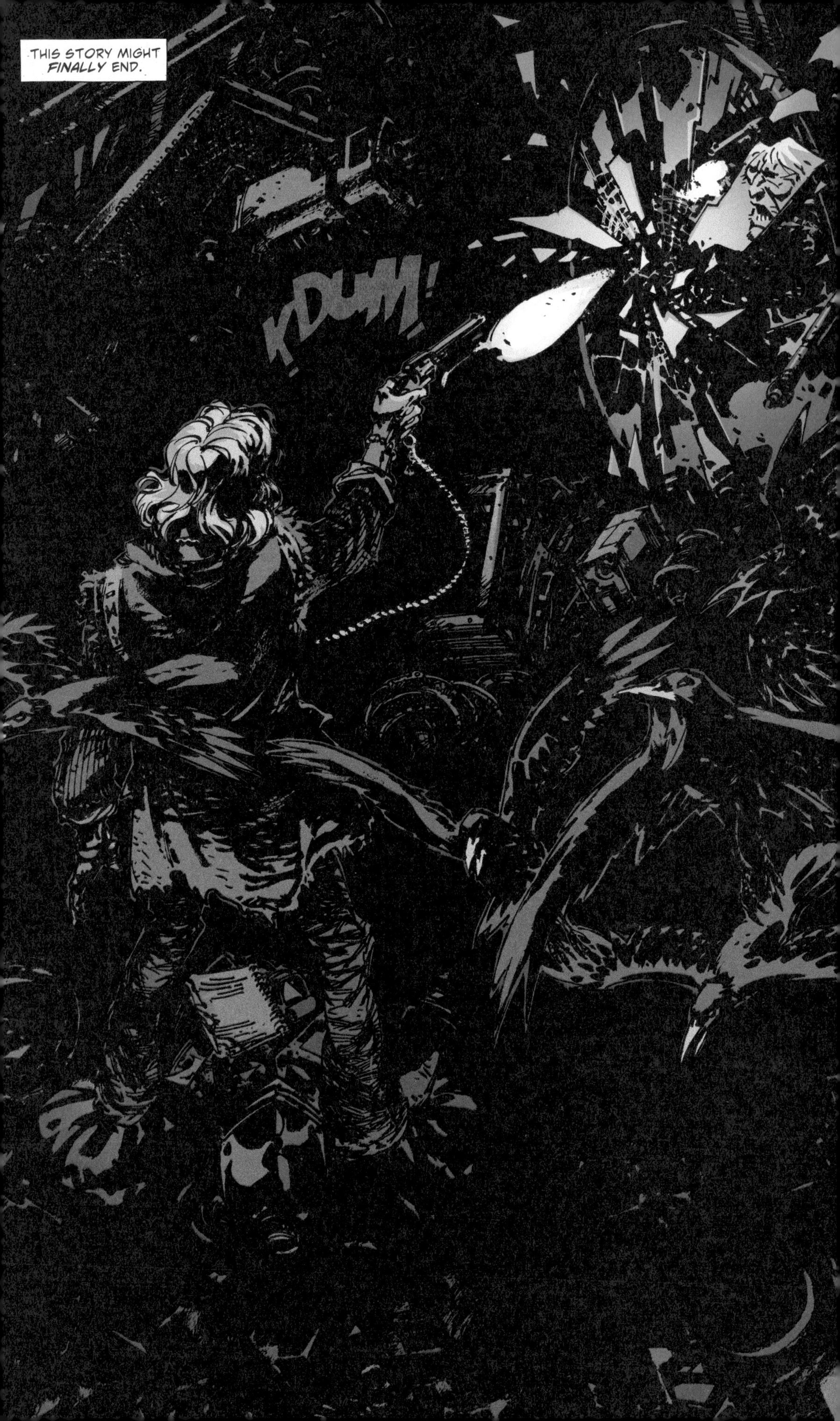
THIS STORY MIGHT FINALLY END.
KDUM!

CASINO BOOGIE PART FIVE: MY AMBITIONZ AZ A RIDDAH

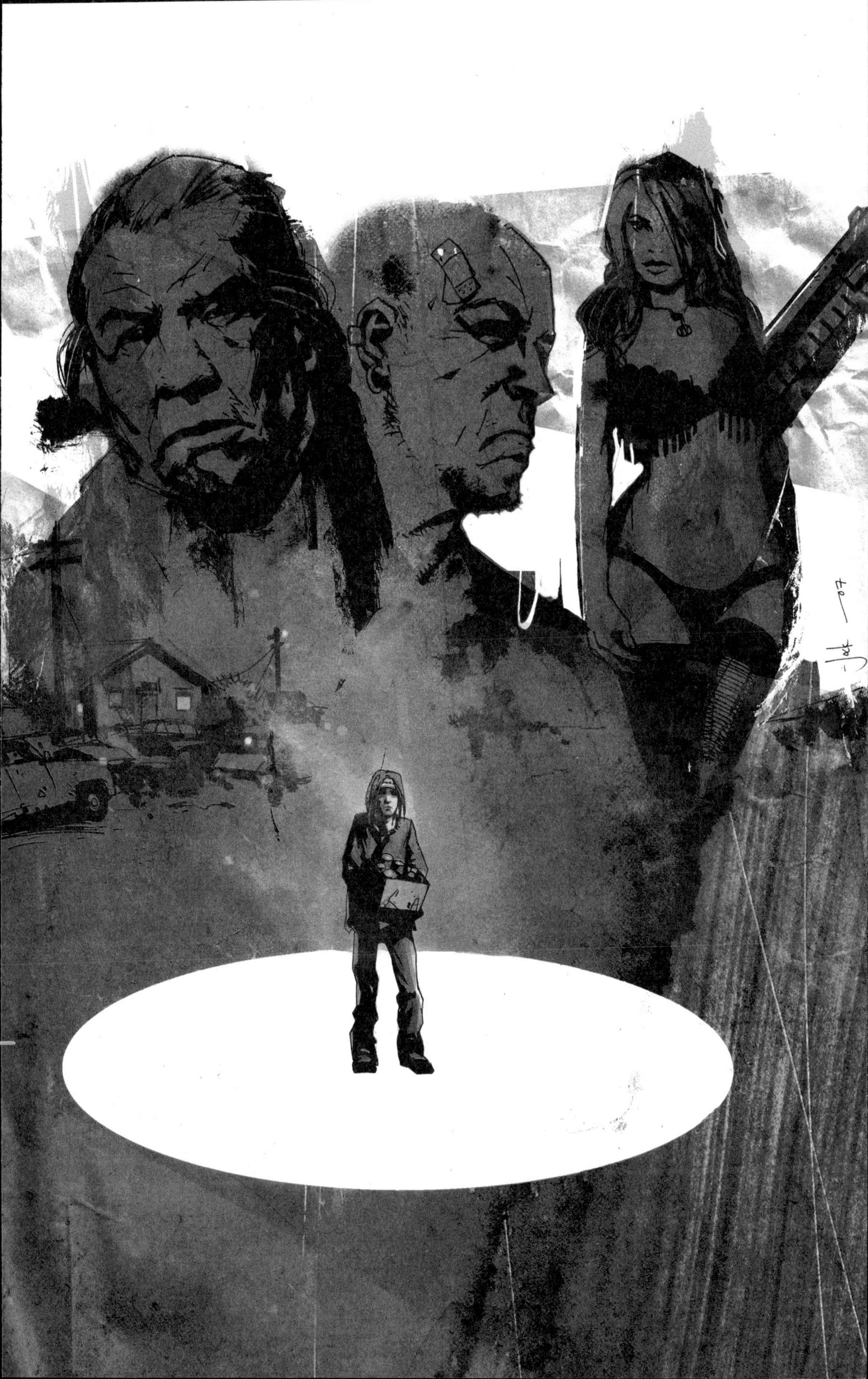

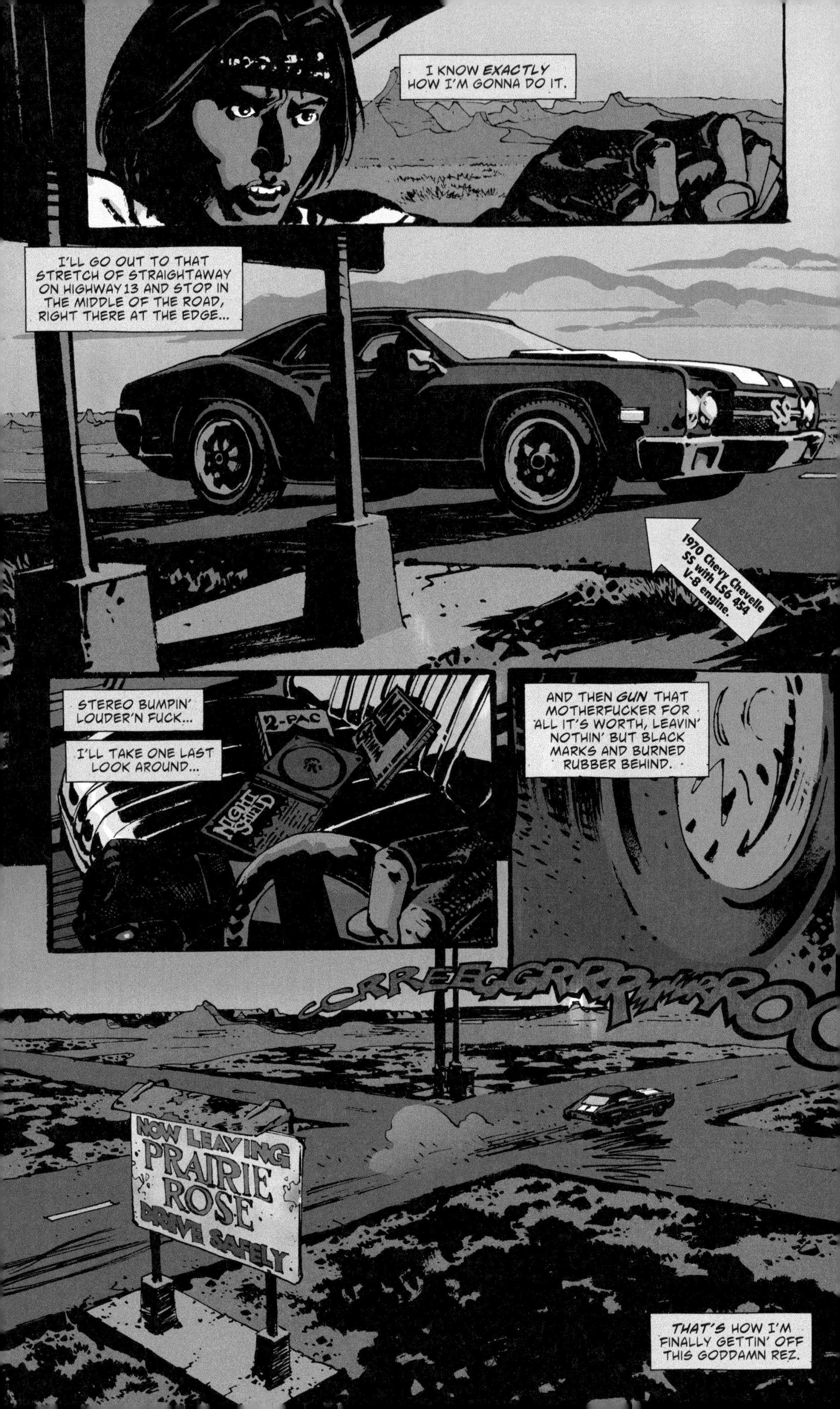
I KNOW EXACTLY HOW I'M GONNA DO IT.
I'LL GO OUT TO THAT STRETCH OF STRAIGHTAWAY ON HIGHWAY 13 AND STOP IN THE MIDDLE OF THE ROAD, RIGHT THERE AT THE EDGE...
1970 Chevy Chevelle SS with LS6 454 V-8 engine.
STEREO BUMPIN' LOUDER'N FUCK...
I'LL TAKE ONE LAST LOOK AROUND...
2-PAC
NIGHT
AND THEN GUN THAT MOTHERFUCKER FOR ALL IT'S WORTH, LEAVIN' NOTHIN' BUT BLACK MARKS AND BURNED RUBBER BEHIND.
CCRREEGGRRRRMMRROO
NOW LEAVING PRAIRIE ROSE DRIVE SAFELY
THAT'S HOW I'M FINALLY GETTIN' OFF THIS GODDAMN REZ.

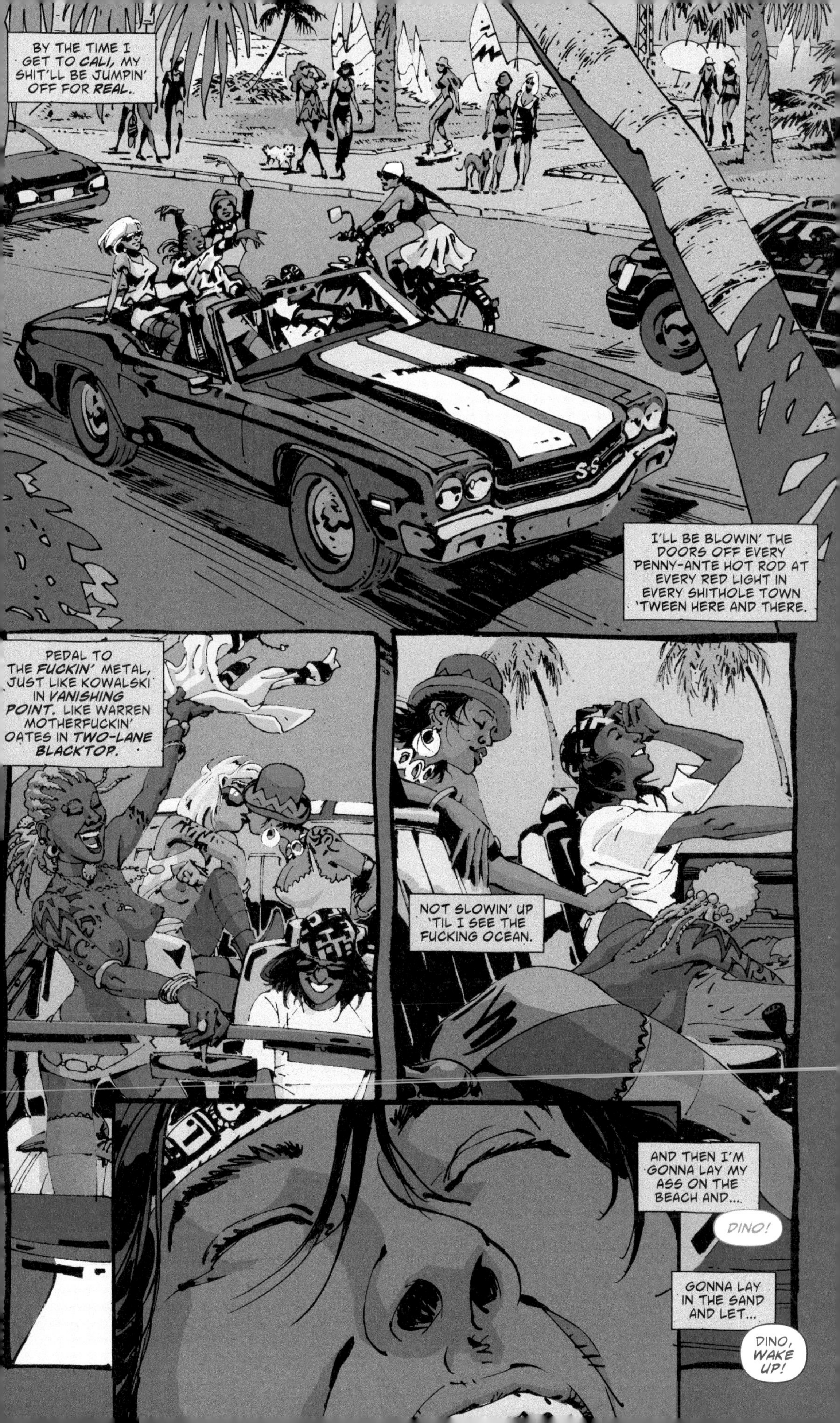
BY THE TIME I GET TO CALI, MY SHIT'LL BE JUMPIN' OFF FOR REAL.
I'LL BE BLOWIN' THE DOORS OFF EVERY PENNY-ANTE HOT ROD AT EVERY RED LIGHT IN EVERY SHITHOLE TOWN 'TWEEN HERE AND THERE.
PEDAL TO THE FUCKIN' METAL, JUST LIKE KOWALSKI IN VANISHING POINT. LIKE WARREN MOTHERFUCKIN' OATES IN TWO-LANE BLACKTOP.
NOT SLOWIN' UP 'TIL I SEE THE FUCKING OCEAN.
AND THEN I'M GONNA LAY MY ASS ON THE BEACH AND...
DINO!
GONNA LAY IN THE SAND AND LET...
DINO, WAKE UP!

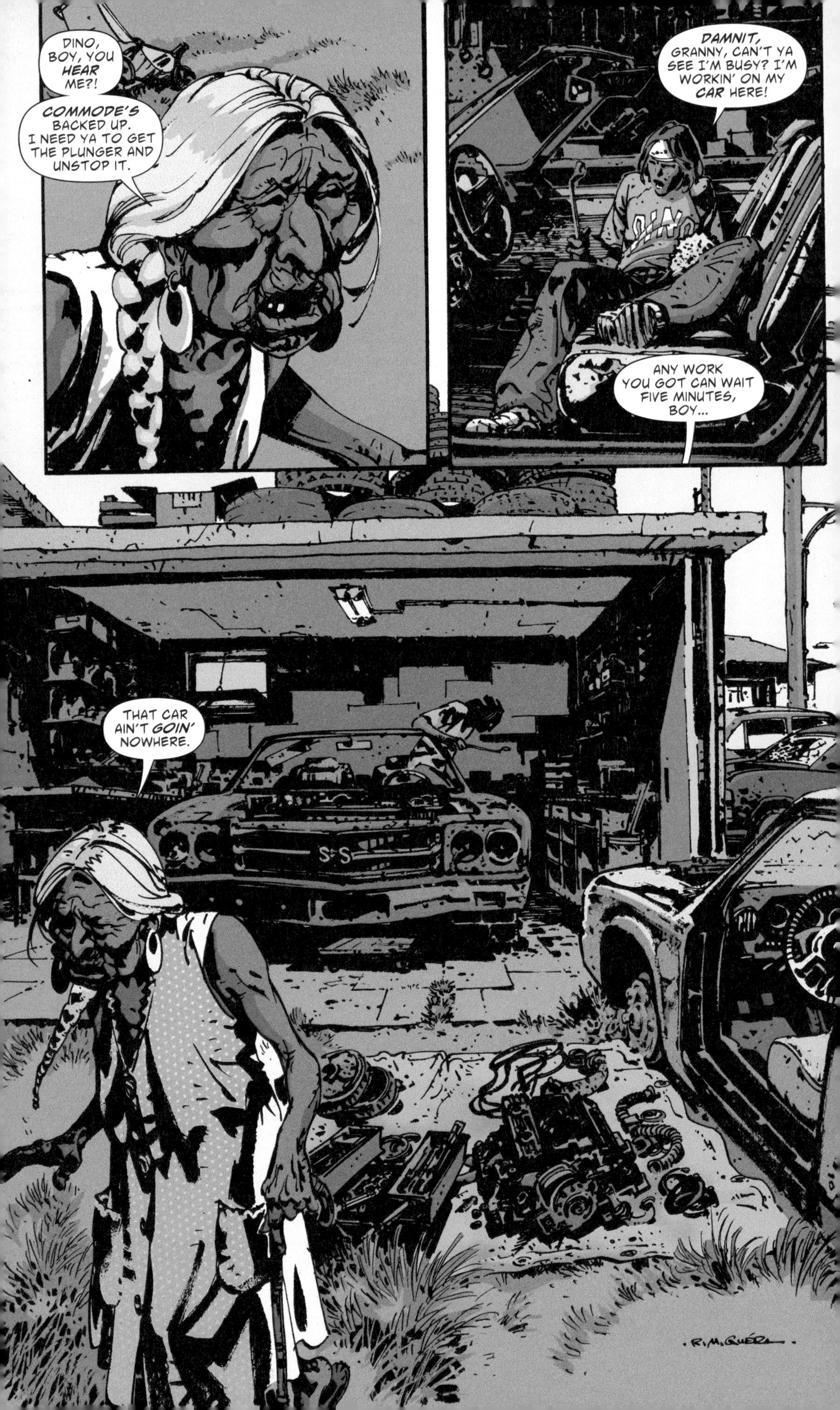
DINO, BOY, YOU *HEAR* ME?!
COMMODE'S BACKED UP. I NEED YA TO GET THE PLUNGER AND UNSTOP IT.
DAMNIT, GRANNY, CAN'T YA SEE I'M BUSY? I'M WORKIN' ON MY *CAR* HERE!
ANY WORK YOU GOT CAN WAIT FIVE MINUTES, BOY...
THAT CAR AIN'T *GOIN'* NOWHERE.
R.M. GUÉRA

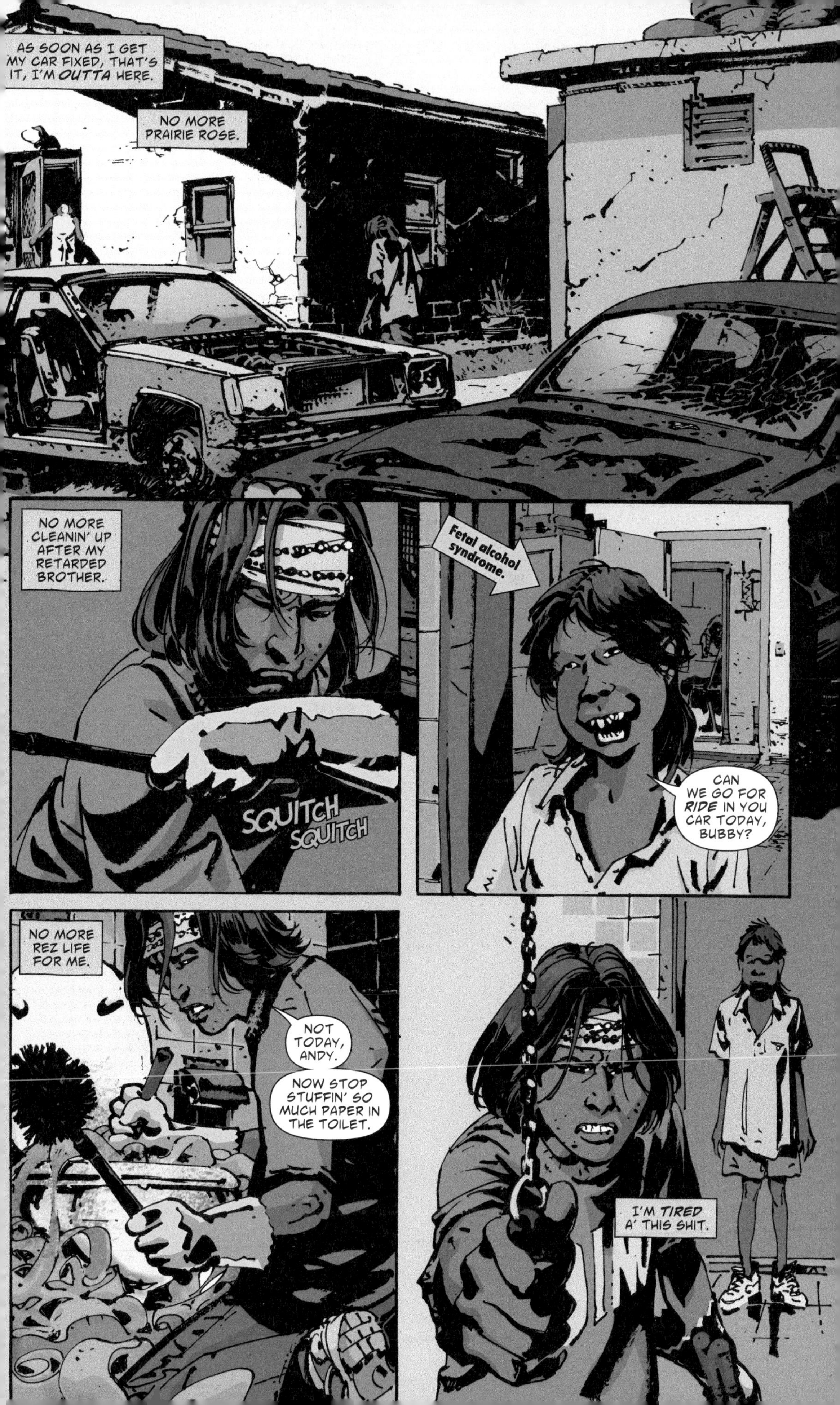

AS SOON AS I GET MY CAR FIXED, THAT'S IT, I'M OUTTA HERE.
NO MORE PRAIRIE ROSE.
NO MORE CLEANIN' UP AFTER MY RETARDED BROTHER.
SQUITCH SQUITCH
Fetal alcohol syndrome.
CAN WE GO FOR RIDE IN YOU CAR TODAY, BUBBY?
NO MORE REZ LIFE FOR ME.
NOT TODAY, ANDY.
NOW STOP STUFFIN' SO MUCH PAPER IN THE TOILET.
I'M TIRED A' THIS SHIT.

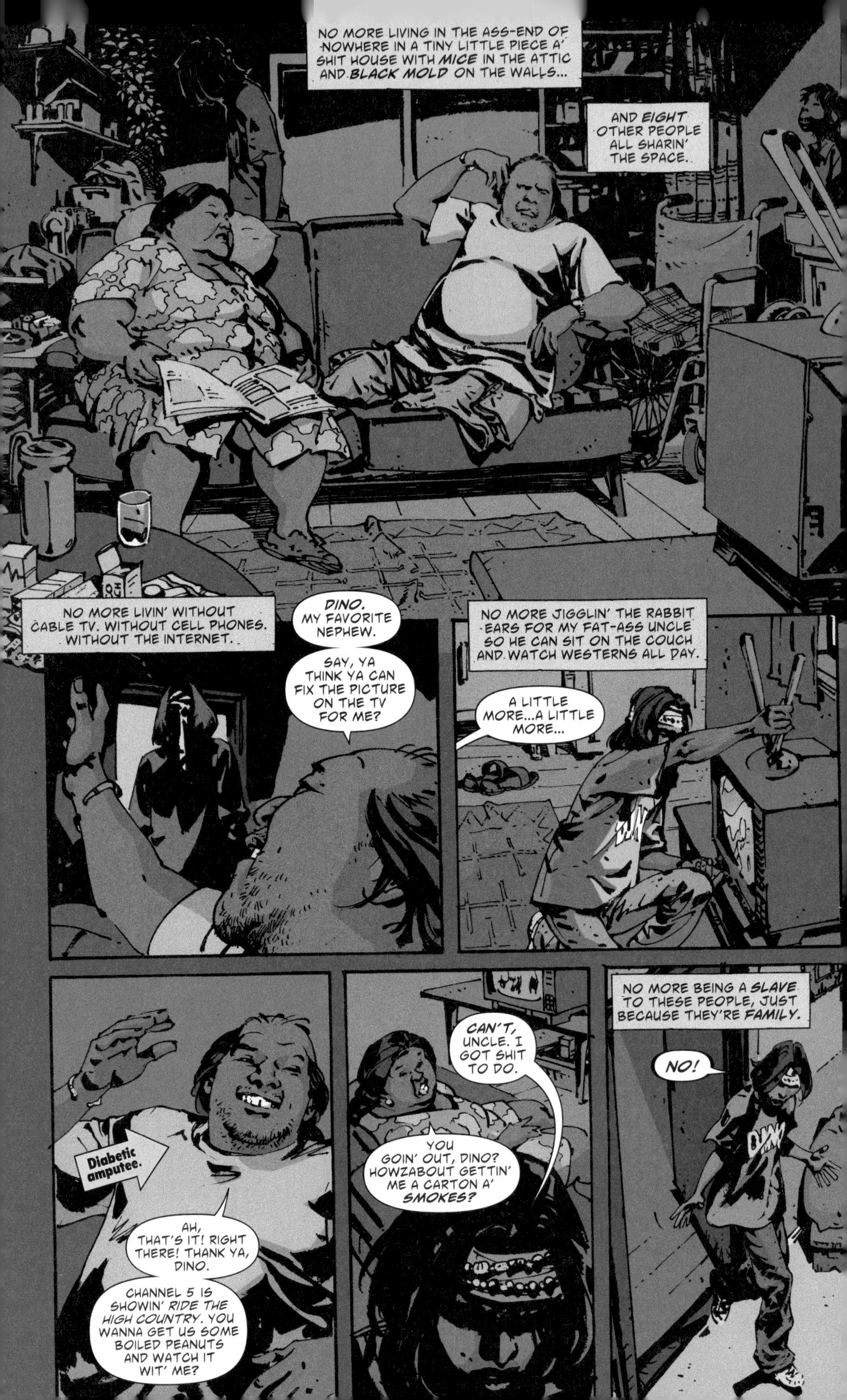
NO MORE LIVING IN THE ASS-END OF NOWHERE IN A TINY LITTLE PIECE A' SHIT HOUSE WITH *MICE* IN THE ATTIC AND *BLACK MOLD* ON THE WALLS...
AND *EIGHT* OTHER PEOPLE ALL SHARIN' THE SPACE.
NO MORE LIVIN' WITHOUT CABLE TV. WITHOUT CELL PHONES. WITHOUT THE INTERNET.
DINO. MY FAVORITE NEPHEW.
SAY, YA THINK YA CAN FIX THE PICTURE ON THE TV FOR ME?
NO MORE JIGGLIN' THE RABBIT EARS FOR MY FAT-ASS UNCLE SO HE CAN SIT ON THE COUCH AND WATCH WESTERNS ALL DAY.
A LITTLE MORE...A LITTLE MORE...
Diabetic amputee.
AH, THAT'S IT! RIGHT THERE! THANK YA, DINO.
CHANNEL 5 IS SHOWIN' *RIDE THE HIGH COUNTRY*. YOU WANNA GET US SOME BOILED PEANUTS AND WATCH IT WIT' ME?
CAN'T, UNCLE. I GOT SHIT TO DO.
YOU GOIN' OUT, DINO? HOWZABOUT GETTIN' ME A CARTON A' *SMOKES?*
NO MORE BEING A *SLAVE* TO THESE PEOPLE, JUST BECAUSE THEY'RE *FAMILY*.
NO!

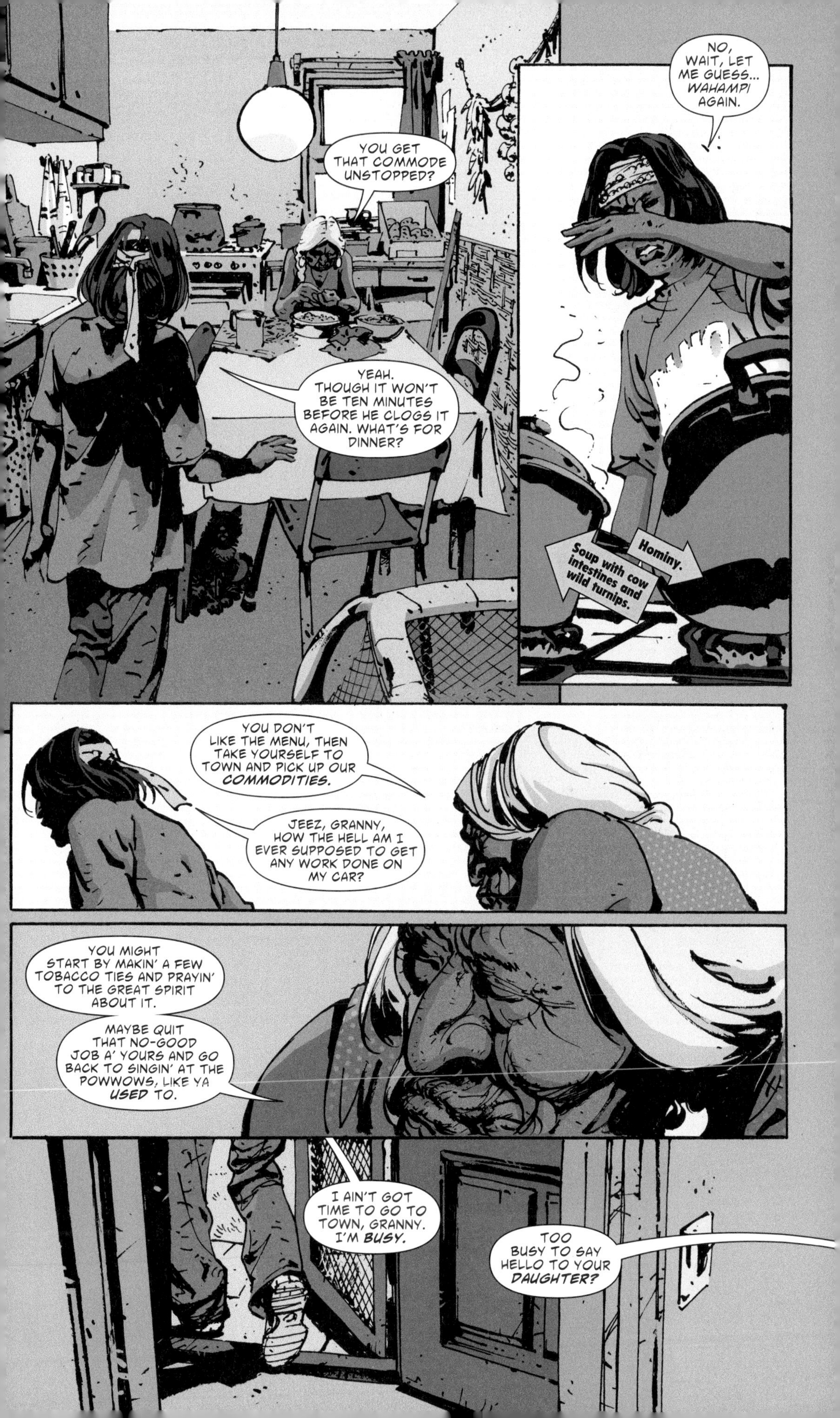
YOU GET THAT COMMODE UNSTOPPED?
YEAH. THOUGH IT WON'T BE TEN MINUTES BEFORE HE CLOGS IT AGAIN. WHAT'S FOR DINNER?
NO, WAIT, LET ME GUESS... WAHAMPI AGAIN.
Hominy.
Soup with cow intestines and wild turnips.
YOU DON'T LIKE THE MENU, THEN TAKE YOURSELF TO TOWN AND PICK UP OUR COMMODITIES.
JEEZ, GRANNY, HOW THE HELL AM I EVER SUPPOSED TO GET ANY WORK DONE ON MY CAR?
YOU MIGHT START BY MAKIN' A FEW TOBACCO TIES AND PRAYIN' TO THE GREAT SPIRIT ABOUT IT.
MAYBE QUIT THAT NO-GOOD JOB A' YOURS AND GO BACK TO SINGIN' AT THE POWWOWS, LIKE YA USED TO.
I AIN'T GOT TIME TO GO TO TOWN, GRANNY. I'M BUSY.
TOO BUSY TO SAY HELLO TO YOUR DAUGHTER?

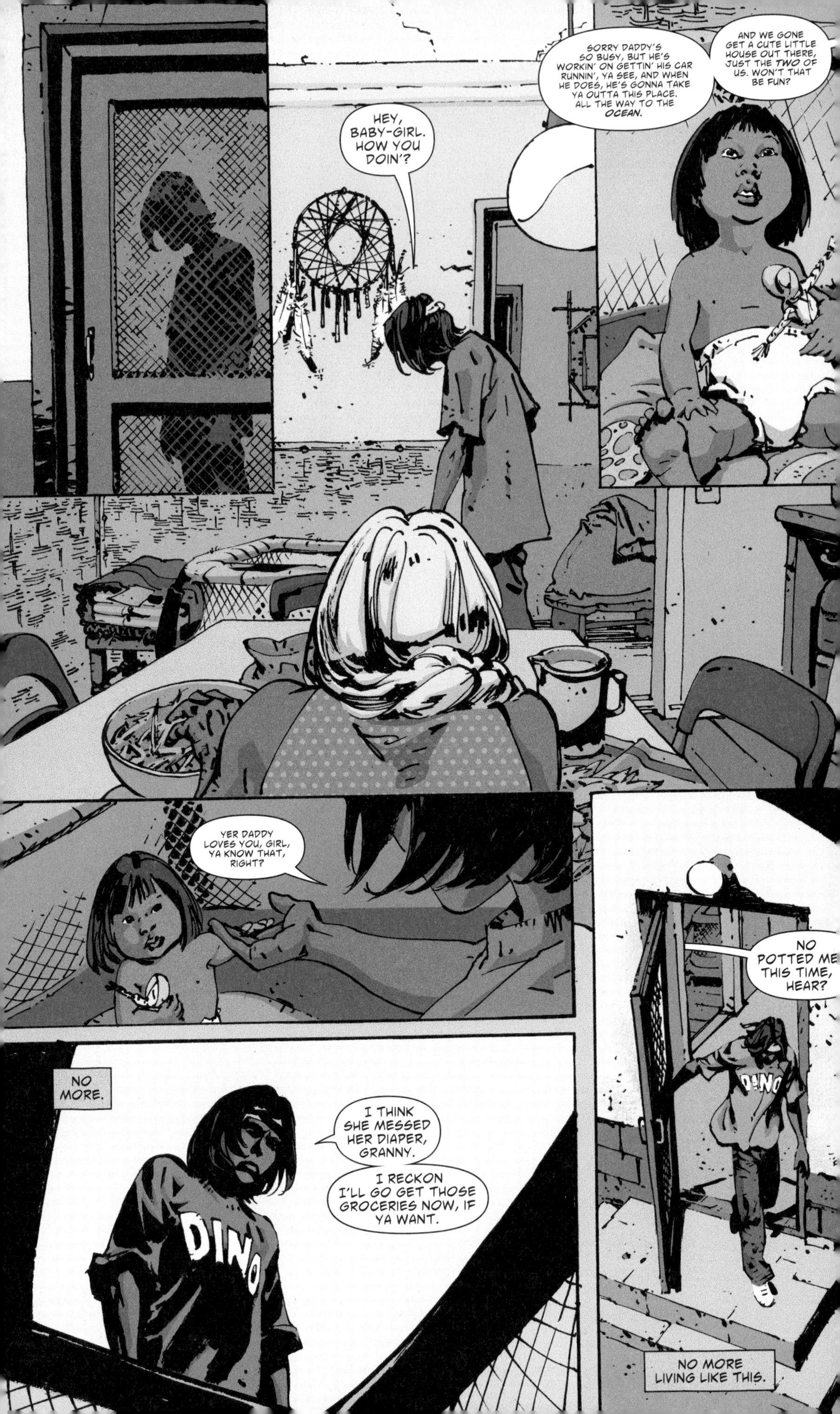
HEY, BABY-GIRL. HOW YOU DOIN'?
SORRY DADDY'S SO BUSY, BUT HE'S WORKIN' ON GETTIN' HIS CAR RUNNIN', YA SEE, AND WHEN HE DOES, HE'S GONNA TAKE YA OUTTA THIS PLACE. ALL THE WAY TO THE *OCEAN*.
AND WE GONE GET A CUTE LITTLE HOUSE OUT THERE, JUST THE *TWO* OF US. WON'T THAT BE FUN?
YER DADDY LOVES YOU, GIRL, YA KNOW THAT, RIGHT?
NO MORE.
I THINK SHE MESSED HER DIAPER, GRANNY.
I RECKON I'LL GO GET THOSE GROCERIES NOW, IF YA WANT.
NO POTTED ME THIS TIME, HEAR?
DINO
NO MORE LIVING LIKE THIS.

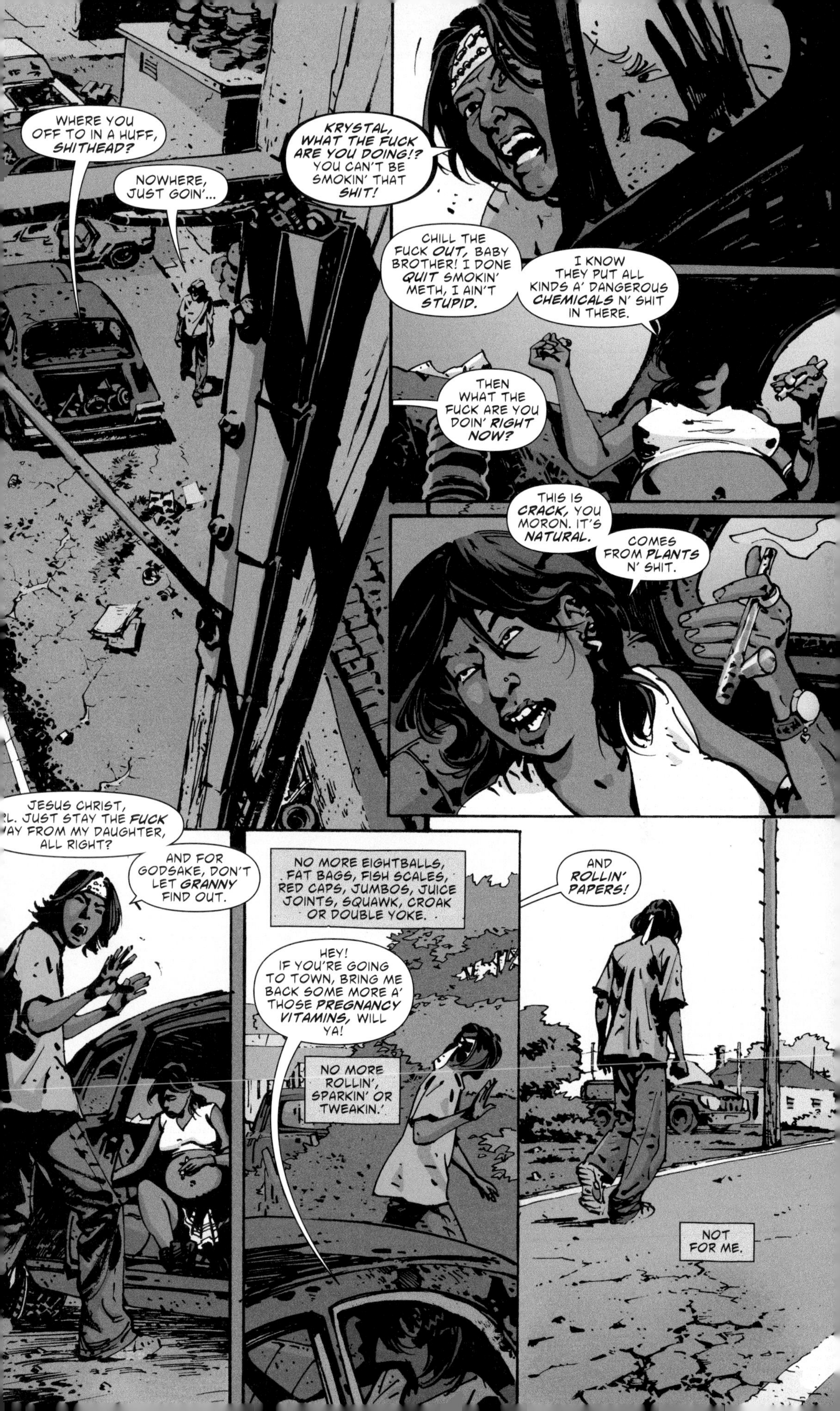

WHERE YOU OFF TO IN A HUFF, SHITHEAD?
NOWHERE, JUST GOIN'...
KRYSTAL, WHAT THE FUCK ARE YOU DOING!? YOU CAN'T BE SMOKIN' THAT SHIT!
CHILL THE FUCK OUT, BABY BROTHER! I DONE QUIT SMOKIN' METH, I AIN'T STUPID.
I KNOW THEY PUT ALL KINDS A' DANGEROUS CHEMICALS N' SHIT IN THERE.
THEN WHAT THE FUCK ARE YOU DOIN' RIGHT NOW?
THIS IS CRACK, YOU MORON. IT'S NATURAL.
COMES FROM PLANTS N' SHIT.
JESUS CHRIST, ...L. JUST STAY THE FUCK ...AY FROM MY DAUGHTER, ALL RIGHT?
AND FOR GODSAKE, DON'T LET GRANNY FIND OUT.
NO MORE EIGHTBALLS, FAT BAGS, FISH SCALES, RED CAPS, JUMBOS, JUICE JOINTS, SQUAWK, CROAK OR DOUBLE YOKE.
HEY! IF YOU'RE GOING TO TOWN, BRING ME BACK SOME MORE A' THOSE PREGNANCY VITAMINS, WILL YA!
NO MORE ROLLIN', SPARKIN' OR TWEAKIN.'
AND ROLLIN' PAPERS!
NOT FOR ME.

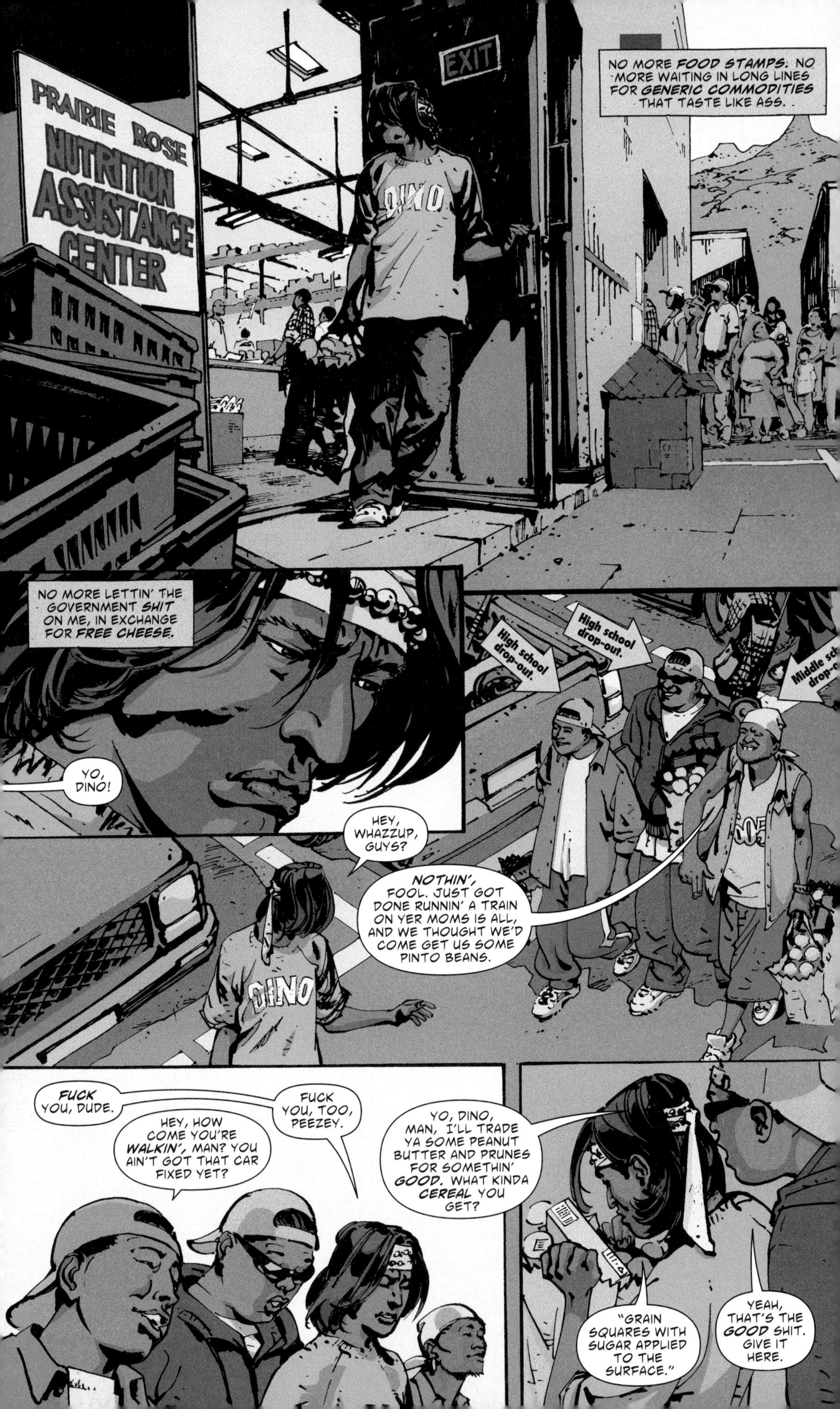

PRAIRIE ROSE NUTRITION ASSISTANCE CENTER
EXIT
NO MORE FOOD STAMPS. NO MORE WAITING IN LONG LINES FOR GENERIC COMMODITIES THAT TASTE LIKE ASS.
DINO
NO MORE LETTIN' THE GOVERNMENT SHIT ON ME, IN EXCHANGE FOR FREE CHEESE.
High school drop-out.
High school drop-out.
Middle sch drop-
YO, DINO!
HEY, WHAZZUP, GUYS?
NOTHIN', FOOL. JUST GOT DONE RUNNIN' A TRAIN ON YER MOMS IS ALL, AND WE THOUGHT WE'D COME GET US SOME PINTO BEANS.
DINO
FUCK YOU, DUDE.
FUCK YOU, TOO, PEEZEY.
HEY, HOW COME YOU'RE WALKIN', MAN? YOU AIN'T GOT THAT CAR FIXED YET?
YO, DINO, MAN, I'LL TRADE YA SOME PEANUT BUTTER AND PRUNES FOR SOMETHIN' GOOD. WHAT KINDA CEREAL YOU GET?
"GRAIN SQUARES WITH SUGAR APPLIED TO THE SURFACE."
YEAH, THAT'S THE GOOD SHIT. GIVE IT HERE.

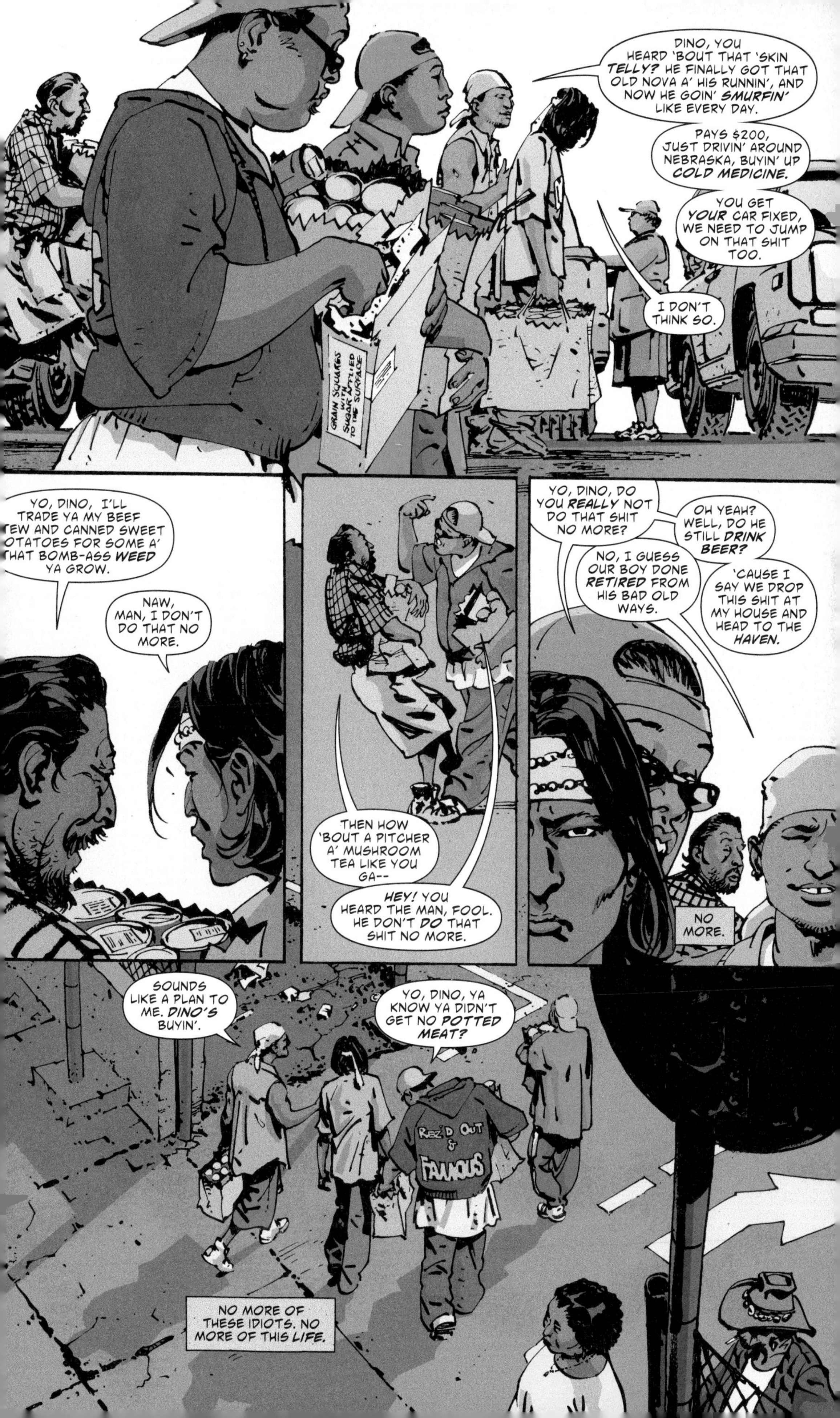
DINO, YOU HEARD 'BOUT THAT 'SKIN TELLY? HE FINALLY GOT THAT OLD NOVA A' HIS RUNNIN', AND NOW HE GOIN' SMURFIN' LIKE EVERY DAY.
PAYS $200, JUST DRIVIN' AROUND NEBRASKA, BUYIN' UP COLD MEDICINE.
YOU GET YOUR CAR FIXED, WE NEED TO JUMP ON THAT SHIT TOO.
I DON'T THINK SO.
GRAIN SQUARES WITH SUGAR APPLIED TO THE SURFACE
YO, DINO, I'LL TRADE YA MY BEEF TEW AND CANNED SWEET OTATOES FOR SOME A' THAT BOMB-ASS WEED YA GROW.
NAW, MAN, I DON'T DO THAT NO MORE.
THEN HOW 'BOUT A PITCHER A' MUSHROOM TEA LIKE YOU GA--
HEY! YOU HEARD THE MAN, FOOL. HE DON'T DO THAT SHIT NO MORE.
YO, DINO, DO YOU REALLY NOT DO THAT SHIT NO MORE?
OH YEAH? WELL, DO HE STILL DRINK BEER?
NO, I GUESS OUR BOY DONE RETIRED FROM HIS BAD OLD WAYS.
'CAUSE I SAY WE DROP THIS SHIT AT MY HOUSE AND HEAD TO THE HAVEN.
NO MORE.
SOUNDS LIKE A PLAN TO ME. DINO'S BUYIN'.
YO, DINO, YA KNOW YA DIDN'T GET NO POTTED MEAT?
REZ'D OUT & FAAAOUS
NO MORE OF THESE IDIOTS. NO MORE OF THIS LIFE.

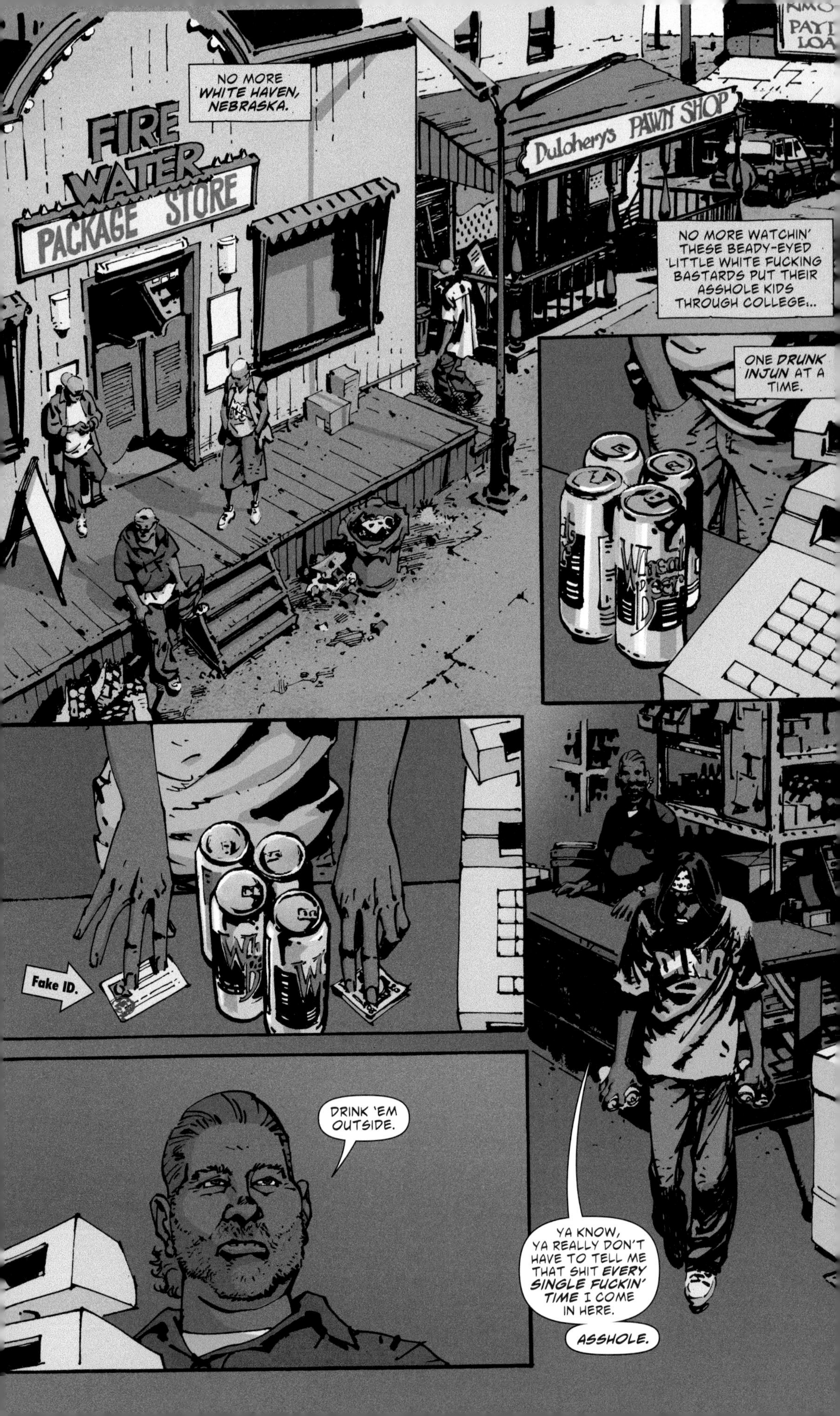
NO MORE WHITE HAVEN, NEBRASKA.
FIRE WATER PACKAGE STORE
Duloherу's PAWN SHOP
NO MORE WATCHIN' THESE BEADY-EYED LITTLE WHITE FUCKING BASTARDS PUT THEIR ASSHOLE KIDS THROUGH COLLEGE...
ONE DRUNK INJUN AT A TIME.
Fake ID.
DRINK 'EM OUTSIDE.
YA KNOW, YA REALLY DON'T HAVE TO TELL ME THAT SHIT EVERY SINGLE FUCKIN' TIME I COME IN HERE.
ASSHOLE.

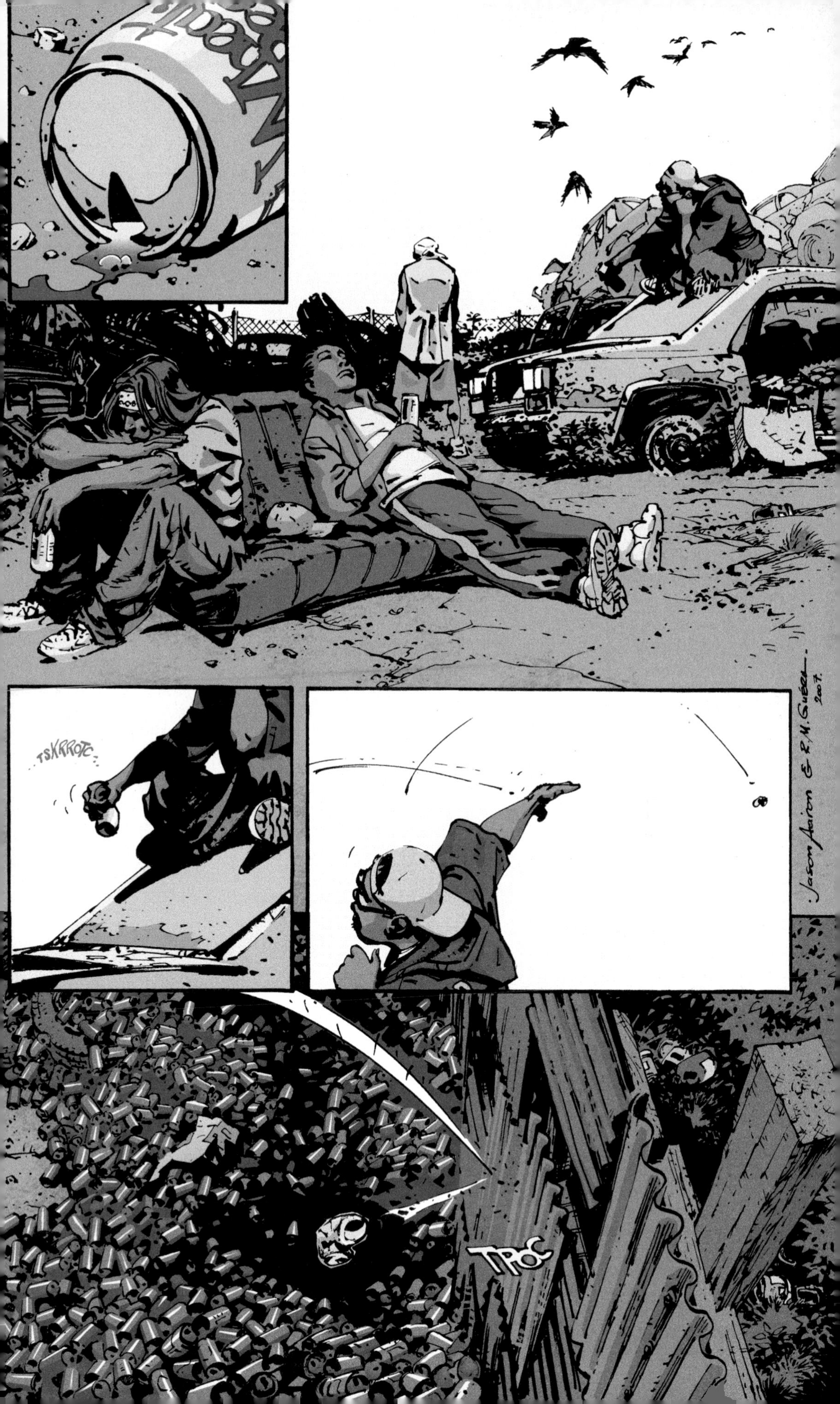
TSKRROTC
Jason Aaron & R.M. Guéra 2007.
TROC

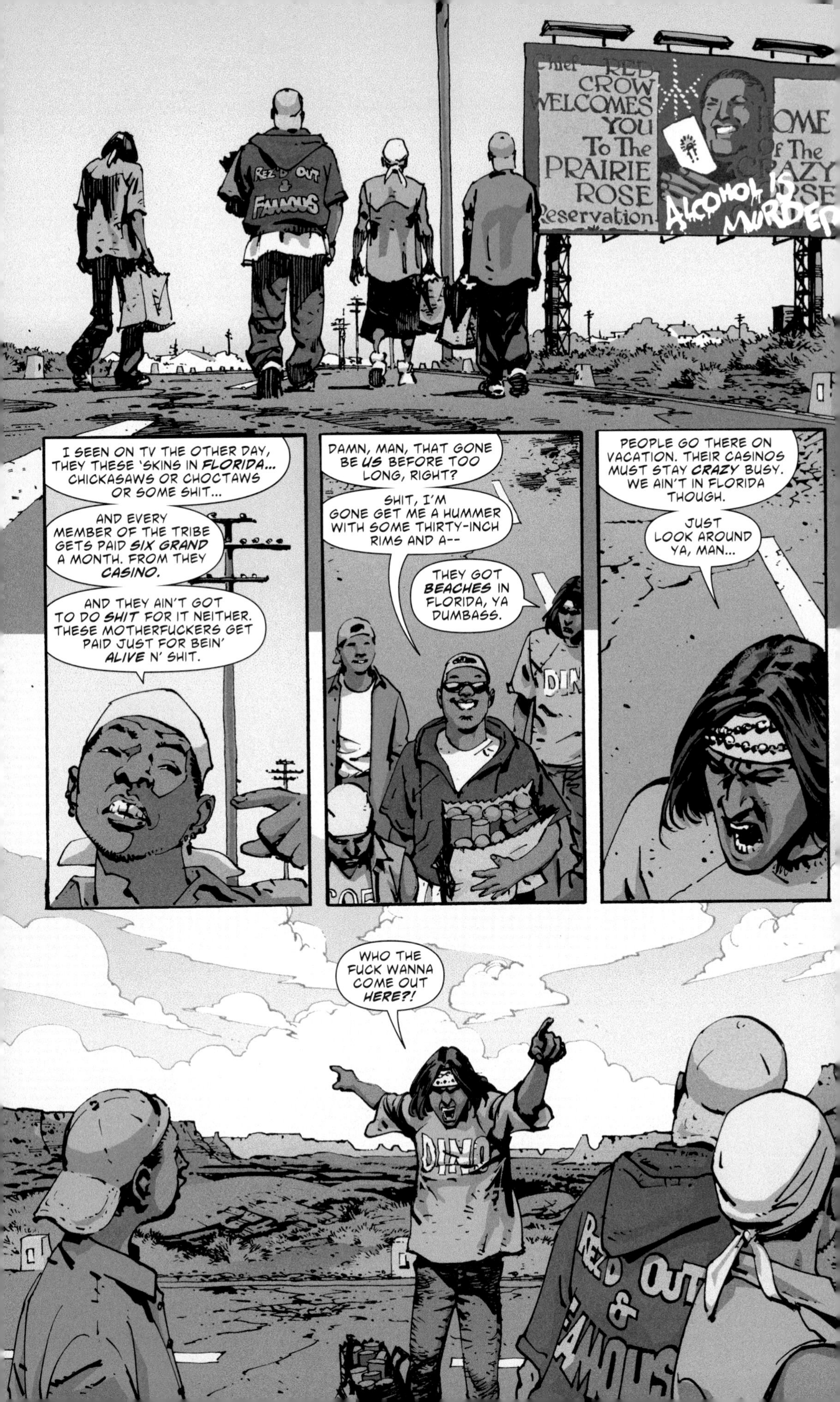
Chief RED CROW WELCOMES YOU To The PRAIRIE ROSE Reservation
HOME Of The CRAZY HORSE
ALCOHOL IS MURDER
REZ'D OUT & FAMOUS
I SEEN ON TV THE OTHER DAY, THEY THESE 'SKINS IN FLORIDA... CHICKASAWS OR CHOCTAWS OR SOME SHIT...
AND EVERY MEMBER OF THE TRIBE GETS PAID SIX GRAND A MONTH. FROM THEY CASINO.
AND THEY AIN'T GOT TO DO SHIT FOR IT NEITHER. THESE MOTHERFUCKERS GET PAID JUST FOR BEIN' ALIVE N' SHIT.
DAMN, MAN, THAT GONE BE US BEFORE TOO LONG, RIGHT?
SHIT, I'M GONE GET ME A HUMMER WITH SOME THIRTY-INCH RIMS AND A--
THEY GOT BEACHES IN FLORIDA, YA DUMBASS.
PEOPLE GO THERE ON VACATION. THEIR CASINOS MUST STAY CRAZY BUSY. WE AIN'T IN FLORIDA THOUGH.
JUST LOOK AROUND YA, MAN...
WHO THE FUCK WANNA COME OUT HERE?!
REZ'D OUT & FAMOUS

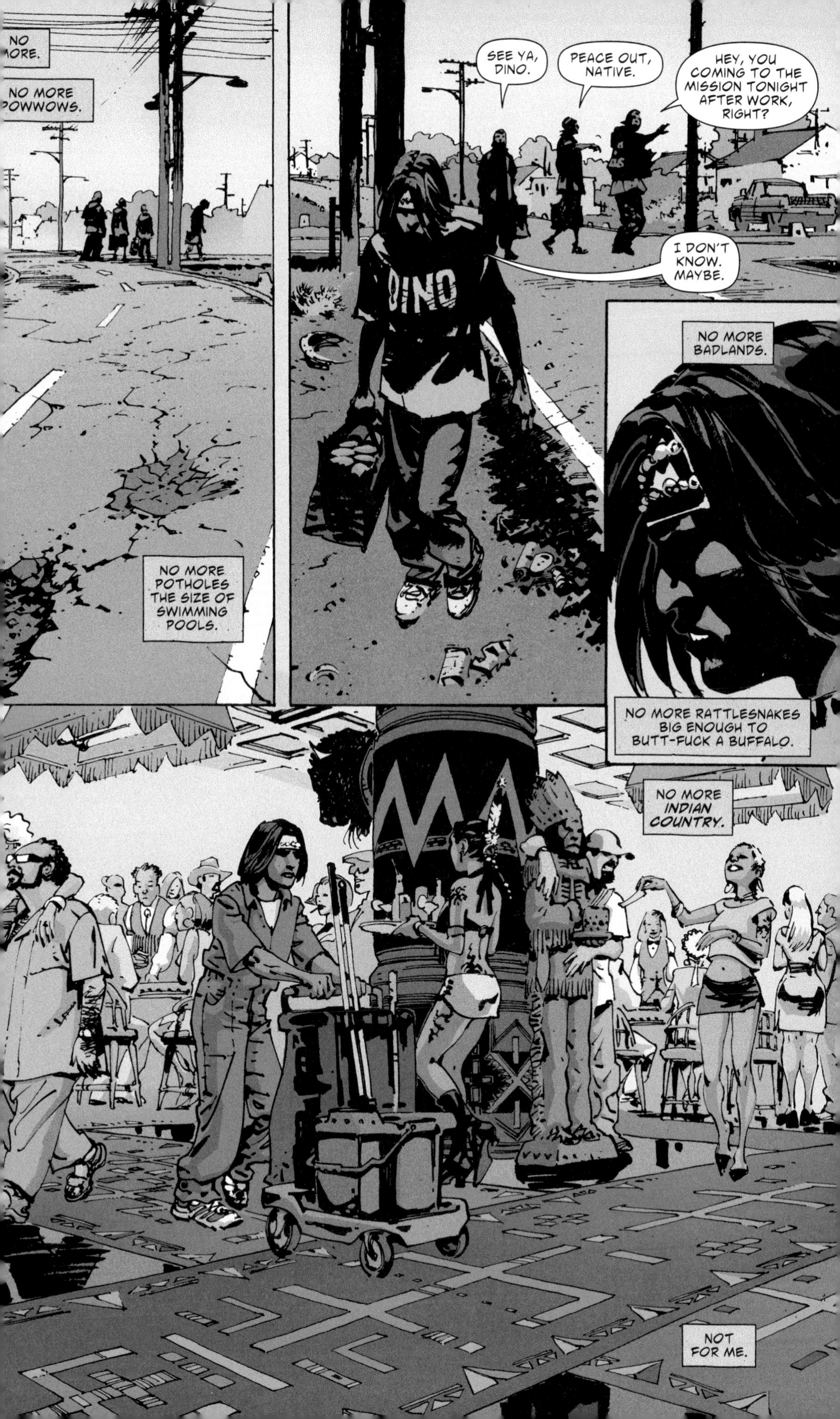
NO MORE.
NO MORE POWWOWS.
NO MORE POTHOLES THE SIZE OF SWIMMING POOLS.
SEE YA, DINO.
PEACE OUT, NATIVE.
HEY, YOU COMING TO THE MISSION TONIGHT AFTER WORK, RIGHT?
I DON'T KNOW. MAYBE.
DINO
NO MORE BADLANDS.
NO MORE RATTLESNAKES BIG ENOUGH TO BUTT-FUCK A BUFFALO.
NO MORE *INDIAN COUNTRY*.
NOT FOR ME.

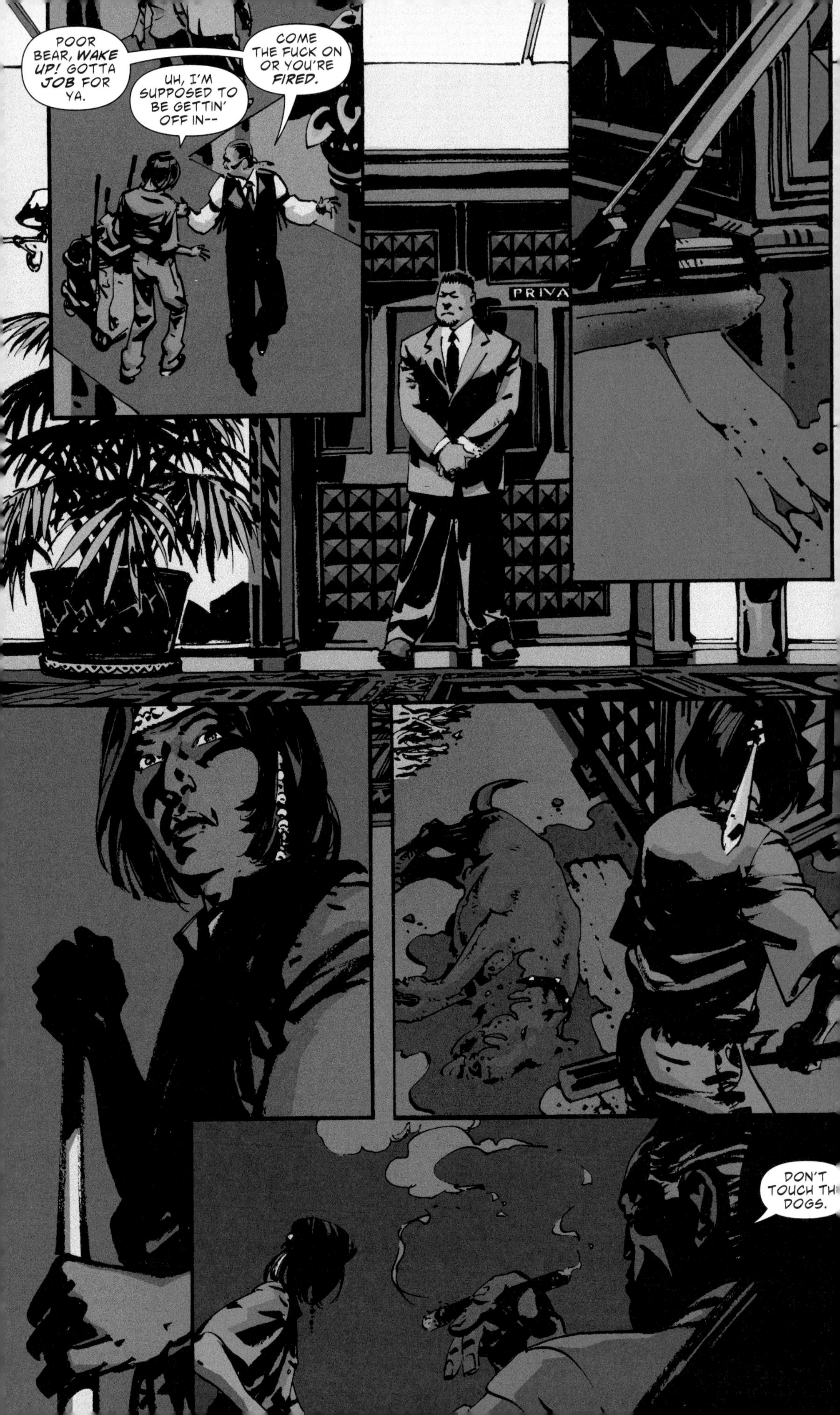
POOR BEAR, WAKE UP! GOTTA JOB FOR YA.
UH, I'M SUPPOSED TO BE GETTIN' OFF IN--
COME THE FUCK ON OR YOU'RE FIRED.
PRIVA
DON'T TOUCH TH DOGS.

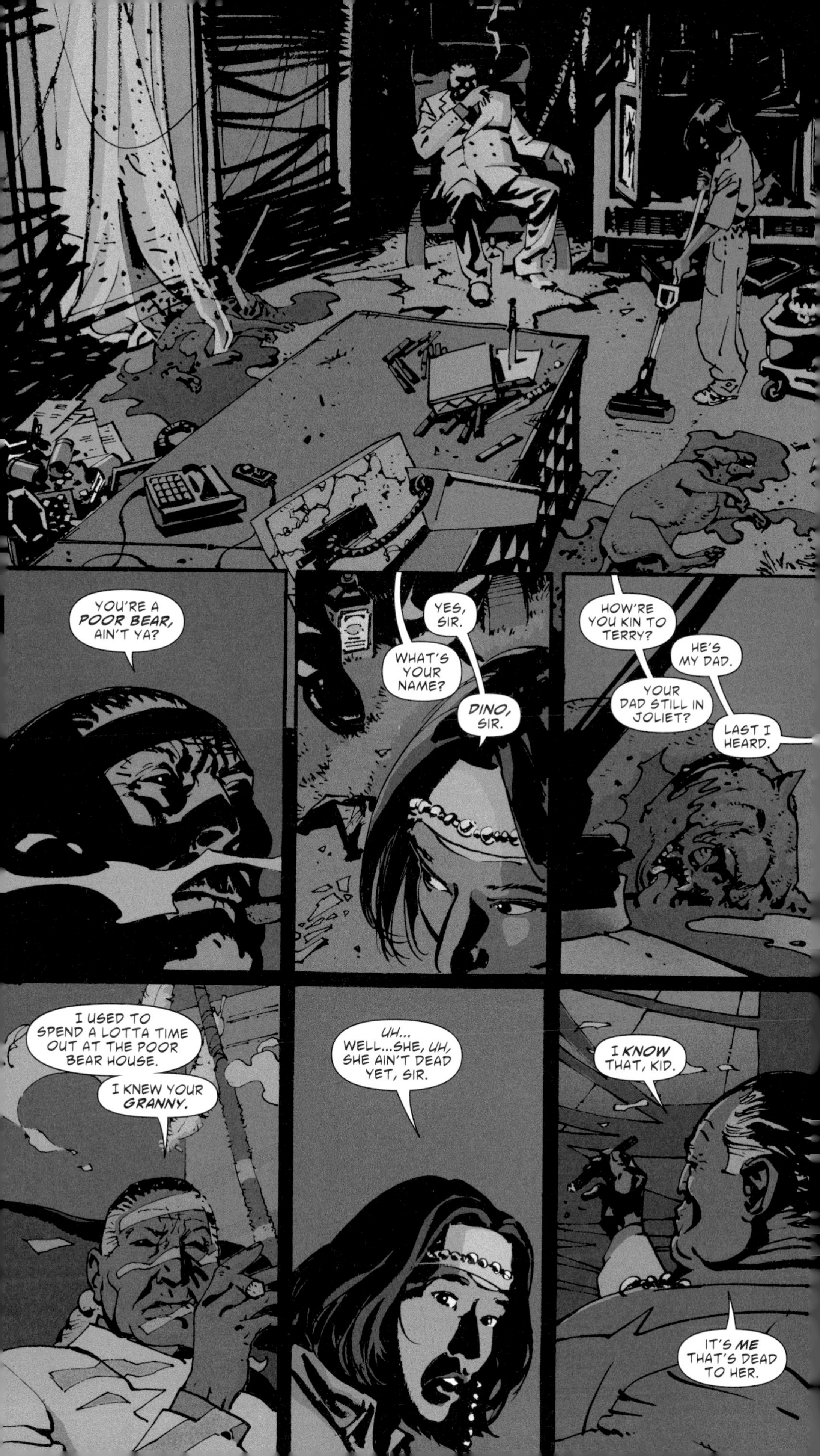

YOU'RE A POOR BEAR, AIN'T YA?
YES, SIR.
WHAT'S YOUR NAME?
DINO, SIR.
HOW'RE YOU KIN TO TERRY?
HE'S MY DAD.
YOUR DAD STILL IN JOLIET?
LAST I HEARD.
I USED TO SPEND A LOTTA TIME OUT AT THE POOR BEAR HOUSE.
I KNEW YOUR GRANNY.
UH... WELL...SHE, UH, SHE AIN'T DEAD YET, SIR.
I KNOW THAT, KID.
IT'S ME THAT'S DEAD TO HER.

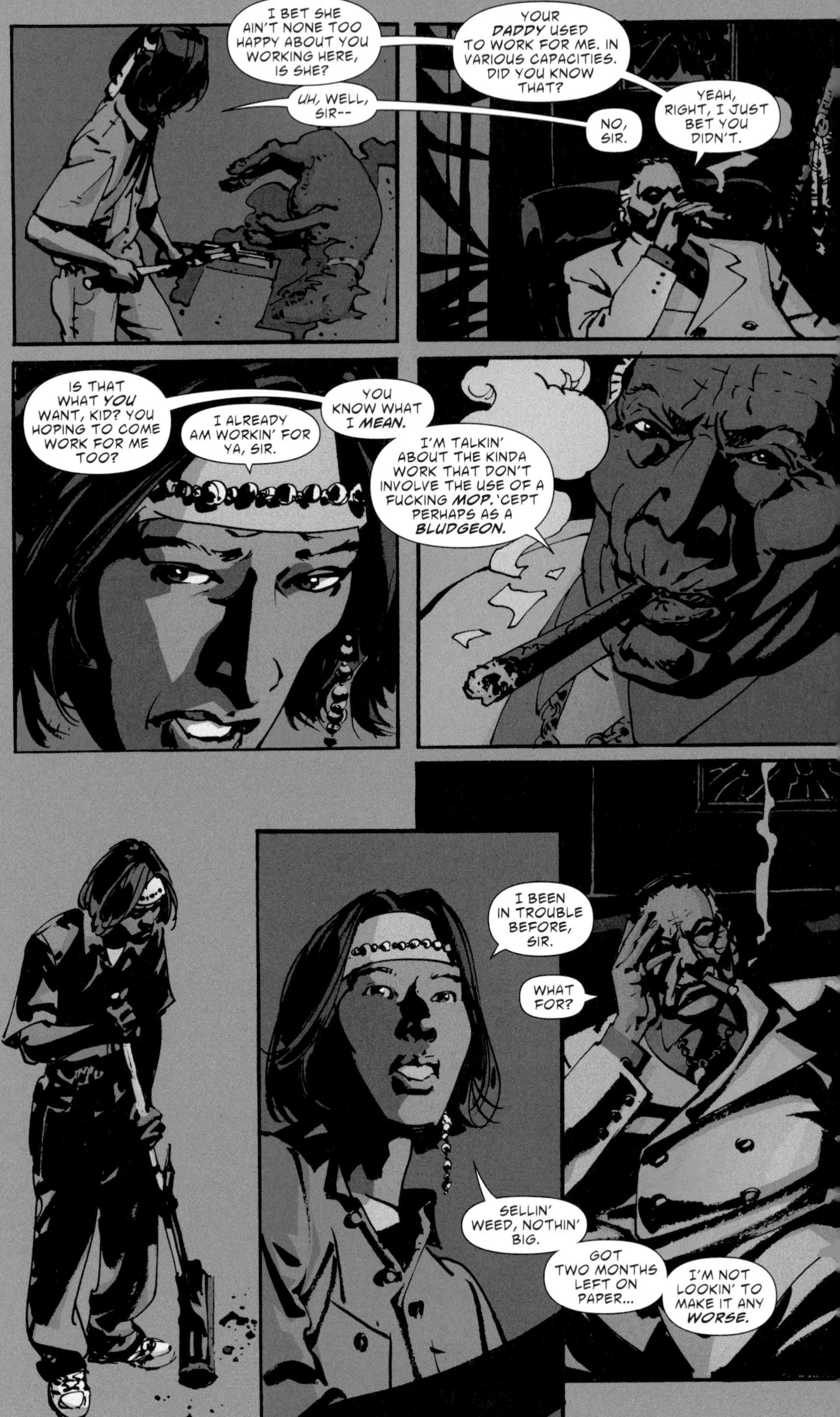
I BET SHE AIN'T NONE TOO HAPPY ABOUT YOU WORKING HERE, IS SHE?
UH, WELL, SIR--
YOUR DADDY USED TO WORK FOR ME. IN VARIOUS CAPACITIES. DID YOU KNOW THAT?
NO, SIR.
YEAH, RIGHT, I JUST BET YOU DIDN'T.
IS THAT WHAT YOU WANT, KID? YOU HOPING TO COME WORK FOR ME TOO?
I ALREADY AM WORKIN' FOR YA, SIR.
YOU KNOW WHAT I MEAN.
I'M TALKIN' ABOUT THE KINDA WORK THAT DON'T INVOLVE THE USE OF A FUCKING MOP. 'CEPT PERHAPS AS A BLUDGEON.
I BEEN IN TROUBLE BEFORE, SIR.
WHAT FOR?
SELLIN' WEED, NOTHIN' BIG.
GOT TWO MONTHS LEFT ON PAPER...
I'M NOT LOOKIN' TO MAKE IT ANY WORSE.

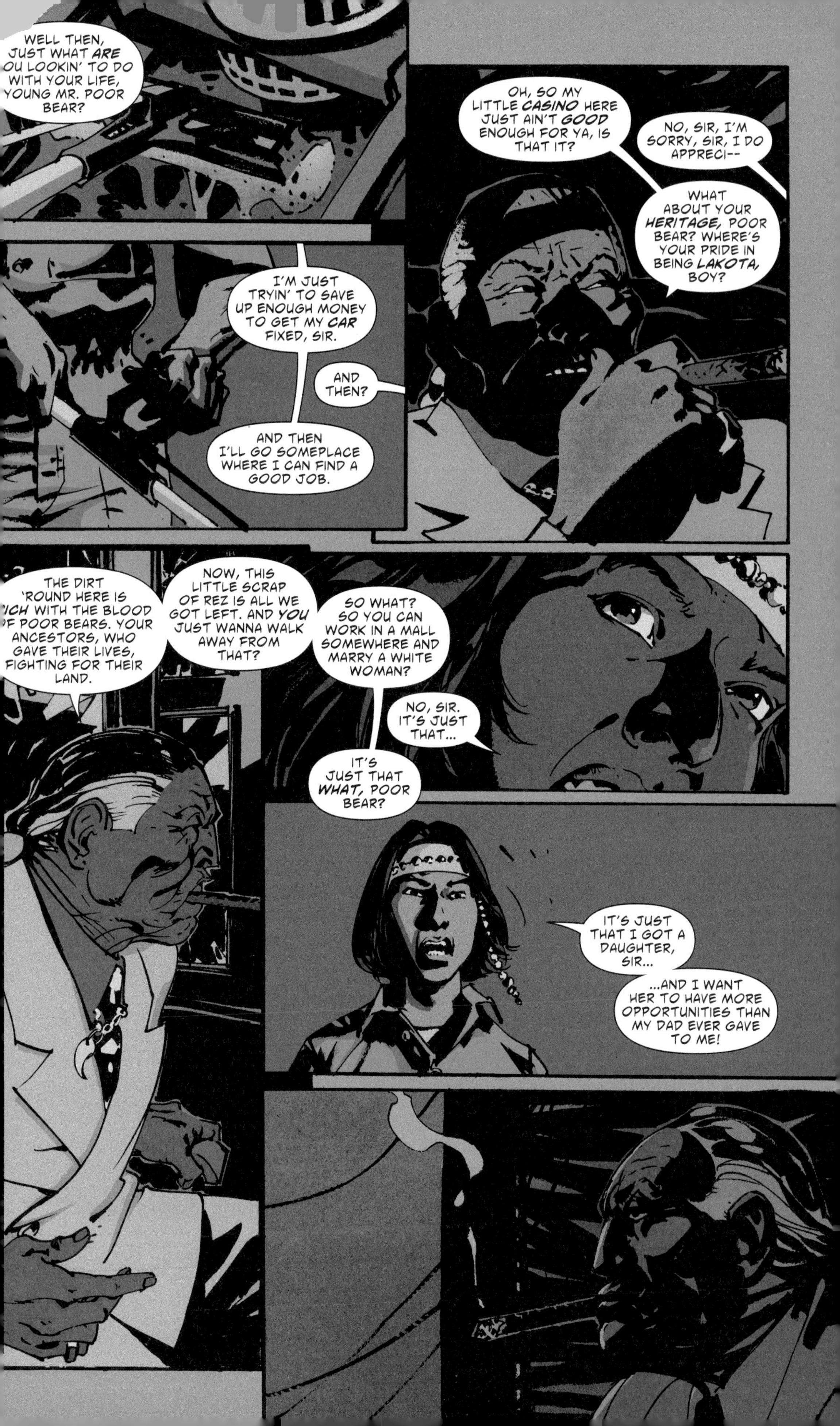
WELL THEN, JUST WHAT ARE OU LOOKIN' TO DO WITH YOUR LIFE, YOUNG MR. POOR BEAR?
I'M JUST TRYIN' TO SAVE UP ENOUGH MONEY TO GET MY CAR FIXED, SIR.
AND THEN?
AND THEN I'LL GO SOMEPLACE WHERE I CAN FIND A GOOD JOB.
OH, SO MY LITTLE CASINO HERE JUST AIN'T GOOD ENOUGH FOR YA, IS THAT IT?
NO, SIR, I'M SORRY, SIR, I DO APPRECI--
WHAT ABOUT YOUR HERITAGE, POOR BEAR? WHERE'S YOUR PRIDE IN BEING LAKOTA, BOY?
THE DIRT 'ROUND HERE IS ICH WITH THE BLOOD F POOR BEARS. YOUR ANCESTORS, WHO GAVE THEIR LIVES, FIGHTING FOR THEIR LAND.
NOW, THIS LITTLE SCRAP OF REZ IS ALL WE GOT LEFT. AND YOU JUST WANNA WALK AWAY FROM THAT?
SO WHAT? SO YOU CAN WORK IN A MALL SOMEWHERE AND MARRY A WHITE WOMAN?
NO, SIR. IT'S JUST THAT...
IT'S JUST THAT WHAT, POOR BEAR?
IT'S JUST THAT I GOT A DAUGHTER, SIR...
...AND I WANT HER TO HAVE MORE OPPORTUNITIES THAN MY DAD EVER GAVE TO ME!

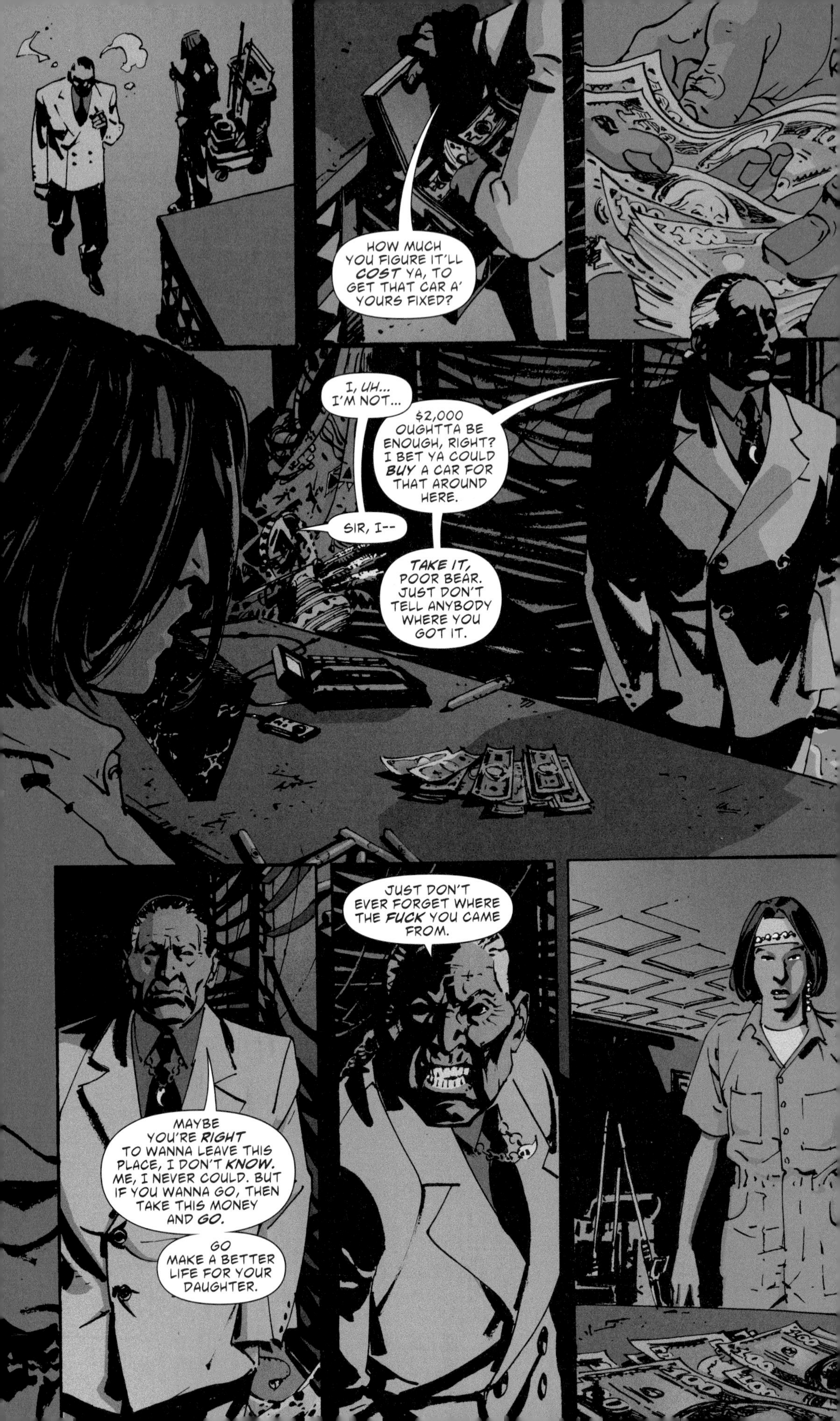
HOW MUCH YOU FIGURE IT'LL COST YA, TO GET THAT CAR A' YOURS FIXED?
I, UH... I'M NOT...
$2,000 OUGHTTA BE ENOUGH, RIGHT? I BET YA COULD BUY A CAR FOR THAT AROUND HERE.
SIR, I--
TAKE IT, POOR BEAR. JUST DON'T TELL ANYBODY WHERE YOU GOT IT.
MAYBE YOU'RE RIGHT TO WANNA LEAVE THIS PLACE, I DON'T KNOW. ME, I NEVER COULD. BUT IF YOU WANNA GO, THEN TAKE THIS MONEY AND GO.
GO MAKE A BETTER LIFE FOR YOUR DAUGHTER.
JUST DON'T EVER FORGET WHERE THE FUCK YOU CAME FROM.

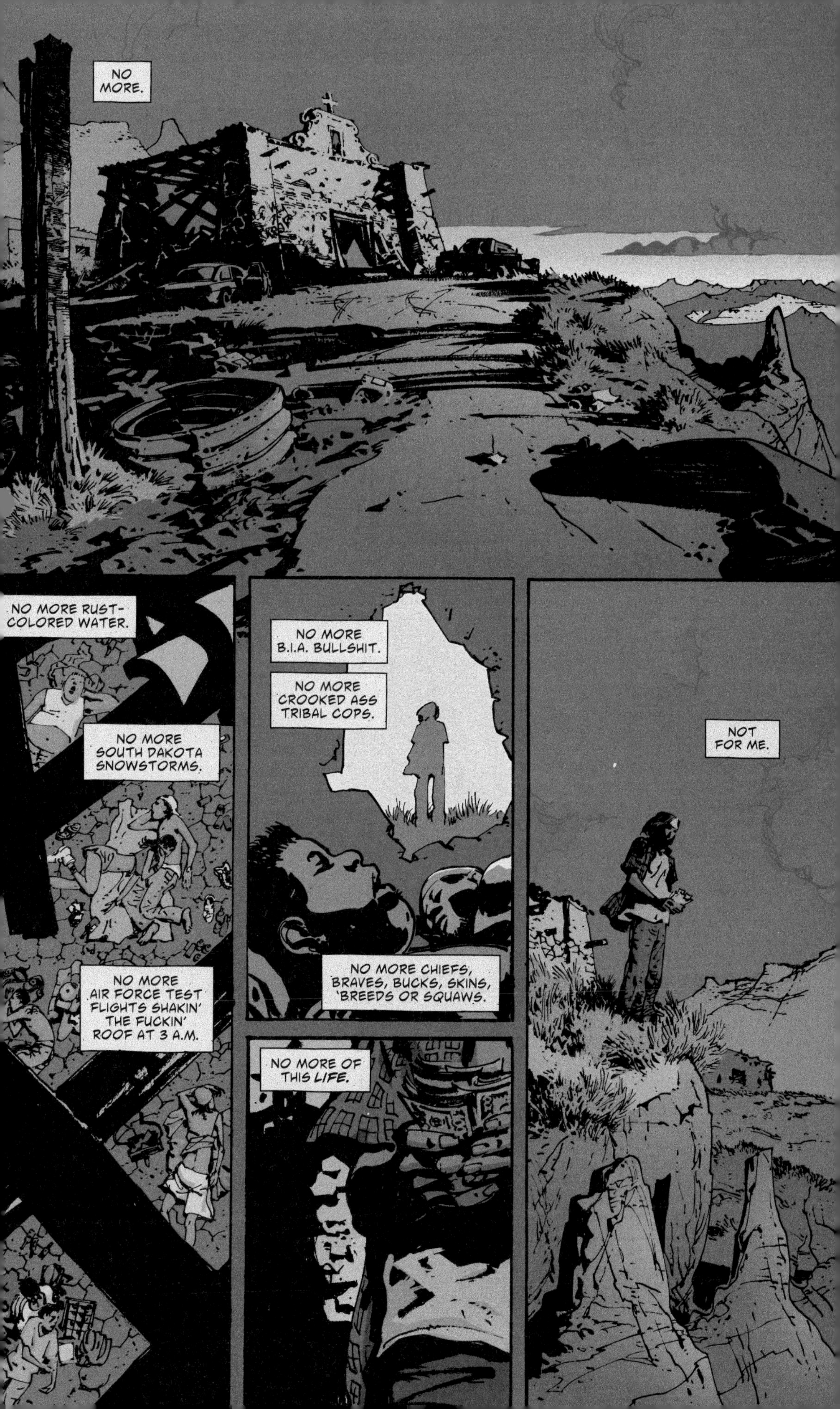

NO MORE.
NO MORE RUST-COLORED WATER.
NO MORE SOUTH DAKOTA SNOWSTORMS.
NO MORE AIR FORCE TEST FLIGHTS SHAKIN' THE FUCKIN' ROOF AT 3 A.M.
NO MORE B.I.A. BULLSHIT.
NO MORE CROOKED ASS TRIBAL COPS.
NO MORE CHIEFS, BRAVES, BUCKS, SKINS, 'BREEDS OR SQUAWS.
NO MORE OF THIS *LIFE*.
NOT FOR ME.

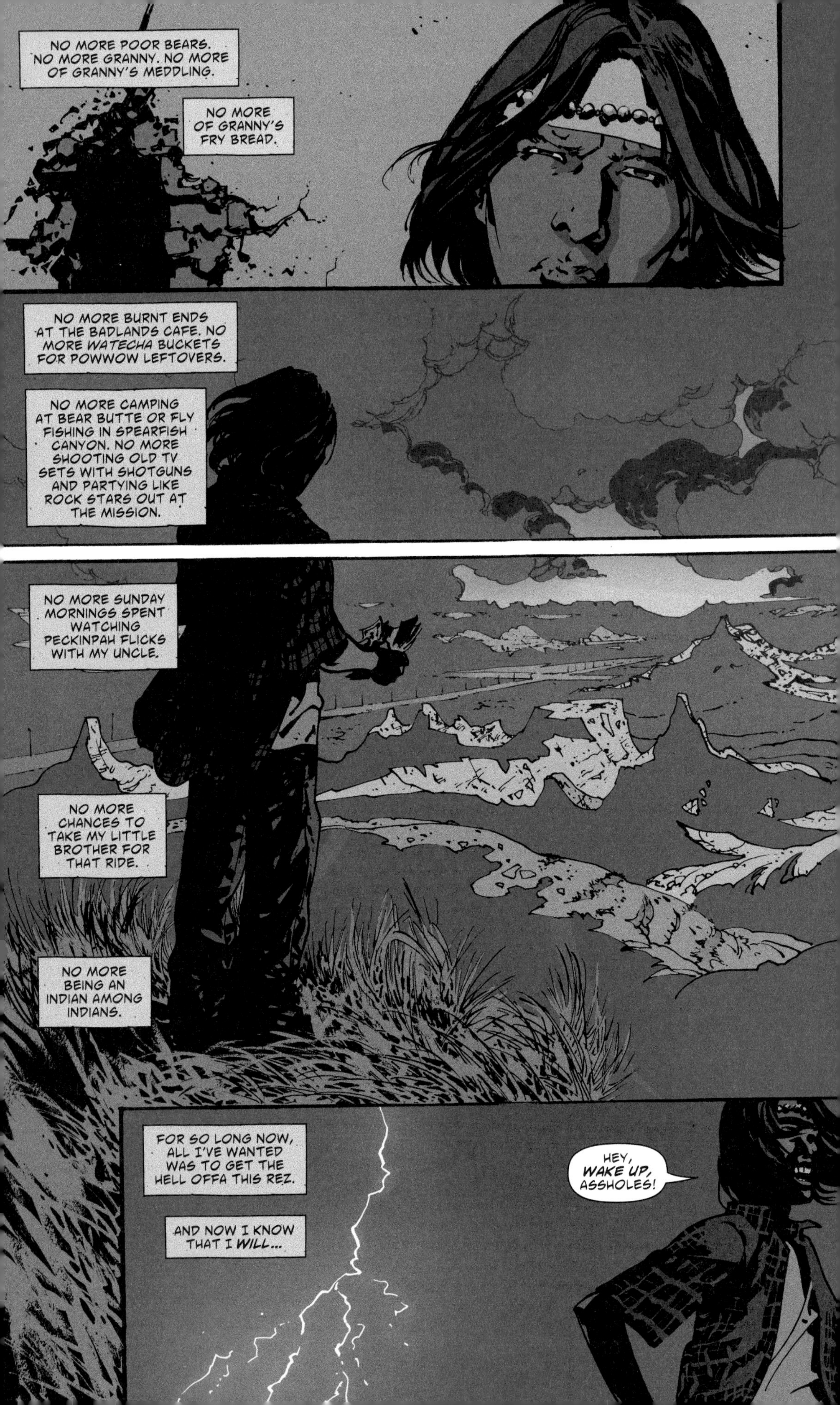
NO MORE POOR BEARS. NO MORE GRANNY. NO MORE OF GRANNY'S MEDDLING.
NO MORE OF GRANNY'S FRY BREAD.
NO MORE BURNT ENDS AT THE BADLANDS CAFE. NO MORE *WATECHA* BUCKETS FOR POWWOW LEFTOVERS.
NO MORE CAMPING AT BEAR BUTTE OR FLY FISHING IN SPEARFISH CANYON. NO MORE SHOOTING OLD TV SETS WITH SHOTGUNS AND PARTYING LIKE ROCK STARS OUT AT THE MISSION.
NO MORE SUNDAY MORNINGS SPENT WATCHING PECKINPAH FLICKS WITH MY UNCLE.
NO MORE CHANCES TO TAKE MY LITTLE BROTHER FOR THAT RIDE.
NO MORE BEING AN INDIAN AMONG INDIANS.
FOR SO LONG NOW, ALL I'VE WANTED WAS TO GET THE HELL OFFA THIS REZ.
AND NOW I KNOW THAT I ***WILL...***
HEY, ***WAKE UP,*** ASSHOLES!

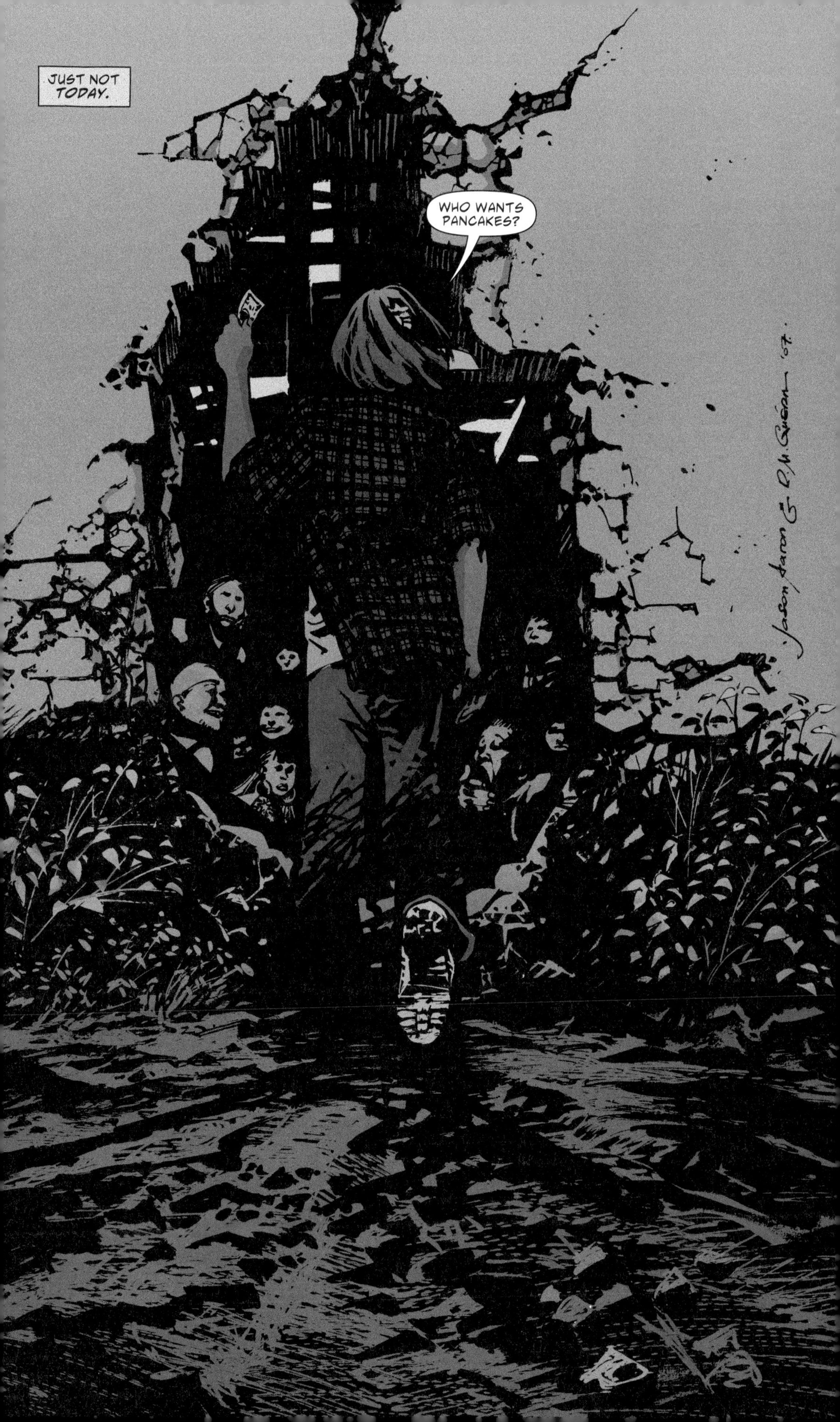
JUST NOT TODAY.
WHO WANTS PANCAKES?
Jason Aaron & R.M. Guéra '07.

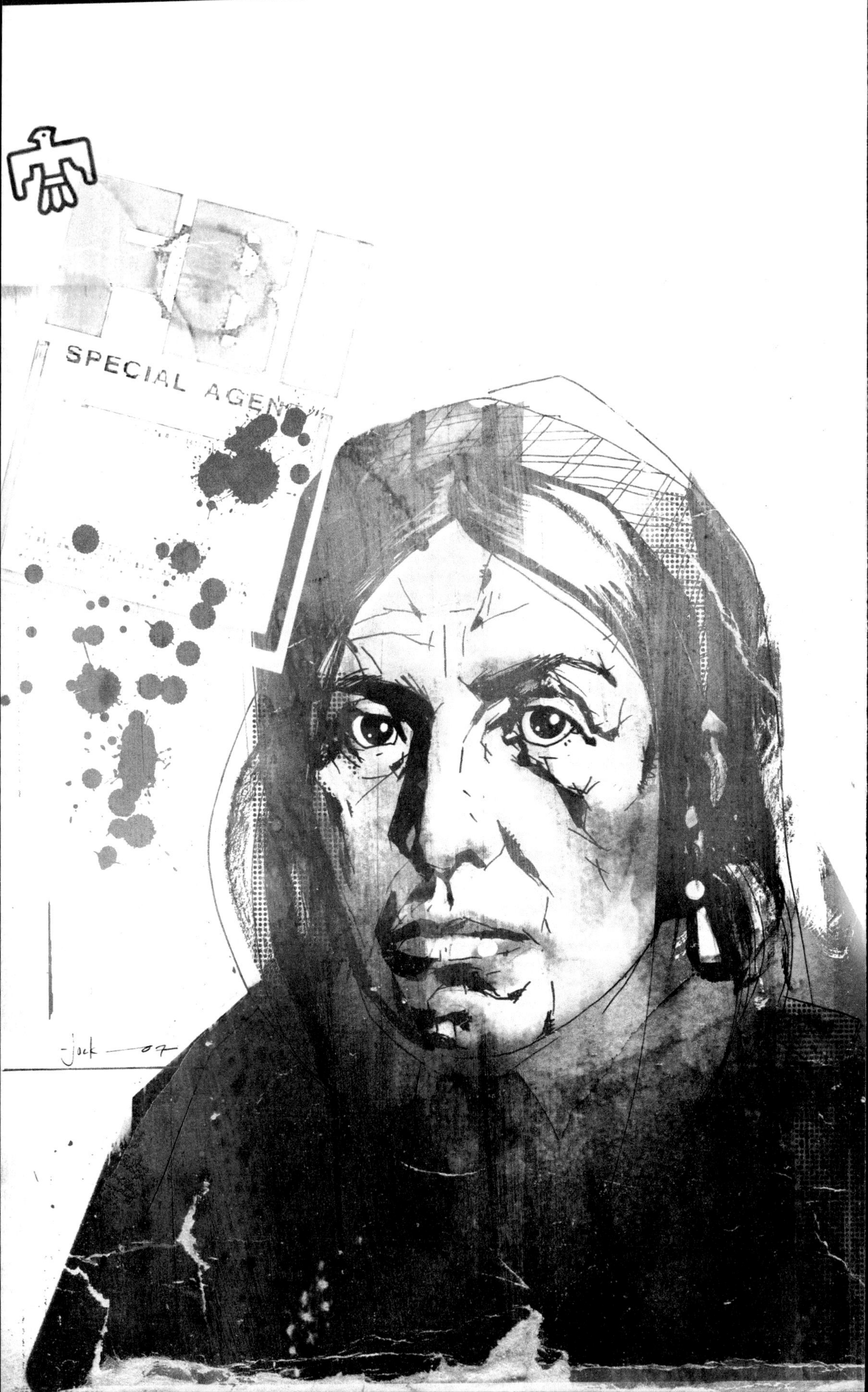
SPECIAL AGEN
Jock 07

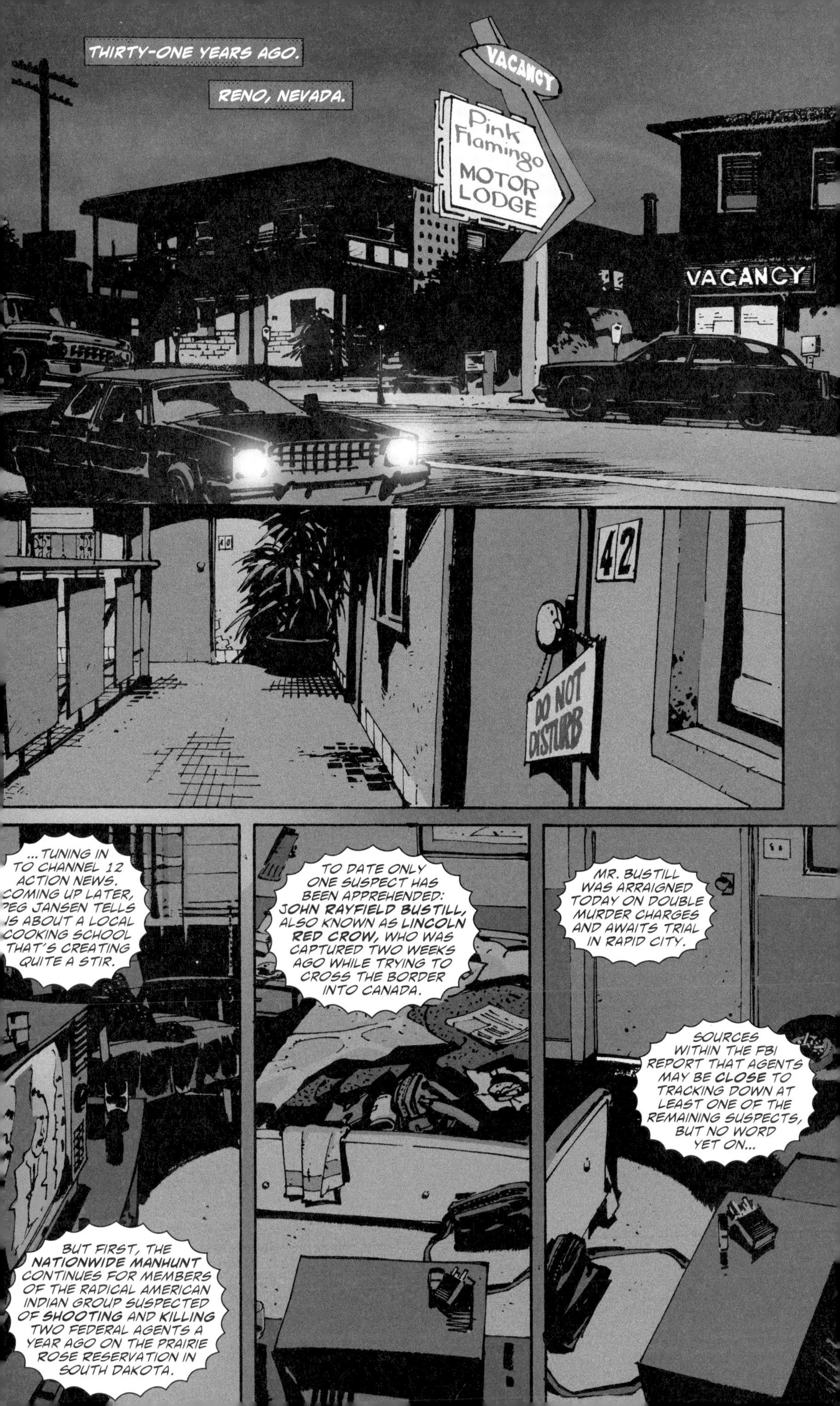

THIRTY-ONE YEARS AGO.
RENO, NEVADA.
VACANCY
Pink Flamingo MOTOR LODGE
VACANCY
40
42
DO NOT DISTURB
...TUNING IN TO CHANNEL 12 ACTION NEWS. COMING UP LATER, PEG JANSEN TELLS US ABOUT A LOCAL COOKING SCHOOL THAT'S CREATING QUITE A STIR.
BUT FIRST, THE NATIONWIDE MANHUNT CONTINUES FOR MEMBERS OF THE RADICAL AMERICAN INDIAN GROUP SUSPECTED OF SHOOTING AND KILLING TWO FEDERAL AGENTS A YEAR AGO ON THE PRAIRIE ROSE RESERVATION IN SOUTH DAKOTA.
TO DATE ONLY ONE SUSPECT HAS BEEN APPREHENDED: JOHN RAYFIELD BUSTILL, ALSO KNOWN AS LINCOLN RED CROW, WHO WAS CAPTURED TWO WEEKS AGO WHILE TRYING TO CROSS THE BORDER INTO CANADA.
MR. BUSTILL WAS ARRAIGNED TODAY ON DOUBLE MURDER CHARGES AND AWAITS TRIAL IN RAPID CITY.
SOURCES WITHIN THE FBI REPORT THAT AGENTS MAY BE CLOSE TO TRACKING DOWN AT LEAST ONE OF THE REMAINING SUSPECTS, BUT NO WORD YET ON...

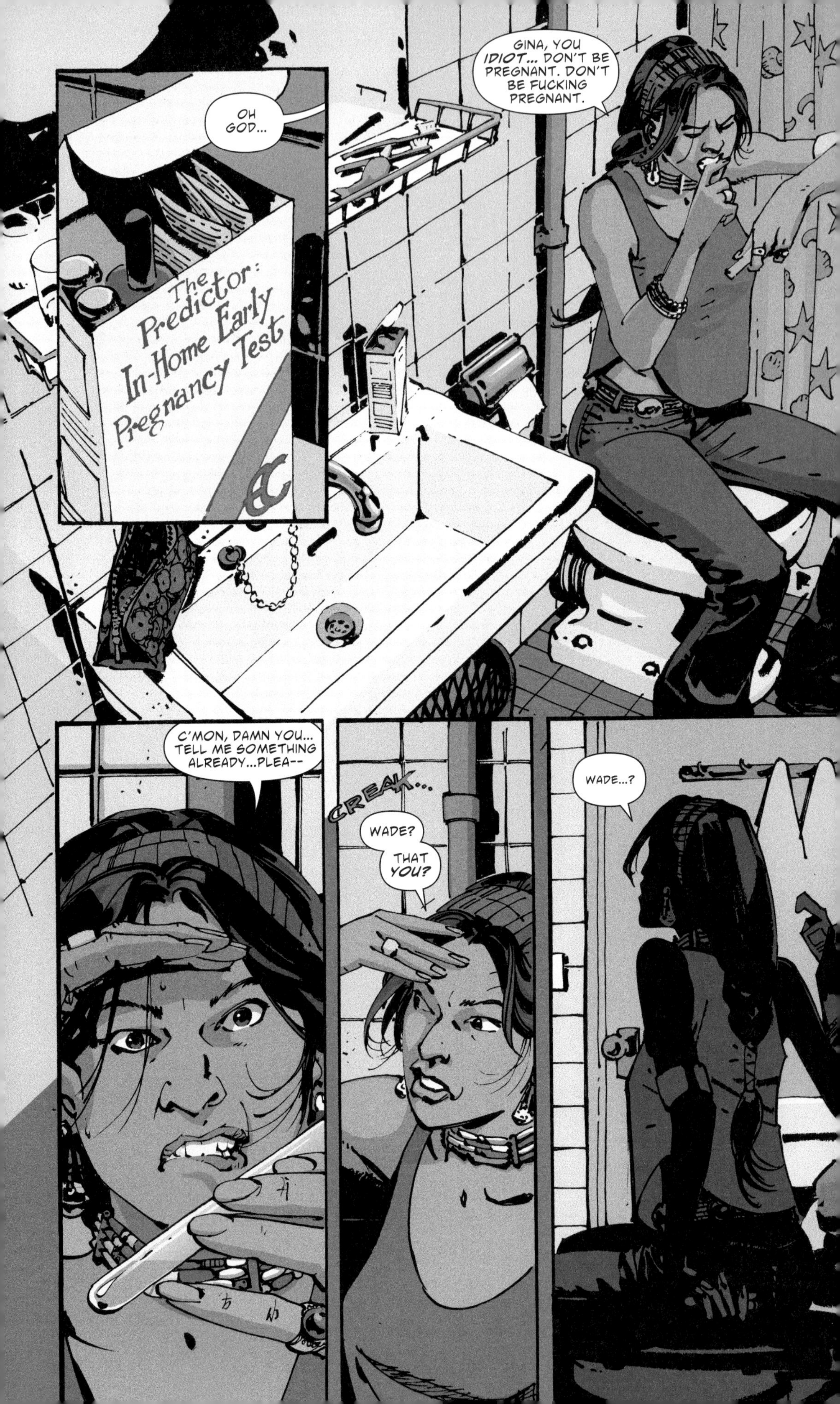
OH GOD...
The Predictor: In-Home Early Pregnancy Test
GINA, YOU IDIOT... DON'T BE PREGNANT. DON'T BE FUCKING PREGNANT.
C'MON, DAMN YOU... TELL ME SOMETHING ALREADY...PLEA--
CREAK...
WADE?
THAT YOU?
WADE...?

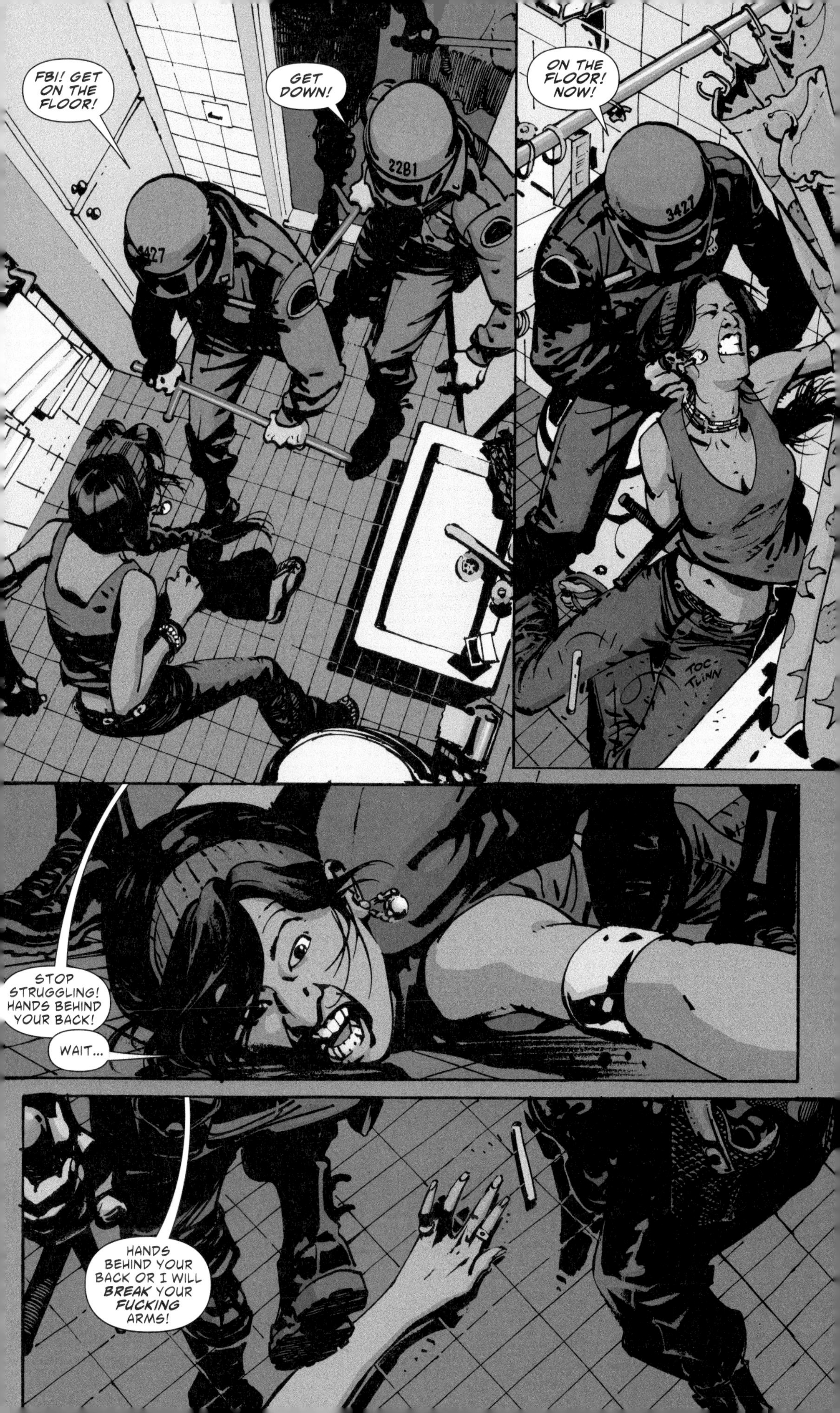

FBI! GET ON THE FLOOR!
GET DOWN!
2281
3427
ON THE FLOOR! NOW!
3427
TOC-TLINN
STOP STRUGGLING! HANDS BEHIND YOUR BACK!
WAIT...
HANDS BEHIND YOUR BACK OR I WILL BREAK YOUR FUCKING ARMS!

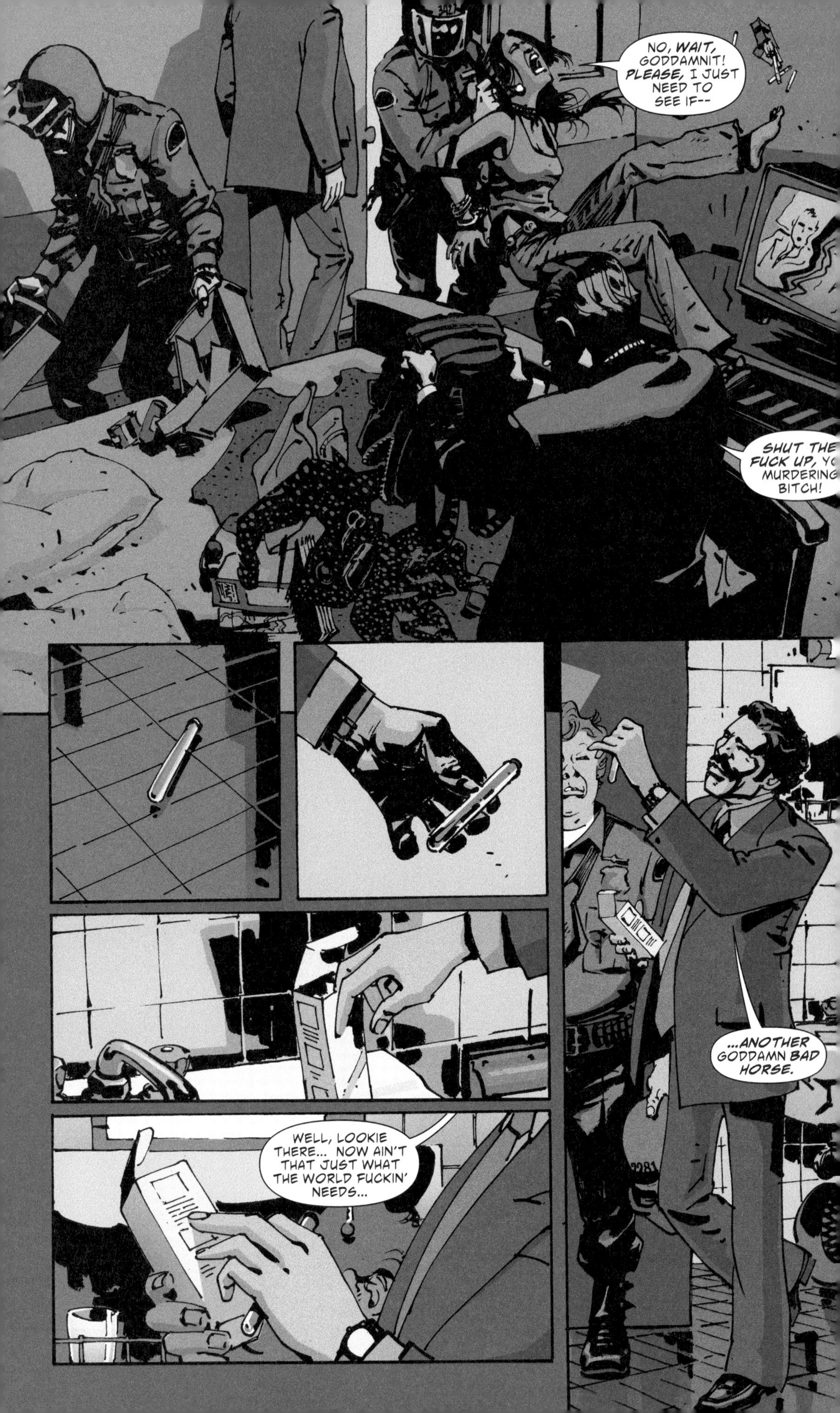
NO, WAIT, GODDAMNIT! PLEASE, I JUST NEED TO SEE IF--
SHUT THE FUCK UP, YO MURDERING BITCH!
WELL, LOOKIE THERE... NOW AIN'T THAT JUST WHAT THE WORLD FUCKIN' NEEDS...
...ANOTHER GODDAMN BAD HORSE.

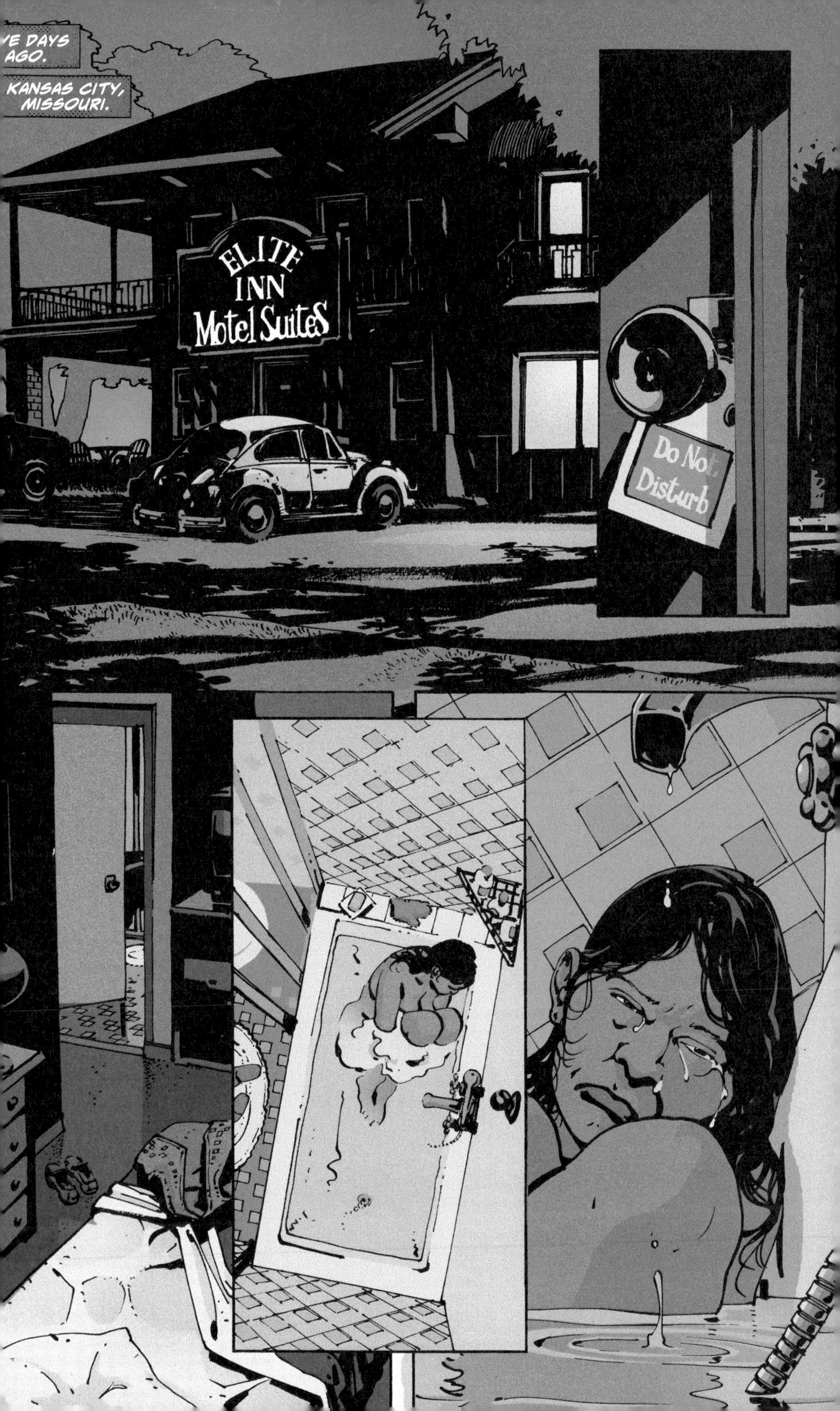

E DAYS AGO.
KANSAS CITY, MISSOURI.
ELITE INN Motel Suites
Do Not Disturb

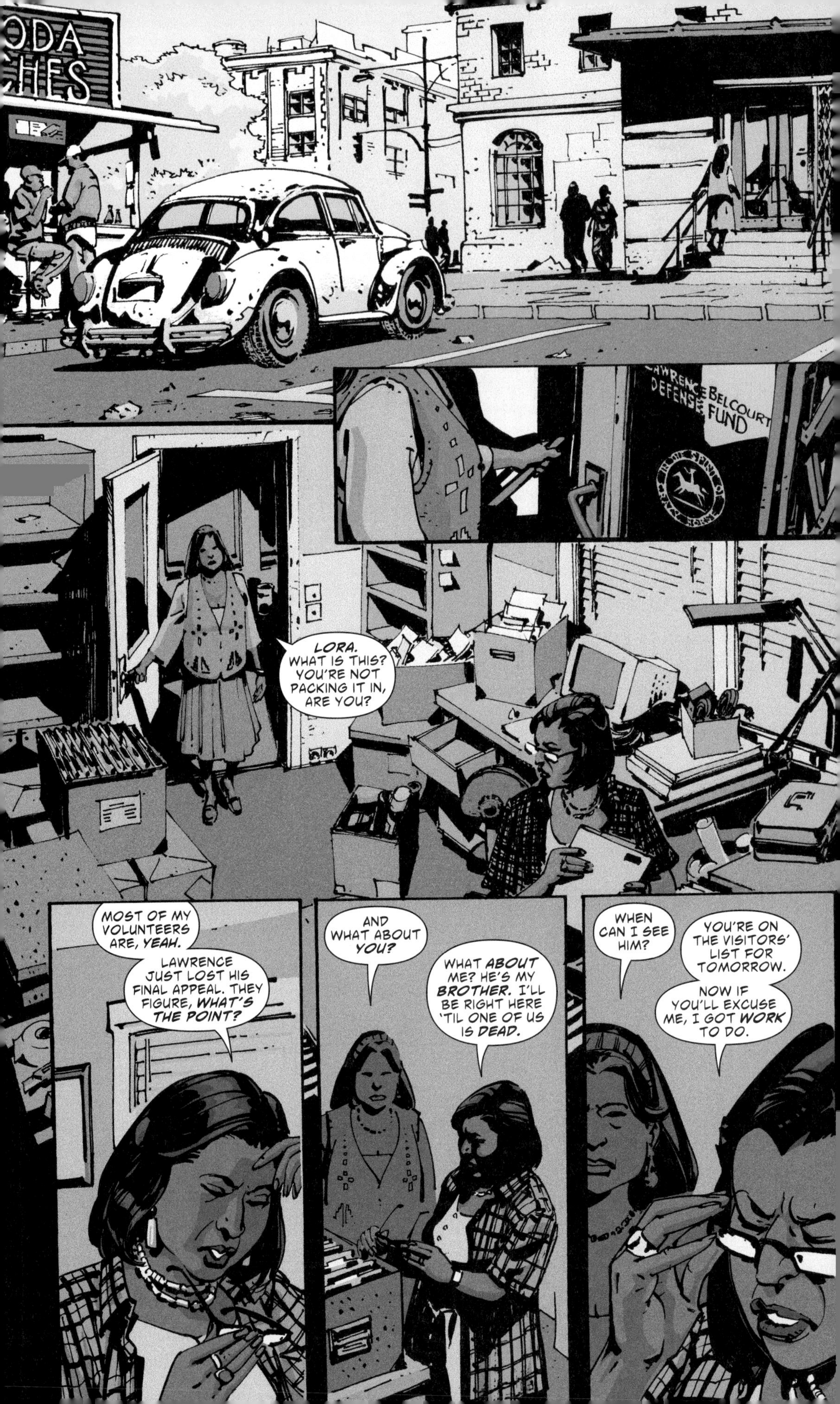
ODA
HES
LAWRENCE BELCOURT
DEFENSE FUND
LORA. WHAT IS THIS? YOU'RE NOT PACKING IT IN, ARE YOU?
MOST OF MY VOLUNTEERS ARE, YEAH.
LAWRENCE JUST LOST HIS FINAL APPEAL. THEY FIGURE, WHAT'S THE POINT?
AND WHAT ABOUT YOU?
WHAT ABOUT ME? HE'S MY BROTHER. I'LL BE RIGHT HERE 'TIL ONE OF US IS DEAD.
WHEN CAN I SEE HIM?
YOU'RE ON THE VISITORS' LIST FOR TOMORROW.
NOW IF YOU'LL EXCUSE ME, I GOT WORK TO DO.

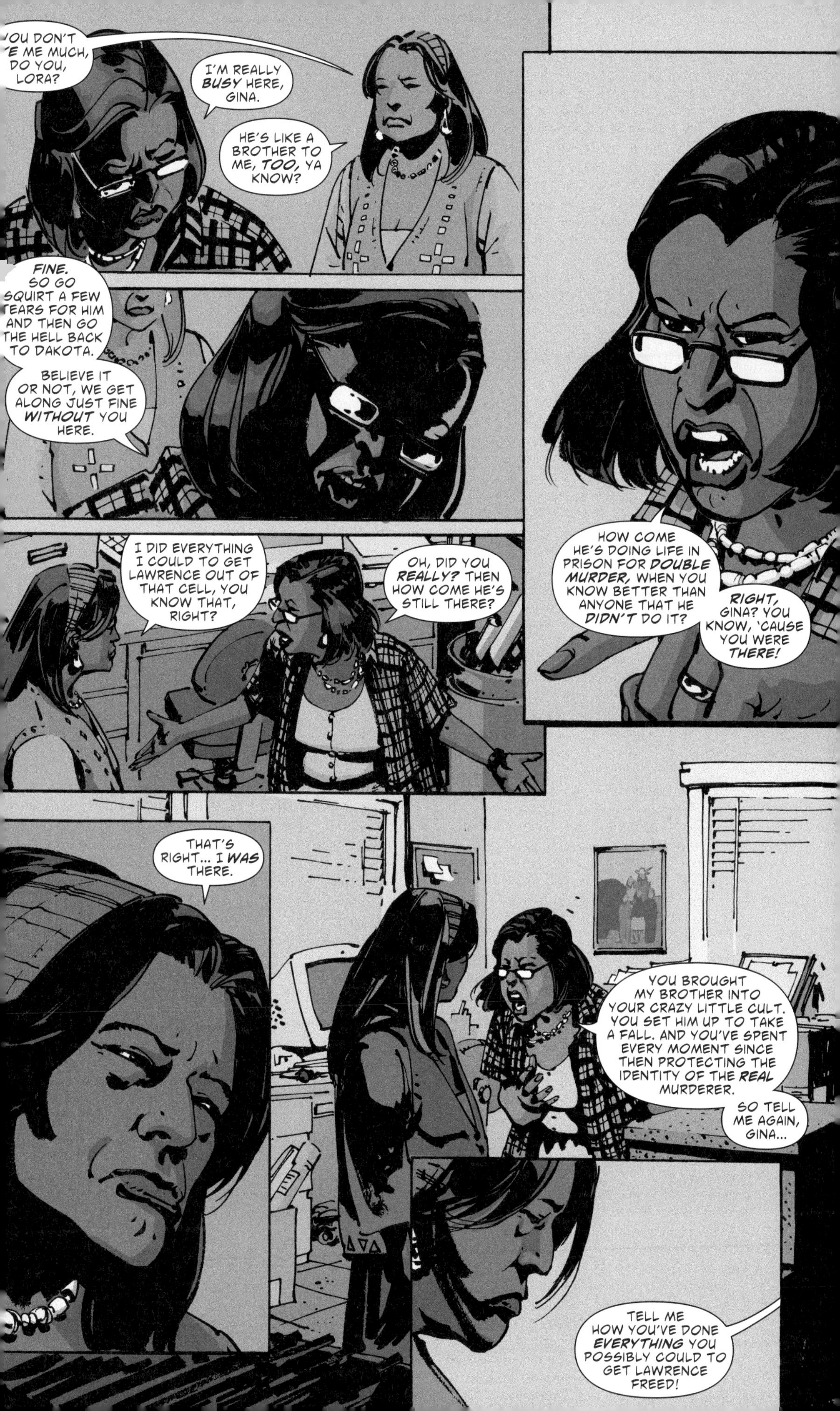

YOU DON'T 'E ME MUCH, DO YOU, LORA?
I'M REALLY BUSY HERE, GINA.
HE'S LIKE A BROTHER TO ME, TOO, YA KNOW?
FINE. SO GO SQUIRT A FEW TEARS FOR HIM AND THEN GO THE HELL BACK TO DAKOTA.
BELIEVE IT OR NOT, WE GET ALONG JUST FINE WITHOUT YOU HERE.
I DID EVERYTHING I COULD TO GET LAWRENCE OUT OF THAT CELL, YOU KNOW THAT, RIGHT?
OH, DID YOU REALLY? THEN HOW COME HE'S STILL THERE?
HOW COME HE'S DOING LIFE IN PRISON FOR DOUBLE MURDER, WHEN YOU KNOW BETTER THAN ANYONE THAT HE DIDN'T DO IT?
RIGHT, GINA? YOU KNOW, 'CAUSE YOU WERE THERE!
THAT'S RIGHT... I WAS THERE.
YOU BROUGHT MY BROTHER INTO YOUR CRAZY LITTLE CULT. YOU SET HIM UP TO TAKE A FALL. AND YOU'VE SPENT EVERY MOMENT SINCE THEN PROTECTING THE IDENTITY OF THE REAL MURDERER.
SO TELL ME AGAIN, GINA...
TELL ME HOW YOU'VE DONE EVERYTHING YOU POSSIBLY COULD TO GET LAWRENCE FREED!

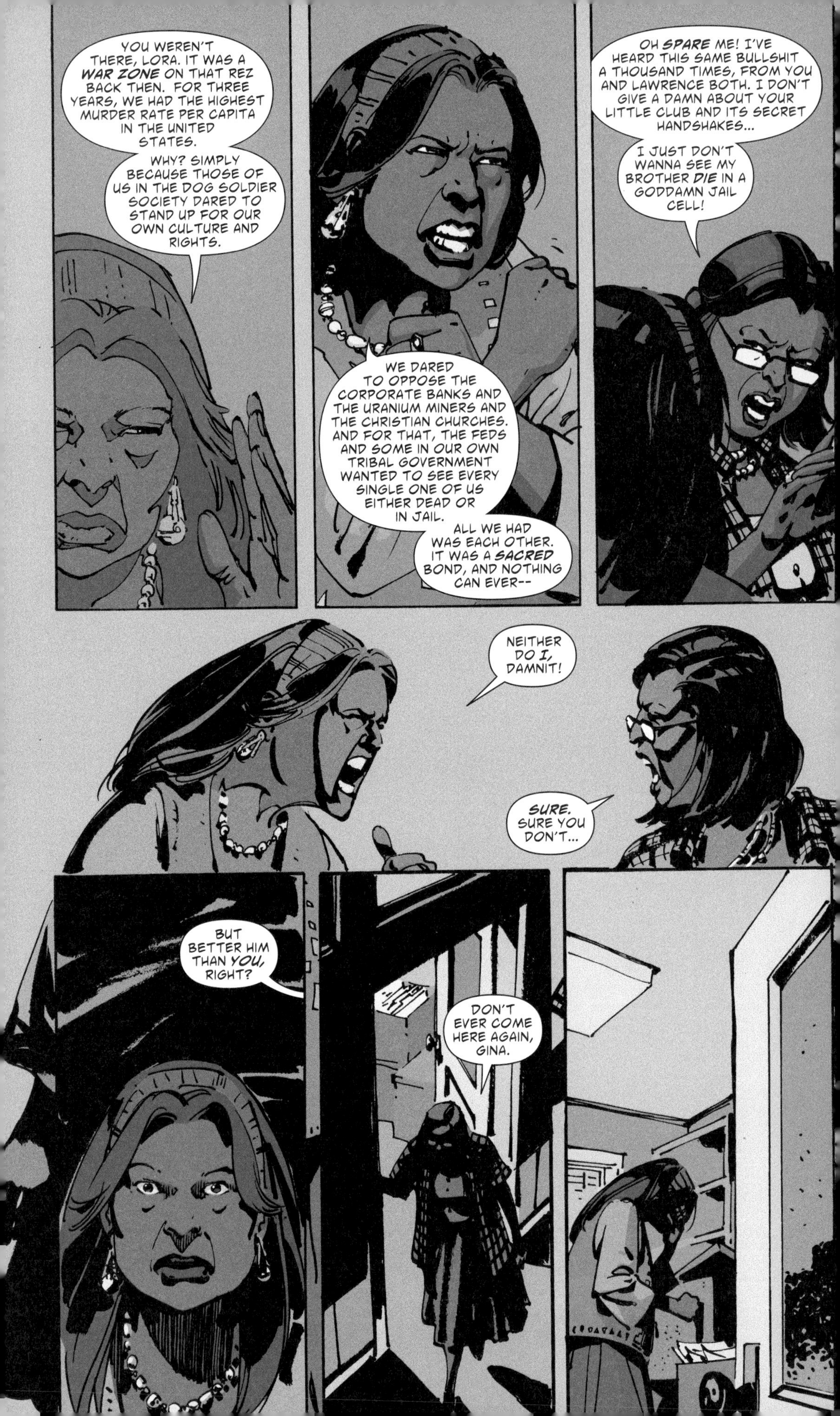

YOU WEREN'T THERE, LORA. IT WAS A WAR ZONE ON THAT REZ BACK THEN. FOR THREE YEARS, WE HAD THE HIGHEST MURDER RATE PER CAPITA IN THE UNITED STATES.
WHY? SIMPLY BECAUSE THOSE OF US IN THE DOG SOLDIER SOCIETY DARED TO STAND UP FOR OUR OWN CULTURE AND RIGHTS.
WE DARED TO OPPOSE THE CORPORATE BANKS AND THE URANIUM MINERS AND THE CHRISTIAN CHURCHES. AND FOR THAT, THE FEDS AND SOME IN OUR OWN TRIBAL GOVERNMENT WANTED TO SEE EVERY SINGLE ONE OF US EITHER DEAD OR IN JAIL.
ALL WE HAD WAS EACH OTHER. IT WAS A SACRED BOND, AND NOTHING CAN EVER--
OH SPARE ME! I'VE HEARD THIS SAME BULLSHIT A THOUSAND TIMES, FROM YOU AND LAWRENCE BOTH. I DON'T GIVE A DAMN ABOUT YOUR LITTLE CLUB AND ITS SECRET HANDSHAKES...
I JUST DON'T WANNA SEE MY BROTHER DIE IN A GODDAMN JAIL CELL!
NEITHER DO I, DAMNIT!
SURE. SURE YOU DON'T...
BUT BETTER HIM THAN YOU, RIGHT?
DON'T EVER COME HERE AGAIN, GINA.

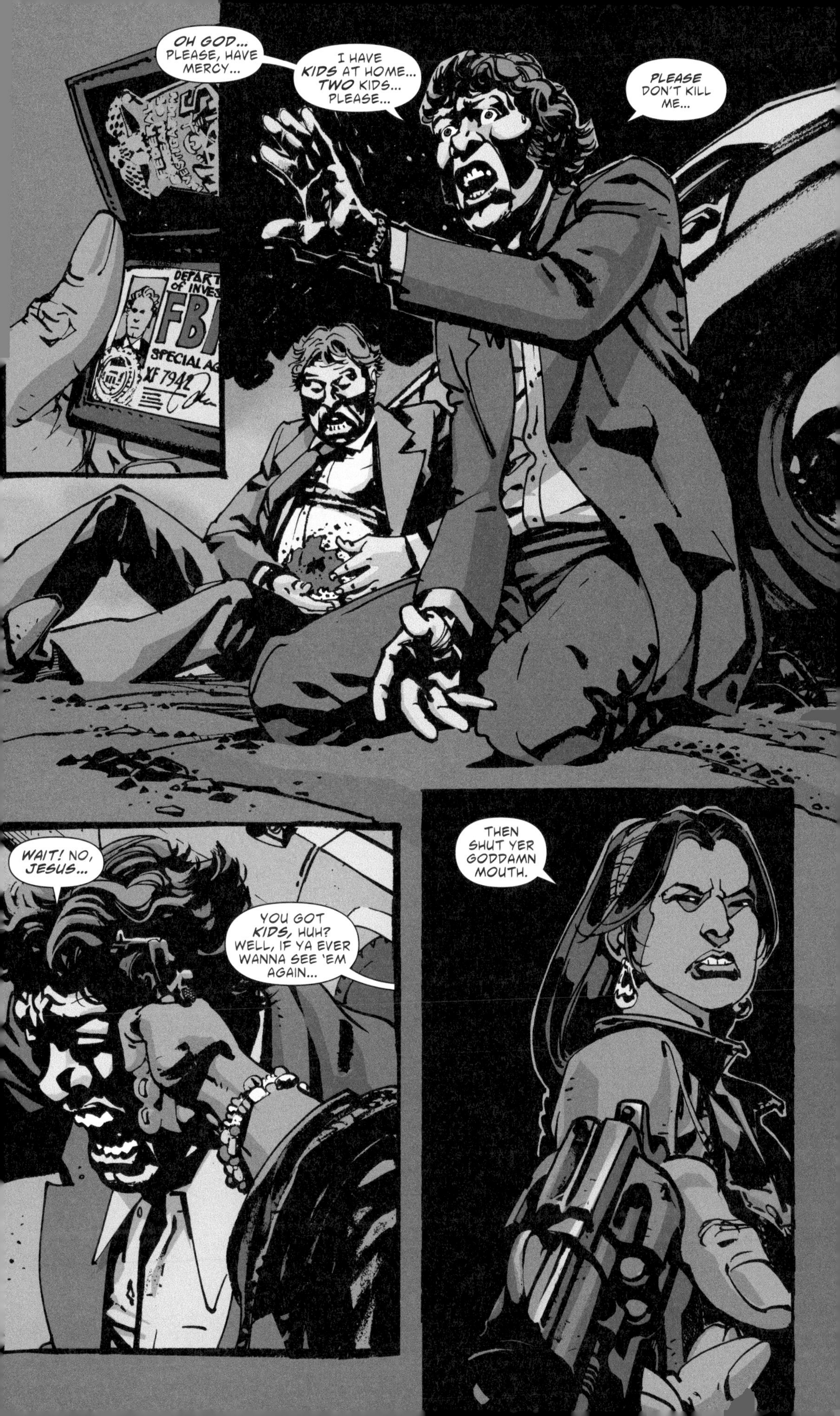
OH GOD... PLEASE, HAVE MERCY...
I HAVE KIDS AT HOME... TWO KIDS... PLEASE...
PLEASE DON'T KILL ME...
DEPART OF INVES
FBI
SPECIAL AG
XF 7942
WAIT! NO, JESUS...
YOU GOT KIDS, HUH? WELL, IF YA EVER WANNA SEE 'EM AGAIN...
THEN SHUT YER GODDAMN MOUTH.

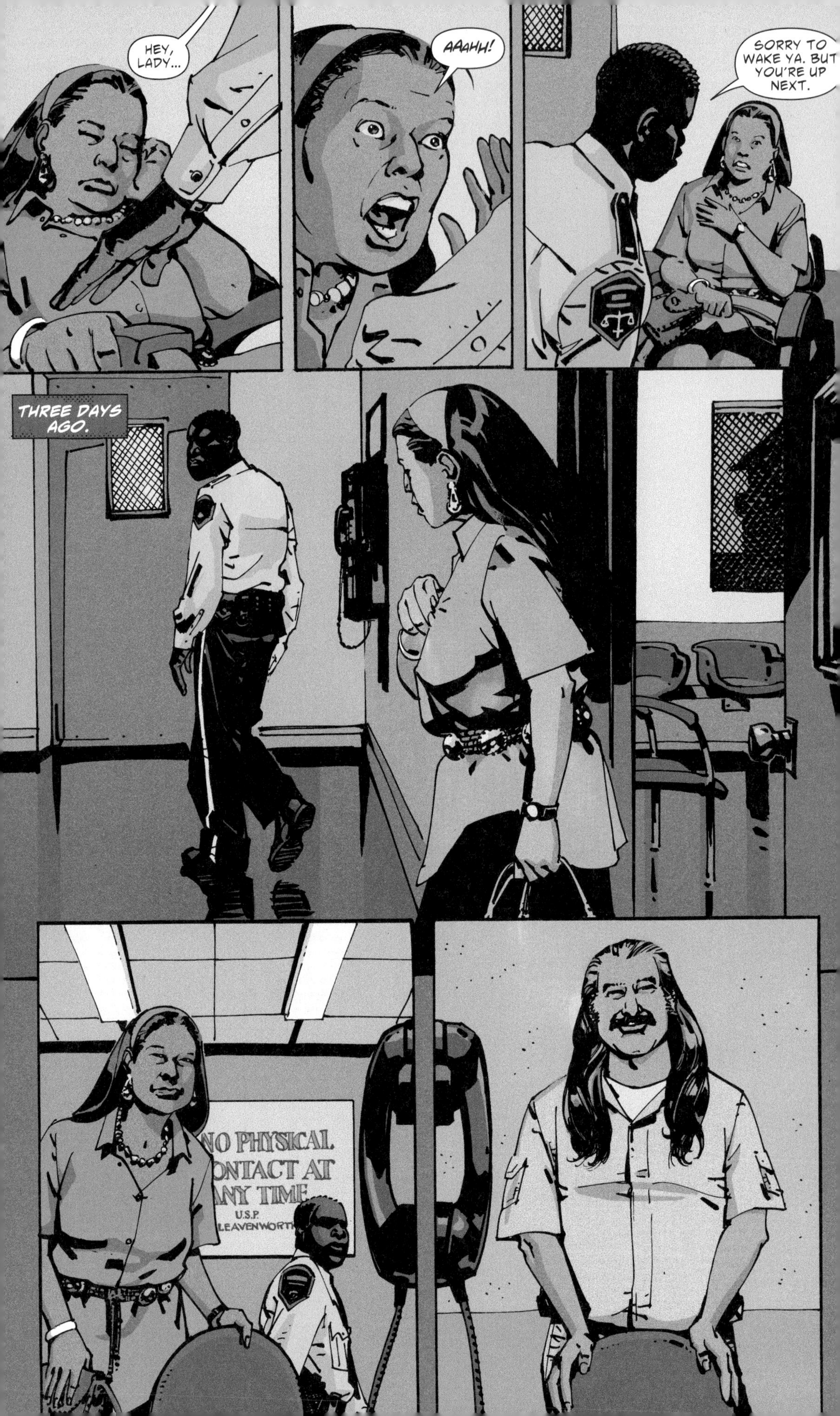
HEY, LADY...
AAAHH!
SORRY TO WAKE YA. BUT YOU'RE UP NEXT.
THREE DAYS AGO.
NO PHYSICAL CONTACT AT ANY TIME
U.S.P. LEAVENWORTH

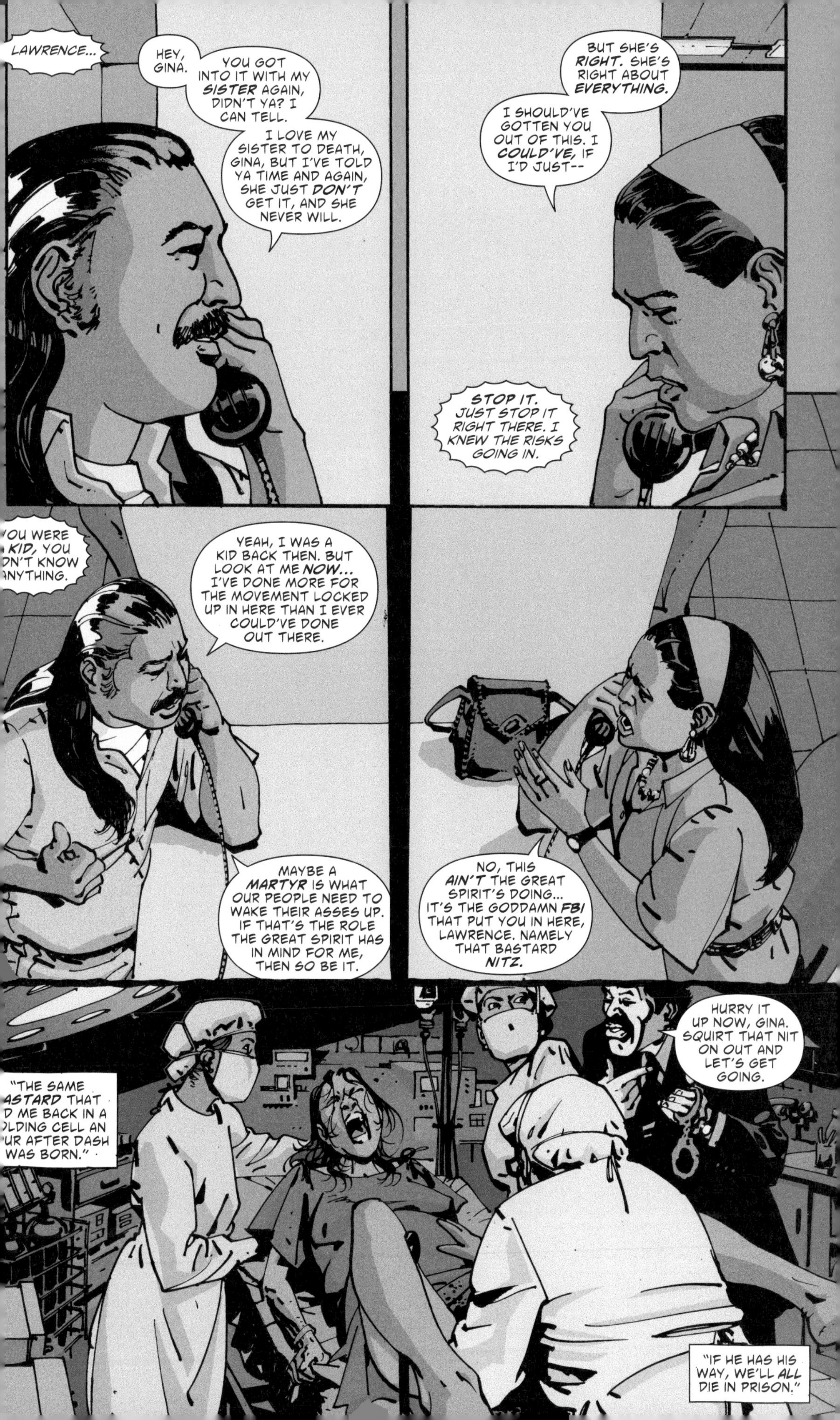
LAWRENCE...
HEY, GINA.
YOU GOT INTO IT WITH MY SISTER AGAIN, DIDN'T YA? I CAN TELL.
I LOVE MY SISTER TO DEATH, GINA, BUT I'VE TOLD YA TIME AND AGAIN, SHE JUST DON'T GET IT, AND SHE NEVER WILL.
BUT SHE'S RIGHT. SHE'S RIGHT ABOUT EVERYTHING.
I SHOULD'VE GOTTEN YOU OUT OF THIS. I COULD'VE, IF I'D JUST--
STOP IT. JUST STOP IT RIGHT THERE. I KNEW THE RISKS GOING IN.
YEAH, I WAS A KID BACK THEN. BUT LOOK AT ME NOW... I'VE DONE MORE FOR THE MOVEMENT LOCKED UP IN HERE THAN I EVER COULD'VE DONE OUT THERE.
MAYBE A MARTYR IS WHAT OUR PEOPLE NEED TO WAKE THEIR ASSES UP. IF THAT'S THE ROLE THE GREAT SPIRIT HAS IN MIND FOR ME, THEN SO BE IT.
NO, THIS AIN'T THE GREAT SPIRIT'S DOING... IT'S THE GODDAMN FBI THAT PUT YOU IN HERE, LAWRENCE. NAMELY THAT BASTARD NITZ.
HURRY IT UP NOW, GINA. SQUIRT THAT NIT ON OUT AND LET'S GET GOING.
"IF HE HAS HIS WAY, WE'LL ALL DIE IN PRISON."

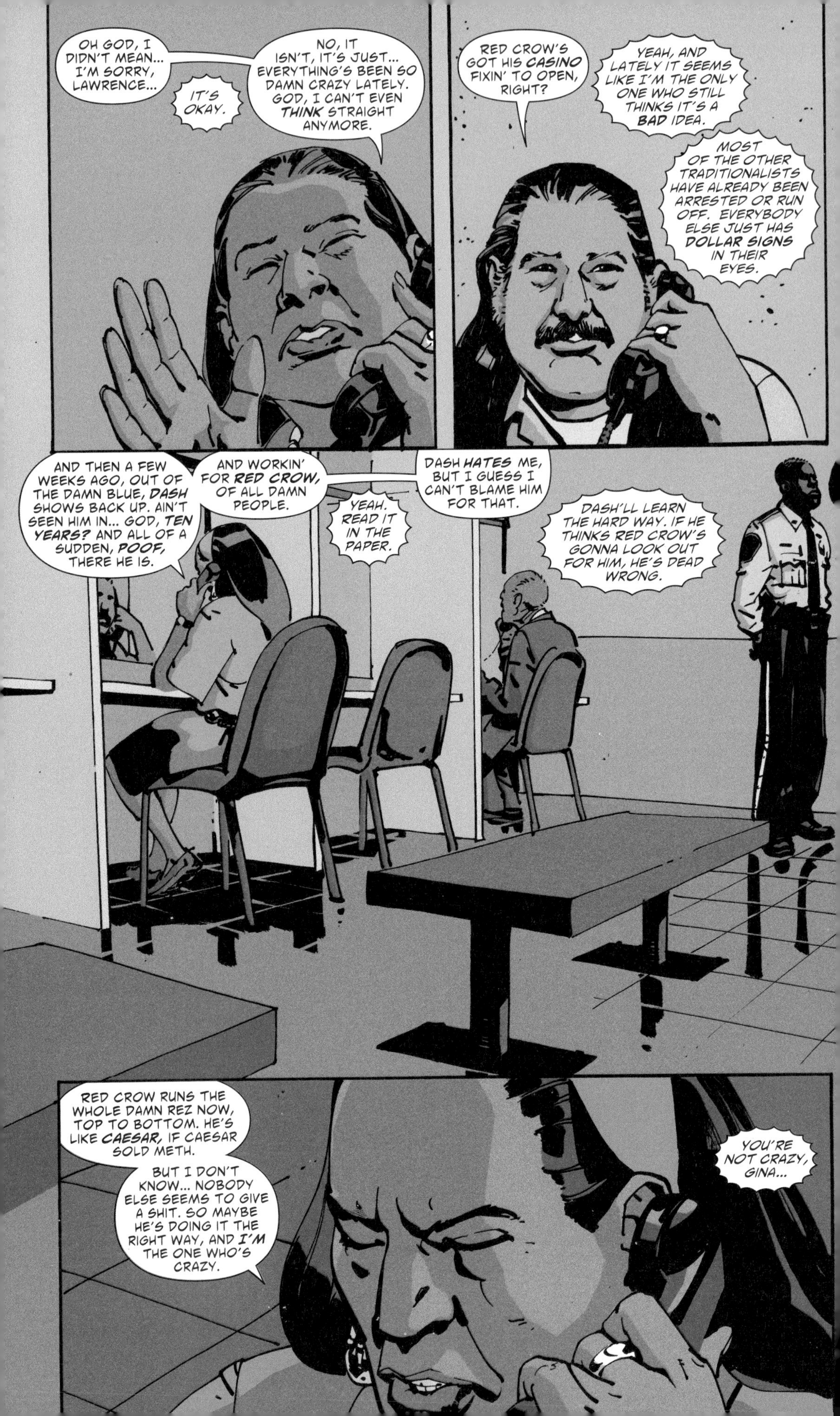
OH GOD, I DIDN'T MEAN... I'M SORRY, LAWRENCE...
NO, IT ISN'T, IT'S JUST... EVERYTHING'S BEEN SO DAMN CRAZY LATELY. GOD, I CAN'T EVEN THINK STRAIGHT ANYMORE.
IT'S OKAY.
RED CROW'S GOT HIS CASINO FIXIN' TO OPEN, RIGHT?
YEAH, AND LATELY IT SEEMS LIKE I'M THE ONLY ONE WHO STILL THINKS IT'S A BAD IDEA.
MOST OF THE OTHER TRADITIONALISTS HAVE ALREADY BEEN ARRESTED OR RUN OFF. EVERYBODY ELSE JUST HAS DOLLAR SIGNS IN THEIR EYES.
AND THEN A FEW WEEKS AGO, OUT OF THE DAMN BLUE, DASH SHOWS BACK UP. AIN'T SEEN HIM IN... GOD, TEN YEARS? AND ALL OF A SUDDEN, POOF, THERE HE IS.
AND WORKIN' FOR RED CROW, OF ALL DAMN PEOPLE.
YEAH. READ IT IN THE PAPER.
DASH HATES ME, BUT I GUESS I CAN'T BLAME HIM FOR THAT.
DASH'LL LEARN THE HARD WAY. IF HE THINKS RED CROW'S GONNA LOOK OUT FOR HIM, HE'S DEAD WRONG.
RED CROW RUNS THE WHOLE DAMN REZ NOW, TOP TO BOTTOM. HE'S LIKE CAESAR, IF CAESAR SOLD METH.
BUT I DON'T KNOW... NOBODY ELSE SEEMS TO GIVE A SHIT. SO MAYBE HE'S DOING IT THE RIGHT WAY, AND I'M THE ONE WHO'S CRAZY.
YOU'RE NOT CRAZY, GINA...

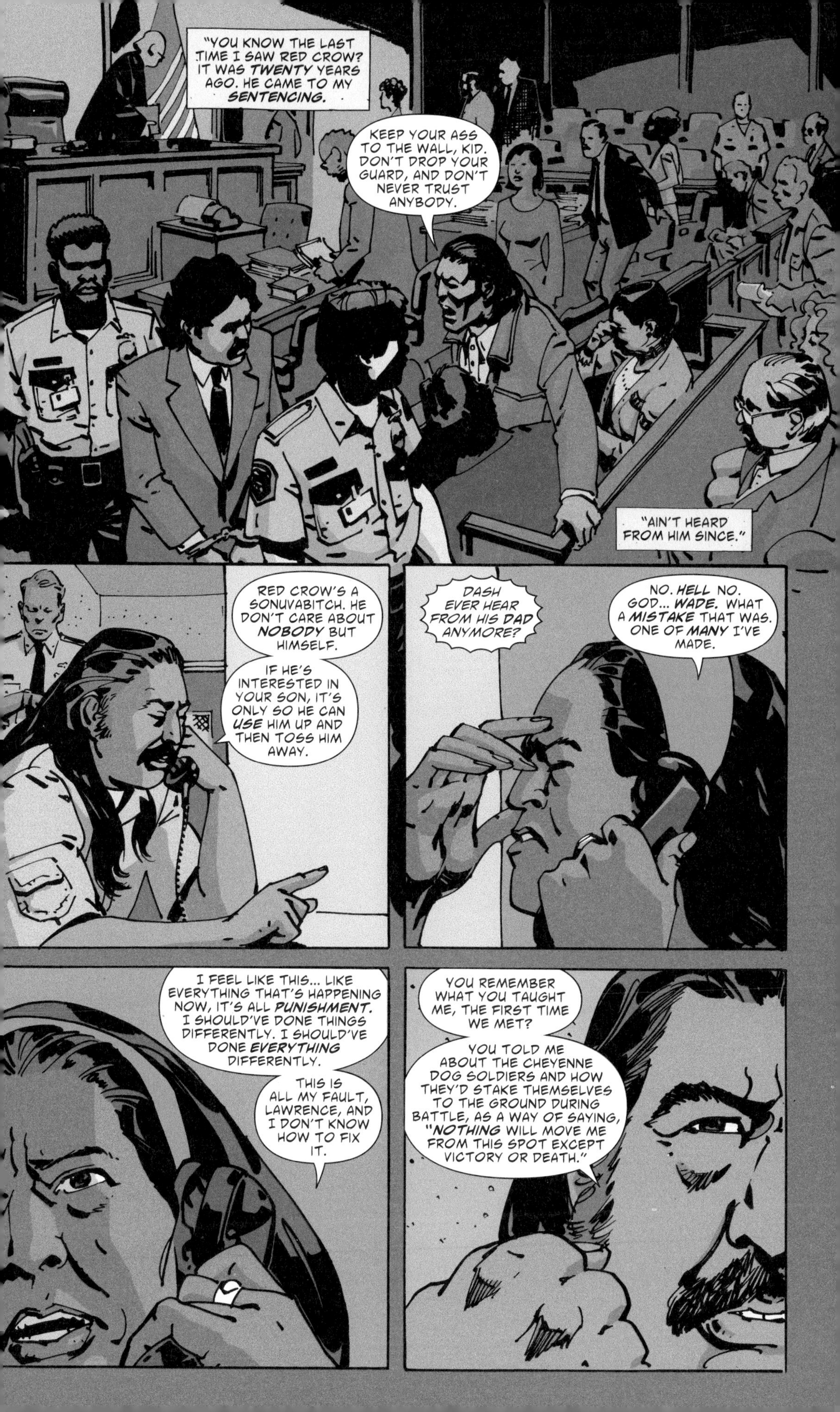

"YOU KNOW THE LAST TIME I SAW RED CROW? IT WAS *TWENTY* YEARS AGO. HE CAME TO MY *SENTENCING.*
KEEP YOUR ASS TO THE WALL, KID. DON'T DROP YOUR GUARD, AND DON'T NEVER TRUST ANYBODY.
"AIN'T HEARD FROM HIM SINCE."
RED CROW'S A SONUVABITCH. HE DON'T CARE ABOUT *NOBODY* BUT HIMSELF.
IF HE'S INTERESTED IN YOUR SON, IT'S ONLY SO HE CAN *USE* HIM UP AND THEN TOSS HIM AWAY.
DASH EVER HEAR FROM HIS DAD ANYMORE?
NO. *HELL* NO. GOD... *WADE.* WHAT A *MISTAKE* THAT WAS. ONE OF *MANY* I'VE MADE.
I FEEL LIKE THIS... LIKE EVERYTHING THAT'S HAPPENING NOW, IT'S ALL *PUNISHMENT.* I SHOULD'VE DONE THINGS DIFFERENTLY. I SHOULD'VE DONE *EVERYTHING* DIFFERENTLY.
THIS IS ALL MY FAULT, LAWRENCE, AND I DON'T KNOW HOW TO FIX IT.
YOU REMEMBER WHAT YOU TAUGHT ME, THE FIRST TIME WE MET?
YOU TOLD ME ABOUT THE CHEYENNE DOG SOLDIERS AND HOW THEY'D STAKE THEMSELVES TO THE GROUND DURING BATTLE, AS A WAY OF SAYING, "*NOTHING* WILL MOVE ME FROM THIS SPOT EXCEPT VICTORY OR DEATH."

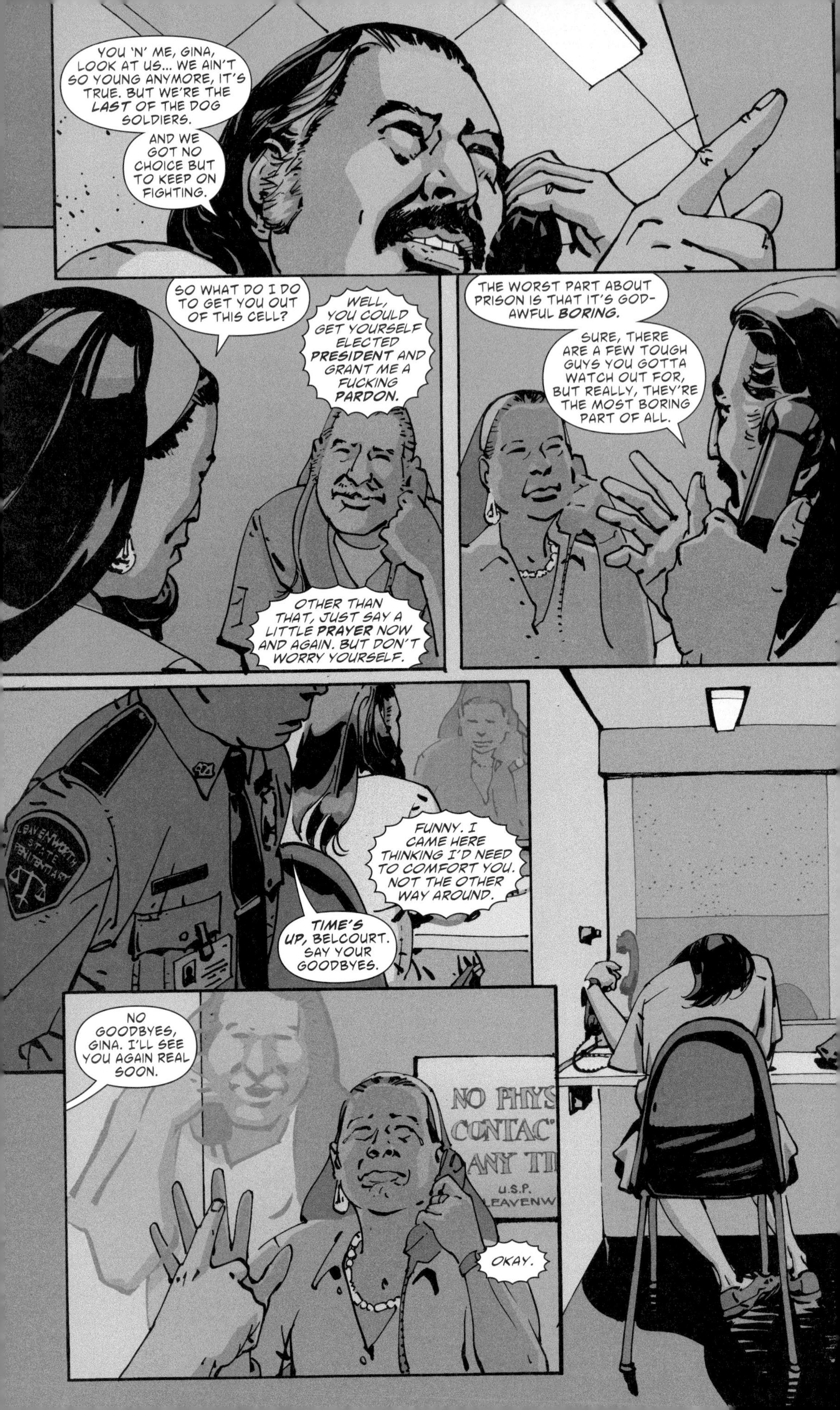

YOU 'N' ME, GINA, LOOK AT US... WE AIN'T SO YOUNG ANYMORE, IT'S TRUE. BUT WE'RE THE LAST OF THE DOG SOLDIERS.
AND WE GOT NO CHOICE BUT TO KEEP ON FIGHTING.
SO WHAT DO I DO TO GET YOU OUT OF THIS CELL?
WELL, YOU COULD GET YOURSELF ELECTED PRESIDENT AND GRANT ME A FUCKING PARDON.
OTHER THAN THAT, JUST SAY A LITTLE PRAYER NOW AND AGAIN. BUT DON'T WORRY YOURSELF.
THE WORST PART ABOUT PRISON IS THAT IT'S GOD-AWFUL BORING.
SURE, THERE ARE A FEW TOUGH GUYS YOU GOTTA WATCH OUT FOR, BUT REALLY, THEY'RE THE MOST BORING PART OF ALL.
LEAVENWORTH STATE PENITENTIARY
FUNNY. I CAME HERE THINKING I'D NEED TO COMFORT YOU. NOT THE OTHER WAY AROUND.
TIME'S UP, BELCOURT. SAY YOUR GOODBYES.
NO GOODBYES, GINA. I'LL SEE YOU AGAIN REAL SOON.
NO PHYS
CONTAC
ANY TI
U.S.P.
LEAVENW
OKAY.

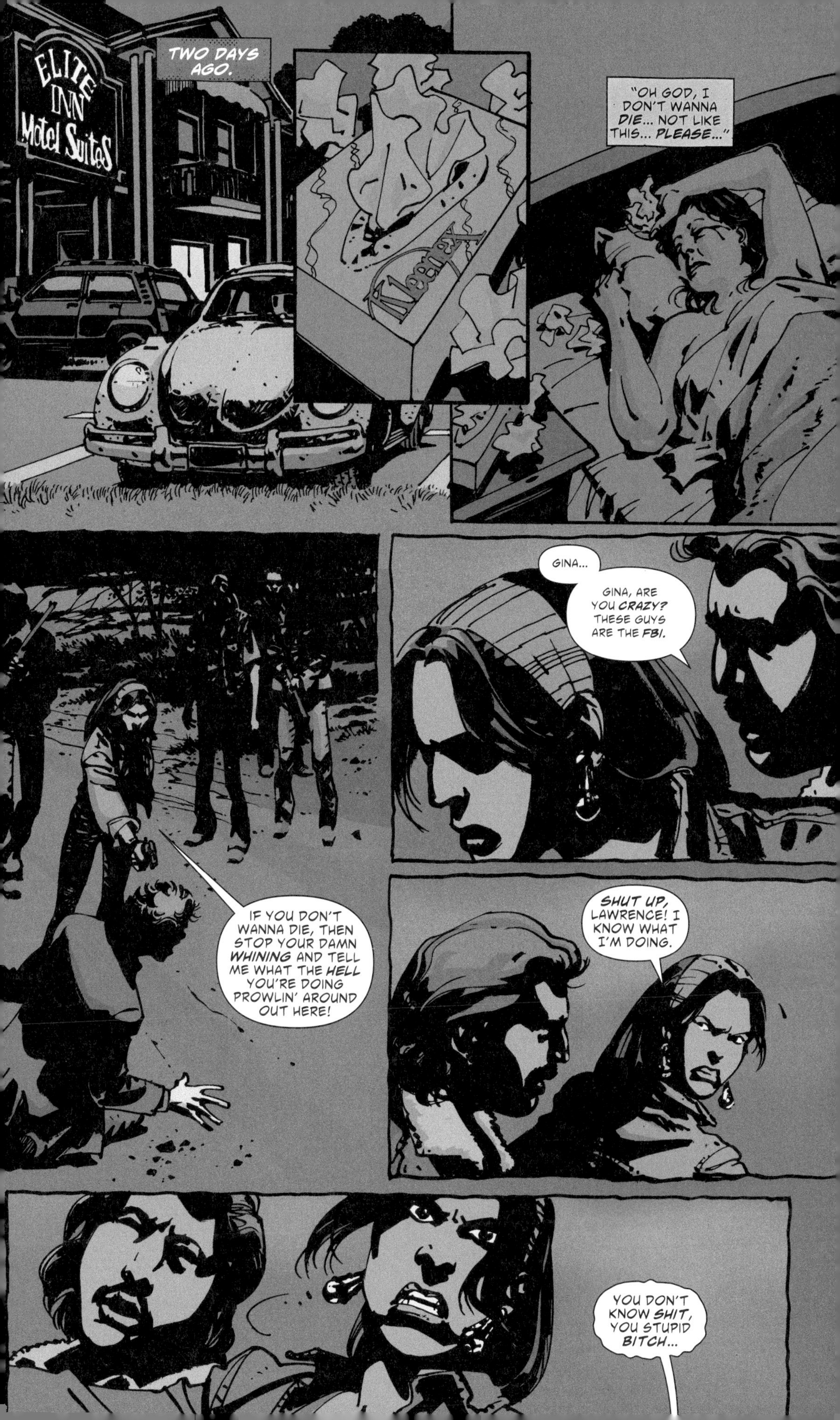
ELITE INN Motel Suites
TWO DAYS AGO.
"OH GOD, I DON'T WANNA DIE... NOT LIKE THIS... PLEASE..."
GINA...
GINA, ARE YOU CRAZY? THESE GUYS ARE THE FBI.
IF YOU DON'T WANNA DIE, THEN STOP YOUR DAMN WHINING AND TELL ME WHAT THE HELL YOU'RE DOING PROWLIN' AROUND OUT HERE!
SHUT UP, LAWRENCE! I KNOW WHAT I'M DOING.
YOU DON'T KNOW SHIT, YOU STUPID BITCH...

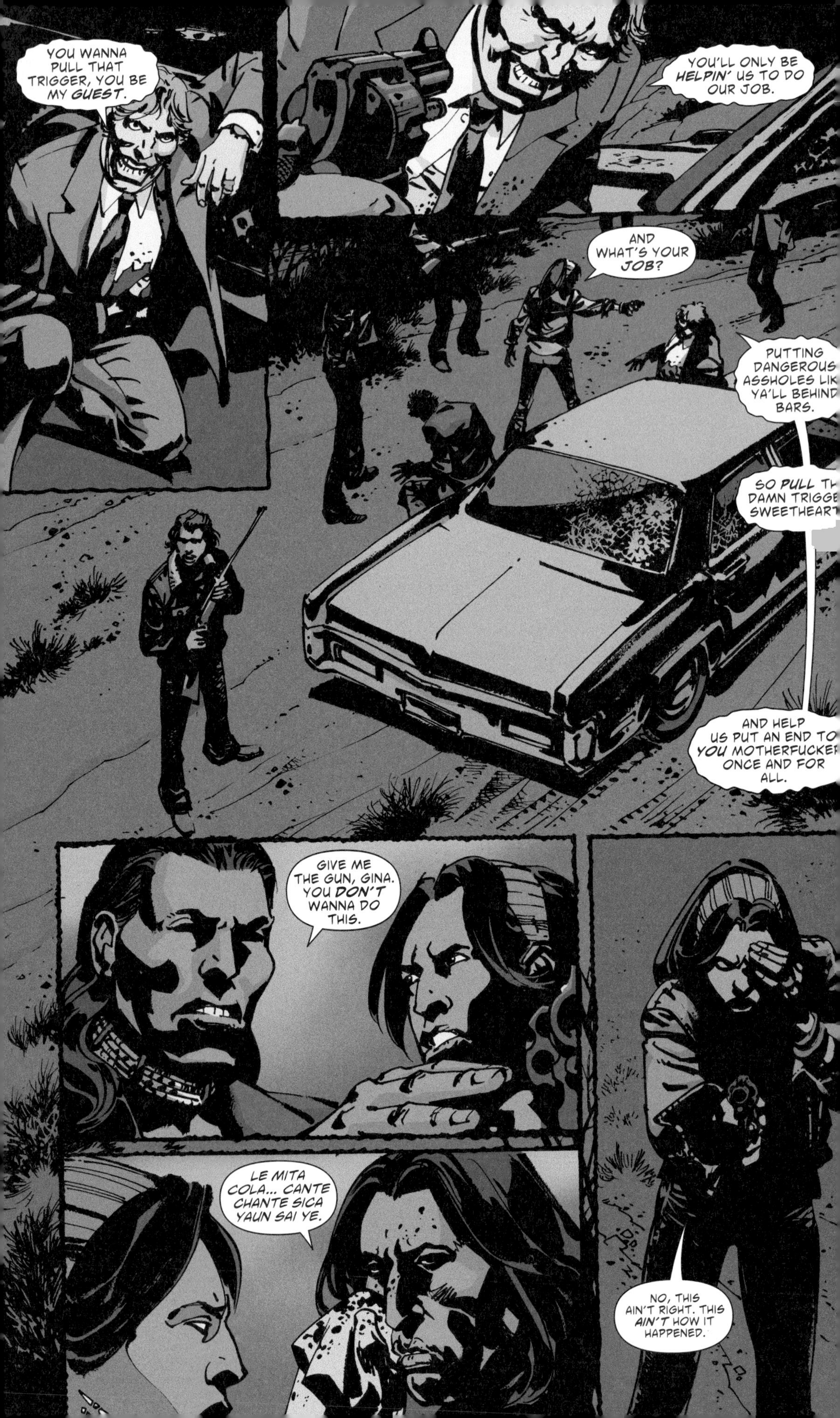
YOU WANNA PULL THAT TRIGGER, YOU BE MY GUEST.
YOU'LL ONLY BE HELPIN' US TO DO OUR JOB.
AND WHAT'S YOUR JOB?
PUTTING DANGEROUS ASSHOLES LIK YA'LL BEHIND BARS.
SO PULL TH DAMN TRIGGE SWEETHEART
AND HELP US PUT AN END TO YOU MOTHERFUCKER ONCE AND FOR ALL.
GIVE ME THE GUN, GINA. YOU DON'T WANNA DO THIS.
LE MITA COLA... CANTE CHANTE SICA YAUN SAI YE.
NO, THIS AIN'T RIGHT. THIS AIN'T HOW IT HAPPENED.

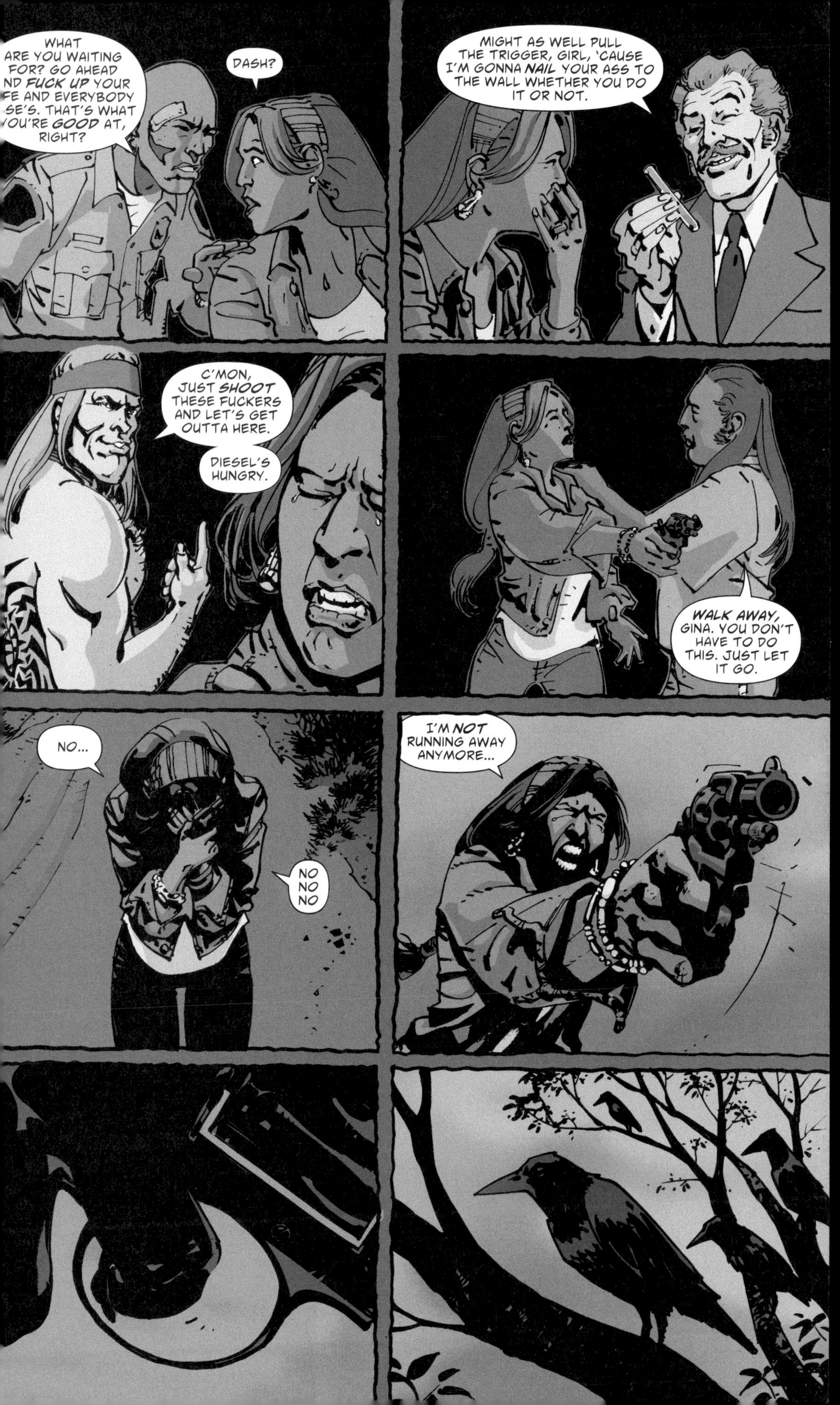
WHAT ARE YOU WAITING FOR? GO AHEAD ND FUCK UP YOUR FE AND EVERYBODY SE'S. THAT'S WHAT OU'RE GOOD AT, RIGHT?
DASH?
MIGHT AS WELL PULL THE TRIGGER, GIRL, 'CAUSE I'M GONNA NAIL YOUR ASS TO THE WALL WHETHER YOU DO IT OR NOT.
C'MON, JUST SHOOT THESE FUCKERS AND LET'S GET OUTTA HERE.
DIESEL'S HUNGRY.
WALK AWAY, GINA. YOU DON'T HAVE TO DO THIS. JUST LET IT GO.
NO...
NO NO NO
I'M NOT RUNNING AWAY ANYMORE...

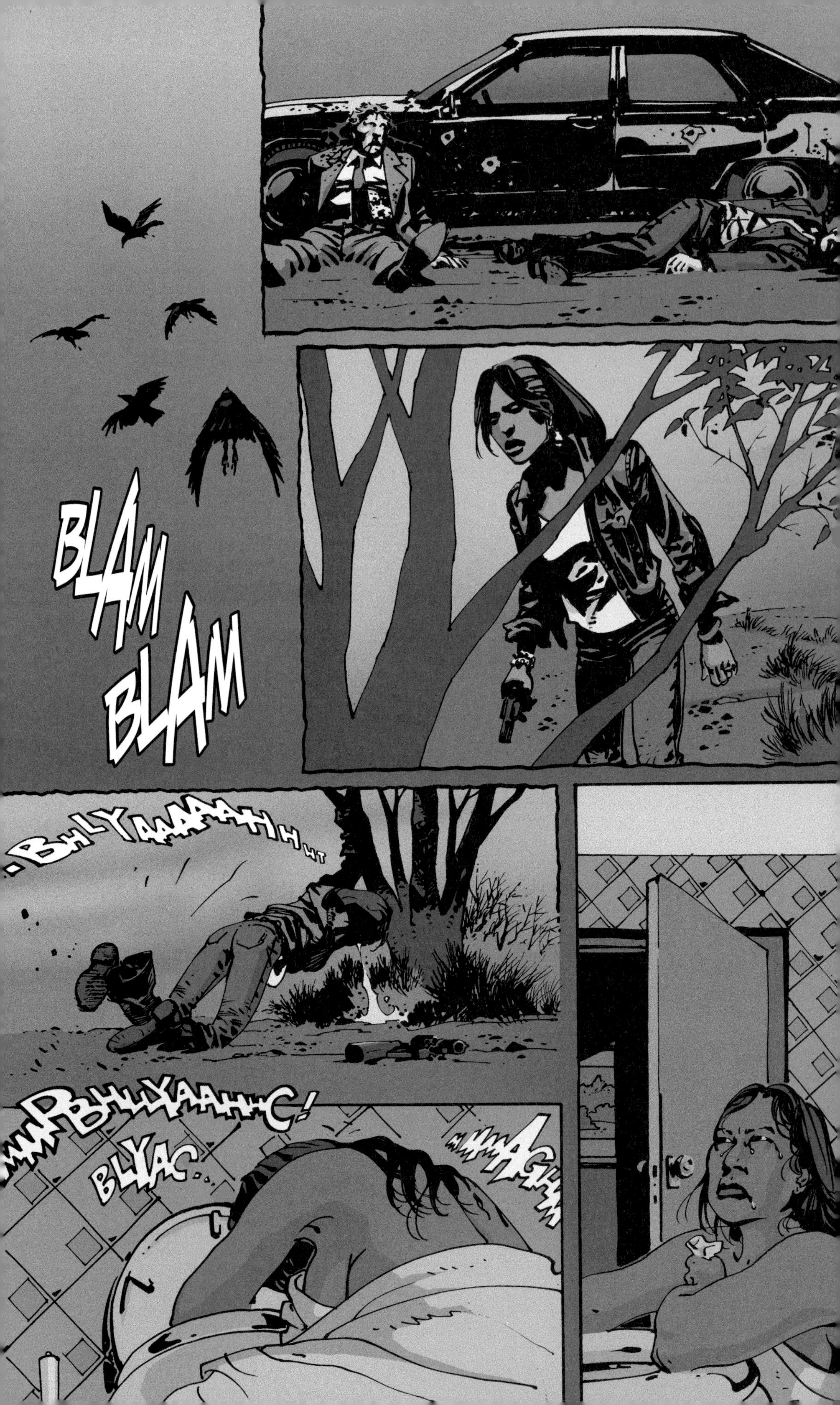
BLAM BLAM
BHLYAAAAAHHHT
RBHLYAAHHC!
BLYAC...
AGH

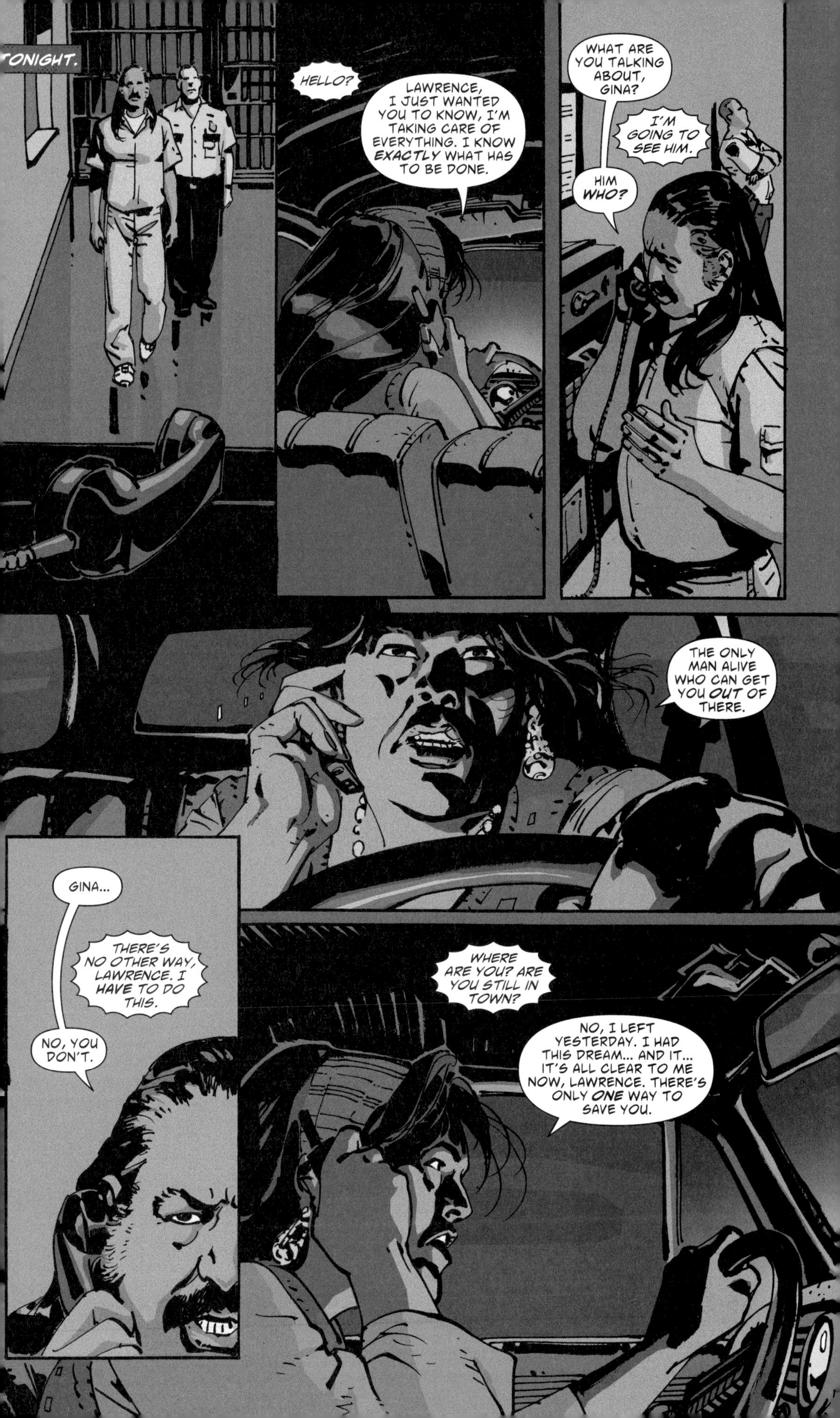
TONIGHT.
HELLO?
LAWRENCE, I JUST WANTED YOU TO KNOW, I'M TAKING CARE OF EVERYTHING. I KNOW EXACTLY WHAT HAS TO BE DONE.
WHAT ARE YOU TALKING ABOUT, GINA?
I'M GOING TO SEE HIM.
HIM WHO?
THE ONLY MAN ALIVE WHO CAN GET YOU OUT OF THERE.
GINA...
THERE'S NO OTHER WAY, LAWRENCE. I HAVE TO DO THIS.
NO, YOU DON'T.
WHERE ARE YOU? ARE YOU STILL IN TOWN?
NO, I LEFT YESTERDAY. I HAD THIS DREAM... AND IT... IT'S ALL CLEAR TO ME NOW, LAWRENCE. THERE'S ONLY ONE WAY TO SAVE YOU.

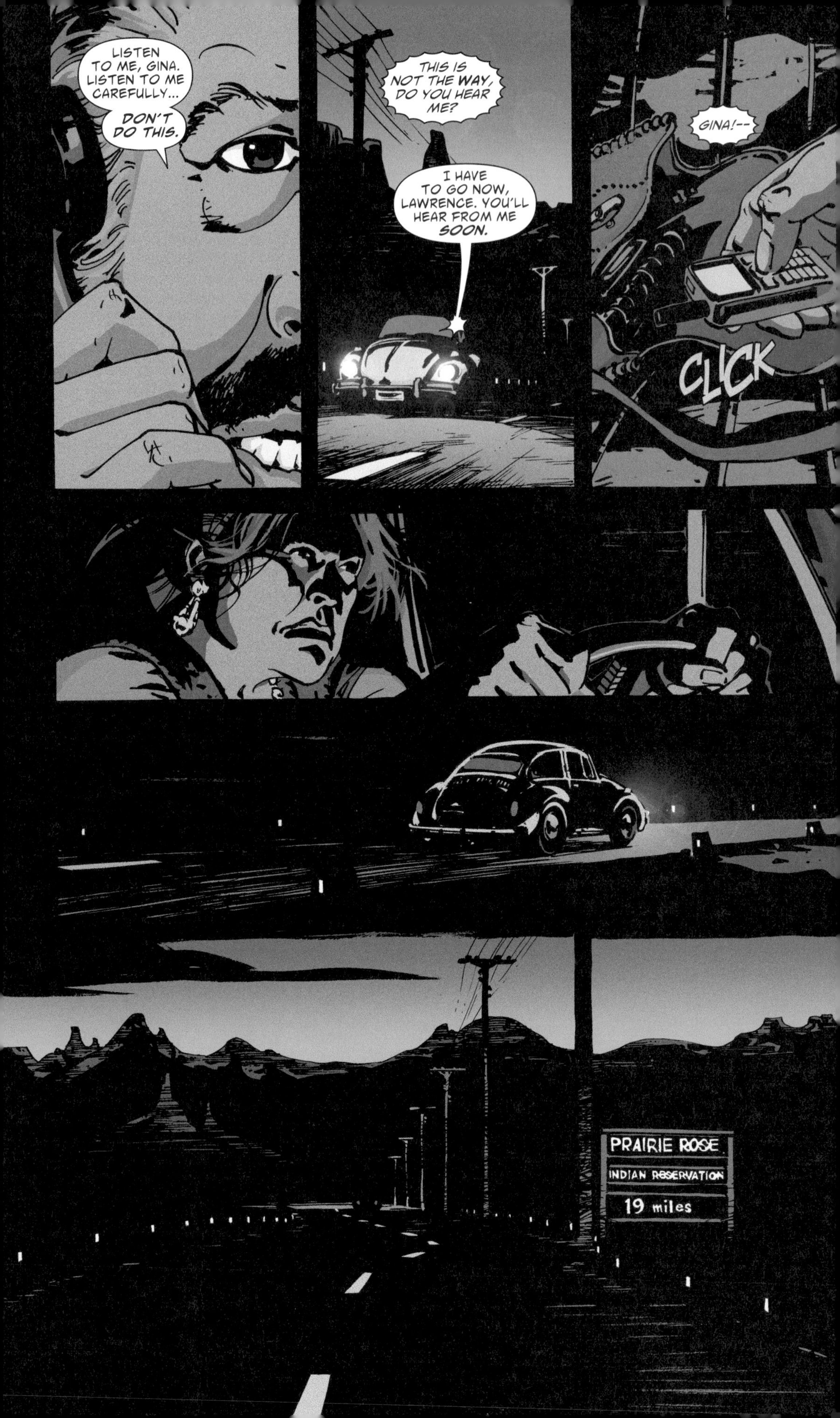
LISTEN TO ME, GINA. LISTEN TO ME CAREFULLY...
DON'T DO THIS.
THIS IS NOT THE WAY, DO YOU HEAR ME?
I HAVE TO GO NOW, LAWRENCE. YOU'LL HEAR FROM ME SOON.
GINA!--
CLICK
PRAIRIE ROSE
INDIAN RESERVATION
19 miles

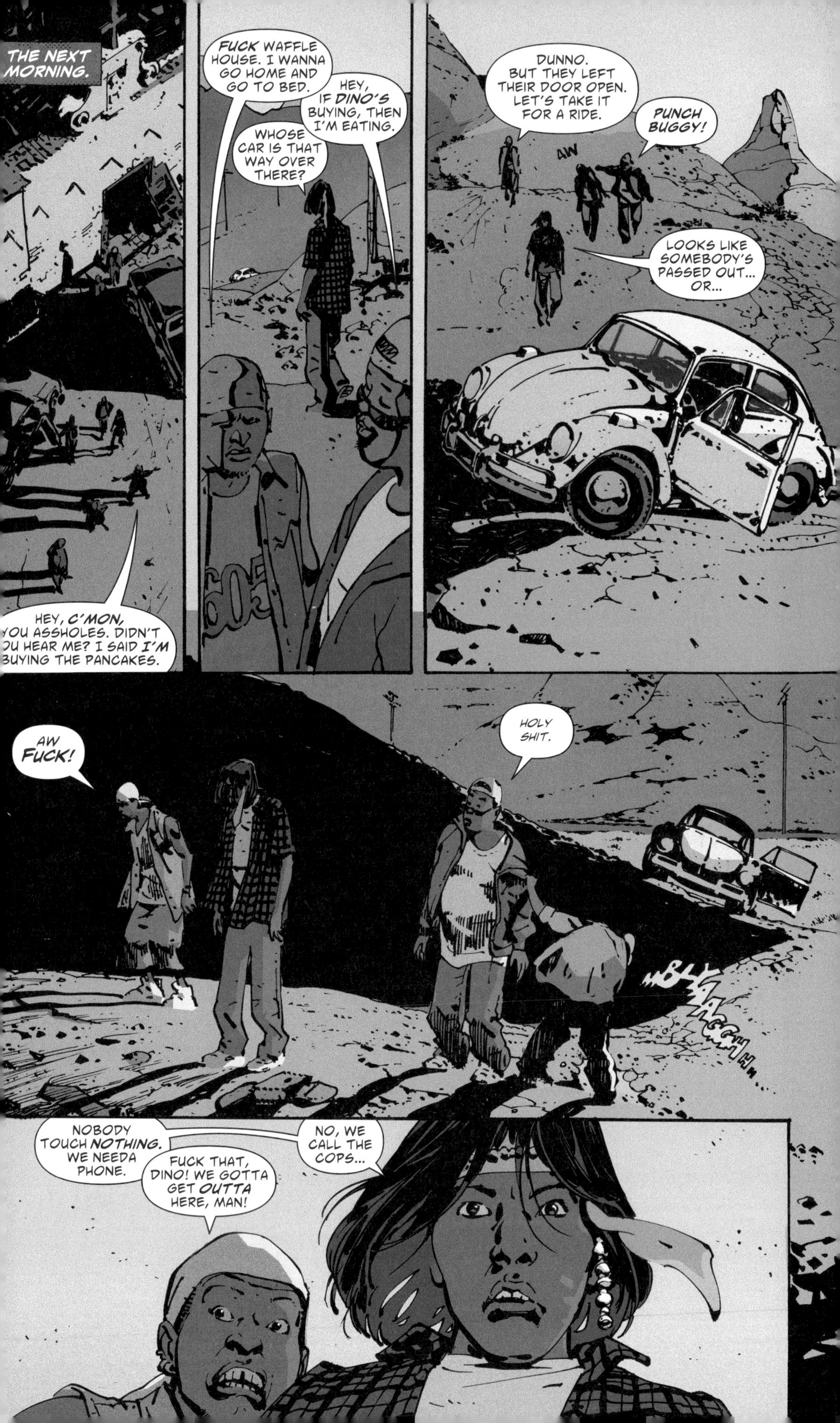
THE NEXT MORNING.
HEY, C'MON, YOU ASSHOLES. DIDN'T YOU HEAR ME? I SAID I'M BUYING THE PANCAKES.
FUCK WAFFLE HOUSE. I WANNA GO HOME AND GO TO BED.
HEY, IF DINO'S BUYING, THEN I'M EATING.
WHOSE CAR IS THAT WAY OVER THERE?
DUNNO. BUT THEY LEFT THEIR DOOR OPEN. LET'S TAKE IT FOR A RIDE.
PUNCH BUGGY!
AW
LOOKS LIKE SOMEBODY'S PASSED OUT... OR...
AW FUCK!
HOLY SHIT.
NOBODY TOUCH NOTHING. WE NEEDA PHONE.
FUCK THAT, DINO! WE GOTTA GET OUTTA HERE, MAN!
NO, WE CALL THE COPS...

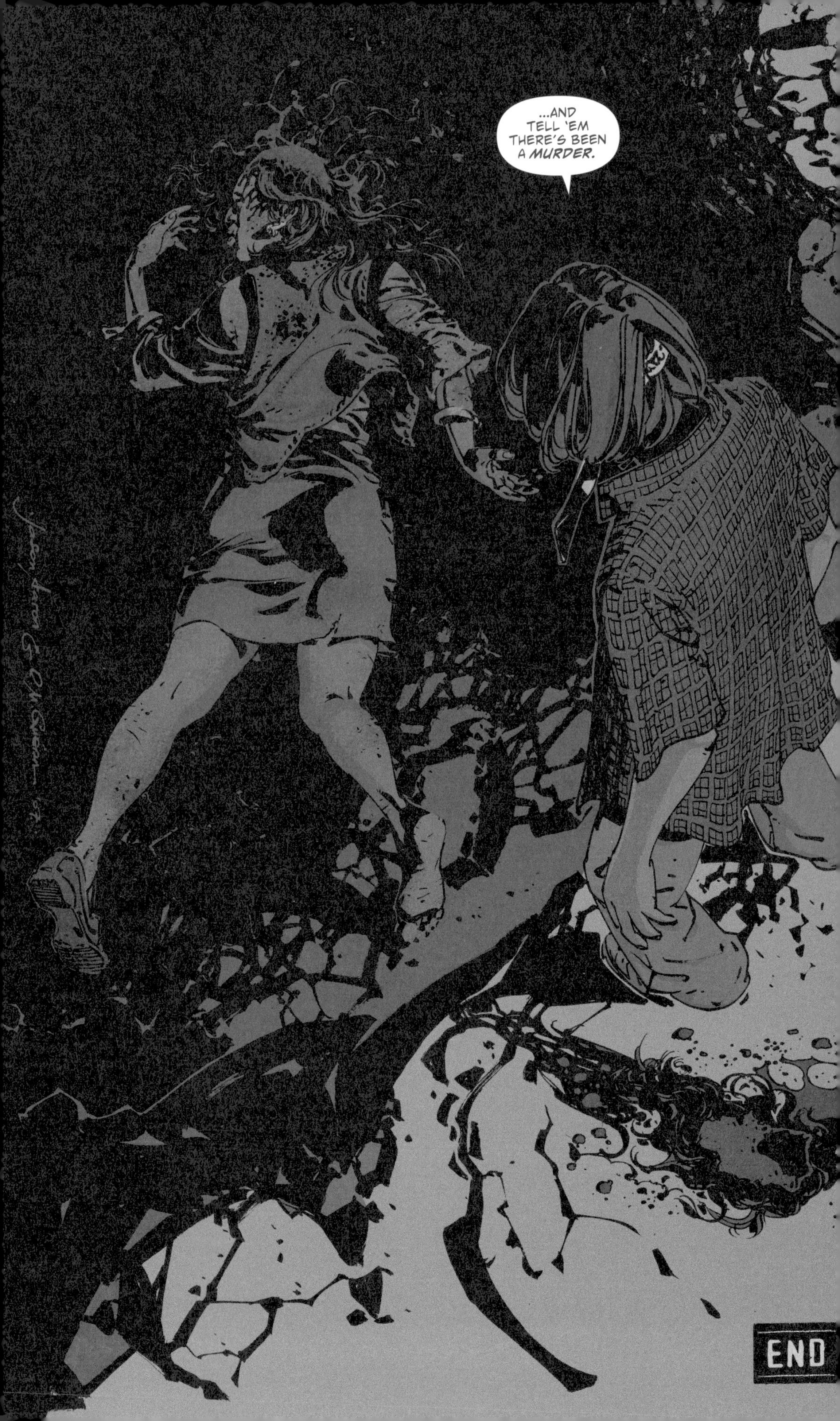
...AND TELL 'EM THERE'S BEEN A MURDER.
END

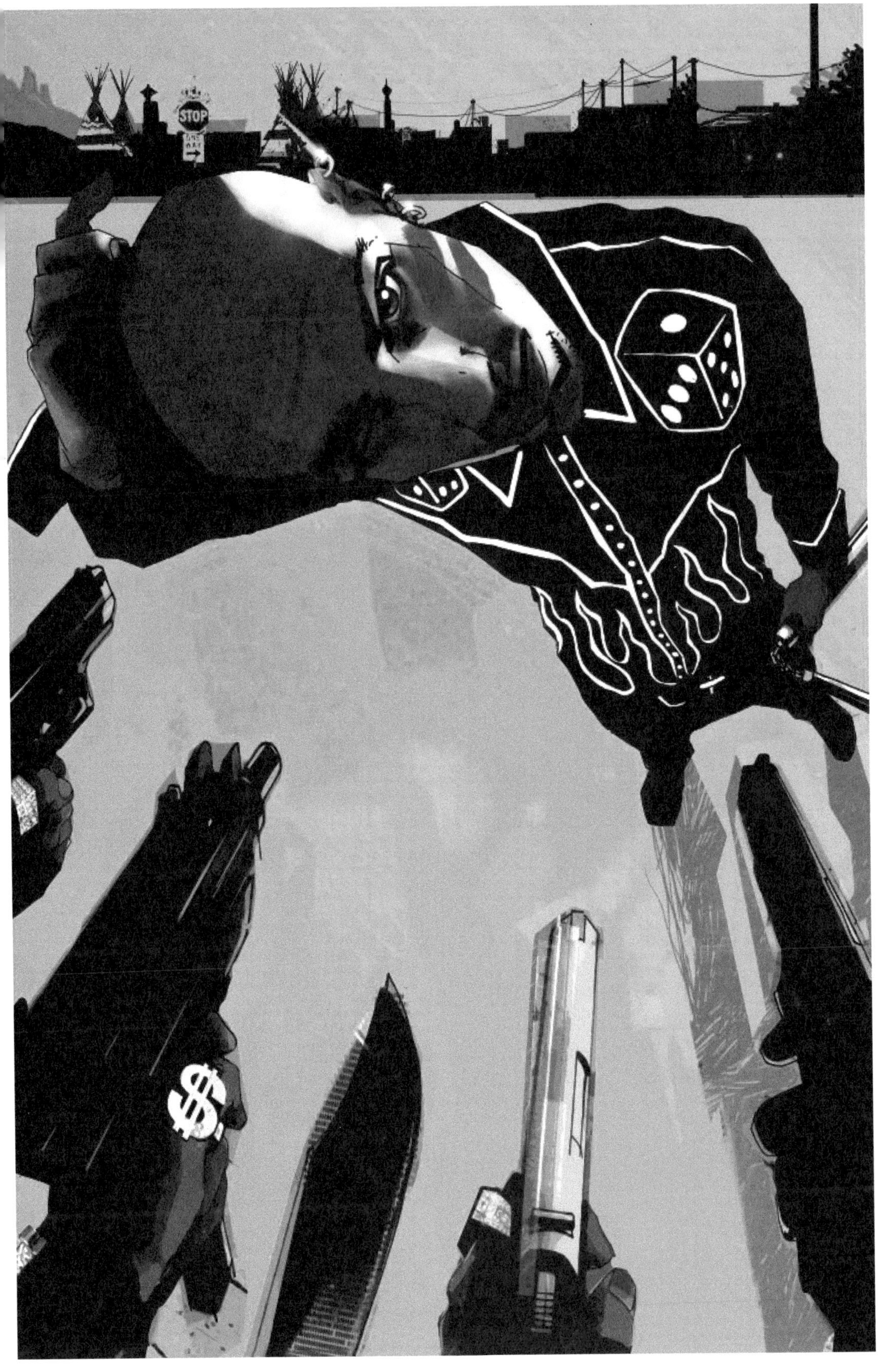
STOP

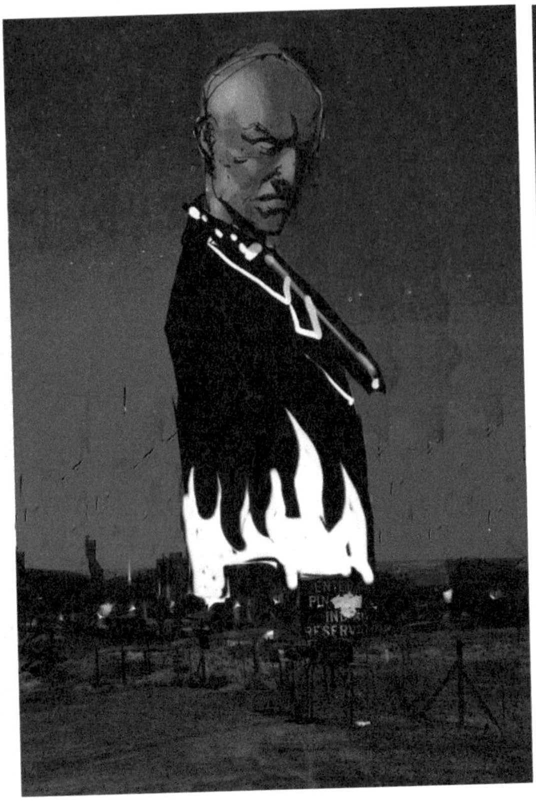

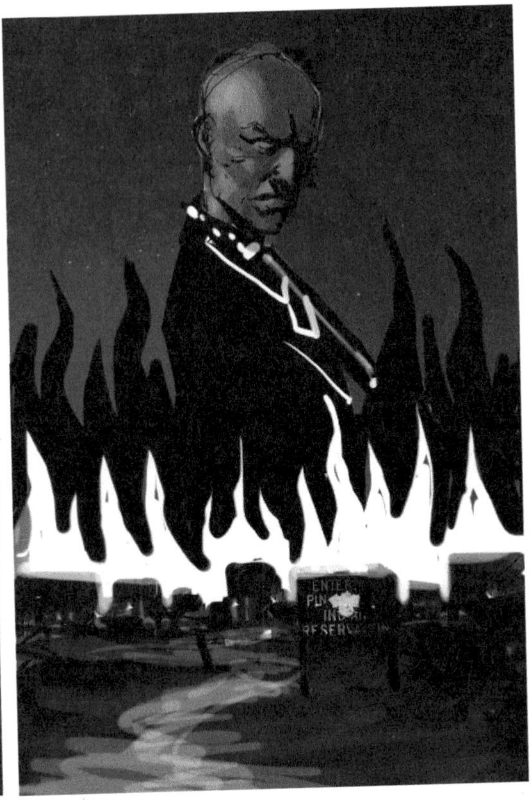

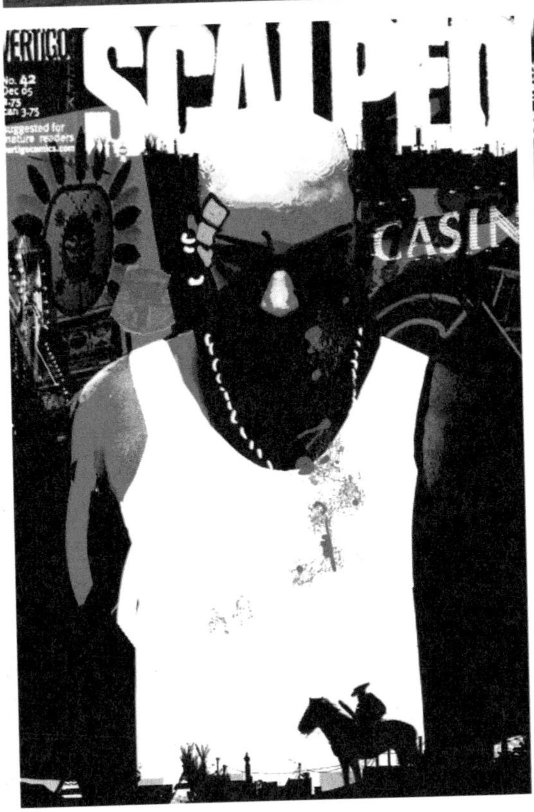

VERTIGO
SCALPED
No. 42
Dec 05
suggested for
mature readers

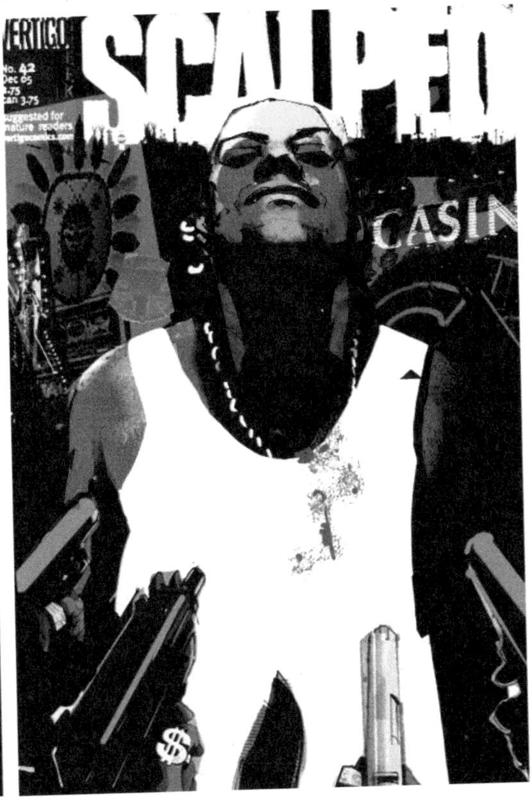

VERTIGO
SCALPED
No. 42
Dec 05
suggested for
mature readers

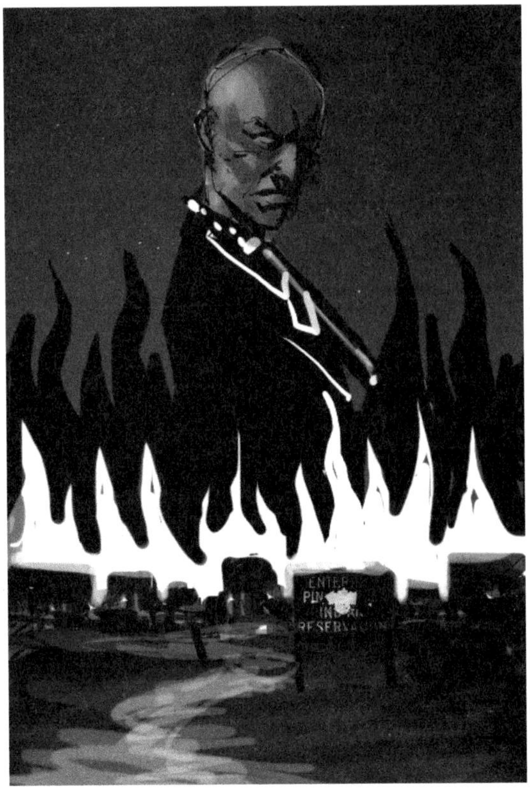
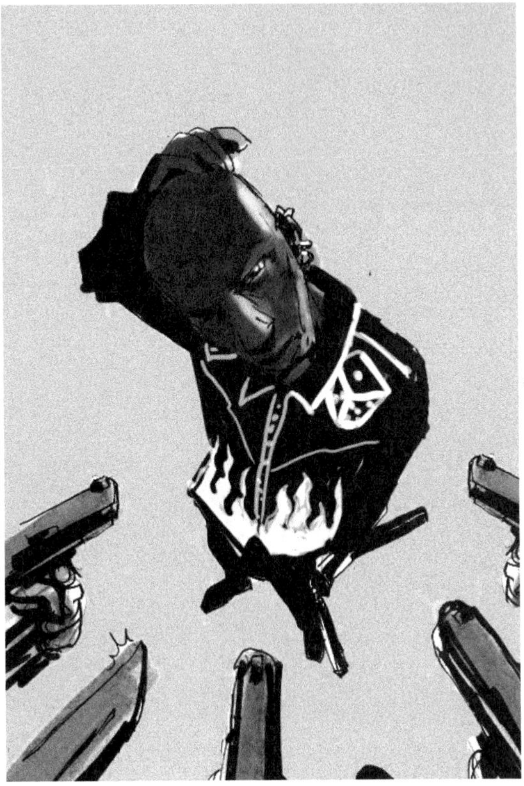
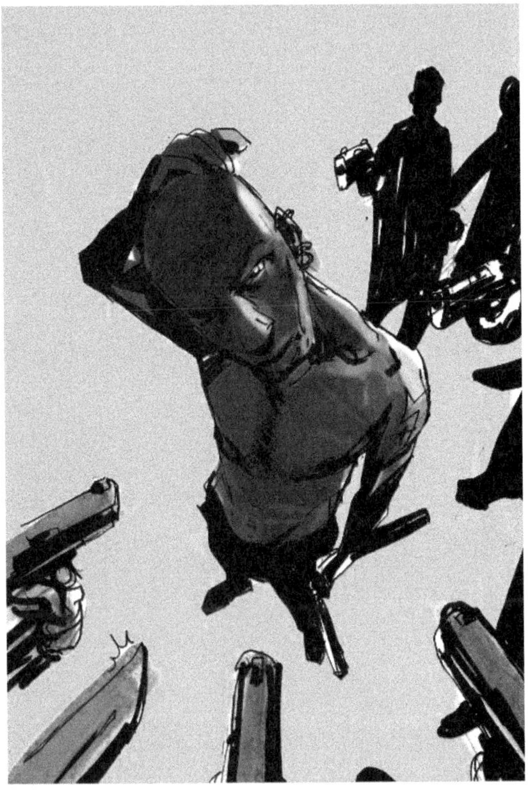
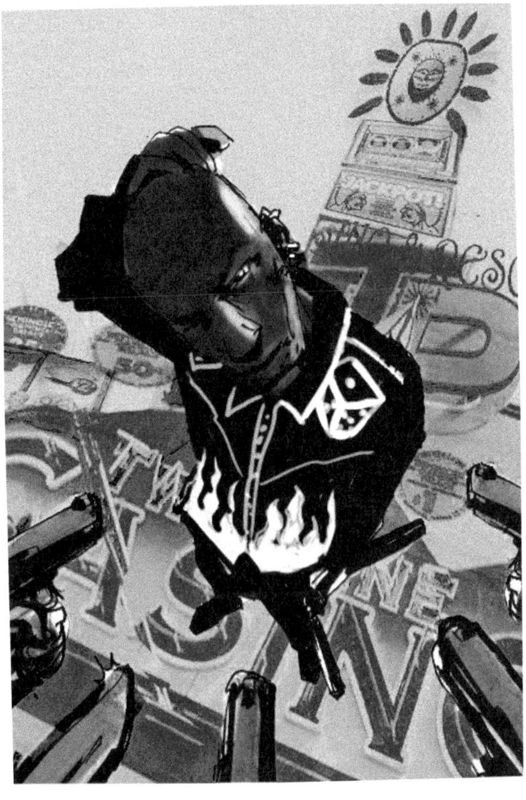

SCALPED

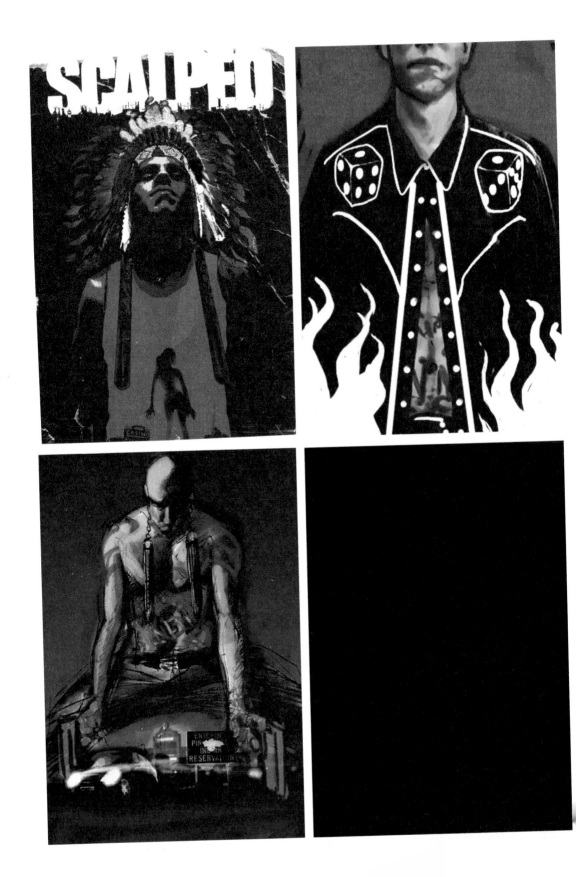

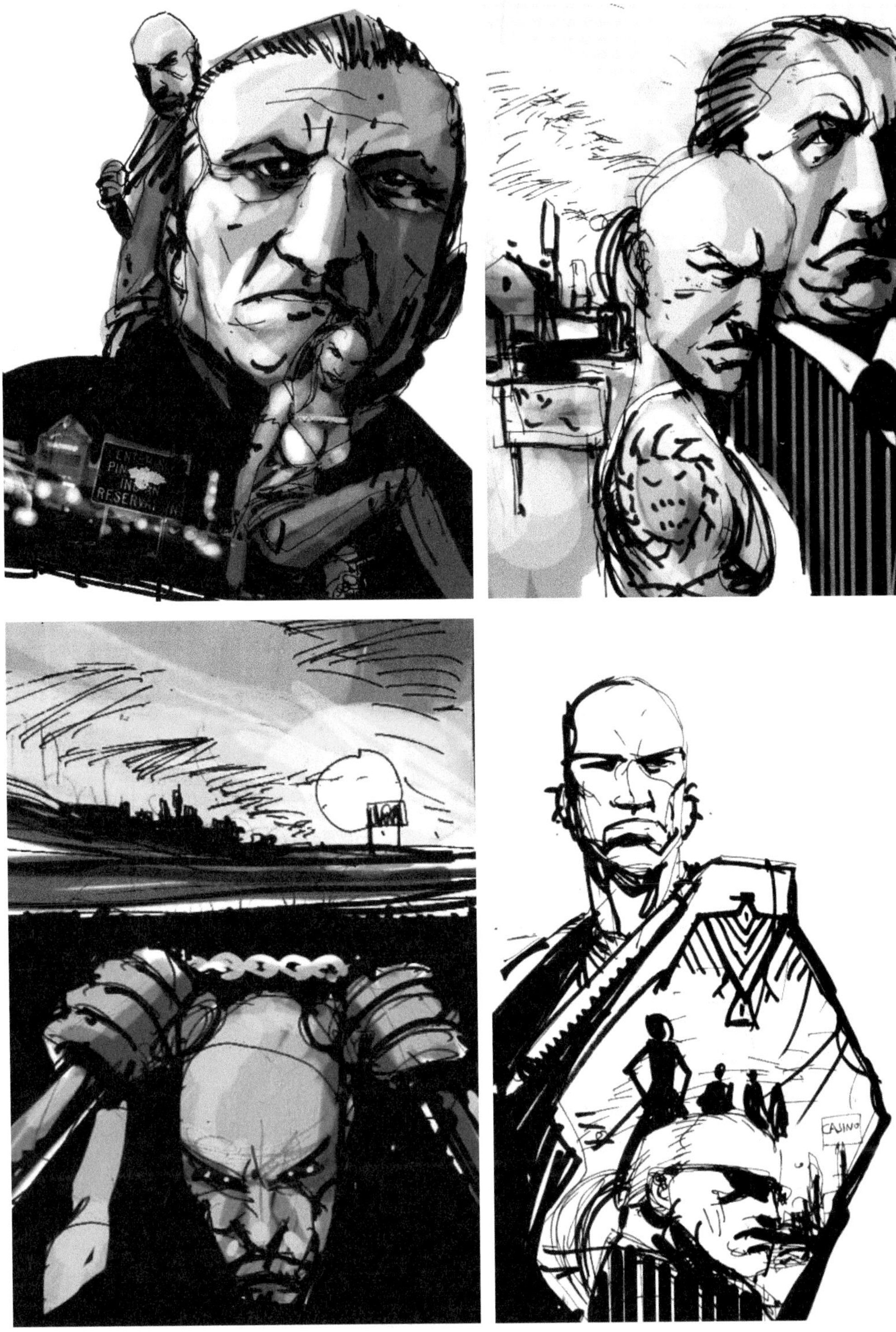
CASINO

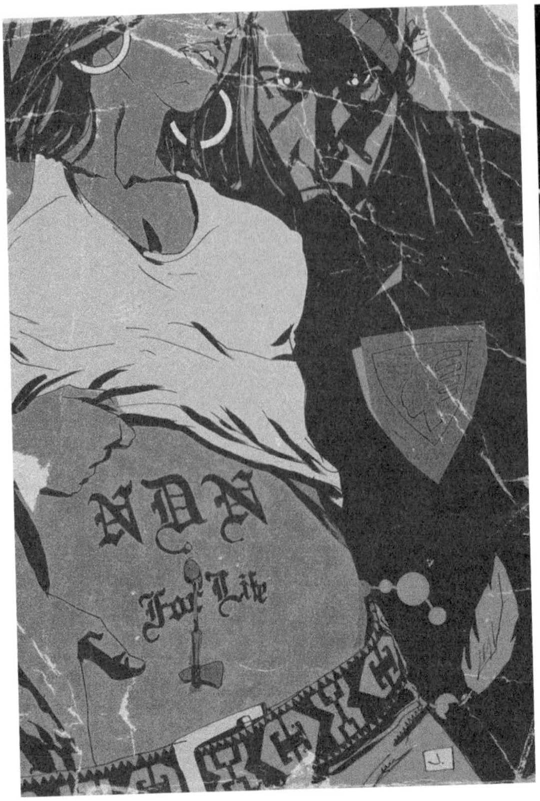
NDN
For Life

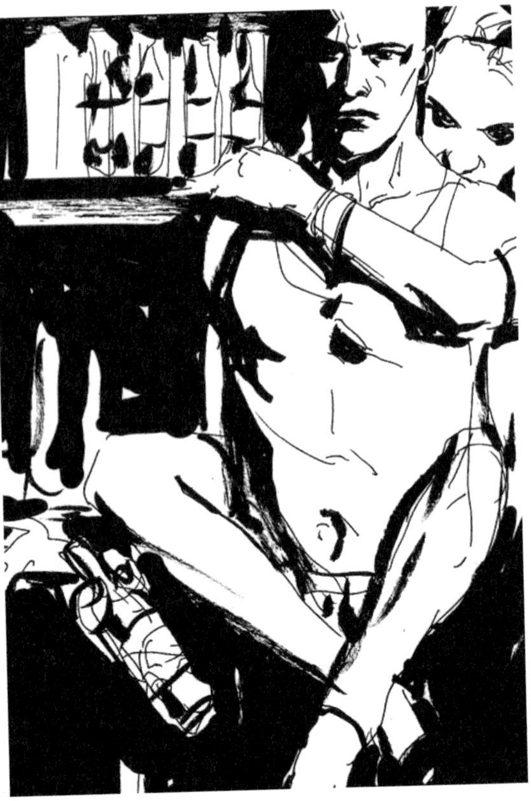

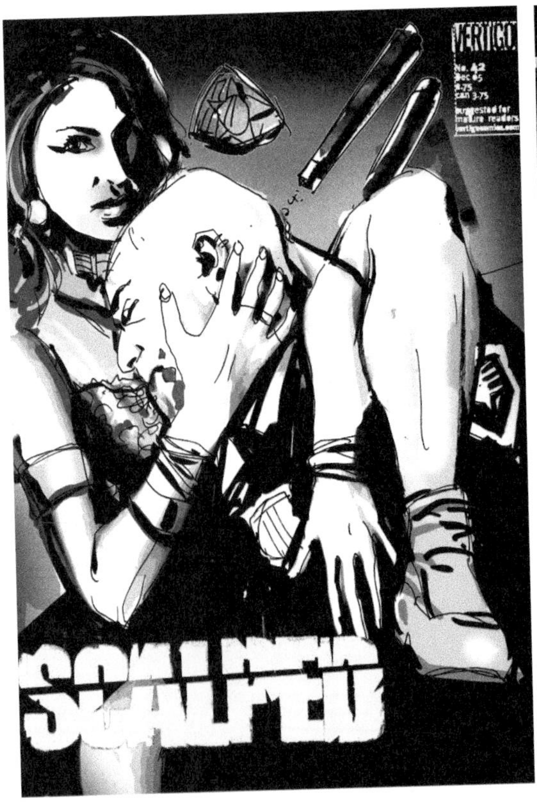
VERTIGO
No. 42
SCALPED

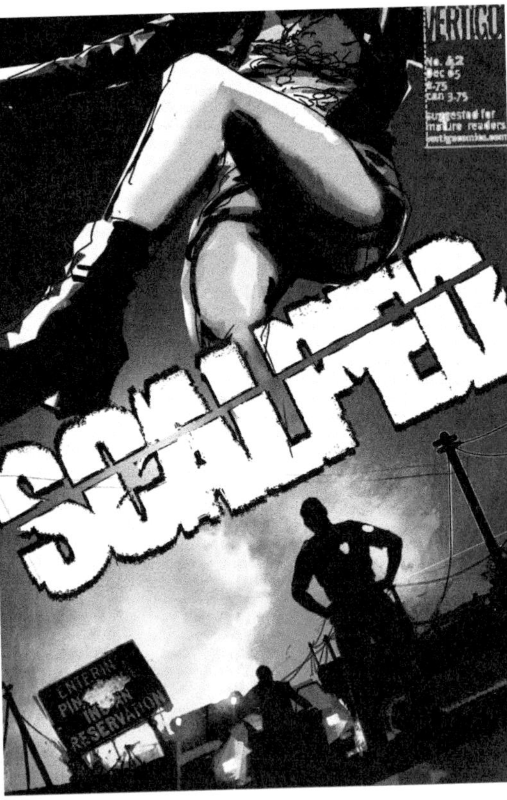
VERTIGO
No. 42
SCALPED

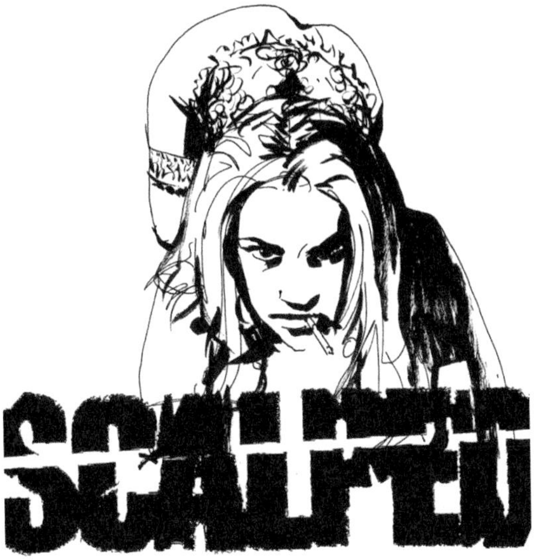
SCALPED

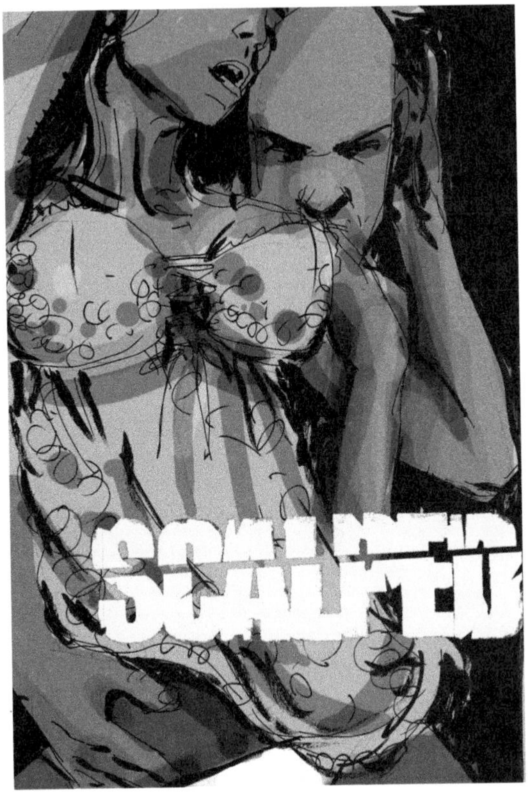
SCALPED

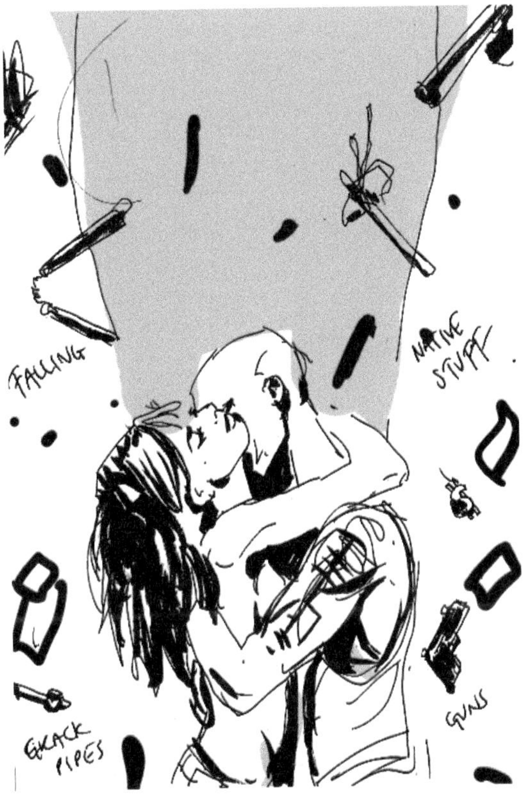
FALLING
NATIVE STUFF
GUNS
CRACK PIPES

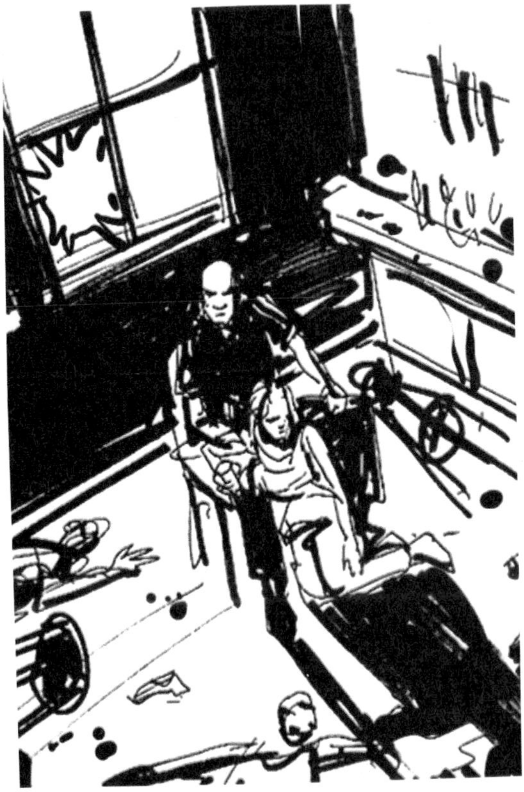

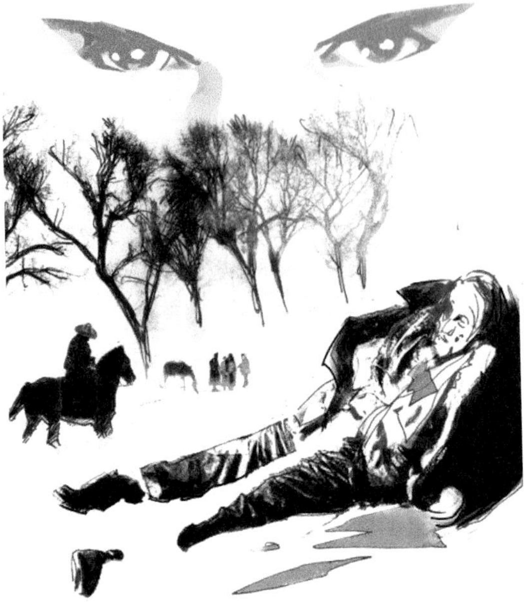

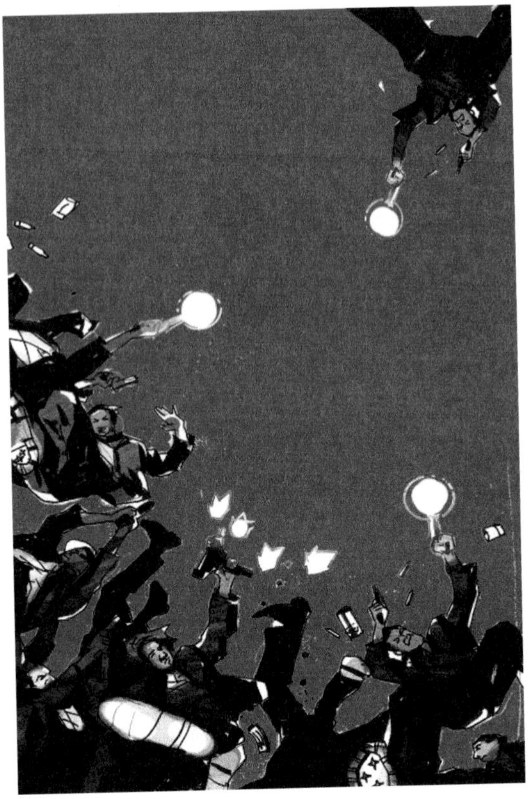

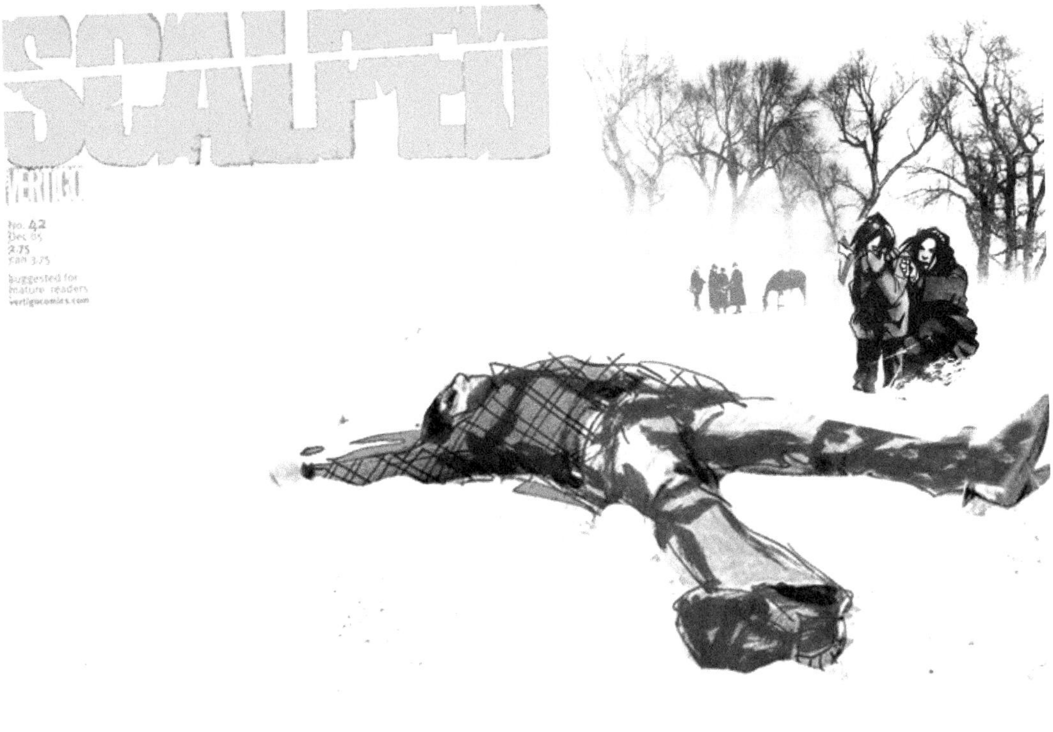
SCALPED
VERTIGO
No. 42
Dec 05
2.75
Can 3.75
Suggested for
mature readers
vertigocomics.com

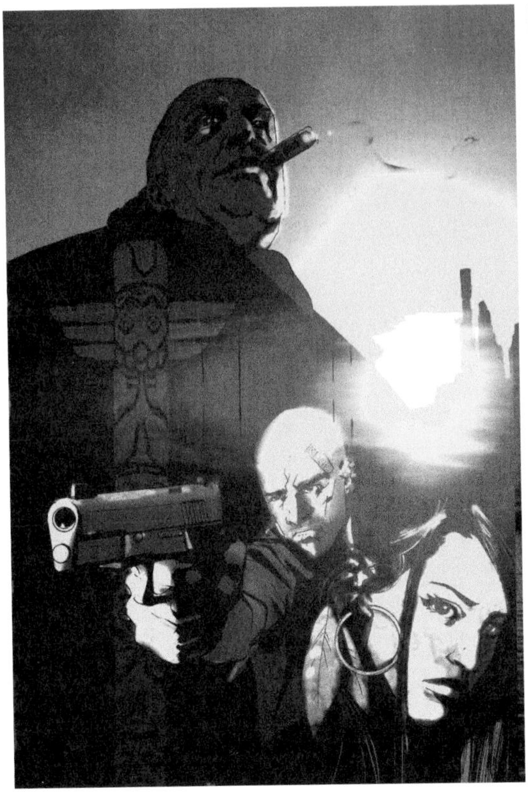

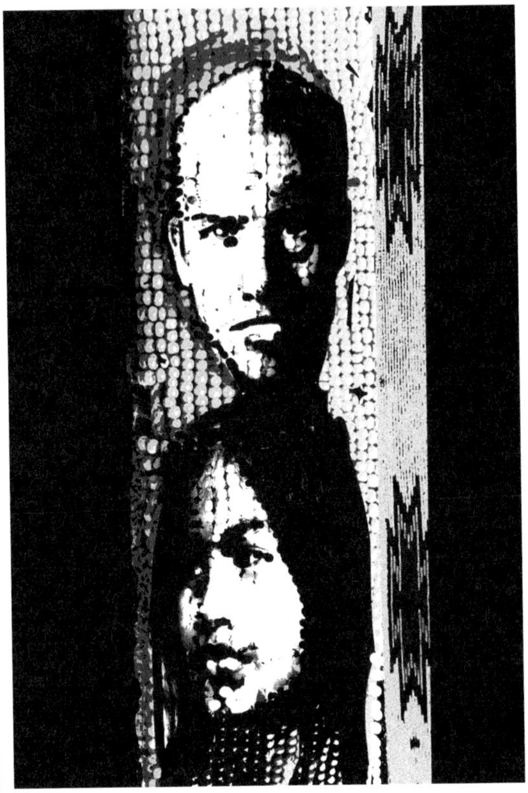

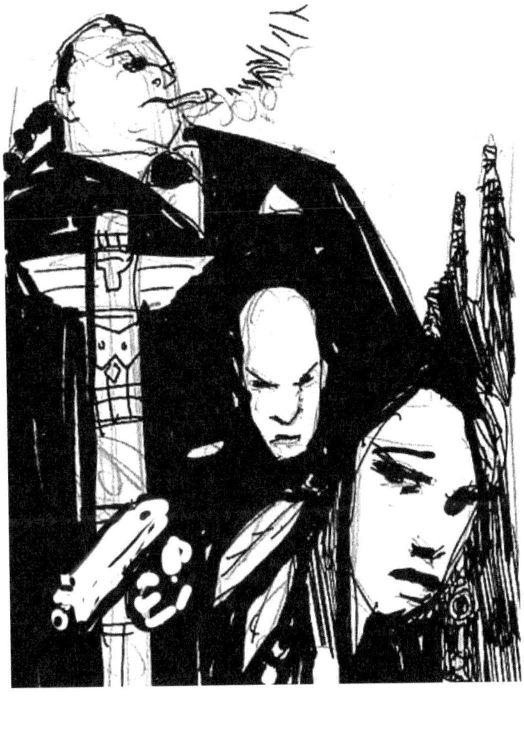

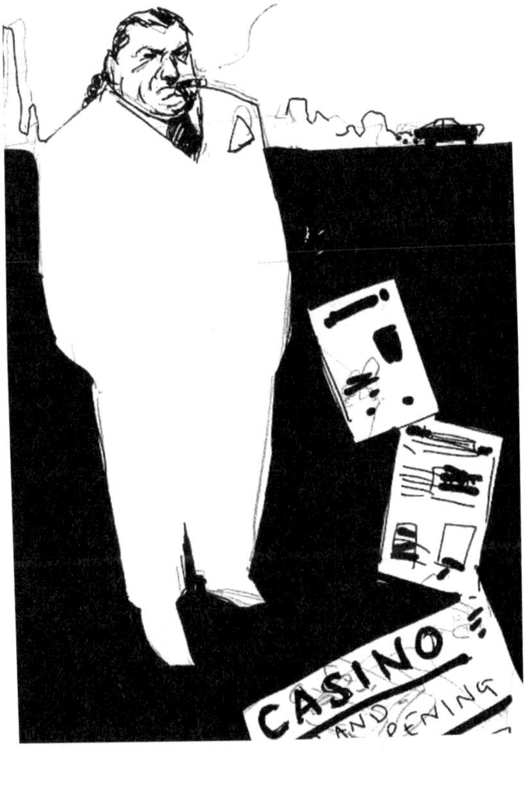
CASINO

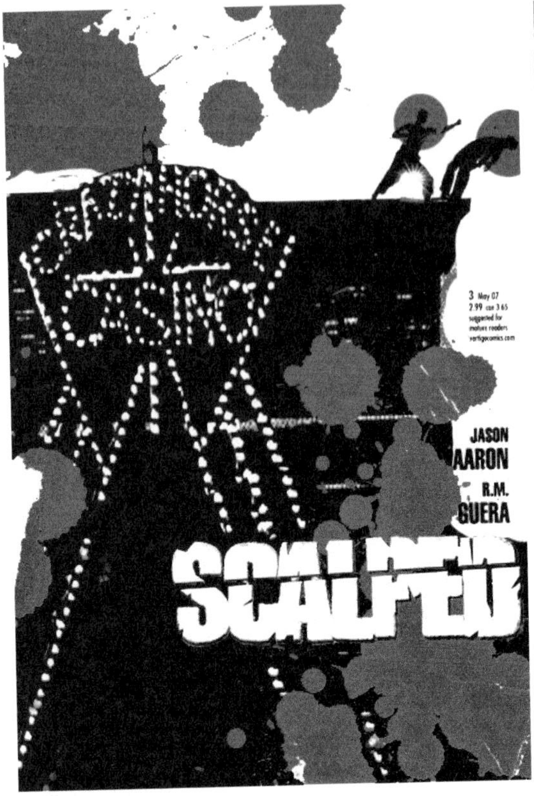
CASINO
3 May 07
2.99 can 3.65
suggested for
mature readers
vertigocomics.com
JASON
AARON
R.M.
GUERA
SCALPED

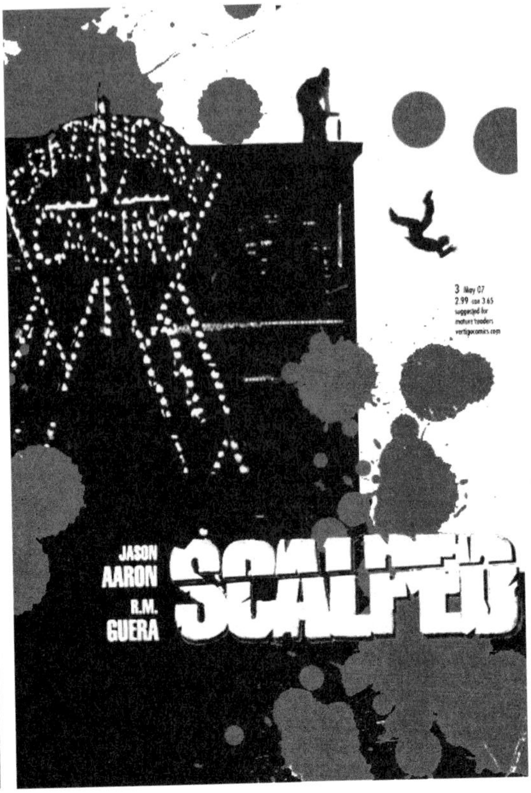
CASINO
3 May 07
2.99 can 3.65
suggested for
mature readers
vertigocomics.com
JASON
AARON
R.M.
GUERA
SCALPED

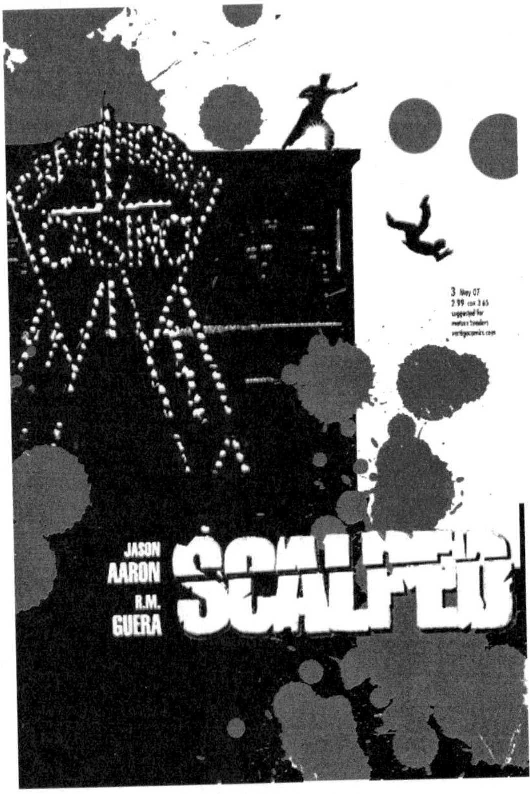
CASINO
3 May 07
2.99 can 3.65
suggested for
mature readers
vertigocomics.com
JASON
AARON
R.M.
GUERA
SCALPED

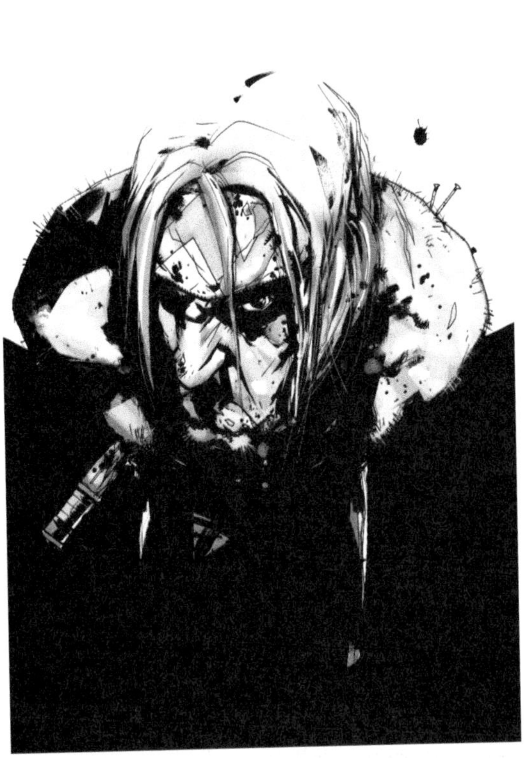

Full Script
#1 of an Ongoing Series
For Will Dennis & Casey Seijas
Vertigo Comics

"Indian Country"
Part One of Three

Written by
Jason Aaron

1) Long range shot of the Battle at Little Bighorn. Lt. Colonel George Armstrong Custer and the 647 men of his 7th Cavalry have been overwhelmed by Oglala, Blackfeet, Minneconjou, Hunkpapa, Brule and Cheyenne Indians, all on horseback. The fighting still lingers in pockets. In other spots, men and horses lie dead or dying, pierced with arrows. Soldiers are being dragged from their horses and scalped. Old women are stripping the bodies.

CAPTION: June 25, 1876

2) Focus on Custer, on his hands and knees, crawling out from under his wounded horse, Comanche (Comanche was actually one of the battle's survivors, and his stuffed hide is still on display at the University of Kansas). Custer's dressed in buckskin and has been shot through the side. There's blood coming from his mouth. Scalped corpses litter the ground around him.

CAPTION: Crazy Horse dreams himself into the real world…

CUSTER: Aaaa, God damn…**God damnit**…

3) Custer looks down, searching in the tall grass for his guns. Indians enter the frame, moving toward him on foot, though we only glimpse them. Legs and feet maybe.

CUSTER: God fucking damnit…

INDIAN BRAVE: **Pahuska!**

4) Custer looks up in horror, having found his pistol, but it looks useless in his hands, drooping limply. We see him through the throng of Indians, as they're closing in from all around, men, women and children now, all reaching out. Weapons are gripped tightly. We can see a long, bone-handled knife in one Indian's hands, the one who's speaking. It's the same bone-handled knife we'll see later this issue in Red Crow's office.

CAPTION: And Long Hair pays for his sins against the Paha Sapa…

CUSTER: Oh God.

INDIAN BRAVE: Let go your holy irons…

5) The throng closes around Custer and we're right in there with them. Someone has his arm, pushing it up as the pistol goes off. Someone else has him by the hair. He's trying to scream, and we're all clawing at him, raising our weapons, the bone-handled knife higher than the rest, poised, ready to strike. We're going to scalp him, then cut off his ears and stab out his eyes, and leave his corpse on the battlefield for the buzzards.

CAPTION: all along the banks of the Little Bighorn.

INDIAN BRAVE: You are not man enough to do any harm.

This page represents our version of the events that took place on the Pine Ridge Reservation in 1975, when a firefight broke out between two FBI agents and members of the militant Indian Rights movement, AIM. In our version, the militants present included Gina Bad Horse, Lincoln Red Crow and Catcher, among others, though we won't see their faces on this page and won't know for several issues exactly which one of them fired the fatal shots.

1) We're inside the front seat of a Bureau car. There's a police radio on the dash. The side windows are all shot out. The front windshield is pockmarked with bullet holes. The front seat is littered with broken glass and spent shells. Through the open passenger's door, we see rolling prairie with maybe the figures of armed Indians moving toward us in the sun's glare.

CAPTION:	June 26, 1975
RADIO:	**Bayer**, come in… **Who** is firing? What is the situation?
RADIO:	Agent Bayer, who is **hit**, over?

2) We're moving along the side of the car now. The whole thing is peppered with bullet holes. Both front tires are flat. The emergency flashers are flashing. FBI Agent Dulohery lies on the ground alongside the door. He's barely conscious and looks like he's trying to rise or pull himself up, his right arm wrapped in a bloody rag. The Indians are moving past the car, though we don't see their faces.

CAPTION:	The Bluecoats again fall like grasshoppers…
AGENT DULOHERY (faint):	Uuuuuhh…
AGENT BAYER (from off):	Please, Jesus…don't kill me, don't kill me, please…

3) The second agent, Bayer, leans back against the rear wheel, wounded in the chest. He has one bloody hand in front of his face to block out the sun. The trunk is open and pierced with bullets. The Indians are gathering around the agent.

CAPTION:	ike gifts from Wakan Tanka, the Great Spirit…
AGENT BAYER:	Please…
AGENT BAYER:	I have **children**.

4) The barrel of a pistol is pressed against Bayer's palm.

INDIAN (from off):	So do **we**, asshole.

5) The gun fires, blowing apart Bayer's hand and blasting a hole in his face.

CAPTION:	all because the wasichus have no ears.

1) We cut to a nighttime view of Red Crow's new Crazy Horse Casino and Entertainment Palace. It's a few weeks away from opening, so there's still evidence of construction, maybe a big Coming Soon sign. Around the neon marquee, there's the large image of an Indian brave giving a war whoop with his tomahawk raised. The vast wasteland of the reservation stretches out beyond the casino. A customized Hummer with tons of chrome is pulling up outside the casino, kicking up trails of dust. This is one of the rides of the Dawg Soldierz, Red Crow's gang of muscle. Since the thugs themselves are a cross between Indian braves of the past and hip hop gangsters of the present, maybe we could put some sort of paint job on their cars that's a mix of modern graffiti and traditional Indian war paint. Nothing too gaudy, just a few touches.

CAPTION:	Today.
CAPTION:	he Prairie Rose Reservation in South Dakota.

2) The Hummer empties while another customized car pulls up (the car's like something you'd see on www.dubpublishing.com). The thugs getting out are dressed like gangstas, like the rapper 50-Cent, with do-rags, tilted caps, designer bulletproof vests, pants hanging off their asses, gold teeth and heavy gold jewelry. Some are shirtless and tattooed. They're all muscle-bound and intimidating, all mixed-blood Indians. And they're all painted like Indian braves going into battle. You can also mix in feathers, beaded chokers, whatever, just a mad collision of Native American and hip hop cultures. They're fired up as they get out of the Hummer, even though they all show signs of having been through a heavy duty battle. Lots of bumps and bruises. Some are slamming beers. Some are armed with baseball bats and tire irons. Their leader, Shunka (means "dog" in Lakota), slides out the passenger's door, yelling at the others to fire them up.

SHUNKA:	This punk thought he could fuck with **us**?
SHUNKA:	**Nobody** fucks with us and lives to fuck again! Not in our house!
RANDOM DAWG SOLDIER:	Hell yeah! We run this!

3) Two carloads of thugs all gather around the trunk of the car. There are ten of them all together, all armed with bats and metal pipes and such, real menacing, ready to beat the holy shit out of someone. They look like they're ready to go to war. "Dawg Soldierz" is painted on the car, along the bottom of the trunk, where Shunka stands, about to pop it open.

RANDOM DAWG SOLDIER:	Get his punk ass out here! I wanna crack his fucking head some more! C'mon!

4) They all crowd in as the trunk pops. It's a tangled mass of people and limbs as they drag Dash from inside the trunk. The thugs are all yelling, all threatening.

RANDOM DAWG SOLDIER:	You mangy piece a' shit! You're in for a world of hurt!
RANDOM DAWG SOLDIER:	I'm gonna slice your dick off and stick it in your mouth, ya bald-headed faggot looking bitch!

5) They're swarming around Dash, kicking him, dragging him to his feet. In the mass of people, we can't get a clear look at him.

RANDOM DAWG SOLDIER:	Get up, motherfucker! **Move**, before I skin you alive!
DASH:	You know, all this sweet talk's giving me a hard-on the size of **Plymouth Rock**.
DASH:	What say we skip the foreplay, ladies…

The dramatic entrance for our hero. Dash stands revealed. But he's sure seen his better days. He's shirtless and barefoot, dressed only in jeans, and he's beat to shit, bruised and swollen, but still defiant. He's angry as hell, in fact, and ready for another go round, no matter how bruised he might be. His hands are bound and he's being shoved along by the throng of scowling Dawg Soldierz, heading toward the casino.

DASH: Let's just fucking **do** this.

TITLE: Indian Country

TITLE: Part One

CREDITS:

1) They move in through the front doors of the casino, framed by fake totem poles.

SHUNKA: You sure talk big, but you're up **shit creek** now, sweet pea.

SHUNKA: Your family—**fucked**. Your friends, neighbors and ex-girlfriends—fucked, fucked and **double** fucked.

2) They move past rows of slot machines and gaming table. There are still ladders and scaffolds up, signs of construction. Dash looks around like a tourist checking out the sights, seemingly not even hearing their threats.

RANDOM DAWG SOLDIER: You done pissed off the **big boss**, shithead. I'm lookin' at a dead man. The boss is gonna fuck your ass up royally.

3) They move toward a door marked Office, around which a couple of beefy Indians stand guard, dressed in Casino Security shirts.

RANDOM DAWG SOLDIER: The boss got **crazy** strong medicine. He'll probably cut you from asshole to elbow, then pull your heart out and **show** it to your ass before you die.

4) They move through the office door, shoving Dash along. Shunka beams proudly.

SHUNKA: Boss, **lookie** what we brung ya.

5) Inside the office, Red Crow stands with his back to us, washing up in a sink next to his bar. The office is dark, with lots of dark woods and light from small lamps. The décor is a study in contrasts. There's antique, hand-carved furniture from Mexico, like a table made from 100 year old hacienda doors, but the lamps are art deco and the bar is sleek, stainless steel. There are traditional Indian blankets and thick fur rugs, painted buffalo skulls and native masks, but also a flat screen TV and state of the art sound system. Very elegant, sophisticated surroundings, but then there are also cigar store Indians and gory paintings of settlers being scalped by half-naked Indians. Red Crow has two vicious looking pit bulls roaming around, but he also has a massive, gorgeous aquarium filled with delicate, exotic fish. There's a guy dressed in rain gear who's mopping up around RC's desk.

RED CROW: Be with you in a minute, boys. Make yourself comfortable.

1) The guy with the mop pauses to stare at us. His rain gear is splattered with gore, as he mops up a pool of blood.

SHUNKA (from off):   You heard the man, dick weed.

2) The two massive pit bulls at Red Crow's feet turn and stare as well.

NO COPY

3) Dash is handcuffed in a chair, right in front of Red Crow's desk. The chair is a heavy stone or adobe structure with ornately carved armrests that Dash's hands are cuffed into (one pair of cuffs for each hand). Dash is looking down at the fresh splatters of blood on the chair. Shunka and the Dawgs are gathered behind. Shunka slaps him in the back of the head while he talks.

DASH: Your chair's **sticky**. Did somebody spill Kool-A—
SHUNKA: Shut the fuck up.

4) Back to Red Crow. He's still bent over the sink, washing blood off his hands. His back is to Dash and the Dawgs. We don't see his face.

SHUNKA: This is him, boss. **Bad Horse.** The asshole who's been startin' fights at the pool hall every night.

HUNKA: Motherfucker's ass is sure **feisty,** I'll give him that.

5) Blood going down the sink.

RED CROW: Yes, it appears so. Either **that**…
RED CROW: or you're a bunch of half-wit **incompetents**, who could barely overcome a man you outnumbered **ten to one.**

6) Shunka holds out Dash's nunchucks.

SHUNKA: He uh, he was **armed**, boss.

7) Focus on Dash, head down, apparently finally feeling the pain of all the beatings he's endured.

RED CROW (from off):   You're **kidding** me, right?
RED CROW (from off):   Jesus kid, your mother should've **never** taken you to see Billy Jack.

DASH: My mother shoulda never done **alotta** things.

1) Tight on Dash. He looks serious, like he's actually gonna make a sincere appeal for sanity in the midst of all this violence.

DASH: Listen, dude, I have no idea **who** you are or what the deal is or **anything**,

DASH: but let's get **one thing** straight, okay, before any of this gets out of hand…

2) Tighter on Dash. No appeal for sanity, after all. He may be tired but there's still plenty of gravel in his guts and fire in his eyes. He seriously doesn't give a fuck what Red Crow's gonna do to him.

DASH: **Fuck you.**

3) The Dawgs are incensed, ready to rend Dash limb from limb.

SHUNKA: You are **so** unbelievably **dead**, you fucking—

RED CROW (from off): **Outside!** Wait outside, boys.

4) Red Crow dries his hands as the thugs all reluctantly turn to go. We still don't see Red Crow's face.

RED CROW: And I'd take it as a personal favor if you wouldn't **bleed** on anything.

5) The blood splattered guy who was mopping turns to leaves, grinning a sadistic grin at Dash as he goes. He's convinced the kid is about to lose some flesh.

MOP GUY: I'll come back later, Mr. Red Crow.

MOP GUY: To clean up the **mess**.

6) Dash watches as the door closes and he's left alone with Red Crow.

NO COPY

7) Red Crow stands with his back to us and Dash.

NO COPY

1) He's still standing there, behind his desk. The wall there is covered with historical Native American weapons. Tomahawks, axes, lances, arrow heads, gun stock war clubs, coup sticks, knives and shields. There are Indian weapons from tribes all over the country, not just the Lakota.

RED CROW: Among Native tribes, the practice of **scalping** predates the arrival of that syphilitic, ginney **fuck**, Columbus.

2) Tighter on the wall of weapons. We see the bone-handled knife from page 1 hanging there.

RED CROW: Though it was spick settlers who popularized it by offering bounties for the scalps of their enemies…man, woman and child.

RED CROW: Among the **Lakota**, the scalps of our enemies, like The Crow, Shoshone and Pawnee, would adorn our staffs during the sacred Sun Dance.

3) Red Crow takes the knife down.

RED CROW: I am tribal president of the **Oglala** Lakota, the people of Red Cloud and Crazy Horse.

RED CROW: I'm also **sheriff** of the tribal police force, head of the Prairie Rose planning committee, treasurer of the Highway Safety Program and Managing Director of the Crazy Horse Casino.

4) Red Crow holds the knife.

RED CROW: I'm a **Dog Soldier** and **War Chief**, a descendant of the Plains Indian warriors of legend.

RED CROW: My name is **Red Crow**.

5) From behind Red Crow, we see him turn to face Dash. Red Crow's long hair cascades down his back.

RED CROW: But I reckon all that don't mean jack shit to a badass like you, right?

RED CROW: All **you** need to know, kid, is that **around here**…

1) Full reveal on Red Crow. He stands at his desk, holding the knife like he wouldn't mind using it. Even though he's dressed in a slick, tailored suit and his hairline is receding a little, he still looks like a majestic Indian chief of old.

RED CROW: I'm the guy who can make it so you never even existed.

RED CROW: You savvy?

2) Cut back to Dash, still not showing any signs of fear.

DASH: So, you called me up here just to **introduce** yourself?

DASH: Coulda put that on a **postcard**, chief.

3) Red Crow moves toward him with the knife. He moves like a panther, always calm and collected.

RED CROW: You take after your mother in the **smart-ass** department, don't you?

DASH: What the fuck do you know about my mother?

4) Red Crow slithers around the chair where Dash is chained.

RED CROW: I know she's a **mouthy** bitch. I know she can handle herself alright with an **AR-15**. I know she likes you to pull her hair when you're **riding** her from behind.

RED CROW: And I know she was always a poor excuse for a mother, though she did try.

5) Dash still doesn't show any signs of fear, though he's pulling at the cuffs a little, like he'd love to get a piece of Red Crow, knife or no knife.

DASH: What now, you gonna tell me you're my long-lost **daddy**?

RED CROW: No. Your father was a right fine waste of space.

RED CROW: Is that you, kid? Are you a chip off the ole **worthless** block?

1) Red Crow has the knife right in Dash's face.

DASH: You're not my PO too, are you?

RED CROW: To you, young Mr. Bad Horse, I'm the father, the son and the holy fucking ghost all rolled into one.

RED CROW: Do you know how simple it is to scalp a man?

2) Cut to the two pit bulls, licking at the blood and flecks of gore around the bloody mop.

RED CROW (from off): You make an incision around the hair, from the forehead to the back of the neck...

3) Tight on Dash's eyes, the knife gleaming in front of them. He finally looks a little worried. A little frantic.

RED CROW: Then you flip 'em facedown...

RED CROW: brace your foot on their shoulder...

4) Tighter on the pit bulls. We can see there's a clod of scalp on the floor where they're licking.

RED CROW (from off): and yank the hair off with both hands, in one quick movement, from back to front.

5) Looking down at Dash from Red Crow's perspective. We see Dash's sweaty, bald head gleaming in the light. He's bending back, looking up to meet our gaze.

DASH: You gonna scalp **me**, chief, you got your work cut out for you.

6) Red Crow stands behind Dash, examining the blade of the knife.

RED CROW: Maybe I could do like the **Iroquois** and simply break your fingers with my teeth, yank your nails out, slit your scalp and stuff sand in the wound, burn you with torches throughout the night...

7) Tight on Dash's hands, pulling hard on the cuffs.

RED CROW (from off): and then eat whatever's left.

RED CROW (from off): See this knife?

Page Eleven
Five Panels

1) Red Crow dangles the knife in front of Dash.

RED CROW:	You **see** this knife?
DASH:	It's kinda hard to miss.
RED CROW:	This knife is 200 years old. It's claimed more men's lives than **typhoid**. **Your** life either begins or ends right here in this room, **right now**.

2) Focus on Dash, wiggling uncomfortably in his chair a little bit. And it ain't part of his undercover act.

DASH:	Look, man, I came to town just to lay low for a little while. I was never looking for no **trouble**.
RED CROW:	Yet here we are.

3) Focus on Red Crow, still fiddling with the knife's blade, testing its sharpness.

RED CROW:	You ran away from the Rez when you were what, **thirteen**? Been home just **two weeks** and already started half a dozen fights in local bars.
RED CROW:	Okay, so you got my attention.

4) Red Crow at his sternest, gesturing with the knife.

RED CROW:	I will not abide any half-crazy **buffalo-jockey** who thinks he can wave his dick around and make trouble on **my** Rez. Especially not when this casino is three weeks away from opening.
DASH:	Look, your boys out there are cowards who like to run their mouths and push people around.
DASH:	Lord knows I ain't no saint myself, but shit like that tends to **annoy** me.

5) Red Crow gestures with the knife like a teacher waving a ruler around.

RED CROW:	In this place, there are **Skins**, like you and I. **Full-blood** Lakotas. The real natural human beings.
RED CROW:	And then there are **Breeds**, like those mixed-blood fuckwits out there. These days, all I have to work with are watered-down Injuns.
RED CROW:	That's why **you** work for me now.

Page Twelve
Five Panels

1) Dash knows he's inside now, but still tries to play the reluctant badass.

DASH: No thanks. I like my unemployment checks just fine.

RED CROW: Those'll buy you a nice unmarked grave in the Badlands. And maybe someday, somebody somewhere will actually **notice** you're gone.

2) Red Crow turns on Dash, reminding him he still has the knife and is still willing to use it.

DASH: Get me outta this chair, **then** we'll talk.

RED CROW: I'll **cut** you out of that chair, **piece by piece**, unless I hear what I wanna hear.

3) Dash looks more comfortable in the chair now, even a little cocky.

RED CROW: You think I don't mean business? Try asking the guy whose **blood** you're sitting in.

DASH: C'mon, ain't you already well-stocked with thugs and degenerates? What the hell you need **me** for?

4) Red Crow's walking back toward his desk with a sly look on his face.

RED CROW: Oh, I got something **special** in mind for you. Once in a lifetime opportunity, you might say. After all...

5) Cut to a few days later. Dash is dressed in his tribal police uniform. His cuts and bruises have partly healed but he still has some band-aids here and there on his face. He's standing in front of a rowdy throng of Traditionalists who are angrily protesting Red Crow's casino. They have hand-painted signs with slogans like "Red Crow is a Liar!" "No Casino—Not Now, Not Ever!" "We Won't Trade Our Heritage for $$$" Dash has his back to a wooden police barrier, his arms out, trying to hold back the mob. He doesn't appear to be enjoying his new job.

CAPTION: "When else is a scumbag like you gonna get the chance to be a **cop**?"

Page Thirteen
Four Panels

1) We're out in front of the casino. At a safe distance from the mob, Red Crow leans against a tribal police car. Construction continues, despite the protestors. Several tribal cops and Dawg Soldierz are manning the barrier, keeping the dozens of protestors at bay. Dash approaches, wiping sweat from his brow. He looks uncomfortable in his new duds.

RED CROW: How goes the first day?

DASH: It'd go a lot better if you'd give me back my nunchucks.

2) Red Crow and Dash stand talking. Beyond them, Gina Bad Horse has just pushed her way past the barrier.

RED CROW: Can you believe the **balls** on these blanket-ass, prairie niggers? They call themselves "**Traditionalists**" and accuse **me** of betraying **The People**?

3) Same view. They're still talking while Gina stalks toward them. Neither of them notices her.

RED CROW: How many of them have ever **pierced** at a Sun Dance? How many of them even speak their own language?

RED CROW: All they know about being Lakota they learned from watching *Dances With Wolves.*

4) She's right on top of them, looking pissed. Red Crow notices her at the last second. Dash never sees her.

RED CROW: Buncha fuckin' wahoos. They only...

RED CROW: Uh oh.

1) Gina slaps the shit out of her momentarily surprised son, knocking his hat off.

GINA: You **asshole**!

2) Dash grabs her by the shoulders. They're both raging.

GINA: Dashiell, you fucking ingrate! You make me **sick**!

3) He slams her around into the side of the car. Hard.

NO COPY

4) He's right on top of her, his finger in her face. She's shocked and out of breath.

DASH: You crazy bitch, you just slapped an officer of the law! You're **lucky** I don't run your ass in right now and bury you under the goddamn jail!

1) She shoves him away, holding her side.

GINA: Get off me!

GINA: You're not the law here. You're just another one of Red Crow's **flunkies**.

2) She gives Red Crow a deathly stare as she stalks past him, heading back toward the mob, still holding her side.

RED CROW: Evenin', **Gina**. Lookin' **lovely** as ever.

GINA: Go fuck yourself, Lincoln.

3) Red Crow moves toward Dash, watching Gina. Dash is bending over to pick up his hat.

RED CROW: That there's one fiery filly.

DASH: Really? Seems like a **psycho bitch** to me.

4) Tight on Dash. He's putting his hat back on. Trying to regain his composure. His reaction to being slapped wasn't just an act for Red Crow's benefit. He truly hates that woman.

RED CROW (from off): Well, **you'd** know, I guess. After all…

RED CROW (from off): she's your **mother.**

5) Tight on Red Crow, watching Dash out the corner of his eye with a sly grin on his face.

RED CROW: In case you didn't know, she's also the **leader** of this here mob.

6) They stand together, looking out at the protestors.

RED CROW: She's a real **ball-buster**, your mom. How long since you two saw each other last?

DASH: Not nearly long enough. Only **15 years**.

7) Red Crow gives Dash a friendly slap on the shoulder.

RED CROW: Well I'd say that's enough tearful reunions for one day. I'm starting to feel like Oprah…

Page Sixteen
Five Panels

1) Dash and Red Crow are pulling up to the Fire Water Package Store in Dash's police car. They're just across the state line in White Clay, Nebraska, where all the Rez Indians come to get drunk. It's a town of about 20 people that manages to sell about four million cans of beer each year. The parking lot is packed with plenty of "Rez Mobiles," junk cars held together with duct tape, rust and prayers.

CAPTION: "How 'bout a beer?"

2) Inside the store, we're looking at someone's items moving down the conveyer belt to be rung up. There's a box of condoms, a carton of cigarettes and a sixpack of beer.

CASHIER: Will this be cash or charge, ma'am?

3) Carol stands over the items, holding out a page of food stamps, a sour look on her face, like she's a debutant who's disgusted to even be there. A cigarette dangles from her mouth. She's dressed in cut-off jeans, flip-flops and a ratty t-shirt that's too small. The waistband of her thong underwear pokes up over the frayed, low cut top of her shorts. Her shirt reads "Oglala High School Cheerleading Squad, 1990." Her hair is messy. No make up. She needs a bath. She's been rode hard and put up wet. But still, she exudes sexuality. She's the kind of woman who'd either fuck your brains out or just steal your wallet. Maybe both. The gorgeous body and devious eyes: she's got femme fatale written all over her. One look and you know she's nothing but trouble, but goddamnit, something inside you can't help but wanna make a run at her.

CAROL: Food stamps.

4) Red Crow and Dash come waltzing in.

RED CROW: And here we have the one store in the area that's guaranteed to never go out of business.

RED CROW: Alcohol's **illegal** on the Rez, so…

5) They're right by Carol before Red Crow notices her. She flips him a bird without looking.

RED CROW: Oh hell.

CAROL: Why if it ain't big chief **Eat-Shit-n'-Die**.

Page Seventeen
Six Panels

1) Dash stands in front of the beer cooler, looking back at Carol. Red Crow's reaching in for some beer.

DASH: I **know** her, don't I?

2) Carol's finishing up her purchase, not paying any attention to Red Crow and Dash.

RED CROW (from off): I'd say so. You were in **love** with her when you were twelve.

3) Cut to a flashback of young Carol, maybe 12 or 13 years old, seen from Dash's perspective. She's looking deep into our eyes with mischievous glee.

CAROL: You can see **me** pee, Dash, if I can see you first.

4) Red Crow's holding the beer, looking at Dash with a serious stare.

RED CROW: That was a **long** time ago though. These days, Carol there's the type of cooze what drags men down **black roads**.

RED CROW: She's also married. To a goddamn **wasichu**, if you can believe it.

5) Dash is still staring after her, a little transfixed.

DASH: She's your **daughter**, ain't she?

RED CROW (from off): She's a **whore** and a **liar**. And if you got a lick o' goddamn sense…

6) Carol's glances back at him, over her shoulder as she's walking out the door with her bag. She's got a great looking ass and she knows it.

RED CROW (from off): you'll stay **way** the hell away from her.

1) Dash and Red Crow sip beer as they cruise in Dash's patrol car, kicking up clouds of dust. They're passing a large sign as they cross the border onto the Rez. The vast emptiness of the Badlands stretches around them in every direction.

SIGN:	Prairie Rose Indian Reservation
SIGN:	Est 1889
SIGN:	Home of the Oglala Lakota
RED CROW:	So what do you think of our beloved **Rez** so far, Officer Bad Horse?
DASH:	Not much, really.
RED CROW:	Yeah, well, the happy hunting grounds it definitely **ain't**.

2) Cut to a shot of tarpaper shacks in a field of dirt. A toddler wearing only a filthy diaper stands in the yard, crying, surrounded by flies. A shirtless old man watches, emotionless, from the open door of one shack. He's wearing a stained t-shirt that says "Redskins," and he has a prosthetic hook for a hand.

CAPTION:	"Welcome to the **poorest** county in the United States. This is where the **Great Sioux Nation** came to die."
CAPTION:	"Household income averages around $3,000 a year, with 80% unemployment."

3) An ancient looking lady is hanging her laundry out to dry between several dilapidated houses. The area is cluttered with trash. Old refrigerators. Washing machines. Bags of garbage. There's a totaled car nearby that someone's sleeping in, curled up with blankets. There's no grass. Only dirt.

CAPTION:	"The rate of fetal alcohol syndrome is thirty-three times higher here than for whites."
CAPTION:	"Our children reject their culture, then turn to inhalants and methamphetamine. One in five will attempt **suicide** by the end of high school."

4) A man's passed out drunk, lying in his own vomit, with a mangy looking dog sniffing at him. Over them looms a historical marker commemorating the site of a Ghost Dance in 1890. The marker is pock-marked with bullets and defaced with graffiti that reads "Nits make lice."

CAPTION:	"The **alcoholism** rate here is the highest in the country. We're twice as likely as non-Indians to be **murdered**. Our overall life expectancy is fifteen years less than the national average."
CAPTION:	"We are a thoroughly defeated people."

1) Dash and Red Crow cruise past the Poor Bear family home. It's a trailer with a collapsed porch and a dirt yard cluttered with Dino's collection of junk cars, all of them in various stages of "almost running." Dino Poor Bear's working under the hood of one, dressed in a gas station attendant's shirt with a name tag that reads "Dino."

RED CROW:	Fifteen years after he survived the massacre at **Wounded Knee**, my grandfather was shot dead by his best friend, during an argument over some cowboy boots.
DINO:	Okay, I got it now. Juanita, turn it over one more time!

2) Flashback. Red Crow's father lies facedown in a muddy ditch on the side of a dirt road, in the middle of nowhere. A whiskey bottle lies at his side. Nothing else in sight except the dreary emptiness of Nebraska. For these flashback panels, which I'd like to sprinkle in from time to time, maybe we could use a muted color palette or more of a painted look, in order to denote them as flashbacks.

CAPTION:	"My father survived the trenches of WWII only to die in a ditch in **Nebraska**, so drunk he drowned in three inches of water."

3) Back to the Poor Bear home. Dino's pregnant sister, Juanita, sits behind the wheel of the car, smoking a cigarette, turning the key. Dino's waving at the smoke coming from the engine. Their mentally-retarded younger sister, a victim of fetal alcohol syndrome, stands in the yard, waving at the passing police car.

CAPTION:	"My older brother moved to Rapid City, married a white bitch and joined the Marines.
CAPTION:	"He stepped on a land mine in some godforsaken place I can't even pronounce, because he thought **he** was John Wayne and the **Vietnamese** were the Indians."
JUANITA:	Good job, Dino. Another **Rez Mobile** for your collection.

4) Another flashback. Dashing, young Lincoln Red Crow as a Red Power activist in the 70s, alongside Gina Bad Horse and Catcher. The three of them are holding an American flag upside down, crying out in rage, while they fight off the riot police trying to wrestle them to the ground. Beyond them, on the steps of the BIA office in Washington DC, there are several other long-haired Indian militants fighting with the cops. The building's façade is covered with graffiti: "Sioux, Nez Perces, Cheyenne, Hoka Hey, Dog Soldier Society." The militants are wearing a mix of traditional Indian dress (feather, chokers) and ragged hippie wear (bellbottom jeans, fringe vests).

CAPTION:	"**Me**, I chose a different course for my life."

1) Cut back to Red Crow in the car, staring off into the distance as he conjures up the past.

RED CROW: I once defended the Rez with **rifle** in hand. I was there when the Dog Soldier Society occupied the Bureau of Indian Affairs office in DC.

RED CROW: We flew the flag upside down. Much to our surprise, living conditions on the Rez did not improve overnight.

2) Flashback. Aftermath of the events on page 2. Both FBI agents lie dead after being executed.

CAPTION: "I was there in '75 when some feds **accidentally** caught a few stray bullets…"

CAPTION: "point blank in the face. "

3) Dash and Red Crow drive past rows of government built housing, all fallen into disrepair.

RED CROW: We were naïve children, thinking the key to our independence lay in the treaties of the past. I moved on. People like your mother never did.

4) Tight on Red Crow, very stern look on his face.

RED CROW: These days, I'm not fighting for the Rez. **I am** the Rez. And this casino is the future.

RED CROW: The wasichus stole the Black Hills from us, they stole our hunting grounds and our way of life. But the **free ride's** over.

5) The police car heads off into the distance, between rows of trailers, shacks and rusted car frames. The wall of one house, apparently abandoned, is spray-painted with the words "Indian Country."

RED CROW: This time, when they come calling…

RED CROW: they better bring their debit cards.

Page Twenty-One
Five Panels

1) Late at night. A Bureau car sits in the middle of the Badlands with two agents inside.

AGENT #1: How you liking your new assignment, kid? A real **shithole**, right?

AGENT #2: Uh, I don't know, sir. I guess.

2) Close-up of a gun and FBI badge sitting on the dash.

AGENT #1: Wasn't too long ago this place had the highest **murder rate** per capita in the country.

AGENT #1: Trust me, with what we got going on, it won't be long and these Native American fucks'll be dropping like flies.

3) Straight on shot of the two agents. Agent #1 is older, saltier. Agent #2 is fresh and green.

AGENT #1: You just stick by me, do **exactly** what I say, no questions asked, and you'll have **promotions** coming out the ying yang.

4) Tight on Agent #1.

AGENT #1: **RED CROW'S** the one we want. He's crooked as a barrel of fish hooks, always has been. And I'm so looking forward to shitting in his cereal.

5) Another car comes toward them out of the darkness. It's a rusty looking pick-up with only one headlight.

AGENT #1: All right, here's our boy.

Dash steps out of the pick-up into the headlight's glow. He's angry and exasperated, yelling at the agents.

DASH: Forget it. I can't fucking do this.

DASH: I want **out!**

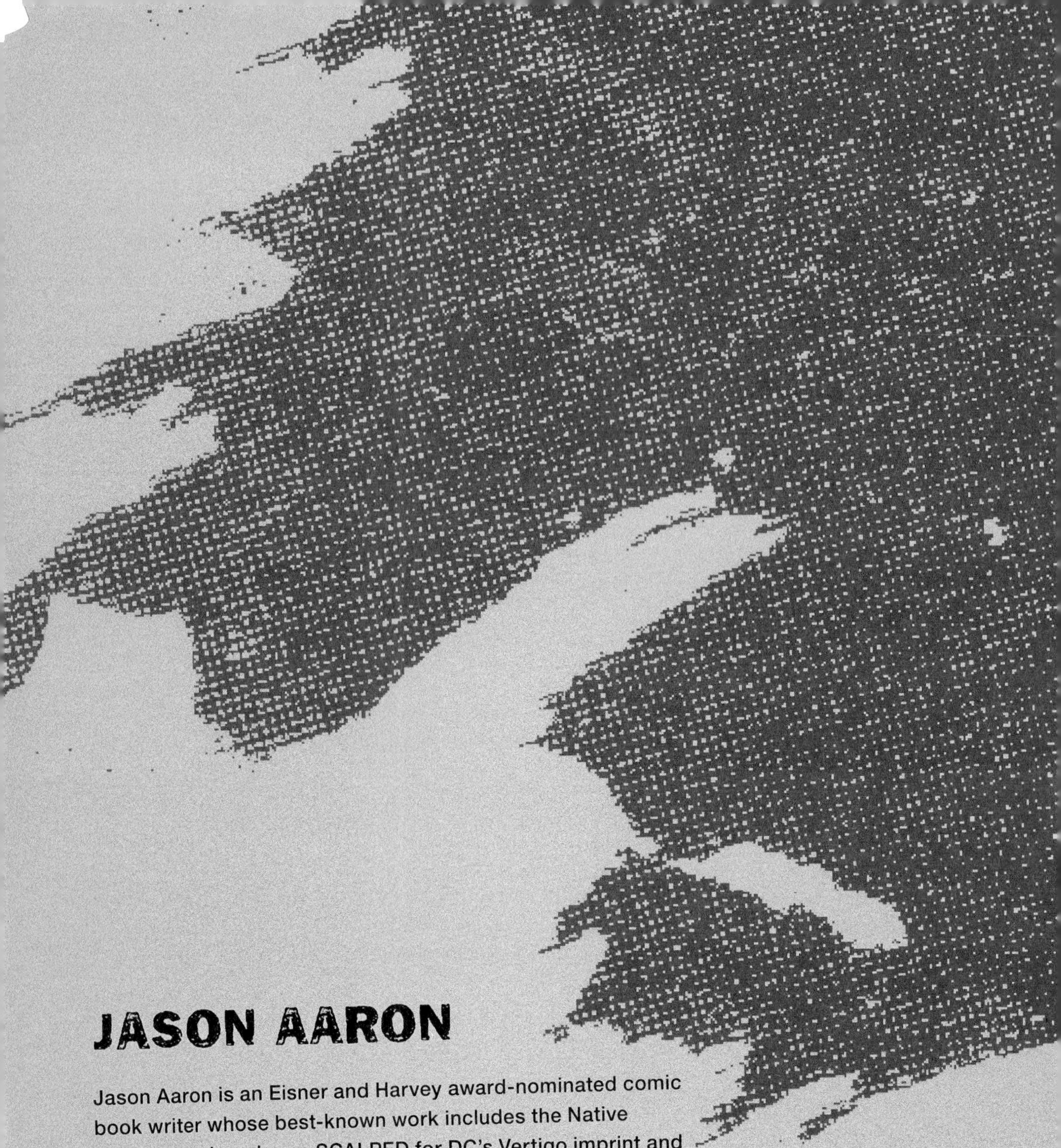

JASON AARON

Jason Aaron is an Eisner and Harvey award-nominated comic book writer whose best-known work includes the Native American crime drama SCALPED for DC's Vertigo imprint and the acclaimed *Southern Bastards* (co-created with artist Jason Latour) for Image. He also wrote several well-regarded runs on a number of titles for Marvel Comics, including *Wolverine*, *Ghost Rider* and *Thor*. Aaron was born in Alabama and currently resides in Kansas City. He enjoys many things, but shaving is not one of them.

R. M. GUÉRA

Born in Yugoslavia, comic book artist R.M. Guéra has lived in Spain since 1991. His internationally published work includes two volumes of the French series *Le Lièvre de Mars*, written by Patrick Cothias and published by Glénat, and the critically acclaimed Native American crime series SCALPED, written by Jason Aaron and published by Vertigo. He has also illustrated BATMAN ETERNAL for DC Comics, as well as the comics adaptation of Quentin Tarantino's DJANGO UNCHAINED for Vertigo.